W9-ADT-199

Architecture's New Media

Architecture's New Media

Principles, Theories, and Methods of Computer-Aided Design

Yehuda E. Kalay

The MIT Press   Cambridge, Massachusetts   London, England

This book was set in Adobe Garamond, Din, and Symbol by The MIT Press and was printed and bound in the United States of America.

Library of Congress Cataloging-in-Publication Data

Kalay, Yehuda E.
    Architecture's new media : principles, theories, and methods of computer-aided design / Yehuda E. Kalay.
        p. cm.
    Includes bibliographical references and index.
    ISBN 0-262-11284-1 (alk. paper)
     1. Architectural design—Data processing. 2. Computer-aided design. I. Title.

NA2728.K35 2004
720'.28'040285—dc22

2003066646

To my wife, Riki, without whose patience, encouragement, support, and professional help this book could not have been completed.

Contents

Foreword

Designs are descriptions of things that don't yet exist. They may be stored in your head, on paper, or in digital format. The tasks of recording and editing designs; sorting, searching, filtering, and formatting them; visualizing, analyzing, and interpreting them; drawing inferences from them; and translating them into sequences of construction operations are all forms of information processing.

You might hold a design entirely between your ears, process it internally, and execute it directly with your own two hands. This works for sand castles and snow forts, but larger and more complex projects require division of labor among members of design and construction teams. These teams may be distributed over wide geographic areas, and design and construction processes may extend over months or years. Information technology—the subject of this book—provides ways of externalizing and preserving designs, linking team members across time and space, coordinating their efforts, and automating various of their tasks.

On ancient and medieval construction sites, the creative, design role of the architect was rarely clearly distinguished from that of the craftsmen who followed instructions. Nor were design and construction processes separated geographically. The designer was right there on site, and he relied upon a combination of demonstrations and verbal instructions with rudimentary forms of externalized design representation—templates, rough sketches, and physical models—to express design intentions and convey them to workers responsible for execution. There was no intellectual, managerial, or legal need for the sort of comprehensive design documentation we know today.

The interrelated technologies of parchment and paper, Euclid's theorems and geometric construction procedures, and technical drafting instruments, eventually changed all that. They allowed the design atelier to distance itself from the construction site, so that conceiving, developing, evaluating, and documenting building designs became a specialized type of office work. Design ideas were now explored on paper, discussions and presentations were organized around drawings and scale models, and the outcome of a design process became a comprehensive, detailed set of construction documents. These documents acquired legal significance: they established responsibility for design decisions (and liability if something went wrong), they were employed in bidding processes, and they became the basis of construction contracts.

Designs on paper were portable; they could be carried around under your arm or sent through the post. They were also relatively permanent and could be kept in files or at site offices until needed. And they could be copied, with increasing ease as graphic reproduction technology evolved, in order to support the work of multiple designers and consultants in parallel. So it became possible to organize large-scale design and construction processes, involving numerous participants at geographically dispersed locations, and to coordinate these processes through transfer of information on paper.

In most parts of the world, this pattern of architectural practice remained unchallenged until the 1950s. It was inseparable from the image of architects in society, the pride and prestige that architects derived from their graphic skills, fee structures for architectural work, and prevailing strategies of architectural education and licensing. Then, as digital technology appeared and burgeoned in the postwar decades, the revolutionary idea emerged of replacing drawings on paper as primary representations of designs with digital representations that were stored in computer memory and manipulated by means of interactive computer graphics interfaces.

It was obvious from the beginning that this application of digital storage and computation capabilities had many potential advantages. It might speed the production of design documents, reduce errors and omissions, provide inexpensive and vivid visualizations, and enable the direct application of engineering and cost analysis software to stored digital representations. A few adventurous thinkers even saw the possibility, in suitable contexts, of automated design synthesis. By 1963 Ivan Sutherland's Sketchpad system had demonstrated that these ideas were indeed practical, and by the early 1970s, computer-aided architectural design systems were beginning to penetrate everyday architectural practice.

These early systems were, of course, limited by the computer technology of the time. But, as with systems to support other types of information work, they evolved rapidly to take advantage of the explosive growth in digital information-processing capability that characterized the second half of the twentieth century. As computer memory dropped in price, and raster graphic displays became commonplace, interactive computer graphics developed from a laboratory curiosity to an indispensable part of everyday life. As digital storage devices and associated database technology became increasingly powerful, it became possible to store, edit, and process large, detailed, complex, three-dimensional digital models of buildings. As microprocessor technology followed the curve of Moore's Law, powerful personal computers displaced typewriters, drafting boards, audio and video recorders, and other predigital desk accessories—then shrank to lightweight, wireless laptops. As the Internet and the Web grew explosively, transferring design information among team members evolved from mailing or carrying drawings to downloading files. And as intelligence was embedded in fabrication and construction machines, it became possible to drive them directly from the CAD models produced by architects. By the mid-1990s—about three decades after the first working demonstrations of CAD technology—architectural practice without CAD technology had become as unimaginable as writing without a word processor.

However, just as the new materials and manufacturing processes of a century earlier had awaited designers who could break with tradition and adventurously explore the possibilities of industrial modernism, so the cultural possibilities of the computer in design and construction were not immediately obvious. CAD technology was undeniably useful, and it had made design work more efficient, but it had not opened up new domains to the architectural imagination. The possibilities of "paperless studios" were largely framed in terms of existing conventions and practices, like those of "horseless carriages" and the "wireless telegraph." But as Y2K approached, this changed dramatically, when a few architects began to produce powerful works that would have been impossible without innovative use of advanced information technology. The defining moment was the construction of Frank Gehry's Guggenheim Museum in Bilbao—a huge popular and critical success that depended directly upon shrewd use of three-dimensional CAD modeling, CAD/CAM fabrication, and a globalized design, fabrication, and construction process that was coordinated through electronic information transfer.

In my 1977 book *Computer-Aided Architectural Design* (New York, Van Nostrand Reinhold) I summarized an emerging research literature, described some pioneering practical applications, and proposed that architects should consider a new way of working. (To put this moment in context, recall that it was well before the emergence of the first successful personal computers.) Now, the research literature is enormous and divided into highly specialized subfields; the architectural applications of computer technology are supported by a vast, global industry; architectural practice and education have been transformed; and innovative, exciting projects are emerging from computer-savvy practices. Yehuda Kalay's new introduction to the field provides the perfect starting point for those who want to participate in this ongoing intellectual adventure.

William J. Mitchell

Preface

Architects, according to John Archea, consider design a "search for the most appropriate effects that can be attained in a unique context."[1] Horst Rittel characterized this search as "an activity aimed at achieving certain desired goals without undesired side- and after-effects."[2] But how can we tell what are the "desired goals" and "most appropriate effects" in a given context? How can we tell if a proposed design solution will achieve them? How can we measure its "goodness" and uncover its undesired side and aftereffects before constructing the building? How can we begin the search for design solutions in the first place?

These questions perplexed architects and philosophers for thousands of years. In the first century BC, the Roman architect Vitruvius offered some answers, in the form "best practices," that would guarantee a "good" solution. Since then, many architects and researchers have tried to come up with theories, methods, and tools that will make the results of architectural design more predictable and the design process itself more tractable, teachable, and open to analysis and improvement.

The advent of computers in the 1950s provided new hopes—and fears—that the age-old questions may finally be answered; that by using computers an architect could access multitudes of prior solutions, obtain help when generating new ones, test them, even fabricate them at the touch of a button.

Early success in applying computers to solving complex mathematical problems—of the kind found in engineering analyses—encouraged researchers and architects to seek computational means that would help them solve architectural design problems as well. These hopes were bolstered by Ivan Sutherland's 1963 Sketchpad program—the first interactive graphical design tool—which demonstrated that computers could be used for drafting and modeling, not merely for number crunching.

But the drafting and modeling systems of the 1970s that followed Sutherland's example could meet only a few of the original objectives, namely, visual appraisal of the emerging design solutions and certain geometry-based evaluations (e.g., energy consumption, cost). They still could not tell whether the design was really "good," nor did they provide much help in generating the design solutions themselves, except in highly limited domains such as the design of prefabricated hospitals and housing units.[3]

In the 1980s the search for computational methods and tools that could assist architects in their quest for "good" solutions was strongly influenced by the general euphoria associated with artificial intelligence—a branch of computer science dedicated to solving problems in ways that would be considered "intelligent" if done by humans.[4] A large number of "expert" and other types of knowledge-based systems were developed, purporting to package design expertise and to bring it to bear on design problems without the experts who generated the knowledge in the first place. Few of these systems lived up to their creators' expectations. However, the advent of computer graphics at about the same time provided architects a rich tool kit of drafting, modeling, and rendering systems. While these tools could not help architects design, at least they made the production and communication aspects of the process easier.

The globalization of the building industry in the 1990s, coupled with the increasing capabilities of computers as telecommunication devices (due largely to the rise of the Internet), brought about the birth of computer-aided collaboration. The first uses of computers to facilitate collaboration were purely technical: it was easier and faster to send digital design information through the Internet than to send physical drawings through the mail. But this ability, along with accelerated schedules for designing and building, raised serious problems of interoperability, concurrency, authority, and version control. Some systems that can manage the multifarious data formats used in a typical building project have emerged, raising difficult questions about the design process itself along the way.

At the dawn of the third millennium it is pertinent, therefore, to take stock of what has been accomplished in the last half of the twentieth century as far as the use of computing in architectural design is concerned and to assess the directions in which these accomplishments have been leading the discipline and the profession of architecture. But however interesting it may be to review the history of a fast moving field such as computing in general, and computer-aided architectural design in particular, such study holds limited promise to understanding the future of the discipline. To be of relevance, the assessment must look deeper—at the *principles* underlying the evolution of computer-aided design, and at the *impacts* these developments have had on the practice of architecture and its products. Only then can we draw meaningful conclusions from the past, understand the successes and failures of information technology as far as architecture is concerned, and help guide future developments in this field.

Consider, for example, the impact computing has had on architecture's sister disciplines—electrical, mechanical, and civil engineering. They have taken advantage of the increasing power of computers to develop CAD software that can manipulate much more sophisticated representations than graphical depictions alone: they manipulate rich data sets that allow models of computer chips, airplanes, automobiles, and buildings to behave much like the physical objects they stand for. As a result, hypothetical electrical, mechanical, and civil engineering design propositions now can be subjected to a vast array of evaluations that help engineers test and optimize them before they are fabricated. Nor has CAD software simply improved the design of conventional mechanical and electrical engineering solutions; it also made possible the design of artifacts that could not have been designed, fabricated, or even used without the aid of computers. As such, it is no longer possible to design a car, an airplane, a ship, or a computer chip—with its tens of millions of transistors—without the use of computers.

Computers have transformed not only the design (CAD) and manufacture (CAM) of many artifacts, but have also changed the way we operate and use them. The average automobile now has more than twenty-six embedded microprocessors, connected through a sophisticated data "bus." They have radically altered the way we maintain (engine failure diagnostics) and operate automobiles (ignition timing, ABS, traction control, collision sensors, etc.) and even how we keep track of them (using GPS and the On-Star system). More profoundly, for the first time since Henry Ford introduced his famed Model T, computers have allowed the automotive industry to change its business model from mass production to mass customization.

In short, computer-aided design has allowed these disciplines to reinvent themselves and their products and to advance their professions into what we now call the post-industrial age, or the age of information technology.

Compare these advances to the progress made in architectural design: although 2D and 3D graphics software proved to be a remarkable departure from pencil and tracing paper and has been adopted almost universally as the predominant, if not exclusive, means of production in architectural practice, it merely represents the commercialization of the simplest and most obvious application of information technology in architectural design: the automation of traditional processes like drafting, modeling, and communicating. Most generative and evaluative software that have been developed over the past five decades failed to gain a foothold in architectural practice, hence to add value to professional design practices and its products. As a result, architectural design solutions are still crafted manually, much the same way they have been for the past 500 years, except that the drawings and models that represent them can now be edited more easily and communicated more expeditiously among the members of the design team. In other words, information technology has had—so far—relatively little *qualitative* impact on the profession of architecture itself and on the way buildings are constructed and used.[5] At best, it has improved the *efficiency* of designing buildings, when in fact it has the potential to *reinvent* the architectural design process itself, much as it has helped to reinvent other disciplines.

Why has architecture been slower than other disciplines to take advantage of information technology? The complexity of the discipline is certainly an important factor, as are its lack of a rigorous research tradition and scientific basis, the conservatism of professionals, and the paucity of funding for research and development. Still, much work has been done in computer-aided architectural design over the past fifty years. Tremendous advances have been made in developing data structures that can support more than just the graphical appearance of architectural objects like walls and windows. Many new methods have been developed to simulate and evaluate how buildings perform with respect to energy usage, lighting, acoustics, traffic, emergency egress—even habitability and aesthetics. Advances have been made in automating standard design procedures and in facilitating collaboration among architects, engineers, contractors, and clients. These advances are intimately tied to the basic tenets of architectural design—from the principles of design methods themselves to the modalities of evaluation, communication theory, and the practices of professional collaboration.

As the first step in overcoming the aforementioned factors that hold back advances in computer-aided architectural design, this book aims to help readers understand the *principles*, the *theories*, and the *methods* that underlie the application of information technology to architecture. It discusses the principles of information technology that are pertinent to architectural design, analyzes the benefits and drawbacks of various computational methods purporting to support designers, and explores the potential of emerging computational techniques to affect the future of the discipline and its products.

The book covers five main topics, each comprising the principles, theories, and methods pertinent to its subject matter, with examples and case studies of their application:

1. *Introduction*	What is design, what are computers, and what are the relationships between them? This topic covers the nature and history of computing in general and CAAD in particular and presents a computational view of the design process.
2. *Communication*	Communication has two distinct roles in the process of design: an intra-process role, in which the designer communicates with himself or herself (a process known as "ideation"); and an extra-process role, in which the designer communicates with other members of the design team. This topic covers the principles of communication and representation, including computer graphics, databases, and product models.
3. *Synthesis*	How can computers be used to generate design solutions, and what are the advantages and limitations of their synthetic abilities? This topic covers procedural and heuristic design methods, knowledge-based CAAD, neural networks, and genetic algorithms.
4. *Evaluation*	What are the roles of evaluation and prediction in design, and how can computers be of assistance?

	This topic covers the two modalities of computer-aided evaluations of buildings (multicriteria and multilevel) and provides examples from their application to structures, energy, acoustics, human factors, and aesthetics.
5. *The Future*	How will developments in computing and telecommunications affect the processes and the products of architecture? This topic covers multidisciplinary collaboration, design and construction automation, the significance of the Internet for architecture, and the impact of computers on the discipline and its products in the future.

The range of topics covered by this book is much too broad to allow their in-depth treatment. Instead, it is the explicit purpose of this book to provide a comprehensive overview of the subject matter, tying the separate developments to one another and to the principles underlying architectural design. To support in-depth inquiry of specific topics, the book provides over 500 carefully selected references to both classical and cutting-edge publications. Together with this text, they provide a comprehensive treatment of computer-aided design and its related topics.

It is hard to predict the impact of information technology on any discipline, especially one like architecture, because technology tends to create its own uses and often changes established methods and practices in the course of its adoption. Yet understanding the principles on which architectural design and computing are founded is a necessary first step in bringing about these changes. Only then will the development of methods and tools progress in a direction that can truly help the discipline and the practice of architecture, and only then can their relevance, impacts, and desirability for the profession of architecture and the environment(s) it creates be fully understood.

Acknowledgments

A comprehensive book of this kind could not have been written without the help of numerous colleagues, students, researchers, and corporations involved in various aspects of computer-aided architectural design.

Foremost, I wish to thank the Graham Foundation for Advanced Studies in the Fine Arts for its generous support of this project. I also wish to thank architect John Marx, Design Principal of Form4, of San Francisco, Calif.; and Dr. Chris Yessios, president and CEO of AutoDesSys, of Columbus, Ohio, for their support and encouragement.

Special thanks to Wei Yan and Jae-Wook Lee for their help in preparing the illustrations for this book.

I also wish to acknowledge the help of and thank: Robert Alvarado and his coworkers at Charles Salter & Associates of San Francisco; Scott Arvin of AutoDesk; The Asian Elephant Art & Conservation Project; Gordon Bell of Microsoft Corporation; Santiago Calatrava SA; Gianfranco Carrara of the University of Rome "La Sapienza"; Justin Cassell, Terry Knight, and Kent Larson of the Massachusetts Institute of Technology; Tom Coffin, Donna Cox, and Bob Patterson of The National Center for Supercomputing Applications at the University of Illinois at Urbana-Champaign; Becky Cohen, photographer; Harold Cohen of the University of California, San Diego; Tanya Das Neves of Immersense; Tim Dietz of Fairchild Semiconductor International; Charles Eastman of Georgia Institute of Technology; Charles Ehrlich, Konstantinos Papamichael, Greg Ward, and Fredrick C. Winkelmann of the Lawrence Berkeley National Laboratory; the San Francisco Exploratorium; Ulrich Flemming of Carnegie Mellon University; John Gero and Mary Lou Maher of the University of Sydney, Australia; Gabriela Goldschmidt, Rivka Oxman, Edna Shaviv, and Avraham Yezioro of the Technion, Israel Institute of Technology; Jay Graham Photography, San Francisco; Donald Greenberg of the Computer Graphics Laboratory, Cornell University; the Solomon R. Guggenheim

Museum, New York; Alicia Haber of the MUVA Virtual Museum of Arts El País, Uruguay; Lenor Leeds of Harry Teague Architects, Aspen, Colorado; Kraftmaid Corporation; Jaime Locquiao of the Mineta San Jose International Airport, California; Claus Lynge Christensen of Odeon, Lyngby, Denmark; Christin Minnotte of Asymptote Architecture, New York; Gordie Morgan of First Technology Safety Systems; NASA Ames Research Center; Rick Noll of Activeworlds, Inc.; Lionel March of the University of California, Los Angeles; Paul Richens of the Martin Center, Cambridge University; Jens Pohl of the California State University and Polytechnic, San Luis Obispo; Janette Rosebrook and Frederic Silber of the Experience Music Project, Seattle; Philip Steadman of the Bartlett School, University College London; Stephen Tobriner of the University of California, Berkeley; Tsou Jin-Yeu of the Chinese University of Hong Kong; Heidi Williams of Koning-Eizenberg, Architects, Santa Monica, California; Z Smith; and Dr. Haitham El-Zobaidi, Middle East Online, London.

Introduction

According to science philosopher Jacob Bronowski,[1] design is the epitome of intelligent behavior: it is the single most important ability that distinguishes humans from other animals. Although some animals can use tools to help them accomplish certain tasks—such as extracting termites from a mound, or breaking coconuts—no other animal is capable of analyzing a problem to uncover its root causes, which can help it to consistently and deliberately devise the means to solve the problem even when these means are not immediately obvious.

Problem analysis is a rational behavior—formal deductive, inductive, and abductive logical methods combine with experience-based heuristic reasoning to uncover the roots of a problem and indicate a course of action that will lead to its successful resolution. It relies on the problem solver's familiarity with formal reasoning methods and ability to frame the problem in a manner that will make it amenable to solution.

Problem analysis plays a major role in the process of design, but it is not the only ingredient. Unlike other problems—such as those posed by a game of chess—that rely solely on the problem solver's ability to reason and can, therefore, be solved through rational behavior alone, design problems are "ill-structured," according to Herbert Simon,[2] and downright "wicked," according to Horst Rittel.[3] They often do not contain enough information to be solved rationally, and they confront the designer with uncertainties that must, nonetheless, be dealt with. They typically must achieve multiple, often conflicting, goals, requiring the designer to make difficult tradeoffs whose outcome cannot be reliably predicted. And they always have side effects and aftereffects, which may render the solution unacceptable for reasons not directly associated with the problem itself.

To overcome these difficulties, designers must rely on intuition and creativity: the cognitive facilities of "knowing" without the use of rational processes, culminating in the celebrated "intuitive leap"—when all the pieces of the puzzle somehow seem to fall into place, and an overall order descends upon the problem. Neither of these facilities can be well defined, let alone codified or taught. They are innate abilities, which distinguish the artist from the mere artisan, the genius from the merely competent.

But unlike art, which must often conform only to the artist's self-imposed goals and constraints, architectural design is an activity that deals, in equal measures, with externally imposed constraints (e.g., site conditions, climate, functionality, cost, building codes, and so forth) and internally drawn inspirations. It thus relies on both sides of the brain—the analytical and the creative—to produce solutions to problems that cannot be solved with one facility alone.[4]

Computers, by their nature, are superb analytical engines. If correctly programmed, they can follow a line of reasoning to its logical conclusion. They will never tire, never make silly arithmetical mistakes, and will gladly search through and correlate facts buried in the endless heaps of information they can store. They will do all that quickly and repeatedly, by following a set of instructions called a program, which tells them in minute detail how to manipulate the electrical impulses in their circuits. They can present the results of these manipulations in the form most suitable for human comprehension: in textual reports, tables of numbers, charts, graphical constructions—even in dynamically changing images and sounds. But while they can follow instructions precisely and faultlessly, computers are totally incapable of making up new instructions: they lack any creative abilities or intuition.

What, then, is the use of computers for the process of design, which requires both rational and creative abilities, if they lack one of the two key ingredients needed to solve design problems? Why do we even bother to draft them into the service of designers? Is it because we humans, who possess both rational and creative abilities, are easily bored, distracted, and tend to make mistakes when confronted with large and complex problems? While our memories are vast enough to store the experiences of a lifetime, our ability to recall these memories at will is limited. This is precisely where computers excel. If we could find a way to take advantage of the abilities of computers where ours fall short, and use our own abilities where computers' fall short, we would create a very powerful symbiotic design system: computers will contribute their superb rational and search abilities, and we humans will contribute all the creativity and intuition needed to solve design problems.

Computers, for example, could list and keep track of all the goals and constraints the design solution must accomplish. They could group them into related issues,[5] search for precedents, even propose possible alternative standard solutions. The designer could then use these as the basis for developing new solutions that better fit the problem, which the computer could analyze and compare to the stored list of goals and constraints. Once a solution has been found, the computer could help represent it graphically and numerically and communicate it to other partners in the design process. It could then keep track of changes and updates, even alert the designer to potential inconsistencies and errors. Furthermore, computers could help fabricate and construct the resulting buildings, much like robotic machines now help fabricate cars, airplane parts, and integrated circuits. They could even help us manage the buildings once they have been constructed, much as they control the engine of a car or monitor elevators in buildings. And, further still, computers could provide an alternative "space" for human inhabitation—the so-called cyberspace—which could offer a new stage for human activities, from education to commerce to entertainment.[6]

Such a symbiosis is predicated on *communication*: the ability to share information between humans and computers. But communication, as discussed in part 2 of this book, is a process that relies on shared knowledge, which the communicating parties use to interpret the information. It is relatively easy to communicate information from computers to humans, who posses the intelligence needed to understand textual, numerical, graphical, and auditory messages. But it is frustratingly difficult to communicate information from humans to computers, who lack the intelligence and the ability to interpret messages, unless they are coded in a completely unambiguous manner. Communicating the nuances of an idea—especially a design idea—from humans to computers is, therefore, a very tall order. Although some attempts have been made to solve this problem,[7] most researchers have opted to avoid it by placing the entire design process within the computer's electronic realm.

Hence, the majority of computer-aided design research over the past fifty years has been directed toward developing computational systems that provide varying levels of assistance to human designers by taking care of smaller or larger parts of the design process. They range from drafting and modeling systems, where the role of computers is limited to supporting human designers in drawing lines and other geometrical entities that have no meaning to the computer; to analytical systems with enough "understanding" of the data to be able to provide rational appraisal of human designers' solutions (e.g., energy, cost, fire egress, acoustics, and so forth); to knowledge-based, "intelligent" design systems that can actually propose design solutions for appraisal and further development by human designers. Along the way, systems have been developed that offer design information storage and query capabilities and systems that help human designers communicate with one another. Each type of system has found its niche and provides useful service to its users, but because of their widely different objectives, these systems can rarely communicate with one another, although attempts have been made since the 1960s to develop interoperability protocols.

The following chapters discuss the nature of design, the nature of computers, and how the two have been combined in the form of computer-aided design systems over the past fifty years.

Design

Design is a process we engage in when the current situation is different from some desired situation, and when the actions needed to transform the former into the latter are not immediately obvious. For example, if we were caught hiking on the snowy slopes of a mountain in an unexpected snowstorm, we would engage in a process whose purpose is to change our unsheltered situation into a sheltered one. If adequate shelter presented itself in the form of a cabin, a cave, even a grove of trees, the process of seeking shelter would not be characterized as design: the solution would be immediately apparent. However, if there was no adequate shelter in sight, we might have to devise one by digging into the snow, gathering rocks or branches, or undertaking some other process whose outcome would allow us to solve the original problem, namely, becoming sheltered. The process of devising the shelter itself will not solve our problem: it is only an intermediary step, whose results—if successful—will create conditions that can solve the shelter problem. What makes it a process of design, rather than a haphazard undertaking of digging or gathering of materials, is foresight: each step in the process will be *evaluated* by considering its potential for solving the original problem. If and only if it shows promise, it will be undertaken. Otherwise, another action will be sought. If more than one action is possible, the one chosen will be that which is expected to have a better payoff or is less costly to undertake. Design, accordingly, is a *purposeful* activity, aimed at achieving some well-defined goals. This means that the original problem must be analyzed for the purpose of setting goals, which, when achieved, will solve the problem. The analysis will also reveal the constraints on accomplishing the goals. Subsequently, actions that may lead to accomplishing the goals must be devised. Furthermore, there must be a way to predict and evaluate the potential of each action to accomplish the goals. If executing the actions requires the participation of people other than ourselves, there must also be a way for us to communicate with our partners to get their opinions, agreement, and assistance for each of the above activities.

Analyzing problems, setting goals, devising actions that might accomplish them, evaluating the efficacy of these actions, and communicating with others involved in the process is what designers do. Professional designers, like architects, differ from laymen in that they have been trained in solving a particular class of problems, have experience doing so, and often have demonstrated an aptitude for coming up with effective solutions. Part of their training involves becoming familiar with methods that have proved effective in accomplishing any or all of these actions. Learning such methods helps designers direct their efforts toward successful solutions rather than waste their time searching for unsuccessful ones; find and use shortcuts; understand the affordances of the situations they face; and understand the implications of their actions beyond the immediate solution of the problem at hand.

The search for effective general methods of design—ones that can be taught, learned, and applied with some assurance of success in every case—was begun with the ancient Greeks, who recorded their successful design methods in a teachable manner. The very richness and complexity of the problems that require design methods for their successful solution has extended that search to the present day, when computers have been enlisted in support of the effort. In fact the search for design methods has become an activity in and of itself, much like research in other scientific fields has, with the added complexity that there is no agreement on the demonstrated effectiveness of any given method.

1.1 The Evolution of Architectural Design

Architectural design as we know it today is a relatively recent phenomenon. It became a form of professional practice only in the 1450s, when Italian noblemen, like Leon Battista Alberti, renounced the technical utilitarianism of Gothic architecture in favor of aesthetic principles derived from humanism and governed by a system of rules based on the vocabulary and the syntax of the ancient Greek orders. Thus, whereas thirteenth-century buildings were built by master masons who left much of the buildings' details to the specification of an army of craftsmen, the Renaissance's holistic approach required a strict adherence to fixed building plans and elevations, whose every detail was planned in advance by the newly established discipline of architecture. To facilitate the design process, architects had to invent design methods, which included the use of scale drawings and models, and encode their newly formed body of knowledge in books that could help them disseminate it among their colleagues all over Europe. Architecture became a profession, rather than a craft, and its practitioners became some of the most respected and educated members of society, rather than artisans, gifted as they may have been.

Craftsmanship

Buildings, prior to the Renaissance, were *constructed*, not *planned*: a master mason developed a simple schema, often by following the traditional patterns he learned as an apprentice and as a journeyman. Facades were derived by way of deducing the elevation from the plan, applying the master builder's "trick"—a system of proportions based on triangles or squares—with the help of a compass and a ruler. Much of the building was unplanned, or undesigned, in the modern sense of the term; other than templates for columns and vaults, there were no drawings and no models to follow. Rather, an extraordinarily talented and well-trained (though uneducated) army of craftsmen were entrusted with every detail of the building. Organized in guilds, or lodges, their skills were honed by long apprenticeships and governed by the strict rules of conduct of their lodges. Becoming a mason or a carpenter—the two major crafts needed to construct a building—was a way of life, not a vocation. Masons carried their own tools, moved from building project to building project (where, depending on the type of building, they may have lived for many years), and shaped the building according to their own skills and training—often signing their names in the stones they cut.[1]

Craftsmanship produced spectacular results—the product of training, specialization, and strict rules of conduct. But it was also a slow process, which could not easily adapt to new technologies or styles. While strictly hierarchical, it made overall control over the building project difficult, if not impossible.

Scale Drawings and Models

To assume control over the building process, so they could shape it according to the new spirit and principles of their time, the architects of the Renaissance needed the means of representation that would allow them to plan the entire building before construction started and to communicate with builders. The primary means of representation became the scaled drawing—a set of blueprints that depicted the building as it would be once constructed, in all its details, proportions, and dimensions. With the introduction of scale drawings, architects ceased to be *technicians* supervising the construction project on-site and became *designers*, who expressed their professional skills through drawings. Training in painting, drafting, and theory became more important than practical experience in construction, opening the profession to "dilettantes"—amateurs compared to the craftsmanship-trained master builders—who came from the ranks of the nobility and the intelligentsia rather than the trades. The first among them was Leon Battista Alberti, a Florentine. Not only did he lack practical building experience, but he was also reluctant to travel to the actual building site of his first building in Rimini—some 100 miles outside Florence. He had to rely on professional builders at the site, with whom he communicated through scaled drawings. Alberti has thus come to symbolize the separation of *conception* of a building from its *construction*.

The growing use of drawings as a means of communication between the architect and the builder required the development of drawing conventions—a language—which helped the communicating parties interpret the message conveyed by drawings in an unambiguous way. A system comprised of plans, elevations, and sections was developed, along with conventions for laying them out on paper in a manner that would allow easy correlation of the respective elements in each mode of representation. In a letter he wrote to Pope Leo X in 1519, Raphael—who took over Bramante's work on St. Peter's cathedral in Rome—suggested that the elevation and section should be drawn directly above the plan in order that they should conform to the same scale. He emphasized the need for a geometrical drawing to show the measurements accurately and rejected the perspective view, which he regarded as deceptive.[2]

The technical evolution of scale drawings has, paradoxically, increased the importance of scale models, because clients became less able to interpret the growing abstraction of architectural drawings. Scale models have always been a preferred mode of communication in architecture, as they can show buildings in a three-dimensional, volumetric manner. With the advent of scale drawings, they became tools for planning and design, not merely souvenirs for the patron who commissioned the building. Scale models of whole buildings and of building details were produced to test the visual effect of such important components as domes. Training in cabinetmaking has become as important a part of architectural education as drawing.

Drawings and scale models allowed architects not only to communicate with the builders and their clients, but also to experiment with alternative design solutions and test them on paper for form and function before they were committed to stone. They allowed more people to become involved in the design process, and allowed the architects to develop more intricate designs.

Design as a Profession

The separation of designing from building established architects as independent agents in the design-build-use continuum: by mastering the art of design, professionals in charge of building projects moved away from the craft of making buildings and became theoreticians skilled in drawing and making models. To emphasize their distinction from the master builders, who continued to be in charge of construction, they adopted the name *architect*, derived from Greek. As the name took hold, and as the designers became more and more separate from the builders and the engineers, architecture became a profession of its own, with its own educational process, conventions, language, and governing institutions. Architects became revered members of society, with status similar to artists. They befriended monarchs and popes, signed their names in prominent locations on their buildings, and were even accorded burial honors similar to the aristocracy's.[3] Architecture became a profession, with skills that needed to be learned and perfected by experience and practice, worth protecting through licensure, providing a service people were willing to pay for.

1.2 The Process of Design

Separating the conception of the building from its construction, however, did not come without penalties. Drawings, which are the products of the architect, are a different medium than the buildings they represent. They obey different laws and allow for the design of buildings that cannot exist in reality, as depicted so well by the lithographs of the Dutch artist Morris C. Escher (fig. 1.1). By severing the craftsmanship closed-loop feedback

1.1 Morris C. Escher lithograph *Relativity* (1953), depicting an impossible reality. (Copyright 2002 Cordon Art B.V., Baarn, Holland. All rights reserved.)

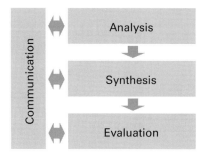

1.2 The major components of the architectural design process.

between an idea and its realization, design errors may go unnoticed until the building is under construction, when it is too late—or too expensive—to correct them.

To compensate for this deficiency, while taking advantage of the obvious benefits of design vs. craftsmanship, architects adopted a design process that would ensure that their creations met the design goals, abided by its constraints, and reduced the likelihood of errors. This process, which has been practiced for hundreds of years but was only formalized in the 1960s,[4] consists of four intertwined phases (fig. 1.2):

- Problem analysis
- Solution synthesis
- Evaluation
- Communication

Problem Analysis

Problem analysis, also known as feasibility analysis, is the phase of the process where the designer tries to identify all the elements of the problem, including the goals to be achieved (along with their performance measures), the constraints that the solution will have to abide by, and the possible side effects and aftereffects that potential solutions might create. For example, the client may specify her wish to build a new headquarters for a company on a given site, for a given number of employees, under a certain budget. Using this information as a starting point, the architect must determine the size of the building, its desired configuration (in terms of room adjacencies, traffic patterns, and so forth), orientations, and other factors that will guide the solution development process. The architect must also uncover the constraints with which the solution will have to contend and the opportunities it might take advantage of, such as site conditions (weather, topography, views, proximity to existing buildings), code requirements, socioeconomic factors, cultural factors (e.g., the nature of the neighborhood), and so on. Side effects and aftereffects are typically determined through an environmental impact study, which attempts to forecast the effects of such things as adding more traffic to a given site, covering it with pavements, and shading adjacent buildings and open spaces. The result of this phase of the design process is a list of specifications, often in the form of a book, which spells out in great detail what the building ought to be like without actually designing the building itself.

It is an analytical, rational process, which relies on information obtained from client interviews, precedents, surveys, building codes, economic and physical forecasting, and other sources. In fact the difficulty associated with this phase is not obtaining the information itself, but rather organizing it in a manner that will be useful for the subsequent steps in the design process, as will be discussed in chapter 11.[5]

Solution Synthesis

This is the creative phase of the design process, where the architect forms ideas and possible solutions that might address the goals, constraints, and opportunities established during the problem analysis phase of the process. It is not a rational process, for despite Louis Sullivan's famous proclamation that "form follows function," no such causal relationship has ever been found (at least not in architecture) between form and function.[6] Instead, this is an intuitive step, in which the designer finds an arrangement of forms, materials, views, orientations, lighting conditions, and other elements that come together into a holistic ensemble, where the parts support one another and have an intrinsic structure of their own.

Although it is not a rational process, the synthesis of design solutions benefits from familiarity with precedents, metaphors, reflective sketching, as well as formal knowledge of rules of composition and style. It can be induced by searching through solutions that conform to the specifications in a mechanical manner (e.g., all possible room arrangements that conform to some adjacency requirements,[7] or that follow some formal rules of composition). It can also be induced by placing the designer in a "creative" state, such as strolling through the woods, or by depriving him or her of distractions—as practiced by the Ecole des Beaux-Arts in the nineteenth century, where students were literally locked in a closet so that they could come up with solutions to their sketch exercises (the *esquisses*).[8]

Evaluation

The solutions that emerge from the synthesis phase of the design process are often incomplete, may not address all the requirements, and contain internal conflicts. They must be evaluated rationally, which is the purpose of the third phase of the design process.

The evaluation compares the proposed solution to the goals, constraints, and opportunities developed in the problem analysis phase of the design process, to discern compatibilities and conflicts and to establish the degree to which the proposed solution achieves the performance criteria.

Evaluation is a rational process. However, not all performance criteria can be evaluated rationally: aesthetics, human behavior, and the overall "feel" of a building are qualitative aspects that have defied attempts at rational measurement and assessment. Nonetheless, a host of means to help designers predict and measure the potential of the solution to meet the goals and abide by the constraints have been developed. They include calculation, reasoning, simulation, extrapolation, even guessing.

Evaluation of the proposed solutions is further complicated by conflicts among competing qualities: it is possible that a proposed design solution will meet all the needs of the client but impose too much traffic on the neighborhood; or that its panoramic windows, which take in a magnificent view, also allow too much energy to escape. Sometimes such conflicts can be resolved without compromising other performances, but often they require sacrifices. Choosing among such tradeoffs is an integral part of the design process.

The results of the evaluation are communicated back to the previous steps for improvement or adjustment of the solution, or for changing the requirements. It is possible that a deficiency detected by the evaluation process can be fixed by changing the solution. Or, if the deficiency is not due to a shortcoming of the solution, but rather to incompatible goals or overly restrictive constraints, the goals and the constraints must be adjusted if a satisfactory solution is to be achieved.

Communication

Communication allows all participants in the design process to become informed of the evolving goals and solutions, to help generate solutions (or partial solutions), and to evaluate them. The expertise needed to assess all the different factors contributing the performance of a modern building are too numerous for the architect alone to master. Rather, a host of consultants, including structural engineers, mechanical engineers, economists, lawyers, building code specialists, and many contractors and subcontractors need to be involved in the process. They communicate through a wide range of representational means, including drawings, specifications, renderings, models, and notes. Communication also helps the architect record his or her thoughts, so that they can stimulate reflection and improvement. Communication is thus the "glue" that connects the different parts of the design process to one another and serves as its record and as its stimulus. That is why so much effort has been devoted to developing effective means of communication to support architects, and why, to the uninitiated, "design" has become synonymous with "drafting."

Communication is much more complex than is evident in any one means chosen for its representation: it is a process of encoding and decoding information, using a medium that can best afford the transfer of ideas, information, and messages between the different parties associated with the design process, and across the different phases of the process itself. The evolution of means of communication has had a direct impact on the process of design, as discussed earlier: the invention of drawings in the fifteenth century made it possible to separate design from construction and contributed directly to the establishment of the profession of architecture. The recent addition of computers to the repertoire of means of communication has expanded access to information and opened up the design process for more people to become involved.

1.3 Paradigms of Design

Moving from one phase of the design process to another can take different forms, depending on the direction of the transition. When trying to find a solution that accomplishes given goals and abides by their attendant constraints, designers are said to be *problem solving*—a paradigm[9] according to which alternative solutions are generated and tested against the goals and the constraints, until a "satisficing"[10] solution is found. On the other hand, when trying to formulate goals that match the spatiotemporal context of the design problem and can be achieved by emerging solutions, designers are said to be *puzzle making*—the paradigm of fitting given parts into a coherent whole. Since the goals and the solutions are interdependent and cannot be separately determined, the overall design process necessarily oscillates between these two cognitive modalities, forming a kind of dialogue between goals and solutions (fig. 1.3).

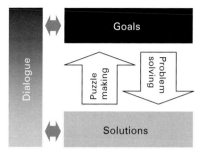

1.3 Two paradigms of the architectural design process.

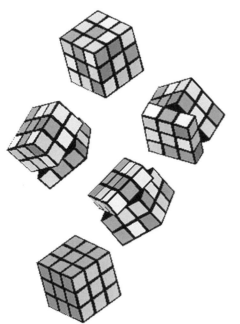

1.4 The Rubik Cube, an example of problem-solving behavior.

Problem solving is a general paradigm for producing solutions to ill-defined problems. It was first introduced by Herbert Simon and Allen Newell in the early 1960s, who implemented it in their General Problem Solver (GPS) computer program.[11] It was even suggested that a refined version of the paradigm can explain all human cognition.[12]

In problem solving, the desired effects of some intellectual endeavor are stated in the form of goals and constraints at the outset. To find the solution, the problem solver generates successive candidate solutions and tests them against the stated goals and constraints, until one is found which meets them. The goals and the constraints thus "guide" the search for a solution right from the beginning of the process, causing new information to be generated effectively, in a goal-directed manner, rather than in a random trial-and-error search. The process itself tells the designer what to do, when to do it, and how. For example, solving the Rubik Cube puzzle (fig. 1.4) is a problem-solving activity: it is clear from the beginning what the goal state looks like, and every move can be evaluated for its progress toward that state.

Problem solving assumes that knowing what should be accomplished can be separated from the process of accomplishing the goals. Such knowledge can be acquired through an independent inquiry (analysis), which should be completed before the search for a solution can begin. For example, selecting a structural system to span some opening follows an analysis of forces, cost, and other characteristics that need to be accomplished by the structure.

Since the characteristics of the solution, according to the problem-solving paradigm, are known prior to initiating the search for the solution, the search is goal-directed and can be guided to the desired solution by means-ends analysis. Thus the skills employed when following the problem-solving paradigm are mainly analytical. They include the ability to compare the current state of the designed artifact to its desired state and to draw operational conclusions from this comparison so that the differences can be reduced (hence the term "means-ends analysis"). Such goal-driven approaches have been computationally represented as backward-reasoning search strategies: operators are applied to the goal statement in order to convert it to a set of subgoals that are relatively easy to solve (which is the common method for solving the Rubik Cube puzzle). This method can be applied recursively until a set of subgoals that can be solved without further reduction is found.[13]

Puzzle Making

It is not always the case, however, that the characteristics of the desired solution can be formulated prior to and independently of the search for the solution that satisfies them. For many problems, including some phases of the architectural design process, such knowledge cannot exist prior to the search itself, since the sought-after solution is unique, and the process of finding it is characterized by missing information and uncertainty. For example, the brief that architects are given by their clients is much too vague, in most cases, to form a complete statement of goals. It is in general merely a statement of intents that defines a general framework for the solution and some of the constraints by which it must abide. Instead, architects develop the statement of goals gradually as they proceed through the design process itself. The additional information needed to complete the goals statement must either be invented as part of the search for the solution or adapted from generalized precedents, metaphors, and symbols. Since the relationship between these generalizations and the particular needs of the problem can be discovered only as the problem becomes clearer, the adaptation itself is context-dependent and cannot be accomplished prior to engaging in the search for solutions.

According to this paradigm, design is a process of discovery, which generates insights into the problem that were not previously known. The process may be compared to puzzle making: the search for the most appropriate effects that can be attained in unique spatiotemporal contexts through the manipulation of a set of components, following a set of combinatorial rules. For example, using the seven basic pieces of the Tangram puzzle, one can make new shapes, each one leading to other new shapes (fig. 1.5).

The main skills employed by designers following the puzzle-making paradigm are, therefore, synthetic—the ability to compose given parts into new, unique wholes. Such data-driven approaches have been computationally represented as forward-reasoning search strategies: operators are applied to the current state of the problem with the aim of transforming it according to predefined sets of rules.

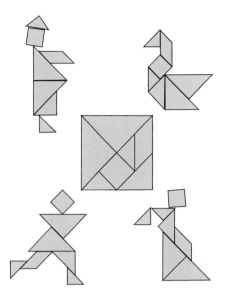

1.5 The venerable Tangram puzzle—making new shapes from the seven basic pieces.

1.6 Design as a dialogue between goals and solutions.

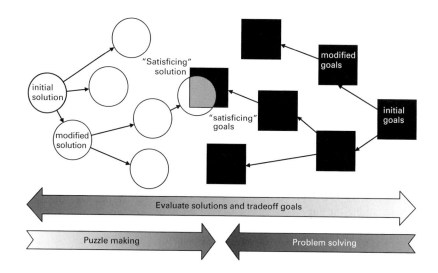

A Dialogue

The interdependency between the goals, the solutions, and the design context creates a cyclical relationship between the two paradigms: design goals are developed that provide the process with a direction, then solutions are proposed that purport to accomplish them. As these solutions emerge, they often help uncover opportunities and limitation that have not been addressed when the goals were first developed. To accommodate these discoveries, the goals must be modified and the constraints relaxed or new ones added. The modified goals and constraints induce changes in the design solutions, which may, in turn, change the goals, and so on until a solution is found that accomplishes an acceptable set of goals. The designer must continuously predict and evaluate the expected performances of the emerging solutions along the criteria established by the goals and must be willing to modify both the solutions and the goals to bring about their convergence.

The process of design thus resembles a dialogue between the goals and the solutions within the context of the problem. Like a dialogue between

Introduction

two people, each side learns from and informs the other, and the discussion weaves itself between the positions of the two parties until a consensus emerges. The design equivalent is the "satisficing" solution, which is often somewhat different from the original solution and meets goals that are somewhat different from the ones that were determined at the outset of the process (fig. 1.6).

1.4 Design Methods

The difficulty and unreliability of the design process, especially when trying to bridge the gap between the first step (setting the goals and the constraints) and the second step (devising potential solutions) has been a source of irritation—and delight—to architects for the past two and a half millennia. They have been irritated by the unpredictability of the process, where much effort may be expanded with no apparent results, while at the same time they have derived much satisfaction from a novel solution finally presenting itself. To try to overcome this unpredictability, without compromising the delight of discovery, architects have developed methods that can be relied upon to produce satisfactory (albeit perhaps not spectacular) results in every case, much like a cookbook provides recipes that can be relied upon to produce adequate dishes for every occasion.

The starting point for many design methods has been the notion that design is a process of *searching* for a solution that satisfies a given set of goals and constraints. The sought-after solution, according to this notion, "exists" within a universe of potential, or candidate, solutions—a so-called *solution space*. Some of these candidate solutions (or perhaps only one, or even none) may meet the goals and satisfy the constraints (fig. 1.7). It is the task of the designer to find those solutions (or determine that none exists, in which case the goals and the constraints must be modified). The methods are intended to make this search more effective.

The quest for such methods has been at the core of architectural design since the time of the ancient Greeks. Different answers suggest different approaches to how candidate solutions can be found (or produced) for evaluation against the goals, and how the goals themselves may be modified to make the search more effective. They have taken the form of trial-and-error searches, constraint-satisfaction methods, rule-based design, and precedent-based design methods.

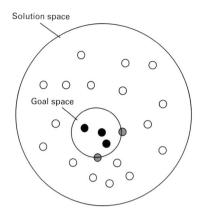

1.7 Design as a process of search. Some of the solutions meet the goals and abide by the constraints (black), while most do not (white) or do so only partially (gray).

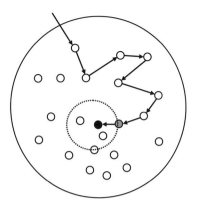

1.8 Examining existing candidate solutions for compliance with the goals and constraints.

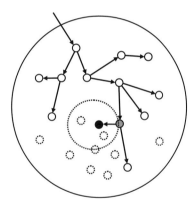

1.9 Developing new candidate solutions and testing them for compliance with the goals and constraints.

Search

Search is a process we engage in when the outcome of an action cannot be fully ascertained in advance. It consists of finding, or developing, candidate solutions, and evaluating them against the goals and the constraints. For example, determining the precise shape of an auditorium, such that it will have desired acoustical qualities, cannot be determined by analytical means alone. It can only be done by trial and error: a shape is picked and is subjected to mathematical or physical simulation of sound propagation. Evaluating the results of the simulation reveals how well the specified shape meets the desired reverberation objectives. We may find that the predicted reverberations meet the desired performance characteristics specified for this auditorium, thus validating the proposed shape. More often, however, the evaluation will reveal that the simulated acoustical effects do not achieve the objectives, in which case the shape or the materials proposed for constructing the auditorium must be modified so that they will meet the desired performances.

Search processes involve two steps: (1) producing candidate solutions for consideration, and (2) choosing the "right" solution for further consideration and development. The process repeats itself until the considered solution is deemed satisfactory in all relevant manners. If it turns out that process has reached a dead end, it must be backtracked, and another solution must be chosen for consideration and development, or the goals and the constraints must be modified, as discussed earlier.

Candidate solutions may present themselves in the form of a given, limited set of solutions, as in the case of looking for a house to buy within a given real estate market: we can only choose from the houses currently available for sale. In that case, it is often possible to examine each one (or a sufficiently large number) of the candidate solutions for compliance with the goals and the constraints, until one that meets them is found (fig. 1.8).

Alternatively, if no candidate solutions exist that can be examined, they have to be produced by the designer before they can be compared with the goals. This is the prevailing case in architectural design. Solution development is a process of informed search: one solution leads to another, better developed solution, until one that satisfies all the goals and abides by all the constraints has been reached. It is likely, of course, that a given line of development will lead to more than one solution, or to a dead

Introduction

end. In the first case, one of the candidate solutions must be chosen for further development. In the second case, the designer must backtrack and start again (fig. 1.9). This process is demonstrated by the common Tangram puzzle depicted in figure 1.10: putting the pieces back into the box they came from entails placing piece after piece in the box, gradually "developing" a solution through trial and error.

Search processes are so common in solving problems that they have received special attention in the field of artificial intelligence, a branch of computer science that has devoted considerable energy to the study of search methods,[14] including:

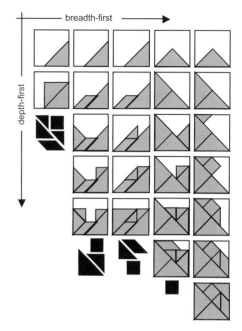

1.10 Backtracking is a common feature of search processes, as demonstrated by the task of fitting the seven pieces of the Tangram puzzle into a square box.

- *Depth first.* In this method a promising candidate solution is explored to its logical conclusion (either it meets the goals, or it fails) before another candidate solution is examined (demonstrated in fig. 1.10 when reading it top-to-bottom, left-to-right).
- *Breadth first.* In this method several alternative ways to develop a candidate solution are explored before any one of them is taken to its logical conclusion (demonstrated in fig. 1.10 when reading it left-to-right, top-to-bottom).
- *Best first.* In this method all currently available candidate solutions are evaluated, and the one which appears most promising is chosen for further development.

Architectural design typically uses a combination of search methods. Designers use whichever methods seems most prudent at any time, often without being cognizant of whether it is "depth first," "breadth first," or otherwise. They follow the path outlined by the solution that is currently under consideration or put it aside to explore possibilities offered by other candidate solutions, only to come back to the first one when it appears to hold more promise than later solution.

Constraint Satisfaction

The conceptual and technical difficulties associated with generating and examining a large pool of candidate solutions to find one that meets the goals and abides by the constraints of the problem have led designers to develop a different method: instead of searching the solution space for the

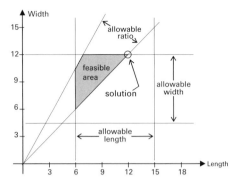

1.11 Finding the maximal dimensions of a rectangular room subject to given constraints. (Adapted from W. J. Mitchell, *Computer-Aided Architectural Design* [New York: Petrocelli/Charter, 1977].)

solution to a problem, they look for a solution to the problem.[15] This can be accomplished by reducing the size of the solution space by adding constraints until all but a few or perhaps only one solution remains, making the selection of the satisfactory solution trivial.[16]

This method, called constraint satisfaction, is derived from a branch of mathematics known as linear programming, which was developed during World War II to deal with logistical problems involving multiple variables and constraints.[17]

Consider, for example, the simple problem of determining the maximal dimensions of a rectangular room, subject to the following constraints:[18]

1. Its width W must be not less than 4.5 meters and not more than 12 meters.
2. Its length L must be not less than 6 meters and not more than 15 meters.
3. The proportions of the room L/W must be in the range of 0.8 to 1.0.

The problem can be represented in graphical form as depicted in figure 1.11, where the area defined by the constraints represents the feasible solutions. The desired solution is for the longest length and width of the room, delivering the maximal area, subject to the constraints.

The problem could still be solved if we removed some of the constraints, say the minimal length and width requirements, or the ratio requirement. However, if we remove too many constraints, or some critical ones, the problem becomes underconstrained: the number of solutions to choose from will be too large. Likewise, if we added more constraints, or if the existing constraints conflicted with one another, the problem becomes overconstrained: there will be no solution that can satisfy all the constraints. If the constraints leave exactly one solution to the problem (as is typical in solving mathematical problems), then the problem is said to be uniquely constrained.

Most design problems are underconstrained as formulated by the clients who commission them. Designers, therefore, must impose upon them additional constraints to make the selection process more tractable. Such constraints may include abstract aspirations, such as aesthetics, political or social messages; or they can be concrete, such as using a regular grid or a particular structural system. The systematic addition of constraints and the assignment of values to initially undefined design parameters gradually reduces the size of the solution space and guides the process toward a particular solution. The addition of new constraints may, however, unintentionally affect other design parameters through constraint relationships and, therefore, require retesting solutions that have previously been deemed satisfactory. The constraint satisfaction approach thus incorporates problem-solving-like, goal-directed search, as well as puzzle-making-like addition of new constraints as insight is developed during the search process.

Rule-Based Design

The oldest recorded design method can be found in Marcus Vitruvius Pollio's *De architectura* (known as his *Ten Books on Architecture*), written during the reign of the Roman emperor Augustus (first century BC). Using a narrative style and no drawings, Vitruvius provided "recipes," or rules, for all aspects of Roman design, including architecture, engineering, and city planning. For example, his recipe for designing the walls of a city is:

> From the exterior face of the wall, towers must be projected, from which an approaching enemy may be annoyed by weapons, from the embrasures of those towers, right and left. An easy approach to the walls must be provided against: indeed they should be surrounded by uneven ground, and the roads leading to the gates should be winding and turn to the left from the gates. By this arrangement, the right sides of the attacking troops, which are not covered by their shields, will be open to the weapons of the besieged. The plan of a city should not be square, nor formed with acute angles, but polygonal; so that the motions of the enemy may be open to observation. A city whose plan is acute-angled, is with difficulty defended; for such a form protects the attacker more than the attacked.[19]

Vitruvius's treatise greatly influenced Renaissance architects, whose new status as professional designers, rather than builders, required them to develop or adopt some kind of a design method to stay ahead of their clients and be informed of all matters that might require their professional intervention. As a first step they translated and adopted Vitruvius's *De*

1.12 Vignola prescribed, in great detail, how to construct columns of each of the five major Roman orders (1562).

architectura, which they then expanded and improved upon, while continuing to use his rulelike style. Architects like Leon Battista Alberti, Sebastiano Serlio, Andrea Palladio, and Giacomo Barozzi da Vignola developed their own rule-based design methods. For example, in his 1562 treatise on the five orders of architecture, Vignola formulated—in minute detail—rules of proportion for the classical orders appearing in Roman buildings (fig. 1.12).[20]

Indeed, rule-based methods are one of the most popular—and effective—ways to instruct (and learn) how to complete a task, as evidenced by the modern proliferation of cookbooks and how-to manuals. This method often (although not always) dispenses with the rationale underlying the rules in favor of presenting in a concise, stepwise manner the process of effectively accomplishing some task. Since rules can be used to capture any well-known process, they have become the method of choice for programming computers, instructing them how to accomplish given tasks, as is discussed in chapter 3.

It is, however, their deterministic, unequivocal nature that also makes rule-based design methods questionable. Design, as discussed earlier, is not a well-understood process, and therefore encapsulating it in deterministic rules is, at the very least, rather ambitious. Moreover, any set of rules necessarily also encapsulates its author's views, biases, and convictions, without allowing any room for argumentation or dissent. For example, in their well-known book *A Pattern Language*, Christopher Alexander and his coauthors prescribe a four-story limit to the height of buildings, offering the following explanation:

> High buildings have no genuine advantages, except in speculative gains for banks and land owners. They are not cheaper, they do not help create open space, they destroy townscape, they destroy social life, they promote crime, they make life difficult for children, they are expensive to maintain, they wreck the open spaces near them, and they damage light and air and view. But quite apart from all this, which shows that they aren't very sensible, empirical evidence shows that they can actually damage people's minds and feelings.[21]

Rule-based design thus derives its authority from the reputation of its author, which the disciples acknowledge and accept.

Case-Based Design

Given that many design problems must meet similar goals (e.g., provide shelter, a place to educate students, heal the sick, and so on), it is natural that the solutions that meet them are similar too. While the particulars of a solution may vary due to specific needs, site conditions, and other variables, the overall structure and the components are largely the same. This phenomenon, which is not unique to architectural design, gives rise to an important design method—precedent-based design.

In architecture, law, medicine, business, and engineering, past experiences—encapsulated in the form of "cases"—provide a rich, empirically validated host of "canned" solutions to complex problems. If the new problem facing the designer, the lawyer, or the physician is similar to a problem that has been faced in the past, there is a good chance that it might be solved by similar means. In jurisprudence, precedents have become known as case law, which legally obligates judges facing similar cases to deal with them in the same manner the precedents were dealt with. In other professions past experiences have not attained quite such a binding status, but they do, nevertheless, constitute an important part of the curriculum of professional schools and practices. In architecture we often refer to the work of the great masters, such as Mies van der Rohe, Louis Kahn, Le Corbusier, and Frank Lloyd Wright. Professional journals are devoted, by and large, to disseminating new "cases," and in design studios students are exposed to specifically tailored cases of design, intended to build up the knowledge base on which they will draw when they become practicing architects.

Practically any experience—directly observed or learned through professional education—can become a case, which can be reused in other circumstances. The application of a case to solving a particular design problem, however, depends on the relevance of the situation from which the case was derived to the current situation. Their degree of similarity characterizes cases as prototypes, precedents, analogies, symbols, or metaphors—each category further removed from the particulars of a specific design situation.

Prototypes are the most common formalism used to capture and apply architectural cases. They are generalized groupings of elements in particular design domains, including prerequisites, sets of elements (syntax), knowledge about these elements (semantics), relationships among the elements, and, in some cases, parameterized design descriptions, or description generators.[22] For example, a bathroom can be prototyped as having a core that includes a bathtub, one or more sinks, a toilet, and possibly a bidet, with certain desired adjacency relationships among them, certain minimal size requirements, and a choice of styles, materials, and finishes. To use a prototype the architect must first identify the proper characteristics of the problem at hand, then select a prototype that has similar characteristics. The prototype can then be "instantiated," a process that applies it to the particular circumstances of the present problem by copying its general features while modifying its less important ones. Thus, for example, the bathroom prototype can be instantiated into a particular house by identifying the cardinal dimensions, orientations, and accessibilities of the specific room, and furnishing it according to principles derived from the prototype.

The use of prototypes in design is predicated on the similarity between the present design problem and the one encountered previously. Such similarity, of course, is often hard to find, because every design problem is different from all other problems, due to the unique spatiotemporal and social contexts in which it takes place. Hence, the conditions for selecting a prototype must often be relaxed to admit cases that might not be considered prototypical yet bear enough similarity to the present problem to provide useful information.

Such cases might be considered precedents. Precedents are themselves embedded in the particular, often nonsimilar, spatiotemporal contexts that shaped them and are essential for their interpretation. The use of precedents in design leaves more room than prototypes for interpretation by the architect, who must choose the characteristics that are similar to the present problem while ignoring those that are not. For example, the Greek temple has been used as precedent for many secular buildings, imparting to them grandeur without the original religious connotations. The very richness of precedents may hinder their reuse in new design contexts. Therefore, the application of knowledge derived from precedents in the design process is indirect: precedents serve to stimulate the creation of new ideas rather than to dictate them.

As the design case used for knowledge transfer becomes further removed from the present problem, its application becomes less certain of reaching desirable results. This is the case when using analogies, symbols, and metaphors, each representing cases of progressively lesser direct relevance to the problem at hand, yet still yielding enough useful information to make them viable.

Much like other design methods, the use of prototypes, precedents, and metaphors is intended to provide the designer with a starting point from which to develop the new design. Each design method uses a different approach to accomplishing this task, whose purpose is to bridge the gap between the three main components of the design process: the analysis of the problem, from which design goals and constraints can be developed; the synthesis of design solutions; and their evaluation vis-à-vis the goals and constraints.

Bibliography

Akin, Ö. "How Do Architects Design?" In *Artificial Intelligence and Pattern Recognition in Computer Aided Design,* ed. J. C. Latombe. New York: IFIP, North Holland, 1978.

Aksoylu, Y. "Two Different Systematic Approaches to Design." Technical Report, University of California, Berkeley, 1982.

Archea, J. "Puzzle-Making: What Architects Do When No One Is Looking." In *Computability of Design,* ed. Y. E. Kalay, 37–52. New York: Wiley Interscience, 1987.

Archer, B. "The Structure of the Design Process." In *Emerging Methods in Environmental Design and Planning,* ed. Gary T. Moore, 285–307. Cambridge: MIT Press, 1968.

Bijl, A. "An Approach to Design Theory." In *Design Theory in CAD,* ed. H. Yoshikawa and E. A. Warman, 3–31. Amsterdam: North Holland, 1987.

Broadbent, G. *Design in Architecture.* London: John Wiley and Sons, 1981.

Cross, N., H. Christiaans, and K. Dorst. *Analyzing Design Activity.* Chichester: John Wiley and Sons, 1996.

Dorst, K., and J. Dijkhuis. "Comparing Paradigms for Describing Design Activity." *Design Studies* 16 (1995): 261–274.

Gregory, S. A. *The Design Method.* London: Butterworths, 1966.

Newell, A., and H. A. Simon. *Human Problem Solving.* Englewood Cliffs, N.J.: Prentice-Hall, 1972.

Venturi, R., D. Scott Brown, and S. Izenour. *Learning from Las Vegas.* Cambridge: MIT Press, 1972.

Zeisel, J. *Inquiry by Design.* Cambridge: Cambridge University Press, 1984.

Computing 2

Computing devices—machines that can aid in making calculations and manipulating information—were developed as early as civilization organized itself into permanent, agriculture-based settlements, with a need to keep track of different quantities of property (parcels of land, crops, animals, slaves, and so forth). Clay counting tokens, whose shape and markings designated a certain quantity of a particular commodity, have been found in Israel, Syria, Turkey, Iraq, and Iran at sites of the Neolithic age. Dating back some 9,000 years, they predate the invention of writing by about 3,000 years.[1] They were replaced by more reliable accounting tools—such as the abacus—about 4,000 years later. It took nearly another 4,500 years before the first mechanical calculator—Blaise Pascal's Pascaline—was invented, in the seventeenth century. From then on, new computing devices were invented and improved in rapid order, responding to the growing needs for calculation to aid navigation, warfare, economics, and information management.

The engineering breakthrough that led to the development of the modern digital computer was the brainchild of Charles Babbage, an English mathematician, who in 1822 proposed to build a steam-powered machine the size of a locomotive to aid in the production of arithmetic tables for the Royal Navy. Babbage's Difference Engine—which was never completed—was superseded by his Analytical Engine (which also was never completed)—a more powerful and more general version of the Difference Engine. Its design, requiring over 50,000 parts, would have allowed the machine to receive its instructions (the "program") in the form of perforated cards, perform calculations in its "mill" (the equivalent to modern computers' CPU), and print the results automatically.

Modern computers were developed in Germany during World War II by Conrad Zuse, who built an electromechanical computer called Z3; at Harvard University by Howard H. Aiken (in cooperation with IBM), who developed the electromechanical Mark-1; and at the University of

2.1 ENIAC, the first vacuum tube computer, developed by Eckert and Mauchly at the Moore School of Engineering, University of Pennsylvania (1945).

Pennsylvania Moore School of Engineering by J. Presper Eckert and John W. Mauchly, who developed ENIAC—the first vacuum-tube computer (fig. 2.1).

Since then, at least four "generations" of progressively more capable computing devices have been developed, differentiated mostly by their underlying technology. Most of them were based on similar principles, outlined by the Princeton mathematician John von Neumann in the 1940s: a set of instructions—called a program—applied one at a time (though increasingly more rapidly) to a data set that is stored separately from the instructions themselves. By changing the program, the same device can perform different tasks, making it a "universal" machine.

2.1 The History of Modern Computing

Modern computing thus began during World War II, when great needs produced many technological innovations, including the radar and the atomic bomb. Originally meant to help the military break enemy codes and to calculate artillery firing tables, computers were drafted into the service of economic, social, political, and scientific needs at the end of hostilities. The first among them was the U.S. Census Bureau's need to tabulate

Introduction

the results of the 1950 census before the 1960 census came around. It relied on the Universal Automatic Computer (UNIVAC), designed by Eckert and Mauchly's Computer Corporation (which they founded after leaving the University of Pennsylvania) but built and delivered by the Remington Rand Corporation, after Eckert and Mauchly's company folded.

UNIVAC was the first general-purpose electronic digital computer designed for commercial use. It was built of 5,600 vacuum tubes, 18,000 crystal diodes, and 300 relays; it operated at a 2.25 MHz bit rate and had an internal storage capacity of 12,000 characters (12K). It measured twenty-five by fifty feet and had to be housed in an air-conditioned space. A total of forty-six machines were built, at a cost of $1 million each (fig. 2.2).[2]

First-Generation Computers (1946–1959)

The UNIVAC is considered to be a first-generation computer, characterized by vacuum tubes and made-to-order operating instructions, written in a language developed specifically for the purposes of one particular machine (so-called machine language). Vacuum tubes accounted for the machine's colossal size, enormous power consumption (up to 160 megawatts—enough to power 16,000 homes), and slow speed. Writing instructions in machine language was a tedious and error-prone task, making the machine difficult to program and of limited versatility.

2.2 UNIVAC, the first commercially available computer, built in 1951–1952.

2.3 IBM 650—the best-selling
first-generation computer,
introduced in 1955.

The commercial benefits of first-generation computers, and especially UNIVAC's success in predicting the results of the 1952 U.S. presidential elections (which Dwight Eisenhower unexpectedly won in a landslide), helped to convince the business community of the usefulness of computers and created a demand that surprised even the few companies that produced them.[3]

UNIVAC was delivered on June 14, 1951. It was followed by the CADAC, produced by Consolidated Engineering Corporation (which was later absorbed by NCR); the Datatron, produced by ElectroData Corporation (which was absorbed by the Burroughs Corporation); and IBM's 650 (fig. 2.3), which became the most widely used of all first-generation computers (several hundred machines were delivered between 1955 and 1959). Its success owed as much to the machine's technical abilities as it did to IBM's marketing skills, capitalizing on its customers' familiarity with existing punch-card systems, which IBM has been marketing since 1924.

Second-Generation Computers (1959–1963)

The second generation of computers, much like the first, was prompted by military needs, coupled with a major technical breakthrough. The need was the Cold War, which put pressure on the USA to develop nuclear weapons and the means to deliver them, especially after the Soviet Union demonstrated its technical prowess by putting into orbit the first artificial satellite, Sputnik, on October 4, 1957. The technical breakthrough was the invention of the transistor at Bell Labs by physicists William B. Shockley, Walter H. Brattain, and John Bardeen, on December 23, 1947.

Consisting of solid-state materials (mostly silicon), whose conductivity could be changed by inducing a control current (hence the term semiconductor), transistors performed the same function as the large, heat-emitting, power-hungry, and slow vacuum tubes. They found their first uses in televisions and radios, but by 1959 they also became the primary component of computers, making computes smaller while boosting their speed and reliability.

The second generation of computers is also characterized by advances in magnetic-core memory and the invention of higher-level programming languages like COBOL and FORTRAN, which made writing instructions for computers much easier than in first-generation machine language.

Second-generation computers were smaller, faster, more reliable, and more energy-efficient than their predecessors. Although they found their first uses in a few large-scale machines (supercomputers), which were developed explicitly for atomic energy research (Philco's TRANSAC S-2000, IBM's STRETCH, and Sperry-Rand's LARC), by the mid-1960s most large businesses routinely processed financial information using second-generation computers. Companies like Burroughs, Control Data, Honeywell, IBM, NCR, RCA, Sperry-Rand, and others were developing new hardware and software for business, engineering, and other uses. A new industry was born, along with new careers (programmer, analyst, and computer systems expert).

Third-Generation Computers (1964–1975)

The major technical advancement that differentiates third-generation computers from their predecessors was the invention of the monolithic integrated circuit (IC), by Texas Instruments engineer Jack Kilby, on July 24, 1958. The IC combined resistors, capacitors, and transistors in one block ("chip") of semiconductor material.

By 1959 Kilby's invention was improved upon by Jean Hoerni and Robert Noyce at Fairchild Corporation, who developed a silicon structure that replaced the gold wires used by Kilby to connect the components (fig. 2.4). Their invention, which won them the Nobel Prize in physics in 2000,

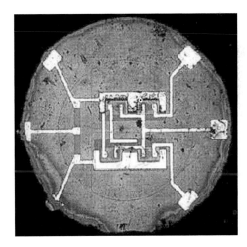

2.4 The first integrated circuit (a resistor-transistor logic product) available as a monolithic chip, developed by Jean Hoerni and Robert Noyce at Fairchild Semiconductor International in 1959. (Courtesy of Fairchild Semiconductor International.)

set the stage for complex integrated circuits and the processes used today to manufacture them. Integrated circuits allowed large-scale integration (LSI), a process that used photolithographic methods of manufacturing; no longer was it necessary to solder individual components on a circuit board one at a time. LSI made the components smaller, therefore consuming less power and emitting less heat. This allowed for packing more components on each chip, and made computers faster and more powerful. It also made the manufacturing process much cheaper and the computers themselves more robust, thus availing them to a broader market.

The most significant computer that took advantage of the new technology was IBM's 360, introduced on April 7, 1964. It used eight-bit "words" to represent characters and nine-track tapes and removable disk packs for information storage—features that were adopted by many other systems. It also introduced *time-sharing*: the ability to run many programs, by different users, on the same machine at the same time, where each program was given a small slice of the computer's processing power in small time intervals. Many thousands of the Model 360 were sold to businesses and universities, further increasing the demand for computing in many fields that henceforth did not use computers.

The growing demand for computing power spurred the development and marketing of minicomputers, which were not as powerful as their larger cousins but consumed much less space, were much more affordable, and could be operated by personnel who were not dedicated computer technicians, thus making them accessible to small firms—including architectural offices. The most successful among the minicomputers was the PDP series, introduced in 1970 by Digital Equipment Corporation (DEC). They marked the beginning of *distributed computing*—where a company or a university could afford to have many smaller computers in lieu of one big computer, each dedicated to the tasks of and operated by one group of researchers or office workers, instead of the "priesthood" of a central computing center.

Modern Computers (1975–present)

The concept of computer generations does not extend beyond the third generation, since there is no generally accepted definition of fourth-generation computers. Rather, computers produced since the late 1970s are known as modern. Their major distinguishing characteristic has been very large scale integration (VLSI)—packing hundreds of thousand, even millions of components onto a single chip. This technology allowed Intel Corporation and others (Motorola, AMD, Zilog) to develop an entire microprocessor—a whole computer, including its central processing unit (CPU), memory, and input/output controllers—on a single chip. Because the design of VLSI chips is expensive, they must be produced in large quantities to be cost effective. Large quantities make individual processors relatively cheap, allowing the trend of distributed computing, which was started by third-generation minicomputers, to continue to its logical conclusion—the development of personal computers.

Among the first VLSI chips was Intel's 4004, a 4-bit processor of limited power that was meant to power calculators. In March 1972 Intel introduced an 8-bit version of the chip, the 8008, which was adequate to power stand-alone computers. A few computers were designed around this chip, including the French Micral and the American Scelbi.

The introduction of Intel's 8080 chip in 1974, with an enhanced 8-bit processor that operated at a speed of 2 MHz and was able to address 64K of memory, opened the doors to the design of true stand-alone microcomputers. The first among them was the Altair 8800 (fig. 2.5a), developed by Edward Robert and his Micro Instrumentation and Telemetry Systems Corporation (MITS) of Albuquerque, New Mexico. It was sold in kit form for $395, mainly to hobbyists. Similar computers followed, like the IMSAI, Commodore Pet, the TRS 80, and the Apple I and II.

The success of personal computers, especially the Apple II, which was introduced in 1977 (fig. 2.5b), was due to their usefulness in accomplishing everyday tasks, like word processing and accounting—and game playing. The introduction of IBM's personal computer (PC) in 1982, based on Intel's 8088 chip, literally put the power of computers in the hands of nontechnical individuals and made PCs an indispensable appliance for office work and, later, home use (fig. 2.5c).

The advent of personal computer hardware was accompanied by an explosive growth in the writing of software that made them useful. First among them was the programming language BASIC, developed by John Kemeny and Thomas Kurtz at Dartmouth College in the mid-1960s and adapted by Paul Allen and Bill Gates to run on the Altair 8800 in 1974. It was followed by Microsoft's adaptation of the programming language

a

b

c

2.5 Early personal computers: (a) Altair 8800, (b) Apple II, (c) IBM PC.

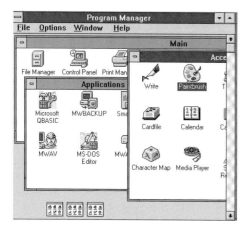

2.6 Windows 3.0, the first successful version of Microsoft's best-selling operating system.

FORTRAN; UCSD's Pascal; MicroPro's word processing software WordStar; Ashton-Tate's database software dBase; and other programs that ran on an operating system developed by Gary Kildall for microcomputers, called PC/M-80. QDOS (Quick and Dirty Operating System) was developed by Seattle Computer Products in early 1979 to support the newly introduced Intel 8086 chip. It was licensed by Microsoft and developed into the MS-DOS operating system that has powered most personal computers well into 2002.

The introduction of personal computers by a major corporation like IBM "legitimized" their use for business applications and triggered a demand that was quickly filled by clones of the IBM PC, making personal computers even more affordable. The number of personal computers in use more than doubled from 2 million in 1981 to 5.5 million in 1982. By 1992 an estimated 65 million PCs were in use. Computers continued to be downsized, from desktops to laptops to palmtops. In 1984 Apple Computer introduced its Macintosh line, popularizing the graphical user interface (which was invented by Xerox PARC in 1972 for use in their Alto computer). This user-friendly design offered an operating system that allowed users to manipulate the computer by using a mouse instead of typing arcane command lines. It was adopted by Microsoft in the form of its Windows operating system. Since the introduction of Windows 3.0 in 1991—its first successful version—it has become the standard for all human-computer interface designs (fig. 2.6).

The World Wide Web

The proliferation of personal computers had the unintended side effect of isolating users from one another. In contrast, earlier-generation computers connected users who shared the same machine. This separation was particularly bothersome to scientists and business people, who had become accustomed to the convenience and added productivity of being able to share files and communicate through their computer terminals.

Efforts to develop communication networks that would connect computers started in 1973, funded by the U.S. Defense Advanced Research Projects Agency (DARPA). Called the Internetting Project, its objective was to develop communication protocols that would allow networked computers to communicate transparently across multiple, linked networks. The system of networks that emerged from this research was known as the Internet, and the protocols that supported it became known as the TCP/IP Protocol Suite, named after the two initial protocols that were developed to support it: Transmission Control Protocol (TCP) and Internet Protocol (IP). In 1986 the U.S. National Science Foundation (NSF) initiated the development of the NSFNET, which today provides a major backbone communication service for the Internet.

Since the Internet was originally part of a federally funded research program, it was used almost exclusively by scientists and government agencies, and has, subsequently, become a major part of the U.S. research infrastructure. During the late 1980s, however, the population of Internet users and network constituents expanded internationally and began to include commercial facilities. By the end of 1991 the Internet had grown to include some 5,000 networks in over three dozen countries, serving over 700,000 host computers used by more than 4,000,000 people (fig. 2.7). But it was still a text-only network, used to transmit files and facilitate e-mail.

The World Wide Web was conceived in 1989 by Tim Berners-Lee and his colleagues at CERN (now called the European Laboratory for Particle Physics), in Geneva, Switzerland. The initial work centered on the development of a shared information space to support collaborative work, including the sharing of image data. Berners-Lee defined the HyperText Transmission Protocol (HTTP)—a network protocol for requesting and transmitting files and documents that Web servers and browsers can understand—and HTML (Hyper-Text Markup Language) for writing the shared documents themselves. By December 1990 CERN had developed a Web server and a text-based browser for NExTStep computers. In January 1992 an updated version of the browser (version 1.1) was made freely available on the Internet. By January 1993 there were fifty Web servers in existence and freely available graphical browser software had been made available for the Apple Macintosh. By February 1993 the Web was accounting for 0.1 percent of all Internet traffic.

The main factor in the rapid acceptance and growth of the Web was the work done by Marc Andreessen and his colleagues at the National Center for Supercomputer Applications (NCSA) at the University of Illinois in Urbana-Champaign. Their software development group created a graphical Web browser, called Mosaic. In September 1993 they released

2.7 A visualization of inbound traffic, measured in billions of bytes, on the NSFNET T1 backbone, September 1991. (Courtesy of Donna Cox and Robert Patterson, National Center of Supercomputing Applications, University of Illinois.)

versions of this software for Microsoft Windows running on PCs, Apple Macintosh, and Unix computers running X Windows. Each of the versions handled files in a very similar manner, with images and text interspersed in the same document, allowing organizations to create visually exciting documents that could be viewed in very similar formats on the three main types of computers in use at that time.

In 1994 Marc Andreessen cofounded Netscape Communications Corporation, the company that developed the Netscape Navigator, a Web browser that quickly became the de facto standard for Web communication. In addition, they developed methods of file transmission details, such as credit card numbers, which would lead to a rapid growth in using the Web for electronic commercial transactions.

Microsoft Corporation introduced its own Web browser, Internet Explorer, in 1995, which competed head to head with Netscape's Navigator. With the release of Internet Explorer 5.0 in 1998, Netscape's Navigator was displaced as the dominant Web browser, a result of aggressive marketing by Microsoft combined with technical improvements.

The development of the Internet, and even more so the development of the World Wide Web, have changed the concept of computers from machines that *calculate* to machines that *communicate*. Communication occurs between people and other people and between people and data. The majority of the applications that are being developed and used now are geared to facilitate these two types of computer-assisted communication, with a growing trend to merge the two by providing software that helps several people access and work collaboratively on the same data.

2.2 Hardware

The digital computer is a machine that processes information it is given as input, according to a given set of instructions, and produces the results in the form of text, images, sounds, or motion. The two major characteristics that make computers different from other machines are automation and general-purposeness.

Automation implies that, once started on some task, the machine can operate without human intervention until the task is complete. The instructions on how to carry out the task are stored within the machine itself and are performed sequentially until the task is done. In contrast, a

Introduction

handheld calculator needs a user to initiate each individual arithmetic operation by pressing a key. Automation allows computers to operate at very high speeds, unlike machines that require human intervention.

Computers are general-purpose machines: they can perform any task for which there exists an appropriate set of instructions (a program). Thus the same machine can be used to calculate payroll, type letters, draw pictures, play music, and perform scientific and engineering calculations. By comparison, single-purpose machines, like automobiles and televisions, are designed to perform one task only: the results of that task (the destination of the automobile or the show displayed on the TV screen) may be different from occasion to occasion, but their differences are due to differences in the input, not the actions of the machine itself.

A digital computer consists of six main logical components (fig. 2.8):

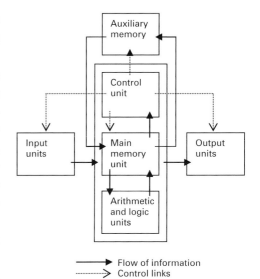

2.8 General structure of a digital computer. (After A. Ralston and E. D. Reilly, *Encyclopedia of Computer Science and Engineering* [New York: Van Nostrand Reinhold, 1983].)

- *Input units.* These are the conduit through which information and instructions are communicated to the computer. Input units are keyboards, mice, touch screens, joysticks, microphones, and so forth.
- *Control unit.* The control unit interprets the instructions received from the input units and refers them to the proper units for execution (e.g., addition, storage, display). It does so by means of built-in microprograms, or instruction sets, which define the characteristics of the computer: some computers use a relatively small set of complex instructions and are referred to as CISCs (complex instruction set computers). Others have a large set of simple instructions and are referred to as RISCs (reduced instruction set computers).
- *Main memory unit.* Also known as random-access memory (RAM), the main memory unit is where the currently executing instructions and data are stored. It is a very fast memory, which is connected directly to the control unit and the arithmetic-logic unit.
- *Arithmetic-logic unit.* This unit performs the four arithmetic operations of addition, subtraction, multiplication, and division, as well as logical operations of comparing two numbers and determining if a number is positive or negative.
- *Output units.* Output units are the conduit through which the results of a computation are communicated to the outside world. Output units include video display terminals, speakers, plotters, printers, and robotic actuators.

- *Auxiliary memory units.* These are units where information can be stored for prolonged periods of time, even when the computer itself is not powered. Auxiliary memory is relatively slow, compared to the main memory, but much larger in capacity. Hard disks, floppy disks, CD-ROMs, DVDs, and magnetic tapes are auxiliary memory units.

The control unit, the main memory, and the arithmetic-logic unit are often bundled together and form the computer's central processing unit (CPU). The CPU also includes a clock, which synchronizes the operations of all the other units, and determines how fast the computer as a whole operates. The major components of the computer outside the CPU are connected through a data "bus," the pipeline that communicates data and instructions among them.

The physical implementation of these components keeps changing as new technologies are being developed. On the whole, they keep getting smaller, faster, and more capable, and their cost keeps shrinking (see part 5 for a more complete discussion of this trend).

Von Neumann Machines

The overall structure of virtually all modern digital computers is attributed to the Hungarian-born mathematician and physicist John von Neumann, who in a 1945 paper, titled "First Draft of a Report on the EDVAC," described the basic elements of cellular automata and the stored program concept. It established the notion, originally suggested by Charles Babbage for his Analytical Engine, that if the instructions (the "program") were stored in the computer's memory, rather than fed to it one at a time, their sequences of execution could be modified by the computer itself, based on other instructions and on the nature of the data being processed at the time. This would allow the computer to alter its own behavior as needed rather than be locked into performing an inflexible set of instructions that could only be modified through human intervention.

To facilitate such abilities, the von Neumann machine, as the architecture came to be known, would need to have random-access memory—a kind of memory comprised of individual memory "cells," each of which is designated by a unique numerical address that could be used to access or replace the contents of that cell in a single step. This random-access memory holds both the data that is being operated on and the instruction being executed at that moment. The CPU repeatedly goes through a fetch-execute cycle, comprising the following four steps (fig. 2.9):

1. Fetch an instruction from memory into the CPU's register (its local memory).
2. Fetch any data required by the instruction from memory into the CPU's register.
3. Execute the instruction (process the data).
4. Store the results in memory.

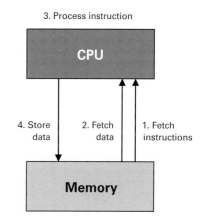

2.9 Schema of a von Neumann machine.

The von Neumann architecture can, in principle, solve any problems that can be stated in terms of an algorithm—a well-defined set of stepwise instructions (a "recipe") which, if carried out precisely, is guaranteed to deliver the answer to the problem, much as a recipe for baking a chocolate cake, if followed faithfully, will deliver the desired cake.

This very reliance on single-step processing of the data is also, however, the von Neumann architecture's major disadvantage, for two reasons:

1. The machine must be told in advance, and in great detail, the exact series of steps required to perform the task: if such an algorithm cannot be devised, as is the case for problems like evaluating the aesthetic appeal of a building, then a computer based on von Neumann's architecture cannot be used.
2. The speed of a computer based on the von Neumann architecture is necessarily limited, because it executes only one instruction at a time. Although tremendous advances have been made over the past five decades in developing faster and faster processors, and building them into bigger, faster computers—known as supercomputers—their speed is still linearly dependent on the complexity of the task: a task that requires twice as many instructions to complete as another task will take twice as long to execute (all other factors being equal).

Additionally, the von Neumann architecture is very susceptible to errors in data or the instruction set: "noisy" data can confuse the machine, and a single error in the instruction set will cause it to produce erroneous

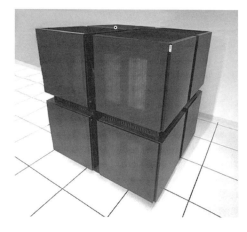

2.10 Thinking Machines' CM-2 massively parallel computer. (Photograph by Wade Sisler, NASA/Ames Research Center, California, 1990.)

results, or to crash (cease operating). These disadvantages of the von Neumann machine have prompted researchers to seek other computer architectures that are free from them.

Parallel Processing

The first obvious way to speed up the execution of any task is to break it up into many small pieces that can be executed in parallel. Highways, for example, consist of multiple lanes of traffic, so several cars can travel side by side rather than one after the other, thereby adding capacity to the throughput of the road. An auditorium or a stadium can be evacuated more rapidly, in case of an emergency, if people can use multiple exits rather than just one. Similarly, computational tasks such as the multiplication of two vectors or matrices—an operation used extensively in graphical applications—is an inherently parallel operation that could be significantly accelerated through parallel processing, yielding faster animations.

Executing more than one instruction at a time requires multiple processors working in concert. Parallel processing can only be applied to tasks that possess a sufficient degree of logical disconnectedness that they can be broken into tasks that can be operated on independently for some period of time. This kind of processing also requires an organizational structure that can synchronize the independent tasks and integrate their results into a composite whole.

The first requisite—having multiple processors—is a problem that has become easy to solve. The shrinking size and cost of computer chips has made the development of computers comprising hundreds, even thousands, of individual processors, a relatively simple task. Single machines made of hundreds of individual processors emerged in 1985, with the introduction of Massachusetts-based Thinking Machines Corporation's CM-1 Connection Machine, which was made of 65,536 individual 1-bit processors—the brainchild of Danny Hillis, conceived while he was a graduate student under Marvin Minsky at the MIT Artificial Intelligence Lab (fig. 2.10). It was followed in 1985 by Intel's iPS C/1 Hypercube, made of thirty-two processors, each an Intel 286 processor with 512KB of memory, Cray Research's T3D in 1993, and others. They were employed by large research organizations and government agencies in support of numerically intensive tasks, such as weather forecasting, nuclear engineering, and fluid-dynamics calculations. Smaller parallel computers were built for special purposes, such as IBM's Deep Blue (for playing chess) and SGI's Origin 2000 (for processing graphical information).

An alternative to these expensive, special-purpose machines has been to network together hundreds of small, relatively cheap computers that were not individually designed for parallel computing. This was the route taken by animation studios like Pixar (maker of such movies as *Jurassic Park* and *Toy Story*) and Industrial Light & Magic (*Star Wars* and *The Mummy*), who found that computing the thirty individual frames needed for each second of animation is a task that can be speeded up considerably by sending it to a "rendering farm"—a cluster of PC-class or workstation-class machines, managed by a central server. Similarly, a network of sixty Sun Microsystems' UltraSPARK workstations powers UC Berkeley's NOW-2 cluster, another network-based massively parallel computer.

The ultimate massively parallel computing effort is harnessing millions of home computers through the Internet, through such projects as UC Berkeley's SETI@home project, which "borrows" the idle computer time of millions of subscribers. By downloading and processing little packets of data, then uploading them back to a central server for integration with other such packets, they help search for evidence of extra terrestrial intelligence.

The major shortcomings of parallel processing are finding problems that are parallelizable then writing the programs to process them as such. Parallelizable problems are those that can be broken down into many autonomous units, whose solution does not depend on the solution of other units. While many such problems exist, it is often not easy to ascertain in advance that the units indeed are independent of each other. Moreover, writing programs that can process many independent units and integrate the results is much more difficult than writing single-stream programs—ones that process one instruction at a time.

Neural Network Computing

A different approach to parallel processing, which can circumvent the difficulties associated with programming parallelizable problems, was derived from the cognitive theory of connectionism—a theory that tries to explain

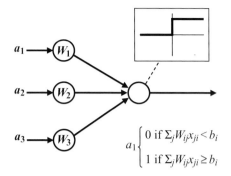

$$a_1 \begin{cases} 0 \text{ if } \Sigma_j W_{ij} x_{ji} < b_i \\ 1 \text{ if } \Sigma_j W_{ij} x_{ji} \geq b_i \end{cases}$$

2.11 A threshold logic unit (TLU) is a signal processor that integrates the weighted inputs and produces an output signal 1 if the result exceeds its threshold of activation b_i.

how complex behavior arises from the connection of many simple units.[4] The engineering version of this theory, whose origins are attributed to Aristotle, models computation after the human brain rather than mechanical symbol processing. It argues that the brain does not process information by executing explicit instructions one at a time or even many at a time. Rather, it behaves like a signal processor—a machine that compares input patterns to stored patterns and derives meaning from matched patterns. According to this approach, each individual signal is meaningless in and of itself (e.g., an individual photon of light striking the retina or an individual note picked up by the ear), as are the individual units that process that signal (the individual neurons in the brain). What matters are the patterns that collections of such signals make when they are picked up and processed by a network of connected processors.

In biological networks of processors (i.e., brains), each processing unit is represented by one neuron: a nerve cell that has the capacity to sense the presence of a neurotransmitting chemical at one of its ends and—if the intensity of the concentration of the chemical exceeds a certain (predetermined) threshold—to release neurotransmitting chemicals of its own at its other end. The neurotransmitting chemical—acetylcholine, dopamine, serotonin, histamine, epinephrine, and many others—acts as a signal that stimulates the cell to transmit a signal of its own. Because there are over 20 billion cells in the (human) brain, connected to one another through synapses, a stimulus generated by one cell can generate signals that are amplified and distributed, stimulating many cells, or it can decay and subside after a few steps. The route traveled by the stimulus and the cells it activates along the way are thought to be the locus of the human (and other animals') cognitive mechanism.

Artificial neural networks mimic this biological structure. Instead of neurons, they comprise threshold logic units (TLUs), and instead of chemical neurotransmitters they use electrical signals. TLUs (fig. 2.11), which were originally proposed by McCulloch and Pitts as early as 1943,[5] are signal processors that operate on the all-or-none principle: the signals a_j that appear at TLU_i input nodes are multiplied by some weights w_j, indicating the strength of each signal. The weighted signals are accumulated to produce an overall unit activation value a_i. If this value exceeds TLU_i threshold of activation b_i, the output signal equals 1, else it equals 0. The TLU's output signal is picked up by other TLUs it is connected to,

Introduction

where the process is repeated. Thus, the only processing that occurs within the TLU is filtering: signals are either allowed to proceed, or not. The signal itself has no meaning. The determination whether to transmit a signal (called "firing") or not is made by the weights each TLU assigns to incoming signals and its threshold of activation.

Although the structure of the network is fixed, the weights each TLU associates with incoming signals from its neighboring TLUs, and the threshold of its own activation, are variable. By setting the weights and threshold of each TLU to respond to one set of signals but not to another, the network as a whole performs signal, or pattern, recognition.

The weights and the thresholds need not be set manually, one TLU at a time. Rather, the network can be trained to recognize patterns by trial and error. During a training session, the network is presented with input/output pairs and put in a mode where it can modify the weights and the thresholds of its TLUs until the desired output matches the input. Once that state is achieved, the weights and the thresholds are locked, and the network is ready to process new patterns. If a new pattern triggers input signals that will filter through the network as trained, a match will be reported, otherwise the pattern will go unrecognized.

Such programming by training avoids the need to describe explicitly the relationship between input patterns and output values. This is especially useful when the relationship is difficult to explicate, as in the case of recognizing handwriting, speech, and, to a limited extent, even aesthetic values. A neural network could be shown examples of "beautiful" buildings and be expected to infer from these examples what we mean by "beauty," or similar nonquantifiable characteristics of a building (chapter 20 discusses this subject in more detail). Needless to say, the network does not "understand" what it does. Nor does it understand the concept of beauty or anything else for that matter: it simply applies the pattern recognition it has been trained to perform, matching an output pattern to some input. Any interpretation regarding the "meaning" of the match is purely artificial.

The pattern recognition knowledge is not stored in any one of the nodes of the network. Rather, it is stored in the network as a whole, in the form of weights and threshold values. Clearly, this style of processing is completely different from programming in the tradition of a von Neumann computer, where the pattern recognition algorithm would have to be programmed explicitly.

Another advantage of neural network computers is their robustness in the presence of "noise": small changes in an input signal will not drastically affect a node's output. Neural network computers are also robust in the presence of hardware failure: a change in a weight may only affect the output for a few of the possible input patterns. Clearly, however, such a processing model is not applicable to all problems, leaving a great need for von Neumann–type computers.

Bibliography

Dreyfus, H. L. *What Computers Still Can't Do.* Cambridge: MIT Press, 1992.

Feigenbaum, E. A., and P. McCorduck. *The Fifth Generation: Artificial Intelligence and Japan's Computer Challenge to the World.* Reading, Mass.: Addison-Wesley, 1983.

Freiberger, P., and M. Swaine. *Fire in the Valley.* New York: McGraw-Hill, 1984.

Gardner, H. *The Mind's New Science: A History of the Cognitive Revolution.* New York: Basic Books, 1985.

Hofstadter, D. R. *Gödel, Escher, Bach: An Eternal Golden Braid.* New York: Basic Books, 1979.

Ralston, A., and E. D. Reilly. *Encyclopedia of Computer Science and Engineering.* New York: Van Nostrand Reinhold, 1983.

Weizenbaum, J. *Computer Power and Human Reason: From Judgment to Calculation.* San Francisco: W. H. Freeman, 1976.

Weyhrich, S. "Apple II History." Ver. 2.0. <http://apple2history.org/history/ah01.html#99> (12 November 2001).

Wulf, A. W., M. Shaw, P. N. Hilfinger, and L. Flon. *Fundamental Structures of Computer Science.* Reading, Mass.: Addison-Wesley, 1981.

Introduction

Programming 3

The idea of separating the operating instructions from the machine these instructions control, thereby enabling the same machine to perform different tasks, was conceived by the French toy maker Jacques de Vaucanson in 1745. He used punched cards to control a mechanical flute playing machine, allowing it to play different tunes for each set of cards. The concept was improved and put to large-scale industrial use by Joseph-Marie Jacquard in 1801. He used punched cards to control the patterns woven by automatic looms, allowing production of intricate patterns that, until that time, could only be woven by hand. Charles Babbage adopted the idea in the 1830s to control his Analytical Engine. He enlisted the help of Ada Byron, Countess of Lovelace and Lord Byron's daughter, who worked out the instructions such cards needed to calculate Bernoulli numbers on Babbage's machine and who is considered, therefore, to be the first programmer.

Conrad Zuse's Z3 electromechanical computer used perforated film to store and control its operations in the late 1930s. In their design of ENIAC, the first electronic computer, Eckert and Mauchly reverted to hardwiring. To change its function their machine had to be literally rewired, a lengthy and cumbersome process during which time the $3 million machine sat idle.

John von Neumann's theoretical work helped Eckert and Mauchly design UNIVAC, the first commercial electronic computer, which use punched cards to store the programs it performed. But the instructions had to be written in machine language—a collection of alphabetic symbols and memory addresses that is specific to a particular computer. This made programming very difficult and error prone, and required rewriting the program for each new machine.

The growing need to write programs that would make computers useful led to the development of more capable, higher-level programming languages, which were closer to human language than to machine language. These programs also required the development of compilers and interpreters—programs that could translate the high-level programs into machine-understandable instructions (0s and 1s)—the only kind of instructions actually "understood" by the hardware.

The history of programming is synonymous with the quest to develop more efficient ways to instruct computers how to perform their tasks. Hundreds of programming languages have been developed, along with theories and methods that helped software engineers to design programs that would be effective, efficient, and most of all, correct. Collectively, these theories, methods, and practices have come be known as the discipline of computer science.

Computer science—originally a branch of mathematics—has devoted itself largely to developing methods that, much like architectural design methods, make the task of composing large instruction sets tractable, reliable, efficient, and effective. Unlike architectural design, the methods developed by computer scientists can be proved to produce correct or incorrect results, thanks to a theoretical model developed by the British mathematician Alan Turing in 1936.[1] Still, there is much in common between the development of computer programs and architectural design: both are scientifically based, yet their successful accomplishment is a matter of art.

3.1 Algorithms

The hardware of a digital computer is activated by a list of instructions—a program—which controls the different hardware components of the computer in a sequence specified by the programmer. Consider a simple computational task: adding a number stored in memory address A to the number stored in memory address B, then storing the result in memory address C. This can be written as the following program:

```
LOAD A
ADD B
STORE C
```

The first instruction, LOAD A, reads the content of a memory cell whose address is A and brings it into the computer's arithmetic-logic unit (ALU), overwriting any data previously stored there. The second instruction adds a number stored in memory address B to the current content of the ALU. The third instruction stores the sum held in the ALU into memory address C.

Note that the contents of memory addresses A and B are not mentioned explicitly in this program: they are considered to be the data on which this program operates. Hence, unlike a calculator—where the numbers punched in are part of the instruction set—this little program can add any two numbers—whichever numbers have been previously stored in memory locations A and B.

Such a generalized instruction set is known as an algorithm—a procedure for solving a given problem. The name is believed to be derived from the name of the Arab mathematician Mohammed ibn-Musa Al-Khowarizmi, who was part of the royal court in Baghdad from about 780 to 850, and whose work is considered to be the likely source for the word algebra as well.

The essence of programming can be demonstrated through a simple task like folding an origami paper duck (fig. 3.1): it is the ability to write a concise list of instructions that can be used on any set of (appropriate) data for the purpose of accomplishing some well-defined task. The task itself (folding the paper, in this case) must actually be solved before it is ever presented to the computer (or the novice paper folder, in this case) and must be written down (or illustrated) in the form of a concise, correct, and effective list of simple instructions. Writing programs thus requires expertise both in the domain of the problem itself and knowledge of effective ways to write and test the programs that encode the solution.

The task of finding an algorithm that can effectively solve a given problem has troubled mathematicians since the beginning of the twentieth century and led to the development of the theory of computability by Turing in 1936. Apart from the philosophical question of which problems lend themselves to mechanical (i.e., computational) solution, the difficulty involves finding the most effective algorithm to solve them. In general, an algorithm must fulfill five requirements:

- It must be unambiguous.
- It must be deterministic (i.e., produce the same results whenever it is applied to the same data).
- It must be finite (i.e., terminate after a reasonable amount of time).
- It must be simple (i.e., given in terms of elementary instructions).
- It must be effective (i.e., produce the desired results).

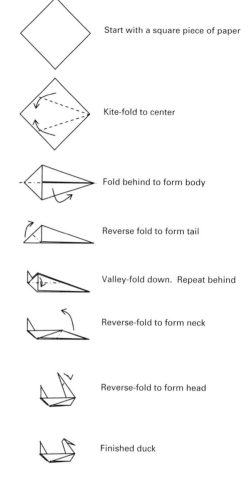

Start with a square piece of paper

Kite-fold to center

Fold behind to form body

Reverse fold to form tail

Valley-fold down. Repeat behind

Reverse-fold to form neck

Reverse-fold to form head

Finished duck

3.1 Algorithm for folding an origami paper duck.

Computer programs, unlike recipes in a cookbook, cannot rely on common sense or on knowledge outside the algorithm itself. Hence, the instructions must be unambiguous. Instructions such as "add a dash of salt" or "bake until golden brown"—which rely on the cook's familiarity with the art of cooking in general—are too ambiguous for computers.

Computer algorithms must terminate, or they will run forever in what is known as an infinite loop. This typically happens when the programmer fails to anticipate some conditions of the problem. For example, if the solution calls for repeating a calculation until some condition is satisfied (a so-called loop), yet that condition is never satisfied by some data set, the calculation will never terminate.

The instructions given to a computer cannot be complex, like "design a three-bedroom house." Rather, they must be spelled out in great detail, where every step of the solution can be executed without any further elaboration (e.g., the LOAD A and ADD B in the example above). For convenience, software engineers often develop their programs in modular, hierarchical way, where complex instructions are elaborated gradually through the use of subprograms called subroutines. They may also call upon commonly used instruction sets stored in software libraries, such as instructions for drawing doors or windows in an architectural drafting program. Still, the program as a whole must include the elaboration of all the instructions the computer is expected to perform.

Finally, and most importantly, the algorithm must accomplish the task it has been designed to accomplish and do so within a reasonable time frame, using reasonable computing resources. The search for ever more effective solutions to known problems is one of the driving forces of computer science.

3.2 Programming Languages

Once an algorithm for solving a problem has been developed, it must be translated into instructions that can be understood by the hardware. This translation process is called programming. It uses some artificial language, called a programming language, in which instructions are written in a manner that can be automatically translated into 0s and 1s.

Like natural languages, programming languages are comprised of symbols (syntax) and rules (grammar). For example, the program depicted in figure 3.2 instructs the computer to draw a rectangle. It is written in the programming language PASCAL and is augmented with a library of graphical subroutines that elaborate such instructions as READ_CURSOR_LOCATION; MOVE_TO; AND DRAW_TO.

Like many other programs, it begins with a header, which gives it a name that will enable the computer to find it, when so instructed, and tells the computer that the program will be using some input and output services.

The second line is the declarations section. It tells the computer to reserve memory space for four integers, which the program will be referring to by the names X1, Y1, X2, and Y2. This instruction also enlists the computer's help in assuring that the content of the reserved memory cells will be integer numbers rather than some random piece of data that might interfere with the proper execution of the program.

The set of instructions between the words BEGIN and END is called the main body of the program. It is here that the sequence of instructions needed to draw the rectangle is listed. The first two instructions tell the computer to read the two locations of the cursor, indicated by the user, that mark opposite endpoints of the rectangle. The next five instructions tell it to move to or draw to the four vertices of the rectangle, which are determined by the coordinates of the cursor.

The overall structure of the program, as well as the syntax and the grammatical rules it uses, is determined by the PASCAL programming language. For example, the semicolons at the ends of many instructions are mandatory: they separate one instruction from the next. Failing to include one of them will prevent the program from executing properly.

These instructions, as written by the programmer, constitute the source code of the program. Before the computer can execute them, they must first be translated into binary notation, called object code, comprised of 0s and 1s. Such translation is accomplished through another program—the compiler. It verifies that the instructions given in the program are grammatically (although not semantically) correct, that no variables are used that have not be reserved ("declared") ahead of time, and that all the instructions are well formed and correctly separated from each other. If they pass all the verifications, the compiler translates them into object code.

The object code can be executed by "running" it on the given hardware, at which time the user will be prompted to indicate two points on

```
PROGRAM  RECTANGLE  (INPUT,  OUTPUT);
VAR      X1,  Y1,  X2,  Y2:  INTEGER;
BEGIN
         READ_CURSOR_LOCATION  (X1,  Y1);
         READ_CURSOR_LOCATION  (X2,  Y2);
         MOVE_TO  (X1,  Y1);
         DRAW_TO  (X1,  Y2);
         DRAW_TO  (X2,  Y2);  DRAW_TO  (X2,  Y1);
         DRAW_TO  (X1,  Y1);
END.
```

3.2 PASCAL program to draw a rectangle.

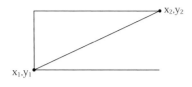

```
PROGRAM RECTANGLE (INPUT, OUTPUT);
VAR X1, Y1, X2, Y2: INTEGER;
BEGIN
    READ_CURSOR_LOCATION (X1,Y1);
    READ_CURSOR_LOCATION (X2,Y2);
    MOVE_TO (X1,Y1);
    DRAW_TO (X1,Y2);
    DRAW_TO (X2,Y2);
    DRAW_TO (X1,Y1);
END.
```

3.3 Transposing the last two DRAW_TO instructions causes a logical error in the program, which will fail to draw the desired rectangle.

the screen, and the computer will draw the rectangle that fits them—unless the programmer made a logical error in writing the program, which would result in either total failure ("crash") or unexpected results. For example, if the programmer has mistakenly transposed the last two DRAW_TO commands, the result will look like the one depicted in figure 3.3.

Writing a program, therefore, is a matter of considerable effort. First the problem needs to be solved, and a proper algorithm must be devised to capture the solution. Then it must be coded in some programming language, with proper attention to all the syntactical and grammatical rules of that language. It must then be compiled and executed, and the results must be carefully checked to see that they conform to the programmer's expectations. If there are errors in any one step of the process, all the steps from that point onward must be repeated, in what is called "debugging": getting rid of errors that prevent the successful completion of the task. It is a lengthy, often frustrating process, requiring considerable intellectual effort. Large programming tasks involve hundreds, even thousands of programmers, and take many years to complete.[2]

Procedural Programming Languages

The objective of programming languages is to support the (human) programmer in writing correct code for some task. Since the tasks vary, many different programming languages have been developed, each suited to support some tasks better than others.

The PASCAL programming language demonstrated earlier is typical of so-called procedural programming languages. These are languages where each action of the computer must be fully spelled out and in the correct sequence. Such languages began to be developed in the 1950s, when it became clear that programming in machine language was impractical.

The first true programming language was assembly language, which allowed for a more human-readable approach to writing programs than binary code. Assembly language is not a single language, but rather a group of languages: each processor family (and sometimes individual processors within a processor family) has its own assembly language. Despite its cumbersomeness compared to modern high-level programming languages, assembly language is still used where tight control is needed over the execution time and the resources used by the computer, such as in wrist watches, toasters, and other small appliances (although the Java programming language was originally conceived to explicitly support these tasks).

FORTRAN (Formula Translation) was developed for numerical analysis by John W. Backus at IBM in 1954. It was the first high-level language to be widely used, and allowed programmers to write algebraic expressions for arithmetic operations. Its major uses were for engineering and scientific applications. Since the principles on which many of the applications coded in FORTRAN never changed (e.g., structural engineering), and the cost of rewriting the programs is often prohibitively large, FORTRAN remains in use to this day, though it has been revised several times since it was first introduced.

COBOL (Common Business-Oriented Language) was developed in 1960 by the Conference on Data Systems and Languages (CODASYL)—a group of computer users and manufacturers joined with the U.S. Department of Defense. Its major use has been in the business community. It was the first language to attempt to use English-like syntax and was truly machine-independent.

ALGOL 60 (Algorithmic Language) was developed in 1960. It was the first block-structured language and introduced many modern programming concepts that remain at the root of many languages, including PL/1 and PASCAL.

BASIC (Beginner's All-Purpose Symbolic Instruction Code) is a general-purpose programming language developed by John G. Kemeny and Thomas E. Kurtz at Dartmouth College in the mid-1960s. It is one of the simplest high-level languages and can be learned with relative ease even by schoolchildren and novice programmers. Since about 1980, BASIC has become popular for use on personal computers. In the 1990s, Microsoft extended BASIC to include instructions that directly manipulate its popular Windows operating system environment. The new language is known as VISUAL BASIC, and has become one of the most widely used development languages for Windows-based applications.

APL (A Programming Language) was published in 1962 by Kenneth E. Iverson of IBM. It can handle general file formats and, consequently, has been adopted for business as well as for scientific programming. While a very capable language, it is very nonintuitive and requires an extra set of symbols not available on every keyboard.

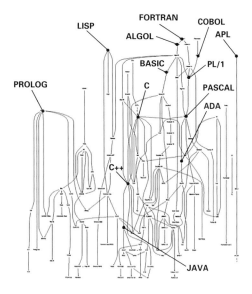

3.4 The history and evolution of programming languages. (Courtesy of GNU Free Documentation License, http://merd.net/pixel/language-study/diagram.html)

PASCAL was developed by Niklaus Wirth of the Federal Institute of Technology, Zurich, Switzerland, in the late 1960s. It was intended to be a good educational tool for the systematic teaching of programming and to have fast, reliable compilers. Since 1974 the PASCAL compiler that was developed by Wirth has been available to the public and has been used by many universities. PASCAL strongly influenced many languages developed later, including ADA.

ADA was developed in 1975 by the U.S. Department of Defense in an effort to provide a uniform programming language for all defense-related applications. While it is similar to PASCAL, it contains many additional features that are convenient for the development of large-scale programs. Its abundant features, however, can overwhelm ordinary programmers, precluding its widespread use for other than U.S. Department of Defense applications.

The programming language C was developed by Dennis M. Ritchie of AT&T Bell Laboratories in 1972. Although it is considered to be a high-level language, C has many low-level features, such as the ability to directly handle memory addresses and bits. It has become, therefore, the programming language of choice for "serious" applications (the operating system UNIX has been written almost exclusively in C).

Java, developed by James Gosling at Sun Microsystems in 1991, was intended to be a language used to program appliances like microwave ovens and toasters. Its small size and machine-independence made it the language of choice for programming Web applications that can deliver not only data over the Internet but also the instructions that manipulate the data.

Many other procedural programming languages have been developed over the years, borrowing concepts from one another while developing their own improvements. Most did not enjoy widespread use but were instrumental in helping other languages to develop (figure 3.4 shows the lineage of most programming languages).

Declarative Programming Languages

A different approach to programming was taken by the artificial intelligence community, whose applications did not lend themselves to the procedural approach used by other areas of computing. Instead, they needed

Introduction

a programming language that was adept at resolving statements concerning relationships among objects and drawing conclusions from those relationships.

For example, determining whether two persons, X and Y, are sisters depends on whether they are both female, and whether they have the same parents. This relationship can be represented in the form of rules and facts. The rules would be:

sisters (x, y):	*X and Y are sisters if*
female (x),	*X is female*
female (y),	*Y is female*
parents (x, m, f),	*M and F are X's parents*
parents (y, m, f).	*M and F are Y's parents*

And the facts might be:

female (jane).	*Jane is female*
female (mary).	*Mary is female*
parents (jane, john, carol).	*John and Carol are Jane's parents*
parents (mary, john, carol).	*John and Carol are Mary's parents*

The computer could then answer the question:

?- sisters (jane, mary).	*Are Jane and Mary sisters?*

Clearly, this example (written in PROLOG), shows a different approach to programming from the procedural approach discussed earlier: it does not spell out *how* to perform the computation, only *what* the facts and rules of some situation are. The computer is then able to substitute the facts in the appropriate rules, so it can answer questions on the subject matter.

Programming languages that facilitate this type of computation have been in use since the 1950s, starting with LISP (List Processor), developed by John McCarthy at MIT. It was followed by SNOBOL in 1962 (developed by D. J. Farber, R. E. Griswold, and F. P. Polensky at Bell Labs), PROLOG in 1971 (developed by Alain Colmerauer and Philippe Roussel at the University of Aix-Marseille), and many others.

They operate on the principle of unification, which is a generalization of pattern matching. The terms in a statement are compared and are deemed equal if they match. If they are comprised of other terms, the process repeats itself recursively until all the terms have been resolved. This approach has proved useful for problem domains dominated by rules and facts rather than procedures and where answers to questions involve descriptive measures, rather than calculations.

Object-Oriented Programming Languages

The notion underlying both procedural and descriptive programming languages is that the data constitutes a separate entity from the functions or the rules that operate on it: one piece of data can be operated on by many functions (or rules), and one function (or rule) can operate on many data items. A different approach was proposed by researchers in the 1980s, based on the observation that similar instructions often operate on similar data for the same purposes. They called this an object-oriented approach: data and the operators that manipulate it were "encapsulated" into a unified entity, called an object. This approach offers two advantages over procedural and descriptive programming—clarity and efficiency. Clarity is gained because all parts of a program that involve handling one kind of object are grouped together, making it easy to spot errors. Efficiency is gained by the ability to easily create new objects by copying similar ones and modifying only those attributes that are different. The new object would then "inherit" all the properties of the older object, except those explicitly modified by the new object.

For example, an electric motor is a complex "object," which consists of components (the rotor, the commutator, the coils, and other components) and actions (how it works, what it can do). The components and the actions are intimately linked to each other: the action of the motor could not be performed if the components where not there to support it, and at the same time the action gives a reason for the components to be included in the motor's package. The user of the motor—an electric fan manufacturer, for example—really need not know what goes on inside the electric motor, only its input requirements and its output characteristics. Packaging the components and actions of the motor into one object, with specified inputs and outputs, can save the electric fan manufacturer from having also to be in the business of electric motor manufacturing. He can switch to another electric motor manufacturer if it better matches his needs (e.g., price, performance, size, weight, and so on), without significantly affecting his own product (the fan). Likewise, the electric motor manufacturer need not know about fans and is free to design the motor as best fits her needs. Moreover, she could develop new motors based on the design of the old one, by copying most of the old motor and modifying only certain components.

Object-oriented programming has thus borrowed the principles of modular engineering—the hallmark of the Industrial Revolution. It attempts to transform the craftsmanship-like practice of software design into a more engineering-like practice: programs can be written at a fraction of the time of comparable procedural and descriptive programs by assembling discrete predefined, self-contained objects from libraries written by other programmers.

To support this approach, object-oriented programming languages (OOPL) had to be developed. SIMULA (developed by Ole-Johan Dahl and Kristen Nygaard of Norway in 1967) and SMALLTALK (developed by Alan Kay and Adele Goldberg of Xerox PARC in 1972) are examples of early object-oriented languages. Their demonstrated high productivity made OOPL extremely popular, prompting the adaptation of procedural languages like C and PASCAL to the object-oriented paradigm. C++ is an object-oriented version of C, developed by Bjarue Stroustrup of AT&T Bell Laboratories in the early 1980s. Objective-C is another object-oriented version of C, developed by Brad Cox in 1984, as is Java, which was developed by James Gosling at Sun Microsystems in 1991. Modula–2 was developed in 1977 by Niklaus Wirth as an object-oriented successor to PASCAL.

Fourth-Generation Languages (4gls)

The experience gathered over the years in software engineering has demonstrated that certain application areas could benefit by adding to them limited, tailor-made programming languages. The first among these were database applications, which had to permit adding and deleting of records to a database, finding information through query operations, and generating reports—all by non-programmers. Database end-users (who are not programmers) needed a task-specific, very high level programming language. The first such language, JPL's Display Information System (JPLDIS), was developed by Jeb Long at NASA's Jet Propulsion Laboratory, in Pasadena. It was termed a fourth-generation language by database expert James Martin, to indicate that it was even closer to English than other high-level programming languages, which are called third-generation to indicate their departure from assembly language and, before that, machine language. Long's invention was implemented in Ashton-Tate's dBASE-II—the most successful database program developed for personal computers in the early 1980s. End-users could type in queries such as: "WHAT WAS THE TOTAL OF ALL REVENUES IN THE THIRD QUARTER SALES OF THE NORTHWEST REGION?" The software would search the database and generate the appropriate report, without encumbering the user with the need to learn computer-like command languages. Other database management systems manufacturers adopted this approach, particularly IBM in its Structured Query Language (SQL) and Information Builders' FOCUS—a database management system that is popular among COBOL users.

Other successful fourth-generation languages are document formatting languages like Metafont (developed by Donald E. Knuth), Adobe's PostScript (developed by John Warnock at Xerox PARC), Wolfram Research's Mathematica (a comprehensive symbolic and numerical mathematics software), and other data visualization languages such as AVS, APE, and IRIS EXPLORER.

3.3 Operating Systems

All the software that runs on a computer must, of course, make use of the CPU, memories, and I/O units of the computer. While early programs managed these resources themselves, it was soon found to be more convenient and efficient to relegate these tasks to a special program called the operating system (OS). Playing the role of both a bridge and a buffer between the software and the hardware, an operating system allocates hardware resources to the running programs, manages the usage of these resources, and ensures that programs do not conflict with one another. As a bridge/buffer, operating systems are hardware-specific: a different operating system—or at least a different version of it—must be developed for

Introduction

every family of computers. As they developed and were assigned additional responsibilities (including management of the graphical user interface), operating systems have grown in complexity and size. Today they are among the largest programs running on the computer, and their capabilities and efficiency are critical to the overall effectiveness of the system.

The Evolution of Operating Systems

The first widely used operating system was the OS/360 system introduced by IBM in 1964. It provided a single platform that could run any program on all the computers in IBM's System/360 family, which allowed users to upgrade their computers to more powerful ones (within the same family) without having to rewrite their application programs. As time-sharing became more popular, IBM introduced its OS/MFT (multiprogramming with a fixed number of tasks) in 1967 and OS/MVT (multiprogramming with a variable number of tasks) in 1973. Its System/370, introduced in 1970, added the ability to use virtual memory (make some of the secondary storage behave like the primary memory), which made it possible to run larger applications, albeit more slowly. It was upgraded to the OS/SVS, introduced 1974, then again to the OS/MVS (multiple virtual storage system). IBM continued to introduce more capable operating systems as the need for larger virtual memory grew and as its computers advanced.

UNIX is an operating system developed by Ken Thompson and Dennis Ritchie of AT&T Bell Laboratories in 1969. Initially it was designed for a single user. The programming language C was subsequently developed specifically for UNIX, and the system was rewritten almost entirely in C. It was improved by the addition of multiprogramming (also known as multiprocessing) and time-sharing capabilities and enhanced portability (the ability to run it on multiple different machines). Starting about 1975, the source code of UNIX had been distributed to universities at low prices—a practice that was discontinued in 1981, when AT&T adopted UNIX as a commercial product named UNIX System III. UNIX became extremely popular in universities, being used mostly on workstations for scientific and engineering processing. Because it can be easily modified, UNIX has been improved in many ways by academic and industrial institutions. The University of California, Berkeley, in particular, added new features, such as text editing on a monitor and communication facilities on a computer network. This so-called Berkeley Software Distribution (BSD) version of UNIX has gained wide popularity. In 1983 AT&T introduced the improved UNIX System V. As computer manufacturers developed their own versions, a few dozen different varieties of UNIX evolved. To promote UNIX, AT&T separated its UNIX business and set up UNIX System Laboratories, with other companies. This company was acquired by Novell in 1993.

The Control Program for Microprocessors (CP/M) operating system was developed by Digital Research, in response to the introduction of the 8080 processor by the Intel Corporation in 1974, which became the core of the first commercially successful personal computer. CP/M became the standard operating system for personal computers during the late 1970s. In 1981 IBM introduced its own family of personal computers, based on Intel's 8088 microprocessor. This new microprocessor handled 16-bit words, and required, therefore, a new operating system. Due to business incompatibilities between IBM and Digital Research, the task of developing an operating system for the new line of personal computers fell to the nascent Microsoft Corporation. The MS-DOS (Microsoft Disk Operating System) was born and came to dominate the personal computing industry for the next twenty years.

In 1987 IBM introduced the PS/2 family of personal computers, using Intel's 80386 microprocessor, which handled 32-bit words. To complement the abilities of the new processor, IBM developed its OS/2 operating system, in cooperation with Microsoft. In addition to MS-DOS features, it includes memory management, multitasking, windowing, database management, LAN management, and the ability to communicate with larger computers. When Microsoft reoriented itself in 1990 to develop its Windows operating system, IBM sought other partners to continue the development of OS/2. This development continues to date, though the operating system has failed to achieve commercial success.

Apple Computer introduced the Macintosh personal computer family in 1984 and popularized a windows-based operating system along with the mouse to control it (both were originally developed at Xerox Palo Alto Research Center for their Alto computer, which never made it into commercial production). They relieved users from having to remember arcane commands and introduced a user-friendly "drag-and-drop" interface, which appealed to non-programmers. This new form of user interaction with a computer dominated the earlier command-line mode.

Microsoft developed its own graphical user interface, called Windows, which was based on MS-DOS but presented the user with an environment similar to that of the Macintosh. Microsoft expanded Windows to Windows NT (New Technology) in 1993, making it a multitasking system. In 1995 Microsoft introduced Windows 95, as an intermediate upgrade for Windows 3.1 users who could not afford the large computers needed to run Windows NT. It was followed by successively more advanced versions, at roughly two-year intervals.

The most recent major operating system is Linux, which started in 1991 as a hobby project by Linus B. Torvalds, a second-year student of computer science at the University of Helsinki. It is based on MINIX, an operating system written for instructional purposes by Andrew S. Tanenbaum, a Dutch professor of computer science. What makes Linux unique is that it is the collaborative product of thousands of programmers worldwide, who answered Torvalds's call and freely contributed their time and talent to make a coherent, full-fledged, yet open-source and copyright-free operating system. Although it has been a Web-based collaborative effort involving many programmers, the Linux development has been well organized. It resulted in a robust operating system that has UNIX-like features, and won the confidence of businesses and universities alike, who consider it the personal computer alternative to UNIX.

The Functions of an Operating System

An operating system has six main functions:

1. *Process management.* The operating system schedules the resources of the computer in an efficient manner to support the needs of the (often many) programs that run on it. This allows computers to run many programs at once rather than only one at a time. Since most computers use only one processor, each program gets a slice of time in which it can execute a few commands, before another program gets the processor's attention. This allows all programs to finish their tasks in a reasonably short and equitable amount of time. The operating system must keep track of each program's progress and the data it

needs for completing its task. If an anomaly occurs, such as a hardware or software malfunction, the operating system interrupts the process, often without interrupting other processes.

2. *Memory management.* The computer's main memory (its RAM) is often too small to accommodate the needs of a running program. Instead, the operating system designates parts of the computer's secondary memory—its hard disk—as a logical extension of its main memory; the additional resource is called virtual memory. The operating system then must constantly shuffle segments of the running program and its intermediate processing results between the main memory and the secondary memory. It allows the user to employ far greater memory space than is available in the main memory, without being aware of the distinction between the two kinds of storage, except in term of the speed of execution: transferring program blocks of either fixed size (pages) or variable size (segments) to and from hard disks to the main memory slows down the execution of the program, something that becomes noticeable in animation and audio applications.

3. *Input/output and file management.* The operating system controls many different types of input and output devices, such as keyboards, pointing devices, printers, monitors, magnetic disks, magnetic tapes, scanners, and audio devices. Whenever a new device is added to the system, the operating system must be notified—either automatically ("plug and play") or manually, so it can add the device to its managed list. Similarly, the operating system also keeps track of the files and directories that reside on hard or floppy disks.

4. *Communication management.* The operating system manages communication among computers connected on a network. Since data exchanged on the network may be received intermittently instead of continuously, it must be combined by the operating system into complete wholes. As local- and wide-area networks (LANs and WANs) continue to become more widely used, management of distributed processing—i.e., execution of computational tasks by many computers and peripheral equipment connected through a network—is becoming an increasingly important role of operating systems.

5. *Security management.* The operating system protects computers from access by illegal users and from data corruption introduced by unin-

tentional mistakes made by legitimate users. Security is particularly important for computers that are connected to a communications network because many users can freely access any computer. The most common way to authenticate authorized users is through individual passwords and encryption "keys," although biometric authentication devices (thumb print, retina scan, or voice recognition) are becoming increasingly more widely used.

6. *User interface management.* The operating system provides an interface between a computer and its users. In the case of personal computers and workstations, graphical user interfaces, such as windows and icons displayed on a monitor, have become the standard "face" of the operating system. Each program runs in a rectangular area on a monitor—a "window"—that displays a file or part of a file. Many applications can be run concurrently, each in a different window. Icons—small pictures displayed on a monitor—represent visual mnemonics for specific command or objects that can be manipulated by a user, typically by clicking on them with a hand-controlled device like the mouse.

The evolution of computers into this highly differentiated yet integrated complex of hardware, software, and operating systems marks the birth, growth, and maturation of the device that saw it beginning in Sumerian counting tokens some 9,000 years ago. And while its abilities have evolved and expanded, its primary function has remained the same: to assist people in accomplishing tasks whose complexity taxes the abilities of the human brain. Yet, for all their abilities, and for all the fanciful imagination of science fiction writers,[3] computers have not yet been able to exceed, even equal, the abilities of the human brain. Some researchers think it is only a matter of time before they do.[4]

Bibliography

Aho, A. V., J. E. Hopcroft, and J. D. Ullman. *The Design and Analysis of Computer Algorithms.* Reading, Mass.: Addison-Wesley, 1974.

Bentley, J. *Programming Pearls.* Reading, Mass.: Addison-Wesley, 1986.

Elson, M. *Concepts of Programming Languages.* Chicago: Science Research Associates, 1973.

Graham, G. *Introduction to Computer Science: A Structured Approach.* New York: West Publishing, 1982.

Gries, D. *The Science of Programming*. New York: Springer Verlag, 1981.

Harel, D. *Algorithmics*. Reading, Mass.: Addison-Wesley, 1987.

Horowitz, E. *Fundamentals of Programming Languages*. Rockville, Md.: Computer Science Press, 1984.

Horowitz, E., and S. Sahni. *Fundamentals of Computer Algorithms*. Rockville, Md.: Computer Science Press, 1978.

Knuth, D. E. *The Art of Computer Programming*. Reading, Mass.: Addison-Wesley, 1973.

Polya, G. *How to Solve It? A New Aspect of Mathematical Method*. Princeton: Princeton University Press, 1973.

Sedgewick, R. *Algorithms*. Reading, Mass.: Addison-Wesley, 1983.

Wirth, N. *Algorithms and Data Structures*. Englewood Cliffs, N.J.: Prentice-Hall, 1986.

Computing in Architectural Design

Architecture, as a practical form of art, has been in need of computation—and computational aids—since ancient times. While computation has no doubt played an important role in the design of even the humblest of dwellings, it came to the fore in such monumental undertakings as the ziggurats of Mesopotamia (5000–2000 BC), the Neolithic stone circle at Stonehenge (2750–1500 BC), the pyramids of Egypt (2570–2500 BC), the temples and the cities of the Greeks and the Romans (600 BC–400 AD), the Great Wall of China (300 BC), and the stepped pyramids of Central America (100 BC–800 AD). In particular, architects had a great need for geometry as a means to calculate sizes, proportions, areas, and volumes, and the tools to create geometric constructions and communicate them to the builders.

Computation acquired added importance during the Renaissance, when contemporary interpretations of the Vitruvian ideal—that the proportions of the human figure should be reflected in every temple—coincided with the Renaissance focus on humanism and the harmony between man and God. Vitruvius's simple description of a man with outstretched hands and feet fitting exactly within the most perfect geometrical figures—the circle and the square—seemed to reveal a deep and fundamental truth about man and the world (fig. 4.1). It so captivated the imagination of Renaissance architects that training in geometry became prerequisite for a career in architecture, and architecture itself became obsessed with finding the most appropriate geometric relationships between the components of a building.

The tools architects used to aid them in determining these geometric relationships were primarily the compass and the straightedge. They developed ingenious methods (algorithms) to "square the circle" (that is, to find a square whose perimeter is exactly equal to the perimeter of a given circle, or a square whose area is exactly equal to the area of a given circle); to calculate the "proper" dimensions of a space, given its width (the *ad quadratum* method); and to calculate the golden section (the most "beautifully" proportioned geometric form).

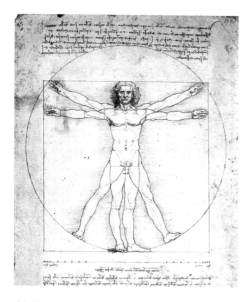

4.1 Vitruvian man, by Leonardo da Vinci (c. 1490).

The focus on a human-centered universe also promoted the use of perspective drawings, thought to have been invented by Filippo Brunelleschi (1377–1446), although it had been previously mentioned by Vitruvius (c. 40 BC). Linear perspective provided a means to communicate the illusion of depth by foreshortening objects further away from the observer. It also provided a "natural" spatial organization and structural focus to images as opposed to the pre-Renaissance, liturgical view.[1] The popularity of perspective drawings prompted a search for scientific methods for constructing them, which were provided first by Leon Battista Alberti in his book *De pictura* (1435), in which he gave practical advice on how to construct perspective paintings by observing a scene through a thin veil, as illustrated by Albrecht Dürer's 1527 treatise *Underweysung der Messung* (fig. 4.2).

While computation served the needs of architecture in terms of laying out building plans and elevations, and in terms of communicating them to clients and to builders in a formalized graphical manner, its major impact on buildings themselves occurred in the eighteenth century, with the advent of building and material science—particularly the elastic theory of structures. Beginning with the Swiss mathematician Leonhard Euler's theory of column buckling in 1757, and more so with the advent of the English scientist Thomas Young's modern definition of the modulus of elasticity in 1807, it became possible to predict the structural performance of buildings with considerable accuracy, provided there was adequate control over the materials used. The concept of statically determinate structures—structures whose forces could be determined from Newton's laws of motion alone—was set forth by Otto Mohr in 1874, and dominated nineteenth-century structural design. But it was not until the advent of computers (and the evidence gathered from the behavior of bombed-out buildings in World War II) that equations describing the behavior of statically indeterminate structures could be solved.

4.1 The History of Computer-Aided Design

The first use of computers in the service of the building industry was thus through engineering analysis, for the purpose of solving the differential equations that describe the transfer of forces through determinate and indeterminate structures. The process of design was carried out in the

Introduction

usual (manual) manner, except that at certain points in the process quantities were taken off the drawings and fed to the computer for "crunching numbers," the results of which were then applied (manually) to the evolving design. While such numerical analysis considerably sped up the number crunching itself, it was a tedious and error-prone process to prepare the input and to apply the results to the otherwise manual design process.

Sketchpad

In 1963 Ivan Sutherland, as part of his Ph.D. dissertation at MIT, developed a way to integrate the evolving design and analysis programs. Sutherland and his mentor, Steven A. Coons, thus invented both the modern concept of computer-aided design and the tools to implement it. The concept was summarized by Coons in his 1963 AFIPS conference paper:

> We envisioned even then the designer seated at a console, drawing a sketch of his proposed device on the screen of an oscilloscope tube with a "light pen," modifying his sketch at will, and commanding the computer slave to refine the sketch into a perfect drawing, to perform various numerical analyses. . . . In some cases the human operator might initiate an optimization procedure.[2]

4.3 Ivan Sutherland and the Sketchpad system, running on MIT's TX-2 mainframe computer (1963).

The tools were Sutherland's Sketchpad program and the specially modified TX-2 computer system at MIT's Lincoln Laboratory (fig. 4.3). Built by IBM for the U.S. Air Force in 1959, the TX-2 was a giant machine by the standards of the 1960s: it had 300 kilobytes of random access memory (about twice as much as commercial systems of its day) and occupied 1,000 square feet of space. It was slow (1/12 MIPS) and had no operating system and no language compiler, but it did have a 7-inch, 1024 x 1024 pixel graphical display device, and was equipped with a light pen (which was first developed for the SAGE system at MIT's Lincoln Lab in 1955). Sutherland used it to write a program that allowed entry of graphical information by indicating points directly on the screen rather than through a keyboard. Since data entered this way was not very accurate, Sketchpad could straighten the lines and squares drawings using built-in assumptions about the shape the user intended to draw.

Sutherland's approach was emulated by Don Hart and Ed Jacks at General Motors Research Laboratory, who, in collaboration with IBM, developed the DAC-1 system in 1964. By the end of the 1960s, similar systems were operational in most other automotive and aerospace companies.

Interest in using computers for architectural design first emerged in academic circles.[3] It received considerable credence in 1964, with the publication of Christopher Alexander's influential book *Notes on the Synthesis of Form*,[4] which described a systematic utilization of a computer-based architectural design method. A number of conferences were organized around this topic (in 1964 at the Boston Architectural Center and in 1968 at Yale), and a number of computer-aided design systems were developed, such as Negroponte's URBAN5 (fig. 4.4) and Souder and Clark's COPLANNER.[5]

Computer systems began to appear in architectural practices in the early 1970s. Perry Dean & Stuart in Boston used a combination of a PDP-15 computer, a Gould 4800 printer, and a Computek cathode ray tube and tablet to run a family of programs developed by Design Systems. It included a database of spaces, called Compugraph, which included their required dimensions, ceiling heights, and cost per square foot. An adjacency-matrix-driven bubble-diagram generator, called Compurelate, produced optimal arrangements of the spaces and was able to generate squared "rooms" that could be further manipulated to arrive at a floor plan (fig. 4.5).

Introduction

First-Generation CAD Systems

The development of computer-aided design in the 1970s took two different routes: a geometric modeling route, geared toward supporting the needs of mechanical engineering applications in the automotive and aerospace industries; and a building-specific route, geared toward supporting the needs of the construction industry. The first was lead by industry giants like General Motors, who saw the need for computer systems that could assist engineers in drawing complex curves, construct complex geometries through Boolean operations, and test their designs for manufacturability by planning milling machine paths and sheet metal folding tolerances. The results of these R and D efforts were commercialized by companies like Computervision, Applicon, Calma, Autotrol, Intergraph, and CADAM.[6]

In contrast to this industry-sponsored, general-purpose geometric modeling approach, building-specific CAD in the early 1970s was spearheaded by university-based research groups in the United States and Britain. In the U.S., research at the Institute for Physical Planning at Carnegie Mellon University, headed by Charles M. Eastman, focused on developing systems for building description and space planning that would support, in one package and using one database, all building-related operations. In 1974 the group developed the Building Description System (BDS)—a solid modeler and a building-specific database. It was expanded and modified in 1977 to form the Graphical Language for Interactive Design (GLIDE), which was based on an interpreted programming language and supported geometric operations on parametric building descriptions. At the same time, researchers at the University of Michigan, led by Harold Borkin and supported by the Army Corps of Engineers Construction Research Laboratory, developed the Computer Aided Engineering and Architectural Design System (CAEADS)—a large architectural and engineering design system that could support habitability analysis, energy analysis, and building specification verification analysis.

At MIT, the Architecture Machine Group, founded by Nicholas Negroponte in 1967, took an artificial intelligence approach to developing architectural computing applications. It rejected the division of labor by which human and machine would be assigned tasks they were supposed to be respectively better at, and suggested, instead, a joint venture

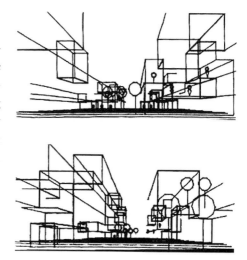

4.4 URBAN5 was an early computer-aided urban planning system, designed by Negroponte and Groisser at MIT in 1964 to support urban planning.

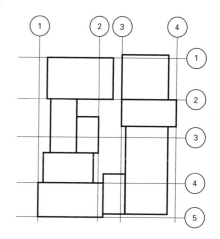

4.5 Compurelate, an early architectural CAD program developed by Design Systems, was used by the architectural firm Perry Dean & Stewart in Boston in the early 1970s to help design floor plans from bubble diagrams (after ARK-2, BIG Production, 1971).

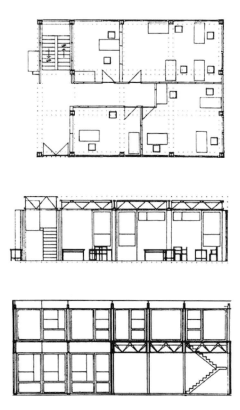

4.6 The OXSYS hospital design system. (P. Richens, in *Bulletin of Computer-Aided Architectural Design* 25 [1977].)

model, in which the environment itself—the "architecture"—could initiate actions on its own accord for the purpose of fulfilling the needs of its inhabitants. Thus, the group strived to develop computing devices that could sense the presence and needs of the inhabitants and respond to them without the intervention of an architect, whom they considered to be an unnecessary, even detrimental middleman between the continually changing needs of the inhabitants and the continuous incorporation of those needs into the environment.[7]

In the United Kingdom the development of building-related computational applications has been mostly associated with large-scale public building projects, capitalizing on modular coordination and industrialized building components. Such closed building systems, which naturally lent themselves to computational application, were used by the British Post Office administration, the Health and Social Security administration, and by the Scottish Special Housing Association. Among their most significant developments were OXSYS[8] (fig. 4.6) and HARNESS (1970), developed by Applied Research of Cambridge for the design of hospitals made of prefabricated components; CEDAR, for the design of post offices; and SSHA (1969–1973), developed by Aart Bijl at the University of Edinburgh, for the design of housing.

These early approaches to developing computational systems to support the design and construction of buildings originated in architectural design departments of universities—the research arm of the building industry. They approached the problems from an intuitive, architectural design point of view, rather than a formal computer science point of view. As a result, their solutions tended to encompass more of the architectural design process but were often too cumbersome to be useable in practice or too closed in nature (like OXSYS and SSHA) to be of general use. The popular diffusion of CAD in architecture had to await the invention of cheap computing hardware (the personal computer and the color raster scan display), and the development of general-purpose drafting and modeling systems.

Second-Generation CAD Systems

Early CAD systems required large and powerful computers like mainframes, or at least minicomputers, to support the calculation-intensive computations needed to manipulate and display geometrical constructions. They also required expensive display hardware (graphics-capable CRT screens and plotters) and specialized (hence expensive) input devices (light pens or tablets). The introduction of (relatively) cheap personal computers, display technology, and graphics-oriented input devices (the mouse) made CAD systems affordable to the larger architectural community and created a demand for useful software.

The needs of the architectural community appeared, from outside the profession, to consist primarily of drafting, or at most, modeling applications. Hence, the first CAD-like software to be written for the increasingly popular personal computer (first the Apple II, then the Macintosh) consisted of drafting systems. In particular, the introduction of the Macintosh in January 1984, with its overall graphics-oriented approach and input device, made drafting on a personal computer both feasible and accessible to non-researchers. Early CAD systems that were developed for the Macintosh included MacDraft, MacDraw, Dreams, MiniCAD, and PowerDraw. Although intuitive and easy to learn, their capabilities were far too limited to support professional architectural drafting (even in two dimensions).

The advent of the IBM PC, which first made its way into architectural offices as a business machine, and the growing capabilities of the Macintosh encouraged companies to develop professional-grade CAD software. New companies, or divisions of existing graphics software (and hardware) companies like AutoDesk, VersaCad, Summagraphics, Microstation, and others began to write software that was intended explicitly to support the drafting aspects of architectural design. Initially, these systems were slow, suffered from poor user interfaces, and were prone to crash. With the advent of faster processors, like Intel's 80386 in the late 1980s, growing storage capacity, and especially the advent of windows-like multiple views on the screen, professional-grade drafting software became available and widely used (fig. 4.7).

The continuing growth in the power of processors, the growing resolution of computer display screens, and the advent of cheap raster color printing with the introduction of ink jet printers by Epson and Hewlett-Packard made it possible to introduce affordable modeling systems. Such capabilities, which were previously the exclusive province of high-end workstations, began to appear on PC-class machines. They allowed users to display, manipulate, and print shaded, translucent and reflective sur-

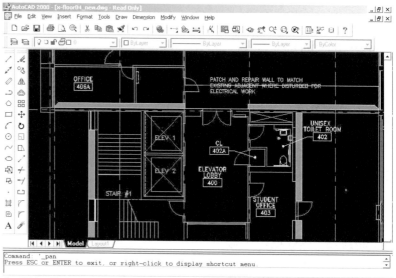

faces. Architects were able to use computers not only for the drafting phases of their work, but also to conceive and to communicate their designs to their clients in the form of photo-realistic renderings. Companies like Auto·Des·Sys, Kinnetix, Graphisoft, Revit, and others begun to develop modeling and rendering software for architects and, later, for the more lucrative market of digital movie making (fig. 4.8).

Paradoxically, these second-generation CAD software systems were less capable than the earlier, graphically poorer first-generation CAD systems. In fact while the first-generation systems were introduced as "building design systems," the second-generation were known as drafting and modeling systems: the emphasis on the unique attributes of buildings was sacrificed for the sake of generality. No longer did the software handle such building-specific objects as doors, windows, columns, and stairs. Rather, second-generation CAD software dealt with polygons, solids, NURBS,[9] and "blobs." To interpret the building's performance from these representations required expensive manual translations into specialized evaluation software, where a human operator identified and distinguished the various building components. Architects thus gained computer-assisted drafting and rendering capabilities but lost the analytical capabilities that formed the basis for the introduction of computing into the profession in the first place.

Introduction

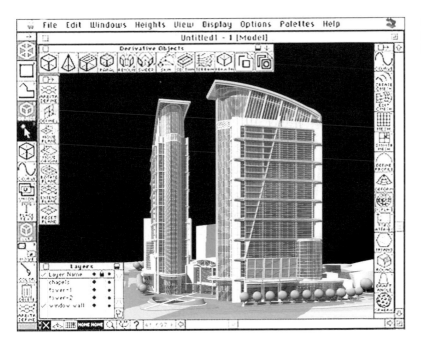

4.8 Form·Z, developed by Aut·Des·Sys of Columbus, Ohio. (Courtesy of John Marx, Form4 Inc., San Francisco, California.)

Third-Generation CAD Systems

This "dumbing down" of architectural CAD happened while other disciplines—most notably the electronics industry—were making their own CAD software more intelligent. First in university research labs, and later in corporate research labs, graphics-oriented software that handled "objects," not merely "shapes," began to emerge. Projects like SPICE, at Carnegie-Mellon University (1980s), showed that it was possible to add nongeometric attributes that made even simple geometric shapes—like rectangles—be treated by the computer as transistors, capacitors, and resistors. The computer, in turn, could be made to use this added data to reason about the design: it could inform the designer when certain design rules were being violated, such as the proximity of different layers of silicon represented by the rectangles, causing excessive heat build up. Furthermore, the computer could be instructed to carry out certain design operations on behalf of the human designer, such as laying out well-known electronic components like memory units. These abilities relieved the human engineer from having to lay out and check every component

Computing in Architectural Design

of the circuit, and concentrate instead on orchestrating its overall behavior. The result was improvement by orders of magnitude in the productivity of electrical engineers and a comparable increase in the number of components—hence the capabilities—of the integrated circuit itself. We have now reached a point where it is no longer possible to design an integrated circuit—of any reasonable complexity—without the assistance of computer-aided circuit design software: humans are simply not able to process all the information needed to design devices made of millions of individual components. Similar advances, though with less dramatic results, also occurred in the automotive and aerospace industries, where specialized design software helps engineers design, analyze, and fabricate complex machines.

The success of the electronics industry in developing software that can truly assist in the design, not only the communication of complex artifacts, inspired similar efforts in the architectural research community. In 1983 a research group at the University of Buffalo, under the leadership of Yehuda Kalay, started the development of a knowledge-based architectural CAD system called WorldView (fig. 4.9).[10] Sponsored by the Maedl Group of Buffalo, N.Y., the software addressed architectural objects such as walls, doors, and windows and had the ability to manipulate their geometric and

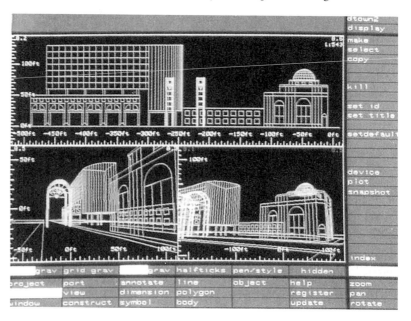

4.9 WORLDVIEW, an early knowledge-based CAD system. (Y. E. Kalay, "WORLDVIEW: An Integrated Geometric-Modeling/Drafting System," *IEEE Computer Graphics & Applications*, 2[7]:36-46, February 1987.)

Introduction

nongeometric attributes. It was intended to support an open-ended range of architectural analyses (energy, habitability, cost, and so on). In 1989 it was turned over for commercial distribution to Intelligence Artificielle, SA, of Lausanne, Switzerland, under the name AiSys.

A parallel development was undertaken in Italy by a research group headed by Gianfranco Carrara at the University of Rome "La Sapienza" (fig. 4.10).[11] Supported by the CARTESIANA consortium, it was aimed at developing knowledge-based software to aid in designing hospitals. Implemented as a frame-based system in LISP, the system, called KAAD (Knowledge-Assisted Architectural Design), was able to represent architectural building and space units like walls, doors, and rooms, and to detect violations of rules concerning such qualities as containment for infectious disease units, fire egress, and the placement of furniture. An advanced version, called MetaKAAD, has been under development since 2002.

Another knowledge-based design system was developed by Jens Pohl at the California Polytechnic and State University, in San Luis Obispo. Called ICAAD, the system consisted of a host of design "agents," each responsible for one aspect of the design. It thus emulated the argumentative nature of the design process, where the agents made design propositions and evaluated the propositions made by other agents.[12]

A project headed by Ulrich Flemming at Carnegie Mellon University in the 1990s produced the SEED system, intended to support the preliminary design of buildings.[13] It partitioned the design process into tasks, each supported by a separate module of the system, such as architectural programming, schematic layout design, and schematic configuration design. SEED was a case-based system, deriving its knowledge from precedents stored as prototypes, which were selected for their match with the specific conditions of a problem and modified as needed.

In the late 1990s, a research group headed by Konstantinos Papamichael at the Lawrence Berkeley National Laboratory developed the Building Design Advisor (BDA), a system intended to support the analysis of various energy-related building performance measures. At its core, BDA had a comprehensive, object-oriented building model, which included all the attributes of building materials, climate data, and other knowledge bases.[14]

Such third-generation systems seem very similar to the first-generation CAD systems, which were centered on architectural objects and were

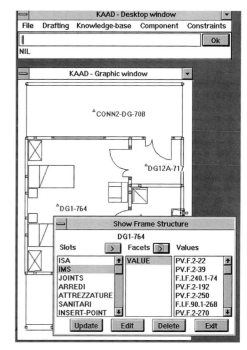

4.10 KAAD, a frame-based knowledge representation system for the design of hospitals. (G. Carrara et al., in *Automation in Construction* 3, nos. 2–3 [1994].)

intended to support the design, not merely the representation of buildings. The difference is in the manner the newer systems go about achieving the original goal: two decades of research and experience in developing large computer systems have taught developers the principles and the methods that ought to be used when undertaking complex software development tasks. In particular, recent advances in object-orient programming (OOP), artificial intelligence (AI), and database management systems (DBMS) are the underpinnings of third-generation CAD systems.

Efforts to develop such third-generation CAD systems continue to date, but they have yet to emerge as commercially viable design tools. Their tardiness can be attributed, in part, to the difficulty of constructing comprehensive building-specific data- and knowledge bases and harnessing these nongeometric attributes into an effective design support system. Their ineffectiveness as practical design tools is combined with the reluctance of the architectural community to relinquish any part of the design process to the computer (as evidenced by the slow acceptance, compared to other professions, of *any* computer aided design tools in architecture). Still, the success of knowledge-based, object-oriented CAD in other disciplines beckons architectural CAD system developers, who have mostly exhausted the purely geometric route taken by second-generation systems and are looking for ways to enhance the capabilities of their tools.

4.2 The Roles of Computing in Architectural Design

The evolution of computer-aided design in architecture can be viewed as the search for technology that can fulfill certain preconceived roles. Alternatively, it can be viewed as the search for the most appropriate role, or combination of roles, that technology can play in the architectural design process.

The first view sees architectural design as the driving force behind a technology struggling to meet the needs of a profession. Beginning with the need for more powerful computers to handle complex geometrical operations, for high-resolution graphical input and display devices, and for methods that can accommodate very large data sets, the needs of CAD have always been one step ahead of prevailing technological solutions. CAD was directly or indirectly responsible for the development of computer graphics, minicomputers, and input devices we now take for granted. And while those developments have found use in many areas, CAD continues to set the goals for computing technology. Even now a complete car, let alone an airplane, is too large to be stored in one computer model. The representation of a complete building is even more difficult. Solving such problems as simulating the dynamic behavior of buildings, the movement of people, and the natural environment will continue to require not only more powerful computers, but also new methods for managing the data.

It is, however, the second view that is of greater interest to the profession and discipline of architecture, possibly even to society at large. The search for the roles that technology can play in the architectural design process may actually change how the built environment is conceived, constructed, and used, because computers, much more so than any other tool, have the power to change the tasks they are applied to, creating new roles for themselves along the way.

Design Tools

The first and most obvious role computers have assumed in the design process has been as tools—instruments with no intelligence or volition of their own, that can augment the abilities of an experienced designer, making the execution of some specific task more efficient, more precise, or more effortless. Drafting and modeling tools are examples of computers fulfilling this role: they replace traditional paper and pencil with electronic implements, but do not fundamentally change the task of drafting or modeling. The designer must still instruct the computer to draw each line, construct each object, change its color, and position the viewpoint. The computer, like paper, does not understand the evolving design. It cannot comment on its qualities, nor does it know when the architect has made a mistake.

Like other instruments, such as telescopes and microscopes, computers can help designers see what cannot be seen by the naked eye. For example, they can help realistically visualize buildings that do not yet exist. In that capacity they go beyond drafting and modeling tools, because the visualization can reveal details and nuances that formerly only a very talented artist could draw.

In a more advanced state of their role as tools, computers can function as measuring instruments—light meters, thermometers, accelerometers,

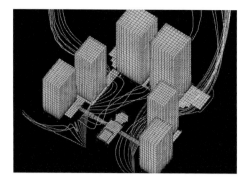

4.11 Computers can help designers and engineers visualize and measure natural phenomena like wind patterns around tall buildings. (Courtesy of Tsou Jin-Yeu, Department of Architecture, The Chinese University of Hong Kong.) (See color plate 13.)

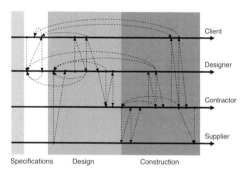

4.12 Communication is key to the success of design projects. (Xiaolei Chen, University of California, Berkeley.)

and more. In this capacity they can collect data from the model and convert it into measurements of light levels, temperature maps, and displays of wind patterns around tall buildings (fig. 4.11). Still, they function only at the direction (and discretion) of the human designer. The information they provide must be interpreted by the designer then acted upon in the form of design changes.

Tools, of course, have a glorious and important role in the advent of civilization, and their importance and impact on the design process must not be underestimated. Still, their ability to affect a qualitative change in the task they are applied to is limited by their need to be activated and supervised by their human operators.

Means of Communication

Another role of computers as design tools is provided by their communication abilities: by connecting individual computers through communication networks, like the Internet, members of a design team can share information quickly and efficiently. And since buildings have long been the result of joint efforts of many specialists who must coordinate their individual contributions, computers' ability to enable communication between sometimes distant collaborators is as important as their contributions in support of individual designers. Moreover, their processing abilities allow computers to be active tools, rather than simply dumb conduits, like telephones and fax machines. They can, for instance, help assure the proper distribution of design information, track changes proposed by individual members of the design team, and enforce access and version control (fig. 4.12).

Design Assistants

To go beyond the limitations imposed by a human operator, tools must be infused with intelligence and volition of their own. Secretaries, travel agents, and stock brokers provide a service that cannot be matched by mere tools: they are able to take a general instruction, fill in missing details, negotiate obstacles, find alternatives, and present the results of their work in a processed form to their "masters."

Introduction

Computers have the capacity to become such assistants. In the design process, the role of computational assistants may be likened to that of a junior designer who can take generic instructions such as "design a staircase between these floors" and carry out the task without further intervention by the senior designer. They could elaborate details, watch out for known problems and resolve them. They could answer questions submitted by less capable tools and supervise their operations (fig. 4.13).

In their capacity as design assistants, computers would relieve designers from the need to perform mundane tasks and thus augment their ability to supervise complex projects. Of course the boundary between interesting and mundane must be negotiated between the design partners, human or computational, much like it is being negotiated today between human designers in an architectural office. The same task may appear more interesting one day, deserving the full attention of the human designer, and less so another day, when it is relegated to the computer assistant.

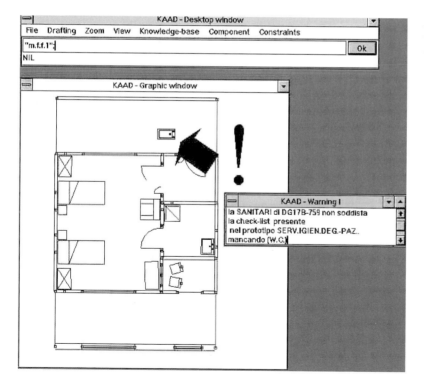

4.13 The KAAD system can detect and flag the designer's mistakes. (G. Carrara et al., in *Automation in Construction* 3, nos. 2–3 [1994].)

By endowing them with the intelligence necessary to carry out complex tasks and the volition to do so on their own, computers can go beyond the abilities of their human operators. Their unlimited patience, infallible memory, and enormous speed may help them develop interesting and novel design solutions, find answers to baffling questions, and contribute to the development of new knowledge, as is discussed in part 3 of this book.[15]

Design Environments

The inability of computers to comprehend any design activities that take place outside the computational environment itself, hence the need to design "in" the computer, had the unintended but critical effect of transforming the computer from a design "tool," in the traditional sense of the word, into a design environment: a "place" where design occurs. Instead of following the designer, like a pencil does, allowing him or her to design wherever and whenever desired, computers force designers to "come to them." Consequently, designers must fiddle with all sorts of knobs, switches, and gadgets to set the machine up so it can begin to support the design activity and, in general, are constrained and shoehorned into the machine's environment.

By becoming the environment where design occurs, the computer has changed the culture of the design profession. In the early days, when computers were too expensive to sit idle, designers had to work in shifts—a most unnatural imposition on the oft intuitive and serendipitous process of design. Later, the addition of Internet communication abilities extended their design environment to encompass not only the individual designer, but also other members of the design team—the manufacturers of the objects that are used to assemble the design, the clients, the public, and other interested parties. It has contributed to creating a global design environment, diminishing the importance of colocation and transcending time zones. As a consequence, there is better integration of the various parts of the design. But there is also a need to accommodate the schedules and work habits of others, to control the flow of information, and sometimes the loss of ownership of the final product.

Introduction

Habitable Physical Environments

Changing the culture of the design profession by placing it within the domain of the computer is, however, only the first of three emerging effects of computers as environments. The second effect—computers as inhabitable physical environments—has been envisioned by the Architecture Machine Group at MIT in the early 1970s. In its twenty-first-century incarnation, the vision of inhabitable environments infused with many computational devices has taken the form of computer-controlled temperature, humidity, and lighting, security systems, elevators and doors, even electronic building "skins" (fig. 4.14), creating seamlessly networked and ever changing electronic landscapes. The typical automobile now sports some twenty-six individual computers, controlling everything from fuel injection to temperature to traction to air bags, brakes, and pre-tensioned seat belts. We expect the door at the supermarket to "recognize" us and open before us as we approach, and are becoming accustomed to the presence of ever vigilant security cameras, tied to automated face recognition systems in airports and sport stadia. Public pay phones have lost their cachet because almost everyone is now connected by a wireless communication device, which can deliver not only sound but also text and video messages. Consequently, we no longer know where, even when, the target of our phone call is.

4.14 Times Square, New York, is a physical environment infused with ever-changing media that blur the boundaries of space and information. (See color plate 2.)

The diffusion of computers into our everyday environment has the effect of making the environment more "intelligent"—at least more cognizant of our presence and activities—and enabling "it" to take action on our behalf. Such actions can be based on simple feedback loops, such as the control of temperature though a thermostat or the opening of the supermarket doors as we approach; or it can be model-based, such as scheduling elevators to meet the needs of rush hour traffic in an office building based on expected activities rather than evident ones.

Virtual Environments

The third and potentially most radical effect of computers assuming a role of inhabitable environments is the advent of cyberspace—a term coined by William Gibson to denote the information space created by the Internet—and its steady assertion of itself as a "place."[16]

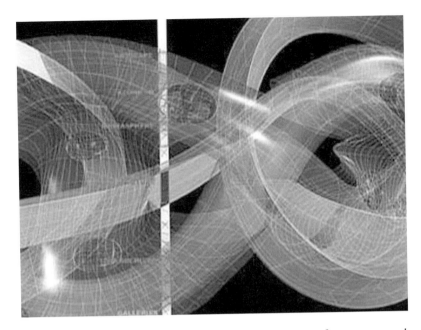

Although it can only be accessed through the mediation of computers and
can only be inhabited by proxy, cyberspace is fast becoming an extension
of our physical and temporal existence, offering a common stage for everyday economic, cultural, educational, and other activities (fig. 4.15).
Unlike other networks that preceded it, for example the telephone network, cyberspace has become more that just another means of communication. It has become a destination in and of itself. We shop "there," are
entertained "there," and get educated "there." To rephrase Gertrude Stein,
"There is a there there."[17]

Making places for human inhabitation in a nonphysical space raises
interesting questions concerning presence, authenticity, adaptability, orientation, and suspension of disbelief. What kind of activities can be supported by nonphysical spaces? What will it take to support them in a
socially and psychologically appropriate manner? Already video conferencing, e-commerce, and video entertainment are migrating to cyberspace, leaving behind the agoras, bazaars, and amphitheatres of the past.
The new "space" is virtual, the construction of computers. But we humans
have not changed, nor have our relationships with other human beings.
The opening of a new kind of space made possible by computers and networks promises to revolutionize our perception of reality like no other

Introduction

invention before it and challenges the professions of architecture, town planning, and interior design which have been striving to accommodate human activities in the physical domain for thousands of years.

The roles of computing, with regard to architecture, are thus multifarious and have varying degrees of impacts. They range from being tools that can augment certain traditional design activities, with little impact on the activities themselves, to more pervasive (and invasive) impacts as environments within which design and even inhabitation itself occurs.

The changes are occurring very rapidly compared to the sedate pace of past evolutions in architectural design, thus shaking the foundations of the profession as no other invention has done before—not even the invention of scale drawing in the Renaissance, which established the profession of architecture in the first place.

Bibliography

Agre, P. *Computation and Human Experience.* Cambridge: Cambridge University Press, 1997.

Coyne, R. *Designing Information Technology in the Postmodern Age: From Method to Metaphor.* Cambridge: MIT Press, 1995.

Coyne, R. *Technoromanticism: Digital Narrative, Holism, and the Romance of the Real.* Cambridge: MIT Press, 1999.

Gero, J. S., and H. Tang. "Concurrent and Retrospective Protocols and Computer-Aided Architectural Design." In *CAADRIA'99,* ed. J. Gu and Z. Wei, 403–410. Shanghai: Shanghai Scientific and Technological Literature Publishing House, 1999.

Gross, M. D. "Why Can't CAD Be More Like Lego? CKB, a Program for Building Construction Kits." *Automation in Construction* 5, no. 4 (1996): 285–300.

Kalay, Y. E., L. M. Swerdloff, B. Majkowski, and C. Neumberger. "Process and Knowledge in Design Computation." *Journal of Architectural Education* 43, no. 2 (winter 1990): 47–53.

Mitchell, W. J. *The Logic of Architecture.* Cambridge: MIT Press, 1990.

Mitchell, W. J. "The Theoretical Foundation of Computer-Aided Architectural Design." *Environment and Planning B* 2 (1975): 127–150.

Mitchell, W. J. "Three Paradigms for Computer-Aided Design." *Automation in Construction* 3, nos. 2–3 (1994): 239–245.

Mitchell, W. J., and M. McCullough. *Digital Design Media.* New York: John Wiley and Sons, 1995.

Communication

Design is a social act. Buildings, like most other artifacts we use daily, are much too complex to be designed by one individual alone. Their technical, social, regulatory, and financial complexities require the joint efforts of a team of specialists, each educated in one particular aspect of the collaborative enterprise. Yet a building is the sum total of all these specializations. To achieve the necessary integration, specialists must coordinate their own work with other specialists, on whose efforts they rely and whom they affect through their own efforts. The architect, for example, relies on the client's input to guide the design toward a solution that will meet the client's needs and produces drawings and specifications that direct the contractors who construct the building. The architect also relies on the expertise of specialists like structural engineers, electrical engineers, and mechanical engineers to help develop a complete, functional, and economically feasible solution. These specialists take their cues from the architect's initial designs, which their own contributions will subsequently modify.

Coordination among the participants in the design process is facilitated by *communication*—a means for sharing information among individuals. In the animal world, a cry represents the awareness of an animal to some danger, coupled with the intent to alert other members of the troupe to its presence. A bird's display of brightly colored feathers is a communication of the desire to mate. A honeybee's complex dance communicates the location of a rich source of nectar.

Humans, over the past 50,000 years, have expanded this rather limited, genetically encoded repertoire of communications used by animals to include speech, painting, writing, and a large number of symbolic means, which are transmitted through a vast array of physical and electromagnetic media. Not surprisingly, communication has been the subject of much study, especially since Marshall McLuhan famously proclaimed "the medium is the message."[1] Communication is much too broad a subject to discuss in the context of this book. Instead, we will examine only its characteristics that are pertinent to the problem of promoting coordination among the participants of a design project.

Communication is comprised of a message and a medium: the sender of the information must encode the message in the form of some symbolic language, which is then transmitted, through a suitable medium, to the receiver of the information. To retrieve the information, the receiver must access the medium of communication and decode the message. In a conversation, for example, the information may consist of an idea or an instruction. It is encoded by the sender in the form of spoken language and transmitted through the medium of sound. The receiver must be able to hear the sound and decode the message by interpreting the language into ideas or instructions. In order for this complex transaction to take place, the communicating parties must establish an agreed-upon shared meaning of the symbols used in the coding language and must have access to the medium used to transmit the message. The shared meaning assures that the message will be understood by the receiver in the way it was intended to be by the sender, once it has been retrieved from the medium used to transmit it. The medium that is used to transmit the message not only provides the connection between the sender and the receiver but also dictates, to a large degree, its nature and hence the level of abstraction that must be used to encode the message. A telephone conversation, for example, limits the communicating parties to the use of sounds, hence a coding based upon some spoken language or auditory cues (e.g., laughter). A letter, on the other hand, which uses visual symbols to encode the message, offers a richer means of communication, including text, numerals, and graphics.

Each one of the professions participating in the design of buildings has, over the years, developed its own coding conventions to facilitate discourse within its own subculture. But these conventions may be different from those adopted by another profession, even when referring to the same object or concept. For example, architects typically use the term "strength" to designate most of the structural qualities of buildings. Structural engineers, on the other hand, assign a much more narrow meaning to this term, alongside other terms such as stiffness, ductility, toughness, stability, redundancy, and robustness, to name a few. Conversely, architects use the term "movement" to mean the passage of people through the building, or a rhythm evoked by repeating elements such as columns or windows. Structural engineers typically interpret the same term as the result of forces like earthquakes and wind loads on the building. And while structural engineers can encode their messages in precise mathematical formulae, architects must often use the much less precise, yet in many ways more meaningful, media of drawings and illustrations to express their ideas.

When these specialized languages must be used across disciplinary boundaries, as they are in a multidisciplinary design team, they can lead to errors and misunderstandings. But while it is understandable that the absence of an adequate means of communication led, thousands of years ago, to the demise of the biblical construction project known as the Tower of Babel, it is less obvious why miscommunication persists today, since we have a notational means of communication introduced in the fifteenth century in the form of scale drawings. Or have scale drawings, three-dimensional models, and written specifications missed the mark, as far as communication is concerned? If so, are our current efforts in developing computational means of communication also destined to fail? To answer this question we need a better understanding of the essence of communication as it pertains to the architecture-engineering-construction (A/E/C) industry, and the nature of the means that have been developed to address it.

The Nature of Communication 5

Communication is a process whose purpose is to transfer information from a sender to a receiver through some intermediary medium of transmission. In architecture, communication allows architects, engineers, contractors, clients, and other participants in the design process to share information so they can consider it, analyze it, debate its merits, and act upon it in a coordinated manner. A telephone conversation, a drawing, a list of specifications, and a physical or digital model are all forms of communication used in architecture.

Before the message can be communicated, it must be *encoded* to fit the medium of transmission. In the case of a conversation, the encoding is a common language, like English, and the medium of transmission is speech. In the case of written specification, the encoding is some written alphabet or numerals, and the medium of transmission is paper (or its electronic equivalent). In every case, the language that is used to encode the message must be understandable by both the sender and the receiver, otherwise the message cannot be *decoded* and hence cannot be interpreted by the receiver.

Encoding is necessary because the message must be made to fit the medium of transmission—a process known as representation (to present an idea or a person in a different form). The information must be put into words or images so it can be conveyed from one person to another. Representation changes the information, often condensing it, through a process known as abstraction. It leaves out some of the original information, which subsequently must be made up by the receiving party on its own from resources that are not included in the communicated message itself. Thus the proper decoding of the message depends on the ability of the receiving party to add the missing information in a manner consistent with the intentions of the sender.

How much abstraction the sender may use when encoding the message, and what information needs to be added by the receiver to properly decode it, depend on the nature of the message and on the nature of the medium that is used to communicate it. A message such as "Mr. Watson—come here!,"[1] encoded in English and transmitted through the medium of the telephone, is simple enough to decode, although it assumes that Mr. Watson understands English and knows where "here" is. A more complex message, like the plans for a building, requires more extensive means of encoding—representation through scale drawings and written specifications. Consequently, they rely on considerably more knowledge on the part of the receiver to decode, which is typically acquired through extensive professional training.

The capacity of the transmitting medium to carry more or less information—its "affordance"—affects the amount of abstraction needed to encode the message. A book, for example, can only represent text and static, two-dimensional images. The reader must actively interpret the text and build a mental image commensurate with the unfolding narrative. Much of the interpretive burden thus rests with reader—the receiver of the information. A movie, on the other hand, can represent moving images and sounds, along with the nuances of utterances and the facial expressions of the actors. The viewer of the movie, therefore, must exert much less effort to interpret the message: the burden has been shifted to the movie's director and the actors—the senders of the information.

As the reliance on the receiver to fill in missing information grows, so does the potential for the message to be misinterpreted, or interpreted differently from the way it was intended by the sender. In some cases, such interpretations add an artistic flare to the communication, as in musical interpretations. In other cases, as in architecture, they may lead to errors, cost and schedule overruns, and dissatisfaction with the results.

5.1 Encoding: The Process of Abstraction

The main mechanism that transforms a reality or an idea into a communicable message is abstraction—the purposeful omission of certain details, or their aggregation into one "chunk." Abstraction extracts and distills the meaning of the message, focusing attention on its salient characteristics. Which details are preserved, and which ones are omitted, depend on the subject of the communication, on its purpose, on the knowledge of the receiver, on the context of the communication, and on the medium used for its transmission.

Consider, for example, the floor plan shown in figure 5.1a. Its subject is a kitchen, and its context is a proposal for remodeling that kitchen. Its purpose is to communicate the proposed layout to the client and to the contractor. As such, it is comprised of information about the number and sizes of the cabinets and the island in the proposed kitchen, and about their relative locations. The method of representation used to communicate this information is graphical, more specifically a scale drawing of the kitchen's floor plan. This is a highly abstract representation, which omits much information. It provides no information about the height of the cabinets, nor about the materials to be used, their colors, or the costs of the project. Moreover, decoding the information contained in this message requires the receiver to be able to read architectural floor plans. Without such ability, the message will appear as little more than a structured collection of colored lines, rectangles, and circles.

Figure 5.1b depicts the same kitchen using a different abstraction—a perspective rendering, taken from a particular point of view. It still uses graphics as the means of representation, but the encoding of the information is far less abstract than the floor plan in figure 5.1a. It is much easier to decode the message, requiring no particular skill on the part of the receiver, who may be a client not versed in reading floor plans. But the reduced level of abstraction is not without cost: the message is much more difficult to construct. It will take the sender more effort to encode the message (i.e., produce the perspective rendering) than it takes to produce the floor plan. Moreover, the rendering contains considerable ambiguity: it is difficult to know how big the depicted objects really are and how far apart they are from one another.

Figure 5.1c also communicates information about the same kitchen. The content of the message is, however, different from that of the first two: it communicates cost information. The method of representation relies on text and numbers rather than graphics. It assumes the receiver can read English and will be able to understand shorthand symbols like "w/2" and "$." Obviously, figure 5.1c contains no information about the spatial qualities of the kitchen and would be useless as a means to communicate to the client what the kitchen might look like. But it is invaluable for communicating the budget needed to carry out this project—information that neither figure 5.1a nor 5.1b is capable of communicating.

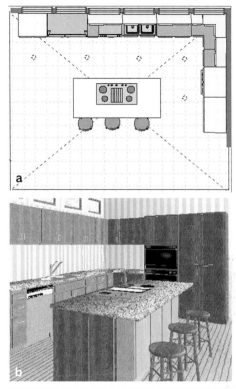

Name	Size	Quantity	Unit Price	SubTotal
Base cabinet with 3 drawers	12.00" Width x 34.50" Height x 24.00" Depth	1 lin. ft.	$300.00	$300.00
Base corner cabinet	36.00" Width x 34.50" Height x 36.00" Depth	3 lin. ft.	$190.00	$570.00
Sink cabinet w/ double doors, false drawer	36.00" Width x 34.50" Height x 23.71" Depth	3 lin. ft.	$160.00	$480.00
Base cabinet, single door	18.00" Width x 34.50" Height x 24.00" Depth	1.5 lin. ft.	$150.00	$225.00
Base cabinet w/ double doors, 2 drawers	36.00" Width x 34.50" Height x 24.00" Depth	3 lin. ft.	$210.00	$630.00

5.1 Different symbolic representations of the same kitchen: (a) floor plan, (b) 3D view, (c) bill of materials. (3D Kitchen, by Books That Work, Palo Alto, California, 1995.)

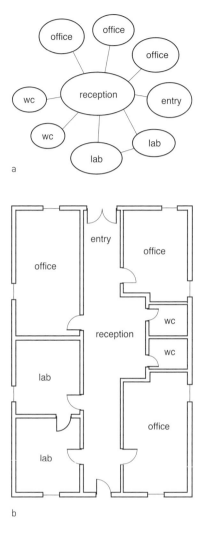

a

b

5.2 Two different abstractions of the same floor plan.

A high degree of abstraction, therefore, makes communication more efficient, though not necessarily more effective. It relies more heavily on shared knowledge between the sender and the receiver than communication at a lower level of abstraction. In effect, the receiver of a highly abstracted message is "coerced" by the sender to be an active partner in the communication, supplying the missing information from his or her own resources.

Abstraction not only makes communication more efficient, but it also helps to focus the receiver's attention on the parts of the message that the sender considers most important. Figure 5.2a is a bubble diagram, a type of representation commonly used in architectural design to communicate the nature, the relative size, and the connections among different rooms in a building. Figure 5.2b is a scaled drawing of the floor plan of the same building. It communicates the exact dimensions of the rooms and the location of the doors and windows. While it contains more information than figure 5.2a, it conveys less about the building's major spaces and their connectedness than can be inferred from the bubble diagram.

Clearly a balance is needed between loss of information due to abstraction and the need for verbosity to ensure proper interpretation. There is, however, no "right" degree of abstraction: each level of abstraction omits some information, thereby requiring the receiver to complete the message. It also focuses the attention of the receiver on some specific characteristics of the design—the relationships among spaces in the bubble diagram and, in the floor plan, their exact dimensions.

Within the field of architecture, which is primarily focused on developing and communicating the idea of a building to other people, a significant amount of abstraction must be used—there is simply too much information to be communicated. Some information must be omitted. But too much abstraction may confuse the receiver of the information if important characteristics of the message are omitted or if the sender relies too heavily on the ability of the receiver to interpret the message.

5.2 Representation: The Vehicle of Communication

Representation is the means used to encode information: it is an abstracted, symbolic means, chosen for its parsimony and its ability to convey, with reasonable effort, as many of the characteristics of the message as the sender cares to communicate. It must faithfully capture all the relevant and essential characteristics of the message, so its interpretation by the receiver will be consistent with the intents of the sender.

Consider the well-known "smiley" button—a simple geometric construction comprised only of a circle, two ovals and a curved line (fig. 5.3a). This representation, which is intended to convey a facial expression, communicates, in fact, much more than that—it also communicates a state of mind. The meaning it conveys can be easily changed into an expression of surprise by substituting another oval for the curved line (fig. 5.3b) or of sadness by flipping it upside down (fig. 5.3c). "Smiley" is obviously not a smiling human face. Rather, it is a message encoded through a geometric representation. The power of this representation is derived from its simplicity—it is highly abstract and therefore easy to encode and to represent. Yet it is also easy to decode and to interpret with no special training; one relies, instead, on the inherent human trait of anthropomorphizing the geometric pattern and "reading" it as an expression of the human face.

The representation that is chosen to convey a particular message can take many forms. It can be a spoken language, like English, in which case the message is represented in words. Or it can take the form of text, where the message is represented through special graphical symbols (an alphabet) with which the communicating parties are assumed to be familiar (i.e., they know how to read). Graphics of different kinds are appropriate for conveying visual information, but they require much more effort to encode the information and a higher bandwidth for transmission. Scale models represent information in three-dimensional, material form, affording transmission of volumetric and tactile information, but they are very time-consuming to encode (i.e., to build the model) and hard to communicate to a large number of receivers (who must come to a designated place where the model is on display). The choice of representation thus depends on the characteristics of the message, on the purpose of the communication, and on the effort the sender and the receiver are willing and able to make. A verbal communication is appropriate for short messages, if the communicating parties are known to be able to receive (hear) the representation (spoken words) and able to decode it (understand the spoken language). A written message is appropriate when more detailed or precise information is involved, thereby affording the parties the ability to go back and reread parts of the message or to refer to it in subsequent actions. Graphics are appropriate when the information involves spatial elements

a

b

c

5.3 The smiley button—a symbol that communicates a state of mind.

and the relationships between them, which would be hard to describe in words; and 3D models are appropriate when the materiality of the message is of consequence or when the receiver of the message is not versed in interpreting more abstracted information, such as scale drawings.

The Medium of Representation

Representation requires the use of some medium to capture the information in a tangible manner. In architecture, drawings and scale models have traditionally been the most important and frequently used media for capturing design information. Each medium can communicate certain kinds of information and not others. Affordance is the ability of a medium to communicate information.[2] Speech, as a medium of communication, affords the communication of sounds, but not images. Paper, on the other hand, affords communication of images, but not sounds. The affordance of the medium has a direct impact on the message it conveys: drawings, because they have no tactile quality and cannot be viewed interactively from various perspectives, convey a more "detached" message than scale models, which allow the viewer—rather than the sender—to determine the point of view.

The representation of a message, along with the medium in which it is recorded, is often the only tangible component of the communication—the link that connects the sender to the receiver. Thus, although the representation is only a proxy between the sender and the receiver, it acquires an importance of its own: it becomes the embodiment of the message itself. Consider, for example, the crash test dummies that are used in the automotive industry to test the safety of cars (fig. 5.4). Their purpose is to communicate the direction and magnitude of the forces that will be applied to different parts of the human body in case of an accident. Thus they are, in effect, a collection of sensors. Although sensors could be placed individually in the tested car to measure forces and accelerations, it is easier to package them in reusable sensor-packs. And since they must be placed in very specific locations in the car, which correspond to a human's head, torso, and limbs, this sensor-pack is built in a form that resembles the shape, weight, and joints of a person. It is a rather small step from there to begin treating the sensor-pack as an embodiment of a human being. Dress it up, as figure 5.4 shows, name it, even use it for car commercials, where the representation literally takes on a life of its own.

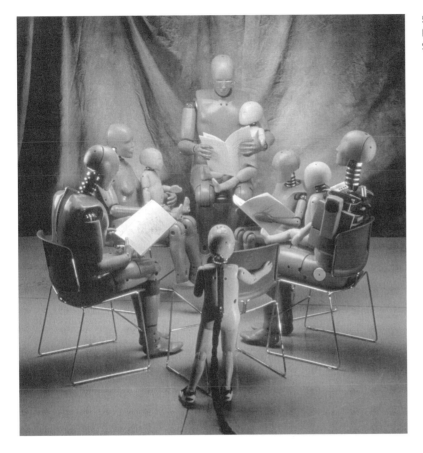

5.4 A "family" of crash test dummies. (Courtesy of First Technology Innovative Solutions, Plymouth, Michigan.)

The ability to treat the representation as the embodiment of the communication makes it easier, in many cases, to interpret (i.e., understand) the message. But it may also make us forget that the representation is only a proxy—a medium for transmitting a message—not the message itself. A crash test dummy helps us to understand more easily the crash-worthiness of a car than a non-anthropomorphized sensor-pack might have, but it may also lead us to associate properties with the manikin that are not part of the communicated message, as the "family" group in figure 5.4 suggests. At best, these extraneous properties may be irrelevant for the purpose of the communication; at worst they may distract from the communication and lead us to a false interpretation of the message.

As the representation takes on a meaning of its own, it can be manipulated in a manner that is similar to operating on the reality it stands for, but with much greater ease and economy. It is possible to subject a crash test dummy to destructive tests that cannot be applied to the actual passengers of the car; and it is possible to show a client what a building will look like before it has been constructed through drawings or scale models. On the other hand, because the representation is only a proxy, it can also be manipulated in ways that are inconsistent with the reality or idea for which it stands, further distorting the message. The "family" portrait of crash test dummies in figure 5.4 may make us sorry to see them "hurt" in an accident. Similarly, architects (and clients) often "fall in love" with scale models of their buildings. It is important, therefore, to maintain the proper correspondence between the representation and the reality or the idea for which it stands. Without this correspondence it would not be possible to learn about the reality or idea from its representation.

5.3 Decoding: The Meaning of Meaning

How people extract the meaning of a communicated message is a question that has intrigued philosophers and linguists for thousands of years.[3] The debate has centered on two problems:

1. The same message (a word, a picture) can have more than one meaning, thereby allowing different interpretations (by different people).
2. Two different messages can have the same meaning.

Communication requires, of course, adherence to agreed-upon meanings of words, graphics, and other forms of representation. But who establishes those meanings? The sender? The receiver? How is meaning "established" in the first place?

In his book *A Preface to Logic*, Morris Cohen states that "anything acquires meaning if it is connected with or indicates, or refers to something beyond itself, so that its full nature points to and is revealed in that connection."[4] Meaning, he argues, is not a property inherent to "things," but rather arises from the three-way relationship between: (1) the object (the "stimulus"); (2) its referent (the "consequent"); and (3) the conscious observer. Accordingly, meaning is both *referential* and *inferential:* objects (and concepts) acquire meaning by association with other objects (and/or concepts), after this reference has been established by an observer. This definition explains why the same message may hold different meanings to different receivers: the *referential* nature of meaning permits different receivers to associate the message with different referents, while the *inferential* nature of meaning allows them to interpret the reference differently. The potential for different interpretations grows if we also factor in the dynamic nature of the process of inferring: the same receiver may associate the same message with different referents under different circumstances and interpret the reference differently at different times.

Reference

Reference may be direct, as in "this is a door," which indicates that the referring object ("this") is an instance of a class of objects known to have doorlike properties, such as an adjustable opening in a wall that allows the passage of people-sized objects. A consequence of this reference may be the inference that, in case of an emergency, "this door" will afford egress— an inference that may prove to be false if the door has been locked, thereby modifying its referent's premise of allowing passage.

The reference may be even more specific, as in "this is a sliding door," which would indicate a specific subtype of the class of all doors. On the other hand, the reference may be more abstract, as in "this is an opening," which refers to a prototypical entity that may include, in addition to doors, also windows and skylights, for example.

Obviously, the more abstract the reference, the more difficult it is to ensure that the meaning it conveys will be interpreted by the receiver as it was meant to be interpreted by the sender. The common solution to this problem—reliance on shared cultural, educational, and experiential backgrounds—is risky, at best, because it involves assumptions that are themselves rarely communicated and are not always shared by different people (especially professionals, who have been educated to understand the world around them in specific, narrow ways).

Frame of Reference

The extraction of meaning is further complicated by the fact that both reference and inference are influenced by the frame of reference within which an observation is made. The frame of reference can be local, as in the

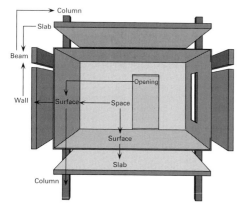

5.5 An assembly as the local frame of reference of a wall. (L. Khemlani, "Building Representation for Collaborative, Multi-Disciplinary Design," Ph.D. diss., University of California, Berkeley, 2000.)

5.6 A project of students from San Francisco's Academy of Art College. Objects have been removed from their customary frame of reference, thereby altering their meaning.

specific relationship between the observed object to other objects in its vicinity; or it may be global, as in the relationship between the object and its overall context (sociological, cultural, temporal, economical, and so forth). We refer to the local frame of reference of an object as its "assembly relationship" to other objects, implying that an object is, in most cases, part of a larger whole. For example, a WALL is part of a ROOM assembly, which includes other walls as well as spaces, columns, surfaces, and so on (fig. 5.5). This assembly can itself be part of a larger assembly, which includes the whole wing of a building, a particular floor, and so on. Consequently, when an object is taken out of its customary frame of reference it may lose much of its meaning, as was demonstrated by the students of San Francisco's Academy of Art College, who fixed various pieces of furniture to the facade of an abandoned building in San Francisco (fig. 5.6).

As an example of changing the meaning of an object or a message by changing its global frame of reference, consider the meaning we associate with bedrooms. In her paper on the history and evolution of modern bedrooms, Elizabeth Cromley describes how, in addition to providing a place for sleeping, bedrooms in the seventeenth century also functioned as parlors, dining rooms, and as places for entertaining guests.[5] Inviting someone to a lady's bedroom had a rather different meaning than it does today. . . .

An object, much like a message, can reference more than one referent at a time, thereby raising the possibility for multiple different interpretations. For example, in Philip Johnson's Glass House the walls, which are made of glass, also act as windows (fig. 5.7). Their meaning, in this case, cannot be derived from their composition and context alone, but rather from the function they perform. Considered as walls, they must provide protection from the elements. Considered as windows, they must afford view and, possibly, openability. Different observers may consider the design more or less satisfactory from their specific points of view. Clearly, this type of "wall" provides less privacy than a comparable wall made of standard, opaque materials. As a "window," however, this design provides more view and integration with the outdoors than smaller, more conventional openings. Together, the design may exceed the individual performance criteria of its partial references and provides an overall better solution to the combined functionality. Or it may clash with conventional

Communication

5.7 Philip Johnson's Glass House, New Canaan, Connecticut (1949), allows for different interpretations of its enclosing walls. (Photograph by Michael Moran, New York.)

expectations, delivering a less-than-acceptable performance from either or both points of view, as evidenced by the controversy centered on Johnson's creation.

An object or a message can be understood from within more than one frame of reference at the same time, thereby raising the possibility for multiple different interpretations. For example, the walls of a building can be understood within an architectural frame of reference as partitions and boundaries of spaces. At the same time, they can be understood as part of the building's structural system, where they are interpreted as load-bearing or non-load-bearing structural elements. The choice of frame of reference may be based on the observer's disciplinary affiliation. Where an object has more than one referent or frame of reference, and where these references are in conflict with each other, interpretations that are based on these different inferences may lead to radically different understandings. An architect, for example, would be ill advised to move or change the composition of wall that has been designated a bearing wall by the structural engineer.

Bibliography

Akin, Ö., and E. Weinel. *Representation and Architecture*. Silver Spring, Md: Information Dynamics, 1982.

Anderson, J. R. *Language, Memory, and Thought*. Hillside, N.J.: Lawrence Erlbaum, 1976.

Argyle, M. *Cooperation: The Basis of Sociability*. London: Routledge, 1991.

Borgmann, A. *Holding On to Reality: The Nature of Information at the Turn of the Millennium*. Chicago: University of Chicago Press, 1999.

Ericsson, K. A., and H. A. Simon. *Protocol Analysis: Verbal Reports as Data*. Rev. ed. Cambridge: MIT Press, 1993.

Gero, J. S., and T. M. McNeill. "An Approach to the Analysis of Design Protocols." *Design Studies* 19, no. 1 (1998): 21–61.

Goel, V. *Sketches of Thought*. Cambridge: MIT Press, 1995.

Khemlani, L. "Building Representation for Collaborative, Multi-Disciplinary Design." Ph.D. diss., University of California, Berkeley, 2000.

Lawson, B. *How Designers Think: The Design Process Demystified*. Oxford: Architectural Press, 2001.

McLuhan, M. *Understanding Media: The Extensions of Man*. New York: McGraw-Hill, 1964.

Nilsson, N.J. *Principles of Artificial Intelligence*. Palo Alto, Calif.: Tioga Publishing, 1980.

Searle, J. R. *The Construction of Social Reality*. New York: Free Press, 1995.

Searle, J. R. *Mind, Language and Reality*. New York: Basic Books, 1998.

Winston, P. H. *Artificial Intelligence*. Reading, Mass.: Addison-Wesley, 1977.

The Roles of Communication 6

Communication plays two distinct roles in the process of architectural design: an *intra-process* role, where the designer communicates with him or herself during the search for and formation of design ideas in a process known as ideation; and an *extra-process* role, where the designer communicates with other members of the design team.

Ideation can be considered a form of communication because the complexity of the design enterprise requires the use of some means of representation external to the designer's mind: a napkin sketch, a list of issues to be considered, a travelogue, and some samples of materials to be used in the design are such external memory aides and can therefore be considered "representations."

The globalization of the architecture, engineering, and constrction (A/E/C) industries and the specialization of design activities have created a need for communication among a growing number of professionals who participate in the design process. These experts may be dispersed geographically, often across many different continents and time zones. An important role of communication is the timely sharing of information generated by other experts on whom the designers rely to do their part of the process.

Sharing information is, however, not enough. One of the consequences of professional specialization has been the fragmentation and distribution of building-related knowledge among a growing number of disciplines. Each one these disciplines has, over the years, developed its own professional language, means of representation, belief systems, even worldviews, which may be different from those of other disciplines involved in the design process. Each discipline might use a language that, while clear to its own members, can be misunderstood or misinterpreted by members of other disciplines. Different worldviews and beliefs can hinder one profession from understanding another profession's priorities and concerns. Hence, beyond sharing information, communication across disciplinary boundaries also involves engendering shared understanding of the project's goals and constraints—an attempt to disseminate the values, beliefs, and priorities of each participating profession to the others.

Engendering shared understanding is hard to do. When it fails, conflicts arise. Communication then takes on the role of finding common ground, compromises, and others ways of resolving conflicts so the project can move on.

6.1 Ideation

Design problems, according to Horst Rittel, are "wicked" problems: they do not have unique solutions; the solutions are never optimal (since each has undesirable side effects and aftereffects); and the search for them, in and of itself, changes the problem, hence the goals it seeks to accomplish.[1] The process of design, therefore, is different from other problem-solving processes that typically consist of finding the best solution to a well-defined problem. The process of design comprises the simultaneous activities of understanding the problem, generating potential solutions, evaluating those solutions, and possibly modifying the problem to avoid obstacles or take advantage of emerging opportunities. How do designers cope with the complexity of their tasks? Or, as John Archea put it, "What do designers do when no one is looking?"[2]

Researchers have been looking for answers to that question for the past fifty years.[3] Their observations and recordings of the cognitive process that occurs while designers do their work have shown that designing is a kind of conversation between the designer and the designed object. This dialogue between the designer and his or her work has been defined by Donald Schön as a "reflection-in-action."[4]

Imagine, for instance, that the task of an architect is to design a house: the client may have told her something about the site where the house will be located, his needs—in terms of family size and number of rooms—and his budget. Yet there is much uncertainty about what ought to be done for this particular client. The goals are not completely specified, and the number of potential solutions (the "solution space") is far too large for a solution to be developed in some systematic way. The design problem is stated in terms that are much too abstract and needs to be developed into something more concrete from the goals and the context as part of the design process itself. Starting from the initial requirements, the architect would typically go through a process of framing the problem within the social, cultural, economic, and other contexts in which the project takes place. Some of this work may be done with the client or other people involved in the process, but most of the task will consist of an internal dialogue between the architect and herself.

As she starts sketching the solution (metaphorically and figuratively), the architect searches her memory to invoke a repertoire of expectations, images, prior solutions, and techniques that can give her added specifications to incorporate in the design. Like a jazz musician who "feels" the flow of the music, the architect improvises a scenario for further moves. This procedure can be thought of as a system of productions, in which the elements that have already been evoked from memory serve as the stimuli for evoking the next set of elements.[5] While progressing in her work, the architect gets a better understanding of the problem itself. She is able to better appreciate the initial situation, reframe the problem, and "negotiate" with herself the direction she should take. As Schön states: "The designer reflects-in-action on the construction of the problem, the strategies of action, or the model of the phenomena, which have been implicit in his moves."[6] Each decision that she makes is aimed at satisfying a particular requirement, but it impacts other design variables. The architect's task, therefore, is to think of the specifics without losing sight of the whole. Lloyd described the act of designing as a balancing act, where the architect is juggling many issues and subproblems simultaneously.[7]

This ideation process (i.e., the process of forming design ideas) has been documented in so-called protocols, where designers were asked to verbalize their thoughts as they were sketching solutions to a design problem. Figure 6.1 depicts one such protocol, which recorded the thoughts of an architect designing a small library:

1. If I look at the form again . . . it seems that spatially, these are the larger directions (w, x).
2. I am getting one, two, three spaces here (p) and one, two (q) there.
3. They're about square, so there is a tendency to try and see them as spaces.
4. These are secondary directions within the space (y, z), so the entry (3) is actually moving in along the secondary directions.[8]

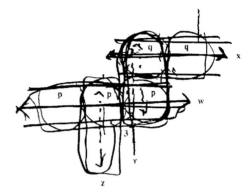

6.1 Sketch of a small library. (G. Goldschmidt, in *Evaluating and Predicting Design Performance*, ed. Y. E. Kalay [New York: Wiley Interscience, 1992].)

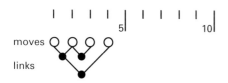

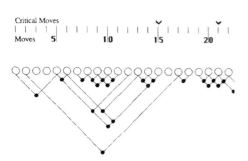

6.2   The Linkograph of the protocol shown in figure 6.1. (G. Goldschmidt, in *Evaluating and Predicting Design Performance*, ed. Y. E. Kalay [New York: Wiley Interscience, 1992].)

6.3   A longer Linkograph. (G. Goldschmidt, in *Evaluating and Predicting Design Performance*, ed. Y. E. Kalay [New York: Wiley Interscience, 1992].)

The protocol can be further analyzed by marking the design "moves" as circles on a linear graphical sequence called a linkograph (fig. 6.2). In addition to the moves themselves, this notation also shows the links among them—the reliance of a move on previous moves (hence the name linkograph). For example, it shows that move 2 follows from move 1, and move 3 follows from move 2. It also shows that move 4 does not follow from move 3. Instead, it follows from move 1 and represents a logical "jump" in the designer's reasoning, who went back a few steps in developing the solution.

Figure 6.3 shows a longer sequence of design actions and displays some of the characteristics of the ideation process. It shows that the links are unevenly distributed, forming so-called chunks, webs, and sawtooth patterns. The chunks represent blocks of links among successive moves that form links almost exclusively among themselves (e.g., moves 2–17 in fig. 6.3). Along with the webs, which represent a large number of closely related links, they indicate an intensive, concentrated design activity. The sawtooth patterns, on the other hand, which are made of relatively long but shallowly linked moves, indicate a relatively consistent flow of ideas, which are based on the immediately preceding ones.

The protocol and its related linkograph offer a visual snapshot of the design ideation process. They show that ideation can be considered a sequence of "moves" that rely on previous moves to a greater or a lesser degree. The designer's ability to pick up and continue the development of an idea, or move, which was made several moves in the past is directly related to the representation used—most often the sketch. The sketch, therefore, becomes the external means of communication that supports the designer's own ideation process: it may mean little to outside observers, who would be hard pressed to make sense of such sketches as depicted in figure 6.1. Yet, to the designer, it is a highly abstracted but fully interpretable record of her thinking process.

6.2 Shared Information

Since the dawn of history, the technical complexity, large scale, and far-reaching social, political, and economic implications of buildings have made their design and construction a social enterprise. From the group activity of a nomadic tribe converting a cave into a place suitable for human habitation, to the organized construction efforts that produced temples, pyramids, and other major civic projects, to the modern collaboration of many experts involved in designing buildings, the number of individuals involved in design and construction projects has risen. A typical building project today may require the coordinated efforts of hundreds, even thousands, of individuals who posses unique elements of the overall skills, knowledge, and expertise needed to complete the task (fig. 6.4).

But while the knowledge and expertise that are needed to complete the design of a building are distributed among many design professionals and suppliers of building components and services, the overall result of their activities—the building itself—is a highly integrated composite of interlocking parts. Hence, the actions and the decisions made by the participants are highly interdependent, requiring close coordination of individual design decisions.

The participants in the design and construction process come together (often for the first time) for the duration of the project, in what is known as a "temporary multi-organization."9 They join the multi-organization when the need for their services arises. When their part in the project is complete, they go their own ways, perhaps to collaborate with each other again in a future project. While joined in the multi-organization, the participants work toward accomplishing the goals of the overall project, contributing from their own expertise, while making sure their part meshes with parts contributed by other specialists to make a coherent whole. Hence, the actions and decisions made by each participant affect, and are affected by, every other participant. Moreover, the decisions made by participants who joined the multi-organization earlier in the project's life cycle impose constraints on downstream participants, who must incorporate them into their own contributions to the project. The upstream participants must, in turn, anticipate the effects their decisions will have on downstream participants. What makes this loose, temporary, and dynamically changing organizational structure work is communication—a means to inform participants of the actions and decisions made by other participants.

When the design team is colocated, and when the task is relatively small, words and sketches provide sufficient means of communication. Communication, in this case, provides the team not only with a way to share information, but also a stimulus to help them generate new ideas

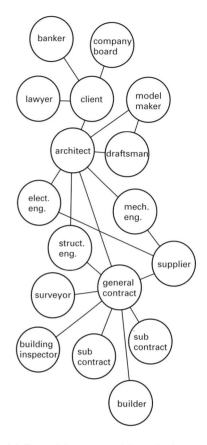

6.4 Some of the many participants in the design project.

based on proposals, observations, and criticisms made by other participants (much like the process of individual ideation discussed earlier).

Communicating across Space and Time

When the design team is dispersed over a large geographic area and across multiple time zones—an increasingly prevalent way of designing large and complex buildings—a tangible means of representation that can be communicated among the participants and can serve as a record of the design process (or at least its main decisions) becomes indispensable. Architecture invented such a means of communication in the fifteenth century, which not only made communication among the participants in the design process possible, but also transformed the profession of architecture itself.

In the Middle Ages buildings were often constructed from a simple schema, denoting the major parts of the building (e.g., the size of a church and the number and placement of its columns). The master builder, who was really the chief technician on the building site, would use his "secret trick" of deducing the elevation from the plan, using a simple system of proportions based on a triangle or a square (*ad triangulum* or *ad quadratum*).[10] This method worked well while the master builder—himself a master mason, stoneworker, or carpenter—spent all his time on the construction site and while the building process consisted of much experimentation and improvisation. Once buildings had to follow strict geometric and stylistic rules, as became the practice during the Renaissance, it was no longer possible to improvise on site: all aspects of the building had to be planned in advance. And as the importance of theory grew, replacing practical building experience as the preeminent skill needed to design buildings, the people who took on that task started to come from the ranks of the nobility rather than the crafts. The first of these *dilettanti* (amateurs, as they were considered by the master masons), was Leon Battista Alberti (1404–1472). His lack of practical competence in construction, combined with his distant residence (in Florence) from the building sites (mostly in Rimini and in Mantua), forced him to rely on other professionals for the actual construction of his buildings. A tangible, persistent means of communication had to be developed to communicate building information between architects, as the new professionals called themselves, and the builders. That means was the scaled drawing.

A whole set of blueprints had to be developed, along with conventions for their consistent interpretation. In 1519 Raphael—a painter turned architect—recommended in a letter to Pope Leo X that three types of drawings be used: the floor plan, the orthogonal elevation, and the section. All three should be drawn to the same scale, and include dimensions to indicate accurate measurements. Moreover, Raphael recommended that the elevation and the section, which he defines in great detail, should be drawn directly above the plan to allow easy reference of the elements they depicted (although, as can be seen in figure 6.5, his recommendation was not always heeded). Raphael rejected the perspective drawing, invented about sixty years earlier, "because the architect cannot obtain measurements from perspective drawings; it is essential in his art that the measurements be absolutely exact and all the lines parallel, conveying the reality and not the semblance."[11]

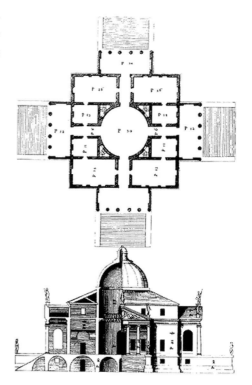

6.5 Andrea Palladio's drawings for the Villa Rotonda (Vicenza, 1560s), floor plan and section/elevation.

Synchronization, Versioning, and Concurrent Updates

As the number of drawings grew, along with the number of participants in the design process who needed to access them, managing the communication process became an issue in and of itself. Two specific problems surfaced: (1) how to ensure that everyone who needed to see a drawing has seen it, and (2) how to ensure that all the participants have seen the latest set of drawings.

The first problem was solved by employing good secretarial skills: an aide was instructed to make a distribution list and ensure that everyone included in it received the newly released drawings in a timely manner. The second problem was solved by adding a bookkeeping component to the drawing itself—a title block (fig. 6.6). It lists information about the drawing itself rather than the building it represents. This meta-information allows architects and engineers to know when a drawing has been released, what, if any, changes from the previous version it contains, and who has seen and approved it.

With the advent of electronic drawing distribution methods, the bookkeeping abilities of computers have supplanted these rather simple, but tedious manual processes. The computer can be programmed to distribute the drawing to a predefined list of recipients, alert them to the arrival of a new drawing, even require them to acknowledge that they have seen it.

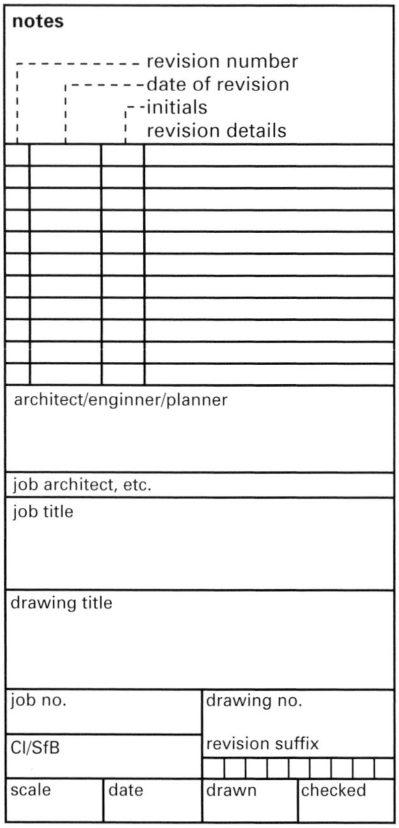
notes
revision number
date of revision
initials
revision details
architect/enginner/planner
job architect, etc.
job title
drawing title
job no.
drawing no.
CI/SfB
revision suffix
scale
date
drawn
checked

6.6 The title block conveys information about the drawing itself, not the building it represents.

No satisfactory solution, either manual or electronic, has yet been found to the problem of concurrent updates to drawings, where two individuals might be making changes to the same drawing (or rather, the building it represents) at the same time. For example, if the architect changes the location of a door in a part of the building that is, at the same time, used by a structural engineer to calculate the load bearing capabilities of the wall in which the door is located, errors will ensue. It is a situation similar to the case of two travel agents attempting to book the same seat on the same flight for two different clients at the same time—a case that might leave one of the passengers stranded. In the air travel industry, such concurrent transaction are quite rare, because it takes only a fraction of a second to complete the booking, and thus block the seat from further bookings. In the process of designing buildings, however, the "transaction" can be lengthy—measured in days or even weeks, not fractions of a second—thus making the likelihood of concurrent updates quite real.

6.3 Shared Understanding

Sharing information among the participants of a design team is a necessary but not a sufficient condition for effective communication—it only addresses the first two components of the communication pipeline (encoding and representation). If the information is to be useful, it must also be interpreted correctly by the recipients. But the fragmentation of the A/E/C industry into many subdisciplines makes correct interpretation of shared information a difficult task.

To master the intricate issues for which it is responsible within the overall building enterprise, each subdiscipline requires increasing amounts of knowledge in very specialized fields. Architects are educated to be responsible for the allocation of spaces and for specifying the materials of the building; structural engineers are educated to be responsible for making it resistant to gravity and lateral forces; mechanical engineers are educated to be responsible for heating, cooling, and ventilating the building, and so on. Their specializations are reinforced by educational practices and socioeconomic trends that promote and reward excellence in ever narrowing fields. In turn, specialization fuels the discovery and development of better understanding, improved methods, and refined products for accomplishing specific tasks, leading to even greater specialization.

Consider the case of such disciplines as law and medicine: once composed of general practitioners, they are now bustling with hundreds of specialists. Even architecture, the most "general" of all disciplines, has yielded to specialization, as evidenced by the proliferation of professional interest groups within the American Institute of Architects (AIA), each concerning itself with one specific set of issues, for example, with health care, codes and standards, construction management, or housing.

Worldviews

One of the consequences of professional specialization is the emergence of specialized worldviews: the socially constructed belief systems through which discipline-specific knowledge is developed, transmitted, and maintained.[12] These worldviews facilitate communication within each discipline and foster the development of a subculture and a unique language that distinguish one profession from another, and the professionals from the laymen. Through professional education and practice—the process of "socializing" into a specific discipline—disciples are taught the profession's own way of seeing the world, which guides their thoughts and actions. Over time, like a religion, this worldview becomes no longer open to challenge.

Each one of the professions participating in the design and construction of buildings has developed its own worldview, which upholds and promotes certain values over others. In general, architects tend to emphasize the *quality* of artifacts over their function, purpose, and the processes of making them. Engineers tend to emphasize the *function* or *purpose* of the artifact, placing less emphasis on the process of making, and still less on its formal qualities. Construction managers are interested mostly in the process of *making*, whereas facilities managers are interested in the process of *maintaining*. Building owners and end-users are usually relatively uninterested in their environment as long as it does not impinge on their activities and interfere with the achievement of their personal or institutional goals (i.e., how well the place supports the education of students, the fabrication of goods, or making people well).

Their different worldviews prevent the participants in the design process from forming a shared, objective basis for understanding design communication. The importance, meaning, and value of objects, concepts, situations and action are understood differently by each participant,

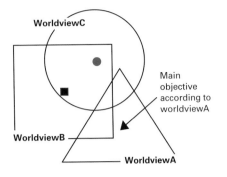

6.7 Different worldviews promote different objectives: what is central to Worldview A does not even enter the universe of Worldview B, and what is central to Worldview B is peripheral to Worldview C.

seen through the lens of its own socially constructed reality. What might be considered central to one participant's worldview may be secondary to, or even completely absent from, another's (fig. 6.7). In the best case, their different worldviews can cause the participants to misunderstand each other. In the worst case, they can lead to conflicts that must be resolved if the design process is to yield successful results.

Facilitating Shared Understanding

To facilitate shared understanding it is necessary, therefore, to introduce each participant to the worldviews of the other participants. Normally, this is an educational process that takes many years to accomplish and is, therefore, impractical for the temporary nature of a multi-organization formed by the participants for any particular design project. Still, limited shared understanding can be achieved by augmenting the communicated message with information that conveys the rationale and the background for the decisions and the actions, in addition to communicating the actions themselves. One such method is participatory design.

Participatory design is a process used by architects who wish to involve the users of the intended facility in its design. Such involvement often promotes better acceptance of the resulting facility by its users and may generate insights and ideas that the architects can use for shaping it. As an example of such participatory design process, consider the experiment conducted by the San Francisco Exploratorium—a hands-on science museum housed within the Palace of Fine Arts. It was founded in 1969 by noted physicist and educator Dr. Frank Oppenheimer. By the early 1990s the Exploratorium filled its banana-shaped exhibit hall to capacity and embarked on an expansion project that would add new floors within its cavernous space. As befitting a leader in the movement to promote museums as educational centers, the Exploratorium's curators decided to invite the public to participate in the process of its design.

The shared means of communication chosen for this purpose was the Internet. A Web site was designed that allowed the public to register their views on various aspects of the existing exhibit space and the proposed one. Very quickly it became apparent that shared communication was not the main problem—shared understanding was. The public was not familiar with the main design issues, the constraints the designers had to con-

Communication

tend with, the goals set by the curators, and good practices in museum design. The flood of information provided by an enthusiastic public became unmanageable and useless.

In an effort to educate the public in matters related to the expansion of the Exploratorium, a shared understanding was facilitated through a revised Web site, called the Virtual Atelier. It provided visitors with background information about five topics that were deemed to be the most important for the Exploratorium: light, sound, way finding, the entrance, and the machine shop (fig. 6.8).

By clicking on one of the appropriate symbols, visitors were introduced to the selected topic. For example, the entrance topic explained that the entrance to a museum like the Exploratorium fulfills many functions in addition to being the gateway to the exhibits: it is where money is collected, where parties meet, where the visitor transitions from the public to the private realm, where security is enforced, and so on. The content of this topic, simple as it may have been, provided the public with much better understanding of the issues. Similar explanations, in the form of text, graphics, and animations, provided visitors with a basic understanding of the other chosen topics. The quality of the input received from the public once this Web site was activated improved dramatically and provided useful feedback to the designers and the curators, confirming the importance of shared understanding.

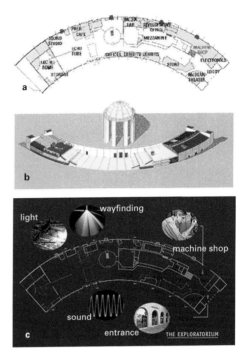

6.8 The Virtual Atelier was developed to facilitate shared understanding in the design of the San Francisco Exploratorium (1998).

6.4 Conflict Management

Given that all the participants in a building enterprise have been educated into their own ways of viewing the world, it is inevitable that conflicts will arise as they begin to understand what is being proposed by other members of the design team. Accordingly, conflict is defined as "a situation of competition in which the parties are aware of the incompatibility of potential future positions and in which each party wishes to occupy a position that is incompatible with the wishes of the other."[13] To arrive at a consensual plan, the conflicts among the participants in a design process must be resolved.

According to Kuhn, conflict resolution among different professionals (as opposed to conflict resolution among feuding parties, whether nations, corporations, or individuals) involves reconciliation of differently constructed worldviews or different paradigms.[14] He proposed three ways in which such paradigmatic conflicts can be resolved: (1) persuading one side of the conflict to adopt the position of the other side; (2) compromising the beliefs inherent in both sides' paradigms; and (3) jointly arriving at a new, "super-paradigm"—a process that requires a leap of faith on the part of all parties involved. The first and second strategies risk reducing the commitment of one or both parties to the shared enterprise because of their diminished "ownership" or influence. Finding a mutually acceptable super-paradigm is the optimal but most difficult way of resolving a conflict. It requires a more extensive understanding of the worldview of the "other side" and a willingness to compromise one's own position, if not one's entire worldview, for the benefits of enhancing the performance of the project as a whole.

Not surprisingly, conflict management has been studied by almost all the social sciences, including economics, political science, sociology, and psychology. Economists have studied conflict among firms, unions, and other economic entities. Political scientists have focused on conflicts among states,[15] and sociologists have looked at conflicts within and among families and racial and religious groups.[16] Anthropologists study the conflict between cultures, and psychologists study conflict within the person.

Although conflict management behavior exhibits many different patterns, these patterns are not entirely different from one another because they are all based on common human traits. Thus conflict management models that have been developed in such fields as industrial relations, international relations, and interpersonal relations are, to a large extent, interchangeable, with suitable adaptation to the particular context. And, although the nature of architectural design is different from other fields, the generalized model of conflict management is applicable to resolving conflicts within the process of designing buildings.

A General Model of Conflict Management

A general model of conflict management has been proposed by Serag-Eldin.[17] It includes two major components: avoidance and procedural resolution (fig. 6.9). The first component is the most common, though by its very nature it is also the least noticeable: the parties to the conflict simply remove themselves from each other's company, increasing the distance between them to the point where the conflict ceases to exist. An engineer who has strong views that are incompatible with the architect's can quit and leave the project team. An architect who does not get along with the client can be fired (a form of removal, in the context of conflict management). Such conflict management is characterized by lack of communication—there is often little effort to try to reconcile the differences between the parties.

If the parties can neither avoid each other nor remove themselves or each other, some form of procedural resolution is likely. It is here that communication plays a central role. Since the parties will continue to work together, there must be some agreement, based on mutual understanding, on how to resolve the conflict. Such agreement may take one of three forms:

1. *Reconciliation.* Both parties discard their original, incompatible preferences in favor of new, common ones. This is the condition Thomas Kuhn called "paradigm shift."
2. *Compromise.* Each party is willing to settle for something less than its original (ideal) position rather than continue the conflict. In case of a compromise, a mutual settlement is reached through bargaining between the parties themselves. This form of conflict resolution is different from reconciliation in that the parties reduce their original expectations rather than adopt new ones.
3. *Award.* A settlement is reached because both parties have agreed to accept the decision of an outside person or agency rather than continue the conflict. Compromise and award are essentially similar in that they both represent less than the ideal situation for each party; they differ mainly in the method of arriving at the settlement.

Reconciliation is thus the result of communication that leads to modifications in the preferences of the parties involved in the conflict. Compromise is the culmination of a bargaining process. An *award* is the end result of arbitration.[18] None of the three forms of settlement is completely separate in practice, though there is a tendency for one form to dominate in any particular case. Frequently, both reconciliation and compromise occur simultaneously. Some reconciliation may be necessary

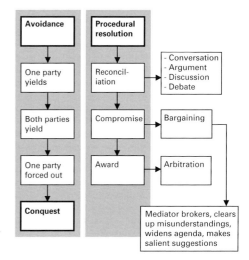

6.9 A general model of human conflict resolution. G. Serag-Eldin, "Applying a Human Conflict Management Model to Architectural Design Collaboration," Ph.D. diss., University of California, Berkeley, 2003.

before compromise is possible. Similarly, in arbitration cases, there are often elements of both reconciliation and bargaining before the award is handed down; indeed, the award is unlikely to be accepted unless it has been preceded by informal reconciliation and bargaining. In every case, however, communication takes the form of argumentation—the process where issues are raised, debated, and shared through discussion. Argumentation increases the chances that the participants in the design process will perceive views other than their own, thereby reducing the "symmetry of ignorance"—the tunnel vision of professionals who view the world through a particular disciplinary knowledge base and set of beliefs. Through the play and counterplay of questioning and arguing, participants form and exert their judgments continuously, developing a better understanding of the problem, its origins, and its solutions.

Representing the Conflict

In the 1970s Horst Rittel proposed that communication leading to shared understanding or conflict resolution can be facilitated by explicitly representing and structuring the argumentation process itself.[19] He developed a computational tool, called IBIS (Issue-Based Information System), to represent the argumentation process. It was intended to be used by government agencies, administrative bodies, and planning groups who were confronted with complex planning and design problems and had to arrive at a consensual plan for action. By breaking down complex problems into more manageable components, called issues, positions, and arguments, and by recording the argumentation process in a retrievable form, IBIS provided a means to represent the argumentative process, promoting the transparency of the decision-making process and illuminating, if not avoiding, conflicts.

An issue in IBIS is stated in the form of a controversial question, about which people may have differing points of view. Examples of issues might be: "What color should this building be?" "Should another skyscraper be built downtown?" "What aesthetic style is most appropriate for this building?"

A person's response to an issue is called a position. For some issues, including deontic issues (issues of what ought to be), such responses include two opposing viewpoints: "Yes, that should be," and "No, that should not be." For other issues, there may be an open-ended list of positions, consisting of alternative courses of action.

The evidence offered in support of or in opposition to a position is known as argument. A position might have any number of arguments to support or object to it, and some arguments may support more than one position. There are several general responses to a position or other argument:

- agree
- concede
- concede hypothetically ("Let's assume that you are right . . .")
- ask "So what?" ("What is the significance of your proposition?")
- request justification ("How do you know?")
- request further evidence ("Explain!")
- question ("Is this so?")
- doubt
- object or contradict
- question or deny the significance or relevance of the proposition ("What does that have to do with the problem?")

The structure of an IBIS protocol is established by the various types of relationships of its issues, positions, and arguments. Positions can be linked to their issues through the verb "to respond." Arguments can be said to "support" or "object to" someone's position. When documented, these linguistic relationships structure the argumentation in a manner that make it traceable, assist in pointing out where distinct issues may be interrelated, and assist designers in discovering where entire types of issues have been neglected.

Visualizing the Conflict

Every participant in the design process is interested in a particular set of important design issues to which he or she associates relative values with respect to how well they are accomplished by a given design solution. This set of issues is called a view. Conflicts arise when one participant's view differs from another's. To resolve the conflict, the participants' views must be aligned. But how can the participants communicate their views to each other?

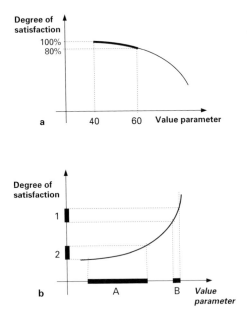

Degree of
satisfaction
100%
80%

a   40   60   Value parameter

Degree of
satisfaction

1

2

b   A   B   Value
                      parameter

6.10 Satisfaction curves represent the correlation between the degree of change in the value of some design parameter and the satisfaction it elicits.

A visual method of communicating views, called "satisfaction functions" (fig. 6.10), was first introduced by Gustav Theodor Fechner in 1871 in relation to his work on experimental aesthetics.[20] Simply stated, this theory proposes that the satisfaction (or utility) derived from a commodity varies with the quantity of that commodity but increases less rapidly as the quantity of the commodity increases. The theory was updated by Musso and Rittel in the late 1960s and applied to the evaluation of buildings.[21] Satisfaction curves facilitate the communication of the relationship between the *parametric value*—the degree to which an issue has been satisfied by a specific design solution—and the participant's relative *degree of satisfaction* with that accomplishment. As depicted in figure 6.10a, this representation also communicates the value at which the participants would have been completely satisfied (100%), the threshold below which the issue is considered to be not satisfied at all, and the degree of flexibility of the participant with respect to this issue—the participant's willingness to relax the requirements.

For example, an architect may be interested in a noise level issue, with respect to a window, that ranges between 40 dB and 60 dB. These numbers correspond to degrees of satisfaction that range from 100% to 80%, respectively (i.e., the optimal degree of satisfaction will be reached when noise level of noise reduction achieved by the window is 40 dB). The architect will not be satisfied at all if the level of noise transmitted by the window exceeds 60 dB (too noisy) or is less than 40 dB (feels isolated).

The degree of flexibility in relaxing the requirements is represented by the slope of the curve: the steeper the slope the more abrupt the change, which means that even a small change in the object's parametric value will result in greatly increased satisfaction or dissatisfaction. On the other hand, a shallow slope indicates a wider satisfaction latitude, which allows for more room when negotiating with other participants in case of a conflict related to this issue. Figure 6.10b shows how two changes in performance—A and B—induce the same amount of change in satisfaction, although A represents a greater change in the value parameter than B does.

Each participant must independently define and set the satisfaction curves that represent his or her subjective values with regard to the performance of the design solution. As shown in figure 6.11, these curves might be different for each participant, even with respect to same value. Figure 6.11 also shows how the same parameter value (the dotted vertical line connecting all three curves) can elicit different degrees of satisfaction. While for participant A the achieved value represents an optimal solution, it is barely acceptable for participant B, and for participant C is it not acceptable at all. The figure also shows that either participant B or C will have to change their satisfaction curves (i.e., their position with regard to this issue), because there is no overlap in their curves that will admit a common value that is acceptable to both.

The goal of each participant is to find a design solution that optimally satisfies all issues of concern, within the acceptable range of satisfactions, at the highest possible end of that range. This is unlikely to happen, because there are probably incompatibilities even among the issues that are of interest to the individual participant, let alone among issues of different participants. Hence, each participant will have to prioritize issues and maintain different negotiation strategies to be adopted at certain points during the negotiation process. These may include reprioritizing the various criteria to be satisfied, and willingness to modify the satisfaction curves themselves.

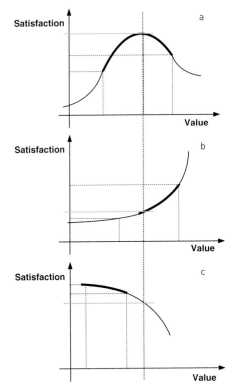

6.11 Comparing degrees of satisfaction for the same parameter value.

Bibliography

Foz, A. "Observations on Designer Behavior in the Parti." In *Design Activity Conference*. London, 1973.

Goldschmidt, G. "Criteria for Design Evaluation: A Process Oriented Paradigm." In *Evaluating and Predicting Design Performance*, ed. Y. E. Kalay, 67–79. New York: Wiley Interscience, 1992.

Graves, M. "The Necessity for Drawing: Tangible Speculation." *Architectural Design* 47, no. 6 (1977): 384–394.

Hitchcock, R. "Improving Life-Cycle Information Management through Documentation of Project Objectives and Design Rationale." Ph.D. diss., Department of Civil Engineering, University of California, Berkeley, 1996.

Larkin, J., and H. A. Simon. "Why a Diagram Is (Sometimes) Worth Ten Thousand Words." *Cognitive Science* 11 (1987): 65–99.

Lloyd, P., B. Lawson, and P. Scott. "Can Concurrent Verbalization Reveal Design Cognition?" *Design Studies* 16 (1995): 237–259.

Rowe, P. G. *Design Thinking*. Cambridge: MIT Press, 1987.

Tufte, E. R. *The Visual Display of Quantitative Information*. Cheshire, Conn.: Graphic Press, 1983.

Zimring, C., E. Y.-L. Do, E. Domeshek, and J. Kolodner. "Using Post-Occupancy Evaluation to Aid Reflection in Conceptual Design: Creating a Case-Based Design Aid for Architecture." In *Design Decision Support System,* ed. H. Dimitripoulos. The Netherlands: Vaals, 1994.

Habitual Methods of Representation 7

Given the complex and multifaceted roles of communication in design, it is not surprising that so many different methods of representation have been developed for use by architects and other professionals involved in the design of buildings. Although the array of all possible representational methods is huge, in common practice the number is limited. Methods range from general modes of communication like speaking, writing, and sketching, to highly specialized modes of representation like drawings and three-dimensional scale models, to full-size prototypes of kitchens, apartments, and even whole buildings. They differ in their affordances and levels of abstraction, as shown in figure 7.1. Some are highly abstract, such as scale drawings and so-called arbitrary codes (including text and numerical notations), requiring considerable mental gymnastics to decode the messages they communicate. Others are highly expressive, like illustrations, photographs, and scale models. At the same time, some of these modes of representation allow the receiver to be an active participant in the communication process, like scale models that afford many different points of view. Others convey a single, highly organized message determined by the sender (like scale drawings). There is, of course, no single mode of communication that is superior to all other: if there were, there would not be so many. Each is better suited to some needs than other methods. The difficulty lies in ensuring that the right method is used for a given communication needs.

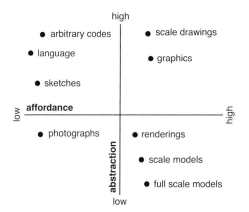

7.1 A taxonomy of habitual methods of representation.

7.1 Arbitrary Codes

Arbitrary codes are highly abstract means of communication, both in form and in content. They are based on a common notational language that can represent ideas and information very concisely. Alphabets, musical notes, mathematical symbols, computer code and iconic signage are examples of arbitrary codes. Each one comprises a kind of "language" into which the message must be encoded. Only those who know the language can decode the message (one must be able to read English to decode the message in this book). The efficiency of the communication depends on the affordance of the language: some languages are well suited for communicating mathematical equations, others for communicating music. Architectural drawings are such arbitrary codes. They include graphical conventions that represent walls, doors, and other elements of buildings, as well as mathematical notations of quantities such as floor areas, and abbreviations or numbers that are used to identify materials, colors, and other properties of building elements.

The advantage of arbitrary codes is their brevity, which focuses attention on content rather than on form. They allow communication of much more information in less time and space and with less effort than the more verbose forms of communication, often with great accuracy. They also have three major shortcomings:

1. The communicating parties must share a common language in order to understand the content and meaning of information. The time and effort required to learn this language limit the number of people who can understand the communicated message.
2. The encoding and decoding processes themselves require a great deal of effort.
3. There can be a significant loss of information and meaning due to the high level of abstraction involved.

The first limitation is quite obvious: a message written in English has meaning only to people who can read English. Like other languages, English requires years of learning before it can be used for communication. For example, neither the textual symbols that are used to form the words "door" and "wall" nor the words themselves—which denote the *objects* WALL and DOOR—look anything like doors and walls in reality: the conversion from symbol to object is a mental one and relies on a shared agreement to interpret the symbols according to a shared decoding method, called the English language.

The second limitation involves the cost of coding and decoding the message, which makes some forms of communication more effortful and time-consuming than others. Much effort, for example, must be spent in architectural and engineering offices on drafting—a process that does not really contribute to the development of the design, only to its representation in a communicable way. That is one of the reasons why draftsmen are the lowest-paid employees in architectural offices and why some offices now out-source the production of drawings to places like Manila, in the Philippines, where the labor force is skilled but inexpensive by American standards.

The affordance of the language may limit the expressiveness of the communication. The adage "A picture is worth a thousand words" aptly expresses how difficult it is to describe an image in words. Likewise, it is difficult to describe musical expressions verbally. On the other hand, some notational languages are very well adapted to communicating the subject of their discourse. Mathematical notation is the preferred way of describing numerical relationships since it is concise and clear. Likewise, programming languages are very good for describing processes of the kind that can be executed by computers. Their affordance, however, is not the same for all tasks: some programming languages are good for coding scientific formulae (e.g., FORTRAN), others for coding semantic relationships (e.g., LISP), and others for coding business transactions (e.g., COBOL).

The choice of using arbitrary codes in the first place, and the kind of code used, depend on the subject of the communication, its context, the required amount of precision, and the amount of time allotted for encoding and decoding the message. In the professional context of architecture, for example, it is necessary to use conventional scale drawings, both as a common means of communication and as the legal document for assigning responsibilities. In the context of computer programming, it is necessary to use arbitrary codes, because computers' ability to understand human language is very limited. In other domains the choice is not always that clear. How many figures, for example, should be used to illustrate a text such as this one? What about photo-journals, where the amount of pictures far exceeds the text? How many video clips should illustrate a news item on television? Here the decision must be made by evaluating the cost of providing illustrations and video clips versus the affordance of words on paper or spoken by the news anchor, and the ability of the public to understand the spoken story versus the video clips.

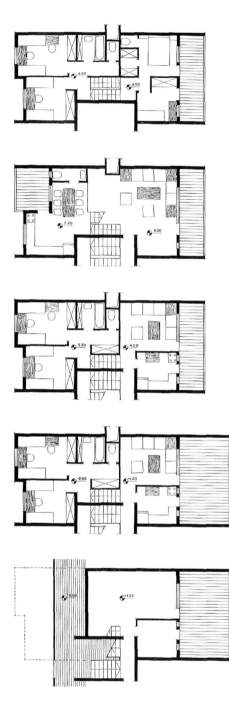

7.2 Architectural scale drawings are arbitrary codes. (Y. E. Kalay, architect.)

Communication

Scale Drawings

Scale drawings are the most common form of arbitrary codes used as means of communication by professionals involved in the design and construction of buildings (fig. 7.2). Drawings provide a parsimonious notation for conveying detailed and exact building information. Since they have been in continuous use for over 500 years, drawings have developed conventions that govern their style and content. However, much of the information that is conveyed by drawings is implicit and relies on interpretation. The ability to interpret them correctly depends on the receiver's knowledge, which must be acquired through professional education. But professional education, as we have seen before, does not guarantee that all the participants in the design process can read each other's drawings: different professions may have developed different conventions. For example, most scale drawings do not explicitly show the spaces (rooms) of a building: they only show the walls that bound them. The relationship between the walls and the spaces they enclose is a matter of interpretation, which may be obvious to an architect, educated to "read" drawings in that manner, but not at all obvious to a structural engineer, who is educated to read them as structural plans. Additional symbols, annotations, and specifications can help to narrow the range of possible interpretations, but they cannot completely eliminate it.

The heavy reliance on interpretation, and the need to augment the explicit information conveyed by a drawing with implicit assumptions, hinders their effective use as a means to engender shared multidisciplinary understanding. In fact, despite overlaps in notational conventions, each one of the participating A/E/C professions has, over the years, developed its own notational symbols, as well as its own interpretations, which are rarely understood outside its own discipline. It is common, therefore, for structural engineers to redraw the drawings they receive from the architects, in effect "translating" them into their own notational symbolism. Construction managers similarly "translate" the drawings they receive from the architects and the engineers, using their own interpretations and symbols. Like every other translation, redrawing invariably involves the loss of information due to incompatible interpretations and the reliance on implicit, uncommunicated assumptions.

Moreover, frame-of-reference information that is conveyed by drawings is limited to the immediate physical context of the project and does not include cultural, economic, and other types of contextual information. Hence, drawings lack the ability to accommodate changing frames of reference and the ability to identify and propagate such changes; they are completely passive instruments of communication.

Efforts to reduce the amount of personal knowledge needed for the correct interpretation of drawings have focused on developing shared symbol sets, in the form of standardized notations. Examples of such standards range from the ubiquitous (but architecturally biased) Architectural Graphic Standards[1] to more general computational standards like IGES and STEP (which are discussed in section 8.5).[2] While these methods have helped to reduce errors that are due to translation from one profession's notational conventions into another's, they have done little to help eliminate interpretive errors due to the paucity of frame-of-reference information. Therefore, drawings are often accompanied by other means of communication, such as natural language.

7.2 Language

Language, unlike arbitrary codes, requires no special professional education: it is spoken by the majority of people in one country. Natural language is used heavily in architecture, as in all other fields of human endeavor, but its primary purpose is to augment the other methods of professional communication.

Language is indispensable for providing instructions such as building regulations, explanations of drawings, and specifications that explain how a building ought to be built. Language is extensively used in the early stages of design to develop problem statements, and it is used to describe the process of design and construction in the form of contract documents. Language is also used for public relations purposes, when the proposed design is presented to the public or to the client.

Natural Language

Languages have variable levels of abstraction. Some are more appropriately termed arbitrary codes, while others require no shared understanding beyond the everyday meaning of the words they use. The former are used, for example, in legal documents that can be read by lay people but often cannot be fully understood without legal training. The latter, on the other hand, require no special training and are, therefore, called "natural languages" (although there is nothing natural about them). They are very flexible and easy to understand but are also open to much misinterpretation, as demonstrated by ambiguous sentences like "time flies like an arrow." Does this sentence denote the swiftness of the passage of time? Or does it denote the diet of a species of insect? (The answer depends, of course, on whether 'flies' is used as a verb or as a noun.) The major advantage of natural languages is therefore also their major disadvantage: while they can be used to communicate anything, they require a great deal of effort to communicate something—especially something as complex as a building—with enough preciseness to allow its construction.

Nonverbal Language

Language, of course, does not have to be verbal. In fact, much of the communication among humans is nonverbal, a phenomenon that explains the expressive poverty of a telephone conversation compared to a face-to-face meeting or even to video-conferencing. In a telephone conversation, much of the redundancy, nuance, and richness of communicating a message is lost, requiring more explicit verbalization—shrugging, nodding, or shaking one's head cannot be heard over the telephone. The same is true when the verbal part of language is completely removed and only the visual part of the communication remains, as in pantomime: both the sender of the information and its receiver must exert considerable effort to encode the information and decode it in a manner that will properly convey the message—so much so that this type of communication has been elevated to a form of art. (People who attend mime shows often comment on the intellectual effort needed to understand the performance, which is the reason they attend the show in the first place.)

7.3 Graphics

Sketches, renderings, perspective drawings, and photographs are important modes of communication in architecture. Visualization has advantages over other modes of communication: it allows designers and clients (and more recently, scientists in many different disciplines as well) to apply what Jacob Bronowski called "visual cognition"—the ability of humans to infer more meaning from visual stimuli than from any other form of communication.[3] Graphical representation helps designers to reflect upon the emerging solution, appraise it in its totality, and observe the relationships between the parts and the whole. Sketches and drawings are to designers what paper and pencil are to mathematicians—an extension of their short-term memory (STM). They provide a means to consider complex components of the artifact in more detail than the limited capacity of short-term memory allows, without the risk of forgetting other parts of the solution on which the designer does not currently focus. And the client, who is often the other principle target of graphical communication, can understand the message in a natural, cognitively unencumbered manner.

Like language, graphics have a wide range of affordances and can represent almost any level of abstraction. Figure 7.3a depicts a highly expressive sketch of Le Corbusier's famed chapel of Notre-Dame du Haut at Ronchamp, France, which leaves little doubt about the form of the building. Figure 7.3b, on the other hand, represents a rather abstract drawing that could be interpreted as the floor plan of the chapel (which it is) as easily as some two dimensional decorative pattern. The rendering uses easily recognizable graphical elements to communicate information, such as shrubs, a footpath, and a sloping landscape. The abstract drawing, on the other hand, is really an arbitrary code that requires special knowledge for its decoding. There is a fine line, however, between an arbitrary code and an illustration. The level of abstraction in an illustration may become so high that a shared convention may have to be established before anyone can understand it.

Illustrations are very good communication tools because they contain a great deal of information that can be readily comprehended even by people not trained in reading professional architectural drawings. Little information and meaning is lost between the sender and the receiver, and little effort needs to be expended for their decoding. Illustrations, however, are very time-consuming to create and very difficult to alter. Furthermore, they convey only inexact information—it is hard to judge precise dimensions, distances between objects, and sometimes even the relationships between them.

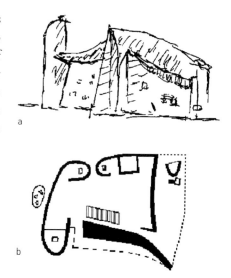

7.3 Le Corbuseir's Notre-Dame du Haut, Ronchamp, France: (a) perspective sketch, (b) a highly abstract floor plan (Le Corbusier's own sketches, c. 1951).

7.4 An optical illusion sculpture in Caracas, Venezuela. Although it appears to be three-dimensional, the sculpture is actually an almost flat sheet of painted metal.

Probably the greatest drawback of graphics (including photographs) as a means of communication is that, in addition to the message itself, the medium of representation also encodes—quite literally—the sender's point of view. Perspective images, photographs, even sketches, are recorded as they are seen from a specific vantage point, determined by the sender. This encoding, which is the hallmark of perspective rendering and was hailed, justifiably, as one of the great contributions of the Renaissance, gives the sender the ability to communicate—in addition to the message itself—also his or her point of view about the communicated information. The receiver of the message cannot tell what the illustrated object looks like from behind, or from the side—only what the sender has decided should be seen. The sculpture depicted in figure 7.4 is a good case in point. It depicts a series of what appears to be three-dimensional boxes, stacked one above the other. But an inspection from the side reveals this to be an optical illusion. The sculpture is actually a largely flat sheet of painted metal. In this respect, illustrations and perspective images are different from scale drawings, which are neutral with respect to the sender's point of view, and from scale models, which allow the viewer (the receiver) to determine his or her own point of view independently from the sender's.

7.4 Scale Models

Three-dimensional comprehension is indispensable for artifacts that are inherently volumetric. Yet, using arbitrary codes and even sophisticated graphics, these qualities can only be inferred through a complex cognitive process. A good example is trying to understand the three-dimensional character of a building through plans, elevations, and sections—a process that requires combining the different views into one comprehensive mental image. Three-dimensional scale models, on the other hand, provide this information in a readily comprehensible manner.

A scale model not only informs the observer of the volumetric properties of the artifact, but allows a choice of vantage point independent of the sender's (fig. 7.5). The observer thus becomes an active participant in the communication process. The sender, in turn, must provide more information than would be required to communicate an image of the building, making the encoding process much more difficult.

Scale models can also be subjected to some actual physical tests, which are difficult to simulate with arbitrary codes and illustrations. For example, physical scale models can be tested in wind tunnels, they can be subjected to a variety of stresses, and they can be tested for daylighting illumination or shadow casting.

Depending on the materials used and the level of detail included, physical models can be very abstract and, like drawings, can cross some imaginary boundary to become arbitrary codes. In that capacity, scale models are often used for the purpose of ideation. Conversely, when they are made from materials that simulate the actual ones to be used in a building, and when the level of detail is high, physical models can become very close simulations of actual buildings. Such models are often constructed (at great expense and effort) once the design is complete and needs to be communicated to the clients and other participants in the design project (as was the case with Sir Christopher Wren's "Great Model" of St. Paul's basilica, which cost the equivalent of building a three-bedroom house in the seventeenth century). Some scale models have attained the status of art objects, such as the one depicted in figure 7.6, which is made of 100 pounds of gold.

The major limitations of physical models are the time and effort needed to construct them, and their bulk, which makes them difficult to transport over great distances. Nor can scale models be transmitted in electronic form (e.g., fax or telephone).[4] This means that fewer people can have access to a model with far less frequency than to other forms of communication.

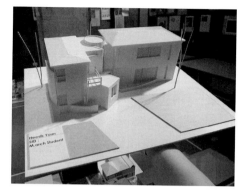

7.5 Scale models allow viewers to choose their own vantage point. (University of California, Berkeley.)

Mock-ups

Full-scale models, known as mock-ups, allow viewers to experience an artifact as close to reality as one can come without constructing the object itself. They allow us to appreciate not only how the object will look, but also how it will feel—the haptic and kinesthetic qualities of the design.

Like scale models, mock-ups are made of materials that are different from the object itself. For example, a mock-up of a full-scale building, made from Lego-like plastic blocks measuring 10 x 10 x 20 cm allows a visitor to experience the spatial enclosure created by the building (fig. 7.7), even though the materials used (plastic) do not mimic reality. Similarly, a desk made of cardboard allows the user to experience the reach and ergonomics of the proposed workstation (fig. 7.8)

7.6 A scale model made of solid gold. (Vatican Museum collection.)

7.7 Mock-up of a building, made of Lego-like building blocks. (Central University of Venezuela, Caracas.)

7.8 Mock-up of a desk, made of cardboard. (University of California, Berkeley.)

Communication

Prototypes

Sometimes mock-ups are made from the actual materials from which the object itself will be made. In that case, they are considered prototypes. Prototypes are, without doubt, the best approximation of the actual artifact: they communicate the visual, spatial, and material properties fully and directly, and can be subjected to all the conditions the final artifact is likely to experience. Yet the time and expense needed to construct them make prototypes a valid form of communication only when the number of artifacts that will be constructed is large (e.g., windows on a high-rise building in Tel Aviv, Israel, as shown in figure 7.9); when the complexity of the artifact is too great to appreciate by any other means, such as the cladding of Frank Gehry's Disney Concert Hall in Los Angeles (fig. 7.10); or in extreme cases, when construction difficulties or safety considerations warrant early experimentation (e.g., in the case of complex laboratory designs, control rooms for nuclear power plants, or hospital operating rooms).

7.9 Prototype windows tested on a high-rise building in Tel Aviv, Israel.

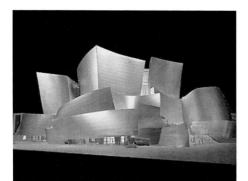

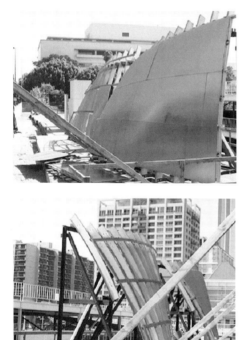

7.10 Prototype of the cladding tested for Frank Gehry's Disney Concert Hall in Los Angeles, California.

7.5 Limitations of Habitual Methods of Communication

Habitual methods of communication pose some serious obstacles to contemporary architectural practices, which in turn create pressures to adopt more effective means of representation and communication. These limitations stem from the following key disadvantages of habitual modes of communication:

1. Lack of flexibility in adjusting the level of abstraction as needed for each stage of the design process.
2. Inability to change and to evolve as the design process progresses.
3. Limited potential for managing the vast amount of information needed to design a building and provide efficient access to that information.
4. Inability to provide adequate information to evaluate the design in progress and to predict its performance.
5. Centralization of control over the design process in the hands of a few people.

Inflexibility

Different phases and aspects of the design process require different levels of abstraction. In the early phases of the design process, drawings and models are used that are, necessarily, highly abstract. It does not make sense to invest a great deal of effort in developing the details of a design when the solution has not yet reached the degree of resolution needed to make decisions about such details. At the same time, a great deal of detail may be useful, in many cases, to spot problems that might hinder the development of a solution later on. For example, early conceptual drawings of a building rarely include furniture. Therefore, planning internal traffic patterns, fire egress routes, and other decisions that affect the design are made without knowing whether the desired furniture arrangements will actually fit in the proposed building.[5]

Too little abstraction, on the other hand, can also lead to difficulties. Clients can be confused by the amount of information provided. Even the architect may be overwhelmed. The abundance of detail may cause the architect to overlook features that are important to some design aspects, while concentrating on others that are perhaps less important. A good

Communication

example comes from the area of fire safety. The ability to evaluate the fire safety performance of a building from early design documents would help in the analysis and optimization of this important design attribute. But doing so too soon in the design process may inhibit the development of novel solutions that might obviate the need for traditional fire safety measures.

Limited Ability to Change and to Evolve

Perhaps the most serious limitation of habitual modes of communication is the lack of continuity between the different representations of the solution as it moves through the phases of the design process. Schematic drawings do not automatically evolve into floor plans and elevations, which in turn do not automatically evolve into renderings, let alone scale models. Rather, at each transition from one mode of representation to another, much manual effort is needed, with the commensurate likelihood of introducing errors due to omissions and oversights. Moreover, there is rarely any effort made to go back and update earlier modes of representation when later ones have been modified, adding confusion to the design documentation which now shows different versions of the same building.

Drawings and scale models are very difficult to change as they grow in complexity and detail, becoming obstacles to revising the design itself in response to new discoveries about the nature of the problem. This inflexibility fuels resistance on the part of the architect to make changes as the project evolves beyond a certain point. Small alterations of details in working drawings, for example, can cause extensive redrawing and transform an economically profitable commission into a loser. Related to this problem is the high degree of redundancy needed to develop successive representations as the project proceeds. Even when sophisticated reprographic techniques are used, much time is wasted redoing representations that have already been created.

Poor Information Management

The complexity of a building requires hundreds, even thousands of drawings, models, and illustrations for its complete representation. It is common to represent the same component of the building (e.g., a window) many times—in plans, elevations, details, and renderings. Naturally, when the design of that part of the building changes as the design progresses, *all* its representations must be updated. Using habitual modes of representation (i.e., paper drawings), such updates require much effort and diligence, lest some representations will go unmodified, thereby making the representation as a whole inconsistent. Updating is a tedious process, which like all tedious processes are prone to errors.

Moreover, changes made to one component of the building are likely to require additional changes, in a process called change propagation: modifying the first floor of the building requires that modifications be made to the second floor, and so forth. The coordination of changes is a delicate process, often requiring going back and undoing some changes made earlier, or redoing changes to accommodate circumstances that were not obvious when the original changes were made.

This process is further complicated when the changes must be communicated to all the participants in the design process in a timely and coordinated manner, and when their responses to changes must be considered and likewise propagated among all the participants in the project.

Limited Support for Performance Evaluation

When using habitual modes of communication, it is hard to predict the performance of the building and the human responses to it, because they are inherently means of representing the product in isolation from the processes of its construction and use. They can resolve only internal compatibilities, not external ones. The designer must, instead, rely on experience and imagination to foresee how the design will respond to external needs—both of which may fail when confronted with novel or different situations. This leads to a design process that is inherently risky and uncertain. Quantitative engineering analyses that are intended to reduce such uncertainty are generally used to predict only a few aspects of design performance and typically do so only toward the end of the design process (when enough information exists for analysis). The full range of sensory feedback that is needed to evaluate how a design will effect the inhabitants of a building is rarely available. For example, it is very difficult, without sophisticated technical knowledge, to appreciate the acoustic or kinesthetic aspects of a design, to appreciate what it might "feel" like sitting in an

Communication

auditorium, listening to a lecture, or enjoying the view once the building has been erected.

Centralization of Control

From the perspective of the client and the public at large, the habitual modes of communication give too much control of information about the problem and its solution to the architect, which is contrary to the social nature of design projects. While the architect is undeniably the major player in the design process, his or her power is augmented—perhaps artificially—by a complete authority over the selection of the method of communication and its contents. Thus, through the use of arbitrary codes and carefully managed information content, the designer can shape the data available to others in the manner most favorable to his or her own point of view. By contrast, when we buy a car, we can climb into it, drive it, look it over carefully, crawl underneath it, open the hood—the proverbial "kicking of the tires." We can even bring the car to an independent mechanic, hook it up to sophisticated electronic testing instruments, and measure its performance quantitatively. However, when a client "buys" a building design (rather than an existing building), the only information available to her is that which is provided by the architect. Clients can request, or demand, additional information, but it will still reflect the architect's point of view.

Despite all these shortcomings, habitual modes of communication have served the building industry well for hundreds of years. They have evolved to a high degree of sophistication, along with conventions that allowed them to contend with, if not overcome, some of their limitations. Computing technology has provided new means of communication and representation, which in many cases has eliminated, or at least alleviated, the shortcomings of habitual methods. Their power flows from those attributes that make computational methods so useful in many other fields: flexibility and the ability to evolve and to change the data to meet the needs of different design phases; powerful information management abilities; new ways to visualize designs; and embedded intelligence that facilitates performance evaluation.

Bibliography

Ching, F. D. K. *Architecture: Form, Space and Order.* New York: John Wiley and Sons, 1996.

Muller, E. J., and J. G. Fausett. *Architectural Drawing and Light Construction.* Englewood Cliffs, N.J.: Prentice-Hall, 1993.

Rapoport, A. *The Meaning of the Built Environment: A Nonverbal Communication Approach.* Tucson: University of Arizona Press, 1990.

Schön, D. A. *The Reflective Practitioner: How Professionals Think in Action.* New York: Basic Books, 1983.

Suwa, M., T. Purcell, and J. S. Gero. "Macroscopic Analysis of Design Processes Based on a Scheme for Coding Designer's Cognitive Actions." *Design Studies* 19, no. 4 (1998): 455–483.

Suwa, M., and B. Tversky. "What Do Architects and Students Perceive in Their Design Sketches? A Protocol Analysis." *Design Studies* 18 (1997): 385–403.

Modeling

Modeling is a form of representation that helps designers make the object of their design tangible enough to be appraised visually and analytically, and enable its sharing with other members of the design team.

Modeling in architecture often (though not always) takes a geometric form, enabling designers to see the shape of the artifact and the relationships between its parts. A model differs from other visual representations, such as renderings, sketches, or even drawings, in that the representation itself is three-dimensional. Hence, while drawings and renderings depict only one view of the object—the view chosen by the sender of the information—both computational and physical scale models give the receiver control over how to view the object. The receiver can turn it around, enter into it, and examine it from any desired vantage point. As such, models communicate much more information than drawings and renderings can. They communicate information about the object itself, not just a selected image of that object.

Computer models share many of the advantages of physical scale models, although not their materiality. The major difference between computational models and physical models is their abstract nature. Computers cannot handle lines, surfaces, and volumes directly, as physical scale models can. Therefore, the shape of the objects being modeled must be translated into a symbolic data structure of the kind computers can operate on. This process of translation is not trivial: it requires the transformation of geometric elements into arbitrary codes, which, as discussed in section 7.1, are a relatively poor form of representation in terms of affordance for communication. The translation carries the risk of information loss, especially with respect to the relationships between the components of the object. Moreover, since arbitrary codes abide by a different set of rules and constraints than physical entities do, it is possible—in fact it is rather easy—to apply changes to an arbitrary-coded representation in a manner that violates some premise of the represented object. If the model is subsequently used to infer or calculate some properties of the represented artifact, such violations may render the results invalid.

How can abstract symbol structures, comprised essentially of 0s and 1s, be made to represent two- and three-dimensional geometric entities? How can they be guaranteed to correspond only to entities that can be realized in physical space? How efficient are these representations? These are some of the issues that computer-aided modeling must contend with.

The search for symbolic data structures that could represent geometric entities in a manner that is amenable to computer manipulation was begun in the 1960s, with Ivan Sutherland's Sketchpad—the first interactive computer-aided design program. Since then, many suitable data structures have been developed, each with its own abilities, efficiencies, and limitations. They include wire frame models that can only represent the edges of an object; surface models that represent the boundaries of an object; and solid models that can represent the object's materiality. Some of the models can only represent planar objects, others can represent curvilinear ones. Many models require considerable computing resources to manipulate, making them viable only for representing partial objects or manipulation on large computers. Others are efficient enough to run on personal computers.

Along with the different approaches to computer-aided modeling, criteria have been developed to assess the abilities of the models themselves, including: *well-formedness,* which denotes the ability of the model to guarantee that it does not violate the rules that apply to the represented (physical) object; *generality,* which gauges the range of shapes the model can represent; *completeness,* which indicates the kinds of information about the represented object that the model supports (e.g., can the volume of the object be calculated?); and *efficiency,* which measures the computing resources needed to run the model.

8.1 Data Structures

Computers are symbol manipulators: machines that can create, manipulate, and query—very rapidly and consistently—vast quantities of very simple symbols (essentially, 0s and 1s). These symbols, or more precisely the structures they make, have no meaning of their own, however. In order for them to acquire meaning, and thus become representations of objects and ideas, they must correspond to some real-world entities. This correspondence, which is known as a mapping, must be constructed and maintained carefully if the symbol structures are to retain their meaning. Hence, not only the symbol structures themselves, but also the operators that create, manipulate, and query them, must be developed in a manner that maintains their well-formedness.

Analytic Geometry

How can geometric entities such as lines, surfaces, and volumes be represented by these symbol structures? How can the operators that manipulate them be represented in a manner that will maintain the correspondence of the symbol structures to the real-world entities they represent? A partial answer to the first question comes from a branch of mathematics known as analytic geometry, in which algebraic notations and operators are used to describe and manipulate geometric entities. Analytic geometry was first introduced by the French mathematician, scientist, and philosopher René Descartes in 1637, as part of his framework for describing the world. Isaac Newton, Leonhard Euler, and other mathematicians extended analytic geometry to the study of conic sections and other families of plane curves. Analytic geometry reached its full development at end of the nineteenth century and the beginning of the twentieth century at the hands of the German mathematician Max Noether and the Italians Corrado Segre and Federigo Enriques.

In its present form, analytic geometry considers every point in space as a unique locus with respect to some frame of reference, known as a coordinate system: a system of two or three axes that are perpendicular to each other, intersecting at one point, called the origin. In two-dimensional space, the horizontal line is called the X axis, and the vertical one is called the Y axis. The distance of a point from the origin, as measured on each axis, provides a convenient way for mapping a geometric entity—the point—into an analytical entity—a pair of numbers referred to as the coordinates of the point (fig. 8.1):

$$P_1 = (x_1, y_1)$$

Using this simple mapping, a line segment can be represented by a pair of connected points, each identified through its own unique pair of coordinates (fig. 8.2):

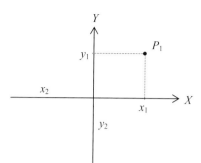

8.1 The Cartesian coordinate system and a point $P_1(x_1, y_1)$ as a locus within its frame of reference.

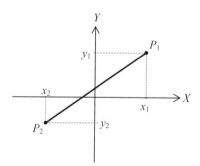

8.2 Analytic representation of a line segment.

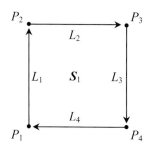

8.3 Analytic representation of a square.

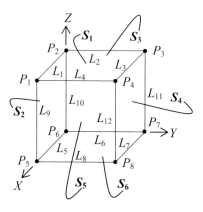

8.4 Analytic representation of a cube.

$$L_1 = (P_1, P_2)$$

Likewise, a quadrilateral can be represented by a sequence of four points (fig. 8.3):

$$S_1 = (P_1, P_2, P_3, P_4)$$

Alternatively, it can be represented as a sequence of four line segments:

$$S_1 = (L_1, L_2, L_3, L_4)$$

Circles and other curves can be broken into many tiny straight-line segments, which can be represented by the same method. In fact, using this simple method, any shape in two-dimensional space can be mapped into an equivalent mathematical notation, which is amenable to manipulation by computers.

Three-dimensional objects can be represented when a third axis—the Z axis—is added to the coordinate system, which affords designation of a third coordinate for every point in space. A cube can thus be represented by six squares (fig. 8.4):

$$C_1 = (S_1, S_2, S_3, S_4, S_5, S_6)$$

Alternatively, it can be represented by twelve line segments:

$$C_1 = (L_1, L_2, L_3, L_4, L_5, L_6, L_7, L_8, L_9, L_{10}, L_{11}, L_{12})$$

It cannot, however, be represented by eight points: there is not enough information in that representation to indicate how the points are connected.

Representing the location of the geometrical components of an object is not enough: it is also necessary to know how the components are connected to one another. Such connectivity information could be implicit, as is the case of the square depicted in figure 8.3, where the sequence of listing the lines or the points determines which line follows which other line, or which point is connected to which other points. Hence, the square can be reconstructed from its mathematical notation by drawing lines from point 1 to point 2 to point 3 to point 4 and then again to point 1:

Communication

$$P_1 \rightarrow P_2 \rightarrow P_3 \rightarrow P_4 \rightarrow P_1$$

It will be a different shape if the lines where drawn in a different sequence, even if the locations of the points (in term of their individual coordinates) were the same. For example figure 8.5 uses the same points as figure 8.3, but a different sequence of connections:

$$P_1 \rightarrow P_3 \rightarrow P_4 \rightarrow P_2 \rightarrow P_1$$

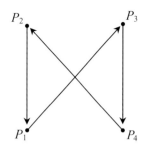

8.5 The manner in which the points are connected determines the shape as much as the locations of the points do.

When the connections, or adjacencies among the components, cannot be inferred from the sequence of their notation, they must be represented explicitly. That is why a cube, or any other three-dimensional shape for that matter, cannot be represented by listing its vertices (points) alone: no simple sequence will suffice to represent the adjacencies between the vertices that comprise the cube.

Topology

The connections among the components of a shape are known as its *topology*—the property that describes which parts of the shape are connected to which other parts and how are they oriented with respect to one another. To represent the topology of an object we need a more complex symbol structure than a sequence of points. We need a notation, often accompanied by a set of rules, or "operators," that tells the reader of the information—the computer, in this case—how to reconstruct the object it represents. Such notations are known as data structures.

The search for a data structure that can describe polyhedral shapes[1] started over 2,500 years ago, with the works of the great Greek mathematicians Hippocrates of Chios, Theudius, Aristotle, and of course Euclid in 300 BC. It took 2,000 years, however, before the German mathematician Leonhard Euler discovered, in the eighteenth century, the simple numerical relationship among the components of a polyhedral solid:

$$F - E + V = 2$$

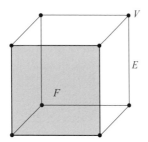

8.6 The components of a cube.

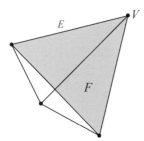

8.7 The components of a tetrahedron.

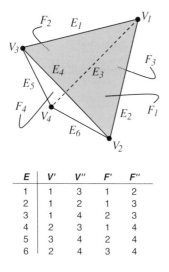

E	V'	V''	F'	F''
1	1	3	1	2
2	1	2	1	3
3	1	4	2	3
4	2	3	1	4
5	3	4	2	4
6	2	4	3	4

8.8 Edge-based topological data structure of a tetrahedron.

where F is the number of faces, E is the number of edges, and V is the number of vertices of the shape. For example, a cube has six faces, twelve edges, and eight vertices (fig. 8.6):

$$6_F - 12_E + 8_V = 2$$

Likewise, for a tetrahedron, which has four faces, six edges, and four vertices (fig. 8.7):

$$4_F - 6_E + 4_V = 2$$

It took another 250 years until a data structure capable of describing these relationships explicitly was discovered by Bruce Guenther Baumgart (1972), a researcher at the Stanford Artificial Intelligence Lab (SAIL).

Baumgart's data structure, which is based on Euler's formula, identifies the edges of a polyhedral solid shape as the carriers of its topological data: every edge connects two faces, and is bounded by two vertices. Accordingly, a data structure that identifies the faces and the vertices that are connected to every edge can describe the structure of the polyhedron (fig. 8.8). Together with geometrical data that locates the vertices within a coordinate system and an appropriate set of operators (called Euler operators), this data structure contains all the information needed to reconstruct the polyhedron in a unique, unambiguous, and complete manner.

The complexity of such data structures grows with the number of edges, the most proliferate geometric element of shape information. It can quickly become unmanageable, in terms of modifications that the designer may want to apply to the objects. The operators help the designer, or the computer, query and manipulate the data structure: they take care of the "bookkeeping" when edges or faces are added or deleted, and when vertices are relocated. For example, if the designer wished to truncate the tetrahedron and transform it to the shape depicted in figure 8.9, the corresponding data structure will have to be changed to reflect the addition of a new face, three new edges, the deletion of V_3, and the corresponding realignment of the connections among many of the new components.

Communication

8.2 Properties of Geometric Data Structures

The complexity of geometric-topological data structures makes them susceptible to errors that would render them useless if left uncorrected. What would happen if the computer transposed a pair of numbers in the table representing the tetrahedron in figure 8.9? It would cease to be a tetrahedron. In fact, it would become a useless collection of numbers, not corresponding to any recognizable shape.

Well-Formedness

Guaranteeing that the representation will always correspond to the shape it represents is one of the most important tasks of geometric modelers. This property, which is called well-formedness, makes it possible to operate on the representations of shapes with the confidence that the data structure will continue to be valid with respect to the shapes it stands for. For example, if it is well-formed, the representation will allow the architect to calculate the surface area of the truncated tetrahedron depicted in figure 8.9, a number that could be used, for example, to order the necessary amount of paint to cover it. A structural engineer could calculate the weight of an object that was shaped like the truncated tetrahedron, with the confidence that the structural loads based on that calculation are correct. Hence, well-formedness has far-reaching ramifications, well beyond the ability of the system to generate images that look like the designed objects.

Generality

The data structure described above, while well-formed, can only represent planar-faced polyhedra. It is not very well suited to representing curvilinear forms such as domes and arches, or free-form shapes such as those preferred by architects like Frank O. Gehry and Greg Lynn. A sphere, for example, would have to be broken down into many small straight lines and planes, rather like a mirrored ball hanging over a dance floor. While this may be acceptable for certain applications, such as designing igloos made of planar blocks of ice, it would not be adequate for applications that require high precision, like representing the body of a car or a smoothly

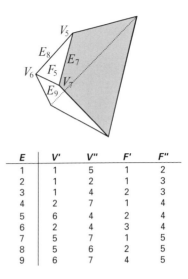

E	V'	V"	F'	F"
1	1	5	1	2
2	1	2	1	3
3	1	4	2	3
4	2	7	1	4
5	6	4	2	4
6	2	4	3	4
7	5	7	1	5
8	5	6	2	5
9	6	7	4	5

8.9 The truncated tetrahedron and its corresponding data structure.

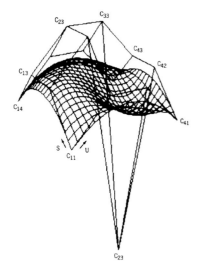

8.10 The bicubic Bernstein-Bézier patch.

curved building. The data structure discussed in section 8.1 is, therefore, not "general." A more general data structure would be needed to represent all kinds of shapes, not only those bounded by planar surfaces.

Many such data structures have been developed, especially for the uses of the automotive and aerospace industries, where curved surfaces are the rule rather than exception. Figure 8.10 shows one such data structure, based on the bicubic Bernstein-Bézier patch.[2] Like other methods for representing geometric surfaces, the Bernstein-Bézier patch explicitly describes the location of each point on the surface through interpolation between a small number of so-called control points (points $C_{i,j}$ in figure 8.10), using the following parametric bivariate polynomial function:

$$P(u,v) = a_{00} + va_{01} + v^2 a_{02} + v^3 a_{03} + ua_{10} + uva_{11} + uv^2 a_{12} + uv^3 a_{13} + \ldots$$
$$= \Sigma\Sigma a_{ij} u^i v^j$$

where $P(u,v)$ is the location of a point in 3D Cartesian space, u,v are functions that define the relationship between the parametric space and the Cartesian space, and $a_{i,j}$ are coefficients that define the form of the curve.[3]

Efficiency

Generality, however, often comes at the expense of efficiency. The data structure described in section 8.1 is already quite complicated. It would have to be made even more complex to represent curvilinear forms. The added complexity would require more computing resources—more storage and faster computers—which might make it unusable on smaller computers. The added complexity would also likely make software based on such a data structure more expensive, putting it out of reach of all but the larger corporations. If the application for which the modeling system is used does not require the added abilities provided by more general data structures, then there is little justification to accept the increased inefficiency and added cost.

Completeness

Much like efficiency, the data structure must also be evaluated on its completeness—what kinds of calculations does it support? Can the surface area of the represented object be calculated? Its volume? Without the ability to support such calculations, the utility of a geometric data structure is very limited. A data structure that cannot support surface area calculations cannot be used to estimate the energy that will be used by a building it represents. If it cannot support volume calculation, it cannot be used for structural analysis, where the weight of the represented objects is of paramount importance. Nor can it be used for estimating the cost of the building or the quantities of the materials it is made of.

An optimal data structure would thus be well-formed, general, efficient, and complete. This combination of properties is, unfortunately, not feasible. The more general the data structure, the less efficient it is, and the more difficult it is to maintain its well-formedness. But a data structure that sacrifices generality for the sake of efficiency is of limited use for representing real-world objects. It would be rather like the blocks of a Lego system, or the cubes of a child's blocks, which support a very limited range of shapes. A good data structure is one that is well-formed, while balancing the attributes of generality, efficiency, and completeness in a manner that matches the needs of the application for which it is used.

8.3 Geometric Modeling

The design of data structures that can represent complex geometric shapes has led over the past forty years to the development and wide use of many geometric models. They fall into three general categories, in ascending levels of generality: (1) wire frame models, (2) surface models, and (3) solid models.

Wire Frame Models

The wire frame modeling approach is the simplest and oldest graphical form of computational representation of shapes. It was developed in the 1960s, when the prevailing display technology—the Tektronix storage tube—could only draw lines on the computer screen, and only in one color (green). Wire frame models represent only the edges of shapes, leaving to the viewer the task of inferring the volume and other properties of the shape from these outlines. Such representations are very familiar to architects and engineers, who are used to representing buildings and

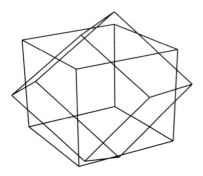

8.11 Wire frame model of two intersecting cubes: where do they intersect?

machines through their contours alone, and are trained to "see" in their mind's eye the surfaces and volumes they represent.

Wire frame models are easy to construct. All that is needed is a data structure capable of representing points and lines. Since such models do not represent the surfaces of the object, they do not need much structure in terms of adjacencies and other relationships between the lines and the points. That makes wire frame models very efficient but also very poor in terms of well-formedness, generality, and completeness. In fact, it is not always easy to tell exactly the shape of the object they represent, nor can wire frame models support surface or volume calculations. Consider, for example, the object depicted in figure 8.11, which shows two intersecting cubes: it is hard to tell what exactly is the relationship between these cubes. Where is the line of their intersection? Are they solid cubes, or are they just made of wires, like a cage? Clearly, it is not possible to discern the volume of the combined object, nor is it possible to calculate its surface area. For that, we need more information.

Surface Models

Surface models represent the vertices, edges, and faces of an object, but the structure they impose on these components is rather limited. They do not convey the adjacency (i.e., topological) relationships between the faces themselves. As such, surface models are essentially collections of unrelated polygons.[4] A cube, according to this data structure, is an unstructured collection of six polygons.

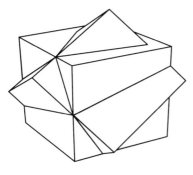

8.12 Surface model of two intersecting cubes.

The inclusion of polygonal information in the data structure makes shapes represented through the surface modeling approach easier to understand, because the surface of the object is readily visible—it does not have to be inferred from the outline alone. Furthermore, since polygons that are closer to an observer may occlude ones that are further away, this approach supports hidden-line removal, the process where only those parts of the shape that are visible from a given point of view are displayed on the screen. Applying this approach to the two cubes shown in figure 8.12 makes it possible to see the relationship between them.

Nonetheless, the visual quality of shapes that are represented through the surface modeling approach is misleading—the surface model does not actually "know" where the two cubes intersect. Therefore it is not possible

Communication

to calculate the surface area of the combined shape, nor to calculate its volume or any of its other overall geometrical properties. For that we need more information. Still, the efficiency and visual quality of shapes represented through the surface modeling approach have made it popular in the video game industry, where fast visualization is of paramount importance. But its usability for design purposes, in architecture and in mechanical engineering, is limited to the visualization of finished products.

Solid Models

Solid modeling is the most complete, well-formed, and general of all methods used to represent shapes. Its efficiency, however, depends on the particular approach used to implement the model. Solid models contain information about all parts of the shape—its vertices, edges, faces, and its volume—though not all elements are necessarily represented explicitly (the parts that are not represented explicitly can be computed from the parts that are). A computational solid model, therefore, is akin to a physical scale model of the object, made of clay or solid wood—its surface, volume, and other geometric properties can be calculated. Moreover, because the representation is geometrically complete, the model can support such operations as union, intersection, and subtraction (the so-called Boolean operations). For example, it is possible to compute the intersection of the two cubes depicted in figure 8.13 as well as their union and their difference(s).

Three approaches have been developed so far for implementing solid modeling of shapes, each with its own advantages and drawbacks. They are: the spatial occupancy enumeration model (also known as the "voxel" model), which is used primarily for medical imaging; the constructive solid geometry model (CSG), which is used in mechanical engineering; and the boundary representation model (B-rep), which is used in architecture and in mechanical engineering of curved-surfaced objects.

Spatial Occupancy Enumeration

Spatial occupancy enumeration considers solids as sets of contiguous discrete "chucks" of matter in three-dimensional space. For practical purposes, the representation imposes a three-dimensional grid on the space and

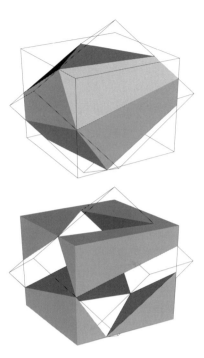

8.13 A solid model supports computation of the intersection and difference of two cubes.

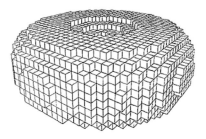

8.14 Spatial occupancy enumeration representation of a doughnut-like object. (A. J. H. Christiansen, *SIGGRAPH '80*. Courtesy of the ACM.)

uses a data structure that lists all the cells in that grid that are occupied by the object (fig. 8.14). These cells are usually cubes of a fixed size. The grid they belong to is known as a spatial array, and the cells are known as volumetric cells, or voxels. This representation is efficient and well-formed. Efficiency is gained because it is very easy to know which points (cells) belong to an object and which do not, thereby simplifying display and query operations. Well-formedness is assured through spatial uniqueness—cells in the grid are either occupied (i.e., they belong to the object) or not. Calculating the volume of the shape is simply a matter of counting the occupied cells and multiplying that number by the volume of a unit cell. Calculating the surface area is a matter of counting the faces of occupied grid cells that have no neighbors on one or more of their sides, and multiplying that number by the area of a unit face.

This method of representation also has two significant shortcomings. It lacks object coherence—the relationship between parts of the shape is not explicitly represented, therefore it must be calculated. And it is extremely expensive in terms of computing resources, especially storage space, because it is highly redundant: any cell is likely to have the same state of occupancy (inside or outside the object) as the cells adjacent to it. Only at the boundaries of the shape is this not so. This redundancy limits the number of cells that can be used for the purpose of representing shapes and, consequently, the accuracy of the representation: to achieve a smooth surface, the cells have to be small. But for each halving of the size of a grid cell, eight new cells (2^3) are created. The number of cells can quickly rise to the millions for even simple, small objects. Spatial occupancy enumeration cannot be used, therefore, where the represented objects are large, as in architecture, nor where high accuracy is desired, as in mechanical engineering. But it has found wide use in medical imaging, where magnetic resonance imaging (MRI) and computerized axial tomography (CAT) scans produce relatively small shapes, whose resolution is limited in the first place by the nature of the image acquisition process.

Constructive Solid Geometry (CSG)

Constructive solid geometry (CSG), as the name implies, is a functional representation: it "constructs" complex solids by combining simpler ones

Communication

through union, intersection, and difference operators. A shape represented by CSG methods is a collection of so-called "primitive" shapes and the operators that combine them. For example, the shape that is depicted at the top of figure 8.15—an L-shaped bracket with a round hole—is the result of a union of two simple blocks from which the cylinder has been subtracted. The CSG model does not actually perform these operations; it only records them as part of its data structure. Later, if we want to calculate the combined object's volume, the calculation operator will follow the instructions coded in the data structure and apply them as needed. A CSG model thus cannot be displayed directly on the screen: it must be processed, through another operator, that determines which parts are visible and which parts are only used to modify the shapes of other components.[5]

CSG is an efficient and well-formed representation, whose generality depends on the set of primitive shapes used. Typically, this set includes rectangular blocks, wedges, cylinders, spheres, and pyramids, which can be scaled and positioned in space with respect to one another as needed. The drawback of this approach is the difficulty of actually using the resulting representation. Each use (e.g., display, volume or surface calculation) requires traversal of the entire data structure and execution of all the operations encoded in it. Therefore, this approach is most suitable for applications that mimic its representation—where the objects are made from identifiable primitive shapes that are added and subtracted to make complex shapes. Machine parts—generally made from stock objects that are turned, joined, and milled to form complex shapes—conform to this paradigm. Architectural shapes, on the other hand, tend to be one of a kind and do not fit the paradigm.

Boundary Representation (B-rep)

Unlike the first two approaches, the boundary representation (B-rep) model recognizes that the likelihood that any two points in space will have the same type of occupancy (either both inside the object, or both outside it) is high, and that changes occur only at the object's boundary. Hence, it uses a data structure that represents explicitly only points on the boundary itself: vertices, edges, and faces (fig. 8.16). It is not a trivial matter, however, to represent the volume of an object through its boundary alone. In essence, this means that a higher-dimensional entity (a volume) is represented

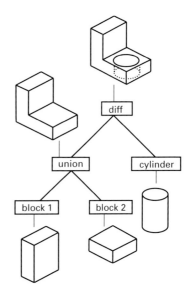

8.15 A constructive solid geometry model of a shape is a construct made of primitive shapes combined through union, intersection, and difference operators.

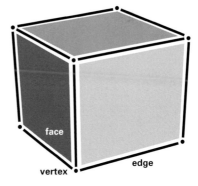

8.16 Boundary representation consists of a highly organized collection of faces, edges, and vertices.

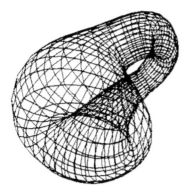

8.17 The Klein bottle—a self-intersecting, single-sided manifold that has no volume.

through a lower-dimensional entity (a manifold). To guarantee well-formedness and to allow for the calculation of such geometric properties as volume and center of gravity, the bounding surface must abide by strict rules: it must be closed, and it must not self-intersect. Only then can it ensure that it divides all points in space into points that either belong to the object (are *inside*) or not (are *outside*).[6] Without such assurance, the representation might cease to correspond to realizable objects and thus lose its roll as a means of communicating design information. One well-known shape that violates these well-formedness rules is the Klein bottle (fig. 8.17): a self-intersecting, single-sided manifold that encloses no volume.

Although this approach to representing solids is more concise than the other two approaches in terms of the storage space it requires, it is more difficult to construct, manipulate, and query. The enclosed volume is represented by inference rather than directly. For example, calculating the volume of all but the simplest objects (ones that conform to some algebraic formula, like cubes, cylinders, spheres, and pyramids) requires the use of procedural techniques such as triangulation—a process where each face of the shape is divided into triangles whose vertices are connected to a point inside the object to form tetrahedrons. The volume of each tetrahedron is easy to calculate. All the tetrahedrons' volumes add up to yield the volume of the overall object.[7]

The B-rep model combines the advantages of surface modeling with volumetric modeling: it provides direct and easy access to the shape's surface for the purpose of visualization. Unlike the surface model, it also carries the information needed for more sophisticated geometric calculations. It has, therefore, become the representation of choice for geometric modeling applications in architecture that are used for visualization and analysis of buildings. However, the complexity of the boundary representation data structure requires that it be augmented by a special set of operators to construct, manipulate, and query the information, and to maintain its well-formedness.

Shape Operators

The need for such operators is not restricted to the boundary representation approach—every data structure of even moderate complexity needs operators to construct, manipulate, and query the information. The oper-

Communication

ators that complement the data structures and support geometric modeling fall into five general categories:

1. Operators that construct and manipulate the *topology* of shapes.
2. Operators that modify the *geometry* of shapes.
3. Operators that *transform* the shapes and position them in space.
4. Operators that create new shapes by combining existing shapes through *Boolean* operations.
5. Operators that create *assemblies* of shapes.

Topological operators create and manipulate the structure of the shapes themselves. Different modelers use different operators for that purpose, depending on their data structures. CSG modelers instantiate shapes from their library of primitive shapes. B-rep modelers use sets of topology-building operators called Euler operators, which correctly handle the complex relationships between vertices, edges, and faces.[8]

Geometric operators assign geometry to the shapes, thereby forming "visible" entities such as floors and columns, as depicted in figure 8.18. For the sake of convenience, in many cases these operators are bundled together with the topological operators. For example, linear (extrusion) and rotational sweep operators allow users to create volumetric shapes by defining a two-dimensional contour and sweeping (extruding) it along a given trajectory or axis (fig. 8.19). *Parametric* geometry operators allow the wholesale manipulation of parts of shapes, of the kind that would change, for example, the column in figure 8.18 into the floor slab by modifying some of its dimensions without affecting others.

Transform operators scale, translate, and rotate shapes, so they assume their desired size and position in space.

Boolean operators combine existing shapes through union, intersection, and difference. They can be likened to sculpting shapes in clay, because they can use one shape to modify another, as was discussed earlier (fig. 8.13). They operate both on the object's topology and its geometry and can be used to create very complex shapes.

Assembly operators combine individual shapes into groups of shapes, so they can be treated as one entity. They are useful, for instance, for creating window assemblies, machines, and other objects that cannot be described by a single shape alone.

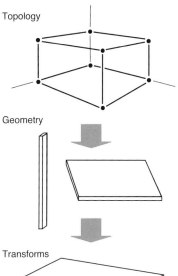

Topology

Geometry

Transforms

8.18 Typology of geometric operators.

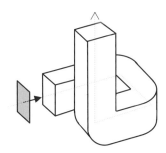

8.19 Linear sweep (extrusion).

Together, the data structure and the operators make a modeling system. Such systems provide users with the ability to create, modify, and query shapes for the purposes of ideation and communication.

8.4 Databases

A model purporting to represent a building or its parts must include more than just geometric information. It must also represent nongeometric attributes, such as the materials it is made of, its cost, the identity of its designers or manufacturers, and even its behavior under certain conditions. Only then can the model support evaluations such as cost estimation, fire egress analysis, energy consumption, and the behavior of the building under earthquake and other conditions. Without such information, the representation can only be used for communicating the visual properties of the building.

Adding nongeometric data to models of buildings, as well as to other products, transforms them from mere geometric models into more comprehensive data models—representations that include information about all or most of the properties of the objects they represent and can, therefore, support many different kinds of queries. Such comprehensive computational representations are called databases.

A database is a structured collection of information that can be used to communicate the properties of some entity. A telephone book can be considered a database that lists, in alphabetical order, the names, addresses, and phone numbers of people or businesses. Unlike unstructured lists of names and phone numbers, the phone book allows rapid search for a specific name. If it is an electronic phone book, its structure can be reorganized so it can be searched by address, by telephone number, or by zip code, rather than by name alone.

A telephone book, however, is a relatively simple database. Databases of the kind that are used in design are far more complex. Consider, for example, the information associated with an everyday product like a DOOR—a person-sized opening, usually made of wood, glass, or metal (or a combination thereof), installed to swing, fold, role, rotate, or slide in order to provide controlled access between two spaces. This deceptively simple definition contains much information about doors, including:

1. *Classification* information: a DOOR is a type of opening, much like a window but not quite the same.

2. *Descriptive* information: size ("person-sized") and materials.

3. *Behavioral* information: the DOOR swings, folds, roles, rotates or slides.

4. *Functional* information: DOORs provide "controlled" access (namely, they can be opened, closed, and locked).

5. *Locational* information: the DOOR is located between two spaces.

6. *Constraint* information: how the DOOR responds to external conditions like fire, weather, vandalism, and maintenance.

A DOORs database would, accordingly, include all this information, and would be organized in a manner that supports easy update and query of the data.

The information about each door will be stored in the form of a "record": a template that consists of attributes, each of which has a name and a value. For example, in figure 8.20, "door type" is an attribute's name, and "full flush" is its value. In many cases, the values can be selected from a predefined list, as in figure 8.20. In other cases, only their type is predetermined (e.g., a number, a text string). This allows the computer to perform some well-formedness tests on the values (e.g., that a text string is not assigned as a value to a numerical attribute).

Flat File

The records that comprise the database can be organized into different structures. The simplest structure is just a list, called a flat file: records are organized alphabetically or numerically, as in a phone book. This simple organization is often not very efficient. Consider, for example, how large the phone book would be if all the residents of the United States were listed in a single volume, without partitions into states or cities. It would take much too long to find a number, unless the person's name were unique among all the entries. When additional structuring information is used, such as states and cities, the phone book can be searched more efficiently.

DOOR RECORD

Name/ID	s-13710011
Instance of	Swing door
Weight	Extremely heavy
Performance level	Extra heavy duty
STC rating	29-32

Door type
_ Full flush
   View
   Narrow
   Glass
   Full Glass
   Dutch
   Panel

Construction
   Full flush
_ Stile & rail
   Stile & panel
   Framed & paneled
   Plywood
   Ledged/braced
   Solid glass

Core
   Plain hollow
   Ladder
   Mesh
   Plastic board
   Stave
_ Mineral composition
   Plain solid

Operation
_ Hinged
   Pivoting
   Balanced
   Pocket
   Double acting
   Pivoting double acting

Elements
_ Stationary panel
   Sidelight
   Transom
   Borrow light

Handing
_ Left hand
   Right hand

Number
_ Single unit
   Two doors

Fire rating
_ Fire rated
   Non-rated

8.20 A record of the DOORs database.

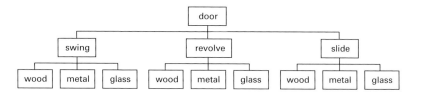

Hierarchy

Organization of data can take many forms. One of the simpler, yet most effective, organizing methods is the hierarchy—a structure where records are grouped into clusters, which are themselves grouped into larger clusters, and so on. It is possible, for example, to group doors according to their operational type—swinging, revolving, sliding—then, within each such operational type, subgroup them according to their material composition—wood, metal, glass—and within each of these subcategories further group them according to size or some other discriminating attribute. The resulting organization resembles the roots of a tree, which branch out from a common trunk (fig. 8.21). Much like a hierarchically organized phone book (according to states, counties, and cities), this structure allows for easy update and query of the DOORs database: to find a particular door, the reader needs only search doors that meet certain criteria. Likewise, adding a new door to the database, or deleting an obsolete one, is easy when one does not have to sift through a long list of doors.

Network

Not all objects can be easily organized into hierarchical structures. In many cases there are no discriminating characteristics that can be used to identify groups. In other cases the most important characteristic of the data is the links among the objects. An organizational structure called the network can more adequately represent such relationships. Figure 8.22 depicts a network structure of the rooms in an infectious diseases suite in a hospital, which consists of the hospital's internal corridor *CI*; an entry room *EN*, which acts as an airlock to filter the air between the patients' room and the rest of the hospital; the patients' room *PT*, with its own bathroom *BT*; and a visitors' room *VS*, which is physically separated from

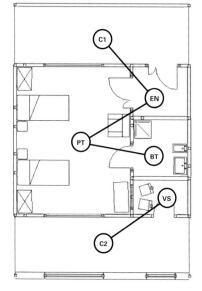

8.22 A network structure helps to communicate the connectivity relationships among the rooms comprising an infectious diseases suite in a hospital. (G. Carrara et al., in *Automation in Construction* 3, nos. 2–3 [1994].)

door/id	type	construction	core	operation	elements	handling	number	fire rating
s-13710011	view	stile & panel	mineral	hinged	transom	right hand	single	120 min
s-33710012	full flush	plywood	hollow	hinged	none	left hand	single	not rated
s-13711011	glass	solid glass	solid	hinged	none	left hand	double	30 min
s-13830067	panel	braced	stave	hinged	Narrow light	right hand	double	60 min

wall/ID	Room 1	Room 2	material	door	window	length
W1	C1	EN	concrete	s-13830067	none	9 ft
W2	EN	PT	stud	s-13830067	none	8 ft
W3	PT	BT	stud	s-33710012	none	9 ft
W4	VS	C2	concrete	s-13710011	none	9 ft
W5	VS	PT	stud	none	r-734500	6 ft

8.23 A relational database connects information of different types.

the patients' room but is connected to the hospital's exterior corridor *C2*. The rooms differ greatly in character and purpose, and it would, therefore, make little sense to try and group them according to function. But the relationships among them, in terms of connectivities, are crucial if the containment of the patients' room is to be preserved. The network structure represents those relationships explicitly, making it easy to identify the conditions that connect pairs of rooms. This information can be used, in turn, in conjunction with the DOORs database, to select doors with the proper attributes for connecting each pair of rooms. For example, the door between the patients' room *PT* and the bathroom *BT* will likely be a simple wooden door, with no window; whereas the doors linking corridor *C1* with the entrance room *EN*, and the entrance room with the patients' room, must allow passage of hospital beds, and are thus much more sophisticated (and expensive) doors.

Relational

Linking different types of data is both common and highly desirable. Yet the representation that is most appropriate for one type of data is not necessarily appropriate for another. For the sake of efficiency, each type of data ought to be organized by the structure that is best suited for its needs. A data organization method that can combine different representations into one overall structure was developed by IBM researcher E. F. Codd in 1970.[9] Called a relational database it represents information in tables, called relations. A relation, as the name implies, connects attributes and their values, as depicted in figure 8.23.

The first table, or relation, in figure 8.23 represents doors. It includes much of the information seen earlier in figure 8.20, namely—the DOOR's name/ID, its type, what is it made of, how it is built, and so on. The second relation represents some of the WALLs that belong to the hospital suite depicted in figure 8.22. It identifies each wall by some unique tag, and describes some of its properties, namely—which rooms it separates, which door it contains (if any), its length, and so on.

While all the information included in each relation is of the same type—doors in the first relation, walls in the second—it is different from the information in the other relation. The difference is not only in the content, but also in its structure—the first relation includes nine attributes, the second only seven. The names of the attributes in the first relation are different from those in the second. That is, the relations represent different types of information.

Yet the two relations are not independent of each other: information that is contained in the DOORs relation is *referenced* in the WALLs relation. Only the key attribute needs to be referenced (in this case, the door's ID number), but its inclusion provides access to all the information about that door, which is represented by the first relation. For example, we can readily tell that wall *W4*, which separates the visitors' room *VS* from corridor *C2*, has a door of type s-13710011, which, according to the information in the first table, is of type "view," has a stile-and-panel construction, is made of a mineral composition that makes it fire resistant up to 120 minutes, and so on. All this information is not included in the WALLs relation, yet it is accessible from it by reference to the DOORs relation. Obviously, such references can be made for each entry in the relation, leading to many other relations, each representing one type of data in the most suitable manner for the content of that information.

Database Management System (DBMS)

Creating, manipulating, and querying such complex databases requires operators that take care of maintaining the well-formedness of the information. Such operators are known as database management systems (DBMS). They include a user interface, which allows users to type in queries such as "What is the fire rating of the door connecting the patients' room and the bathroom?" The DBMS will first search the WALLs relation to identify which wall separates the patients' room from the bathroom, then it will identify which door belongs to this wall. It will then search the DOORs relation, to find the entry that corresponds to this door type, and finally it will identify the door's fire rating attribute. Thus, as long as the information is represented somewhere in the database, and the relationships between data items have been correctly identified, the DBMS can answer any question—even if the sought information has not been represented explicitly as asked for by the query.

8.5 Product Models

It is easy to see that databases that can represent all the components of a building can become very large, exceeding the ability of one designer, or one company, to construct and maintain them. There are literally thousands of different products that come together to make a building, each of which is the specialty of one manufacturer or another. That manufacturer is the one most qualified to develop and maintain the database that represents its products. For example, it is reasonable to expect that the doors manufacturer will be responsible for developing and maintaining the DOORs database; the LIGHTING FIXTURES manufacturer will develop and maintain the lighting fixtures database, and so on. The product manufacturer who develops and maintains the database is likely to choose its own favorite computer system and DBMS software and develop a data schema (structure) that best suits its needs. As a result, the building model as a whole is, in effect, a "distributed database," each of its parts created, maintained, and stored by a different manufacturer. Trying to connect all these different representations into one composite model of the building, so one can obtain timely and accurate answers to queries of the kind listed above, is a daunting task.

The prevailing practice of querying this distributed database has been to call, or send a written request, to the manufacturer of the product in question, or to look it up in paper-based catalogs. Not only is this method inefficient but it is also prone to errors. For example, there is every chance that the person who is looking up the fire rating of door number s-13711011 (which, according to the example in figure 8.23, is 30 minutes) will accidentally find instead the fire rating of door s-13710011 (120 minutes), an error that may put the patients at grave risk in case of fire.

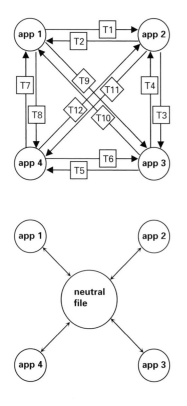

8.24 Translators versus neutral file exchange of data.

This inefficiency and potential for errors has prompted the construction industry, much like the aerospace and automotive industries, to develop databases that can be linked to one another even if they have been developed by different manufacturers, use different computer platforms, and are implemented using different DBMS systems. Such ability to interlink the data, for the purposes of answering queries across different databases, is known as interoperability.

Considerable efforts have been devoted over the past four decades to developing representations that can adequately support interoperability for the purposes of computer-aided design of buildings. These efforts have progressed through three different stages: (1) *translator* systems; (2) *neutral file* systems; and (3) *product models*.

Translators

Translators are computer programs that are independent of any one database. Instead, they "know" how a specific pair of databases represent their information. They can therefore "read" the data in one representation and translate it and "write" it out in the format used by the other system. Writing such translators is a tedious job, which requires expert familiarity with the data structures of both systems. Moreover, whenever either one of the two systems is updated, the translator must also be updated. Many such translators only work in one direction: to facilitate bi-directional data exchange, two translators are needed. And since computer systems are typically updated every one to two years, the effort to keep the translators current never ends. The only advantage of translators is that they do not require the connected databases to agree on a common data format or a common interpretation—the translators take care of the decoding and encoding of the information.

The number of translators grows much faster than the number of systems they connect: if data is to be exchanged between two systems, two translators are needed; among three systems, six different translators are needed. Four systems require twelve translators (fig. 8.24). Clearly, this is a rather poor way of effecting interoperability.

Communication

Neutral File

One way to relieve the problems associated with ad hoc translators is to use a neutral file, an agreed-upon common format and interpretation that all systems can read and write—a kind of "universal language." Efforts to establish such a common data language go back as far as the late 1970s, when the growing use of different CAD systems by different government agencies created a strong demand for product data exchange. Initial Graphics Exchange Specification (IGES)—the first such neutral file format—was released in 1978 and has since become a requirement of all CAD systems procured by the U.S. federal government.[10] It specifies, in great detail, every aspect of the data that can be exchanged, down to the length of the dash (and the space that follows it) in dashed lines.

IGES lived up to its promise, in spite of two major shortcomings of the neutral file method—the necessity to agree upon the definitions it uses, and its rather low-level semantics. The first shortcoming was solved through endless, boring meetings. The second shortcoming could not be solved: by its vary nature, the neutral file format is the lowest common denominator among all the systems that use it. It would do no good for a common file format to represent an entity that many of its users cannot understand. Therefore, if one system can represent an entity called DOOR, along with all its attributes that were listed earlier, but other systems can only represent the geometric form of this entity, there is no reason to burden the neutral file with the higher-level data. As a result, when two systems exchange data through the neutral file, much of the higher-level information is never communicated. Nonetheless, IGES—and IGES-like neutral-file-format data exchange standards—have been developed. The most prevalent one that is used in the building industry is DXF—a standard developed by AutoDesk in response to many of their customers' demands.[11]

Product Exchange Standards

To support true interoperability, the databases must be able exchange the product information itself, not only some watered-down graphical representation thereof. The next phase in interoperability was, therefore, the development of product models and product exchange standards.

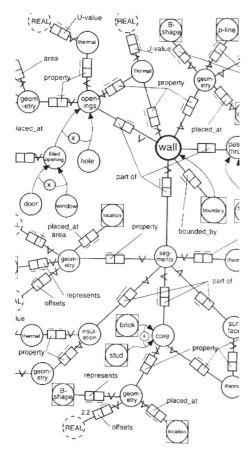

8.25 Part of an ISO-STEP model of a wall. (C. M. Eastman, *Building Product Models: Computer Environments Supporting Design and Construction*, 1999; copyright CRC Press, Boca Raton, Florida.)

Like other representations, a product model is a collection of data and operators that manipulate the data—in essence, a database. It differs from other types of databases in that it adheres to industry-wide, agreed-upon definitions of objects and their attributes: a DOOR in one database that conforms to some interoperability standard will be recognized as such by any another database or application software that conforms to the same standard. This is no small feat. While humans who look at the same representation may be able to interpret it in a similar manner, recognizing a symbol of a door for what it stands for, computers must be explicitly programmed to decode and interpret the data consistently.

The foremost and most widely known such effort was initiated in 1984 by the International Standards Organization (ISO) in Geneva, Switzerland. The ISO commissioned one of its subcommittees (TC184) to develop STEP (STandard for the Exchange of Product Model Data).[12] STEP, like IGES before it, is not limited to exchanging building data. Rather, it is a general engineering product information exchange format, with subsets in many different disciplines (called application protocols).

An ISO-STEP product model starts with a logical data schema, called an application reference model (ARM), which is described through entity relationship diagramming systems like NIAM, IDEF1x, and EXPRESS-G.[13] They produce diagrams of the kind shown in figure 8.25, where the components of the product are represented by the circles, and the relationships between them are represented by links that indicate the nature of the relationship (e.g., part-of, property-of, bounded-by, etc.). This entity relationship schema is automatically converted into a programming language called EXPRESS, which can be read by any system that conforms to ISO-STEP. To simplify the writing of new product models, ISO-STEP uses libraries of predefined components, called integrated resource libraries.

ISO-STEP provided a basis for the development of certain building models that support interoperability among a number of different applications. One such model was developed by the COMBINE project, which facilitates data exchange among various applications within the building industry—primarily energy and HVAC.[14] At its core is an integrated data model that can describe buildings, which can be queried and updated by the applications that use it. The data model underlying the COMBINE project was developed piecemeal, by combining individually developed

Communication

data schemas used by the various applications it connects. Therefore, each time a new application is added to the system, the data model has to be modified too. COMBINE, therefore, does not qualify as an informationally complete building representation: it is only as general and complete as the applications that use it need it to be.

The three major CAD software vendors have recently adopted an approach that supports building information modeling (BIM). This approach provides an industry-wide standard for exchanging more than graphical information. Products like Autodesk's Revit, Bentley Systems' Triforma, and Graphisoft's Archicad now allow architects, engineers, contractors, and owners to access and view information as best fits their needs, synchronize documents automatically, and find information related to materials, fire ratings, and finishes within the same representation.

8.6 Intelligent Objects Models

The ability to link objects to each other, on one hand, and the difficulty of maintaining their well-formedness, on the other hand, coupled with advances in artificial intelligence (AI) and object-oriented programming (OOP), generated interest in what came to be known as intelligent objects modeling.

Intelligent objects combine, in one representation, both data and the operators that manipulate it. As such, an object can automatically calculate some of its own attributes when its other attributes have been changed or when the attributes of another object that affect it have changed. For example, when a wall is moved, all the doors and windows it contains must move along with it. If the object is "intelligent," that is—if it contains operators that are triggered by the move to seek and trigger commensurate moves in the doors and windows that are linked to this wall—then the entire assembly will rearrange itself according to the relocation command. Likewise, if a wall abuts to another wall that has been moved, the "intelligent" wall can recalculate and adjust its own length accordingly, maintaining the abutment condition. In both cases, the responsibility for propagating the consequences of a change are assumed by the representation rather than by the designer, who is relieved of having to manage the consequences of a change and enhancing the overall well-formedness of the model.

```
(dg3 (ako value su))
      (description (value "space unit
  for patient's nursing room" ))
      (ims(value hfur3 ite ))
      (sup(min 22)
            (unit mq)
            (max 28)
            (unit mq)
            (description "minimum and
  maximum net area"))
      (wtemp(range 19 21)
            (unit °C)
            (description "interior winter
  temperature"))
      (stemp range 25 27 )
            (unit °C)
            (description "interior summer
  temperature"))
      (vent(value 2 )
            (unit vol/h )
            (description "number of air
  exchanges"))
      (vela(value 0.2 )
            (unit m/sec )
            (description "air velocity"))
      (sound(max 42)
            (unit dbA )
            (description "maximum noise
  level"))
. . . . . . . . . . . . . . . . . .
```

8.26 Partial definition of a typical SPACE UNIT object
in the KAAD system. (G. Carrara et al., in
Automation in Construction 3, nos. 2–3 [1994].)

Intelligence also allows objects to check the effect of proposed changes before they are executed and to report potential conflicts that may arise. For example, if it is proposed to shrink the length of an "intelligent" wall so that it can no longer accommodate the opening required for the door it contains, the WALL or the DOOR objects can report an error condition.

Intelligence can be embedded in the representation of objects by defining some of the attributes as functions rather than values. For example, figure 8.26 shows part of the representation of an object called a SPACE UNIT, from the modeling system KAAD,[15] which was developed for the purpose of designing hospital suites of the kind shown in figure 8.22. In addition to value-attributes, it includes function-attributes, such as the area of the room (SUP), defined to be between 22 and 28 square meters. This function-attribute can check and see if the room's area falls within the predefined range and alert the designer if it does not.

Objects are connected to other objects through several kinds of semantic links, including "inheritance links" (AKO, ISA) and "association links" (IMS). An inheritance link allows objects to share common attributes, such as their purpose and values, unless explicitly stated otherwise. An association link allows objects to "notify" other objects about changes that have occurred to them, such as relocation or change in dimension.

The inclusion of function-attributes and value-attributes in the same object representation (which is the hallmark of object-oriented programming) makes the model concise and easy to maintain, but it also makes it highly specific—a model that can represent hospital suites cannot represent classrooms or kitchens. To make the representation more general, the function-attributes can be stored separately from the value-attributes. This is the case in systems like EDM,[16] which was developed to support the design of a wide range of buildings using a wide range of construction technologies and variations in building use. By separating the function-attributes from the value-attributes, EDM enforces integrity constraints when needed by each application that uses the model, rather than when the model itself is modified. It makes the model more general, but inconsistencies can only be detected when the data is used, which may be too late. The different approaches taken by KAAD and EDM to solving the same problem demonstrate yet again the tradeoffs that need to be made when developing or choosing a representation between generality, completeness, and efficiency.

Communication

Bibliography

Baer, A., C. M. Eastman, and M. Henrion. "Geometric Modeling: A Survey." *Computer-Aided Design* 11, no. 5 (1979): 253–271.

Baumgart, B. "Winged Edge Polyhedron Representation." Technical Report CS–320, Stanford Artificial Intelligence Laboratory, Palo Alto, 1972.

Eastman, C. M. *Building Product Models: Computer Environments Supporting Design and Construction.* New York: CRC Press, 1999.

Funkhouser, T. A., C. H. Séquin, and S. J. Teller. "Management of Large Amounts of Data in Interactive Building Walkthroughs." In *Proceedings, 1992 Symposium on Interactive 3D Graphics,* 11–20. New York: Association for Computing Machinery, 1992.

Galle, P. "Towards Integrated, 'Intelligent,' and Compliant Computer Modeling of Buildings." *Automation in Construction* 4, no. 3 (1995): 189–211.

Harfmann, A., and S. Chen. "Component-Based Building Representation for Design and Construction." *Automation in Construction* 1, no. 2 (1993): 339–350.

Jacobsen, K., C. Eastman, and T. Sheng Jeng. "Information Management in Creative Engineering Design and Capabilities of Database Transactions." *Automation in Construction* 7, no. 1 (1997): 55–69.

Kalay, Y. E. *Modeling Objects and Environments.* New York: Wiley Interscience, 1989.

Ullman, J. D. *Principles of Database Systems.* Potomac, Md.: Computer Science Press, 1980.

Visualization

Visualization, in the context of computer-aided design, refers to the process of converting the data structures that comprise the geometric model of an object into a graphical form that can be displayed on the screen of a computer or printed on paper. Visualization is part of the larger domain of computer graphics, which has received much attention ever since computers were invented in World War II and has evolved into a prosperous industry that is now as ubiquitous as printed pages and movies.

The importance of visualization as a form of communication derives from our physiological constitution: much of our internal communication (ideation) and external communication (perceiving externally generated information) is eye-related. The evolution of sight has been directly related to the evolution of humans from primates—and more primitive animals before them—who for most of the past 75 million years lived in trees and relied upon good stereoscopic eyesight to survive and to evolve. As a result, at least one third of the human brain is now believed to be occupied by the visual cortex, and we have become almost wholly dependent on sight as a means of understanding the world around us. Consequently, we have become very good at processing visual information; it is processed in a parallel manner, not sequentially, as sound and other sensory inputs are processed. We are able to form a comprehensive understanding of a scene practically at a single glance, recognizing relationships, volumes, directions, colors, and movements in less than one fifth of a second.[1] Compare that to processing music, speech, or text, where comprehension is gained bit by bit, note by note, and word by word. The ease of perceiving information that is presented visually has contributed to great advances in the sciences, helping scientists form models of the cosmos that explain natural phenomena. It has fascinated philosophers and artists since the dawn of history and has prompted some anthropologists to declare the development of the sense of vision to be the greatest culturally formative ability in human beings.[2] Consider the incredible number of metaphors we use in everyday language that are related to the eye and to the sense of sight: vision, visual, visionary, image, imagery, imagination (i.e., making images in the mind). We are said to dream in pictures; fortune tellers are said to be able to "see," not "read" the future; gifted people who are ahead of their time are called visionaries; and even Microsoft called its calendaring system "Outlook."

Vision, more than any other sense, dominates the art of architecture. It allows us to perceive space, the relationships between the components of a building, relative scales, and distances. That explains why advances in computer-aided architectural design—and the tardiness of architects to embrace it—have been closely linked to advances in visualization. Architects are trained to interpret visual information, even incomplete and imperfect visualizations. They can "see" three-dimensional volumes represented by two-dimensional drawings, understand curvatures, and discriminate small variations in shading. Therefore, computer-aided visualization had to reach a relatively advanced level of development before it became acceptable as a tool of the profession.

The development of computer-aided visualization has been tied to advances in both hardware and software. Computer-generated graphics were first achieved by modifying oscilloscopes (instruments used in electrical engineering to visualize the form of time-varying electrical phenomena, like currents and voltages), as demonstrated by Ivan Sutherland's Sketchpad system in 1963. But the device's main component—the cathode ray tube—was capable of displaying only simple line drawings. To help eliminate lines that were occluded by opaque surfaces and cluttered the picture, software had to be developed that could represent polygons and calculate their intersections. The advent of raster scan display terminals promoted the use of color in the rendered scenes, and made possible the development of software that was capable of displaying shaded surfaces, reflections, and translucency. The advent of head-mounted displays and other immersive display technologies offered opportunities that led to the development of virtual reality.

These technical abilities, in turn, spurred research in visual perception, which helped to design better user interfaces for computers and scores of other products where the amount of information that is being communicated can overwhelm even our highly evolved biological visual-processing systems.

9.1 The Human Visual System

The process of human (and many other mammals') vision begins when light, in the form of photons, strikes the rods and cones comprising the retina in the eye. The rods and the cones are filled with a photosensitive fluid, called visual purple (rhodopsin). It is bleached by the light, releasing energy that is translated into an electrochemical signal. The signals from all the rods and cones that have been struck by light travel through the optical nerve to the visual cortex in the back of the brain. The visual cortex aggregates all the signals it receives from both eyes and resolves them into a recognizable image, in spite of the fact the image that falls on each retina is broken into many thousands of individually transmitted signals.

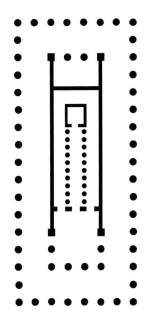

9.1 Temple G in Selinus, Sicily. The columns appear to be components of a straight line.

Perception

To achieve this feat, the processing of visual information begins in the eye itself. It does not simply send to the visual cortex an array of colored dots, but instead picks out and organizes the information according to conjunctions that are meaningful to understanding the scene. Boundaries are such meaningful conjunctions, as are differences in color, contrasts in light, and straight edges. In other words, the eye is predisposed to "see" what it is looking at. For example, it interprets the dots in figure 9.1 as components of straight lines—a phenomenon that has been used extensively in architecture (e.g., in the form of colonnades).

Cognition

The main contribution of the visual cortex to image processing is pattern matching—understanding the image transmitted by the eyes by comparing it to a pattern that has been previously stored in the brain. For example, we commonly understand the image depicted in figure 9.2 as a cube, although in reality it is just a collection of lines on a flat surface. Matching an image to a stored pattern, instead of trying to understand it bit by bit, speeds up and enhances the cognitive process, but it can also be misleading: we see what we are *supposed to see* in a scene, rather than what *there really is* in the scene. As long as the scene conforms to our beliefs, pattern

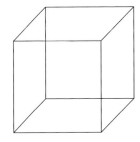

9.2 A collection of lines commonly understood to represent a cube.

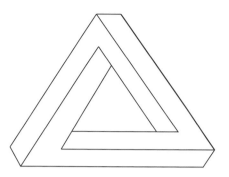

9.3 The pattern-matching process can be easily confounded by presenting it an image that does not match cognitive expectations.

matching is useful. When the scene does not conform to the stored pattern, we may be confused or misled. The first phenomenon is the source of optical illusions of the kind depicted in figure 9.3, where we expect to see a three-dimensional object and are confused when the image does not conform to our expectations. The second phenomenon is used by nature, by the military, and even by architects to hide objects from sight through a process called camouflaging—making the object appear as something other than it is (fig. 9.4).

9.4 "Camouflaging" a building under renovation to hide unsightly scaffolding (Rome, Italy, 2001).

Communication

9.2 The Visualization Transformation Chain

The purpose of computer graphics is to produce images that conform to the expectations of the visual system, thereby fooling it into "seeing" objects when in fact it is only looking at graphical representations of mathematical symbols. Unlike painting and rendering, the source of the image in computer graphics is an abstract data structure, rather than physical paint or charcoal marks on a canvas. Therefore, the image a computer presents to the human visual system is devoid of the rich natural phenomena of light reflecting off a physical object, and must, instead, provide adequate substitutes to compensate for them. That is the role of the various components that make up the visualization transformation chain—from abstract symbols to realistic-looking images.

Geometric Model

Computer graphics thus begin with the data structures discussed in section 8.1—abstract mathematical symbols that have no form whatsoever. The first step in the visualization process is to give them form—preferably graphical form—thereby producing "objects" to be visualized. The conversion of an abstract data structure into a graphical form is based on principles similar to those discussed in section 8.1 in connection with mapping each point of the geometric model onto a specific location in some coordinate system. But unlike the geometric model, the coordinate system used for visualization is two-dimensional; it corresponds to the screen of the display device, or the paper on which the image will be plotted. Once a point has been located within this frame of reference, it can be made visible by directing an electron beam to that location or moving a pen to mark the spot with ink. Two such points can be connected by a line made visible in a similar manner, and whole areas (polygons) can be made visible by "painting" the screen or the paper by moving the electron beam or pen across the area that comprises the polygon.

Lighting Model

Objects in the real world rarely emit light themselves, as neon signs do. Rather, they are visible because they bounce off light that has been gener-

9.5 Lighting makes objects visible (Wei Yan, 2003).

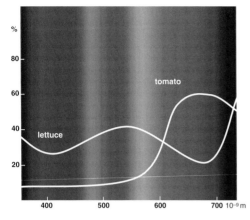

9.6 Surfaces gain their color by reflecting various parts of the visible spectrum in different amounts. (See color plate 1.)

ated elsewhere. The second step in the visualization process is thus to light the scene in a manner that will enable us to see the objects. But light, much like the objects themselves, is an artificial concept as far as computers are concerned—it must be simulated.

Simulating light in a computer-generated scene emulates the principles that govern light in the physical world. The simulation must account for the type of the light source, its shape, intensity, and color. Light sources vary. They can be point sources, like a light bulb, or they can be parallel sources, like sunlight (because of the sun's distance from us). They can be spot lights or ambient light sources (like a window that acts as a light source for a room). They can be shaped in many forms—like long tubes (e.g., neon lights) or discrete objects (e.g., light filtered through a lamp shade). They can take on any number intensities (e.g., a candle versus a 100 W lightbulb) and an unlimited number of colors.

As architects and stage designers know well, light is an extremely malleable component of design, and it can change the perception of a scene as much as the objects themselves. It casts shadows that can help us understand the relative locations of objects (fig. 9.5); and through shadows and colors it can contribute elements to the scene that have no materiality.

Surface Model

Lighting, however, is not the exclusive domain of light sources: it is also affected by the objects being lit, through reflection and translucency. A red object lit by a white light source will appear to be red because it reflects the red part of the visible spectrum, while it absorbs others (fig. 9.6). Reflection reveals the characteristics of the object, or at least the nature of its surface: glass reflects light differently from clay, and a bumpy surface, like that of an orange, reflects light differently from a smooth shiny surface like a Christmas ornament or a soft surface like a tennis ball (fig. 9.7). Reflections also tell us about the relative positions of objects in the world. An object whose reflected image in a pane of glass is visible to us is perceived to stand on our side of the window, whereas one whose image is not reflected is assumed to be on the other side of the window.

Reflection thus reveals an object's materiality: its color, texture, bumpiness, transparency, and shininess. But because neither the computer-represented object nor its surface are "real" in the physical sense, such

9.7 Different materials reflect light in ways that reveal their materiality. (Courtesy of Greg Ward and Isaac Kwo, Lawrence Berkeley National Laboratory, 2002.) (See color plate 6.)

Communication

materiality must be simulated. The simulation only produces visual evidence of the object's materiality, which cannot be verified by touch. Therefore, computer graphics can "fake" materiality without actually modeling it. For example, an object can appear to be made of wood, clay, glass, even water—without changing the object itself. All that needs to be changed is the appearance of the object, through a process called texture mapping. Texture mapping works much like a slide projector that can make an image appear on a blank wall—the chosen surface materiality can be "projected," or mapped, onto an otherwise featureless object. Since the texture map can be adjusted to fit the gross features of the object, the human visual system will be tricked to believe the object is actually made of the mapped material. This feature is very handy for the purposes of design, because architects can easily test the visual effect of using different materials for their building. Of course, the illusion will be destroyed if the texture map conflicts with other visual cues—a feature often used by special effects designers in movies and in the advertising industry.

Rendering Model

Finally, once there exist an object model to be seen, a lighting model to see it by, and a surface model to indicate the object's materiality, the visualization process must find a way to render the scene on the screen of a display device. This process, which depends on the type of computing hardware used, has evolved over the past five decades from simple line drawings, through raster graphics, to photo-realistic imaging and has come to be known as computer graphics. Many different rendering algorithms have been developed, starting with simple but tedious attempt to eliminate hidden lines, followed by flat and interpolated shading algorithms capable of revealing the object's curvature, culminating in ray tracing and radiosity renderers that can display transparencies and reflections in a photo-realistic manner.

9.3 Computer Graphics

Computer graphics (CG) was born in 1946 as a gimmick, when John Mauchly and J. Presper Eckert equipped ENIAC—the first functional, general-purpose electronic computer they built at the University of

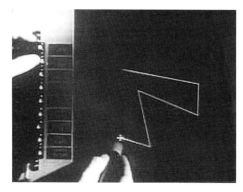

9.8 Sketchpad—the first vector-drawing computer graphics system (1963).

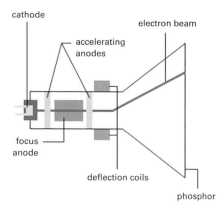

9.9 The CRT picture tube (Wei Yan, 2003).

Pennsylvania Moore's School of Engineering during World War II—with lighted ping-pong balls that helped the media explain to the public what this $3 million machine was doing when it calculated the product of two numbers.

The ability of computers to turn on and off lights that appeared to make graphical patterns did not go unnoticed, and it was soon coupled with oscilloscopes—by then a common device used in electrical engineering (of which computer science was, and in many cases still is, a subdiscipline)—to form vector-drawing display systems. The first such program was Sketchpad, developed by Ivan Sutherland in the early 1960s. It allowed engineers to draw and manipulate drawings displayed on the screen of a cathode ray tube (CRT) using a light pen and a keyboard (fig. 9.8).

Vector Graphics

A CRT consists of an evacuated glass container coated with a phosphorescent substance at one end and an electron gun and a system for focusing and deflecting the beam of electrons at the other end (fig. 9.9). The electron beam that emerges from the gun passes through focusing/deflecting coils—called the yoke—and emerges as a thin beam that can be aimed at any point on the face of the tube, where it excites the phosphorous and causes it to glow for a short time. A point can be drawn by aiming the electron beam to its geometric coordinates after they have been mapped to the coordinate frame of reference of the phosphor-coated end of the container—the "screen." A line can be drawn by aiming the electron beam at one of its endpoints then moving it to the coordinates of its other endpoint—in effect drawing a vector from the first point to the second. Because the phosphorus only glows for a short time, the line needs to be retraced again and again, at least thirty times a second, to keep it from fading away.

Vector graphics, as this method is called, was very adept at drawing lines, hence geometric shapes comprised of lines. The images it could draw where monochromatic—typically light green (the color of the glowing phosphor). Since all the lines had the same intensity, it was difficult to distinguish between lines of the object that were closer to the observer and ones that were further away. Surfaces could only be drawn with great difficulty, by "filling in" the area they delineated on the screen with many

Communication

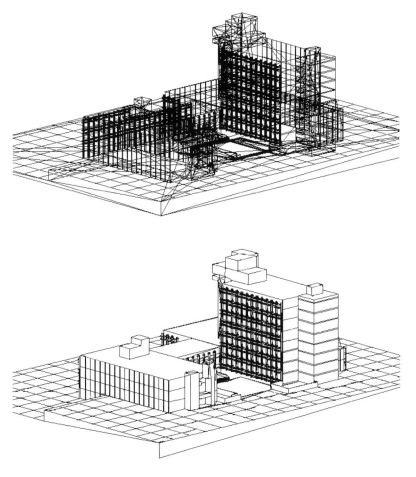

9.10 Hidden-line elimination helps make the image more readable (Wei Yan, 2003).

horizontally drawn "scan" lines, much like a child would color in a line drawing with a crayon.[3] Clearly, a better method was needed.

The method that was developed for this purpose was known as hidden-line elimination. A list of lines to be displayed on the screen—the display list—was constructed from all lines of the object(s). Prior to rendering them on the screen, those parts of each line that were occluded by opaque surfaces were eliminated from the list. If parts of a line were visible, it was cut at the point(s) of occlusion, and the invisible portions were eliminated. The remaining lines in the display list were rendered on the screen, producing an image that is very familiar to architects (fig. 9.10). Calculating which lines were visible and which ones had to be eliminated was predicated on computing the pair-wise intersections of all the polygons that made up the scene—a computationally expensive process that became exponentially worse as the number of objects in the scene and their complexity grew.

Vector graphics became very popular in 1969, when Tektronix—a leading manufacturer of high-quality oscilloscopes since 1945—introduced its model T4000, the first direct view storage tube (DVST) cathode ray tube. Unlike ordinary CRTs, the DVST had *two* electron guns: one to draw the image, the other to "flood" the screen with low-intensity electrons. This flood of electrons caused those parts of the screen that were already excited by the first gun to continue to glow, thus eliminating the need to continually refresh the drawing. As a result, the DVST could draw much more complex images than the single-gun CRT because it did not have to finish drawing each screen in less than a thirtieth of a second. Its main drawback was that in order to delete any one line, the entire screen had to be erased and redrawn from the display list, a process accompanied by an annoying bright flash. This technology considerably simplified the CRT and made it cheap enough to be accessible to universities and companies, which opened the floodgates of computer graphics research and development.

Raster Graphics

The next technological development that had a major impact on computer graphics was the introduction of the raster scan display. Invented in 1973 by Richard Shoup at XEROX PARC, this device used a special memory, called a frame buffer, to store the entire image digitally before it was rendered on the screen. The frame buffer is a large array of individual memory units, each capable of storing one dot that belongs to the image, arranged in a grid. The grid can store anywhere from 400 x 600 dots to 4096 x 4096 dots, or "pixels" (picture elements). By scanning the frame buffer (and the screen) sequentially—from left to right, top to bottom, one array line at a time—the entire image could be drawn all at once, rather than vector by vector, as the DVST did.

The technology has several major advantages over vector graphics, and one major drawback. By eliminating the expensive control mechanism that vector graphics uses to direct the electron beam to specific points on the screen, raster graphics has considerably simplified the display device, making it cheap enough for consumers to buy. By using four frame buffers rather than one, it has made color images possible: one frame buffer stores the black parts of the image, another its cyan (blue-green) parts, the third its yellow (red-green) parts, and the fourth the magenta (red-blue) parts of the image (fig. 9.11). By using three electron guns and three layers of phosphor, each luminescent in one of the three colors (and a perforated display shield to mask each phosphor coating from the other guns), and by mapping each frame buffer to the corresponding gun/phosphor, a colorful image can be displayed. Since the frame buffer can store not only lines, but also areas washed in color, it allows for the display of shaded surfaces. And since the image can be written to the frame buffer much faster than it can be drawn on the screen, changes in the scene can be updated in real time, allowing for what appears to be moving images (animation).

The major drawback of the raster display technology is that lines, and every other element of the image, must be broken into many pixels. The effect of this "pixelation" is an image made of many colorful, discrete dots, rather than continuous lines or areas (fig. 9.12). The appearance of rasterized images, therefore, is much like the grainy pictures in a newspaper—on a low-resolution screen, lines appear stair-stepped (fig. 9.12a). To smooth them, computer graphics relies on the tendency of the human visual system to interpret the scene such that it conforms with the expected image rather than the actual one. In a process called anti-aliasing, a gradation of color is added that blends the foreground color (of the line or area) with the background color, as depicted in figure 9.12b. The effect blurs the edges of the line, which from a distance appears to be smooth (fig. 9.12c).

The ability to display colored areas, not merely their contours, gave rise to simpler display algorithms than the computationally expensive hidden-line-elimination process. Much like seventeenth-century paintings, in which images were "built" layer by layer, from back to front, so can images be displayed on the screen starting with the furthest polygons to the ones closest to the viewer. Since polygons are opaque, the ones drawn later occlude the ones drawn earlier, in effect "hiding" them from view. This so-called painter algorithm is demonstrated by the sequence of images in figure 9.13.

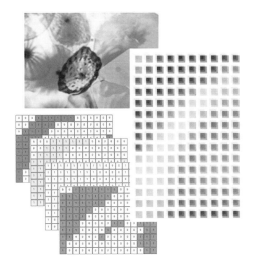

9.11 Raster graphics uses multiple display buffers to render an image in color (Wei Yan, 2003). (See color plate 4.)

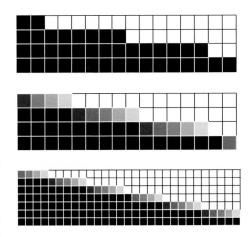

9.12 Anti-aliasing "smoothes" jagged edges by averaging each pixel to the colors of its neighbors.

9.13 The painter algorithm hides invisible surfaces by displaying the polygons of an image back-to-front (Wei Yan, 2003).

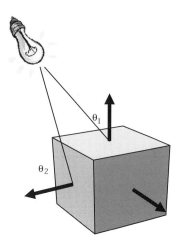

9.14 The flat-shading algorithm computes the shading coefficient by calculating the cosine of the angle between the surface normal and the line connecting the surface to the light source.

Flat Shading

The ability to display shaded areas also required the development of algorithms that could adjust the color of the visible surfaces to conform to the prevailing lighting conditions: surfaces that face the light source illuminating the scene appear brighter than those facing away from it (and, of course, surfaces that face more than 90 degrees away from the light source are not visible at all, unless they are illuminated by reflection from other objects). The so-called flat, or cosine, shading algorithm solved that problem. It calculates the cosine of the angle formed between the normal vector to each surface and the vector connecting that surface with the light source (fig. 9.14). The resulting number (which is always between 1 and 0) is used as a multiplying coefficient for the intensity of the color. Thus, a surface that faces the light source directly will be multiplied by a coefficient of 1 (cos0, or full intensity), whereas a surface oriented 90 degrees to the light source will be multiplied by the coefficient 0 (cos90, or zero intensity). If more than one light source exists, the algorithm becomes more complex: it must take into account the distance and intensity of every light source and calculate their respective contributions to lighting each surface.[4]

172   **Communication**

Interpolated Shading

The cosine shading algorithm contributes much to the realism of the scene, but it is inadequate for rendering smoothly curved surfaces, which appear faceted, like the mirrored ball hanging over a dance floor (fig. 9.15a). An algorithm that smoothly blends the intensities of light reflected by successive points on the surface of a curved object was developed by Gouraud.[5] Gouraud shading—also known as "intensity interpolation shading" or simply "interpolated shading"—begins by triangulating the surface (dividing it into many small triangular polygons). The intensity coefficient for each vertex is calculated using the cosine method described earlier.[6] The intensity of each point along an edge is calculated by interpolating the intensity of the two vertices connected by the edge at that point (e.g., by averaging the weighted intensities multiplied by the distance of the point from each vertex). Finally, the intensity of each point internal to the polygon is calculated by interpolating the intensities of the points on the two edges of the polygon that are intersected by a scan line through that point. The result of this process is a smoothly shaded surface, as depicted in figure 9.15b.

Phong improved Gouraud's shading algorithm by using surface normals instead of the intensities of the vertices.[7] The normals to the surfaces are interpolated as in Gouraud's method, and mapped back into the model coordinate system for calculating their intensities. Phong's method is able to reproduce highlights more faithfully than Gouraud's method.

Both methods, however, only work for the *internal* points of a surface. Boundary points, where there is a sharp change from one surface condition to another, do not support interpolation—there is no intensity or surface normal to interpolate with. As a result, the optical illusion generated through this method breaks down, as seen at the contours of the teapot depicted in figure 9.15b. Moreover, since interpolation is an artificial manipulation of values *after* perspective foreshortening has been calculated, rather than an actual calculation of shading conditions of the object itself, it may produce distorted views. Finally, neither interpolated shading nor the flat-shading algorithms can show surface details; they can only produce smooth looking images, unlike most of the objects we observe in the real world.

9.15 Shading a curved surface: (a) flat shading, (b) Gouraud shading (Wei Yan, 2003).

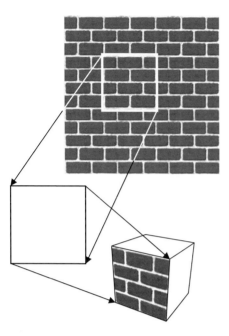

9.16 Texture mapping consists of displaying a scaled and properly oriented image of some texture transformed onto a selected face of the model.

Texture Mapping

Surface details, such as textures and bumps, can be added to the geometric model of the object itself but will quickly overwhelm the complexity of the model, making it too large and too slow for even simple manipulations. Moreover, since many models are used as ideation tools, it is likely that the designer will want to test different materials before deciding on the one to be used in constructing the building. Changing the model's geometry for each material (e.g., stone, brick, concrete) is impractical. Fortunately, the human visual system can be easily tricked to believe it is looking at an object made of stone, brick, or any other material just by making the object appear to be made of that material, clad, as it might be, in a thin veneer, or even just painted to look the part.

Digital texture mapping was pioneered by Ed Catmull,[8] and refined by Blinn and Newell.[9] It consists of displaying a scaled and properly oriented image of some texture (e.g., wood grain, brick, or concrete) on the screen where an otherwise featureless face of an object would have been displayed. Texture mapping consists of applying two sets of transformations to the image of the texture: the set that would map that image (or part of it) onto the selected face of the geometric model, and the set that maps the geometric model to the screen (fig. 9.16). For curved surfaces, interpolation must be applied.

Bump Mapping

If the image being mapped is of a rough surface, like brick, the resulting image will not look quite right, because the direction of the light used to create the image of the texture is likely to be different from the direction of the light used to illuminate the object onto which it is mapped. Bump mapping, a process invented by James Blinn,[10] helps to alleviate this problem by introducing little irregularities into the texture map without changing the geometry of the object itself.

A "bump map" is an array of displacements, each of which is used to move a point on the surface a little above or below its actual position. These little displacements, when matched to the roughness of the texture, are enough to trick the human visual system into "seeing" a roughened surface.

Communication

Transparency

When an object is made of glass, or similar transparent or translucent materials, its appearance must be modified to show both the objects that are behind it, and the reflection of objects in front of it. The simplest method of simulating transparency is to ignore refraction (bending) and display objects that are located behind the transparent one after their color has been interpolated with the color of the transparent object. Without such interpolation, the occluding object will disappear entirely from view. This method of representation is useful when communicating information about the internal parts of a complex object and when visual realism is not important.

To communicate the visual appearance of glass, refraction must be simulated. Refraction occurs when light passes from one medium (e.g., air) into another (e.g., glass), in which it travels more slowly (or faster). The change in speed causes light rays to "bend," making objects appear to be shifted from their true (geometric) location (fig. 9.17). The amount of refraction is given by Snell's Law (also known as Descartes's Law of Sines):

$$\frac{\sin \theta_t}{\sin \theta_i} = \frac{\eta_i}{\eta_t}$$

where θ_i is the angle of incidence, and θ_t is the angle of transmission, relative to the normal to the boundary of the transition plan between the two media, and where η_t and η_i are the indices of refraction of the respective materials (the ratio between the speed of light in vacuum and its speed in that material). Simulating transparency thus means calculating the optical displacement of objects located behind a transparent medium, with respect to the observer's point of view.[11]

Inter-object reflections—when the surface of one object reflects the images of other objects in its vicinity—are calculated using optical laws similar to those of transparency. Reflection can be sharp, as when an image is reflected off simulated glass or metal, or diffused, as when the image is reflected off flat surface materials—such as simulated plastic or plaster. As the number of objects in the scene grows, and as the number of light sources grows, the scene may become too complex for such calculations. Methods that can deal with complex scenes, and at the same time produce visually convincing images, had to be developed.

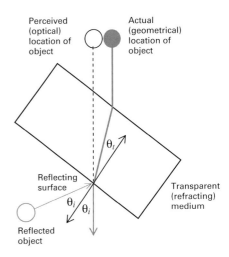

9.17 Refraction and reflection.

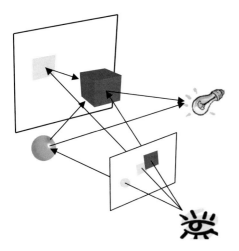

9.18 Ray tracing calculates the color of rays of light reaching the viewer's eye. (See color plate 5.)

Ray Tracing

Ray tracing is the first of the so-called physically based illumination models (radiosity is the second). It is based on the physiological properties of vision that were discussed at the beginning of this chapter, namely that vision is a matter of perceiving different light intensities and colors and occurs only when rays of light arrive at the viewer's eye. Therefore, to generate a synthetic image it is not necessary to model all the reflections and refractions of light in a scene—only those rays that arrive at the viewer's eye matter. By identifying those rays and tracing them back to their origins, we can generate a visible image. Thus if the viewer is looking at a scene comprising a red cube floating in a black void, lit by a single source of white light, many rays of light will never reach the viewer's eye, and need, therefore, not be modeled. Those (relatively few) rays of light that are reflected off the cube and do reach the viewer's eye will appear to be red (fig. 9.18). Their intensities will depend on the inclination of the cube's surfaces with respect to the light source and the viewer's point of view, thus painting the cube's visible surfaces in different shades of red. If there is a white wall behind the cube, the rays reflected off that wall will appear to be white. But some rays will reflect from the red cube onto the white wall before they arrive at the viewer's eye, picking up some of the cube's red color, thus creating a reddish hue approximating the reflection of the cube on the wall (if the wall is made of some shiny material, the cube's reflection will be sharper, as in a mirror). If there is also a yellow ball in the scene, as depicted in figure 9.18, more reflections will occur, further modifying the color of the rays that reach the viewer's eye.

Determining which rays reach the viewer's eye can be simplified if they are traced in reverse—from the viewer's eye to the scene, rather than from the scene to the eye. This is further simplified by accounting for the computer screen's finite size, which comprises a finite number of pixels: only one ray per pixel is visible.

The colors and the intensities of the rays can be calculated by using an illumination model based on the laws of physics governing reflection, refraction, and diffusion. Hence, the basic ray-tracing algorithm is as follows:

1. Generate one ray for each pixel.
2. For each ray:
   2.1 Determine the nearest object intersected by the ray.
   2.2 Compute intensity information for the intersection point (using the illumination model).
   2.3 Calculate and trace reflection ray.
   2.4 Calculate and trace transparency ray (if any).
   2.5 Combine the results of the intensity computation, reflection ray intensity, and transparency ray intensity and set the pixel to the resulting color.
   2.6 If the ray did not intersect any objects, set the pixel color to be the background color.

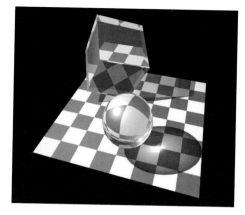

9.19 Ray-traced scenes accurately render reflections and refractions of light (Jae-Wook Lee, 2003).

Ray tracing can handle multiple light sources, reflections, and refractions, shadow casting, and hidden-line removal. It can also be extended to include anti-aliasing, blurred reflections (glossiness), motion blur, and depth-of-field effects. It produces highly realistic images, of the kind depicted in figure 9.19, but it is computationally very expensive: given a typical display screen, over 1 million rays must be traced. Calculating all their reflections and refractions in a complex scene can take a long time (hours, even days), even if optimization techniques and high-speed computers are used. In addition to being visually pleasing, the ray-tracing method can be used to calculate actual light intensity values for evaluation purposes (fig. 9.20).

The major drawback of ray tracing is its view-dependence: it calculates rays cast from the viewer's eye, and its end product is the image seen from the observer's point of view. If the point of view is changed, the entire image must be recalculated. A visualization method that is view-independent—allowing for multiple different points of view—was needed.

Radiosity

The radiosity method is such a view-independent visualization method: it generates a 3D *model,* not an image, that can be viewed from any point in space.

Radiosity was originally developed to study radiative heat exchange. Thermodynamics theory describes radiation as the transfer of energy from

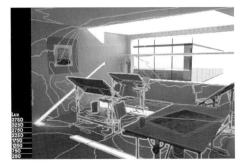

9.20 Radiance, a hybrid deterministic/stochastic ray-tracing program, can be used for lighting evaluation purposes. (Courtesy of Greg Ward, Lawrence Berkeley National Laboratory, 1994.) (See color plate 8.)

a surface when that surface has been thermally excited. This includes surfaces that are *emitters* of energy, such as light sources, and surfaces that *reflect* energy received from other surfaces. This "thermal radiation" theory can be used to describe the transfer of any kind of energy between surfaces, including light energy.

Much like thermal heat transfer, the radiosity method for computer image generation assumes that surfaces are Lambertian diffuse reflectors—emitting and reflecting energy uniformly over their entire surface area.[12] It also assumes that all of the energy in the visualized environment can be accounted for, through absorption and reflection, and that an equilibrium solution can be reached. These two assumptions—which are not valid in reality since surfaces are neither perfectly Lambertian, nor can all the energy be accounted for—allow for modeling the light transfer between the surfaces in terms of the rate of energy that leaves each surface. This rate is called the radiosity of the surface, hence the name of this visualization method. Since the energy used in this calculation is light energy, radiosity is the intensity of light emitted by each surface. This information is stored with each surface and can be displayed in the form of color from any desired point of view after determining the surfaces that are visible from that vantage point. This last step is performed, in most cases, by the hardware video processor, which allows for real-time "walkthrough" in the displayed scene, something ray tracing cannot do.

To achieve Lambertian surface qualities, the surface of each object is subdivided into multiple discrete areas, called patches. Each patch can be considered an opaque Lambertian surface of a finite size that reflects light uniformly over its entire surface. The number of patches affects the accuracy of the computation—the smaller the patches, the more accurate the simulation. However, the more patches that need to be considered, the longer it takes to calculate their mutual reflections.[13]

The radiosity of each surface patch i can be calculated by adding its own emissivity, if it is a light source, to the radiosity of every other patch j whose emitted or reflected light falls on patch i, using the following formula:

$$B_i = E_i + \rho_i \Sigma B_j \, F_{ji}$$
where
$B_i \, B_j$ = radiosity of patches i and j
E_i = energy/area/time emitted by i

Communication

ρ_i = reflectivity of patch i

F_{ji} = the form factor from j to i

The form factor is a ratio, given as a percentage, which describes the geometric relationship between patches i and j. It accounts for the distance between the patches, their relative orientations, and the fraction of each patch that is facing the other patch. For example, two patches that face each other at a close distance, and are roughly overlapping, will have a form factor of 100%. If they face away from each other, their form factor will be 0%; and if they face each other but overlap only partially, their form factor may be 10% or less. Calculating the form factors among all the patches in the scene is the most expensive part of the radiosity method, but since it is a geometric quality of the scene itself, it needs to be calculated only once for all points of view (unless the geometry of the scene itself is modified).

Given the form factors F_{ji} and the reflectivity ρ_i of each patch, the formula listed above can be solved through a set of n simultaneous linear equations:

9.21 Diffuse reflection of light leads to "color bleeding," as the reflected light carries the surface's color to other surfaces. (Courtesy of Donald Greenberg, Cornell University Computer Graphics Program.) (See color plate 7.)

$$
\begin{bmatrix}
1 - \rho_1 F_{11} & -\rho_1 F_{12} & \dots & & -\rho_1 F_{1n} \\
-\rho_2 F_{21} & 1 - \rho_2 F_{22} & \dots & & -\rho_2 F_{2n} \\
\cdot & \cdot & \dots & & \cdot \\
\cdot & \cdot & \dots & & \cdot \\
\cdot & \cdot & \dots & & \cdot \\
-\rho_n F_{n1} & -\rho_n F_{n2} & \dots & 1 & - \rho_n F_{nn}
\end{bmatrix}
*
\begin{bmatrix}
B_1 \\ B_2 \\ \cdot \\ \cdot \\ \cdot \\ B_n
\end{bmatrix}
=
\begin{bmatrix}
E_1 \\ E_2 \\ \cdot \\ \cdot \\ \cdot \\ E_n
\end{bmatrix}
$$

The calculation results in a value of total illumination E_i for each surface. It must be repeated for each one of the primary colors (red, green, and blue), because the reflectivity values are different for each wavelength.

The major advantage of the radiosity method for computer image-generation is the highly realistic quality of the resulting images: no other method can accurately calculate the diffuse inter-reflection of light energy in a scene. Soft shadows and color bleeding are natural by-products of this method (fig. 9.21), just as hard shadows and mirrorlike reflections are natural by-products of a typical ray-tracing algorithm. In addition to being

9.22 Combining radiosity with ray tracing produces photo-realistic images. (Courtesy of Donald Greenberg, Cornell University.) (See color plate 9.)

visually pleasing, the ray-tracing method can be used to calculate actual light intensity values for evaluation purposes (fig. 9.20). The viewpoint independence of the basic radiosity algorithm provides the opportunity for interactive walkthroughs (the ability to navigate the scene interactively), because a single intensity solution serves many views of the same environment.

The costs associated with the radiosity method are, however, substantial: radiosity requires a large amount of storage and long computation times for the form factor calculations and matrix solution. Therefore, radiosity is often performed in "progressive refinement" mode, where images made of courser patches are used to determine if finer refinement is warranted.

The major disadvantage of the radiosity method is its inability to handle specular reflection and refraction. It only works with opaque, diffuse reflections surfaces, where the light leaving a surface (its radiosity) is only influenced by the orientation of the surface patch itself, not by the direction it came from. As a result, the basic radiosity method cannot be used to render glass and shiny surfaces.

It is possible to augment the basic radiosity algorithm to carry directional lighting information, but the method is very expensive in terms of computation.[14] A simpler solution is to combine radiosity with ray tracing. The combined method takes advantage of the strengths of each one of the two methods—radiosity's ability to render view-independent diffuse reflectivity and ray tracing's ability to render view-dependent specular reflection and refraction. Combining ray tracing and radiosity is more complicated than simply adding up the pixel values obtained from each approach. Rather, a two-pass approach is needed, where radiosity is done first and ray tracing second.[15] The results of the combined approach are as close to reality as computers currently can make synthetic scenes appear to be (fig. 9.22).

Kinematics

The scenes we see in the real world are often more than just static snapshots: we move through buildings, doors open and close, lights are turned on and off, and people inhabit the spaces. Visualizing a dynamically changing environment is the province of computer-based kinematics.

Every one of the three main components of the visualization pipeline that were discussed in this chapter can be made time-dependent: the geo-

Communication

metric model can change to show how objects operate (e.g., doors swing, people pass by); the surface model can change to show different surface treatments and lighting conditions (e.g., changes in daylighting); and the rendering model can be changed to show different points of view (e.g., when we walk through the building).

In all cases, the visualization model comprises a sequence of static images, each different from the previous scene by some small, incremental detail (e.g., a slightly different angle of view). When this sequence is displayed at the rate of thirty images per second, the human visual system sees them as one continuous motion.

The images in the sequence can be precomputed, as the frames of a movie, in which case they constitute a predetermined sequence. Alternatively, they can be computed on the fly, responding to some user action (e.g., moving the mouse to go forward and to turn). Precomputed sequences allow for long processing time, hence for superb images that, depending on the rendering method, can be indistinguishable from reality. They can also tell a story, choreographed by the sequence generator. Dynamically changing images, on the other hand, let the *viewer* explore the environment, choosing which passage to take, which door to open, and which direction to look in. To minimize the computation needed to generate each new image in the sequence, changes from scene to scene must kept to a minimum. Still, the quality of a dynamically controlled visualization is generally poorer than the precomputed one, and the "jerkiness" of the motion increases as the complexity of the scene grows, reflecting longer computation times per image.

Modeling dynamic natural phenomena, such as wind, waves, the motion of people and animals, fire, smoke, and so forth, requires careful study of the simulated phenomena and often the development of special software that will help the animator correctly change the image from scene to scene. The demand for such software has grown as the movie industry increasingly uses computer-generated dynamic sequences for special effects requiring a high degree of realism.

In architectural design, where the emphasis is on the environment itself, visualization needs to mimic the way people see and experience reality. The presence of other people, their movements, the noises they make, and the effects of wind and other natural phenomena are important contributors to such experience, but they are secondary to the viewer's ability to control his or her own actions—especially to look around and see the environment at will.

9.4 Virtual Reality

Engendering a sense of "being there," without actually being "there," is hard to do. It requires a considerable amount of mental gymnastics, known colloquially as suspension of disbelief—the act of disregarding the contrary cues provided by the senses, telling the brain that it isn't so. Suspension of disbelief is especially hard when the environment does not really exist and must be described in sufficient detail to paint a comprehensive and convincing mental image. Painting such mental images has been the province of storytellers, actors, and artists for centuries. Good stories are engaging, absorbing, and believable—especially when the listener is in the mood to allow suspension of disbelief, as when reading a book or going to the movies.

Suspension of Disbelief

It is more difficult to suspend disbelief when the mental image corresponds to a nonfictional environment intended to be made part of the viewer's real world, as is the case is in architectural design. The viewer, in that case, is not in a mood to be entertained and is using physiological, not mental, vision to acquire the image. It is hard to ask the viewer of a two-dimensional image, displayed on a (relatively) small, desktop computer monitor, to imagine what it might feel like being inside the depicted three-dimensional space.

Yet the very dominance of the sense of vision in our perception of the world, especially as it pertains to understanding space, is also the key to developing communication technologies that can help engender a sense of "being there." Tricking the eyes into conveying a realistic image to the visual cortex is a big first step toward suspending disbelief.

Tricking the eyes to see an imaginary scene through painted murals (the so-called *trompe l'oeil*) is an art that dates back to the ancient Greeks. It reached its apex during the Renaissance, when the technology of fresco painting was combined with the newly discovered perspective projection to create fictitious landscapes painted on the walls of Italian villas in lieu

9.23 *Trompe l'oeil* is a style of painting in which objects are rendered with extreme realism—in this case, a store in Agripas street, Jerusalem, Israel. (See color plate 10.)

of windows and, more recently, to paint imaginary urban scenes where there are none (fig. 9.23).

In 1880 the Dutch artist Hendrik Willem Mesdag painted the Panorama Mesdag—a 360-degree view of the surroundings of Scheveningen, a fishing village northwest of The Hague. This immense painting (390 feet long and 45 feet high, covering an area of some 17,000 square feet) was a much-loved visual attraction in the nineteenth century. It is accessed through a narrow, dark passage and up a spiral staircase that leads to a visitors' observation deck shaped like a sand dune, creating the illusion of looking out on a faraway landscape (fig. 9.24).

The modern use of virtual reality began in 1928, when Edwin Link started working on a pilot trainer—a device that allowed pilots to take their early flight training safely on the ground. He built an airplane mock-up, complete with an air pump, valves, and bellows to make his trainer move in response to the pilot's actions. Link's trainers led to the development of the modern flight simulator, with visual cues provided by images painted (and later projected) on screens located outside the cockpit.

What allowed *trompe l'oeil,* Panorama Mesdag, and Link's flight simulator to engender a sense of being in a place that does not really exist— a *virtual* place—was their relatively large size and distance from the observer, who was looking at an image that appeared to be roughly of the

9.24 Panorama Mesdag—a hand-painted circular image of 1880 in Scheveningen, a fishing village in the Netherlands, intended to convey a sense of "being there," complete with a sand dune as the visitors' platform. (Copyright the Mesdag Documentation Society, Wassenaar, The Netherlands.)

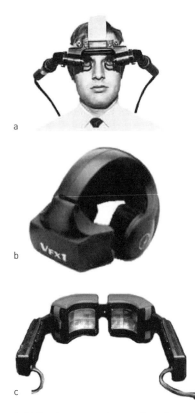

a

b

c

9.25 Head-mounted displays (HMD):
(a) Sutherland's 1968 model, (b) an early
commercial model (Interactive Imaging,
Systems), (c) Keiser Electro Optics (2001).

same size and at the same distance as it would have been had it been a real scene. The observer's relatively fixed point of view, with respect to image, also helped to maintain the illusion: the image did not have to be changed when the observer looked right or left, making it observer-independent.

This, of course, is not the case when the observer is looking at the screen of a desktop computer, where the image is much smaller than reality, is too close for the observer not to notice that it is two-dimensional, and does not change when the observer moves his or her gaze.

Head-Mounted Displays (HMD)

The first attempts to mimic the large, frameless view afforded by life-size images while using digital display technology was made in 1966, when Ivan Sutherland developed the head-mounted display (HMD). It comprised two small cathode ray tubes, each displaying an image close enough to the eye to make it appear large and frameless. The two images were slightly different, producing a stereoscopic effect, which was merged by the brain into a three-dimensional image. The observer's position in space and direction of view were tracked and the image displayed by the CRTs was updated accordingly, maintaining the correspondence between the observer's direction of gaze and the scene. As such, when the observer turned his or her head left, the image rotated to the right, and vice versa. When the observer stepped forward, the image was updated to show the new point of view. All this was done thirty times a second to maintain smooth motion.

The basic technology invented by Sutherland has remained unchanged to date, although it has been much improved. Instead of CRTs, small flat liquid crystal displays (LCDs) are used, making the HMD lighter, cheaper, and safer (fig. 9.25). Audio was added, which helps make the experience more realistic. And tracking makes use of solid state electromagnetic emitters to determine the position and orientation of the observer's location and direction in space, instead of the cumbersome and expensive video-based tracking used earlier. The result is the ability to see a scene much like it would appear if it were real and interact with it in a manner that closely resembles walking through and looking around the real scene. Hardware that allows the observer to indicate objects in space, "grab" them, and move them around, completes the ensemble.

Communication

Still, the experience can be thoroughly disorienting. The lag between moving one's head and having the image updated to correspond to the new position and direction causes a "swimming" sensation that can lead to motion sickness. Depth of field and field of vision problems make it difficult to sort out depth cues and may cause misjudgment of distances. However, the major current limitation of HMD is the solitary experience it affords: it is strictly a one-person view.

VR Cave

To solve that problem, and to allow multiple observers to see the same scene, a theaterlike projection system was developed at the Electronic Visualization Laboratory (EVL) at the University of Illinois at Chicago in 1992.[16] Called the Cave, it provides multiviewer, real-time imaging perspective with a large angle of view, interactive control, and binocular (stereo) display. A typical Cave is a 10 x 10 x 9 ft booth (fig. 9.26). Images are rear-projected onto three, four, even five of its walls, which act as screens. Each one of the images is generated by a separate computer. They are coordinated to provide a seamless display of up to 270 degrees horizontally and vertically. The Cave can accommodate three to five observers, who can all see the same image.

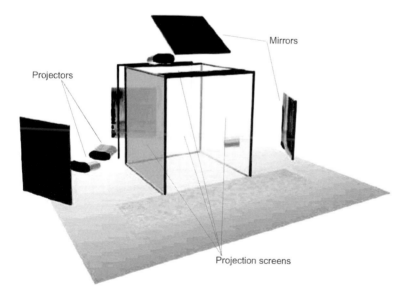

Mirrors

Projectors

Projection screens

9.26 A schema of a typical Cave. (Courtesy of the National Center for Supercomputing Applications, University of Illinois at Urbana-Champaign.)

Stereoscopic views can be generated by projecting separate images for the left eye and the right eye. Viewers wear stereo shutter glasses, which are synchronized with the computer using infrared emitters mounted around the Cave. When the computer renders the left eye image, the right shutter on the glasses is closed, and vice-versa. This happens at least thirty times a second, tricking the brain to perceive a three-dimensional image.

Typically the virtual world is much larger then the physical size of the Cave. Viewers can explore it using some form of navigation, such as simulated "flying" or "walking." To maintain the correct perspective, the viewer's head position and orientation is tracked (though only one user—the driver—can be tracked). Interaction is done through an input device called a wand, which can be thought of as the 3D equivalent of a mouse. It facilitates naviagtion as well as interaction with objects in the scene, which can be picked up by pointing at them with the wand.

The importance of VR for architecture comes from its ability to alter the relationship between the observer and the scene. Architecture can only be appreciated when the observed object engulfs the observer, putting the observer "inside" the observed object. By contrast, in most other design fields (e.g., product design, mechanical engineering, and electrical engineering), the observer is larger than the product, hence displaying a (relatively) small image on a computer screen does not qualitatively affect the viewer's perception. The inverted scale of architecture, where the observer is much smaller than the product, cannot be adeqautely simulated by habitual means (unless full-scale mock-ups or protptypes are built, which is an expensive and rarely used proposition). VR provides the means to simulate being inside a building and provides observers with a qualitative advantage over other means of representation.

Bibliography

Appel, A. "The Notion of Quantitative Invisibility and the Machine Rendering of Solids." In Association for Computing Machinery, *Proceedings of the National Conference,* 387–393. New York: ACM, 1967.

Aukstakalnis, S., and D. Blatner. *Silicon Mirage: The Art and Science of Virtual Reality.* Berkeley: Peachpit Press, 1992.

Bresenham, J. E. "Algorithm for Computer Control of a Digital Plotter." *IBM Systems Journal,* 4, no. 1 (1965): 25–30.

Brooks, F. P. "Grasping Reality through Illusion: Interactive Graphics Serving Science." *ACM Transactions on Computer Human Interaction* (1988): 1–11.

Cook, R. L., T. Porter, and L. Carpenter. "Distributed Ray Tracing." *SIG-GRAH'84* (1984): 137–145.

Foley, J. D., A. van Dam, S. K. Feiner, and J. F. Hughes. *Computer Graphics: Principles and Practice.* Reading, Mass.: Addison-Wesley, 1987.

Glassner, A. *An Introduction to Ray Tracing.* New York: Academic Press, 1989.

Rheingold, H. *Virtual Reality.* New York: Simon and Schuster, 1992.

Weber, R. *On the Aesthetics of Architecture: A Psychological Approach to the Structure and the Order of Perceived Architectural Space.* Aldershot: Avebury, 1995.

Whitted, T. "An Improved Illumination Model for Shaded Display." *Communications of the ACM* 23, no. 6 (1980): 343–349.

The Impact of Computing on Communication in Design

Habitual methods of representation and communication can, and have been, implemented computationally, often yielding faster and more efficient results than their manual counterparts. But computing technology offers much more than improved productivity over existing methods of communication and representation; it has the potential to change communication itself, thereby restructuring the profession of architecture as it has been practiced for the past 500 years.

The possibility of changing communication and representation in architecture with the aid of computing technology is grounded in six properties of computers:

1. *Flexibility*—the ability to change levels of abstraction as needed without having to reconstruct the representation from scratch.
2. *Interlinking*—the ability to link information represented in different ways so that when one representation is modified, the others are too.
3. *Information management*—the ability to organize and access complex information resources.
4. *Visualization*—the ability to produce photo-realistic images of yet nonexistent artifacts and environments.
5. *Intelligence*—the ability to embed design rules, constraints, and goals within the representation itself, making it an active, rather than a passive, partner in the design process.
6. *Connectivity*—the ability to share information rapidly among all the participants in the design process.

These properties can best be illustrated by using the concepts of *internal* and *external* representation, as first proposed by Akin and Weinel.[1] Internal representation refers to the process of ideation—the activity architects use to create and transform a design solution through reflection and action.[2] It involves the creation, evaluation, and revision of mental models with the aid of overt conceptualization and memory aids like sketching and writing. External representation, on the other hand, refers to the process of communicating the evolving design to other participants in the design process for formal evaluation and for constructing the building.

Computing technology allows the "externalization" of internal representations. A model of the problem context and the design solution can be created in a digital form that serves to support the designer's "internal" ideation process in a manner that is similar to—but more powerful than—hand-drawn sketches, drawings, and models. The computer can help the designer analyze the problem and manage the connections between the results of that analysis and the emerging design solution. It can keep track of the progress of the design process and anticipate its future informational needs. It thus becomes a "design partner" that can provide active assistance in the exploration of the problem and the search for an appropriate design solution.[3] When the designer is ready to share the solution with other members of the design team—to "externalize" the solution—computer technology makes it possible to transform the internal representation into an external one—using any number and variety of media that can be transmitted to members of the design team—while maintaining the connection between these external representations and the designer's internal one. Thus, as transformations are made to the internal representation, all the corresponding external representations can be updated automatically. Moreover, the internal representation can be accessed through any one of the external ones, and through it changes made to one external representation can be communicated to all other external representations.

As a result, errors due to manual translations from one form of representation to another are eliminated or reduced, more information (and intelligence) can be brought to bear on the evolving solution, more professionals can be consulted earlier in the design process, and changes can be communicated almost instantaneously to all involved. By reducing errors, oversights, and omissions, as well as allowing for more informed design operations and more design cycles, computer-aided representation and communication can have a *qualitative* as well as a *quantitative* impact on the design process.

10.1 Flexibility

A geometric model—which, after all, is only a collection of abstract mathematical symbols—can be converted into any visual form that suits the needs of the designer. It can be visualized as a bubble diagram (fig. 10.1a), as a fully detailed drawing (fig. 10.1b), or even as a three-dimensional isometric view (fig. 10.1c). Selective visualization entails not much more than omitting the information that is not pertinent to the particular communication—which is what abstraction is all about—and channeling the remaining information through an appropriate rendering pipeline. Of course, the information needed to produce the desired visualization must be resident in the model; no information can be visualized that does not already reside in the representation or that cannot be computed from stored data. The responsibility for providing that information rests with the designer, who might be assisted by the computer, as discussed later in the book. But the responsibility for omitting information that is not relevant for a particular mode of communication can be assigned entirely to the computer, which can be programmed to omit, aggregate, and display only the information that is pertinent to the chosen level of abstraction, and to do so using the proper graphical conventions. To do this, though, the data must be stored in the form of identifiable objects (e.g., walls, windows, doors), not merely lines. Only then can the computer decide which objects to display and how to display them, according to the chosen level of abstraction.

This kind of flexibility works for both internal and for external representation purposes. It allows the designer to start designing at any chosen level of abstraction—bubble diagram, single-line drawings, even a 3D model—and switch at will to any other level of abstraction. It also allows other professionals, who may be accustomed to different visual conventions, to see the same information in the manner that is most suitable to their way of communicating. The ability to automatically adjust the level of abstraction as needed without constructing new representations from scratch reduces the possibility of introducing inadvertent errors when converting from one representation to another and accelerates the design process by eliminating time that is wasted on creating new representations of the same information.

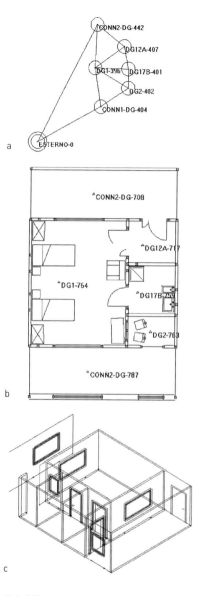

10.1 Different representations of the same information: (a) bubble diagram, (b) detailed floor plan, (c) isometric view. (G. Carrara et al., in *Automation in Construction* 3, nos. 2–3 [1994].)

door	type	construction	core	operation	elements	handling	number	fire rating
s-13710011	view	stile & panel	mineral	hinged	transom	right hand	single	120 min
s-33710012	full flush	plywood	hollow	hinged	none	left hand	single	not rated
s-13711011	glass	solid glass	solid	hinged	none	left hand	double	30 min
s-13530067	panel	braced	stave	hinged	narrow light	right hand	double	60 min

wall	Room 1	Room 2	material	door	window	length
W1	C1	EN	concrete	s-13530067	none	9 ft
W2	EN	PT	stud	s-13530067	none	8 ft
W3	PT	BT	stud	s-33710012	none	9 ft
W4	VS	C2	concrete	s-13710011	none	9 ft
W5	VS	PT	stud	none	r-734500	6 ft

Room	door	Fire rating	To room
C1	s-13530067	60 min	EN
EN	s-13530067	60 min	PT
PT	s-33710012	not rated	BT
VS	s-13710011	120 min	C2

10.2 Interlinking

A complex artifact such as a building requires many representations to be fully communicable. It is common in architectural practice to have hundreds of drawings that represent the building in different levels of abstraction, using different visualization conventions. These include floor plans, elevations, sections, isometric and perspective projections, detailed drawings, and specifications. Obviously all these different views represent the same building and therefore show the same objects, albeit from different points of view. The same window, for example, can appear in several floor plans, at different scales. It will also appear in elevations, sections, detail drawings, and specifications. If at any point throughout the design process the window's size is modified, or it is moved from its original position, or it is eliminated altogether, each and every one of the drawings showing that window must be updated. Failing to do so will introduce inconsistencies in the representation, which can lead to costly design errors and missed schedules. The problem is further exacerbated when professionals other than the architect rely on information that may be inaccurate, leading to building failures and litigations.

Computing technology allows for interlinking all the different representations, so when one is modified, the others are too. This ability is of considerable importance in design, whose nature is to modify the representation of the product until a satisfactory solution is found. It is especially important for architectural design, where the information pertaining to the product is represented in multiple redundancies, all of which must be updated when a change occurs.

10.3 Information Management

Computers are, essentially, information management tools. They have almost unlimited abilities to organize, reorganize, and access complex information resources and to link them in ways that are most useful to the task at hand. For example, the DOOR information that was discussed in section 8.4 was presented in two ways—one convenient for the manufacturer, the other for the contractor who must identify doors by the walls in which they fit. It is just as easy, however, to reorganize the same information according to the needs of the fire marshal, who might want to identify and examine the fire rating of doors according to the types of rooms they enclose (fig. 10.2).

10.3 Visualization of abstract mathematical formulae—fractals based on the Mandelbrot Set ($z_{n+1}: = z_n^2 + c$).

This reorganization can not only save much time in finding the pertinent information, but also can help avoid errors that occur when accessing information presented in a less optimized manner. Since the information can be reorganized at will, the manner in which it is stored does not really matter. The provider of the information can store it in the manner most appropriate for his or her own needs, which may be different from the needs of the information users; all that matters is that the information is organized in the first place.

Because the information *is* organized, it can be easily found when searched for. It is easy, for example to find all doors located in concrete walls, or all concrete walls that have doors. Finding this information in manual databases can be prohibitively expensive and replete with errors due to omissions of pertinent data or the erroneous inclusion of impertinent data.

10.4 Visualization

The ability to communicate information visually, a mode of perception that can be most readily processed by the human brain, has been recognized since the dawn of history, as evidenced by Stone Age cave drawings. Artists and architects have made this most basic mode of communication their primary means of representation, and the advent of computer graphics made it available to a myriad of other disciplines. Scientific visualization, as it has come to be known, is now used to study all manner of information, from weather phenomena to the shape of abstract mathematical formulae such as fractals and chaos theory (fig. 10.3).

10.4 Visualization of daylighting effects reveals unacceptable glare on computer monitor. (Courtesy of Charles Ehrlich, Lawrence Berkeley National Laboratory, 2000.)

For the profession of architecture, which is not a newcomer to visual communication, computers have contributed enhanced realism, easy editing, and dynamic walkthroughs. Realism has been achieved through advances in computer graphics, as discussed in chapter 9. It now permits architects, and their clients, to see the proposed building in a manner that is almost indistinguishable from a photograph of the realized building itself, thus enabling them to better comprehend the design before they commit much effort and capital to its realization. The development of user interfaces that make it possible to easily change lighting conditions (e.g., from day to night, summer to winter) and modify the appearance of materials (e.g., by changing them from stone to brick to concrete) has provided architects with unparalleled opportunities to visually examine alternative design possibilities in a span of time that would otherwise have permitted them to inspect only a few alternatives or had them rely on their imagination to see how they might look. As a result, architects can better match the material selections to the building's functional and aesthetic needs and discover potential problems that might otherwise go undetected (fig. 10.4).

Possibly the most important contribution of computing to the visual communication of design information—which has been practically unattainable by other means—has been the ability to put the viewer "inside"

Communication

the building, through virtual reality technologies. This mode of visualization changes the relationship between the observer and the observed, making the viewer smaller than the designed environment, thus evoking the haptic and kinesthetic sense of "being there." This sense is important for products that humans intend to inhabit, like buildings, cars, and airplanes, which cannot be fully comprehended by looking at a small picture or even a scale model of the intended artifact. But while the automotive and aerospace industries can afford to build full-scale mock-ups of their designs, amortizing their cost over hundreds or thousands of realized products, architecture—which is largely a one-of-a-kind industry—could ill afford to do so. Consequently, architects and their clients often anxiously await the unveiling moment, when their creations are first put to the test of inhabitation: will they look right? Will they "feel" right? VR technology can ameliorate this uncertainty by simulating the look and feel of an inhabitable environment. Adding dynamic walk-through capabilities further enhances the realism of the display, providing the observer with the ability to examine the environment from vantage points other than those chosen by its creator (as perspective renderings tend to do).

10.5 Intelligence

The ability to embed design rules, constraints, even goals within the object representation itself makes it an active, rather than a passive partner in the design process. Embedding rules and constraints in the representation, in the form of "methods" (in the parlance of object-oriented programming)[4] or "parameters" (in the parlance of parametric design),[5] transforms an otherwise "passive" representation into an "active" one: it can "respond" to changes by testing whether a change is permissible with respect to the object's well-formedness or by initiating additional actions made necessary by the first change. For example, in figure 10.5, the program warns the designer that the placement of the sanitary equipment in a corridor is inconsistent with design rules associated with that object.[6] Such "intelligent" objects can save the designer from making simple errors that may otherwise go undetected. Similarly, embedding parametric rules in objects can help speed up their design and modification, by maintaining certain inter- or intra-object relationships, such as abutment of walls, perpendicularity, position of a door in a wall that has been moved, and so on.

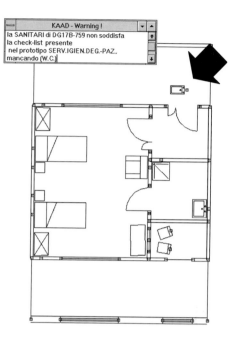

10.5 Intelligent objects. The program warns the designer that the placement of the sanitary equipment is inconsistent with design rules. (G. Carrara et al., in *Automation in Construction* 3, nos. 2–3 [1994].)

Embedded intelligence needs not be elaborate to be effective. Even simple rules can help transform an otherwise "dumb" drawing into an active partner in the design process, responding to changes in a manner that relieves the designer from simple repetitive operations and preventing errors. More complex embedded intelligence can take over certain design tasks—even propose design solutions or "look ahead" several design steps and warn the designer of yet unseen pitfalls (the discussion of such advanced intelligent design assistants is presented more fully in part 3).

10.6 Connectivity

The ability to share information rapidly among all the participants in the design process by sending drawings, models, and specifications electronically, rather than by courier or by mail, adds a qualitative advantage to computer-aided representation: it makes it possible to get rapid feedback from other participants on design propositions, test their feasibility, and get more people involved in the design process in a shorter amount of time than would be possible using traditional modes of communication.

The importance of such collaborative design practices has risen with the increased complexity of buildings, which makes the timely input of specialists indispensable for effective design. The growing globalization of the profession of architecture makes it likely that architects, civil engineers, construction managers, and their clients will be located in different parts of the world, in different time zones. Electronic transmission of design information helps to eliminate the need for the propinquity of all the specialists involved in the design process without sacrificing their ability to collaborate.

Electronic modes of collaboration have evolved from simple e-mail attachments to collaborative virtual design environments, where design information is broadcast, through the Internet, to a list of recipients, who are able to see the new information as soon as it has been "published." It ensures that all parties work off the most up-to-date version of the design, thereby saving time, unnecessary revisions, and reducing errors.

Taken together, these advantages of computer-aided communication combine to make a qualitative difference in architectural design. They allow architects and the other participants in the design process to concentrate on the creation and evaluation of design information rather than spend most of their time representing and re-representing it in many different ways and forms. Computer-aided representation reduces errors that are inevitable when manual translations of the information from one form of representation into another are needed, and it allows for better-informed decision making, whether due to the ability to better "see" the design or due to embedded intelligence in the representation itself.

Bibliography

Akin, Ö. "How Do Architects Design?" In *Artificial Intelligence and Pattern Recognition in Computer Aided Design,* ed. J. C. Latombe. New York: IFIP, North Holland, 1978.

Alexander, C., S. Ishikawa, M. Silverstein, M. Jacobson, I. Fiksdahl-King, and S. Angel. *A Pattern Language.* Oxford: Oxford University Press, 1977.

Anderson, J. R. *Language, Memory, and Thought.* Hillside, N.J.: Lawrence Erlbaum, 1976.

Archea, J. "Puzzle-Making: What Architects Do When No One Is Looking." In *Computability of Design*, ed. Y. E. Kalay, 37–52. New York: Wiley Interscience, 1987.

Carrara, G., Y. E. Kalay, and G. Novembri. "Knowledge-Based Computational Support for Architectural Design." *Automation in Construction* 3, nos. 2–3 (1994): 123–142.

McLuhan, M. *Understanding Media: The Extensions of Man.* McGraw-Hill, New York, 1964.

Mitchell, W. J. "The Uses of Inconsistency in Design." In *Evaluating and Predicting Design Performance*, ed. Y. E. Kalay, 1–13. New York: Wiley Interscience, 1992.

Peña, W. *Problem Seeking: An Architectural Programming Primer.* 4th ed. New York: John Wiley and Sons, 2001.

Rittel, H. W. J., and M. M. Webber. "Dilemmas in a General Theory of Planning." *Policy Sciences* 4 (1973).

Simon, H. *The Sciences of the Artificial.* Cambridge: MIT Press, 1969.

Synthesis

The search for solutions that meet manifested needs and desires while satisfying certain given conditions, can be likened to exploratory search—candidate solutions are examined one at a time to see if they meet the client's needs and desires while satisfying the project conditions. Sometimes candidate solutions are available for examination, as is the case when shopping for a used car or an existing house. If the solutions do not yet exist, as is the case when designing a new car or a new building, they must first be synthesized before they can be examined.

The process of synthesizing, or generating, candidate solutions for consideration is one of the two major activities in any design process (the other being the examination, or evaluation, of the solutions to see if they meet the needs and satisfy the conditions). It is a creative process, which involves processing the information deemed pertinent to the problem and transforming it into a candidate solution.

The synthesis of design solutions is characterized by uncertainty, unpredictability, the joy of discovery, and the frustration of fruitless explorations. It has fascinated, baffled, and challenged designers, researchers, and philosophers for at least 2,500 years. How does a designer know what information is pertinent to the solution, and what is not? How does she or he aggregate seemingly disparate components, attributes, and qualities into complete whole and reconcile their differences? How can the process be made more predictable and its results more consistent? Why are some people better at this task than others? How can their skills be transferred to other people (i.e., taught)?

Answers to these questions have delineated the progress of design inquiry since the time of Aristotle, who—while mainly concerned with "cosmic design" issues (how things come into being in the natural world)—helped frame the discourse on the making of the man-made world as well.[1] Practical answers in the domain of architectural design were first recorded by Vitruvius in the first century BC, who listed "good practice" procedures for successful architectural and urban design projects. However, for the most part, the ability to synthesize design solutions was seen as a "black box," a talent or "knack" some people had while others not, like a talent for composing music or storytelling. Those who exhibited such talent were encouraged to develop it through apprenticeship to others who had demonstrated the same talent, thereby honing their skills by learning techniques and practices relevant to their vocation. They assumed the status of artists or master craftsmen, and the products of their genius have been revered throughout history.

The advent of the Industrial Revolution in the eighteenth century precipitated a need for a more structured approach to synthesizing design solutions—the rapidly growing pace of developing new products was no longer amenable to waiting for ingenuity to strike at random. The "black box" had to be made transparent so the process of synthesizing design solutions could be studied, improved, made more predictable, teachable, and summoned "on demand."

Attempts to rationalize the creative process of design were made in the nineteenth century by architects and theoreticians like John Ruskin, Augustus Welby Northmore Pugin, Gottfried Semper, and Eugène-Emmanuel Viollet-le-Duc. In particular, Viollet-le-Duc's "organic" theory of architecture, as described in his *Dictionnaire raisonné de l'architecture française* and the *Entretiens*,[2] was pitted against the "composition" theory practiced by the Ecole des Beaux-Arts, resulting in distinctly different approaches to creative design. Viollet-le-Duc espoused a "rational" approach to generating design solutions, where the structure emerged from the application of "correct principles" and was conceived to fulfill a functional program—an approach formalized in the twentieth century by Louis Sullivan, who famously proclaimed that form followed function.[3] By contrast, the Ecole des Beaux-Arts espoused a creative process centered on the manipulation of a repertoire of classical forms from Roman antiquity and the Renaissance, structured through a highly symmetrical plan based on two axes laid at 90 degrees.[4]

The search for design methods that would help architects analyze problems, assemble pertinent information, and synthesize "good" solutions intensified with the publication in 1964 of Christopher Alexander's influential book *Notes on the Synthesis of Form*.[5] It provided a theoretical framework for rationally gathering and processing project-related infor-

Synthesis

mation and structuring it in a manner that would be readily accessible for the synthesis of design solutions.

Alexander's method was published at a time when computing technology became accessible and when the field of operations research—a branch of mathematics concerned with the study of optimal resource allocation—was showing remarkable promise in producing solutions to complex, multivariate problems in many fields.

Operations research (OR) methods have been used in Britain for military strategy purposes since before World War II. OR tools like linear programming, quadratic programming, and other optimization techniques were found to be applicable to architectural space allocation problems, allowing the determination of the optimal layout of rooms in a building, given the desired pairwise adjacencies among them. Several different algorithms that implemented such methods were developed, with mixed results: they were exceptionally well suited for the design of warehouselike buildings, including hospitals and schools, but they were not able handle the subtler differences of locating rooms in a house or even appliances in a kitchen.[6]

The advent of artificial intelligence (AI) in the 1970s and 1980s—a field of research concerned with solving problems whose solution appears to involve some intelligence when done by humans—provided architectural researchers with new methods and tools in their quest to rationalize the design synthesis process. AI's heuristic approach to solving problems seemed eminently appropriate to the way designers think, as opposed to the structured, top-down OR methods.

AI inspired the development of rule-based production systems, where knowledge gleaned from highly experienced design professionals was encoded into if-then constructs that described the action that ought to be taken when a certain condition is encountered. When applied to architectural design, such systems were able to tackle more complex layout synthesis problems than the OR-based space allocation algorithms, because they provided a way to handle object-specific knowledge. For example, it was possible to account for the clearances and orientations required by sanitary equipment in a bathroom, or the placement requirements of appliances in a kitchen.[7]

In their geometric form, rule-based production systems constitute a unique class of design synthesis tools called "shape grammars." These substitute both the condition and the action of if-then rules with geometrical constructs, which when applied recursively can form what appears to be architectural floor plans.[8]

The difficulties associated with developing generative design rules—whether algorithmic or heuristic—and the recognition that few designers, if any, use rule-based cognitive processes in the generative phases of the design process, prompted researchers to look for other approaches of synthesizing design solutions. One promising approach was found in the adaptation of previously developed design solutions to the needs and context of a new problem, an approach that came to be known as "case-based" design. According to this approach, most design solutions are not developed from scratch. Rather, they are adapted and evolved from earlier solutions to similar design problems. By starting from an existing solution and modifying it to fit the unique needs, conditions, and context of a new problem, the designer can capitalize on the efforts that went into developing the older solution, learn from its mistakes, and gain a holistic view of the solution instead of the piecemeal view that emerges gradually when developing a completely new solution. Case-based design requires a large database of "cases"—previously developed solutions—on which the designer can draw when confronting a new design situation. The success of case-based design depends on how well the older case matches the new situation, and whether its adaptation to the new problem's unique needs and context will not destroy the characteristics that made the case worth emulating in the first place.

None of these methods, however, has shown much ability to create truly novel solutions. Rule-based methods are trapped in their rule bases, and case-based methods, by definition, are restricted to adaptations of older solutions. That is, using design knowledge that has been codified procedurally or in the form of design cases cannot, in and of itself, emulate the creative leap that designers rely upon when generating novel solutions. A mechanistic (i.e., nonintelligent) approach, which appears to be able to create novel designs from old ones has, nonetheless, been demonstrated by nature itself, in the form of evolution. It has inspired the development of evolutionary, or genetic, algorithms, which have found use in financial and other fields. This approach relies upon the logic of natural selection and "survival of the fittest"—many solutions are generated randomly and subjected to "fitness" tests that weed out those that are clearly

Synthesis

not suitable candidates. The remaining solutions are allowed to mutate and combine, generating new solutions with characteristics "inherited" from their predecessors. These are again subjected to weeder fitness tests, and so on for hundreds, even thousands of "generations." The random introduction of mutations, while weeding out unfit solutions, can generate truly novel solutions, if the solution descriptors and the fitness tests are adequate.[9]

The search for computer programs that generate truly creative designs has been both controversial and difficult. It has been controversial for the very reasons that any "intelligent" computer program has been regarded with skepticism—can a mechanistic handiwork be as "intelligent" as its creator? Or even more so? If creativity is the epitome of intelligent behavior, then developing a computational system that will accomplish it must be very hard indeed. Yet if we succeed, what will it say about us? Will it mean that creative design is not intelligent behavior, after all?

Problem Exploration 11

Design is a problem-solving activity. The problem it sets out to solve arises from the inability of the current situation to satisfy some needs (e.g., shelter, production of goods, and so forth). The solution it produces is a detailed plan of action for achieving a new situation that is expected to satisfy those needs, while it complies with certain constraints (e.g., budget, building codes, environmental conditions, and so forth). The complexity of design problems is such that their solutions are not trivial, otherwise a simple action would suffice to correct the discrepancy.[1] Design problems are further complicated by the fact that they are unique and ill-structured.[2] That is, past experience does not suffice to solve the current problem, and it is unclear how the problem variables interact with one another (improving one may worsen another). Moreover, it is not possible to separate the act of *understanding* the problem from the act of *solving* it.[3] Still, gaining an understanding of the problem is a necessary first step for solving it.

Therefore, the process of design does not begin with the synthesis of design solutions. It starts with an exploration of the problem to be solved. The architect must uncover the issues that are pertinent to solving the problem and the positions that various parties who are involved in the project hold with regard to those issues. Issues and positions include the needs of the participants, their conceptions of how those needs may be satisfied, and their expectations of the solution. The information gathered from this exploratory process leads to the formulation of specific goals for the solution and a plan for accomplishing them.

In addition to establishing the specific goals, the problem exploration also helps the architect understand the context in which the project is embedded—the physical context as well as the social, economic, political, and cultural contexts. Each one of these contexts places certain limitations on the solution. The contexts also reveal opportunities that were not discovered in the goal-exploration stage—views to be incorporated in the solution, orientations that could reduce heating or ventilation costs, indigenous building materials that can be used, even building practices that might help make the solution more appropriate for its site. Typically, the information gathered from the context exploration results in a set of constraints that the solution will have to abide by and additions or modifications to the goals.

All the information gathered during the problem exploration phase must be structured in a manner that will make is useful for the design synthesis phase of the process. In addition, conflicts among competing needs must be uncovered and resolved, and the goals must be prioritized, resulting in a building program that forms the basis for the synthesis of design solutions and for the benchmarks by which candidate solutions will be judged.

11.1 Gathering Information

Architectural design problems are typically stated in a manner that belies their real complexity. "I want a three-bedroom house for under $300,000" is a typical initial problem statement. To begin solving a problem like this, the architect must uncover and gather much more information to develop a solution: What kind of house will it be? Who will occupy it? What are the habits of the prospective occupants? Do they like to cook? To entertain? Where will the house be located? What building codes and regulations govern construction in that area? Are there any views that should be preserved? Are there views that should be avoided? And so on, and so on . . .

Moreover, despite the fact that often only the individual architect is credited for the design of a complex building, in actual practice design depends on the contributions of and agreements between many actors, including the client, the public, and the builder, as well as the architect's consultants. When the client is a complex organization, such as a corporation or a city, many representatives of the organization may be involved in the decision-making process, and they may be replaced with other client representatives before the design process and construction are over. The public often participates directly in design projects when they involve controversial issues pertaining to the use of public funds, or when they might impact their neighborhood. Even when it does not participate directly in the design process, the public is involved indirectly through various regulatory agencies that review and approve the project.

Given the many participants in the design of any building, it is unlikely that there is ever a situation, particularly with complex buildings, when everyone agrees on all the issues associated with the project. The end result is that a building is a negotiated reality that reflect the values and political powers of the various participants in the process.[4]

This social nature of architectural design suggests that organizing the process of gathering all the information that is pertinent to the project would be a particularly effective tool to improve the analysis of the problem and the definition of the project goals. Many leading theorists and practitioners, including Alexander, Habraken, Peña, and Rittel, have proposed such information-gathering and organizing methods.[5] Underlying them is the notion that information and opinions ought to be solicited and gathered from the widest range of parties interested in the project and used as much as possible in formulating the project goals. Such wide consideration will not only ensure that vital concerns and needs are not ignored, but will also increase the satisfaction of the various stakeholders with the eventual product.[6]

Yet the implementation of participatory approaches to design information gathering has traditionally been limited by the extended time frame and increased resources that are required to implement them, both on the part of the design team and on the part of other participants. Moreover, the amount of information obtained from such solicitations is often too large and too difficult to manage to be of practical use (other than public relations purposes—a nontrivial consequence whose failure may doom otherwise worthy projects).

Computer technologies offer opportunities to overcome some of the limitations inherent in participatory design information gathering. They have been used as means of communication, through which information can be collected, and as means for organizing that information.

Computer-Aided Participatory Design

As an example, consider the expansion of the San Francisco Exploratorium, a hands-on science museum located in the Palace of Fine Arts. The original building that houses the museum was designed by famed architect Bernard R. Maybeck in 1915 as part of the Panama Pacific Exhibition. It was converted into a science museum in 1969 by Dr. Frank Oppenheimer, a noted physicist and educator, who was its director until his death in 1985.

Over its three decades of existence, the Exploratorium progressively filled up the entire space of the Palace of Fine Arts and was in need of solutions to accommodate further expansion. Being an educational institution, the curators of the Exploratorium saw the design process as an opportunity to involve the public in a debate over the expansion itself as well as over architectural concepts in general. The process of soliciting public input was initiated in 1997 and was titled *The Permanent Atelier— An Ongoing Design Process.*[7] Like many similar participatory design initiatives, it posed specific topics to frame the discussion. Without such framing, the amount of information and opinions received can easily overwhelm even a simple design problem. Five topics were chosen for discussion: the role and place of the entrance to the museum, wayfinding inside the museum, the location and role of the machine shop, and issues of light and sound. They were presented to the public in the form of a Web page (fig. 6.8) that included a short explanation of each topic as well as "teaser" questions. For example, the "wayfinding" topic comprised the following issues:

- *What is wayfinding?*
  Complex facilities, such as libraries, hospitals, governmental buildings, and museums often present challenges to casual users (i.e., visitors who are not familiar with the facility) who must find their way through them. Research shows that difficulty in finding one's way in a complex building is costly in terms of time, money, public safety, and stress that results from being lost.
- *How do people find their way in complex facilities?*
  People store and retrieve information about the layout of the built environment in a mental representation known as the *cognitive map.* While it is not well-understood how people build and use their cognitive maps, we do know that the process can be enhanced through spatial, environmental, and informational elements, such as:
  —location of key spaces (entrance, auditorium, machine shop, permanent exhibits, etc.)
  —lighting as a means of direction and orientation
  —sound as a means of direction and (dis)orientation.
  —signage

- *Why is wayfinding an issue in the redevelopment of the Exploratorium?*
  —the Exploratorium is based on the principle of discovery, which can benefit from less orderly wayfinding
  —should one's route through the space be left open to chance, or should it be predetermined, and to what degree?
  —what kind of wayfinding system is needed?

The public's responses to this topic-specific solicitation of positions, conceptions, and expectations was collected on the same Web site (fig. 11.1). Along with other information, it formed the basis for proposing design goals for the expansion of the museum.

Background and Context

To fully understand the design problem, the architect must be informed about the context of the building and the background leading to its commission. The context of an architectural design problem comprises two different, but often linked, dimensions: (1) the physical context, which includes the topography of the site, the urban fabric, the climate, and so on; and (2) the sociocultural context, which includes the demographics of the proposed building—who are the intended users?—the institutions or organizations within which they operate, the economic, legal and regulatory contexts of the project, the larger public agenda of the city, and so on.

Photographs, diagrams, notes, interviews, topographic maps, and other similar means, help the design team learn more about the physical and social contexts of the problem. For example, in his design of the Harris Concert Hall in Aspen, Colorado, architect Harry Teague considered the physical setting of the hall in the Aspen hills.[8] He made the roof from a number of staggered concrete plates, which correspond to the rugged topography (fig. 11.2). He also considered the cultural context of the hall, which is located next to the Aspen Music Festival Tent, designed in 1949 by Eero Saarinen (which has since been replaced by the Benedict Music Tent, also designed by Teague). Consequently, he centered the rooflines of the new hall on the Tent's center pole (fig. 11.3). He also considered the social setting of the hall—in a valley rumored to have been occupied by the Ute Indians who were forced by their enemies out of their ancestral home. Following their beliefs, the legend says, they buried a

HOUSEWIFE
from: Jennifer
email: XXXXXXXXXX
Wednesday, August 20, 1997 — 08:02:35 pm

I LIKED THE CHAOS, DON'T CHANGE IT

Chaos vs. Order
from: John
email: YYYYYYYYY
Wednesday, August 27, 1997 — 03:49:07 pm

Serendipity in exploring and discovering the Exploratorium maybe good, but not all aspects of the experience need to be chaotic. The function of the Entrance is rather formal (control, money, security, etc.), hence it need not be part of the overall exuberance of the place.

Entrance
from: Fred
email: ZZZZZZZZZZ
Sunday, November 23, 1997 — 02:13: 46 pm

I like how the space opens up when you enter. I wish the ticket booths were not straight ahead. Could the be off to one side, or even outside. Maybe there will eventually be a way to check people in electronically so there is no waiting in line.

11.1 The public's response to the wayfinding topic in the San Francisco Exploratorium's Virtual Atelier project.

11.2 Physical context. The roofline of the Harris Concert Hall in Aspen, Colorado, is designed to resemble the topography in which it is located. (Harry Teague, architect, 1993. Photograph courtesy of Timothy Hursley.)

musical instrument in the valley's floor so that one day they might return. The resulting building is mostly built below grade, to minimize its impact on the site, and perhaps to remind visitors of the legend.

11.2 Argumentation

The involvement of many different participants in a design process inevitably reveals different opinions, aspirations, conceptions, and beliefs. Any one solution will typically not satisfy all the participants, at least not to the same degree. How can these varying opinions be accounted for, compared, contrasted, argued, and adjudicated to form some consensus for the design?

One such solution, called Issue Based Information System (IBIS), was developed by Horst Rittel in the 1970s.[9] The basic concept behind IBIS was that design is an argumentative process: by gathering, representing, and arguing all the issues related to the project, the chances that something important might be overlooked can be reduced, and the chances are enhanced that connections between issues will be recognized. Recording the results in a manner that makes the argumentation process transparent affords public scrutiny. The designers can use it to formulate their solu-

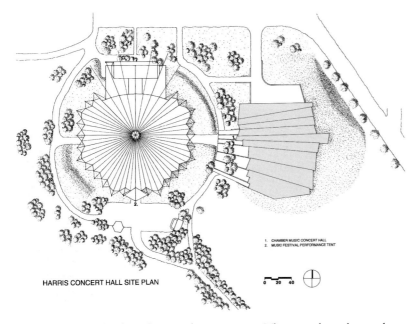

HARRIS CONCERT HALL SITE PLAN

1. CHAMBER MUSIC CONCERT HALL
2. MUSIC FESTIVAL PERFORMANCE TENT

0   20   40

11.3 Cultural context. The rooflines of the new building (right) of the Harris Concert Hall are oriented toward the center pole of the old tent structure. (Courtesy of Harry Teague Architects, Aspen, Colorado.)

tions or backtrack when they reach an impasse. The record can be used to identify the pattern of consensus and conflict as an aid in future design decision making.

IBIS builds a database of issues, positions, arguments, and the relationships between them through dialogues among the participants (fig. 11.4). The process of argumentation can take place any time before or during the design process. The main elements of the database, in simplified form, include:

1. *Issues*—controversial questions such as "Where should the entry be located?"
2. *Positions*—individual responses to an issue such as "Adjacent to the driveway."
3. *Arguments*—evidence to support or oppose a position such as "Yes," "No," or "How do you know?"
4. *Relationships*—linguistic relationships that structure the argumentation, such as "Issue A supports position X," or "Position Y responds to issue B."
5. *References*—referrals to original source material supporting arguments.

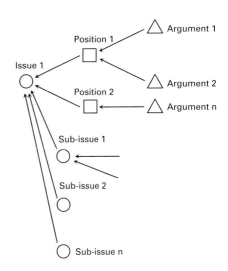

11.4 The structure of an IBIS issue base.

Although IBIS has been used effectively in a manual mode, computer implementation has resulted in some significant advantages: the databases created through the process are easily managed; searches and retrieval of information can be accomplished easily; relationships between the various pieces of information can be identified rapidly; through networking, it is no longer necessary to bring all the participants to the same location or even to the same time frame. Referencing is automated, so that participants' names and the dates of entry can be automatically attached to the records. The structuring of the database through relationships is resolved automatically.

IBIS-like programs have been developed by other researchers as well.[10] For example, the Proceedurally Hierachical Issue Based Information Systems (PHIBIAS), developed by McCall, links an issue base to a CAD system, enabling designers of large, complex artifacts both to design and to store and retrieve the rationale underlying design decisions.[11] PHIBIAS has been used to construct a large issue base of design rationale about zero-gravity habitation, providing an electronic format for NASA's Manned Space Information System documents.

Hitchcock further expanded the IBIS concept to cover the entire life cycle of buildings.[12] By recording the arguments for and against design options, and retaining them after the building has been commissioned, owners could consult information gathered during the design phase of the project for maintenance purposes and retrofits. Furthermore, other projects could tap into the argumentative process as a source of precedent information. They could review the reasons for the decisions that were made and those that were not accepted, see alternative approaches to similar problems, and perhaps apply them to their own projects.

Finally, Noble and Rittel suggested that a further enhancement of the argumentative process would be to include a modeling of a rhetorical process designed to elicit issues and arguments.[13] If automated, such a process could serve as a computerized "devil's advocate" that would challenge the designer to investigate problems thoroughly. It is important to note that IBIS did not provide direct help in making decisions: its primary purpose was only to stimulate discussion and reflection.

11.3 Structuring

Once the information that is pertinent to the project has been collected, it needs to be structured. Contrary to popular belief, at the outset of the process the designer is typically confronted with too much information, rather than too little information. The architect must contend with the wishes of many constituencies: clients, neighbors, regulatory authorities, and his or her own beliefs, to name a few. The designer must impose some order on the information and organize it into a coherent problem statement. This often includes breaking down the problem into manageable subproblems.

In the early 1960s Chermayeff and Alexander stated, "Every problem has a structural pattern of its own. Good design depends on the designer's ability to act according to this structure."[14] To discover this structure, they proposed a method that uses hierarchical structuring to enumerate and organize elementary problem statements—a method that was later further developed in Alexander's seminal book *Notes on the Synthesis of Form*. For example, in solving a typical design problem such as attaching the public and private domains of a house in a city, they list nine major issues:

1. Accommodation and land use.
2. Problems of protection.
3. Responsibility.
4. Climatic control.
5. Illumination.
6. Acoustics.
7. Circulation.
8. Communication.
9. Equipment and utilities.

They go on to list thirty-three more specific issues, including:

1. Efficient parking for owners and visitors; adequate maneuver space.
2. Temporary space for service and delivery vehicles.
3. Reception point to group. Sheltered delivery and waiting. Provision for information; mail, parcel, and delivery boxes; and storage of parcel carts.

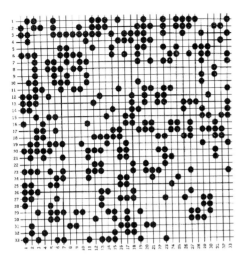

11.5 Identifying the links between the issues of a problem. (S. Chermayeff and C. Alexander, *Community and Privacy: Toward a New Architecture of Humanism* [New York: Doubleday Anchor Books, 1963].)

4. Provision of space for maintenance and control of public utilities. Telephone, electricity, main water, sewerage, district heating, gas, air conditioning, incinerators.

5. Rest and conversation space. Children's play and supervision.

6. Private entry to dwelling, protected arrival, sheltered standing space, filter against carried dirt.

. . .

13. Separation of moving pedestrians from moving vehicles.

14. Protection of drivers during their transition between fast-moving traffic and the pedestrian world.

15. Clear boundaries between the semi-private domain and the public domain.

16. Maintenance of adequate illumination, and absence of abrupt contrast.

. . .

24. Arrangements to protect the dwelling from local noise.

25. Arrangements to protect outdoor spaces from noise generated in nearby outdoor spaces.

. . .

32. Efficient organization of service intake and distribution.

33. Partial weather control between automobile and dwelling.

These statements are written at the same level of generality and deal unambiguously with only one issue each. Together they cover all the issues the designers considered pertinent to the problem.

Once listed, the links between the issues, which give the problem its structure, were identified (fig. 11.5): a black dot indicates that two issues are related, the absence of a dot indicates that they are not related. This structure shows that accommodating one of the linked issues affects the other issues that are linked to it. The links were identified through common sense and through the experience of the designers. Yet the links are not important in and of themselves: it is the *patterns* they make which are important (an issue Alexander developed more fully a decade later in his book *A Pattern Language*).[15]

The large number of such links makes it impossible to consider them all at once. Instead, they can only be considered in groups of related issues, which define subproblems of the original, overall problem. Grouping the links is both difficult and critical to the structuring of the problem. It needs to be done in such a way that the elements within a group are strongly related to one another, but elements in different groups are largely independent of one another (fig. 11.6).

To facilitate the grouping of issues, in the early 1960s Alexander and Manheim developed a computer program called Hierarchical Decomposition of a Set with an Associated Graph (HIDECS), which ran on MIT's IBM 704 computer.[16] HIDECS grouped the issues into "clusters" by considering the number of links between them. The clustering process was based on graph-theoretic methods for partitioning the graph formed by the connected issues into maximally connected subgraphs. It was done by counting the number of connections between each issue and all other issues. A cluster is formed from issues that share many connections. For example, issues 8, 9, and 31 in figure 11.5 form a cluster because each connects to every other issue in the cluster (100% connectedness). More formally, the program determines the connection ratios (CR) for each issue (the ratio between the actual number of connection to the number of possible connections) and forms clusters from issues whose CR exceeds some threshold. The process is iterative—clusters are formed between issues with low CR, then the threshold is increased and subclusters are formed, until it reaches 100%, at which point no more subclusters can be formed. The result can resemble a tree if clusters are not allowed to overlap, or the grouping depicted in figure 11.6 if they are.

The major disadvantages of this and similar methods of structuring problems (e.g., factor analysis) are the considerable amount of effort it takes to collect all the issues and connect them in an interaction matrix. More seriously, the method is not responsive to the dynamic nature of an evolving design process, where issues that were not evident at the beginning are discovered as the search for the solution unfolds, and new connections between existing issues are identified as the work progresses.

Alexander himself rejected this method by 1966, but it continues to be popular for solving large and complex problems. Many similar programs were developed to support clustering (e.g., CLUSTER)[17] and are now used to solve, in addition to architectural design problems, problems in industrial design and in software engineering.[18]

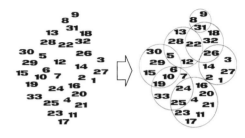

11.6 Structuring the issues into groups. (S. Chermayeff and C. Alexander, *Community and Privacy: Toward a New Architecture of Humanism* [New York: Doubleday Anchor Books, 1963].)

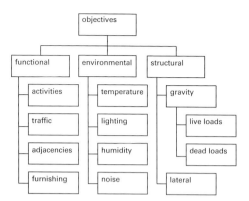

11.7 Hierarchical structuring of goals and constraints.

11.4 Goals and Constraints

The end result of the information gathering and structuring process is a set of goals, or constraints, which represent the negotiated and distilled consensus opinion of the stakeholders about what the solution to the design problem ought to be like. Not only do these goals and constraints help to *identify* a solution once it has been produced, but they also help to *steer* the process of searching for a solution, by providing checkpoints where progress toward a solution can be corrected.

Each goal or constraint is a concise statement of a quality or a characteristic that the solution to a design problem ought to have. The difference between goals and constraints is largely a matter of semantics, representing the ability of stating the requirement more or less precisely. In contrast to design issues that were discussed earlier (e.g., "sufficient parking for residents and visitors"), which are general statements of the desired condition, a goal or a constraint is characterized by preciseness (e.g., "for each dwelling there must be 1.5 parking spaces").

Related goals can be collected into larger classes of goals, each related to a specific aspect of the project. For example, the nature, morphology, and sizes of spaces, their material composition, the equipment and furniture they contain, even the procedures for managing them, can be represented as a class of functional goals. Desired temperatures, humidity, lighting, and other comfort parameters can be represented as a class of environmental goals. Gravity and wind resistance systems can be represented as structural goals, and performance under exceptional conditions such as fire and earthquakes can be represented as safety goals. Such classes of goals can be further divided into subclasses, creating a hierarchical structure of increasingly more specific and detailed requirements (fig. 11.7). Hence, the more general statements at the upper levels of the hierarchy can be considered goals, whereas the more precise ones at its bottom can be considered constraints.

The classification is, of course, highly arbitrary, and can be tailored to the needs and preferences of each project. It represents, nonetheless, the ability to define design objectives explicitly, in terms of testable sets and subsets of goals and constraints. Some of these objectives are derived from the clients' preferences (e.g., budget). Others may be derived from the context (e.g., views, temperature, size limitations). And still other objectives may reflect the architect's own aspirations, style, and ethics.

For example, the dimensions of a hospital nursing suite intended to accommodate two patients, the equipment they need, the temperature, humidity, number of air exchanges, and other spatial and environmental conditions, comprise such a goal hierarchy. The goal set can also include the desired adjacencies of the nursing suite to other parts of the hospital. For instance, when the nursing suite is intended to accommodate patients suffering from an infectious disease, it must abide by certain well-defined access-control constraints intended to protect the patients as well as the staff from the spread of the infectious agents. These goals and constraints can be represented in a concise computer-readable form, such as:[19]

```
DG3
    (description                          of space DG3, which is a nursing suite
        (con                              connections with other spaces
            (adj (value dg6 dg7 ))        must be adjacent to the specified spaces
            (far (value dg2 dg11 dg15 conn2)))  must be far from the specified spaces
        (space
            (min 22)                      boundary values for surface areas(mq)
            (max 28))
    (environment
        (temp (range 19 21)               range of acceptable interior temperatures (°C)
        (rewh (range 40 60)               range of acceptable relative humidity (%)
        (vent (value 2)                   desired number of air changes
        (pura (value 4)))                 desired level or air purity (%))
```

The particular combination of constraints that is considered a goal is established when the goals are first introduced. This forces the designer (and the client) to consider and establish reasonable combinations of objectives, which then guide the design process. Additional goals may be added, or existing goals may be modified or deleted during the design process, thereby providing a measure of flexibility to accommodate changing preferences as the design evolves. (These new goals must, of course, be tested for compatibility with existing goals, as discussed in the next section.)

The specificity of design goals must not be confused with the specificity of the design solutions that satisfy them: different design solutions may achieve the same goal, though each may satisfy the constraints that comprise the goal differently. The different performance levels at which alternative sets of constraints may be satisfied represent tradeoffs in the context of achieving a particular goal.

11.5 Feasibility Analysis

While alternative goals represent desirable combinations of performance levels, some combinations may be preferable to others, and some combinations may not be feasible at all. Weeding out unfeasible goal combinations and prioritizing the remaining goals indicates to the designer which combination of performances she or he should attempt to accomplish first.

Feasibility analysis has traditionally relied on the experience of the architect and her or his consultants (the structural engineers, mechanical engineers, and others). Increasingly, it involves accountants, who weigh in on decisions that have cost implications (virtually all design decisions have cost implications) in a process known euphemistically as "value engineering."

The process of feasibility analysis has benefited considerably from developments in operations research (OR), a branch of mathematics concerned with identifying the optimal allocation of resources. Some techniques that have been borrowed from OR to help weed out incompatible goal sets and prioritize the remaining ones include morphological or incompatibility analysis, optimization, and simulation.

Morphological Analysis

Morphological analysis is a method intended to identify incompatible combinations of goals (or their potential solutions). For example, a budgetary goal (or constraint) can preclude the accomplishment of certain other goals that concern the size of the building, its construction method, or the materials it will be made of.[20]

Morphological analysis entails examining the pair-wise compatibilities of all the goals and constraints, often listed in so-called incompatibility matrices. If a component of one goal is found to be incompatible with a component of another goal, then the two goals are considered incompatible and must be adjusted (or one of them must be eliminated). For example, one of the functionality goals may state that, in order to take advantage of the fabulous view of the San Francisco Bay, a house in the Berkeley hills ought to have large windows facing west. At the same time, one of the environmental goals may state that in order to reduce energy costs the western exposure ought to be minimized. Clearly, the goals are incompatible and need to be reconciled before any design solutions can be contemplated. The resolution of one incompatibility may introduce other incompatibilities among the goals, such as when the resolution to the western-exposure problem calls for using double pane windows that cost more than regular ones and may therefore violate budgetary constraints.

Optimization

Despite its name, optimization rarely finds an "optimal" set of goals. Rather, it is more often used as a means to prioritize goals and constraints. It requires setting some condition, or benchmark, against which goals can be measured. For example, functionality is often such a benchmark, and goals can be prioritized in terms of meeting functionally more important issues. Alternatively, construction costs can be used as a benchmark, and goals are prioritized according to their ability to meet the design objectives at lower costs.

Optimization is an area that has been studied extensively by operation researchers, and consequently, a large number of methods have been developed to support it. They include mathematical modeling such as linear and dynamic programming, integer and zero-one programming, and other methods.[21]

While optimization methods are very useful, they can rarely be applied to architectural design problems that comprise goals and constraints of many different kinds and whose relationships are often intuitive and mathematically intractable. Optimization methods have been used in cases where the goals share a common basis, such as cost. For example, linear programming can be used to determine land use, such as the ratio of expensive to moderate or inexpensive housing in a given development project.

Simulation

The difficulty in comparing goals of different kinds requires the use of methods that can examine the result of the interaction of *all* the goals and constraints in their totality. One such method is simulation, which assumes that certain goals and constraints have been accomplished and looks at the overall result of their interaction.

For example, it is possible to observe the consequences of setting goals for cost, the means of accomplishing some tasks, and the desired performance level of some system. As a case in point, consider the problem of designing a cafeteria to serve a given population within a given time frame—such as serving the occupants of an office building or a factory who go to lunch from 12:00 to 1:30 every day. The goals would be to minimize the number of tables (hence the space needed for the cafeteria and its cost), while serving all the patrons within the given 1.5 hours of their lunch break. How many tables are needed? The answer depends, of course, on many assumptions, such as how many people can (and are willing to) sit at a table, how long it takes for them to eat, and how long it takes to clear the table. However, even when assumptions concerning all these parameters have been made, it is still not possible to determine if the overall solution will be satisfactory. Moreover, it is not clear which of these parameters is more important than the others. For example, is the number of tables more important than their clearing time? If so, how much more?

A discrete event simulation can answer these questions and let the designers know which goals are more important to satisfy than others (or whether the problem cannot be solved satisfactorily at all). It would establish certain ranges of values for each parameter (number of tables, number of patrons seated at each table, the frequency of their arrival, the length of time they eat and clear the tables, and so on). Then for every minute within the allotted time frame for the lunch break, the simulation engine will randomly select a value for each parameter from within the established range. For example, it may decide that a group of three patrons arrives in the first minute and is seated at a table. This table will be out of circulation (i.e., not available for new patrons) for a certain (randomly selected) amount of time, which depends on how long it takes the seated patrons to eat and to clear the table. In the next minute, a group of five patrons may arrive, to be seated at two tables, and so on, until there are no more available tables, in which case the arriving patrons must wait. When a group of seated patrons finishes eating and clears the table, it returns to the pool of available tables. If all patrons have been seated within the allotted time frame, then the performance of the cafeteria is deemed satisfactory, although perhaps too costly (there may have been too many tables). If, on the other hand, not all patrons have eaten, or their waiting time was too long, the number of tables may have been too small—or the amount of time allowed for eating and clearing each table has been too long. By varying the assumptions and running the simulation again and again, it is possible to determine the optimal number of tables and the optimal amount of time they should be occupied.[22] This information will then become the planning guide for the designers of the actual cafeteria.

Simulations can be digital, physical, even hypothetical, and include any number of parameters. Their success depends primarily on how closely the assumptions mirror the reality they are intended to simulate.

11.6 Planning

The prioritization of goals is not only a common practice when architects and clients are faced with limited resources, but it also has a very profound effect on the direction of the design process and on its results. This is due to the fact that all the decisions leading to the specification of a design solution are dependent upon one another, and decisions that were made earlier in the process may limit the options available to the designer in later design phases, sometimes to the point that no options are available at all. For example, choosing a particular construction method early in the design process (e.g., wood frame) imposes many constraints on the building, limiting the options available to the architect in designing its form, details, and construction schedule.

The sequence of accomplishing the goals is sometimes straight forward (it is necessary to complete the programming goal before the schematic design goal can be started and to complete the schematic design goal before design development can be started). However, that is not always the case. For example, the floor plan of the house can be designed before its style has been decided, or afterward. The decision about which set of goals to tackle first will have profound implications for the rest of the process, and must, therefore, be considered a design decision in and of itself.

The decisions that pertain to the sequence of design operations are often referred to as planning; they inform the designer which part of the problem to deal with first. Like the design operations themselves, different plans can achieve the overall goal of designing a single-family house (or any other project) in different yet functionally equivalent manners. Listing possible plans and choosing from among them is a process similar to designing the building itself. Each plan can be assessed on such merits as availability of the information needed to carry it out, timeliness and sequencing of its components, and its likelihood to accomplish the overall objectives of the project. For example, so-called fast-track projects, where it is desirable to start construction before the design has been completed, impose a different sequence of design decisions on the architect than more traditional design-bid-build projects, where all design decisions are completed before construction commences.

The end result of the information gathering, structuring, goal-setting, feasibility analysis, and planning phases of the design process is a set of specifications for the project, called the building program. For complex buildings (which is where a building program is most needed), it takes the form of one or more thick volumes of text and diagrams, which spell out (in as much detail as desired) all the agreed-upon goals, constraints, action-sequences, and preferences of the participants in the project. While the building program does not specify what the solution will look like, it influences it as much as any other design decisions do.

Bibliography

Alexander, C., S. Ishikawa, M. Silverstein, M. Jacobson, I. Fiksdahl-King, and S. Angel. *A Pattern Language.* Oxford: Oxford University Press, 1977.

Cross, N. *The Automated Architect.* London: Pion, 1977.

Forester, J. *The Deliberative Practitioner: Encouraging Participatory Planning Process.* Cambridge: MIT Press, 1999.

Koberg, D., and J. Bangall. *The Universal Traveler: A Soft-Systems Guide to Creativity, Problem-Solving, and the Process of Reaching Goals.* Los Altos, Calif.: William Kaufmann, 1974.

Mitchell, W. J. "Part 4: Problem Solving." In Mitchell, *Computer-Aided Architectural Design.* New York: Petrocelli/Charter, 1977.

Rittel, H. W. "APIS: A Concept for an Argumentative Planning Information System." Technical Report No. 324, Institute of Urban and Regional Development, University of California, Berkeley, 1980.

Habitual Methods 12

The ultimate objective of architectural design is the creation of *form*.[1] Form is the physical arrangement of objects and spaces in such a way that they fit the function and the context of the design project. But, contrary to Louis Sullivan's famous proclamation that "form follows function,"[2] there is no direct causal relationship between the two: having derived a structured list of goals and constraints from an exhaustive exploration of the problem does not, in and of itself, lead to a form that will "solve" the problem. In fact, the struggle that typifies the synthesis of design solutions is largely due to the absence of such causal relationships. Rather, once the design problem has been explored and understood, the designer must undertake a purposeful mental activity, informed by experience and familiarity with precedents and relying on intuition, inspiration, imagination, rational speculation, and subconscious free associations, which will lead to a design *concept*—an image of the solution that might (or might not) prove to be an appropriate combination of form, function, and context. Appropriateness, according to Alexander, means that the form fits the context and supports the functions of the project (fig. 12.1). The search for the proper combination of form, function, and context is hard, and its results are uncertain, since often the only variable under the architect's control is the form itself.

The methods and processes used to design forms that fit particular contexts and support their intended functions have puzzled architectural theorists and philosophers for over two millennia. Many attempts have been made to try and understand the process of design by observing designers "in action" and by recording the external manifestations of the process (the designers' verbal and graphical utterances).[3] And although many different theories have been advanced over the years to explain the process, no one really knows how architects, or for that matter any other designers, synthesize the information gathered in the problem exploration phase into a coherent, holistic, and—most importantly—appropriate

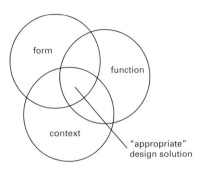

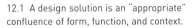

12.1 A design solution is an "appropriate" confluence of form, function, and context.

form. It is not the purpose of this book to explain how designers think in action—that is the realm of design theory and cognitive psychology. Rather, it is the *methods* that designers have relied upon to facilitate their creative abilities and the computational systems that purport to aid them that are the focus of this book. This chapter examines some of the methods that have been used by designers before the introduction of computers, and which—like other habitual methods—have inspired the computational methods that have been advanced over the past fifty years to support the synthesis of design solutions.

Design methods are intended to provide designers with rational means that may help them initiate the design synthesis process and bring it to a successful conclusion. Generally they are not intended to produce "creative" solutions—the kind achieved by some gifted individuals whose creations exceed everyday, routine products of thinking and doing.[4] Rather, they are aimed at helping them accomplish routine design activities, the kind professionals produce day in and day out.[5]

Yet even this humble goal has confounded researchers and designers who, consequently, have come up with many different methods over the years. These include recipelike instructions, attempts to draw inspiration from divine and other sources, "rational" methods, "formalistic" methods, and trial-and-error methods. None has provided a definitive answer—hence their proliferation—to the problem of helping architects synthesize form. Yet even *attempting* to develop design methods has not been universally welcomed by designers themselves. "Method" implies rationalization of the design process, in opposition to "intuitiveness." It implies a "loss of innocence"—a design based on logical premises is easier to criticize than one based on vague artistic ones. Rationalization involves assumption of responsibility, because options must be explicitly evaluated, and decisions must be justified. In contrast, intuition bears no responsibility and requires no explanation.[6]

12.1 Best Practices

One approach to synthesizing form is to rely on design practices that have worked well in the past: if the current problem is similar to a problem that has been encountered in the past, for which a satisfactory solution was found, why not use the same approach again, with suitable adaptations to the current problem and its circumstances? When properly encapsulated, such past approaches to synthesizing form can help not only solve a new problem but also reveal issues and considerations that may have escaped the designer.

The Roman architect and engineer Marcus Vitruvius Pollio, in the first century BC, was one of the first to recognize the value of considering successful solutions to previous design problems and to encapsulate it in the form of "best practices." In his treatise *De architectura* (c. 28 BC) Vitruvius discussed selected practices of Roman architecture, engineering, and city planning. For example, in chapter 1 of book V, Vitruvius discusses how to design a forum based on Greek practices adapted to Roman lifestyle:

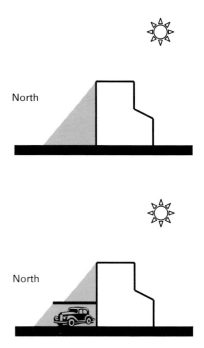

12.2 Alexander's pattern no. 162 for treating the north face of buildings. (Alexander et al., *A Pattern Language* [Oxford: Oxford University Press, 1977].)

The Greeks make their forum square, with a spacious and double portico, ornamenting it with columns placed at narrow intervals, and stone or marble epistylia, and forming walks above on the timber framed work. In the cities of Italy, however, this practice is not followed, because the ancient custom prevails of exhibiting the shows of gladiators in the forum.

Hence, for the convenience of the spectators, the intercolumniations must be wider; and the bankers' shops are situated in the surrounding porticos with apartments on the floors over them, which are constructed for the use of the parties, and as a depot of the public revenue. The size of the forum is to be proportioned to the population of the place, so that it be not too small to contain the numbers it should hold, nor have the appearance of being too large, from a want of numbers to occupy it. The width is obtained by assigning to it two-thirds of its length, which gives it an oblong form, and makes it convenient for the purpose of the shows.[7]

A similar approach was taken by Alexander and his coauthors in their book *A Pattern Language*. Consider, for example, their recommendations for treating the north face of buildings (pattern no. 162, fig. 12.2):

Look at the north side of buildings which you know. Almost everywhere you will find that these are the spots which are dead and dank, gloomy and useless. Yet there are hundreds of acres in a town on the north sides of buildings; and it is inevitable that there must always be land in this position, wherever there are buildings.

These dead and gloomy north sides not only waste enormous areas of land; they also help to kill the larger environment, by cutting it up with shadow areas no one wants to cross, and which therefore break up the various areas of the environment from one another. It is essential to find a way of making these north-facing areas alive, at least in their own terms, so that they help the land around them instead of breaking it apart.

The shadow cast by the north face is essentially triangular. To keep this triangle of shade from becoming a forlorn place, it is necessary to fill it up with things and places which do not need the sun. For example, the area to the north may form a gentle cascade which contains the car shelter, perhaps a bath suite, storage, garbage cans, a studio. If this cascade is properly made, then for most of the year the outdoors beyond it to the north will have enough sun for a garden, a greenhouse, a private garden seat, a workshop, paths.

Make the north face of the building a cascade which slopes down to the ground, so that the sun which normally casts a long shadow to the north strikes the ground immediately beside the building.

Vitruvius and Alexander do not provide encapsulated "solutions" for how to shape and scale, respectively, the forum and the north face of buildings—only instructions and explanations for approaching the problem. Thus their recommendations are "best practices" rather than recipes. The designer who chooses to follow Vitruvius's or Alexander's recommendations will understand their purpose and rationale, and therefore will be able to better adapt them to his or her specific needs than if they were simply given instructions to be followed blindly.

12.2 Recipes

The rediscovery of Vitruvius's text during the Renaissance and the general fascination with all things Roman (including cultural and political ideas) greatly fueled the revival of classicism during that and subsequent periods. Numerous architectural treatises were written to satisfy the hunger for the knowledge of the ancients, beginning with Leon Battista

Alberti's *De re aedificatoria* (presented 1450, printed 1485) and continuing with Giacomo Barozzi da Vignola's *Regola delli cinque ordini d'architettura* (1562), Andrea Palladio's *I quattro libri dell'architettura* (1570), and Serlio's *De architectura libri quinque* (1568–1569). Their approach to encapsulating design practices took a more explicit and recipelike form than the source that inspired them. Indeed, they did not hesitate to provide exact dimensions for various building parts, like columns, vaults, and domes. For example, in his *Four Books on Architecture,* Palladio provides explicit instructions how to construct a "proper" Ionic column (fig. 12.3):

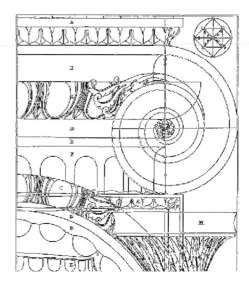

12.3 Andrea Palladio's "recipe" for an Ionic capital.

> To form the capital, the foot of the column must be divided into eighteen parts, and nineteen of these [same] parts is the height and width of the abaco, half thereof is the height of the capital with the volutae, which is, therefore, nine parts and a half; one part and a half must be given to the abaco with cimacio, the other eight remain for the volutae, which is thus made.[8]

The "imitation" inspired by such recipes may not have produced novel creations, but it helped architects avoid new "mistakes."[9] Besides, copying from the "masters" provided good excuses in case something went wrong.

12.3 Heavenly Forms

The search for "appropriate" forms has never been limited to shapes and practices used by architects in the past—if it were, no innovation could be possible. Rather, architects have always looked for new ideas, inspired by a wide range of natural, cultural, even divine sources.

The Renaissance focus on humanism and the harmony between man and God, along with the promotion of a style independent of the underlying building technology resulted in the wholesale rejection of "unharmonious" medieval and technology-driven Gothic forms and fueled the search for new forms that were better suited to revealing the deep and fundamental truth about man's place in the world. This "divine" relationship was found by shifting from the traditional basilica, modeled on the Latin cross, to the centrally planned church, modeled on the pagan temples of the Romans. Even though the new form was unsatisfactory from a liturgical point of view (it did not support the separation of the clergy from

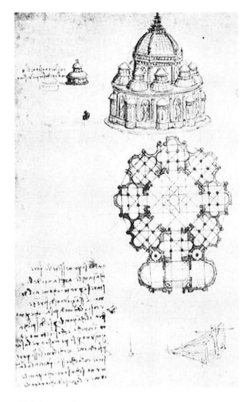

12.4 Leonardo da Vinci's theoretical designs for centralized churches.

the laity and provided no convenient place for the altar), the circular geometric relationships between the components of a building were believed to embody nature's own "ideal" form, revealed through the shapes of the Earth, the stars, trees, animals and their nests, and many other things.[10]

This belief, which was first expressed by Vitruvius in the first century BC and demonstrated by Hadrian's Pantheon in Rome (117–125 AD), was perfectly illustrated in Leonardo da Vinci's famous man with outstretched hands and feet—perfectly proportioned in the image of God—located at the center of the natural universe (represented by the circle) as well as the artificial one (represented by the square), all in complete harmony (fig. 4.1). It so captivated Renaissance architects' imagination that it became central to their synthesis of form from the 1450s to the end of the sixteenth century (fig. 12.4).

Moreover, the church, according to Alberti, had to be the most beautiful building in the city, and its beauty had to surpass imagination. What made it so beautiful? The rational integration of all its parts in such a way that every part had its absolutely "right" size and shape, and nothing could be added or taken away without destroying the harmony of the whole. For example, the height of a wall in round churches, up to the vaulting, should be one-half, two-thirds, or three-quarters of the diameter of the plan—conforming to the Pythagorean harmonious proportions of 1:2, 2:3, and 3:4.[11]

Alberti's divinely inspired recommendations were combined with the practical needs (and traditions) of the church in Francesco di Giorgio's treatise on architecture, *Trattato di architettura civile e militare* (c. 1482), in which he recommends that the circular form—which he considered most perfect—be combined with the (practical) rectangular form of the basilica, composed in such a way that each follows the rules of the type to which it belongs. He demonstrated this composition, and its divinity, by inscribing a human figure on the (now) classical form of a longitudinal church with a central dome above the transept, where all the cardinal lines converge on the human's heart (fig. 12.5).

12.4 First Principles

The Enlightenment of the eighteenth century, which saw the birth of modern science, government, and philosophy, rejected all things authoritarian, including dogmatic religion and its heavenly inspired architectural forms. Thinkers like Voltaire, Newton, Descartes, Pascal, and Rousseau valued reason as the principle by which the world functioned and therefore the proper pursuit for man. Architects and critics embarked on a search for "first principles" of Architecture, inspired by structure, archeology, and philosophy. Of considerable influence was a short treatise titled *Essai sur l'architecture,* written by the Jesuit priest turned author and diplomat Marc-Antoine Laugier, published in Paris in 1753.[12] In contrast with earlier treatises which, according to Laugier, described the measures and proportions of architecture rather than its fundamental principles, the true spirit and the rules that guide architecture could be derived from the construction of the "primitive hut"—a simple structure made of fallen tree branches set upright and arranged in a square, topped with smaller branches and leaves so closely packed that neither sun nor rain can penetrate. The simplicity of this "first model" avoids mistakes and breeds perfection. From this first model architecture can derive such constructs as columns, entablatures, and pediments. It helps to distinguish between parts that are essential to the composition of architectural orders and those that have been added "by caprice." The parts that were introduced by necessity are the cause of beauty, whereas the parts introduced by caprice are the cause of every fault, as the *Essai* goes on to explain in considerable detail. Doors and windows, for example, are parts introduced by necessity, because the "primitive hut" needs walls to protect the inhabitants from inclement weather. Although their shape is determined by necessity, it would be well also to make them elegant. But what is "elegant"? According to Laugier, "elegant" is simple and functional. Hence, curving the top of doors and windows in order to "give them grace" leaves irregular shapes on either side of the wall, which look bad and therefore have been "filled with bizarre ornaments which have been placed there for no other reason than to cover up the fault."[13] Adoption of these first principles would help architects explain their work, justify their choices, and guide their work in a rationale, noncapricious way.

12.5 Francesco di Giorgio's illustration of combining the longitudinal church with the centrally planned one in a harmonious way.

12.5 Formalistic Eclecticism vs. Functional Rationalism

At the beginning of the nineteenth century—a period of political and cultural turmoil in Europe following the French Revolution of 1789–1793, the rise of Napoleon, and the restoration of the Bourbons—architecture

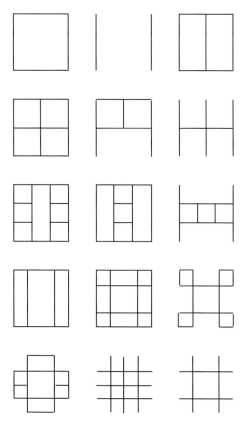

12.6 Some typical *partis* used by the Ecole des Beaux-Arts. (After J. N. L. Durand, *Précis des leçons d'architecture*, 1813.)

was characterized by a search for new styles that would better reflect the changing times and the quest for "empire" architecture. A battle was pitched between two camps, each espousing a different approach to the synthesis of form and the use of construction materials and, consequently, to building styles. One camp was represented by the French Ecole des Beaux-Arts, espousing romantic-classicism and eclecticism and influenced by the "lessons" of Jean-Nicolas-Louis Durand.[14] The other camp was comprised of "rationalists" like Eugène-Emmanuel Viollet-le-Duc in France, John Ruskin and Augustus Welby Northmore Pugin in England, and Gottfried Semper in Germany, who favored a more "organic" approach to architecture.

The Ecole des Beaux-Arts, which was established in 1816 by the Académie des Beaux-Arts for the formal training of young architects (as opposed to the apprenticeship method practiced elsewhere), approached design synthesis as a mapping of the functional requirements of buildings onto abstract, symmetrical geometric patterns, called *partis* (fig. 12.6), which were consequently "dressed up" in an eclectic repertoire of classical forms.

Initially this approach was considered as "revolutionary" as the new Republic itself. But later, with the changing political climate and under the influence of Durand, Beaux Arts-educated architects in France, Germany, and elsewhere began to rely on both precedents and ornamentation, developing a thoroughly formalistic style that included not only the design of the buildings themselves but their presentations as well. Their design process, consisting of composition, distribution, and disposition, reflected this philosophy.

The rationalists, on the other hand, advocated design synthesis based on "organic" form, which would represent the true functional needs of the building. Their model was Gothic architecture, with its clearly expressed force-transferring ribbed vaults and flying buttresses that were conceived to fulfill a functional program, which Viollet-le-Duc (who was in charge of historical restoration of Gothic churches in France, most notably Notre-Dame de Paris), regarded as the ideal rational structure. Inspired by this pragmatic architecture, he developed new principles and innovative ideas that were published in his two major treatises—the *Entretiens* and the *Dictionnaire raisonné de l'architecture française*.[15]

Synthesis

Given their different approached to design synthesis, these two camps ended up with very different design styles. The Ecole des Beaux-Arts usually favored a symmetrical plan, based on two major axes laid at 90 degrees, intersecting at a major central space. Viollet-le-Duc's designs, as those of the other "rationalists," tended to be asymmetrical in plan. In fact, he considered symmetry to be "an unhappy idea for which . . . we sacrifice our comfort, occasionally our commonsense, and always a lot of money."[16] Instead, he advocated that form should be derived from a conscious arrangement of spaces for functional purposes. His design process consisted, therefore, of first establishing the program, then developing the plan, and finally determining the structural program. This idea of "form following function" was rejected by his contemporaries but was adopted later in the in nineteenth century and at the beginning of the twentieth century by the Art Nouveau movement, the Bauhaus, and the modern movement.

12.6 Analogical Methods

Among the most common sources of architectural knowledge—and the method most often drawn upon for synthesizing new design solutions—are completed designs that have proved successful in the past and appear to hold some relevance to the problem at hand. Design from precedents and inspiration drawn from symbols and metaphors provides a "holistic" structure to the solution, rather than the piecemeal, procedural approach of Beaux-Arts formalism and Viollet-le-Duc's rationalism.

Precedents

The rationale behind using precedents for the synthesis of new design solutions is straightforward: if the solution has proved successful in the past, it should be so again in the future, provided that the problem and the circumstances are similar. Hence movie sequels like *Rocky I, II, III,…*, copycat products like Sony's Walkman, and the ubiquitously similar house forms in American cities and suburbs. The precedent embodies the form, the function, and the context of the solution, and benefits from having already withstood the test of reality. Its reuse requires only matching the form, function, and context parameters of the new circumstances to those of the precedent, which—in the case of action movies, portable audio equipment, and suburban housing—is not all that difficult.

The reuse of precedents designed by the same architect is often considered to be his or her "style" because the artifacts exhibit a common set of features, such as the wide overhangs of Frank Lloyd Wright's prairie house roofs.

While each of Wright's prairie houses is considered a masterpiece in it own right, as are many other buildings "designed from precedents," like Palladio's villas, copying precedents often incurs the criticism of lack of originality. Still, the commercial success and effort-saving qualities of this design method are in many cases more than adequate compensation for such lost hubris.[17]

Symbols

Architectonic symbols lend to the present design only a few elements of the "source," often only its form, not its function nor its context. Yet the borrowed form provides not only a holistic framework for the design, it can also confer on the replica some of the conceptions associated with the source. Some of the most frequently "borrowed" building symbols in Western architecture have been copied from Greek temples. They have been used and reused to give form to banks, libraries, court buildings, art galleries, even farmhouses. For example, the Albright-Knox Art Gallery, in Buffalo, New York (fig. 12.7), has borrowed several of its parts from the Acropolis, including its porticoed caryatids. In other cases, the whole building has been shaped like the original—as is the case of the library in the Bahai Temple complex in Haifa, Israel (fig. 12.8), which is shaped like the Parthenon (except for Ionic columns substituting for the original Doric ones), although its function and context are rather dissimilar to those of the original.

Symbolism, of course, works both ways—it helps to organize and give form to a building but also provides commentary, through its form, on the building's function or aspirations. Some of the more famous such commentaries were suggested by Claude-Nicolas Ledoux's projects in the early 1800s, including his "House for Rural Guards," in the form of a giant freestanding sphere; a targetlike shape for the Coopery Company; and "House for the Directors of the Loue River," in the shape of a horizontal cylinder through which floodwater could flow.[18] Likewise, the ubiquitous

12.7 The Albright-Knox Art Gallery in Buffalo, New York, has borrowed many symbols from Greek architecture.

12.8 The library building on the compound of the Bahai Temple in Haifa, Israel, built in the late twentieth century, has been explicitly modeled on the Parthenon in Athens, Greece (except for the building's scale and the style of the columns).

use of the Greek temple facade is often intended to confer stature and respectability upon the "borrower."

Metaphors

In some cases, the source of the form is not a building at all but some object or concept that is so far removed from its application to the current design problem that there can be no question of borrowing its functional or contextual properties. Rather, the source is used only to inspire the current design and lend it some metaphorical value by way of its association with the borrowed source, figuratively or organizationally. Some of the most famous such metaphorical associations have been Le Corbusier's Notre-Dame du Haut in Ronchamp, whose roof is said to have been inspired by the headgear worn by nuns in this part of France; Frank O. Gehry's Guggenheim Museum in Bilbao, Spain, inspired by the shipbuilding history of the town; and Renzo Piano's Parco della Musica, in Rome, in the shape of three giant musical instruments (or giant beetles, in the eyes of some observers).

In those cases, as in many others, the form of one (unrelated) object inspired the shape of another. According to Herbert Simon, such borrowing of form from somewhere else is "legitimate" when the borrowed form does not conflict with the function or the context of the current design problem; it is simply "one way of doing things, chosen from a number of functionally equivalent alternatives." He cites as an example the following analogy:

> Mushrooms can be found in many places in the forest, and the time it takes us to fill a sack with them may not depend much on the direction we wonder. We may feel free, then, to exercise some choice of path, and even to introduce additional choice criteria . . . over and above the pragmatic one of bringing back a full sack [of mushrooms].[19]

Metaphorical analogy is thus a method of imposing a set of constraints on an otherwise chaotic situation, thereby providing the designer with a means to make organizational and formative decisions. Such importing needs not be limited to form. It can also provide functional organization to the project, as is the case when designers liken a nursing home to "quite village," a skyscraper to a "vertical city," or an artificial vacation island in Dubai to a palm tree (fig. 12.9). In such cases the source

Synthesis

helps the architect pay attention to features that might otherwise go unnoticed and explicates the relationships between the parts in some predictable manner.

Analogical and symbolic "borrowing" can also be used to make a point, like advertising the owner's profession or hobby, as in the Saxophone House (fig. 12.10) in Oakland, California, or a company's business, as in the home office of the Longaberger Company in Newark, Ohio—the largest manufacturer of handmade baskets in the United States—which is shaped like a seven-story basket.

Naturally, as the source becomes further removed from the present problem, its application becomes less assuring of reaching predictable results. Hence, the use of metaphors and symbols is less predictable than the use of direct precedents.

Precedents, symbols, and metaphors thus provide a rich source and repository of professional knowledge, which, in the hands of a competent architect, can combine in novel ways to meet current problems and are adapted to fit formative, functional, and contextual requirements. Le Corbusier's Unité d'Habitation (fig. 12.11), which itself has become a source of imitation and inspiration for many other similar buildings, is a case in point. In conceiving the building's spatial concept, Le Corbusier invented a complex, multifunctional, unprecedented form, synthesized from and analogical to a number of precedents—the primitive hut, the passenger ship, the wine bottle rack, the Greek temple, and more. None of these elements were incorporated explicitly in his design. Rather, they were dissected and recombined in new compositions.[20]

The legitimacy of using precedents, symbols, and metaphors has, nonetheless, troubled many architects and theorists over the years. Does "borrowing" forms developed in different contexts, for different purposes, lead to a mere formalistic engagement of the past, or does it also translate meaning? Can we regard historically or otherwise derived typologies as universal elements, regardless of their contextual associations? How is the choice made? Are some images and periods simply more "fashionable" than others? How far can one change the "source" and still retain whatever associations it carries? Can architectural form be treated as an autonomous phenomenon, regardless of significance, context, and purpose?

These questions cannot be properly dealt with in the context of this book, which is concerned with the phenomenon of "borrowing" as a

12.10 The Saxophone House in Oakland, California.

12.11 Le Corbusier's Unité d'Habitation in Marseilles (1947–1952) is the combined product of many precedents, symbols, and metaphors.

method of design synthesis rather than architectural theory and criticism. Still, to quote Eduard Sekler:

> It does not matter in the last resort where models are derived from nor what they are, so long as they become sources of authentic inspiration, catalysts for something genuine. The past as a source for the future need not be feared unless the relation to history is disturbed and unhealthy.[21]

Bibliography

Alexander, C., S. Ishikawa, M. Silverstein, M. Jacobson, I. Fiksdahl-King, and S. Angel. *A Pattern Language.* Oxford: Oxford University Press, 1977.

Argyris, C., and D. A. Schön. *Theory in Practice: Increasing Professional Effectiveness.* New York: Jossey-Bass, 1977.

Cuff, D. *Architecture: The Story of Practice.* Cambridge: MIT Press, 1991.

Drexler, A. *The Architecture of the Ecole des Beaux-Arts.* 2d ed. London: Secker and Warburg, 1984.

Erlande-Brandenburg, A. *Cathedrals and Castles: Building in the Middle Ages.* New York: Harry N. Abrams, 1993.

Hitchcock, H.-R. *Architecture: Nineteenth and Twentieth Centuries.* New Haven: Yale University Press, 1977.

Kruft, H.-W. *A History of Architectural Theory: From Vitruvius to the Present.* Princeton: Princeton Architectural Press, 1994.

Middleton, R. *The Beaux-Arts and Nineteenth-Century French Architecture.* Cambridge: MIT Press, 1982.

Pevsner, N. *Ruskin and Viollet-le-Duc.* London: Thames and Hudson, 1969.

Synthesis

Procedural Methods

Computational methods to support the synthesis of design solutions have fascinated architectural researchers and horrified the practitioners. The first group has viewed computer-aided synthesis as the epitome of rational design,[1] the second as trying to rob human designers of what they consider to be the "protected core" of their profession.[2] The truth, of course, favors neither group. Computational design methods cannot rival the best human designers, nor is every human design effort worth protecting.

Computational design methods have emulated many of the habitual methods used by designers, with the added benefit of the computer's immense processing and storage capabilities. These made the generation and testing of large numbers of potential solutions possible as well as storing and searching vast databases of design "rules" and precedents. The generation of the solutions themselves has been based on first principles of geometry, physics, and nature, and gleaned from human expertise or from precedents developed by human designers.

Procedural methods were the first ones to be employed in the quest for computational design synthesis. They leverage our ability, as human designers, to specify local conditions—like desired relationships between a small number of variables—and the ability of the computer to apply or test for these relationships over much larger sets of variables. Consequently, the judicious application of a relatively small number of conditions can be used to generate complex forms. Obviously, the method, which is based on local conditions, cannot detect, exploit, or avoid global opportunities and pitfalls. For that, human observation (or nonprocedural methods) are needed.

13.1 Complete Enumeration

The likelihood of finding the most appropriate form that fits some prespecified function within a given context increases as the pool of potential forms

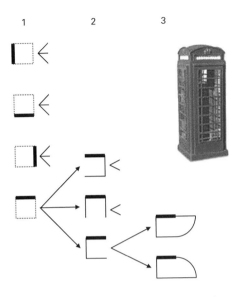

1   2   3

13.1 A method for generating all the permutations of the basic pattern of British telephone booths.

	D1	D2	D3	C1	C2	C3	B1
A1							
A2							
A3							
B1							
B2							
B3							

13.2 Part of the complete enumeration of all possible layouts of a pair of telephone booths. (L. March and P. Steadman, *The Geometry of Environment* [Cambridge: MIT Press, 1974].)

to choose from grows. This is the rationale underlying a computational design method known as "complete enumeration": if having a large number of potential solutions to choose from is good, choosing from among *all* possible solutions is better. Complete enumeration, as the name implies, exploits the ability of the computer to generate a vast number of solutions to a problem—potentially *all* possible solutions—to be examined by the designer (or another computational procedure) one at a time for their fit with the function and the context (or any other conditions, for that matter).

The generation of all potential design solutions is based on using some systematic method that can find all the combinatorially possible arrangements of the basic geometric pattern pertaining to the problem. Such arrangements are often represented as treelike structures, where each level of the tree adds one more design parameter to the level that precedes it. For example, the British telephone booth, designed by Bruce Martin in the 1960s for the British General Post Office (fig. 13.1), consists of a square plan with four elements—a service panel, an entrance, and two window walls. Starting with the four possible locations of the service panel, then adding to each one the three possible locations of the entrance, generates the treelike structure depicted in figure 13.1. In addition, the doors can be hung in either right-handed or left-handed ways, adding two more possibilities to each of the twelve basic configurations, for a total of twenty-four permutations.

Telephone booths are often placed in pairs, arranged back-to-back or side-to-side such that the doors do not open into each other. This allows for seventy-two nonrepetitive arrangements of the booths, as depicted in figure 13.2.

The role of such complete enumeration, even in this rather simple design problem, is to remind the architect of possible geometric configurations that might otherwise escape his or her attention. Complete enumeration is applicable only when the number of potential solutions is too large for the architect to consider but not too large for the computer to manage. The example described above falls into this category. The number of all possible combinations is seventy-two—too many for the architect to remember but certainly manageable by computational means. Had the number of design parameters been much larger and the number of optional values for each greater, then the number of potential solutions would exceed the capabilities of even the largest computers. This phenomenon, known as "combinatoric explosion," increases the number of branches of the permutation tree at each level. For example, if the design problem consisted of ten parameters, each with ten possible values—a relatively modest size when it comes to architectural design—the number of all possible solutions would have been 10^{10} (ten billion)—a number that challenges all but the largest computers.

Consequently, variants on the complete enumeration method have been sought to curb the combinatoric explosion of possible solutions, or bound them in some manageable, finite "envelope." The design of fixed external sunshades demonstrates this approach.

External sunshades are an important climatic control device in hot climates, where the direct penetration of solar radiation into a building increases the heat load and creates visual glare. In the summer, this added heat load must be compensated for by means of artificial cooling. In the winter, direct solar radiation can help reduce the need for mechanical heating. However, if not properly designed, fixed external sunshades can prevent (desired) direct winter sun from entering a room and unnecessarily reduce daylighting throughout the year.

External sunshades are a common, relatively inexpensive way of controlling the penetration of direct solar radiation into a building. They also have a strong visual effect on its appearance, especially if the building is large and has many windows (fig. 13.3). Consequently, in addition to being functionally effective, sunshades must also be designed to be architecturally pleasing.

Sunshades are commonly designed by trial and error: the architect designs an architecturally pleasing form—a small ledge or canopy over the window—and tests its functional efficacy for preventing the penetration of direct solar radiation during prespecified hours of the day and days of the year, while permitting direct penetration at other desired times. Testing is often done by means of computational analysis or, even more often, by placing a physical model of the building on a heliodon (fig. 13.4). In addition to being tedious, this process does not guarantee the best results and may leave many architecturally acceptable forms out of consideration. If physical simulation is used, the need to modify the scale model for each design option severely reduces the number of alternatives that can be tested. Clearly, complete enumeration of all possible designs of sunshades is not feasible.

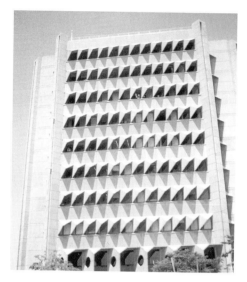

13.3 Pyramidal sunshades, Sackler School of Medicine, Tel Aviv University, Israel.

13.4 The heliodon at the Faculty of Architecture and Town Planning, The Technion, Israel. (Courtesy of Edna Shaviv, Haifa, Israel.)

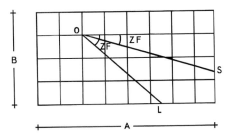

13.5 Calculating the shading envelope for a window located at 32° 7' in the Northern Hemisphere, by placing at each grid point a pole whose length is calculated to cast a shadow that reaches the window's perimeter. (E. Shaviv, in *Proceedings of the Ninth National Passive Solar Conference* [Columbus, Ohio: American Solar Energy Society, 1984].)

A different approach was proposed by Shaviv,[3] which "inverts" the problem: instead of testing the efficacy of a given form for shading the window, it finds all possible forms that adequately shade a given window at the desired hours and dates. It does so by calculating, for every point within the window, the height of the shade needed to prevent the penetration of direct solar radiation on given days and hours. The results of all these shades constitute a shading "envelope," within which all effective sunshades reside.

To find this shading envelope, the window is divided into a grid whose density depends on the complexity of the desired form (simple sunshades can use a coarser grid than more complex ones). The height of an imaginary "pole," placed perpendicular to the plane of the window at each grid point, and which casts a shadow long enough to reach the frame of the window, is calculated (fig. 13.5). The inputs for the calculation include the orientation and inclination of the vector casting the shadow, the geographical location of the building (which determines the position of the sun in the sky), the time and date when shading is desired, and the shape of the window itself. The calculation is performed for the twenty-first day of each month and each hour in which the building is expected to be occupied (thereby eliminating hard-to-shade hours, such as early morning and late afternoon, when there is no need to shade). The maximum length of the shading vector (which differs at each grid point and is reached at different times of the day) is used to generate the shading envelope, depicted in figure 13.6.

The architect can then design a sunshade that fits the envelope. The design is not unique, as depicted in figure 13.6. Different forms can be used, including single or multiple horizontal slates, as well as pyramidal ones. The result is an efficient sunshade, with possibly nonstandard form that enriches the looks of the building while contributing to its climatic well-being.

Interestingly, the same method can be used to compute solar rights—the opposite of sunshades.[4] Solar rights are the rights of existing residents in an urban setting not to have proposed new construction block direct sunlight from reaching them because of the location, orientation, and height of the new buildings. As in the method used to design sunshades, an "envelope" of all possible locations and maximal heights of buildings is generated using the shadow-casting "poles" method. The envelope can then be used to design and locate specific individual buildings within a given neighborhood.

13.2 Space Allocation

One of the early goals of complete enumeration procedures was to generate all possible floor plans from a given set of rooms, from which the architect could choose the most appropriate one for a given design project.[5] It soon became clear, however, that combinatoric explosion rendered this method all but impractical for any but the most trivial arrangements. Yet the lure of computationally arranging rooms in a floor plan did not diminish. It became known as the problem of "space allocation."

Space allocation—also known as "automated floor plan generation," "automated spatial synthesis," and as "quadratic assignment formulation"—is one of the most interesting, difficult, and controversial areas of computer-aided architectural design. Considered by some to be the Holy Grail of CAAD, space allocation is an attempt to enlist the services of the computer in one of architecture's most cherished tasks—the layout of spaces (and the activities they house) in a building according to some rational principles (mostly minimization of distances between spaces that house closely related activities, based on the assumption that such a floor plan would be more "efficient" for the inhabitants using the building).

Space allocation was one of the first design problems to be subjected to computational synthesis, and several solutions have been proposed.[6] Yet, to date, space allocation still only works in very limited areas of architectural design, primarily ones in which quantifiable design objectives can be formulated and where the nature of the solutions is relatively well understood (e.g., the design of warehouses, hospitals, and schools).[7]

In general terms, space allocation can be stated as follows: given a set of spaces (or activities) and the desired adjacencies between them; find the layout that minimizes the distances between spaces that ought to be close to each other. Stated more formally:

$$\min V = \sum_{ij} W_{ij} D_{ij}$$

where V is the "value" of the layout, i,j is a pair of spaces (or activities), W is the weight or relative importance of the proximity between them, and D is the distance between the two spaces.

The relative weights (or importance) of the desired proximities between the spaces can be determined logically, by considering the rela-

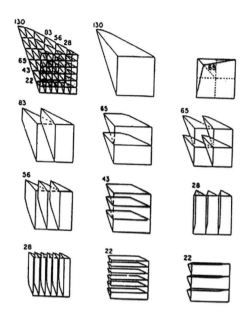

13.6 Alternative sunshades that fit within the same shading envelope. (E. Shaviv, in *Proceedings of the Ninth National Passive Solar Conference* [Columbus, Ohio: American Solar Energy Society, 1984].)

	Reactor	Control	Mech. workshop	Elec. workshop	Cold mach. room	Hot mach. room	Purification	Admin	Utilities	Radiation hazard control	Mech. store	Elec. store
	1	**2**	**3**	**4**	**5**	**6**	**7**	**8**	**9**	**10**	**11**	**12**
1	9	9	2	2	1	8	7	3	6	4	1	1
2	9	9	1	5	3	4	3	1	2	5	1	1
3	2	1	9	8	9	1	1	2	3	1	9	7
4	2	5	8	9	7	1	1	2	3	1	7	9
5	1	3	9	7	9	2	1	1	3	1	8	8
6	8	4	1	1	2	9	7	1	3	2	3	3
7	7	3	1	1	1	7	9	2	9	8	1	1
8	3	1	2	2	1	1	2	9	8	6	2	2
9	6	2	3	3	3	3	9	8	9	4	3	3
10	4	5	1	1	1	2	8	6	4	9	1	1
11	1	1	9	7	8	3	1	2	3	1	9	8
12	1	1	7	9	8	3	1	2	3	1	8	9

13.7 Adjacency matrix for locating the functional spaces in a nuclear reactor. (E. Shaviv and D. Gali, in *Build International* 7, no. 6 [1974].)

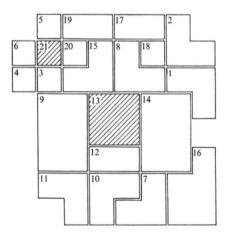

13.8 Whitehead and Eldars's layout of a hospital, using the additive approach. (L. March and P. Steadman, *The Geometry of Environment* [Cambridge: MIT Press, 1974].)

tionships between the activities they house, or empirically, by monitoring a building of the same type as the project at hand and recording the number of trips between each pair of spaces (or activities). The trips can be further weighted according to the different types of users. For example, Whitehead and Eldars, who used a hospital as their target project, gave a considerably higher weight to the number of trips made by surgeons compared to the number of trips made by the nurses. The results are recorded in the form of an adjacency matrix, which lists the weight of the connection between each pairs of spaces (fig. 13.7).

Two general approaches to space allocation have emerged: an additive approach and a permutation-based approach.

Additive Space Allocation

The additive (or "constructive") approach is based on placing the most highly connected space or activity first, typically at the center of a grid. The space or activity that has the strongest connection to the first one is placed adjacent to it. The third space to be placed is the one that is most strongly connected to both the first and the second ones. The algorithm places this space in such a way that that the "value" of the overall layout (the sum of the weighted distances) is minimized. Subsequent spaces are placed in a similar manner, gradually building up the floor plan using less and less strongly connected spaces, until no more spaces are left (fig. 13.8).

The result of this componental buildup is not an architectural floor plan: it is only a generalized mapping of the topological-geometrical relative locations of the component spaces, arranged in a manner that privileges adjacency as a design criterion over all other considerations (e.g., views, orientations, and site-specific issues).

Site-specific considerations can, however, be accommodated, if the grid cells onto which the spaces or activities are placed are given desirability values of their own (e.g., proximity to a road, views, and so forth), as demonstrated by a program called STUNI, intended for the design of university campuses.[8] In that case, each space to be placed must also include its preferential site attributes, and the placement algorithm must take them into account when searching for optimal locations. Conflicts between preferred proximity and preferred site conditions may arise and must be resolved.

Synthesis

Nor is the result of additive space allocation an "optimal" layout, even only from an adjacency point of view. The first-come-first-served approach may cause spaces that have been placed first, due to their higher degree of connectivity, to block the optimal placement of spaces whose overall connectivity is smaller. Furthermore, choosing the sequence of spaces to be placed on the basis of their connectivity with other spaces may cause the bathroom or the entrance to be placed first, since these spaces typically have strong connectivity needs to all other spaces. (This problem can be easily fixed by allowing the architect to specify which space ought to be located first, but it does not solve the mechanical placement of subsequent places.) Moreover, by placing the most highly connected space first, the additive approach tends to generate concentric layouts, clustering subsequent spaces around the "core." This approach is adequate for buildings whose main spaces do not require daylight, like the operating theater chosen by Whitehead and Eldars to demonstrate their method, but is less desirable for buildings composed of spaces that desire daylight, rational circulation routes, and other "macro" considerations that the piecemeal additive approach cannot accommodate.

Permutational Space Allocation

Possibly the major drawback of the additive approach is its inflexibility: once a space has been placed, it stays put. The order of placements thus determines the outcome of the algorithm as much as, or even more than, the adjacency matrix itself.

The permutational (or "improvement") approach to space allocation attempts to solve this problem by allowing spaces to be swapped after the layout has been completed; pairs of spaces may exchange their locations, and the value of the layout is recalculated. If the new layout is better than the former one (i.e., its "value" is smaller), it is kept. Otherwise, the two spaces are unswapped. The swapping of pairs of spaces can be systematic, if the number of spaces is small, testing all possible layouts. However, since the number of all possible permutations is $N!$ (N factorial $= N(N-1)(N-2)\ldots(1)$), systematic swapping (which is akin to complete enumeration) is limited to problems with relatively few spaces (typically, less than 10, which means 3,628,800 permutations), rendering the entire exercise rather pointless. Instead, researchers have proposed that candidate spaces for swapping will be chosen at random.[9] Although such random sampling may miss the optimal layout, or even a large number of good solutions, its results compare favorably to complete enumeration methods.[10] Moreover, since the placement of the spaces is not fixed, there is no need to follow the additive approach of placing the most highly connected space before all others, then the second most highly connected space, and so on. Instead, the permutational approach can start with a random initial layout. The results, nonetheless, are sensitive to the initial layout: better results may be obtained from different starting arrangements.

More formally, the algorithm can be stated as follows:

1. Assign spaces to empty grid cells systematically or randomly.
2. Compute the value of the layout, using rectilinear distances and the weighted connections between pairs of spaces.
3. Randomly choose two spaces for swapping.
4. Recompute the value of the layout (only the change in value due to the swapped spaces needs to be recomputed).
5. If the new value is greater than or equal to the previous value, unswap the spaces; otherwise, keep the new layout.
6. Repeat steps 3 through 5 until the value has not changed in N iterations (e.g., $N = 10$).

Figure 13.9 depicts a simple example of this approach, applied to laying out the twelve functional spaces of a nuclear reactor within a rectangular grid. It shows how an initial, randomized layout, whose value is 6,649, has been improved through swapping to a value of 4,545 (these numbers, of course, have no meaning of their own; they serve only as a measure of improving the layout, relative to initial conditions).

Experimentation has shown that this approach "converges" on a quasi-optimal solution quite rapidly: improvements of the layout tend to be greater at the outset, when the layout is completely randomized, and decrease as the swapping proceeds and as spaces gravitate closer to their desired neighbors. The solution, however, is never fully optimal, because the adjacency matrix may contain internal conflicts (e.g., indicating that space A ought to be close to both spaces B and C, but spaces B and C ought to be far apart from each other) and does not account for geometrical limitations (e.g., there is a limited area around each space, and strongly connected spaces might have to compete for proximity). For the example depicted in figure 13.9, the hypothetical best layout is 1,156 (computed as if all distances were 1), yet the best actual value reached by the algorithm before no further improvements were noticeable was only 4,545. Still, manual inspection of the result reveals that most strongly connected spaces have, indeed, ended up in proximity to one another.

Much like the additive approach, the permutational approach may be trapped in a local optimum—this occurs when swapping (or stepwise placement, in the additive approach), produces a layout that is not optimal but cannot be further improved by swapping individual pairs of spaces. Although some local optima can be avoided by swapping more than one pair of spaces at a time, the problem is inherent to the approach and cannot be totally avoided.

The permutational approach supports allocating spaces within a predefined contour of the building, provided the sizes of all spaces are the same (a limitation not suffered by the additive approach). This means that the architect can design the overall shape of the building before allocating the spaces and that the spaces will fit optimally (or rather quasi-optimally) within the preferred contour, rather than the other way around, as is the case in the additive approach.[11]

If spaces of different sizes are to be used, which would more closely resemble the architectural floor plan that must ultimately be generated from the algorithm's outcome, then one of two approaches can be used:

1. Every space can be subdivided into a number of modular units, each considered a "space" in its own right. The adjacency matrix must be adjusted to reflect the strong "inner" connectivity of these units, by assigning them a much higher affinity than "regular" spaces. This will guarantee that the units that belong to one space "stay together" during the swapping process, although the shape of the area they cover as a group may not be rectangular (this approach is demonstrated in figure 13.9).

2. The grid cells that are used to locate the spaces can initially be made larger than strictly necessary to accommodate the spaces, providing enough room for swapping smaller spaces with larger ones. In addition to swapping, the sizes of the grid cells are gradually "contracted" to more tightly envelope their resident spaces, and the spaces them-

Initial layout

13	8	1	10	1
1	5	1	3	12
11	2	6	1	9
1	7	1	8	5
6	1	4	13	1

V = 6649

Final layout

5	12	11	8	13
5	4	3	9	8
2	1	1	1	10
6	1	1	1	7
6	1	1	1	13

V = 4545

Interpreted layout

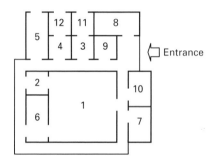

13.9 Improving an initially random layout of activities in a nuclear reactor through swapping, based on the adjacency matrix of figure 13.7. (E. Shaviv and D. Gali, in *Build International* 7, no. 6 [1974].)

selves are translated within their respective grid cells to bring them closer to their neighboring spaces. Such translation may improve the value of the layout, which, combined with the contracting grid cells, will eventually preclude further swapping of the spaces.[12]

Both the additive and the permutational approaches can handle multistory buildings. The additive approach can do so by allowing placement above as well as next to previously placed spaces. The permutational approach can use multiple grids, one per floor. In both cases, the calculation of the value of each layout must account for the added difficulty in moving between spaces that are located on different floors. This can be done by adding an intermediary staircase or elevator space on each floor through which the distance calculation must go, or multiplying the distance by a constant factor. Both methods penalize layouts where spaces with a high degree of connectivity are placed not only far from each other, but on different floors of the building.

The end result of both space allocation approaches is an approximated, not an actual, floor plan. It must be adapted into an architectural floor plan by a human designer, who will take into consideration many additional design criteria, including corridors, colinearity of walls, and more. Figure 13.10 shows how a layout produced by the permutational approach for a three-story high school has been interpreted and adapted into actual floor plans by the architect.

Neither is the result of space allocation programs optimal, or even quasi-optimal, despite claims made to that effect, because any arrangement produced by these programs is optimal only in so far as the criterion of distances is concerned. All other design criteria are not considered. Although attempts have been made to expand the scope of the criteria used by space allocation methods for locating spaces beyond proximity, their uses have been limited to building types where distances are of paramount importance, like large schools, university campuses, hospitals, and especially warehouses, office buildings, and manufacturing plants. In such buildings, the number of spaces (or activities) to be located is large (often over 100), and travel between them has a measurable impact on operating costs. Optimizing their layout, either at the planning phase or at the operating phase, is of great concern to the owners.[13] Their needs have been met through interactive space allocation programs that allow the designer (or

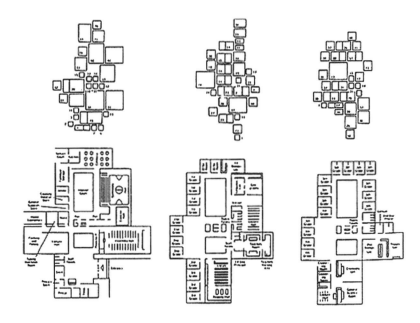

13.10 Manual adaptation of the results generated by the space allocation algorithm for a three-story high school. (E. Shaviv and D. Gali, in *Build International* 7, no. 6 [1974].)

facilities manager) to add or modify constraints and the layout itself, using the algorithm as both a layout generator and a layout evaluator.[14]

13.3 Constraint Satisfaction

For buildings where distances are of lesser importance than other criteria (e.g., privacy in a house), and where additional criteria (e.g., lighting and site conditions) influence the design as much as or more than circulation, space allocation has found little or no use.

Attempts to improve space allocation by including additional design criteria in the decision-making process tend to add constraints to the placement algorithm, sometimes reducing its role to a mere random layout generator, whose results are subject to testing by a much more extensive constraint satisfaction module. The Basic Architectural Investigation and Design system (BAID) demonstrates this approach:[15] randomly generated layouts are tested for compliance with daylight, sunlight, and privacy conditions, expressed in such terms as "a minimum of 1% of the sky [must be] visible at every point on each window face . . . [as] viewed

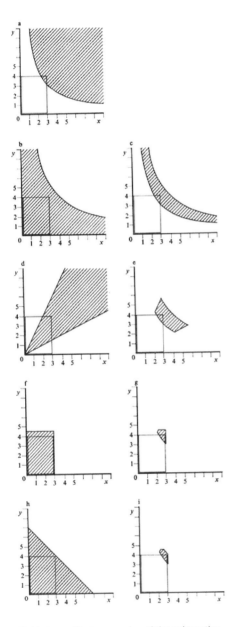

through a standard aperture. . . . It also [must have] a minimum of two hours of sunlight for ten months of the year fall on the full width of one window face, and no window face [must be] closer than 70 feet to any directly opposing window face."[16] The program is intended to produce layouts that stimulate the architects imagination, rather than final designs. The architect is free to modify the layout, which can then be tested again by the program for compliance with the constraints.

Linear Programming

Formal methods for solving such problems with multiple constraints have been developed by a branch of mathematics known as operations research.[17] They are based on solving a system of linear inequalities, each representing one constraint on the solution. For example, the client may specify that the area of a room must not be smaller than nine square meters and not bigger than sixteen, that the ratio of length to width must be less than 1:2, that its length should be less than four and a half meters, its width less than three, and that the perimeter of the room must not exceed fourteen meters. Stated more formally:

$$9 \text{ m}^2 \leq L * W \leq 16 \text{ m}^2$$
$$L \leq 2W$$
$$L \leq 4.5 \text{ m}$$
$$W \leq 3 \text{ m}$$
$$2(L + W) \leq 14 \text{ m}$$

This system of linear inequalities can be solved numerically, or graphically, as depicted in figure 13.11, yielding (in this case) a small range of solutions that satisfy all the constraints. However, such formulaic representation of constraints is typically inapplicable to architectural problems, where the design criteria are not well-defined, individual criteria are rarely independent of each other, and they are often in conflict (which would render the system of linear inequalities unsolvable). A "softer" approach to dealing computationally with multiple design constraints is, therefore, needed.

13.11 A graphical expression of the subtractive role of constraints on a room's dimensions. (L. March and P. Steadman, *The Geometry of Environment* [Cambridge: MIT Press, 1974].)

Synthesis

Constraint Management

One obvious way of handling multiple conflicting constraints is to *manage* them, such that not all constraints need to be solved at once, as in the linear-programming approach. Rather, constraints can be arranged in dependency hierarchies and solved consecutively by assigning values that satisfy individual constraints.

The simplest dependency hierarchy is a list. For example, when designing an office, one might (1) decide how many cubicles are needed, then (2) decide how large each cubicle ought to be (and perhaps what shape it must take), and finally (3) decide the overall layout of the cubicles within the given space. If an earlier decision leads to a conflict or creates an unsolvable situation for a subsequent constraint, it must be modified, and all subsequent decisions must be reconsidered (a process known as "backtracking"). Hence, for example, if the cubicles with assigned sizes and shapes cannot be accommodated within the allotted space (decision no. 3), then either a larger space must be procured for the office or, if that is not possible, the sizes and shapes of some (or all) cubicles must be modified (decision no. 2) and their layout within the given space reattempted (decision no. 3). If that does not solve the problem, and the cubicles still cannot be accommodated within the given space, then their number must be reduced (decision no. 1), after which their sizes and shapes must be reconsidered (decision no. 2) and, finally, their layout within the space reattempted (decision no. 3). Each one of these decisions can be considered a "constraint," both in the sense that it must be accommodated and in the sense that it "constrains" the next decision.[18]

As an example of linear constraint management consider the IMAGE system, developed by MIT's Architecture Machine Group between 1968 and 1974.[19] It is a layout generator that uses various geometric relationships as design constraints. They include such constraints as NEAR and FAR, SHARED WALL, ADJACENT, ON TOP OF, KEEP OUT, and OVERLAP. Each constraint is associated with a computational routine that interprets the evolving layout and its implication for the two spaces related by the constraint and calculates the change that would satisfy it. For example, to alleviate an overlap condition, the KEEP OUT routine might prescribe a positional displacement or a dimensional change for one or both spaces.

13.12 A constraints dependency hierarchy for a single-family house. (Y. E. Kalay, in *ACADIA '85,* ed. P. McIntosh [Tempe, Ariz., 1985].)

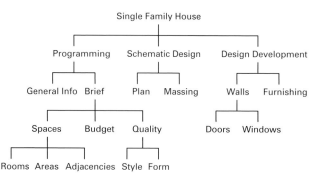

Multiple different constraints can apply to the same space and may require conflicting resolutions. IMAGE manages them by modifying each space in succession, starting with the first one. It then continues the process until all constraints are satisfied. In doing so, IMAGE considers each space, in its turn, as a variable (positionally and dimensionally) and all the others as fixed. It then attempts to satisfy all the constraints that pertain to that space. Suggested changes are stored until all the constraints pertaining to that space have been tested. Then IMAGE calculates a new configuration for that space, which minimizes conflicts among the required changes, using the least-mean-squares-fit method.[20]

This example of constraint management is typical to handling systems of complex constraint networks. More formally, the explicit representation of the constraints is considered a constraint model—a data structure that describes the constraints and their relationships. The method used to resolve them is considered to be a constraint manager—a computational module that can carry out the conflict management, backtracking, and reevaluation of the constraints.

An example of an explicit constraint model and constraint manager is provided by ALEX, a system for designing single-family houses.[21] It was intended to help the client explore the constraints and make decisions about his or her house. ALEX's constraint model is a hierarchical tree (fig. 13.12), where lower levels elaborate the constraints imposed by higher levels of the hierarchy. Thus, for example, the SPACES constraint is elaborated into the ROOMS, AREAS, and ADJACENCY constraints. In turn, the SPACES constraint, together with the BUDGET and QUALITY constraints, are the elaboration of the BRIEF constraint. ALEX's constraint model also includes minimal and maximal room areas and their associated cost per square foot.

Synthesis

ALEX uses an interactive constraint management approach, where the client is asked to make design decisions. They are checked by the program for compliance with earlier decisions as well as with built-in constraints pertaining to the nature of rooms in a house and their areas and to budgetary considerations. For example, ALEX can determine if the budget established by the client has been exceeded by the specifications of rooms and their areas, and, if so, require modification of the budget, the sizes of the rooms, or their number (e.g., go from a four-bedroom house to a three-bedroom house). ALEX can also assume the role of a designer and make decisions on behalf of the client, who is then asked to review and approve them. This role "reversal" qualifies ALEX to be considered a design assistant, not just an automated design generator. Design assistants and ALEX are further discussed in chapter 22.

Successive Approximation

Another way of dealing with multiple conflicting constraints is by means of successive approximation. Rather than fully satisfy all the constraints at the same time, or one constraint after the other (working through a hierarchy or a network of constraints), develop a solution that satisfies most of the constraints well enough to be considered acceptable (what Herbert Simon called a "satisficing" rather than a "satisfying" solution).[22] An approximate yet "satisficing" solution can be generated by starting with an initial solution that is rather far from satisfying the constraints and gradually improving it to better fit the constraints until no further improvements can be made.

This approach was demonstrated by Shaviv in the design of multi-curved shell structures.[23] The traditional method of designing thin shell structures calculates the stresses resulting in an arbitrarily generated geometry under given load conditions. This method inevitably generates stresses in the shell, which must be taken up by relatively thick edge members (beams) or a thicker membrane, thus defying the concept of a graceful, thin shell. Shaviv's approach inverts the process. Rather than calculating the stresses generated by a given structure, it calculates the geometry of the shell that meets given load conditions. It is based on the fact that, for shallow elliptical shells under uniform, gravity-only loads (dead loads), such conditions occur when the altitude $z_{i,j}$ of every point (i,j) on the surface of

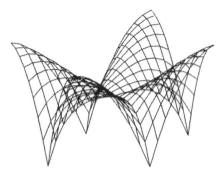

13.13 The form of the shell equilibrates the stresses when each point has the average altitude of its four neighboring points. (E. Shaviv and D. P. Greenberg, in *Bulletin of the International Association for Shell Structures*, no. 37 [1970].)

the shell is the geometric average of the altitudes of its four closest neighboring points (fig. 13.13):

$$z_{i,j} = (z_{i,j+1} + z_{i,j-1} + z_{i+1,j} + z_{i-1,j})/4$$

For n points, this expression requires the simultaneous solution of n equations—much like the linear programming approach required.

Shaviv's method does not attempt to solve any equations at all. Rather, it approaches the correct values by successive approximation. Initially, a flat membrane is assumed, "resting" on the desired boundary conditions. This flat membrane is gradually "slumped" on the boundary, through successive approximations which calculates the $z_{i,j}$ value of each point from the values of its four neighbors. Initially, this value is far off the mark, because only the altitude of the boundary points is correct: the rest are located at some arbitrary level. But as the $z_{i,j}$ values of interior points are gradually adjusted, they approach the correct, sheer-free membrane altitude. The process must be repeated until the value of no point has changed, indicating that the surface has reached its state of equilibrium.

The result is a saddlelike form, which conforms to the boundary conditions set by the architect and which closely approximates the optimal, stress-free form of a membrane stretched over these boundaries, much like a soap bubble membrane does.

The successive approximation method thus does not produce an exact solution to the problem, as an analytical method might do. However, it can handle situations where no analytical solutions are possible and where an exact solution is not really necessary. Architectural design is such a case. The number of constraints is typically too large for analytical methods; and even if exact solutions were available, other factors in the construction process might make them irrelevant.

Overall, attempts to integrate automated synthesis programs into mainstream architectural design have been few. With some exceptions, their results were poor compared to the results obtained by competent architects, and it was difficult to integrate them with other tasks an architect conventionally must perform in the course of a design project. One noted exception has been the use of the automated bubble diagram and floor plan generator Compurelate by the architectural firm of Perri Dean and Stuart, in Boston, Massachusetts, in the early 1970s, as discussed in section 4.1.

Synthesis

Bibliography

Baybars, I., and C. M. Eastman. "Enumerating Architectural Arrangements by Generating Their Underlying Graphs." *Environment and Planning B* 7 (1980): 289–310.

Cross, N. *The Automated Architect.* London: Pion, 1977.

Eastman, C. M. "Automated Space Planning." *Architectural Intelligence* 4 (1973): 41–64.

Eastman, C. M. *Spatial Synthesis in Computer-Aided Building Design.* New York: John Wiley and Sons, 1975.

Galle, P. "An Algorithm for Exhaustive Generation of Building Floor Plans." *Communications of the ACM* 24, no. 12 (1981): 813–825.

Gross, J., and J. Yellen. *Graph Theory and Its Applications.* Boca Raton, Fla.: CRC Press, 1999.

Kalay, Y. E., ed. *Computability of Design.* New York: Wiley Interscience, 1987.

March, L., and P. Steadman. *The Geometry of Environment.* Cambridge: MIT Press, 1974.

Roth, J., and R. Hashimshony. "Algorithms in Graph Theory and Their Use for Solving Problems in Architectural Design." *Computer-Aided Design* 20, no. 7 (1988): 373–381.

Roth, J., R. Hashimshony, and A. Wachman. "Turning a Graph into Rectangular Floor Plan." *Building and Environment B* 17 (1982): 163–173.

The systematic, "mechanical" approach to the synthesis of form, which is at the core of procedural methods, requires a complete understanding of the task at hand. In architectural design, however, such complete understanding is often hard to come by. Design synthesis methods are typically inspired by analogies and guided by the architect's own or another designer's previous experiences. The methods rely on personal and professional expertises accumulated over lifetimes of confronting a variety of design issues. The formalization of such "soft" methods, which draw on approximate rather than precise knowledge, has been the province of heuristic methods of the kind formalized by artificial intelligence research.

Artificial intelligence (AI) is a branch of computer science that was born in the summer of 1956, during a two-month-long meeting of like-minded researchers at Dartmouth College, in New Hampshire. The stated objectives of AI have been to develop computers whose abilities will rival, even surpass, human cognitive abilities, or—as stated by Marvin Minsky—"AI is the science of making machines do things that would require intelligence if done by man."[1] AI's first success was Newell, Shaw, and Simon's Logic Theorist program (later renamed General Problem Solver), which demonstrated the power of recursive search techniques to solve logically complex problems.[2]

AI went on to become a science in its own right in the 1980s, promising to turn computers from mere calculating machines into "intelligent" beings like the famed HAL 9000 computer from the movie *2001: A Space Odyssey*.[3] Such intelligent machines would be able to play chess at world championship level, understand spoken language, reason about complex yet ill-structured problems, even come up with original design solutions— or at least offer designers assistance of the kind they would expect from a fellow human designer.[4]

Although AI has suffered considerable embarrassment and setbacks due to the unfounded exuberance of its early proponents, it has inspired considerable efforts in architectural design research to develop knowledge-based programs that can synthesize solutions on the basis of analogical reasoning, case-based reasoning, design rules derived from the experiences of good designers, even formalized shape transformations that can generate forms within an established corpus of architectural (and other) work.

Unlike procedural methods, heuristic methods cannot guarantee that they will arrive at a solution to the problem they are applied to, nor that a solution they arrive at will be optimal. Their reasoning is not exact, and the knowledge on which they rely may contain logical gaps and inconsistencies. Yet, despite these shortcomings, or perhaps because of them, heuristic methods are able to solve problems the procedural methods cannot. They do so by virtue of relying on a global, holistic view of the problem they deal with rather than the localized one most procedural methods rely upon. This holistic view is derived from human observation and experience. It enables programs that encode it to "see the forest for the trees" and thus overcome localized obstacles that would have stumped procedural methods.

In some cases, as with analogical reasoning, the holistic view—borrowed from other problems or even other domains—sets a new direction for developing a solution that might otherwise have been obscured by the details of the actual problem. Sometimes, as in case-based reasoning, it manifests itself in understanding the whole as more than the sum of its parts. And sometimes, as in expert systems, the holistic view works through generalized "rules of thumb"—conventions gleaned from common sense, observations, and the experience of experts.

14.1 Analogical Methods

One of the most common heuristic methods for synthesizing design solutions is to "borrow" from other knowledge areas that appear to hold some relevance to the problem at hand. Section 12.6 discussed habitual methods of "borrowing" based on the observational powers of the designer. In those cases, the "source" might vary widely from the "target," and its interpretation could be rather free. However, if computational methods are to be used for the purpose of such "borrowing," then the source of the borrowed knowledge and its method of adaptation must be formalized in some manner. Moreover, since the source is obviously rather different from the target (otherwise it would be a case of prototype adaptation rather than analogy), it is often only the generative method, rather than the results of its application, that can be formalized. An example of such analogical "borrowing" is the basing of architectural design solutions on principles of electrical flow and mechanical forces.

Electrical Metaphors

Philip Stedman was the first to propose borrowing a metaphor from electrical networks to guide the computational synthesis of architectural form.[5] He found a surprising similarity between a specially constructed graph representation of architectural floor plans and the physics of electricity, as expressed by Kirchhoff's laws of electrical flow.

Graph-theoretic representation of architectural floor plans is as old as graph theory itself, invented by the Swiss mathematician Leonhard Euler in the eighteenth century. At its core is the use of a network of nodes and edges, which represent architectural elements and the relationships between them. For example, the simple floor plan depicted in figure 14.1a can be represented in graph-theoretic form if each room is considered a node and each wall that connects two adjacent rooms is considered an edge. Obviously, this representation leaves out much information, such as the geometry of the floor plan (e.g. the areas of the rooms, the length of the walls), as well as the locations of doors and windows and other architectural features. It does, however, support (and simplify) all sorts of analyses, such as determining the adjacency relationships between pairs of rooms. Moreover, the nodes and the edges can be labeled, which allows them to carry more information (e.g., the areas of rooms and the length of the walls).

This graph representation is, of course, not unique—many different graphs, representing different features of the floor plan, can be constructed. Steadman chose to represent horizontal walls as nodes of the graph (fig. 14.1b). Each edge in his graph represents the relationship between the two horizontal walls of the same room. The label associated with each edge designates the length of the wall (i.e., the horizontal dimension of the rectangular room). The label associated with each node designates its distance from the bottom-most wall in the floor plan.

This rather nonintuitive representation allowed Steadman to apply Kirchhoff's first law of electrical flow, which states that electricity flows

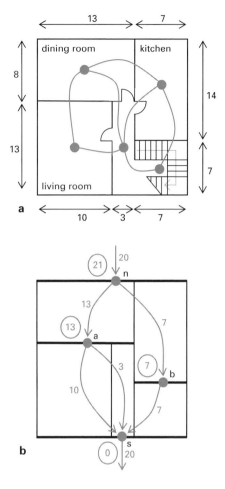

14.1 Two different graph representations of the same floor plan: (a) a conventional graph, (b) Steadman's "electrical flow" graph (after L. March and P. Steadman, *The Geometry of Environment* [Cambridge: MIT Press, 1974]).

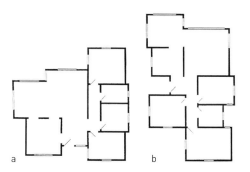

14.2 Floor plans designed by (a) the ABD system, (b) an experienced architect. (A. Schwartz et al., in *Computer-Aided Design* 26, no. 9 [1994].)

from a higher voltage node to a lower voltage node, giving the graph a directionality. Applying Kirchhoff's second law, which states that the total current entering a node is equivalent to the current leaving it, allowed Steadman to use the graph as floor plan generator: it is possible (with the help of some additional constraints, such as the minimal and maximal desired width of each room) to determine the allowable vertical location of the walls. Using a second such representation, for the vertical walls, allows the generative process to determine the vertical dimension of the rooms as well.

A different electrical-flow metaphor, based on techniques developed for the compaction of VLSI layouts, was used by Schwartz to develop his Automated Building Design (ABD) floor plan generator.[6] Very large scale integration (VLSI) is a process used for laying out electrical circuits composed of hundreds of thousands, even millions of electrical components, each represented as a rectangle. Like architectural floor plans, the rectangles of a VLSI circuit must abide by strict adjacency and size constraints. The rules governing their layout are more rigorously defined than the layout of rooms in a building, since they are derived from the laws of physics. This makes the layout of VLSI circuits more precise than architectural layouts. The large numbers of rectangles that make up a VLSI circuit has, however, required the development of automated layout algorithms.[7]

Like Steadman's method, the ABD uses two weighted and directed graphs, one for vertical walls and another for horizontal ones. In addition, it uses a set of constraints to impose design requirements that cannot be represented by the walls themselves, like the placement of doors and windows.

The algorithm uses a branch-and-bound search technique, which generates possible layouts of the floor plan and tests them for compliance with the constraints. It uses a top-down generative process, whereby only branches that comply with the constraints are further developed, curbing the potential combinatoric explosion of indiscriminate generation. The results are realistic-looking floor plans, complete with doors and windows, that are hard to distinguish from human-generated plans (fig. 14.2).

Mechanical Metaphor

Physically based modeling is a technique that applies the principles of dynamic motion and geometrical deformations to rigid and nonrigid

Synthesis

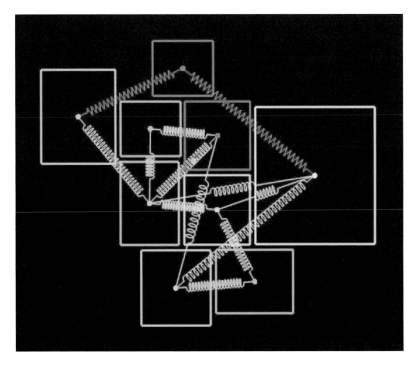

14.3 A spring-based model of the desired adjacencies acting on spaces in a floor plan. (S. A. Arvin and D. H. House, in *Automation in Construction* 11, no. 2 [2002].)

objects for the purpose of simulating realistic behaviors and visual effects.[8] The objects' dynamic behavior is simulated by calculating the forces that operate on them to determine changes in their velocities (i.e., accelerations) and position at discrete time intervals.

The technique was applied by Arvin and House to the generation of architectural floor plans that correspond to a wide range of constraints.[9] They use the analogy of mechanical springs and dampers to connect spaces (fig. 14.3). These springs draw (or repel) the spaces according to prespecified positional and adjacency relationships, expressed in terms of the length of each spring and the location of its attachment to the spaces.

Each spring consists of a mass-spring-damper system (fig. 14.4) of two point masses, m_0 and m_1, connected with a spring whose constant is k_{01}, a dashpot with damping constant d_{01}, and a predefined rest length r_{01}. The forces f_0 and f_1 that are exerted by the spring on the point masses m_0 and m_1 are proportional to the difference between the spring's current length l_{01} and its resting length r_{01} (with a proportionality coefficient k_{01}). The direction of the forces is along the line connecting the point masses.

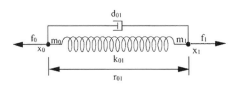

14.4 A mass-spring-damper system.

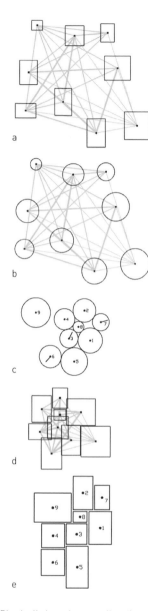

14.5 Physically based space allocation.
(S. A. Arvin and D. H. House, in *Automation in Construction* 11, no. 2 [2002].)

As the masses move farther away from each other, the spring applies an increasing force to try to move them closer, and as they move closer the spring tries to separate them. The dashpot, which is attached in parallel with the spring, acts like the hydraulic piston on a screen door closer: it dampens the motion of the masses by producing forces proportional (with proportionality constant d_{01}) to their relative velocity toward or away from each other, thus reducing the kinetic energy introduced by the spring forces.

Topological design objectives, such as the desired adjacencies between spaces, are represented as forces that operate on point nodes at the centers of the spaces. Geometrical objectives, such as the desired size and proportions of the spaces, are represented by forces operating on line nodes attached to the edges of the polygons representing the spaces.

The springs' rest lengths are set so that they specify the desired adjacencies of the spaces and their desired sizes. The spring constant k_{01} defines the strength of the adjacency requirement. It is set on a scale of –1.0 to 1.0 relative to other adjacency spring constants, where positive numbers represent attraction and negative numbers represent separation.

In addition to adjacencies and size, the representation also supports orientation objectives, such views or daylighting requirements. These are represented by forces "pulling" the designated spaces in the desired directions, using forces whose magnitude can be fixed or inversely proportional to the distance between the space and its desired location. They result in locating the affected spaces on the perimeter of the layout, or conversely, at its center.

Geometric objectives, such as sizes, proportions, alignment or offset of spaces, can be encoded in terms of forces operating on edge nodes, with the springs' rest length set to zero (in case of alignment), or fixed, nonzero in case of offset. Similarly, area and proportion objectives can be encoded by using interrelated springs, whose resting length may increase or decrease proportionally to others, or set to a prespecified magnitude (e.g., one that represents the desired area or proportion). A global "gravity" objective encourages spaces to group together without gaps.

The system first resolves the topological objectives, through a succession of steps in which individual spaces are moved in the direction of the resultant force operating on each (fig. 14.5a–d). The dynamic simulation runs until the system is in equilibrium, which is defined as the point in time when all velocities are zero. Once that state has been achieved, the system resolves the geometric objective (sizes and proportions of spaces) (fig. 14.5e). At the topological resolution phase, the spaces are simulated as circles (fig. 14.5b,c) to allow them to "slide" over each other. In the geometric resolution phase, they are represented as rectangles.

14.2 Case-Based Methods

A common approach to the synthesis of new design solutions, as discussed in section 12.6, is to start with an old solution to a similar problem and adapt it to the needs and circumstances of the current problem. Underlying this approach are the assumptions that: (1) there is a great likelihood that the current problem is not fundamentally different from a similar problem that has been encountered in the past; and (2) starting with a "whole" solution and adapting its parts to the needs of the current problem is preferable to (or at least more practicable than) trying to build up a new solution from scratch, piece by piece.

The first assumption is supported by the nature of design problems themselves, which must often respond to similar human needs (e.g., the need for a place to live, a place to work, a place to study, and so forth). Since the needs are often similar, so are their solutions. Variations are introduced through the details of a particular need (for example, the need for a "place to live" is affected by the size of the family, its habits, its socioeconomic status, and so on), its context (climatic, topographical, demographic, and otherwise), and prevailing "styles," which include both aesthetics and technological innovations.[10]

The second assumption is supported by the added information embedded in the "whole" compared to its "parts": the whole exhibits the relationships between the parts, their mutual effects on one another, and the problems and opportunities they raise and solve by being grouped together. Thus, while knowledge of the "parts" is a necessary condition for good design, it is not sufficient. One may know all that there is to know about the design of a bathroom, but this knowledge is insufficient for incorporating it into a house, as there are contextual problems to solve. Should the bathroom be connected directly to the living room or to a bedroom? Should it be located on the first floor or on the second? How will the answers to these questions change if there are two or three bathrooms in the house?

The two main difficulties associated with this approach to design synthesis are the limited range of prior solutions, or "cases," the architect may be familiar with, and the manner in which they can and ought to be modified to fit the needs of the current problem. The capacity of human memory and recall impose a (rather narrow) limit on the number of cases an architect may be familiar with. This number may be increased, somewhat, through the use of libraries and professional journals, which act as disseminators of "cases," but the fundamental restrictions cannot be avoided. The problem of recall is further exacerbated by the difficulty of matching prior solutions to the current problem. How can one be sure that the cases retrieved from memory are relevant to the current situation? How different may the case be from the current problem before it is deemed irrelevant? And, once a relevant case has been found, how—and how much—can it be modified before it loses its relevance?

Case-based reasoning (CBR), a subfield of artificial intelligence, has tried to formalize and computer-assist the use of experiential knowledge represented as "cases."[11] The added benefit of using computers over similar (manual) habitual methods is that they have vast storage capacities and enormous processing speed. A computer can store (and quickly retrieve) cases the designer is not likely to recall, either because there are too many of them or because they were generated by a different designer.

A case typically consists of a problem definition (what particular need does this case respond to?), a solution (how does the case respond to that need?), and an outcome (how well did it do so?).[12] These three components, in turn, provide the grounds for generating the index(es) that can later be used to retrieve the case. Additional information that may be associated with a case are evaluations, comments, and other information the case-storer deems pertinent and can later be used by the case-retriever to assess the efficacy of the case for a particular design situation. Storing cases, therefore, is a difficult task. It requires the ability to select pertinent cases for storage, their analysis, their proper indexing, and their representation in a manner that will facilitate their adaptation once retrieved.

The retrieval of cases, in turn, is based on comparing the attributes of the current problem (called the target) with the indexes of stored cases. Different methods can be used to affect the comparison that will return cases with different degrees of matched indexes. The simplest is by matching key words to indexes, but this approach is very sensitive to nuances in both the indexes and key words that are used during storage and retrieval, respectively (that is why librarians use only lists of agreed-upon indexes, called authority lists, to classify and index library materials). More flexible retrieval methods search the case library for ranges of values designated "allowable"—adding or subtracting a certain percentage from quantitative indexes, allowing permutations of key words, and even using index classi-fication methods similar to object-oriented programming.[13] Such imper-fect matching requires that found cases be classified according to the strength of their match. Different methods for determining the degree of match have been developed, including preferential ranking of certain attributes.

In both habitual and computer-assisted design processes, the retrieved cases are typically intended only to be a rough draft for subsequent design modifications and adaptations. Once a promising case has been found, it must be adapted to fit the needs of the current problem. In habitual meth-ods, the adaptation is left completely up to the designer. Computational case-based systems, however, attempt to assist the adaptation process. Typically, this adaptation is interactive, provided that the structure of the case allows modification (i.e., that it is possible to add, delete, or modify parts of the retrieved case). Some researchers have combined case-based reasoning with the closely related field of automated prototype adapta-tion.[14] Such systems attempt to generate parametric, even topological vari-ations of the retrieved case by combining some of its attributes with attributes derived from other similar cases. Systems like CADSYN com-prise both a case-retrieval mechanism that finds promising cases and a mutation mechanism that can be invoked to include portions of another case when the adaptation of the case fails (more about this in chapter 15).[15]

To overcome the considerable effort needed to build up a meaningful case library, the case-based design system Software Environment to sup-port Early phases in building Design (SEED)[16] accumulates cases as a "side effect" of design operations. That is, designers who use the system can designate any solution generated during the course of their work as a "case" to be stored by the system. Indexing and other storing-related oper-ations are done automatically. The SEED system is intended to computa-tionally support all aspects of preliminary building design, including problem analysis and generation of specifications, schematic layout design, and schematic configuration of design solutions (which produce three-dimensional configurations and physical building components). The cases it uses must, therefore, span a wide range of issues (e.g., from specifications of requirements pertaining to similar buildings to circulation patterns in an office building). SEED stores cases in purely syntactic terms, independent of context and thus applicable to a wide range of design abstractions.

Both indexing and retrieval are more difficult in spatial domains like architecture than in other disciplines that rely on case-based reasoning, like medicine and law. How can such notions as lines of sight, openness, path-through, and focal point be indexed? And since the likelihood of finding a relevant case depends on the skill of the searcher (in terms of specifying the correct indexes) as well as on the foresight of the person who assigned indexes to the stored cases in the first place, this difficulty is compounded: if either is too broadly defined, the retrieval will return a vast number of irrelevant cases, frustrating the searcher. If they are too narrowly defined, the search may retrieve no cases at all or leave out ones that are relevant but have been improperly indexed.

To overcome these difficulties, researchers have attempted to "soften" the indexing by using both textual and graphical analogical methods or by breaking up the monolithic "case" into components that can be indexed (hence, searched) individually.

Sketch-Based Case Retrieval

A graphical approach to "softening" both indexing and retrieval was demonstrated by Do and Gross.[17] Their Electronic Cocktail Napkin is a pen-based freehand sketching environment with trainable recognition capabilities.[18] Its purpose is to support diagramming as an interface to knowledge-based systems for engineering and architectural design in the early phases of the design process, when designers traditionally use diagrams for laying out building systems. Diagrams allow them to explore ideas and solve problems in an intuitive manner, and—if parsed correctly—they can also be used to retrieve references from case libraries. "Parsing" means associating diagrams or their parts with meaning that can be interpreted by the computer and converted into actions, including linking the diagram with other kinds of information.

Synthesis

For purposes of case retrieval, the Napkin program was linked to the ARCHIE III case-based design aid (CBDA) system, whose case base includes community libraries, courthouses, tall buildings, handicapped access, and service systems in large buildings (pipes, wires, and ducts to provide heating, ventilation, air conditioning, hot and cold water, drainage, gas, telecommunications, and electricity). ARCHIE's domain knowledge comprises case studies of previously encountered problems and their resolution in the form of stories, problems, and responses elicited through post-occupancy evaluation (POE) studies and interviews conducted with design engineers.

A building's service systems diagram comprises simple geometric constructs that abstractly represent the components and connections of pipes, ducts, boilers, and so on. For example, a rectangle can be used to represent a tank, the letter T inside a circle to represent a thermostat or a thermometer, and a line labeled with the letter G to indicate a gas line. The Electronic Cocktail Napkin system recognizes and parses these conventional symbol diagrams and converts them into the proper indexes for retrieval of relevant design cases in the ARCHIE III database. The nature of the symbols and the connections between them form the search pattern that is matched against ARCHIE's case base. The use of diagrams instead of typed keywords alleviates the need for designers to switch from drawing to text input and fits the retrieved cases naturally to the sketched problem with which the designer is presently concerned and for which the case information is needed in the first place.

Chunking Case Information

ARCHIE's story-based approach to storing previously encountered problems and their solutions allows its users to retrieve cases that match either a particular problem or a particular solution. This approach, which is loosely based on Shank and Abelson's theory of memory structures,[19] has been further developed and made into an operational case-based reasoning representational formalism by Oxman.[20]

It is based on the observation that design cases comprise rich and complex information and contain much related information that is often difficult to describe in one all-inclusive unit. Moreover, not all the information in a particular case is relevant for aiding the current design problem.

14.6 James Stirling's Staatsgalerie in Stuttgart, Germany (1984).

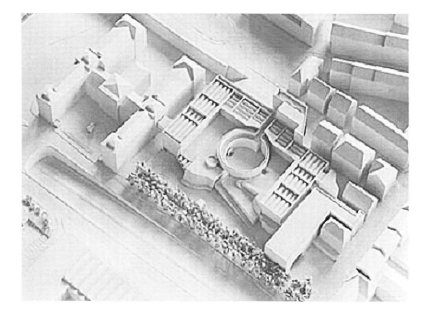

Hence, an approach that is based on "chunking" the information into smaller, independently meaningful units, was developed. Each chunk is considered a "story," which pertains to a specific aspect of the overall case. A design case, therefore, can be made of many "stories."

A typical story, for example, may describe the problem posed by the relationship between the building site and the city, like the one faced by British architect James Stirling when he designed the Staatsgalerie in Stuttgart, Germany, in 1984. The sloped site of the gallery was adjacent to a motorway that cut the old cultural area of the city in two. The program called for using the new gallery—a landmark—as the locus of an urban pass-through between the two parts of the city. Stirling thus had to solve the conflict between urban continuity and the security needs of the gallery itself. His solution was to build a circular courtyard that acted as the focal point of the museum but was open to the public, who could use it to pass through the gallery without entering it. The courtyard, which contains sculptures belonging to the gallery, provides passersby with a glimpse of the gallery, and acts as a landmark in its own right (fig. 14.6).

Oxman's approach to formalizing the information in such stories is based on using three constructs to represent the relevant components of the story: (1) a design issue; (2) a solution concept; and (3) the form used to solve it (fig. 14.7). *Design issues,* as defined by Rittel (see section 11.2), represent specific problems faced by the designer. In the case of the Staatsgalerie, one design issue was the need to maintain urban continuity. The *solution* concept represents the design idea that addresses ("solves") the problem, like Stirling's concept of passing through the gallery without entering it. The *form* represents the particular physical solution used by the architect to implement the concept, as in the Staatsgalerie's circular courtyard (the "drum").

Using these three constructs, the relevant elements that comprise a design case can be represented explicitly and, therefore, searched and retrieved independently. Since the same physical form can be the solution to more than one design issue—as the "drum" of the Staatsgalerie shows—the issue-concept-form (ICF) formalism facilitates finding it when searching both for solutions to different problems (e.g., urban continuity and the design of galleries) and for different design concepts (e.g., pass-through and focal point).

Moreover, the ICF formalism allows different cases to be cross-linked through their constituent components, thus facilitating both "softer" indexing for search purposes and "browsing"—the ability to traverse the case base by moving from one case to another, using similarity either of the issues they address, the solution concepts they use, or the physical forms they employ, thereby finding cases that might otherwise not be retrieved by a more narrow indexing mechanism.

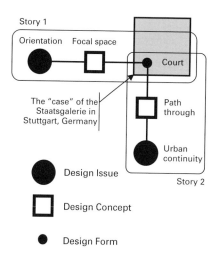

14.7 Two stories related to the Staatsgalerie represented through Oxman's issue-concept-form formalism. (R. Oxman and R. Oxman, in *Automation in Construction* 3, nos. 2–3 [1994].)

14.3 Expert Systems

Rather than attempting to capture the knowledge and expertise of past designers through their work in the form of cases, it is possible to capture it directly in the form of design rules. Habitual design rule systems are as old as Vitruvius's *De architectura* (c. 28 BC), Alberti's *De re aedificatoria* (printed 1485), Vignola's *Regola delli cinque ordini d'architettura* (1562), and Palladio's *I quattro libri dell'architettura* (1570). Their computational implementation has been the province of one of artificial intelligence's most successful applications—expert systems.

Expert systems are computational constructs designed to capture and represent the knowledge of an expert in the form of heuristic "rules of thumb"—encapsulated "chunks" of professional practices, common sense, shortcuts, insights, and other "special-case reasoning characteristic of highly experienced professionals."[21] As such, they can provide expert-level solutions to complex problems, explain why they have arrived at certain conclusions, and are capable of accommodating new knowledge.

Expert systems differ from procedural computer programs in that they use generalized rules and inference instead of hard-coded, stepwise solution procedures. As such, they cannot guarantee that they will arrive at a solution to the problem nor that the solution is necessarily correct. On the other hand, they can handle problems that are intractable by procedural methods. And, although they cannot be "proven true," they are believed to be so on the basis of the reputation of the experts whose knowledge they encapsulate.

The knowledge such systems represent differs from the "data" used in procedural programs. While "data," in its conventional sense, refers to discrete items that are ready for communication or use, and that can be interpreted in different ways, "knowledge" presumes a particular interpretation of the data. For example, the conventions that say a beam's height should be approximately a tenth of the distance it spans, or that to achieve maximal solar gain the building should be oriented ±5 degrees of due south, represent such professional knowledge: they are inexact, unproved in the mathematical sense, and represent a particular interpretation of the facts (one that other experts may disagree with).

The use of heuristic knowledge endows expert systems with more flexibility than procedural programs have, as far as handling missing information and uncertainty. They can even resolve problems arising from conflicting data, by incorporating personal (or expert-specific) preferences. On the other hand, the use of heuristic reasoning rather than procedural methods makes the conclusions reached by expert systems less reliable, to the point where some "certainty factor" must be associated with the conclusion to tell the user how reliable it is. Expert systems, therefore, cannot be "guaranteed" to find a solution to a given problem, as procedural programs can. However, if a solution exists, expert systems can typically find it much faster than procedural programs, because their heuristic reasoning can exploit shortcuts to reach conclusions rather than have to test all solutions exhaustively.

An expert system's knowledge is typically encoded as "situation-action" rules, in the form of IF-THEN couplets, each representing one characteristic of the problem or its solution. The IF part of a rule consists of some generalized condition, which—if fulfilled by the facts that pertain to the current problem—triggers the rule's THEN part, which can add to, delete, or otherwise modify the facts, and derive conclusions from them. For example:

IF there is evidence that A and B are true
THEN conclude that there is evidence that C is true

where A, B, and C are facts pertaining to the problem. The collection of all the rules is known as the system's knowledge base. Its size (number of rules) and quality (how good are the rules?) determine, to a large extent, the usefulness of the expert system. (The knowledge base of a large expert system can comprise thousands of rules.) What makes the design of expert systems particularly attractive is that, unlike procedural systems, the rules need not necessarily be consistent. This makes it possible to add rules to the knowledge base without regard to existing rules, thus expanding its capabilities as more experience with the system is gained over time.

The particular problem to which the rules are applied is represented as a collections of facts (such as A, B, and C in the above example). The application of the rules to the facts may produce new facts or change existing facts. The iterative application of the rules to the changing facts brings them closer to a state recognized by the system as a "solution" or "goal" state, at which point the iteration halts.

The applications of the rules to the facts is done by means of a control mechanism known as an "inference engine," which is akin to the logical processes used by humans to derive conclusions from given facts. It can be done in one of two ways: through deductive reasoning or through abductive reasoning.[22] In deductive reasoning (also known as "forward" reasoning), the inference engine searches for a rule whose premise contains some known fact(s). It then applies (or triggers) that rule, that is, it concludes that the facts mentioned in the action part of the rule are true and adds them to the list of known facts that pertain to the problem. The process is repeated, using the modified list of facts to identify and trigger additional rules. The iteration continues until a rule is triggered whose conclusion part instructs the system to terminate the inference process.

In abductive reasoning (also known as "backward" reasoning), the inference engine chooses a specific fact and attempts to "prove" it as a conclusion that can be derived from other known facts. It thus searches its knowledge base for a rule whose conclusion is the fact chosen to be proved and triggers that rule, that is, it asserts the facts mentioned in the premise of that rule are true and adds them to the list of known facts. The inference process is repeated, choosing the fact that was added to the list of known facts as the one to be "proved." The process continues until some other fact, known to be true, is found, thus terminating the chain of abductive reasoning.

Since expert systems are often used to put experts' knowledge at the disposal of nonexperts, the answers they provide may sometimes be puzzling. To lend credibility to their answers, expert systems are typically equipped with an explanation facility, which makes the reasoning process visible to the user. In the former examples, the user would normally only see the final result to his query (i.e., A→C or C→A). In an "explanation mode," the user will see how A and C are connected through intermediate deductive steps, which include the fact B.

Rule-based expert systems appear to suit design knowledge representation because they are highly modular. They typically encapsulate single chunks of knowledge, therefore the rules can be defined and modified individually on the basis on information observed and discovered during the design process itself and during the operation of the expert system that encodes it. And because rules communicate with one another only through the facts they read and modify, they are operationally independent—the rule base can be built incrementally. Adding or changing a rule does not impact other rules in the knowledge base.

LOOS

An example of a generative rule-based expert system is LOOS and its generalized form, abstraction-based LOOS (ABLOOS), developed by Flemming and colleagues for the design of layouts of objects under an open-ended set of constraints.[23] LOOS comprises a generator of possible floor plans and tester that evaluates them according to a user-extensible set of rules stored in the system's knowledge base. The generator accepts a layout as input and finds all possible ways to add to it a new object (e.g., a

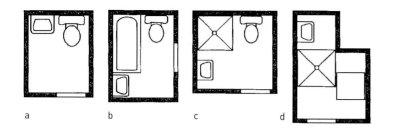

14.8 LOOS demonstrates the ability to incrementally improve the performance of an expert system by adjusting and adding rules. (U. Flemming, in *Knowledge-Based Computer-Aided Architectural Design*, ed. G. Carrara and Y. E. Kalay [Amsterdam: Elsevier, 1994].)

room, a fixture in a bathroom, and so on). The tester evaluates the layout and detects any options that fail to pass one of its "fitness" rules. A controller mediates between the two modules: after each generate-and-test cycle, it selects the next layout to be expanded from among those that passed the tester's evaluation, passes it to the generator, and so on. LOOS also demonstrates the ability to improve incrementally the system's rule base. The user can modify the fitness rules if "good" layouts fail to pass the test or if "bad" ones do. For example, figure 14.8 shows the results of checking for minimal required front clearance of sanitary appliances in a bathroom. Layout 14.8a was accepted by the clearance test, but layouts 14.8b and 14.8c, which are perfectly feasible layouts, were rejected because the system assumed that a clearance area had to have the same width as the object cleared. By modifying the clearance rule, layouts 14.8b and 14.8c were accepted, but so was layout 14.8d, which provides minimal clearances for all objects but no accessibility from the door (a fact that is never mentioned in books or lectures, because it reflects commonsense knowledge rather than expert knowledge). By generalizing the clearance rule and adding accessibility rules, such problems are easily corrected.[24]

PREDIKT

PREliminary Design of KITchens (PREDIKT) is an expert system that captures the knowledge of kitchen designers.[25] Using a knowledge base that comprises both design rules and generalized topological kitchen layouts, PREDIKT can both critique kitchen layouts designed by the user and generate (or complete) kitchen layouts on its own (fig. 14.9). In the first case, it interprets (i.e., converts) graphically represented information into "facts" that can be processed by the rules for verification purposes (e.g., to verify that the area of a window is large enough for ventilation purposes). In the

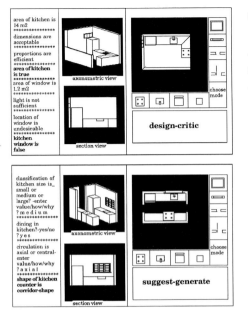

classification of
kitchen size is_
small or
medium or
large? -enter
value/how/why
? m e d i u m
****
dining in
kitchen?-yes/no
? y e s
****
circulation is
axial or central-
enter
value/how/why
? a x i a l
****
shape of kitchen
counter is
corridor-shape

axonometric view

section view

suggest-generate

choose
mode

14.9 PREDIKT is an expert system for the design
of kitchens that can operate both as a critic and as
generator of floor plans. (R. Oxman, in *Evaluating
and Predicting Design Performance*, ed. Y. E. Kalay
[New York: Wiley Interscience, 1992].)

second case, it interprets generalized instructions, such as required activities ("dine-in kitchen"), floor area ("large"), and circulation pattern ("axial") into facts that are used to retrieve a prototype schema from memory and to adapt it to the specifications. The user can interactively modify the design or generate a partial design and instruct the system to evaluate or to complete it. Given that PREDIKT is both an evaluator of given facts and generator of new ones, it operates in both deductive (forward reasoning) and abductive (backward reasoning) modes.

14.4 Shape Grammars

Case-based reasoning, and its closely allied prototype-adaptation method, are based on the notion of finding a well-known "whole" solution to an old problem and modifying its details to meet the needs of the current problem. On the other hand, rule-based methods like expert systems are based on the notion of combining well-defined elements from a "kit of parts" into new wholes. The first approach is akin to reusing a tried-and-true "formulaic" structure of a mystery novel or a Disney movie to create a new one: an evil uncle (*The Lion King*), witch (*Beauty and the Beast*), or queen (*Sleeping Beauty*) does harm to the hero or heroine, who endures the hardships and triumphs over the villain. The second approach is akin to using some effective cinematic ingredients—car chases, explosions, falling off tall buildings or cliffs—and combining them into a new plot. Neither approach is terribly original, but the reliance on proven precedents—either wholes or parts—provides a certain measure of assurance against total failure. In architecture, the first approach is demonstrated by using the image of the U.S. Capitol building as a model for designing state and city halls, endowing them with instant, recognizable "authority." The second approach is demonstrated by using Greek and Roman columns to embellish and lend a "classical" image—along with its conceptions of dignity and stability—to ordinary buildings, such as banks, private homes, and even farm houses.

The "familial" nature of the first approach—and the kit-of-parts nature of the second approach—were recognized as kinds of "languages" by researchers in the late 1970s, who formalized them into systems of rule-based geometrical constructions for designing shapes based on strict compositional rules—an approach that came to be known as the shape grammar method.[26]

A grammar is essentially a set of rules intended to codify some process or knowledge. It typically states how elementary component (e.g., words) in some language may be combined into sentences in that language. A shape grammar comprises a set of rules that can be applied consecutively to a geometrical construct for the purpose of modifying its constituent shapes (e.g., points, lines, volumes, colors) through geometrical transformations (e.g., addition, subtraction, translation, rotation, mirroring).

Much like the rules of an expert system, the rules of a shape grammar include a left-hand side (the condition) and a right-hand side (the consequence). Unlike the rules of an expert system, the rules of a shape grammar, as well as the "facts" on which they operate, are geometrical constructs—points, lines, planes, or volumes. When part of the fact shape matches the left-hand side of a rule, it can be substituted by the shape constituting the rule's right-hand side. For example, an initial shape in figure 14.10b can be transformed by applying the two rules (fig. 14.10a) to any one of the compositions depicted in figure 14.10c. The first rule allows for diagonally translating a square by half its length, the second for diagonally translating an L-shaped form by half its length. The repeated applications of these two rules produces an unlimited number of new shapes, each of which can be examined to identify parts that match one of the two rules and, consequently, be transformed into new shapes.[27]

More formally, a (parametric) shape grammar can be described by a five-tuple (S, L, T, G, I), where S is a set of shape transformation rules (in the form of $A \rightarrow B$) which specifies that whenever the shape A is found in the figure, it can be substituted by the shape B; L is a set of labels that are used to control the application of the rules; T is the set of geometric transformations (rotation, translation, scaling, reflection, or any combination of these) under which rules can be applied; G is a set of functions that assigns values to parameters in rules (e.g., the width and length of a rectangle); and I is the initial shape to which rules are applied to start the shape derivation process. Rules are applied recursively until a termination rule is activated. The shape assignment process can be summarized by the equation:

$$C_{n+1} = [C_n - t(g(A))] + t(g(B)), \ n > 0$$

where C_n is the overall shape at step n. The equation states that for a rule to apply, A (the shape in the left-hand side of the rule) must be a part of

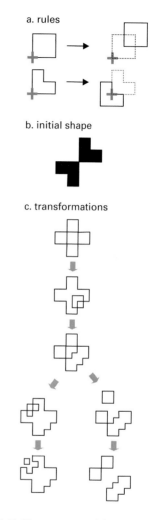

a. rules

b. initial shape

c. transformations

14.10 Shape grammar: (a) transformation rules, (b) initial shapes, (c) successive transformations. (T. Knight, in *International Journal of Design Computing* 2 [2000].)

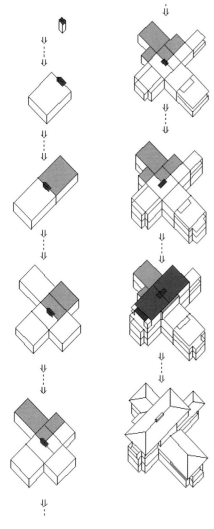

14.11 The Frank Lloyd Wright shape grammar can generate prairie-style houses. (H. Koning and J. Eizenberg, in *Environment and Planning B* 8 [1981].)

C_n, in which case it is deleted and substituted by B (the shape on the right-hand side of the rule).

Much like the sentences generated by a textual grammar, the shapes generated by a shape grammar bear some resemblance to one another, having been all generated from the same "kit of parts" using the same composition rules. Yet the variety of shapes that are generated even by a simple grammar like that depicted in figure 14.10 is derived from treating shapes as nonatomic entities: they can be freely decomposed and recomposed at the discretion of the designer. Moreover, the transformational rules (T in the five-tuple) allow substitutions to be applied to scaled, rotated, even reflected shapes, as long as they match the shape on the left-hand side of one of the rules.

Since the rules of a shape grammar encode descriptions of the shapes that belong to a particular "language," they can be used both to describe forms belonging to the corpus of shapes from which they were derived and to generate new forms that belong to the same "family." Examples of the first (descriptive) role of shape grammars can be seen in their application to analyzing and describing architectural bodies of work like Palladian villas,[28] Frank Lloyd Write prairie houses (fig. 14.11),[29] and Queen Anne houses.[30]

The purpose of using shape grammars to describe forms that belong to a particular corpus of architectural or other works is to extract the essence of the work and to uncover the rules that govern it. By doing so, we gain a measure of control over the knowledge embodied in that work, which is handy if the body of work is to be extended (e.g., for restoration or preservation purposes, as was the case with the Queen Anne houses in Pittsburgh, Pennsylvania).

The generative advantage of shape grammars over other shape synthesis methods derives from their nondeterministic nature: at every step of the process the designer can choose to apply any one of the rules to any matching part of the "fact" shape. Therefore, shape grammars allow for emergence, that is, the ability to recognize and operate on shapes that are not predefined but rather "emerge," or are formed, from any parts of shapes generated through rule applications.

Still, much like other "mechanical" generative methods, the usefulness of shape grammars for design synthesis depends heavily on recognition of "interesting" shapes, rather than on the raw power of the computer to generate them. Simply applying the rules indiscriminately has the potential for generating unlimited numbers of useless shape configurations.

Bibliography

Copland, J. *Artificial Intelligence: A Philosophical Introduction.* Oxford: Blackwell Publishers, 1993.

Gero, J. S., and R. D. Coyne. "Knowledge-Based Planning as a Design Paradigm." In *Design Theory in Computer-Aided Design,* ed. H. Yoshikawa and E. A. Warman, 289–323. Amsterdam: North Holland, 1987.

Heath, T. *Method in Architecture.* Chichester: John Wiley and Sons, 1984.

Lakoff, G., and M. Johnson. *Metaphors We Live By.* Chicago: University of Chicago Press, 1980.

Langley, P., H. A. Simon, G. L. Bradshaw, and J. M. Zytkow. *Scientific Discovery: Computational Exploration of the Creative Processes.* Cambridge: MIT Press, 1987.

Lenat, D. B., and E. E. Feigenbaum. "On the Thresholds of Knowledge." *Artificial Intelligence* 47, nos. 1–3 (1991): 185–250.

Mitchell, W. J. "Reasoning about Form and Function." In *Computability of Design,* ed. Y. E. Kalay, 89–97. New York: Wiley Interscience, 1987.

Navinchandra, D. *Exploration and Innovation in Design.* Berlin: Springer-Verlag, 1991.

Sycara, K., and D. Navinchandra. "Integrating Case-Based Reasoning and Qualitative Reasoning in Engineering Design." In *Artificial Intelligence in Design,* ed. J. S. Gero, 231–250. Heidelberg: Springer-Verlag, 1989.

Evolutionary Methods 15

The methods that were discussed in the preceding chapters are based on the principle of imparting to the computer methods and practices that were first developed by and for human designers, or gleaned from human experience. While effective, these methods are inherently limited by the human condition: they were developed through human-centered socio-cultural practices and customs and made to fit human processing capabilities. The (relatively) small adaptations made to them to take advantage of enhanced processing and storage capabilities offered by computers do not fundamentally change these methods.

The question then rises, could computational design synthesis methods be developed that are free from the shortcomings (and benefits) of human experience? Would they yield novel, "creative" design solutions?

The answer to the first question is yes, for it is possible to develop design synthesis methods that are based on first principles rather than encapsulated practices and experiences in one form or another. These methods can generate forms that were not embedded in them by their programmers, either explicitly or through procedures and rules. The answer to the second question, however, is less certain: it depends on what we consider a "novel," or "creative" solution.

15.1 Creative Design

A design solution is called creative when it exhibits some unexpected characteristics that we have not seen before, in terms of its form, the way it responds to a particular functional problem, or the way it addresses the context in which it is embedded. According to this definition, the source of the solution is of no consequence: it can derive from human ingenuity or the clever programming of a computer. A more strict definition of creative design insists that solutions be the result of processes or methods in which neither the knowledge sources, nor the solution generating strategies, are known in advance.[1]

15.1 *Meeting on Gauguin's Beach*, 1988—a painting produced by Aaron, a computer program written in LISP (oil on canvas, 90 x 68 inches). (Collection of Gordon and Gwen Bell. Photograph copyright Becky Cohen.) (See color plate 11.)

These definitions can be illustrated by the following examples, which demonstrate computer-generated art and elephant-generated art.

Computer-Generated Art

Aaron is a computer program, the brainchild of the British painter Harold Cohen, that produces abstract paintings (fig. 15.1).[2] It produces several images in its memory every night, from which Cohen selects one. For five to six hours during the next day Aaron makes line drawings, mixes colors, executes painting strokes, and even cleans the brushes and paint cups.

Started in 1968, Aaron evolved from a FORTRAN program containing rules about generating simple shapes into its current version, written in LISP, which creates figurative drawings of objects that observers can recognize as people, rocks, and plants. It draws autonomously, relying on rules and feedback paths. Aaron is not a procedural image generator; nor is it a tool for painters to be used as a medium to express the creative ideas of a human artist. Instead, it is a computer program with a software interface to a hardware drawing device that creates original paintings, each different from the next and indistinguishable by the (uninformed) observer from the work of a human artist. Since 1974 Aaron's systems and artworks have been exhibited worldwide and have been auctioned on the Internet.[3]

Elephant-Generated Art

Ruby, an elephant from the Phoenix Zoo, produced works of art since the 1980s that, at one time, generated more than $100,000 a year. Moscow-born, New York-based artists Vitaly Komar and Alexander Melamid seized upon the idea to initiate the Asian Elephant Art and Conservation Project (AEACP), which aims to raise funds for the rescue of Thai, Indian, and Indonesian elephants who became "unemployed" when Thailand banned logging in 1990. Since 1998, their elephants have been given paintbrushes and canvas and taught to produce works of art that have been included in the 1999 Venice Biennale and, in 2000, auctioned at Christie's for thousands of dollars, generating funds to provide proper care for the elephants and support for their trainers (fig. 15.2).

Besides displaying clearly distinct regional and individual styles, the elephants' paintings are said to closely resemble the expansive gestural

Synthesis

work of such abstract expressionist artists as Jackson Pollock, Willem de Kooning, and Franz Kline.[4]

What Is Creative Work?

Clearly, both examples open the debate on whether artistic activity is an inquiry into the nature of art itself and whether intentionality matters, not to mention the question of what art is and what role art institutions play in defining it.

15.2 *KM16*—a painting by Wanalee, an Asian elephant (acrylic on paper, 30 x 22 inches). (Copyright State of the Arts, Palo Alto, California.) (See color plate 12.)

These questions, however, are more appropriately dealt with in the context of theories of creativity—of the kind that concern psychologists and cognitive scientists.[5] This book does not attempt to explain the cognitive process itself. Rather, our interest here is in computational processes and whether computational design synthesis can produce creative solutions. It is somewhat akin to the famous Turing test: all we ask is that the results, obtained by whatever means, pass some test of "creativity."[6] Hence, the questions that need to be answered are: (1) how can computational (and other) methods produce results that will be considered creative in their own right; and (2) how will we recognize the results as such?

In both Aaron's and the Asian elephants' cases, the generative processes were capable of—and apparently did—produce results that were deemed creative by their respective audiences—one through clever programming, the other through the actions of a trained animal. However, the *recognition* of the results as creative works of art required human evaluation: in Aaron's case, initially by the program's creator; in the elephants' case, by their human trainers and patrons.

Can procedural generate-and-test methods like space allocation, and heuristic methods like case-based reasoning and expert systems produce creative solutions—ones that we did not expect, even though the processes they use are well known and predictable? If we apply the criterion of unexpectedness to the results, then the answer is a qualified yes. They can, occasionally, produce unexpected results thanks to the large number of solutions they generate or search, which is too vast for any one designer to imagine. Hence, such methods may occasionally produce a solution that strikes us as novel, or creative.

However, while they may be unexpected, such solutions are rather predictable. After all, the rules used by such systems encode a great deal of

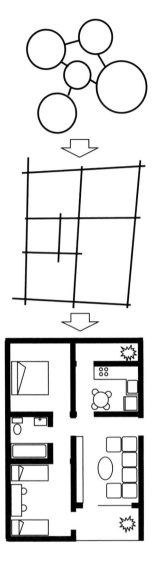

15.3 Architectural elements "emerge" as the design synthesis process progresses.

human problem-solving expertise, or even complete, human-generated solutions. The "unexpectedness" may be in producing a particular solution from among all possible (and expected) solutions.

To qualify as truly creative, or unexpected, we must turn to computational methods that reason from first principles, especially physical causality and biological evolution, and generate innovative solutions without trying to mimic human creativity (as analogical methods do) or embody preprocessed knowledge (as expert systems and shape grammars do).

Reasoning from first principles disregards both the processes employed by human designers and the solutions produced by them. And although they often adopt some form of incremental generate-and-test mechanism, the two components are totally independent of each other and rely on totally different principles.[7] As such, they are able to both generate and recognize configurations that where not evident to begin with. This property is called emergence.

15.2 Emergence

The synthesis of architectural design solutions can be carried out in two different ways. It can start with a set of predefined architectural components (rooms, walls, columns, and so on), which are assembled into meaningful structures that conform to the "fitness" criteria of form, function, and contextual appropriateness. Or it can proceed in a more "intuitive" way, where the definition of the components "emerges" during the problem exploration process (as described in earlier chapters).

The first approach is common to computational systems that rely on well-formed structures of elementary components and equally well formed procedures for assembling them (e.g., drafting systems, modeling system, and product modeling systems, as discussed in section 8.5). The meaning is embedded in the components and the assembly procedures rather than the overall structures themselves, which is why computers have had a difficult time assessing the essence of whole design compositions.

Architects, on the other hand, often work the other way around. They create whole structures then identify within them parts and assemblies of parts to which they assign meaning. Figure 15.3 demonstrates this process. The design synthesis begins by sketching abstract "bubbles" and lines, which represent the rough arrangement (and sizes) of spaces and the connections between them. It progresses by "squaring" the bubbles and adding more lines, representing the strengthening commitment to assigning to them the meanings of "rooms" and "walls." The sketch transforms from a representation of spaces to one that represents walls. In the third step, walls and openings represent explicit commitments to sizes and locations, informed through additional constructs that represent furnishings. This is the essence of sketching, or "thinking with diagrams"—a process where the architect "lets his/her hand do the thinking."[8] Sketching is done within the context of a specific problem and is, therefore, directed toward solving it. But the specific solution—which lines represent walls, which ones represent spaces, and which ones represent some other element or quality of the solution—is not fixed to begin with. Rather, it emerges as the process unfolds.[9]

It has been argued that such emergence of form and meaning from an otherwise unstructured (or differently structured) representation is the essence of creative design. It provides the designer with a visual feedback and a reinforcing mechanism to recognize and understand the possibilities and implications of the evolving design, hence a basis for its further development and evolution into a complete design solution.[10]

The process of emergence is both perceptual and cognitive: the designer must first perceive the conditions that allow for the interpretation of lines as boundaries of spaces or as walls then assign to them meanings as needed. The first modality of the process is syntactical: it is based on "seeing," or picturing, what was not explicitly or intentionally drawn (what Goldschmidt calls "seeing as").[11] The second is an interpretive, "imagining" process, of understanding what the perceived figure does or might stand for (what Goldschmidt calls "seeing that").[12] The two modalities are distinct but not separable. There is a kind of dialog between seeing and imagining; the two feed and reinforce each other.

The notion of emergence is common to architects but alien to computational systems that are based on structured data. Therefore, two problems arise when we come to formalize the process of emergence in a computational method: how to generate unexpected, "novel" forms to begin with; and how to recognize "interesting" or meaningful shapes once they have emerged.

One of the most promising answers to the first problem has been proposed through a technique known as genetic programming. And an answer to the second problem has been suggested through a technique known as neural networking.

15.3 Genetic Algorithms

Methods that are capable of generating novel yet appropriate solution are, necessarily, based on first principles for the purpose of generation and on testing their fitness for validation. Fitness, as defined earlier, is a condition of harmony where each of the three main constituents (form, function, and context) supports and enhances the others—or at least it does not interfere with or contradict them.

Noncontradictory, harmonious conditions are evident in natural physical and biological systems when they are characterized as being in "equilibrium"—the condition when forces are balanced, temperatures are at a steady state, and flora and fauna live in ecologically sustainable harmony.

Possibly the best-known mechanism for creating novel solutions that are, nonetheless, appropriate in terms of fitness between form, function, and context is evolution: the Darwinian process of generating a large number of random "solutions," ruthlessly discarding those deemed "unfit," and replenishing the pool of candidate solutions by copying and modifying the survivors, until—over a large number of intermittent but persistent cycles—one or more solutions exhibit a greater degree of fit, internally (between form and function) and/or externally (with their context). The fit is never quite optimal (unless the problem is trivial), and the degree of adaptation is controlled through the number of candidate solutions and the number of generations that adapt it.

Evolutionary processes have proved their ability to generate surprisingly novel solutions, as evidenced by the enormous proliferation of living organisms. The only major drawback is the length of time it takes to complete each cycle ("generation") and evolve a fitting solution.

Computer-simulated evolutionary processes—called genetic algorithms (GAs)—are similarly based on the idea of survival of the fittest. GAs consist of a population of solutions, called phenotypes, which are represented by their genetic code, or genotypes. A so-called fitness function (whose nature depends on the problem) is used to select the fittest phenotypes from within the population of candidate solutions. Their corresponding genotypes are used to create new, and conceivably better, populations of solutions, through mating and mutation. The genotypes that correspond to solutions that have not been selected are discarded. GAs do not suffer from the shortcoming of their biological namesakes—the enormous speed of digital systems can process thousands, even millions of generations in a relatively short time. The results of these nonhuman generative methods can, sometimes, be surprising, i.e., "creative."

Genetic algorithms belong to the class of stochastic search methods that find solutions to problems by randomly sampling within a solution space. Unlike other stochastic search methods (e.g., hill climbing), GAs are nondeterministic. Moreover, since they operate on large populations of solutions rather than a single candidate solution at a time, they are inherently parallel, and their likelihood of finding an acceptable solution is greater than other methods that are susceptible to getting "stuck" in a local optimum.

Chromosomes and Genes

To use a genetic algorithm, both the genotypes and the phenotypes must be encoded in a structure that can be stored and manipulated. Nature uses the DNA molecule as the encoding structure for genotypes. Formed like a double helix (fig. 15.4), it consists of four chemical bases (adenine, thiamine, guanine, and cytosine) that form interlocking pairs (A-T, G-C). Sequences of hundreds of thousands of base pairs along the DNA molecule comprise chemical "control" units, called genes. About six feet of this molecule, made of hundreds of thousands of genes each, are packed into a structure called the chromosome. Forty-six chromosomes, arranged in twenty-three pairs, encode the entire genetic information about a human being and reside in the nucleus of each one of its 100 trillion or so cells (except in red blood cells). The specific composition of each gene determines, through the proteins it controls, the traits (such as the color of the eyes) of the "phenotype"—the individual human who carries it in his or her cells.

Synthetic genetic algorithms closely resemble the natural model. "Chromosomes" are represented as string structures made of "genes" (fig. 15.5). The "body features" that each gene controls are represented by the parameters of the solutions to the problem which the particular GA solves.

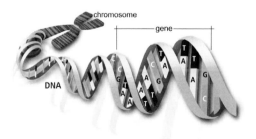

15.4 The double-helix DNA molecule is made of hundreds of thousands chemical bases that form sequences known as genes, which control the features of the body. (Courtesy of U.S. Department of Energy Human Genome Program.)

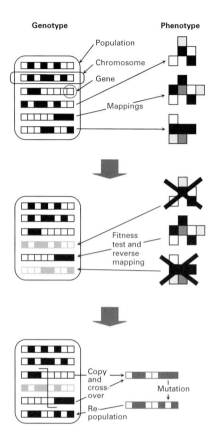

15.5 Genetic algorithms (GAs) use two closely linked representations—the genotype and the phenotype—to model biological-like evolutionary processes. (J. S. Gero and V. Kazakov, in *Advances in Formal Design Methods for CAD*, ed. J. S. Gero [London: Chapman and Hall, 1996].)

More formally, a standard GA problem is represented by means of two separate but related structures. The first structure, *G*, corresponds to the genome (the chromosomes and the genes—the "control" part). The second structure, *P*, corresponds to the phenome (the body features—the "controlled" part). *G* comprises ordered character strings, $g = \{e_1, e_2, \ldots, e_n\}$, whose components e_i are drawn from some fixed finite alphabet *A*. For simplicity, it can be assumed that all genotypes have the same length *n*. *S* comprises the set of solutions that are controlled by genotypes. Each solution *s* is defined by an (unordered) set of parameters $s = \{p_1, p_2, \ldots, p_n\}$, whose components p_i correspond to features of the solution (the phenotype). Each genotype corresponds to a unique phenotype, through a mapping $M: g \leftrightarrow p$, which is given a priori and is fixed.[13]

Selection, Crossover, and Mutation

In nature, when two individuals mate, each parent passes half their paired chromosomes onto their common offspring. The chromosomes combine to form new pairs, which leads to a unique new individual with traits inherited from both parents. GAs employ three operators for manipulating the representation of genotypes to mimic the natural process—*selection, crossover,* and *mutation.*

The selection operator rates phenotypes by means of a fitness function $F(p)$, which measures how well each solution p_i meets some predefined criteria. Subsequently, genotypes g_i are selected for survival based on the ratings of their corresponding phenotypes p_i. The number of surviving phenotypes (and their corresponding genotypes) in any population can be determined a priori or by the threshold of the fitness function. Either way, those genotypes whose corresponding phenotypes did not survive the selection process are deleted, and the population is "built up" to its original size by "mating" the survivors.

The crossover operator *C* generates new genotypes from parts of the character strings of two mating genotypes: $C(g_1, g_2) \rightarrow gc$. It does so by taking parts of g_1 and g_2 and concatenating them into one new genotype g_c of equal length to the original ones. The "cut" point in the character strings of each of the contributing genotypes is the same and is selected at random. The primary purpose of the crossover operator is to get "genetic material" from the previous generation to the next generation.

The mutation operator introduces additional changes into the resulting genotype, by randomly changing one (or more) of its characters e_i. As in nature, a high rate of mutation can lead to disastrous results. Hence, the rate is kept low.

These three operations are applied repeatedly to a population of genotypes and their corresponding phenotypes. Thus, at each cycle a new population is formed, where each genotype represents (controls) the parameters of one phenotype (solution). The process repeats itself, and the dynamically evolving population of genotypes (and their corresponding phenotypes) runs through a predetermined number of iterations.

Since every new generation of genotypes is made of the "best" ones of the previous generation, the traits that make them the "fittest" survive and are passed on from generation to generation, whereas traits that contributed to making less fit phenotypes disappear. The random mutations that are introduced each time a new genotype is created not only keep the population from stagnating but also add a measure of innovation, which can result in the "emergence" of new features in the corresponding solutions.

Applications

The (basic) genetic algorithm is thus rather simple, yet it performs well on many different types of problems. Genetic algorithms have been applied to a variety of problems, including criminal suspect recognitions, music composition, scheduling problems, game playing, structural optimization, aircraft design, and more.

In architectural design, the innovative abilities of GAs have been demonstrated in part through their application to art and to the generation of floor plans. These applications tend to combine GAs and shape grammars, the former as the control mechanism of the latter. For example, a large subset of Mondrian's paintings can be described by recursive rectangle divisions. These divisions can be mapped into a genotype, whose "genes" correspond to a set of values that represent the position and direction of the division, the color of one of the resulting rectangles, and the thickness of the separating line (fig. 15.6). A fitness test evaluates how close these values are to an "ideal" Mondrian painting, in terms of the described parameters, completeness, and absence of additional divisions.[14]

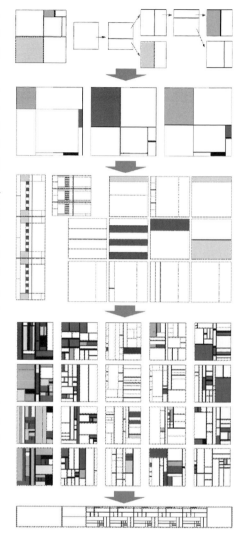

15.6 "Flondrian"—the combination of a GA that can generate Mondrian-like patterns and a GA that can generate Frank Lloyd Wright-like window patterns. (T. Schnier and J. S. Gero, "From Mondrian to Frank Lloyd Wright: Transforming Evolving Representations," Key Center for Design Computing, University of Sydney, 1997.) (See color plate 13.)

The ability of such GAs to innovate has been demonstrated by combining the Mondrian GA with a Frank Lloyd Wright GA to generate FLW-like windows. "Genes" from both GAs were combined (with some measures to assure that they would not be diluted by the crossover and mutation operators) to generate "Flondrian" windows (fig. 15.6). Similar approaches have been used by Jagielski and Gero and by Gero and Kazakov to generate hospital floor plans that compare favorably—in terms of "innovation"—to similar space-allocation-based methods.[15]

Advantages and Drawbacks

Based on self-guidance, self-repair, and reproduction, biological systems are known for their remarkable robustness and flexibility. Genetic algorithms, which are modeled closely on the biological system, enjoy similar traits: they have been proved robust, flexible, and efficient in many fields. In particular, they have demonstrated their ability to search large, "noisy" spaces, with a multitude of local peaks and valleys that stump more traditional search methods. GAs do not assume that the problem space being searched is continuous or monotonic in nature (i.e., that derivatives of the function representing the problem space exist and that they are unidirectional). As such, GAs are not likely to get "stuck" in local optima. By searching a population of solutions, rather than testing one at a time, GAs are inherently parallel and thus increase their chances of finding an optimal solution, especially in noisy spaces littered with local optimum points.

Still, GAs have shortcomings as well. For one, they are sensitive to dependencies between multiple genes in a chromosome—a condition known as epistasis. A genetic representation with high epistasis may have many genes whose phenotypic effect relies to a large degree on the values of other genes. For example, the same shape rule in a rule-based representation may have very different phenotypic effects, depending on which other shape rules precede and succeed it. Conversely, a representation with low epistasis has few or no genes whose phenotypic effect relies on the effects of other genes. With high degree of epistasis, where many genes are linked to other genes, any attempt to improve just one small area of the solution would result in changes to the rest of the solution, making evolution to acceptable designs very difficult, if not impossible. On the other hand, systems with low epistasis (where the effects of genes are largely independent of each other) are well suited for evolving small-scale details, but the evolution of large-scale characteristics, which depend on "wholesale" changes, becomes very difficult.

Another problem dogging GAs is dealing with constraints: constraints, which are ubiquitous in design problems, can limit the effectiveness of evolutionary search by blocking off useful areas of the search space. Alternatively, if the constraints are too relaxed, there can be no guarantee that all the solution will meet the expectations of the problem.

While these two problems derive from the nature of the genetic algorithm itself, most other weaknesses of GAs are associated with their fitness function: it is inherently difficult to develop a comprehensive, sensitive, yet opportunistic function that can discriminate "good" from "bad" solutions yet encourage "experimentation." For example, the relative coarseness of artificial fitness functions, unlike natural selection, makes it difficult for GAs to evolve designs with interdependent parts.[16] Likewise, GAs have a tendency to evolve structural solutions first, rather than details, because the higher payoff of structural improvements has considerably more impact on the survivability of designs. In some instances evolution may prematurely converge on an inappropriate structure, which is hard, if not impossible, to overcome by the evolution of details.

Hence, finding better ways to judge the fitness of solutions has been a major research topic in the design of genetic algorithms.[17]

15.4 Neural Networks

One of the solutions to the problem of recognizing promising, if not altogether innovative solutions, has been found in a computational construct called artificial neural networks (ANNs).[18] As described in section 2.2, neural networks are derived from the cognitive theory of connectionism, which argues for processing information as patterns, by means of networking many independent small signal processors, rather than by executing explicit instructions one at a time (or even many at a time). It is their pattern recognition abilities that make ANNs suitable for the task of recognizing innovative design solutions.

ANNs are based on an information-processing paradigm inspired by the way the densely interconnected, parallel structure of the human brain

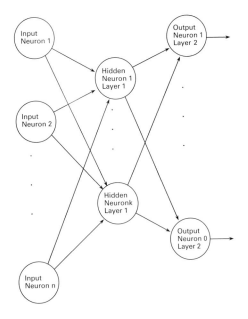

15.7 The general structure of an artificial neural network. (D. B. Fogel, *BLONDIE24: Playing at the Edge of AI* [San Francisco: Morgan Kaufmann, 2002].)

processes information. ANNs emulate some of the information-processing and adaptive-learning processes observed in biological nervous systems. They are composed of a large number of highly interconnected processing elements, called threshold logic units (TLUs), which are analogous to neurons and are tied together with weighted connections analogous to synapses. As described in section 2.2, ANNs operate on the all-or-nothing principle. The signals a_j that appear at TLU_i input nodes are multiplied by some weights w_j, indicating the strength of each signal. If this value exceeds TLU_i threshold of activation b_i, the output signal equals 1, else it equals 0. The signals are summed up according to some activation function to produce an overall unit activation value a_i (which is often modulated to avoid sharp "jumps" in the TLU's activation, using a Gaussian or another statistical distribution function).

The TLU's output signal is picked up by other TLUs it is connected to, where the process is repeated. Thus, the only "processing" that occurs within the TLU is filtering: either the signals picked up are allowed to proceed, or they are blocked. The signals themselves have no meaning. The determination to transmit a signal (called "firing") or not is made by the weights each TLU assigns to incoming signals and its threshold of activation.

A typical ANN consists of three layers of TLUs: an *input* layer, an *output* layer (which may consist of only one TLU), and one or more *hidden* layers (fig. 15.7). It is the hidden layers where the learned "knowledge" of the system is stored (i.e., the adjusted weights of the connections). One hidden layer often suffices for most applications. Two-layer architectures are more powerful than single-layer architectures and can be shown to be able to learn any pattern recognition mapping.[19]

Learning in biological systems involves adjustments to the synaptic connections that exist between the neurons. This is true of ANNs as well: learning typically occurs by "training" the system through examples of paired sets of input/output data where the training algorithm iteratively adjusts the weights between the connections. Thus, although the structure of the network as a whole is fixed, the weights each TLU associates with incoming signals from its neighboring TLUs and the threshold of its own activation are variable. By setting the weights and threshold of each TLU to respond to one set of signals but not to another, the network as a whole performs *signal* or *pattern* recognition.

The network can be trained to recognize patterns by trial and error. During a training session, the network is presented with input/outputs pairs, and put in a mode where it can modify the weights and the thresholds of its TLUs until the desired output matches the given input. Once that state is achieved, the weights and the thresholds are locked, and the network is ready to process new patterns. If a new pattern triggers input signals that will filter through the network as trained, it will be "recognized," otherwise the pattern will go unrecognized.

Such programming by training avoids the need to explicitly spell out the parameters of recognition, which is equivalent to the fitness function in the case of genetic algorithms. This is especially useful when the sought pattern is difficult to explicate, as is the case in recognizing innovative designs. Instead, the neural network could be shown examples of designs we would consider "innovative," and be expected to infer from these examples what we mean by innovative design or similar nonquantifiable characteristics of a building. Needless to say, the network does not "understand" what it does. Nor does it understand the concept of creativity or anything else for that matter: it simply applies the pattern recognition it has been trained to perform, matching an output pattern to some input. Any interpretation regarding the "meaning" of the match is purely artificial.

It is even possible to develop ANNs that can learn on their own, without the guidance of an instructor. Such ANNs essentially perform clustering of the data into similar groups, based on measured attributes or features that serve as inputs. One such system, called BLONDIE24, trained itself how to play championship-level checkers, being told only how many of every five games it played "won" or "lost" the match.[20]

ANNs were first introduced in the late 1950s, but only in the mid-1980s have their algorithms become sophisticated enough for general applications. Today ANNs are being applied to an increasing number of real-world problems of considerable complexity, such as speech, character and signal recognition, as well as functional prediction and system modeling where the physical processes are not well understood or are highly complex, such as trading commodities on the stock market. They are particularly good at solving problems that are too complex for conventional technologies (e.g., problems that do not have an algorithmic solution or for which an algorithmic solution is too complex to be found).

One such application, called Parallel Distributed Processing Analogical Architectural Modeler (PDP-AAM), was developed by the late Ivan Petrovic and his associate Igor Svetle, of the IMS Institute in Belgrade, Yugoslavia. It was intended to support the design of single-family houses built from the prefabricated, catalogued components of the GIMS building system. The GIMS system was developed by the Yugoslav government to address its need for mass housing. Like many similar building systems, GIMS provide both structural and architectural solutions. Unlike other prefabricated housing systems, the GIMS system has no premade building plans or types: a new solution is designed to match each new design problem.

Since the GIMS system is intended to provide semi-custom houses, it is characterized by two-stage design process. First, when the user is unknown, a prototype design comprising an assembly of the building structure and the roof is developed. Second, when the user is known and involved in the design process, specific building components from the catalog are instantiated and the design is finished. Thus, although mass-produced, the GIMS system offers semi-custom-built houses to individual customers.

The GIMS system allows construction of structural spans between 3.0 and 7.20 m in two directions. However, experience has shown that most designers using the system prefer the standard span of 4.20 x 4.20 m, which is technically the most economical solution. Moreover, study of modest-income housing built around Belgrade in recent years led designers of the GIMS system to adopt a standard, 3 x 3 modular grid for their houses, all of which have two floors, a sloped roof, and a minimum of five built-space modules on both floors.

Several computer programs were developed to facilitate the first phase of the GIMS design process, including GIMS-EXPERT (an expert system), GIMS-DDS (a distributed design system), and PDP-AAM (a neural network system).[21]

PDP-AAM is a back-propagation ANN, which uses a 3D viewer and a semantic differential matrix as the means to affect the subjective assessment of a GIMS-type building.[22] After suitable learning from examples, PDP-AAM works in two ways: it can produce a semantic differential for

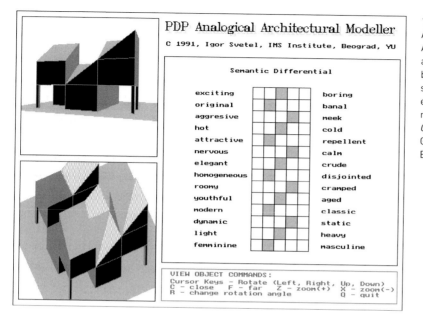

PDP Analogical Architectural Modeller

C 1991, Igor Svetel, IMS Institute, Beograd, YU

Semantic Differential

exciting						boring
original						banal
aggresive						meek
hot						cold
attractive						repellent
nervous						calm
elegant						crude
homogeneous						disjointed
roomy						cramped
youthful						aged
modern						classic
dynamic						static
light						heavy
feminine						masculine

VIEW OBJECT COMMANDS :
Cursor Keys - Rotate (Left, Right, Up, Down)
C - close   F - far   Z - zoom(+)   X - zoom(-)
R - change rotation angle   Q - quit

15.8 Parallel Distributed Processing Analogical Architectural Modeler (PDP-AAM) is a neural network that can evaluate and produce spatial configurations of buildings in the GIMS system that correspond to a list of semantic attributes, listed in the form of a semantic differential matrix. (I. Petrovic, in *Knowledge-Based Computer-Aided Architectural Design*, ed. G. Carrara and Y. E. Kalay [Amsterdam: Elsevier, 1994].)

an unknown GIMS building form (fig. 15.8); and it can produce a new GIMS building form from a given semantic differential. The interaction with the system is done through a simple 3D viewer and allows the user to specify (or inspect) the building's foot print and roofs.

The system has been used to assess a client's preferences and to observe his or her reaction to GIMS building forms generated by the ANN that reflect those preferences. The system can be trained with as little as ten examples. The more examples used, the more predictable the response. Even so, the system is not likely to repeat the training samples when put in design generation mode. Rather, it would come up with "new" forms. While the creativity of the PDP-AAM system is a matter of opinion, its designs conform to the preferences indicated by its semantic differential matrix.

Of particular interest in this context of creative design is the possibility of combining genetic algorithms with neural networks—the first being good at generating unexpected solutions, the second at evaluating solutions in nonprocedural ways. Thus, each method would complement the other.

Such a combination is at the core of systems like BLONDIE24, which uses a genetic algorithm to evolve the neural nets themselves that can evaluate the status of a given board of checkers. When combined with a move generator, BLONDIE24's evolved neural network provides the necessary evaluative power to choose from among alternative possible moves. The intent of this system was not to develop the best checkers-playing computer system but rather to discover if a combined GA-ANN process could learn how to play the game and do so on its own (i.e., without imparting to it human checker-playing expertise). Along the way, it was observed that some of the more successful moves generated by BLONDIE24 could be considered "original," ones that a human player would not have chosen in similar circumstances.

It might be difficult to imagine the need for a computational design system that could generate "creative" design solutions—the "sacred" province and "protected core" of human designers.[23] It is, however, a legitimate goal for a design system that is meant to assist humans by coming up with possibilities they may not have thought of themselves. Nor is the manner in which the solution was generated of practical importance. It can be the result of carefully considered procedural methods or carefully encapsulated design rules or practices. It can come from a search of extensively archived prior design solutions or be generated by evolutionary processes modeled on some natural phenomena. What matters is that computers can generate design solutions, some of which might be considered sufficiently "innovative" that, had they been generated by a human, they would garner the praise reserved for an artist.

Bibliography

Coyne, R. D. "Creativity as Commonplace." *Design Studies* 18, no. 2 (1997): 135–141.

Coyne, R. D. "Tools for Exploring Associative Reasoning in Design." In *The Electronic Design Studio,* ed. M. McCulloch, W. J. Mitchell, and P. Purcell. Cambridge: MIT Press, 1990.

Coyne, R. D., M. A. Rosenman, A. D. Radford, M. Balachandran, and J. S. Gero. *Knowledge-Based Design Systems.* Reading, Mass.: Addison-Wesley, 1990.

Gero, J. S., and M. L. Maher. "Mutation and Analogy to Support Creativity in Computer-Aided Design." In *Computer Aided Architectural Design Futures '91,* ed. G. N. Schmitt, 241–249. Wiesbaden, Germany: Vieweg Verlag, 1992.

Gero, J. S., and M. Yan. "Shape Emergence by Symbolic Reasoning." *Environment and Planning B* 21 (1994): 191–212.

Stiny, G. "Emergence and Continuity in Shape Grammars." In *Computer Aided Architectural Design Futures '93,* ed. U. Flemming and S. van Wyk, 37–54. Amsterdam: Elsevier, 1993.

Evaluation IV

Evaluation, in the context of architectural design, is a term that has many meanings and is, therefore, subject to many interpretations. To some, evaluation means measuring the performance of the buildings themselves (emphasizing technical aspects), to others it has to do with measuring the performance of the people who use them (emphasizing social and behavioral aspects) or measuring the effectiveness of the design process itself (emphasizing cognitive and psychological aspects).[1] Interpretations of evaluation range from retrospective diagnosis (in the sense of post-occupancy evaluation of completed projects)[2] to predictive assessment, aimed at choosing a course of action that will yield the most beneficial results.[3] Generally, evaluation can be considered the measure of how well a given or proposed design solution fits the set of goals it is intended to meet.[4] In the context of this book, we shall only consider evaluation as part of the design process, that is, as a predictive assessment of the expected performances of design solutions.

Evaluation is a direct consequence and derivative of the uncertainty that is inherent to the process of design. Since there are no formulae or procedures that can be followed by designers that would guarantee that a given design solution will meet the goals and expectations of the project, design is necessarily a process of trial and error—solutions are synthesized, and their expected performances are predicted and judged by comparing them to the project's goals and constraints.

Evaluation is the process that performs such predictions and comparisons and determines if the solutions meet the goals and abide by the constraints. If they do—the search for a solution is over. If not, evaluation can provide information on what can be done to improve the fit by modifying either the solutions, the goals, or both. Since the fit is never perfect—there are always desires, expressed as goals, which go unfulfilled and features of the solution that have not been accounted for by the goals—the primary purpose of evaluation in the context of design is to determine if the solution is adequate (as defined by the stakeholders).

The process of evaluation is complicated by four main factors. First, the representation of the solutions is typically given in physical terms, such as geometry and materials. On the other hand, the goals to be met are typically stated in functional terms—level of comfort, desirable views, resistance to earthquakes, and so forth. Hence, to evaluate the fit between the expected performances of a proposed solution and the specified goals, a translation between the physical representation of the solution and the functional representation of the goals must occur.

For example, to evaluate the functionality of a proposed office building, it is necessary to predict the psychological effects of the layout, the materials, the lighting scheme, and other physical components of the building on the physical and mental disposition of the intended users. This prediction can be used to deduce how well the office worker will function, how much the visitors to the building will be impressed by its appearance, and what the environmental effects of the building on the prospective urban site will be.

The derivation of functional assessments from the building's physical representation is error-prone, because it relies on assumptions and generalizations about the effects of the physical environment on the behavior of people, which is complicated by considerations such as memory, prior experiences, and capacity for learning, in addition to being context- and time-dependent. Similar translations must be made for the other attributes being evaluated, each with its own set of predictions and assumptions.

The second factor that complicates the evaluation of complex artifacts such as buildings is the multitude of goals and constraints they must achieve and abide by (e.g., budget, aesthetics, functionality, environmental impact, contextuality, and so forth). Inevitably the goals will compete with one another. At worst, they may be in direct conflict with each other. The designer must, therefore, choose among competing needs. Selecting the "right" set of compromises is a matter of judgment—what appears to be "good" from one point of view may not appear so from another. This is due to the different belief structures of the parties involved in the design process. Architects, for example, may consider the aesthetics of the building more important than engineers do; construction managers may consider the building process more important than the finished product; and the clients often consider its functionality most important.

The third complicating factor is the need for expert knowledge in a wide range of areas. Such expertise can no longer be possessed by a single individual but must reside within a large number of often dispersed experts. Evaluation, therefore, relies heavily on communication among experts. Yet these experts do not always have all the facts they require to make their assessment, and they compensate for their lack of information by making assumptions. However, the assumptions made by one expert may not be identical to those made by another expert about the same missing information, due to different professional backgrounds and expertise. This will inevitably lead to errors because the experts are, in essence, evaluating different products.

The fourth complication is due to the long duration of the design process: it often takes years to complete the design of a building. During this time, evaluations may change because the goals may have changed, or our state of knowledge about them has—consider, for instance, the continuing changes in seismic design codes, due to new knowledge gained from experience with earthquakes. Thus, evaluations that were valid in the past may cease to be valid.

Computational methods that can help predict the effects of design decisions on the state of fitness between a solution and the goals of the project can free the designer from the tedious evaluative aspects of a project to the great advantage of his or her creative powers.[5] They can provide instant feedback on the effects and side effects of decisions made through the creative process and allow the designer to adjust these decisions to achieve better fitness between the solution and the goals. Consequently, proponents of many evaluative methods have tried to model them in ways that would take full advantage of computers.[6]

Yet five decades of research have resulted only in partial realization of this aspiration. The considerable knowledge gained in predicting and evaluating specific aspects of design (including such well-developed areas as energy, cost estimation, and behavior in space) remains largely inaccessible in everyday architectural practice, except to experts in the respective fields, who are often ill-equipped to aggregate them into composite assessments of the overall "goodness" of proposed design solutions.[7] Furthermore, the judgmental part of the evaluation process has remained largely unaided, except for better representation of alternative tradeoffs, as discussed in the following chapters.

The Nature of Evaluation 16

The process of design comprises three major activities, performed iteratively:

1. Analyzing the problem and developing a set of goals that the proposed solution ought to achieve, alongside a list of constraints by which the solution must abide.
2. Synthesizing one or more solutions that, in the opinion of the designer, will achieve the goals and abide by the constraints.
3. Predicting and evaluating the various performances of the proposed solutions to verify that they are consistent with one another and that, when realized, they will achieve the goals.

Evaluation is the "glue" that binds together the components of this triad—the feedback part of each design cycle. Evaluation reveals how well the solution achieves the goals and which side effects and aftereffects it might have. It guides the generative process toward achieving the stated objectives, uncovers opportunities that were not apparent at the outset of the process, and indicates tradeoffs that must be made in order to improve the overall quality of the solution.

16.1 Design as Exploratory Search

Design is a mental activity that recognizes our ability to influence the future and our responsibility to do so in the "proper" way. It is the process of purposefully and consciously specifying the actions that ought to be taken at the present in order to achieve some desired conditions in the future. Specifying the actions that will lead to achieving certain desired human wants or needs by complex systems such as buildings is, however, difficult, for it involves political, psychological, social, economic, environmental, technical and many other considerations. There is no formula or procedure that can guarantee that our actions will have the desired effects.

In fact, it has been argued that even our best-intentioned actions will always have undesired side effects and aftereffects.[1]

The process of design can be likened, therefore, to exploratory search, a process where alternative courses of action are hypothesized and their effects are predicted and evaluated by comparing them to the desired objectives. Each step in the process may lead to further steps, until one is deemed either "successful," in which case the process terminates, or "dead end," in which case the process backtracks to the a previous state.

Search is a process we engage in when the outcome of an action cannot be fully ascertained in advance—when we cannot be certain that the proposed action will result in the desired state. For example, determining the precise shape of an auditorium such that it will have desired acoustical qualities can only be done by trial and error. A shape is picked and subjected to mathematical or physical evaluation. The evaluation determines how well the specified shape achieves the desired reverberation objectives. We may find that the predicted reverberations meet the desired performance characteristics, thus validating the proposed shape. More often, however, the evaluation will reveal that the predicted acoustical effects do not achieve the performance objectives, in which case the shape or the materials that were proposed for the auditorium will have to be modified and reevaluated. This iterative trial-and-error process is complicated by the fact that acoustical performance is only one of several design objectives for the auditorium. Visual comfort, handicapped accessibility, audience capacity, fire egress, and budget are additional common performance characteristics, which may conflict with the optimal acoustical shape or with other design objectives. In such cases, which comprise the majority of design situations, a solution must be sought that achieves *all* the desired objectives—though perhaps none of them optimally. A balanced compromise is often preferable to maximization of a few performance characteristics at the expense of others.

Moreover, the process of evaluation may reveal that the desired objectives themselves cannot be achieved, because they conflict with one another, or for other reasons. For example, it is possible that the desired capacity of the auditorium can only be achieved by a structure whose construction costs will exceed the specified budget or require supports that obstruct lines of sight. In such cases the desired objectives will have to be modified to allow for an acceptable solution.

Architectural design, however, is not a random, trial-and-error search. Rather, it is a goal-directed search, a process that is itself informed by the success or failure of the designer's ability to achieve the desired behavioral and spatial characteristics of the project while conforming to and relying upon cultural, social, environmental, and other norms. That is why we refer to the object that is being designed as the *solution* and to the desired behavioral and spatial characteristics it strives to achieve as the *goals*. The goals provide a definitive direction to the search, a yardstick by which its progress can be measured and its course steered. Design can thus be considered a dialogue between the goals and the solutions within the particular social and cultural context of the project (fig. 16.1). The dialogue adapts and modifies the initial goals and solutions until they converge in a solution that achieves an acceptable set of performance characteristics (what Simon called "satisficing").[2] The designer must continuously predict and evaluate the expected performances of the emerging solution against the desired behavior represented by the goals and change both the solution and the goals in an effort to bring about their convergence.

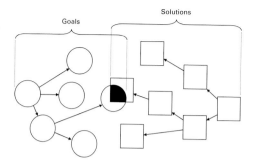

16.1 The process of valuation compares the proposed solutions to the goals and provides direction to the search process, which continues until an acceptable convergence has been found.

The design process often starts by defining a set of needs (what we refer to here as goals), representing the client's general wants and wishes of the sought solution. These are translated into statements that define more specifically the expected behavior of the sought solution, expressed as requirements and preferences. At the same time, the designer often forms a mental image that represents a preliminary solution to the client's wants and needs as well as the designer's own beliefs, which are derived from cultural and social contexts as well his or her personal style. Often there is no direct link between the wants and needs as expressed by the client and the preliminary solution offered by the architect—other than the common cultural and social context within which both operate. The task facing the designer and the client is to find a link, bringing the two into substantial convergence. This is done by way of abstraction and specification— abstraction of the solution, and specification of the goals. The expected behavior of the solution can then be predicted and compared to the desired behavior expressed by the goals (fig. 16.2).

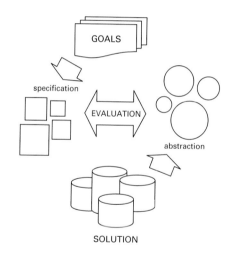

16.2 Specification and abstraction in the design process.

The process by which the goals are generated is, essentially, analytical and deductive. It starts by defining a set of needs representing the wants and wishes of the client and the architect. These are translated into statements that define more specifically the expected behavior of the solution, expressed as structured sets of requirements or constraints. On the other hand, the process by which solutions are synthesized is intuitive and inductive. It begins with the architect's inventing or adapting a solution that appears to have performance characteristics that will achieve the stated objectives as well as other desired attributes (form, cost, materials, and so forth). The expected performance of this initial solution is predicted by means of deductive and other reasoning processes, which generate abstractions that can be evaluated by comparing them to the desired behavior as stated by the goals. The evaluation can result in modification of the solutions and goals to overcome irreconcilable conflicts and to accommodate emerging opportunities that are discovered as the process unfolds, until it is determined that the predicted behavior is close enough to the desired behavior.

16.2 The Role of Evaluation in the Design Process

Given the process described above, design can be said to be comprised of three major activities, performed iteratively: (1) defining a set of goals that the proposed solution ought to achieve; (2) developing a solution that, in the opinion of the designer, will achieve the goals; and (3) predicting and evaluating the performances of the proposed solution to verify that they are consistent with each other and that, when realized, they will achieve the goals (fig. 16.3).

The central role evaluation plays in design stems from the fact that it is responsible for the basic iterative structure of the process—it constitutes the feedback part of the design cycle, the "glue" that binds together the other two components of the triad. Developing a solution that will achieve a given set of objectives cannot be separated from predicting and evaluating the expected performance of the solution. Only by testing and evaluating the effects of each part of the solution can the next step be determined. The evaluation guides the generative process toward achieving the stated objectives, uncovers opportunities to be explored, and indicates tradeoffs that must be made in order to improve the overall quality of the solution.

Prediction and evaluation are, therefore, important means for defining and clarifying the goals of the design process, as well as for guiding the development of the solution. They rely on the designer's ability to predict the environmental, psychological, social, economic and other effects that will ensue from realizing the specified solution, evaluate the desirability of these effects, and derive operational conclusions from that evaluation.

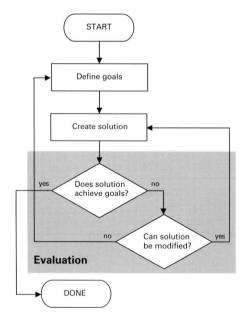

16.3 The iterative structure of the design process, and evaluation's central role in it.

Evaluation

To alleviate the difficulties associated with prediction and assessment of the performance of design solutions, the search for methods to predict the effects of design decisions began in the 1960s, seeking a synthesis between the designer's creative and rational faculties. Five decades of research have, nevertheless, failed to realize this aspiration, even though considerable progress has been made in developing the knowledge needed to predict and evaluate certain building-related factors (e.g., energy, behavior in space). This failure is due in large part to the difficulties inherent to the processes of evaluation and prediction and the isolation of their study from the other components of the design process, which subsequently led to the failure of integrating them seamlessly with other components of the design process. In fact, it can be argued that the very centrality of evaluation to the design process actually precludes its study (and the implementation of computational methods that result from it) independent of the study of the design process as a whole. On the other hand, each type of evaluation requires deep knowledge in a specific, often narrow area, which—like any other kind of specialization—progresses at its own pace and according to its own rules.

Still, methods that recognize the complexity of evaluation and its dependency on other components of the design process have been developed. To understand the motivations behind these methods and how they can be integrated into a comprehensive, computational framework it is necessary first to better understand the principles underlying evaluation and prediction and how they are used in the design process.

16.3 The Principles of Evaluation

Evaluation is a complex, multiphased process, comprising several integrated components. It begins with data provided by the design solution. This data must be processed to extract from it those characteristics that are relevant to the evaluative process. It must also be augmented by additional data that are not part of the specific design solution itself but common to all (or many) solutions of its kind (e.g., the cost of certain building components, their thermal and acoustic characteristics, and so forth). Once processed, the performance and behavioral characteristics of the information derived from the solution must be predicted, since the object being evaluated does not yet exist. The predicted performances must be compared to those specified by the goals. The results of the comparison must then be judged to derive an overall performance assessment and to identify areas that need improvement, or areas whose performance can be compromised to better achieve other qualities of the design. All these integrated steps must be performed both across multiple performance characteristics (e.g., energy, cost, aesthetics), and at various levels of detail (e.g., schematic design, detailed design, and so forth), as supported by the available data and dictated by the needs of the design process.

Representation of Design Solutions

Evaluation can only be as good as the data it operates on, which is provided by the emerging design solution. Hence, the first necessary component of a comprehensive evaluation is a good data model to represent the attributes of the emerging solution as accurately and as completely as possible. As discussed in section 8.2, such a data model must have the following characteristics:

- *Well-formedness.* The model must be semantically correct, to avoid conflicting information that might jeopardize the evaluation. For example, all the walls that bound a room must be explicitly (or implicitly) represented so its area and volume can be calculated as well as its thermal, and other, conditions. This calls for a representation far more semantically rich than the one, for instance, provided by drafting programs, which do not support the notion of walls, rooms, or even materials.
- *Completeness.* The ideal building representation describes as closely as possible the actual building itself. This means that all the architectural elements—spaces, walls, doors, windows, staircases, and so on—are represented along with all their attributes, not just as individual elements but also in terms of their relationships to one another.
- *Generality.* A building representation should be general enough to be able to interface with many different evaluation software packages. While this quality does not pertain to evaluation in principle, the reality of the state of the art of evaluation software is such that most evaluation packages are developed separately and look for information in the model in different ways.

- *Efficiency.* The evaluation software must be able to find the information it needs in the model quickly and efficiently. This can be facilitated by representing the information explicitly or by equipping the evaluation software with the tools to calculate the information it needs from the data provided by the model. Needless to say, the more explicit the information provided by the model, the less time it will take to evaluate it. Nonetheless, it is unlikely that all the information needed for an evaluation will be explicitly represented by the building model. Augmenting the model with query tools that can facilitate the extraction of the relevant information for making implicit data explicit will make the evaluation software itself simpler and more efficient.

Representation of Design Goals

In addition to explicitly representing the design solution, the goals against which it is measured must also be explicitly represented. Design goals can be stated as the desirable performance measures of the sought solution. Alternatively, they can be stated as the constraints that the proposed solution must satisfy. Such performance measures, or constraints, fall into two categories:

1. Externally imposed constraints, such as gravity, wind resistance, building codes, and norms.
2. Internally imposed constraints, such as budget, number of rooms, function, and style.

The first kind, called "hard" constraints, are the ones the designer cannot or chooses not to question (although some might be changed, e.g. through political action—like rezoning or adopting new building codes). They are either satisfied by the solution or not; they are pass-fail constraints.

The second kind, called "soft" constraints, may be satisfied to different degrees. The degree to which a particular soft constraint is satisfied may depend on other constraints, thereby introducing the important concept of tradeoffs. For example, the intent of constructing a four-bedroom, single-family house may not be achievable if the budget only allows for a three-bedroom house. Such tradeoffs are the hallmark of architectural design and are dependent on judicious decision making on the part of the architect and the client.

Each constraint indicates the specific level of performance a design solution should achieve in a particular category or an acceptable range of performance values. It can be represented formally using the following general notation:

constraint (value | range).

where the vertical bar stands for "or": a constraint can be stated in terms of a specific value it must satisfy or a range of values. For example:

number_of_bedrooms (4)
total_living_area (2300–2400 sq ft)
budget ($350,000–450,000).

The conditions under which a constraint is considered satisfied must be established by the designer (or the client) at the outset of the design process but may be changed as the process unfolds and the circumstances of the particular design manifest themselves by the designer's ability to satisfy the constraints. They may consist of desired targets, minimal or maximal values, or any other statement of measure.

A set of constraints indicates a particular combination of desired performances that must be satisfied by a design solution in order to achieve a specific design objective. We call this set a goal. Goals provide a context for satisfying the constraints: they bind together a number of related constraints, which achieve some higher-level intent. For example, the number of bedrooms in a single-family house determines the number of bathrooms it should have, because it is often indicative of the size of the family that will occupy the house. Likewise, the adjacencies of the rooms cannot be separated from their number and the types of activities they contain. The number of rooms and total floor area are directly related to the budget, which is also influenced by the quality of the construction. The function of the goals is thus to group a number of related constraints that should all be satisfied together.

More formally, goals can be represented by this general notation:

goal ({ goal } | { constraint })

The curly braces used in this notation stand for repeating groups: a goal can consist of multiple goals, or multiple constraints. For example:

Office_Lighting
(Performance ((illumination_level (150 fc)),
    (lighting_system (task and ambient)),
    (spatial_impression (privacy))),
(Budget ($2500),
(Design ((pattern (distributed)),
    (density (medium)),
    (source (fluorescent)))).

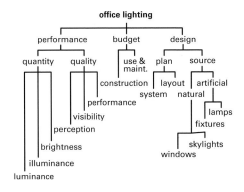

16.4 A goal hierarchy for office lighting.

The goals are considered to be achieved if all their constraints have been satisfied. The particular combination of constraints that is considered a goal is established when the goals are first introduced. This forces the designer (and the client) to consider and establish "reasonable" combinations of objectives, which then guide the design process. Additional goals may be added, or existing goals may be modified or deleted altogether during the design process, thereby providing a measure of flexibility and a means to represent changing preferences as the design process unfolds.

This definition of goals is recursive: a goal can be stated in term of constraints or in term of other goals. There is no inherent difference between goals and constraints. Rather, they form a hierarchical structure where terminal nodes represent constraints, and where intermediate nodes represent goals. An example of a goal hierarchy is depicted in figure 16.4.

The specificity of design goals must not be confused with the specificity of the design solutions that satisfy them: different design solutions may achieve the same goal, though each may satisfy the constraints comprising the goal differently. The different performance levels at which alternative sets of constraints may be satisfied represent tradeoffs in the context of achieving a particular goal. For example, the specifications in the design of the lighting system in an office typically include a performance characteristic, a lighting system, a budget, a style, a form, and so on. A design solution that achieves the office lighting goal would have to satisfy all these specifications. It is likely, however, that alternative solutions will satisfy the constraints at different but equally acceptable performance levels. To accommodate such tradeoffs, alternative goals can be stated, each representing the satisfaction of the same constraints at different performance levels, thus reflecting different preferences. For example, the two following goals represent different acceptable, alternative performance levels for achieving the goal of office lighting, reflecting a price-performance tradeoff. They comprise an equivalence class of context-dependent, related sets of constraints defining the conditions that ought to be met by an acceptable design solution:

```
Office_Lighting
    (Performance ((illumination_level (150 fc)),
        (lighting_system (task and ambient)),
        (spatial_impression (privacy))),
    (Budget ($2500),
    (Design ((pattern (distributed)),
        (density (medium)),
        (source (fluorescent)))).

Office_Lighting
    (Performance ((illumination_level (150 fc)),
        (lighting_system (task and ambient)),
        (spatial_impression (privacy))),
    (Budget ($1500),
    (Design ((pattern (distributed)),
        (density (high)),
        (source (fluorescent)))).
```

While alternative goals represent acceptable combinations of performance levels, some combinations may be more desirable than others. A prioritization of goals, reflecting a descending order of preferences, may be imposed by the designer or by the client. It will indicate which combination of performances the designer should attempt to accomplish first. If that combination cannot be achieved, then the designer should attempt the next preferred combination, and so on until he has reached an acceptable combination of performances.

Prioritization of preferences is not only a common practice when designers and clients are faced with limited resources, but it also has a very profound effect on the direction of the design process and on its results. This is due to the fact that all the decisions leading to the specification of

A. CHAIR COMFORT AND EFFECTIVENESS
Support for Office Work A.1

Requirement	Threshold	Relative Importance		
8	5	E	Comfort A.1.1	
6	4	I	Durability A.1.2	
3	3	M	Stack ability A.1.3	
9	9	E	Cost A.1.4	
8	6	E	Aesthetics A.1.5	
7	7	I	Workmanship A.1.6	

a design solution are linked to one another, and decisions made earlier in the process may limit the options available to the designer in later design phases, sometimes to the degree that no options are available at all. For example, choosing a particular construction method early in the design process (e.g., brick masonry) imposes many constraints on the building, limiting the options available to the architect in designing its form, details, and construction schedule.

Preferences can be represented by adding to the goal notation described earlier a prioritization factor, such as a number on a scale of 1 to 10. Or it can be done more simply (and effectively) by listing the goals in descending order of preferences and constructing the goal-satisfying search algorithm such that it will process the list from top to bottom and terminate as soon as any one goal has been satisfied. This method is easier to implement computationally and allows for additions and deletions of goals without renumbering the remaining ones. Each requirement must also include:

- The desired *level of performance,* expressed quantitatively on an ordinal scale of 0 to 9. This desired level of performance is relative to that of other requirements.
- The *threshold level* of performance, below which the design solution as a whole will be considered unacceptable (some requirements may not have such thresholds).
- The relative *importance* of this requirement, with respect to other requirements.

Figure 16.5 shows an example of the above, as implement in the BestFit software, developed by Serviceability Tools and Methods of Ottawa, Canada.

Evaluation of performances such as energy or cost can only be applied to manifest performance characteristics, which do not exist if the building has not yet been constructed. Hence the information provided by the building model must be processed in such as way that it will describe the building as if it already existed. Such description is done figuratively for the purposes of aesthetic evaluation (by observation) or analytically for nonvisual evaluations, like energy performance and cost estimation.

Prediction typically relies on expert knowledge in particular disciplines and subdisciplines, such as energy, acoustics, structures, cost estimation, social factors, and behavioral psychology. It involves a translation of the physical structures that comprise the emerging design solution into data that is meaningful in their particular domain. For example, cost estimators must count the number of doors and windows, calculate the areas and materials that are used in the design, and multiply them by their respective unit costs to derive an overall estimate of the cost of the building. They must also account for the difficulty in construction, availability of standard components versus their customized manufacture, economies of scale, labor costs, and many other factors that are either "hidden" in the design solution or are not particular to it at all. Likewise, structural engineers must determine the ability of the structure to withstand vertical and lateral loads based on geometry, materials, construction methods, and local conditions like type of soil, earthquakes, and weather.

Prediction thus involves the ability to infer and extract from the solution project-specific characteristics that are relevant to the particular evaluation and augment that information with project-independent data. It also relies on specialized disciplinary knowledge to tell how this data translates into performance characteristics, such as formulae, rules of thumb, and precedents.

Many methods have been developed for, or drafted into the service of prediction. They include calculation, reasoning (logic), simulation, extrapolation, and even intuition. "Stronger" methods, like calculation and reasoning, are preferable to the "weaker" ones but are not always applicable due to the incompleteness of the data or its complexity. Naturally, the accuracy of the prediction depends on the strength of the method used as well as on the data. However, there is no point in using a "strong" method on inaccurate data, and it would be a waste of effort to use accurate data with weak methods.

Judgment and Tradeoffs

Once the expected performance characteristics of the emerging design solution have been predicted, they can be compared to the desired ones, as stated by the goals. For example, the cost estimator might predict that the design solution proposed for a single-family house will cost $500,000. But this figure is meaningless in and of itself until it is compared to the budget established by the client as the goal for building the house. If the amount predicted by the cost estimator exceeds the budget, the design must be revised, or the budget must be increased (likewise, if the cost estimation falls short of the budget, it might indicate that the client is not getting the full benefit of his or her investment).

Drawing conclusions from this comparative process is rather straightforward, as long as only one goal is to be achieved and as long as achieving it depends on a single, independent variable. It becomes much more complicated when several design goals must be met simultaneously and when that depends on multiple, interconnected variables—as is often the case. For example, if reducing the cost of constructing the house involves reducing the number of bedrooms from four to three, another goal set by the client, namely the desire for a four-bedroom house, will no longer be met. Likewise, if reducing the budget could be accomplished either by using less expensive materials (thus reducing the quality of the building) or by reducing the sizes of the rooms, which one of the two design parameters should be compromised? How can the multiplicity and interconnectedness of all these components be managed? More precisely, how can tradeoffs among competing performance characteristics be judged against one another?

Tradeoffs are the hallmark of every design activity because typically all the desired characteristics of a building cannot be satisfied by any one design solution. Often certain needs are achieved at the expense of others. Hence, the degree to which some needs are satisfied may have to be compromised so that others may also be satisfied. But how much should any one need be compromised?

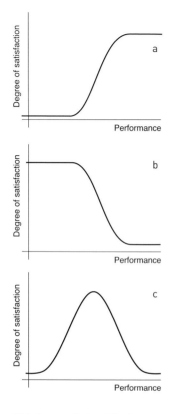

16.6 Some typical satisfaction curves.

Methods have been developed that can help guide the designer through judging tradeoffs.[3] Such methods are based on factoring in the context, in addition to goals and solutions, in the evaluation process. The context, which includes physical, political, cultural, and other parameters, provides a way to judge the degree of satisfaction a particular evaluator (the client, for example), derives from a particular design solution. This degree of satisfaction can be represented in the form of satisfaction curves—mappings that express the specific relationship between the predicted performance of a system and the subjective measure of its desirability under specific circumstances, introduced in chapter 6. Figure 16.6 depicts several typical satisfaction curves. On one axis, they measure the performance of some aspects of the design solution, such as cost or noise level. On the other, they measure the degree of satisfaction each performance value elicits in the evaluator.

The curves demonstrate several phenomena commonly associated with satisfaction. Figure 16.6b, for example, demonstrates that the client may generally be satisfied with the performance of the solution, until it reaches a certain threshold. Then satisfaction drops, but the rate of change, from 100% (completely satisfied) to 0% (not satisfied), is gradual. The curves accommodate such notions as "quite satisfied," "more or less satisfied," or "barely satisfied." The slope of the curves expresses the rate of change: the steeper the slope, the more abrupt the change, which means that once the threshold has been reached even a small change in the system's performance will result in considerable change in satisfaction. On the other hand, a shallow slope indicates a wider latitude in satisfying the evaluator, which allows more room for tradeoffs with other satisfaction curves that may need to be modified.

The satisfaction curves must, of course, be set by the client or by the designer. They are unary functions in the sense that each curve pertains to satisfaction derived from one building characteristic only. This makes it possible to set them individually. To aggregate the separate satisfaction curves into one composite measure of performance, they can be added. But since different behaviors have different importance in the overall performance measure, it is necessary first to assign each of them a relative weight. This method is well established, and has been used by other disciplines to develop aggregates of multicriteria evaluations.[4] The composite result of the summation of weighted, normalized satisfaction curves represents the overall performance of a given design solution. They facilitate the assessment of tradeoffs in three ways:

1. By explicitly showing how well any one need or desire are being satisfied, as a percentage between full and zero satisfaction.
2. By expressing the tolerance for satisfying the expressed need or desire, in terms of the steepness of the curve.
3. By prioritizing the relative importance of each need, in terms of the weights assigned to it.

Using these three measures, it is possible to identify needs and desires that are not being satisfied as well as those that are oversatisfied. It is possible, therefore, to choose a design solution that better achieves the undersatisfied needs, while reducing the achievement of oversatisfied needs.

16.4 Modalities

Architectural design usually must meet a wide range of design objectives—technological, environmental, social, economic, and others. Each one of these objectives has its own requirements, and each has been the focus of intensive study, even specialization, over the years. For example, the objective of making buildings energy-efficient has enjoyed great popularity since the late 1970s because of the worldwide energy crisis. Likewise, work in the area of designing earthquake-tolerant structures has become the focus of considerable research efforts as our understanding of seismic responses of buildings has grown over the years.

These individual objectives are, however, dependent on one another. When they are combined in the context of the built environment, design decisions that are intended to meet one objective may support or interfere with other objectives. For example, to achieve optimal energy efficiency, buildings have been earth-sheltered. (Cellars are considered the best environment to store wine under constant temperature and humidity conditions.) But this design solution interferes with objectives such as accessibility and view. It also creates many technological problems and may have severe psychological drawbacks for the occupants. The designer must, therefore, achieve the individual objectives while reconciling their conflicting effects and side effects with other objectives, to the overall benefit of the design solution as a whole.

The difficulties induced by these often conflicting demands are further exacerbated by the hierarchical nature of the design decision-making process: broad, general solutions are contemplated first and are gradually refined as the design process progresses. Alternatively, designers combine desired details into new wholes. In both cases, constraints are propagated "up" and "down" different levels of the abstraction hierarchy: high-level organizational decisions constrain lower-level details, while decisions that concern details limit the designer's freedom in selecting high-level organizational schemes.[5]

For example, a circulation system in a building is typically first planned out schematically (using such terms as "circular," "linear," "radial"). It is then gradually refined and articulated into a hierarchy of major and minor traffic zones, which are further refined into a hierarchy of public and private circulation spaces. These are later detailed by adding doorways, fire zones, means of egress, and so on.

Design theorists refer to different levels in the design abstraction hierarchy as design phases. These include feasibility studies, conceptual design, design development, detailing, and design documentation. While the exact definition of each phase differs from one researcher to another, their existence has been widely accepted since the early 1960s.[6]

Taken together, the composition of design processes can be said to consist of two separate modalities:

1. The modality in which the designer focuses on one phase of the solution development, searching for a composite solution that achieves multiple design objectives.
2. The modality in which the designer moves between different levels of abstraction, searching for a solution to a particular design objective.

Designers engage both modalities alternately and in parallel. Indeed it is often difficult to engage one modality without, at the very least, being cognizant of the other (although the experts whom the designer consults are typically oblivious to design objectives other than their own).

Given the different modalities of design, and given the centrality of evaluation to the design process, it should come as no surprise that the

Evaluation

evaluation of design solutions follows closely the modalities of the design process itself. Hence, we distinguish between multicriteria evaluation and multilevel evaluations. The multicriteria evaluation modality examines a given design solution from several different points of view (e.g., energy, cost, structural stability). Because it evaluates a particular design solution, this modality is limited to a single design phase. The multilevel evaluation modality examines how the design solution, or a succession of design solutions, satisfy a particular design objective (e.g., energy) at different phases of the design process.

While it is possible to consider multiple different aspects of the design solution at a particular phase of the design process, it is virtually impossible to consider all aspects at all phases. It is possible, however, and even desirable to consider individual design characteristics in depth, from top to bottom, anytime in the design process. In early design phases such consideration will help to select approaches that are likely to prove productive later on, while later design phases will benefit from reflection upon the reasons for adopting a particular approach rather than another, thereby helping the designer to select details that better support the chosen approach.

Bibliography

Augenbroe, G., and F. Winkelmann. "Integration of Simulation into Building Design: The Need for a Joint Approach." Technical Report, Building Physics Group, Delft University of Technology, The Netherlands; and the Simulation Research Group, Lawrence Berkeley Laboratory, University of California, 1990.

Broadbent, G., and A. Ward. *Design Methods in Architecture*. London: Lund Humphries, 1969.

Cross, N. *The Automated Architect*. London: Pion, 1977.

Gregory, S. A. *The Design Method*. London: Butterworths, 1966.

Johns, C. *Design Methods: Seeds of Human Futures*. New York: John Wiley and Sons, 1980.

Kalay, Y. E., ed. *Evaluating and Predicting Design Performance*. New York: Wiley Interscience, 1992.

Rittel, H. W. J. "Evaluative Methods to Measure the Performance of Buildings." Technical Report, College of Environmental Design, University of California, Berkeley, 1966.

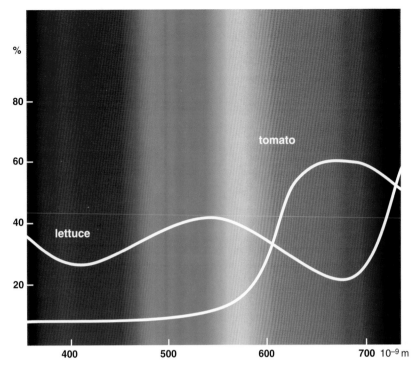

Plate 1 Surfaces gain their color by reflecting various parts of the visible spectrum in different amounts. (See corresponding image 9.6.)

Plate 2 Times Square, New York, is a physical environment infused with ever-changing media that blur the boundaries of space and information. (See corresponding image 4.14.)

Plate 3 The NASDAQ MarketSite Tower in Times Square, New York, is draped in a 10,800-square-foot cylindrical media wall, which transforms the building into an active participant in the environment. (See corresponding image 23.4.)

Plate 4 Raster graphics uses multiple display buffers to render an image in color (Wei Yan, 2003). (See corresponding image 9.11.)

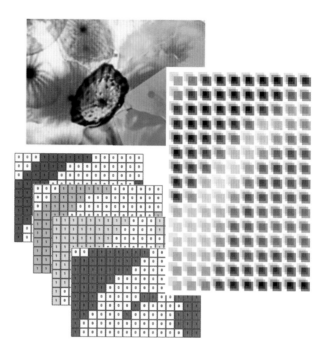

Plate 5 Ray tracing calculates the color of rays of light reaching the viewer's eye. (See corresponding image 9.18.)

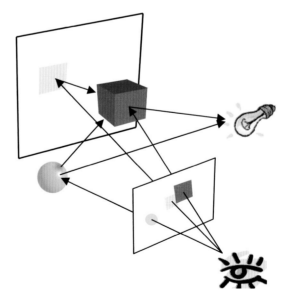

Plate 6 Different materials reflect light in ways that reveal their materiality. (Courtesy of Greg Ward and Isaac Kwo, Lawrence Berkeley National Laboratory, 2002.) (See corresponding image 9.7.)

Plate 7 Diffuse reflection of light leads to "color bleeding," as the reflected light carries the surface's color to other surfaces. (Courtesy of Donald Greenberg, Cornell University Computer Graphics Program.) (See corresponding image 9.21.)

Plate 8 Radiance, a hybrid deterministic/stochastic ray-tracing program, can be used for lighting evaluation purposes. (Courtesy of Greg Ward, Lawrence Berkeley National Laboratory, 1994.) (See corresponding image 9.20.)

Plate 9 Combining radiosity with ray tracing produces photo-realistic images. (Courtesy of Donald Greenberg, Cornell University.) (See corresponding image 9.22.)

Plate 10 *Trompe l'oeil* is a style of painting in which objects are rendered with extreme realism—in this case, a store in Agripas street, Jerusalem, Israel. (See corresponding image 9.23.)

Plate 11 *Meeting on Gauguin's Beach*, 1988—a painting produced by Aaron, a computer program written in LISP (oil on canvas, 90 x 68 inches). (Collection of Gordon and Gwen Bell. Photograph copyright Becky Cohen.) (See corresponding image 15.1.)

Plate 12 *KM16*—a painting by Wanalee, an Asian elephant (acrylic on paper, 30 x 22 inches). (Copyright State of the Arts, Palo Alto, California.) (See corresponding image 15.2.)

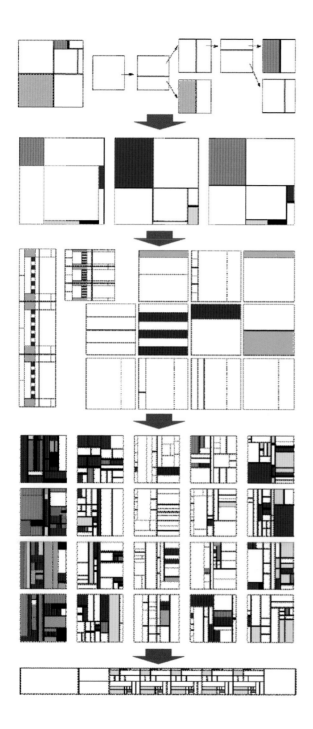

Plate 13 "Flondrian"—the combination of a GA that can generate Mondrian-like patterns and a GA that can generate Frank Lloyd Wright-like window patterns. (T. Schnier and J. S. Gero, "From Mondrian to Frank Lloyd Wright: Transforming Evolving Representations," Key Center for Design Computing, University of Sydney, 1997.) (See corresponding image 15.6.)

Plate 14 Computational fluid dynamic (CFD) simulation of summer wind patterns around tall buildings in Hong Kong. (Courtesy of Tsou Jin-Yeu, Department of Architecture, The Chinese University of Hong Kong.) (See corresponding image 17.3.)

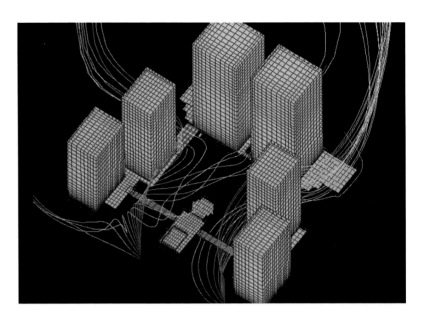

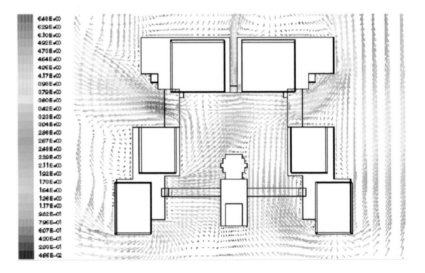

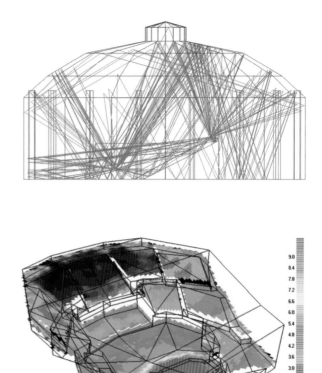

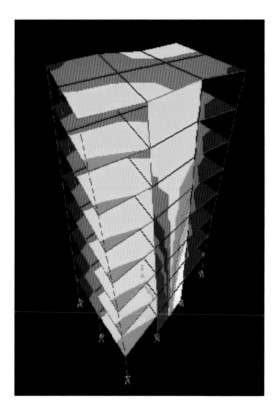

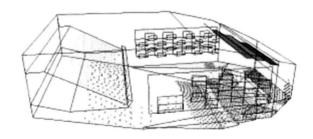

Plate 15 SAP2000 produces color-coded stress maps showing how the building responds to earthquake and wind loads (Computers and Structures, Berkeley, California). (See corresponding image 19.1.)

Plate 16 The outputs of ODEON: (a) ray-traced sound propagation, (b) absorption map, and (c) reflector coverage map. (Courtesy of ODEON, Lyngby, Denmark.) (See corresponding image 19.6.)

Plate 17 Virtual Museum of Arts El País. (Courtesy of MUVA Virtual Museum of Arts El País, Uruguay, 2002.) (See corresponding image 24.7.)

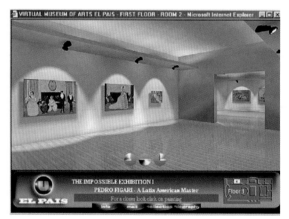

Methods of Prediction 17

Futurist Alvin Toffler wrote in the introduction to his seminal book *Future Shock:*

> Prediction is a risky business, especially about the future. . . . No serious futurist deals in "predictions." These are left for television oracles and newspaper astrologers. No one even faintly familiar with the complexities of forecasting lays claims to absolute knowledge of tomorrow. . . . The inability to speak with precision and certainty about the future, however, is no excuse for silence.[1]

This paradoxical, tongue-in-cheek statement by arguably the greatest "predictor" in recent history is indicative of the dilemma facing designers: on one hand, they must predict the consequences of their proposed design propositions, so they can be evaluated and acted upon with some degree of confidence in their results. On the other hand, all such predictions are risky at best, and may lead to false conclusions.

Prediction typically relies on deep knowledge in a particular discipline or subject matter, such as environmental factors, structures, economics, acoustics, psychology, and others. It involves the translation from one symbol system—the one used for representing the emerging design solution (typically drawings and models)—into another symbol system that is meaningful in the particular domain of prediction (typically numerical data). This involves the ability to infer and extract the characteristics of the emerging solution that are relevant to the particular prediction. Project-specific information must be combined and augmented with project-independent data, drawn from the domain of the prediction. For example, in estimating the cost of a building, the prediction process must identify each door in the drawing, then combine this project-specific information with the unit cost of the appropriate door type, which come from project-independent manufacturers catalogs.

The methods that facilitate the process of prediction range from strong to weak. Strong methods use mathematics or other hard sciences to translate the inputs into reliable forecasting. Timetables for airplane and train schedules are examples of such predictive methods. Although there is no guarantee that a plan or a train will arrive on time, airlines and transportation authorities can predict (with relatively high degree of confidence) the arrival time of their plans and trains. By contrast, predicting the numbers that will win the state lottery is based on guessing—a very weak predictive method—and is therefore highly unreliable. In between these two extremes lie many phenomena that are amenable to prediction with different degrees of confidence. For example, loaning money to someone is often based on her or his credit history: if the person is known to have paid back previous loans on time, there is a good chance, though no guarantee, that the new loan will also be repaid. Similarly, life insurance companies set their premiums (i.e., cost of the risk they assume) based on general trends of longevity of the population to which the insured belong (e.g., age, gender, lifestyle).

The complexity of architectural design requires the use of many different types of prediction. Some aspects, such as cost, can use calculation or reasoning-based predictors. Others, such as energy consumption, daylighting, and fire egress, use simulations. Still other aspects, such as aesthetics, can use only extrapolations from previous experiences. Each method has its uses but must be accompanied by a measure that indicates the degree of confidence in which its result can be held.

17.1 Calculation

One of the most common methods of prediction is by way of calculation. The arrival time of an airplane, for example, can be "predicted" by knowing its time of departure, the distance from origin to destination, and its speed. The cost of a particular construction or remodeling job can typically be predicted (with different degrees of accuracy) by adding up the costs of the components that comprise the building and the cost of labor needed to put them together, and multiplying the results by certain coefficients to account for interest rates, delays, and other factors.

Calculation is a method that is applicable whenever prediction is based on some concise list of simple components, each of which is itself unambiguous and certain, and when the dependencies between the components are well known. When applicable, calculation is the preferred method of prediction, because it is guaranteed to lead to a result that can be trusted, in the sense that it is backed by rigorous mathematical reasoning. It is a method that can be subjected to analysis and verification, can be "proved," and tested for sensitivity to changes in the data.

Cost estimation is a good example of calculation-based prediction. At an appropriate time in the design process, the drawings and specifications provide a basis for estimating the final cost of construction. When information needed to complete the prediction is missing, default values, rules-of-thumb, and estimates are used. Thus, even though it is based on calculation, the results of predicting the cost of construction cannot be entirely accurate as long as the project is still unresolved and in a state of development.[2]

Calculation-based prediction is typically implemented in the form of spreadsheets, where individual entries are connected to each other through mathematical formulae. Upon input of the solution's parameters (e.g., door schedule), the spreadsheet can produce the requisite summaries by substituting the symbolic materials with their appropriate unit prices, which are stored in a database that must periodically be updated. More complex calculations can be implemented in the form of algorithms, which can account for loops and recursion.

Other than its (relative) rigor, calculation-based prediction offers the advantage of interrogating the data for sensitivity to changes in the values of one or more parameters. This so-called sensitivity analysis allows the decision maker to see how much changing one parameter will affect the overall outcome of the project. If, in response to a unit change in the value of some parameter the overall result will change only a little, the project is considered insensitive to changes in the value of that parameter. If, on the other hand, the effect on the overall result will be considerable, the project is considered sensitive to changes in the value of that parameter. For example, a difference of 10% in the cost of a typical unit window in a skyscraper, which contains thousands of windows of the same type, can result in considerable cost variances and can affect the decision as to which window system to choose, whereas the same difference in window costs would hardly affect the choice when considered in the context of a single-family house.

The quality of calculation-based prediction is, of course, only as good as the data on which it is based, and the operations applied to it. In fact, the very belief in the "correctness" of calculation-based prediction can be it is worst enemy, leading to over-reliance and misplaced confidence. When it fails, calculation-based prediction often has significant and embarrassing consequences, such as the failure of the 1,090-foot-long Millennium Footbridge over the Thames River in London, which closed due to excessive sway on the same day it was opened on June 11, 2000. The predictive calculations for the bridge, designed cooperatively by architects Foster and Partners, sculptor Sir Anthony Caro, and structural engineers Ove Arup and Partners, did not account for the harmonious vibration induced by lockstep pedestrian traffic, a problem that plagues all narrow long-span footbridges.[3]

17.2 Reasoning

Reasoning is the process of extending a set of known facts, beliefs, or observations by applying to them rules that combine the known facts in a manner that produces new facts and rules.

The iterative application of rules to facts for the purpose of deriving new facts and rules is called inference. The known facts, beliefs, and observations are called premises, and the new facts derived from them by way of inference are called conclusions. Reasoning produces conclusions that can be verified, even proved to be true, if the premises from which they are derived are known to be true, and if the rules of inference are known to be true.

Reasoning is closely associated with logic (from the Greek word *logos* [reason])—the science that deals with the conditions under which conclusions follow from given premises. Many kinds of logic exist, ranging from the classical or first-order (predicate) logic that dates back at least to Aristotle, to modern kinds of logic such as many-valued logic, modal logic, temporal logic, and fuzzy logic.

In general, the process of prediction by logical reasoning can be applied in three ways:

1. By deduction, with reasoning applied to known facts and rules to derive new conclusions (also called classical or predicate logic).
2. By abduction, with reasoning applied to observed conclusions and known rules to uncover the facts on which they rest (much like what detective do in crime novels).

Evaluation

3. By induction, with reasoning applied to known facts and observed conclusions to derive the rules that connect them (the process on which much of science is based).

The strength of reasoning is derived from (and depends upon) the degree of confidence we have in the premises and the rules. If either is uncertain, then the conclusions derived from applying the rules to the facts are also uncertain. Furthermore, only deduction is "guaranteed" to be certain, given facts and rules that are known to be true; neither induction nor abduction shares this degree of certainty, even when the observed conclusions and the rules are true.

Classical Logic

Classical, first-order, logic is defined by a finite set of axioms, or facts, that are known to be true and a set of inference rules that are applicable to these facts; application of the rules produces new facts that are also true. For example:

Socrates is human	(a fact known to be true)
All humans are mortal	(a rule known to be true)
Socrates is mortal	(a new fact derived from combing the first fact and the rule)

This example makes use of a logical construct known as a syllogism, a form of deductive logic where a generalization (the rule) is applied to a particular fact (the premise) to derive the conclusion. Stated more formally, the rule can be written as:

$$x \in A \rightarrow x \in B$$ (if x is member in class A, then it is also member in class B)

where $X \in A$ is the premise, and $x \in B$ is the conclusion.

This form of inference is the one used most often, whenever new facts must be inferred from existing facts and an existing body of knowledge, formulated as rules applicable to the existing facts. It is generally known as deduction, or as forward chaining, in the AI branch of computer science. An example of its application in architecture is provided by Energy Expert, a system designed by Bharati Jog for predicting seasonal energy use by a proposed building and providing advise on improving the design of that building to make it more energy-efficient (to learn more about this system, see section 18.2).[4]

Other Kinds of Logic

Unresolved logical problems and advancements in our understanding of human reasoning have contributed to the invention of new logical systems in the past century.

For example, classical logic employs only two truth-values: true and false. There are cases, however, where a third truth-value might be useful. This third value may indicate *undecidedness, ignorance,* or *meaninglessness.* Undecidedness could be useful in, for example, a murder mystery, when a character in the novel is suspected of being the villain but there is not enough evidence to prove guilt or innocence. Ignorance might be useful in describing military reconnaissance cases where the intelligence-gathering officer may not have enough information to determine the size of the enemy force. Meaninglessness may be applied to newly acquired information that conflicts with some previously held beliefs, which, unless discarded, lead to a paradox rendering the information meaningless. For example, the following inference introduces a contradiction:

Socrates is human	(a fact known to be true)
All humans are mortal	(a generalization known to be true)
Socrates is NOT mortal	(a new fact, which does not follow from the premise and the rule)

The contradiction causes all facts and rules to be suspect, unless it can be settled in some manner, such as by explaining the difference between Socrates' physical mortality and his metaphysical immortality, as the father of modern philosophy.

Three-valued logic is particularly applicable to design, because of the uncertainty and complexity of the design process, which involves stepwise decision making and choosing between alternative options. The incremental nature of the design process means that not all decisions are made at the same time, leaving the designer in a state of partial ignorance until the very end. The fact that the "correctness" of design decisions depend on subsequent decisions as much as they depend on past decisions may lead to negation of previously held beliefs, hence to their meaninglessness. Finally, the need to evaluate the relative desirability of the design objectives themselves at every step of the process may leave the designer undecided about the truth value of certain design decisions.

The sequential nature of design, where old beliefs are discarded in favor of new beliefs, can be regarded as non-monotonic logic. For example, we might plan to construct a four-bedroom, 2,300-square-foot house, only to discover that the choice of materials, which is typically made later, exceeds the budget, necessitating redesign.

Redesign, and indeed any retracing of the steps taken earlier, is known as backtracking—the process of undoing, reversing, or remaking the latest decisions. If that measure fails to remove the contradiction, earlier decisions are revisited, and so on. Backtracking is a form of non-monotonic logic and is characteristic of human problem solving when we have only partial information of the state of the solution.

Fuzzy Logic

The most radical departure from classical logic (in all its forms) is advocated by proponents of so-called fuzzy logic, who claim that standard logical formalisms are incapable of handling informal arguments.[5] Such arguments arise when we discuss relative attributes, such as fast, tall, rich, beautiful, and small. For example, we might consider a race car traveling at 200 miles per hour very fast, but a jet airplane traveling at the same speed would be considered very slow.

To handle such imprecise arguments, fuzzy logic has modified the two basic premises on which classical logic is founded:

1. The premise of the set.
2. The premise of universal truth and falsehood.

The first premise is based on the notion that every shareable property determines a set, namely the collection of all things that share the same property. For example, all the buildings designed by Frank Lloyd Wright form a set, which distinguishes its members from all the buildings he did not design.

More formally, the classical notion of a set can be stated as a function that classifies all objects of some abstract universe U into objects that have property P and those that don't:

$f(Pu) = \{0,1\}$; $u \in U$ (1 means that object u, which is an object in universe U, shares the property, and 0 means it does not. The curly braces mean that 0 and 1 are the only two values available to u.)

The fuzzy notion of sets, on the other hand, claims that the boundary between objects that have the property and those that don't is ill-defined; objects may share the property to different degrees. For example, all the buildings whose design has been *influenced* by Frank Lloyd Wright form a set, which distinguishes its members from all the buildings whose design has not been influenced by him. Since "influence" is not a well-defined term, critics may differ in their opinion as to which buildings were influenced by Wright and which were not. Furthermore, some buildings may have been influenced by him more than others, hence the boundary that distinguishes the two sets is fuzzy.

More formally, the fuzzy notion of a set can be stated as a function which classifies all objects of some abstract universe U into objects that share property P to a degree that varies between 0 (not at all) and 1 (fully):

$f(Pu) = [0,1]$; $u \in U$ (The square brackets mean that the value of u can vary between 0 and 1.)

In other words, according to fuzzy set theory, a set is no longer a collection of objects alone, but rather a collection of objects with an *index* that indicates the degree of their membership in the set.[6]

The second premise of classical logic that has been modified by fuzzy logic concerns the notions of truth and falsehood. In classical logic, only two values are available (true and false). This narrow range has been extended by three-valued logic into three (true, false, and undetermined). In fuzzy logic, a much broader range is available, including true, false, not true, very true, not very true, more or less true, rather true, and so on. Lotfy Zadeh, the inventor of fuzzy logic, calls them linguistic truth-values. The assignment of any one of these truth-values to an argument in the logical system is rather arbitrary, and, according to Zadeh, depends on the domain of discourse.

Fuzzy truth-values allow inferences that can only be considered "approximate." For example:

A is small	(*A* belongs to a set of objects considered to be small)
A and *B* are approximately of equal size	(a binary fuzzy relation)
B is more or less small	(the semantic consequence which follows from the premise and the relation)

It is apparent that the truth-value of the conclusion in this example is only as certain as the assumptions underlying the assertions themselves (i.e., the definitions of small and approximately equal). Furthermore, some of the cornerstones of classical logic, as defined by Frege and Russell, are not applicable to fuzzy logic, including the important notions of completeness, consistency, axiomatization, and even the rules of inference themselves. Nonetheless, the absence of "hard" logical foundations and the reliance on subjective, domain-dependent semantics actually enhances the applicability of fuzzy logic to representing real-world situations, many of which involve handling incomplete, unreliable, and subjective data.

Normative Logic

Another kind of logic that appears to hold special relevance to design is normative logic: unlike ordinary types of logical reasoning, which are well suited to describing how things *are,* normative logic—much like design—is concerned with describing how things *ought to be.*

Herbert Simon has demonstrated how introducing the term "should" changes the meaning of otherwise simple logical propositions.[7] Consider the difference between the following ordinary inference:

Dogs are pets	(a premise known to be true)
Cats are pets	(another fact known to be true)
_____	
Dogs and cats are pets	(a new premise derived from combining the premises)

and the following normative inference:

Dogs are pets	(a premise known to be true)
Cats are pets	(another premise known to be true)
_____	
You *should* keep dogs *and* cats	(a new fact derived from combining the premises)

Though many people might disagree with the conclusion, this is the kind of "logic" used by designers much of the time.

17.3 Simulation

Simulation is a method of predicting the performance of an artifact (or phenomenon) under some prescribed conditions by way of experimentation. Its goal is to validate (or disprove) a hypothesis—in the form of a model or prototype of the designed artifact—and uncover unintended consequences of its design (e.g., the survivability of passengers in a car during an accident, the thermal properties of a building, or its behavior under earthquake conditions). As such, simulation requires either the artifact itself or a model of it to be experimented on. It also requires a model (or description) of the conditions under which the artifact's performance is tested. For example, to test how well a given car protects its passengers during a collision, the simulation can put the car (and its passengers) in a controlled test environment where it is crashed into a wall (fig. 17.1). More often, however, when the artifact is not available for testing—because it is too valuable to be experimented on (like the passengers in the crash-tested car) or is still under design (like a proposed building)—a physical or a digital model is used instead. Such models can be as elaborate as crash-test dummies equipped with sensors to record what kinds of injuries the passenger might sustain during a collision, a cardboard scale model of a building to be used in daylighting evaluation, or its mathematical (digital) model for energy or structural evaluation.

Simulation is a preferred method for evaluating the performance of designed artifacts when the relationships among the decision variables are too difficult to establish analytically because they interact in complex ways or there are too many of them; and when real system experimentation is too expensive, time consuming, or dangerous. Simulation allows replacement of the actual system by a functionally equivalent abstraction, which can "function" while it is being observed and its performance is being recorded.

Simulation is predicated on having a model of the artifact—a car, a building, even an economic model—and having a model of the conditions under which the artifact is to be tested. Both models must be functionally equivalent to the reality that they mimic, but need not be as complex or as complete as that reality, when such complexity does not significantly change the expected behavior. For example, a crash test dummy must have the same size, weight, and articulation of the human body, but it need not be able to walk or even stand on its own. A cardboard scale model is often sufficient to test how daylight will illuminate a proposed building, but it is not sufficient to test the building's energy performance or its structural integrity. Likewise, the speed, mass, and angle of a car crash must be realistic, as must be the source of the daylight (i.e., real or artificial sun located at the correct position in the sky relative to the building), or the heat transfer model that describes the thermal behavior of buildings.

A simulation thus consists of three main components:

1. An input model, comprising both the artifact to be tested and the environment in which it is embedded.
2. A "simulation engine," comprising the dynamic stresses to which the artifact will be subjected.
3. Output, comprising the performance data.

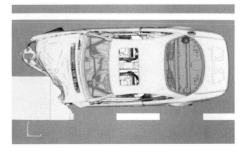

17.1 Digital versus actual simulation of crash test cars to predict the survivability of their occupants (European New Car Assessment Programme).

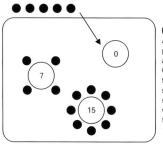

Minute 2:
A group of five patrons arrives. One of the tables is free so they can be seated. They will occupy the table for 15 minutes.

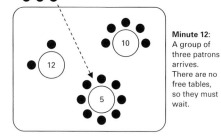

Minute 7:
A group of two patrons arrives. All the tables are occupied, so they must wait to be seated. After 2 minutes a table will clear, and they will be seated.

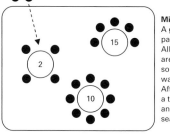

Minute 12:
A group of three patrons arrives. There are no free tables, so they must wait.

17.2 Three snapshots of the cafeteria simulation.

Consider, for example, the problem of determining the number of tables needed in a cafeteria to adequately serve a given target patronage.[8] Clearly, dividing the number of patrons p by the capacity of a table would result in many wasted tables, since not all patrons go to lunch at the same time. On the other hand, providing too few tables would result in long queues and unhappy customers. There is, however, no formula that can translate the number of patrons into the number of needed tables.[9] The best method to answer the question is simply by allocating a certain number of tables, and observing the behavior of the patrons. Discrete event simulation can help to do exactly that without actually building the cafeteria: it provides minute-by-minute "snapshots" of the number of patrons arriving and the tables they occupy (fig. 17.2). The input parameters include the number of tables n, the range of the number of patrons p arriving at the cafeteria at any given moment, and the range of time t they occupy a table. The simulation engine determines the actual minute-by-minute pattern of patrons' arrival, distribution to available tables (if there are any), and the time it takes each group to eat and clear the table (by choosing a random number within the range of each parameter). The "snapshots" of the interaction of these parameters are the output of the simulation. These cumulative snapshots reveal when the number of tables is inadequate (patrons queuing up), too many (tables are empty), and point out the actual bottlenecks of the situation.

Simulation, if properly done, is a powerful predictive tool. It can show the expected behavior of a complex system, with many interacting components (fig. 17.3). Naturally, it is only as good as the input models and the simulation engine used. These are limited by our knowledge of the phenomenon and by the need to simplify it so it can be simulated in a reasonable amount of time using a reasonable amount of resources. For example, the digital simulation of automobile accidents requires accurate geometric information about the crashing cars, the properties of the materials they are made of, the relative speeds, angle of impact, and much more. While crash tests can and have been done on super computers, the results are still poor compared to those obtained by crashing "real" cars. The latter are also able to show the injuries sustained by the occupants of the cars, who are simulated by highly complex (physical) manikins.

Most of the effort in developing simulations is devoted to programming the simulation engine, which is responsible for combining the input

Evaluation

values and affecting the interactions among them. Over the years, different approaches have been used to program simulation engines. Today, they include event-driven simulation engines (such as traffic simulation); goal-driven simulation engines (ray tracing, which was discussed in section 9.3, is such a simulation engine—it traces one ray per pixel until the image is complete); steady-state simulation engines (used when the input model and simulation parameters do not change during the simulation, as in radiosity models); and dynamic simulation engines (used when the input model and/or the simulation parameters change during the simulation, as in the cafeteria example and in energy evaluation of buildings, as discussed in section 19.2).

Simulation must, as much possible, be calibrated against the phenomena it attempts to predict. Thus, comparing the thermal performance of actual buildings to their simulated performance prior to construction has helped validate and calibrate thermal performance simulation.[10] Earthquake simulation models have been updated based on data gathered from actual earthquakes, and fire simulations have been improved by gathering data in actual and test fires.[11] Such validation procedures help increase the confidence the designer may place on the results of a simulation, and correct errors due to overlooking some critical parameters or the interactions among them.

For a simulation to be considered "successful" its predictions must be consistent with the reality it stands for. Thus, for instance, visual simulation is considered successful when it is indistinguishable from a photograph of the same scene. However, simulation of designed artifacts can do more than that; it can help reveal formerly unseen design parameters or establish the relative importance of known parameters. For example, in the cafeteria example, simulation can show that the required number of tables is influenced most by patronage turnaround: the faster they eat and return occupied tables to the pool of available tables, the fewer tables are needed (a fact well known by fast food chains, whose operational motto is, therefore, "eat it and beat it"). In addition to providing useful design information and a better understanding of the simulated phenomena, simulations also provide a nonnegligible entertainment value, as proven by such popular computer and video games like SIM-CITY, Roller-Coaster Tycoon, Civilization, and many others.

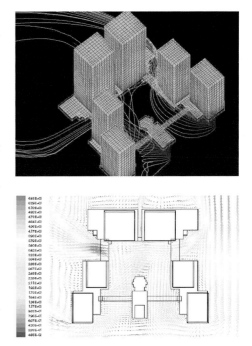

17.3 Computational fluid dynamic (CFD) simulation of summer wind patterns around tall buildings in Hong Kong. (Courtesy of Tsou Jin-Yeu, Department of Architecture, The Chinese University of Hong Kong.) (See color plate 14.)

17.4 Extrapolation

Extrapolation is a method of prediction based on experience gained from previous similar experiences: if a proposed design solution is similar to one that has been built in the past, it is possible to predict the performance of the proposed solution by comparing it to the old one and adjusting for the differences between the two.

Past experiences come in different forms. Some are precedents, which are situations similar to the present one in most of their details. Others are analogies—similar in their gross features but not in detail. Still others are metaphors, which may bear only remote resemblance to the present situation yet could impart some relevant information to it. These three broad categories (and their many subcategories) form a body of past experiences whose relevance to the present design situation becomes progressively more remote: metaphors are less relevant than analogies, which are less relevant than precedents. As such, predictions drawn from metaphors are likely to be less reliable than those drawn from analogies, which are likely to be less reliable than those drawn from precedents.

Although past design experiences are readily available, identifying one that is applicable to the current design problem is a difficult task, subject to interpretation of both the past experience and the current problem. Furthermore, the adaptation of the experience to the current needs is a nontrivial task, which calls for judgment and intuition, more so than the other approaches to predicting the performance of design solutions that were discussed earlier.

Precedents

Precedents form the rich, empirically validated core of architectural experience. They can be visited, and their performances can be experienced rather than merely imagined. However, extrapolating performance expectations from precedents to new, unbuilt projects is predicated on the similarity between the present design problem and the precedent. Such similarity is often hard to define, because every design problem is different from every other problem due to the unique spatiotemporal and sociocultural contexts in which it is embedded and which shaped it and gave it its unique character. Still, precedents carry, by definition, also nonunique information that is transferable to other (similar) design situations. For example, the uniquely shaped footbridges pioneered by architect-engineer Santiago Calatrava show enough resemblance to one another to provide a measure of predictability—in terms of aesthetic and functional appropriateness—to allow municipal design committees who visit one bridge to extrapolate the experience to their own locale (fig. 17.4).

Not all precedents carry such strong resemblance to one another—nor to the current design problem. Hence, the conditions for selecting a precedent must often be relaxed to admit experiences that might not be considered prototypical in the sense discussed in section 12.6 yet bear enough similarity to the present problem to provide useful information. Moreover, the use of precedents as performance predictors leaves much room for interpretation by the architect, who must choose those characteristics that are similar to the present problem while ignoring ones that are different. Thus the very richness of precedents often hinders their use as predictors for new design problems.

Analogies

Analogy is a method of applying carefully chosen examples from other experiences, sometimes far removed, to clarify and predict the behavior of a present situation. It works in two ways, as far as prediction goes. First, analogy can transform a new, unfamiliar design situation into one with which the designer is familiar. The designer can then predict the expected performance of the new situation by extrapolating from his or her experience with the familiar case. Second, analogy can help predict performance by extrapolating test results gleaned from a situation that is different from the case at hand but deemed applicable to it. This method is widely used to predict the effects of drugs on human beings by first testing them on animals whose response to the drug is taken to indicate how humans will respond to it. Unlike the first method, such analogical reasoning extrapolates the results of the past experience to the new situation; it does not transform the new situation as a whole into the old one. Using the image of a quiet village as an analogy when designing a nursing home is an example of the first type of prediction by analogy in architecture. Visiting a completed project to infer from it the expected performance of a new design proposal, even when the new project is different from the old one,

17.4 Santiago Calatrava's asymmetric, inclined, single-mast, cable-stayed Trinity footbridge (top) over the river Irwell in Salford/Manchester, England (1993–1995), which served as a precedent for a similar bridge (bottom) over the Hoofdvaart Canal in Haarlemmermeer, Holland (1999). (Courtesy of Santiago Calatrava, SA, Switzerland.)

is a method often used by architects, landscape architects, and interior decorators to demonstrate to their clients what they mean in their design propositions for the new case.

Metaphors

The etymological meaning of the term metaphor (Greek *metapherein*) is to transfer or to bear; a metaphor is a figure of speech in which a word or phrase is used in place of another to suggest a likeness or similitude between the two. However, as demonstrated by George Lakoff, a metaphor is much more than a superficial rhetorical device that decorates speech: it is a cognitive agency that organizes thoughts, shapes judgments, and structures language.[12] Metaphors, according to Lakoff, have a generative capacity: they facilitate thought by providing an experiential framework (a "schema," in cognitive psychology terms) linking a conceptual representation to its sensory and experiential ground, by which new concepts can be accommodated and understood.[13] Metaphors connect a source domain to a target domain, thereby causing the target to become grounded in spatio-physical experience via the source. The result is that the new concept (or design proposition, in our case) can be understood through the conceptual and physical properties of the source. For example, the story about the plight of Native Americans who had to leave their home in what is now Aspen, Colorado, and who buried one of their musical instruments in the ground to assure their return provided a metaphor that helped architect Harry Teague to design the mostly buried Aspen Concert Hall at the same location (see section 11.1).

The predictive powers of a metaphor accrue from the same connection between the source and the target: the performance of the source can be mapped to the performance of the target. Such mapping, however, becomes more tenuous as the distance between the source and the target, connected by the metaphor, grows wider. Often a metaphor can only be used to predict the general state-of-mind the observer of the new situation is expected to have when experiencing the new design. It was such a metaphorical prediction that prompted changes in the 1990s in the design of the Nissan Altima's front grill, which was metaphorically interpreted by the company's Japanese directors to represent a frowning, "unhappy" face.[14]

A symbol is a reference that connects a physical object, image, sound, word, or action with the memory of some past experience. The experience evoked by the symbol may be physical or conceptual. It may be personal or shared by many. The relationship between the symbol and the experience depends on the meaning of the original experience for the observer: a personal experience evoked by a symbol will typically carry more meaning for the observer than a shared, impersonal experience, learned through teaching or reading. One symbol can have many different layers of meanings, which may be interpreted differently by different observers.

A Japanese garden, for example, is an object full of symbols. As a whole, it is a metaphor of the universe. Its elements—stone or iron lanterns, rocks, water, and plants—symbolize fire, earth, water, and life in different forms. The meandering garden path *(roji)* symbolizes the meditative journey that separates the visitor to the garden form the day-to-day world. This is the reason for the stones being placed with careful irregularity, leading indirectly, rather than directly, to often hidden or obscure places. Bends in the path, or larger stones, are stopping points for vistas or views, symbolizing meditative pauses in the journey. Jagged stones symbolize mountains, and islands in a pond or a stream symbolize everlasting life, or Nirvana—a place without time, a place of ultimate retirement in peace and tranquility.

These symbols gain their meaning through the philosophy of Zen. As such, they mean nothing to the uninitiated—yet many different things to a Zen master. Moreover, no one symbol alone contains the whole meaning on its own. It is their ensemble into a whole that invests them with meaning.

The evocative powers of symbols that reference shared experiences can be used to elicit—hence predict—expected behavior. The unabashed appropriation of place-specific, time-specific, even fiction-specific symbols by the architects and developers of Las Vegas, Nevada, are a case in point (fig. 17.5). They used hotel-size symbols of an Egyptian pyramid, New York City skyscrapers, the campanile and the Doge's Palace in Venice, and other landmarks, as well as medieval castles and Italian resorts—albeit resized, exaggerated, and dressed up—to elicit the suspension of disbelief and the state of mind people slip into when on vacation, when they are

17.5 The New York, New York hotel in Las Vegas, with wings modeled after New York City's skyscrapers and landmarks, is an example of themed hotels in Las Vegas.

more willing to part with their money and pay extravagant fees and charges that they never would have consented to in their non-vacation state of mind.

When applied correctly, analogies, metaphors, and symbols provide a powerful means of drawing conclusions from past experiences. However, identifying the "correct" analogy, metaphor, or symbol is not a simple matter. Furthermore, adapting the chosen experience to the present problem is subject to much interpretation and judgment. In this respect, analogies, metaphors, and symbols provide much less certain predictive abilities than other methods of prediction. Still, all three provide a means to transfer a seemingly unrelated experience to a new situation, and can be used to predict performances that cannot otherwise be forecasted.

17.5 Intuition and Guessing

When more formal methods of prediction cannot be applied, architects—like many other professionals—use their intuition for guidance. Statements like "it does not feel right," or "this ought to do it," are commonly heard during design sessions.[15] Although they may appear to be no more than educated guesses, they are, in fact, based on designers' tacit knowledge. The more experienced the architect is, the more often these informal modes of prediction are correct.

Donald Schön has argued that this tacit knowledge is, in effect, the essence of professionalism. It is the knowledge that has been accumulated over years of practice, observed first hand, or acquired through professional training.[16] This knowledge distinguishes the professional from the lay person, the veteran from the novice. In architecture, law, medicine, business, and engineering, experience provides a rich, empirically validated host of "canned" solutions to complex problems. If the new problem facing the professional is similar to a problem encountered in the past, there is a good chance that its solution by similar means will lead to similar results.

Bibliography

Akin, Ö. "How Do Architects Design?" In *Artificial Intelligence and Pattern Recognition in Computer Aided Design,* ed. J. C. Latombe. New York: IFIP, North Holland, 1978.

Clipson, C. "Simulating Future Worlds." Technical Report, Architecture and Planning Research Laboratory, University of Michigan, Ann Arbor, 1988.

Coyne, R. D., M. A. Rosenman, A. D. Radford, M. Balachandran, and J. S. Gero. *Knowledge-Based Design Systems.* Reading, Mass.: Addison-Wesley, 1990.

Norman, R. B. "Intuitive Design and Computation." In *Computability of Design,* ed. Y. E. Kalay, 295–301. New York: Wiley Interscience, 1987.

Oxman, R., and R. Oxman. "Cognitive Models in Design Case Libraries." *Automation in Construction* 3, nos. 2–3 (1994): 113–122.

Ozel, F. "An Intelligent Simulation Approach in Simulating Dynamic Processes in Architectural Environments." In *Computer Aided Architectural Design Futures '91,* ed. G. N. Schmitt, 177–190. Wiesbaden, Germany: Vieweg Verlag, 1992.

Rosenman, M., J. Gero, and R. E. Oxman "What's in a Case?" In *Computer Aided Architectural Design Futures '91,* ed. G. N. Schmitt, 285–230. Wiesbaden, Germany: Vieweg Verlag, 1992.

Stahl, F. "Computer Simulation Modeling for Informed Design Decision Making." In *Proceedings of the Thirteenth Annual Conference of the Environmental Design Research Association,* ed. P. Bart, A. Chen, and G. Francescato. Washington, D.C., 1984.

Modalities of Evaluation 18

Architectural solutions must frequently meet a wide range of design objectives, imposed by technological, environmental, social, economic, and other considerations that the solution incorporates or with which it interacts. Each one of these objectives imposes its own requirements, which over the years have become the subject of focused studies, even specialization. For example, the objective of making buildings energy-efficient has enjoyed great popularity since the late 1970s, due to the worldwide energy crisis. As a result, we now have a much better understanding of thermal and visual comfort parameters, and the tools to predict and evaluate building performances relative to energy and light. Some of these understandings have even been codified in the form of minimal energy performance standards, such as California's Title 24.[1] They have resulted in energy evaluation tools, lighting simulation and evaluation tools, numerous conferences, curricula, books, and professional associations.

These individual design objectives become, however, dependent on one another when they are combined in the context of the built environment: design decisions that are intended to meet one objective may support or interfere with others. For example, to achieve optimal energy efficiency, it has been proposed that buildings be located underground, a solution that interferes with other design objectives such as accessibility and view.[2]

Designers must therefore achieve the individual design objectives while reconciling their conflicting effects and side effects with other objectives, to the overall benefit of the design solution as a whole.

The difficulties induced by these often conflicting demands are further exacerbated by the hierarchical nature of the design decision-making process, where broad, general solutions are contemplated first and are gradually refined as the design process unfolds. High-level organizational decisions that were made early in the process will constrain lower-level details, while decisions that concern details limit the designer's freedom in selecting high-level organizational schemas.[3]

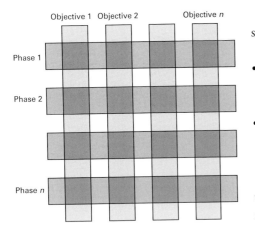

Objective 1   Objective 2   Objective *n*

Phase 1

Phase 2

Phase *n*

18.1 The dual modality of design: multicriteria and multilevel.

Taken together, the synthesis of design solutions can be said to consist of two separate but related modalities:

- The modality in which the designer focuses on one phase of the solution development, searching for a composite solution that achieves multiple design objectives.
- The modality in which the designer moves between different levels of abstraction, searching for a solution to a particular design objective.

Figure 18.1 depicts (schematically) this dual modality. Each horizontal band represents a particular design phase, while each vertical band represents a particular design objective. The bands are overlaid to show the close coupling between the two modalities. Designers engage both modalities alternately and in parallel; it is often difficult to engage one modality without, at the very least, being cognizant of the other.

Given the different modalities of design, and given the centrality of evaluation to the design process, it should come as no surprise that the evaluation of design solutions follows closely the modalities of the design process itself. Hence, we distinguish between multicriteria evaluation and multilevel evaluations.

The multicriteria evaluation modality examines a given design solution from several different points of view (e.g., energy, cost, structural stability). Because it evaluates a particular design solution, this modality is limited to a single design phase. Hence, it corresponds to a horizontal band in figure 18.1.

The multilevel evaluation modality examines how a design solution satisfies a particular design objective (e.g., structural stability), albeit at different levels of abstraction. A schematic design solution may at first appear to satisfy some design objective, but it may be found at a later phase that some design details prevent it from achieving this objective (e.g., the structural solution may appear to be satisfactory at first, but later be found unbuildable due to construction-related obstacles, such as the difficulties or costs associated with the need to sink the piers of a bridge in deep waters). It corresponds, therefore, to a vertical band in figure 18.1.

While it is possible to consider multiple different objectives of a design solution at a particular phase of the design process, or a specific objective across multiple phases, it is virtually impossible to consider all objectives at all phases. Still, a "good" design solution depends on satisfying all the objectives of the project by the time it is considered complete. In fact, "completion" depends on achieving all the objectives of the project to some satisfactory degree.

18.1 Multicriteria Evaluation

Proposed design solutions, as well as realized design projects, exhibit many performance characteristics that meet a variety of design objectives (e.g., budget, comfort, habitability, and so forth). Still, their performance with regard to each objective may vary: a design proposal can excel with regard to some performance objectives yet prove deficient on other counts. This is to be expected, since all performance measures rely on the common physical attributes of the building (e.g., layout and materials). Attempts to maximize performance with regard to one objective influences and impacts performance with regard to other objectives.

Figure 18.2 shows an example of this problem. Two alternative proposals for the design of a school are depicted, along with a visual representation of their performances for each of a number of design objectives (visual impact, circulation, structural performance, and so forth).4 Each segment in the respective pie chart represents the performance of the proposed solution for one design objective. The circle represents normalized desirable performances. A segment that exceeds the circumference of the circle means that the solution performs better than expected with regard to that objective, whereas a segment that does not reach the circumference of the circle means that the solution does not perform as well as desired.

In most cases, the designer must strive to balance the overall performance of the solution, achieving desired performance levels while not inadvertently compromising the performance of other characteristics. When the evaluation shows that all the design objectives cannot be equally well satisfied, the designer must establish the relative importance of competing or conflicting objectives. Such prioritization will allow the designer to determine the overall merit of the solution and compare it to other candidate solutions. The designer must also determine the marginal returns of relaxing certain performances in order to gain in others. For example, when the budget that was established for the purpose of constructing a single-family house requires choosing between a third bedroom

18.2 Different design solutions achieve the same set of performance criteria to different degrees, as demonstrated by the relative lengths of the pie sections that correspond to each criterion. (G. Schmitt, in *Computability of Design*, ed. Y. E. Kalay [New York: Wiley Interscience, 1987].)

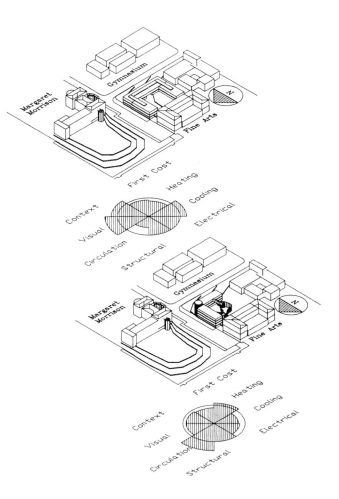

and a family room, which one of the two will the client prefer to have? How will that decision be affected if the choice was between a fourth bedroom and the family room?

Figure 18.3 shows the corresponding pie charts of (a) unweighted; and (b) weighted evaluations of the same design solution, where the width of the segments of the pie chart reflect their relative importance.

Multicriteria Evaluation Software

The examples depicted in figures 18.2 and 18.3 illustrate two problems facing designers of multicriteria evaluation software:

Evaluation

1. Where do the individual performance evaluation programs come from?
2. How can the results of individual performance evaluations be integrated into a composite measure of performance?

The first question pertains to the considerable expertise needed to design any reasonable evaluation software, let alone a software system that can evaluate a design solution in the multicriteria modality. The choice (and the desire) is often to use existing evaluation tools that were developed by experts in their respective fields (some of which are discussed in chapters 19 and 20). Typically, however, each evaluation program requires different input parameters, presented in a particular format, and produces its output in its own unique way that makes it difficult to compare the results of one evaluation to those of another. This makes the use of existing evaluation tools difficult, often to the point where it is deemed easier to redesign each and every evaluation program to fit the integrated system.

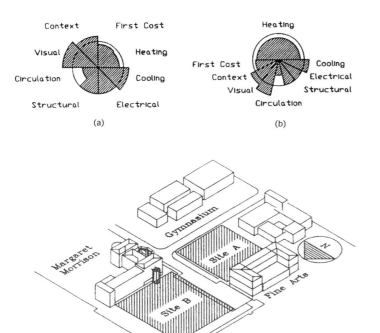

18.3 Visual presentation of weighted multicriteria evaluation. (G. Schmitt, in *Computability of Design*, ed. Y. E. Kalay [New York: Wiley Interscience, 1987].)

Obviously, while redesign solves the second problem, it aggravates the first one, necessitating rewrite of each evaluation program from scratch.

The second problem pertains to integrating the various performance measures into one composite whole, which will qualify as a single, overall measure of the solution's quality. This can be done by weighting the importance of each performance characteristic relative to others or by using some rule-based integration mechanism, based on experience, which can trade one performance against others. It can be argued, however, that the overall value of a design solution is a subjective matter. While that is undoubtedly true (what is important to one designer may be less so to another), it is also true that what designers (and their clients) expect from multicriteria evaluation software is often an overall value, which would help them choose among multiple options.

Wiezel and Becker's Approach

Wiezel and Becker have demonstrated an integration approach based on a specially developed set of evaluation programs that evaluate the thermal, acoustical, fire safety and lighting performance of a building.[5] The results of the individual evaluations were weighted as percentages of the overall evaluation (fig. 18.4). These weights were based on an extensive survey of existing facilities,[6] and careful adjustment of sample test cases to derive composite results that matched the researchers' experience-based assessments. The overall result is the sum Q_k of n individually weighted qualities q:

$$Q_k = \sum_{n=1}^{N} W_n q_{n,k}$$

This method allowed Wiezel and Becker to produce a single composite measure of performance for each design proposal. While recognizing that such a singular measure is meaningful only for comparative purposes, it shows the designer how improving certain aspects of the solution may hurt (or enhance) other performance aspects. The drawback of Wiezel and Becker's method is its lack of extensibility: it is difficult to add additional criteria for evaluation since additions will necessitate reweighting each one of the many other criteria.

	Building parameter	Enhancing criterion ("prevention of")	W_n (%)
1	Acoustic insulation of exterior envelope	Noise penetration from outside	8.5
2	Thermal insulation and resistance to fungi of internal coverings	Mold growth due to condensation in the dwelling	8.5
3	Acoustic insulation of interdwelling partitions and floors	Noise penetration form neighboring dwellings	7.6
4	Balance between thermal insulation and thermal time constant (TTC) of envelope	Excessive expenditures for cooling during summer	7.4
5	Fire endurance of external envelope	Fire penetration into the dwelling from outside	7.4
6	Medium TTC of external envelope	Excessive heat during summer	7.4
7	Low fire spread of interior coverings	Fire spread in the dwelling	7.2
8	Location of thermal insulation close to the inside	Excessive cold in the evening during winter	7.2
9	Low TTC of envelope	Excessive heat in the evening during summer	7.0
10	Thermal insulation of external envelope	Excessive cold at night during winter	7.0
11	Thermal insulation and high TTC of envelope	Excessive expenditures for heating during winter	6.6
12	Location of thermal insulation close to the inside	Excessive cold in the morning during winter	6.3
13	Acoustic insulation of intradwelling partitions	Noise penetrating between rooms within dwellings	6.1
14	Acoustic insulation of intradwelling partitions	Being heard in other rooms (privacy)	5.9

18.4 Weighting factors for individual performance criteria. (A. Wiezel and R. Becker, in *Evaluating and Predicting Design Performance*, ed. Y. E. Kalay [New York: Wiley Interscience, 1992].)

IBDE

In contrast to Wiezel and Becker's approach, the Integrated Software Environment for Building Design and Construction Planning (IBDE), developed at Carnegie Mellon University, relies on a host of existing evaluation programs that deal with spatial configuration, structural design, and construction planning issues in high-rise office buildings.[7] Developed independently, each of these evaluation programs requires a different representation schema and control mechanism. Communication and coordination among the different programs, therefore, is one of the major issues underlying the IBDE. They are provided through shared memories called blackboards, which serve as common data stores (of different kinds) for the various evaluation processes.[8]

The IBDE comprises a number of knowledge-based processes, a controller, a data store and data store manager, message and constraint blackboards, and a user interface (fig. 18.5). The constituent processes are capable of both evaluation and generation of design solutions. The overall process provides each subprocess with data and constraints generated by the other subprocesses. When encountering an unacceptable choice made by another subprocess, processes turn into "critics" and post their criticism to the shared blackboard.

18.5 Overall architecture of the IBDE system. (F. J. Fenves et al., in *Evaluating and Predicting Design Performance*, ed. Y. E. Kalay [New York: Wiley Interscience, 1992].)

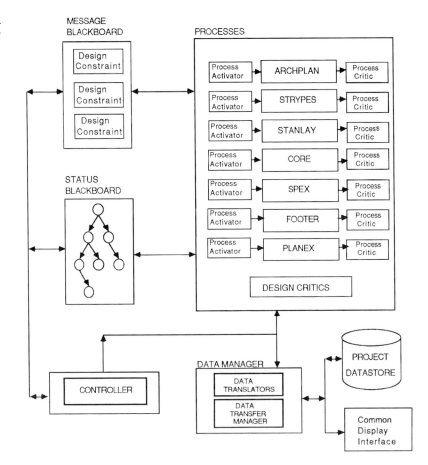

This integration approach allows each process to maintain its identity and follow its own method of evaluation and solution generation, while providing a coordination mechanism that steers the overall design process toward a common goal. Thus, the IBDE does not attempt to derive a composite evaluation, but rather to assure that the evolving design solution complies with the constraints underlying each aspect of performance represented in the overall system. The system invokes individual processes as needed and may reinvoke them if advice (or criticism) are warranted. This is determined by the nature of the postings placed by individual processes on the common blackboards. For example, ARCHPLAN—the module responsible for architectural planning and evaluation—may produce a configuration that includes a service core.[9] This part of the design is evaluated by CORE—the service core evaluator module—which is invoked to generate and test the layout of service core elements (elevators, lobbies, rest rooms, emergency stairs, utility rooms, and so on).[10] If it finds that it is unable to generate an acceptable core, ARCHPLAN will be invoked again to redesign the floor plan, and so on until an acceptable design is reached—or the user intervenes.

COSMOS

A hybrid approach that combines the advantages of both an integrated set of evaluators and stand-alone ones was developed by Hacfoort and Veldhuisen at Eindhoven University of Technology.[11] The system, called COSMOS, provides a quick, rough evaluation of a building using built-in integrated evaluation tools that can assess the design's performance in areas such as cost, energy, acoustics, lighting, construction, and utility. If the building passes this first evaluation, the data is sent to stand-alone evaluators for more comprehensive evaluation (fig. 18.6).

Rather than attempt to derive an overall performance measure, Hacfoort and Veldhuisen chose to establish the relative value of trading off pairs of performance measures that depend on the same design variables. For example, a window is a design variable that is responsible for both the view and the amount of noise that penetrates the building. A larger window will afford a better view but also allow more noise to penetrate (a factor that can be reduced by improving the glazing, but this will increase the cost of the window). The composite value of relative performance measures can be established by using one of two methods: (1) by linear least-square equations (fig. 18.7a); or (2) a contingencies table (fig. 18.7b). The first method produces a "cloud" of points in the space defined by the two variables, indicating datum points (points that correspond to the paired performance of two variables). The least-squares method shows the overall correspondence between the datum points. For example, in figure 18.7a it shows that the cost per cubic meter of mean thermal insulation increases as more insulation is added. This method is applicable when there is a continuous, monotonic correspondence between the variables. The second method is applicable when the correspondence between the variables is not continuous and monotonic. This is the case, for example, in trying to put a value on the view relative to the amount of noise a

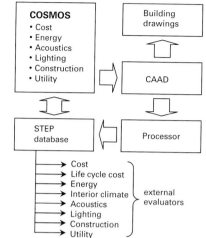

18.6 Overall architecture of the COSMOS system. [E. J. Hacfoort and J. Veldhuisen, in *Evaluating and Predicting Design Performance*, ed. Y. E. Kalay [New York: Wiley Interscience, 1992].]

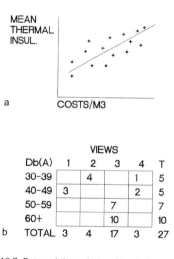

18.7 Determining relationships between various criteria: (a) scattergram, (b) contingencies table. [E. J. Hacfoort and J. Veldhuisen, in *Evaluating and Predicting Design Performance*, ed. Y. E. Kalay [New York: Wiley Interscience, 1992].]

window transmits. While larger windows allow more noise to penetrate the building, doubling the amount of windows does not necessarily double the view. Using this method, the client may indicate his or her preferences (in the form of ordinal values on a scale of 1 to 10) of the combined effects of view and noise.

18.2 Multilevel Evaluation

The difficulty of designing large and complex artifacts such as buildings necessitates the use of hierarchical abstraction and stepwise refinement methods as means of partitioning the design process into discrete, manageable "chunks," called design phases.

Typically, a design solution is first conceived schematically, then further developed and detailed in subsequent design phases. The development and elaboration of detailed design decisions requires considerable effort, and provides a basis for making other design decisions. It may be very useful to know in advance—before much effort is spent on their elaboration—the implications of early design decisions on the overall performance of the solution and on the options they will afford (or exclude) in later phases of the design process.

The emerging design solution needs, therefore, to be evaluated at different levels of abstraction. Early in the design process there may not be sufficient information to allow the application of detailed evaluation procedures, nor would it be meaningful to do so even if it were possible. Rather, a generalized appraisal of the solution may be called for to verify that the approach chosen by the designer is at all on the right track. Conversely, in later phases of the design process it may be possible and desirable to perform a detailed evaluation of the performances of the proposed solution. At intermediate design phases, when the design solution is only partially developed, it may be prudent to use evaluation methods that can operate with whatever information is available and provide results that are meaningful for the specific design phase. In other words, different evaluation methods are needed at different design phases.

The major problem in developing software that can assist designers in performing multilevel evaluation of individual design parameters stems from the different informational characteristics of the design phases they must span. Each phase of the design process typically relies upon and includes a different informational content. Early on the solution may be expressed in generalized, often textual form, which describes the overall qualities of the solution but does not describe its shape, structure, or even the specific materials it is made of. At later design phases, of course, all this information is available. In fact, there may be too much information, and the evaluator must carefully select those facts that are relevant to its assessment.

The different informational characteristics of different abstraction levels determine the kind of software tools that can be used for evaluation. Late design phase evaluations—having to do with such concerns as energy, structures, acoustics, and cost—have been developed over the past five decades and enjoy a considerable body of knowledge to support ever increasing detailed and accurate assessment of fully developed design solutions. Early design phase evaluations, which can assess informationally poor design abstractions, are relatively scarce. And tools that can assess the performance of intermediate design phases are practically nonexistent. How, then, can the performance of design solutions be evaluated at the different phases of the process?

Three approaches have emerged to handle multilevel evaluation:

1. Augmenting the informational characteristics of early design solutions through the use of defaults and approximations.
2. Developing evaluation tools that can deal explicitly with informationally poor design solutions, using heuristics rather than calculations.
3. Using methods that "understand" the implications of early design phase decisions on later design phases by automatically "elaborating" them.

Defaults and Approximations

Decisions that are made in early design phases have a significant impact on the design solution, but do not carry enough information to permit the use of evaluation software developed for later design phases.

Substituting default values for missing information permits the application at early design phases of evaluation software that was originally developed for late design phases. The Building Design Advisor (BDA), developed by the Building Technologies Program at the Lawrence Berkeley National Laboratory (LBNL), uses this approach to support a number of

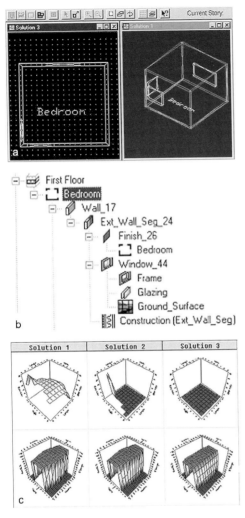

b

c

18.8 Building Design Advisor (a) schematic graphic editor, (b) prototypical values database, (c) decision desktop. (K. Papamichael et al., in *Automation in Construction* 6, no. 4 [1998].)

environmental evaluations at early design phases.[12] To use the BDA, the user specifies the basic geometric attributes of spaces, windows, doors, and other building elements, using a schematic graphic editor (fig. 18.8a). The program automatically assigns default values from a prototypical values database to all the nongeometric parameters that are required for energy and other types of evaluation, such as the thermal properties of walls and windows, and the occupancy schedules of the building (fig. 18.8b). These default values are based on the location, building type, and space type of the specific project. The user can review and change them at any time. The proposed design solution can then be evaluated by late design phase energy evaluation software such as DOE-2[13] and lighting evaluation software like DElight.[14] The results of the evaluations can be viewed on BDA's decision desktop (fig. 18.8c), which allows designers to compare multiple alternative design solutions with respect to the same design considerations.

The advantages of using a default-based approach to apply well-developed, late design phase evaluations at early design phases are twofold: (1) late design phase evaluations are readily available in many fields; (2) they tend to be better developed than evaluations that were developed explicitly to handle early design phases, whose informational characteristics limit the scope of the evaluation.

The use of defaults to fill in missing information does, however, also have two drawbacks: (1) if the building does not conform to the averages from which the defaults were derived, their use may actually be misleading. For example, assuming a default insulation for buildings in hot, humid climatic zones may aggravate the thermal solution rather than improve it;[15] (2) it may not be meaningful to perform precise evaluations and to provide the designer with a false sense of "exact" heat loss information or precise sizing of structural elements—even were it possible to calculate them using default values—when the designer has not yet committed to specific wall materials and openings, or to a particular structural system. Rather, at the early phases of the design process, the designer may be interested only in the effects that the orientation of the building will have on its general energy consumption and whether the chosen structural schema is at all plausible.

To overcome these disadvantages, a less elaborate but effective and commonly used method to derive the details needed to evaluate an unelaborated design solution is to use evaluation procedures that can work with approximated values—determined from the gross, schematic details of the design variables.

Such an approximation-based approach to multilevel evaluation has been used by Robert Johnson to support judicious resource allocation by calculating the cost of alternative solutions early in the design process.[16] His method handles the different informational profiles of design solutions at the different phases of the process by arranging the defaults in a hierarchical object database, where lower levels of the hierarchy correspond to more detailed design solutions. For example, the perimeter of a building depends both on the size of its footprint and its shape. Johnson provides approximation formulae to calculate the perimeter of generic building shapes (fig. 18.9). Clearly these calculations cannot provide accurate measures, but such measures would not be meaningful at the early phases of the design process anyway. Using these formulae, it is possible to compute gross cost per square foot of alternative building forms, which can help the designer to choose from among alternative schemas. The estimates can be refined by adding more accurate dimensioning and material costs as the design solution becomes more detailed over time.

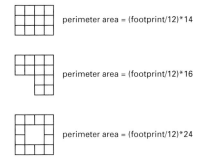

18.9 Example of approximations for calculating the area of the perimeter walls of differently shaped buildings. (R. E. Johnson, in *Evaluating and Predicting Design Performance*, ed. Y. E. Kalay [New York: Wiley Interscience, 1992].)

Heuristics

Rather than automatically fill in details in an unelaborated design solution to match the needs of an existing evaluation tool, it is possible to match the information needs of the tool to available data. The evaluation, in this case, will necessarily be less accurate and less specific than late design phase evaluations, but it may be more appropriate for the needs of the designer at early design phases.

Such an approach has been demonstrated by Energy Expert, a system developed by Bharati Jog.[17] It uses heuristics, or rules of thumb, which are generalized, encapsulated chunks of "common knowledge" gleaned from the experience of experts. It calculates seasonal energy uses of a building in the schematic design phase and provides advice on improving the design of that building to make it more energy-efficient. Unlike many other energy evaluation systems, Energy Expert is able to predict the building's energy performance in its schematic design phase.

The system's database contains information collected from seventy cities in the USA, comprising facts about the temperature and the direct and diffused sunlight each city receives during an average day in four seasons. The information about the building itself is taken from user input or calculated from a schematic drawing. It includes floor and roof areas, floor to roof height, desired interior temperature range, exterior walls and window areas in each direction and their U values, average number of occupants, and fuel costs.

The advice provided by the system concerns design decisions that would reduce the need for artificial heating and cooling while maintaining the internal temperature at the desired comfort range. Seasonal energy performance is tested for six possible conditions, expressed as rules and actions:

1. IF heat loss all day THEN action 1
2. IF some heat loss AND some allowable heat gain THEN action 2
3. IF some heat loss AND some allowable heat gain AND some excess heat gain THEN action 3
4. IF all allowable heat gain THEN action 4
5. IF some allowable heat gain AND some excess heat gain THEN action 5
6. IF all excess heat gain THEN action 6

The action part of the rules directs the system to check for certain subconditions (e.g., the difference in temperatures outside the building and its interior) and advises the designer which actions might be taken to improve the comfort level while reducing energy costs. The advice (called solutions) includes:

1. Increasing/decreasing internal heat generation
2. Increasing/decreasing solar heat gain
3. Increasing/decreasing envelope heat gain and loss
4. Increasing/decreasing ventilation heat gain and loss
5. Storing heat
6. Storing cold

Each solution is accompanied by a list of directives, which form the advice presented to the user. The directives include instructions such as INCREASE EXPOSURE, CONSIDER ACTIVE SOLAR HEATING, and INCREASE

ABSORPTIVITY. Each of these directive is accompanied by a list of suggestions, such as PROVIDE LARGE OVERHANGS, REDUCE FLOOR TO FLOOR HEIGHT, CONSIDER A MORE COMPACT CONFIGURATION, and so on.

For example, if the energy performance of the building is such that during the fall season there is some heat loss, some allowable heat gain, and some excess heat gain, rule number 3 is triggered. Its list of solutions includes DECREASING ENVELOPE HEAT GAIN AND LOSS, DECREASING VENTILATION, HEAT GAIN AND LOSS, and STORING HEAT.

These solutions trigger directives and suggestions which, if followed, would reduce the heat gain of the building in the fall. Suggestions are displayed on the screen, accompanied by graphs that help the designer visualize the problem (fig. 18.10).

One advantage of using a heuristic-based system like Energy Expert is that it lets the designer access evaluations early in the design process in a manner that is most appropriate for improving the design. A disadvantage is that the advice is indeed generalized and not solution-specific.

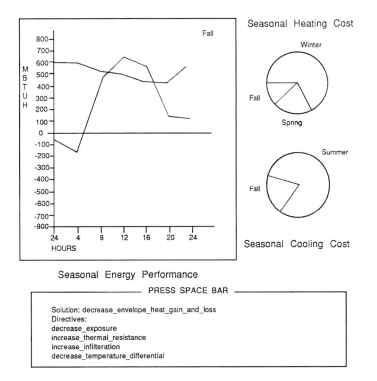

18.10 Energy Expert evaluates the thermal performance of a building in its early design phases and presents generalized information and advice. (B. Jog, in *Evaluating and Predicting Design Performance*, ed. Y. E. Kalay [New York: Wiley Interscience, 1992].)

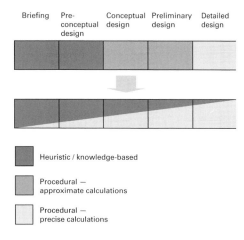

Briefing   Pre-   Conceptual   Preliminary   Detailed
            conceptual design   design   design
            design

■ Heuristic / knowledge-based

▨ Procedural —
  approximate calculations

☐ Procedural —
  precise calculations

18.11 Schematic comparison of the combined
heuristic/defaults approach (bottom) and separate
heuristics and default-based evaluations (top). (E.
Shaviv and Y. E. Kalay, in *Evaluating and Predicting
Design Performance*, ed. Y. E. Kalay [New York:
Wiley Interscience, 1992].)

A Combined Approach

The difficulty associated with choosing the appropriate default values or heuristics needed to perform an evaluation when the design is still in its schematic form have been recognized by Shaviv and Kalay, who developed a system that uses a combination of rules, defaults, and precise simulation to evaluate the thermal properties of a design proposal.[18] In the early phases of the design process, heuristic rules are used to provide generalized advice on energy-related design decisions, such as preferred orientations, overall form attributes, and the relative importance of ventilation versus insulation. In later design phases, the heuristics help the architect select appropriate default values so that simplified but accurate energy simulation models (LCR and SLR) can be used. In late design phases, accurate thermal evaluation software can be used to calculate precise thermal performance.

This approach balances the use of heuristics and default values throughout the design process, providing advice that is appropriate to the level of detail under consideration (fig. 18.11). The data needed to construct the heuristics was generated from hundreds of simulations of different buildings in many climatic zones. The data thus generated was analyzed manually and encapsulated in rules of thumb and defaults.

18.3 Constraint Propagation

To assess the impact of design decisions made in one phase of the design process on decisions made in subsequent phases it is necessary to consider how the "gross" decisions made in early phases will be elaborated later on. For example, if at an early design phase the architect decided to orient the building in a particular direction, perhaps to abide by the site's zoning regulations or to orient it to an access road or views, she or he has in fact determined many of the energy performance characteristics of the building or at least has created certain problems that the energy consultant will have to solve, such as requiring extensive shading devices or specially coated glazing to reduce heat gain. The orientation decision has, therefore, implicitly determined design factors that have not yet been fully considered at that stage of the design process. Any subsequent design details that result from this early decision may turn out to be easily accommodated in later design phases, or they may become the source of costly problems.

DESIGN PHASE	a	b	c	d	e
Total floor area	⊕		+	+	
Volume of building		⊕	+	+	
Number of external walls			⊕	+	
Azimuth of reference wall			⊕	+	
Area of internal mass				⊕	+
Heat capacity of internal mass					⊕
Initial temperature distribution		⊕			
Heat gains: constant	⊕				
Heat gains: schedule	⊕				
Heater: schedule; temperature set		⊕			+
Cooler: schedule; temperature set		⊕			+
Vent: type; schedule, ACH: day; night		⊕			+
Wall No. 1					
Number of layers				⊕	+
Materials (c, Λ, d)				⊕	+
" " "					
" " "					
Wall: azimuth, inclination			⊕	+	
Area of wall			⊕	+	
Wall: albedo, emissivity					⊕
Wall: SC-summer, winter				⊕	+
Number of windows and solar elements			⊕	+	
Window: area			⊕	+	
Window: type				⊕	+
Window: SC-summer, winter		⊕			+
U window: day; night				⊕	+
U window: schedule		⊕			+

18.12 The design phases at which various energy-related design parameters are first considered (⊕), and reconsidered (+). The design phases are: (a) briefing, (b) preconceptual, (c) conceptual, (d) preliminary, and (e) detailed design. (E. Shaviv and Y. E. Kalay, in *Evaluating and Predicting Design Performance*, ed. Y. E. Kalay [New York: Wiley Interscience, 1992].)

To avoid such problems, it is desirable to know in advance what the impact of early decisions on the evolving solution will be on later design phases. To do so, however, it is often necessary to add more design details, which would be needed to make such subsequent assessments. These details have, as we have seen earlier, not yet been decided at the early design phases, when the decisions are made, and it would be impractical to ask the designer to make them at the early stage of the process. How, then, would it be possible to assess the implications of the designer's early-phase decisions on subsequent phases?

Shaviv and Kalay's method provides an answer to this problem by explicitly considering the subsequent effects of each design parameter on the thermal behavior of the building as a whole (fig. 18.12). For example, total floor area is one of the first parameters to be decided in the design process, and it has a considerable impact on the energy needs of a building. As the design process unfolds, the floor area becomes more accurately defined, along with its energy-related implications.

The system's knowledge base contains rules for constraining the selection of building parameters at later phases of the process, given the early-phase decisions. These rules, operating bi-directionally (i.e., top-down and bottom-up), can be used to inform the designer of the consequences (if any) that certain design choices will have on the thermal performance of the building.

The benefits of this approach, however, come at a considerable cost of system development: every design parameter must be considered and reconsidered, and its implications for every other design decision must be explicitly determined.

TOPDOWN

TOPDOWN, a system developed by Liggett and colleagues attempts to (partially) resolve this system-development problem by automating the functional interpretation of architectonic shapes, such as columns and floor plans, and their propagation across design phases.[19] It allows the designer to check the degree to which the evaluated element will fulfill its desired function (e.g. , structural support, floor area) at any phase of the design process. TOPDOWN deals with the problem of interpreting the implications of design decisions made at different levels of the representational abstraction by employing shape grammars that tell the system how to refine an abstract, high-level subsystem into a specific arrangement of detailed, lower-level subsystems, and how to assemble a set of detailed, lower-level subsystems into higher-level ones. For example, the problem of designing a small house can be solved by first enumerating the topological patterns of rooms that satisfy some adjacency requirements, then adding dimensions that comply with standard room sizes and proportions. TOPDOWN emulates this process by elaborating the overall shape of the house from gross configurations to the fine details of its internal layout. At each step, alternative internal room patterns are considered for substitution, and values are assigned to dimensioning variables such that the adjacency, minimum and maximum room areas, and proportions are pre-

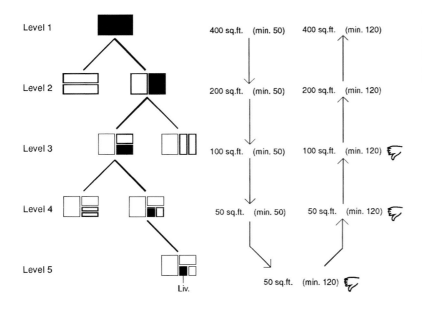

Level 1

Level 2

Level 3

Level 4

Level 5

Liv.

400 sq.ft.　(min. 50)　　400 sq.ft.　(min. 120)

200 sq.ft.　(min. 50)　　200 sq.ft.　(min. 120)

100 sq.ft.　(min. 50)　　100 sq.ft.　(min. 120)

50 sq.ft.　(min. 50)　　50 sq.ft.　(min. 120)

50 sq.ft.　(min. 120)

18.13　Transformation rules and evaluations for TOPDOWN refinement of a schematic design. (S. R. Liggett et al., in *Evaluating and Predicting Design Performance*, ed. Y. E. Kalay [New York: Wiley Interscience, 1992].)

served. Evaluations are applied at every level to determine if one or more rooms have violated some constraints (fig. 18.13).

The user can—even at the very early phases of the process—quickly determine which configurations may work and which not and thus concentrate his or her efforts on developing only those configurations that are likely to succeed. And since TOPDOWN operates in an interactive manner, the user can change dimensions while learning of the implications.

PREDIKT

A different method to support the interpretive transformation of one level of representational abstraction into another was developed by Rivka Oxman, using a rule-based expert system called PREliminary Design of KITchens (PREDIKT).[20]

The system operates both as a design generator and a design critic. In the first mode, the system can, given some input from the user, generate kitchen designs. In the second mode, the system can evaluate design solutions proposed by the user. It uses a rule-based expert system to facilitate both the translation between different levels of abstraction and the generation and evaluation of design alternatives. It can infer implied design decisions—ones not yet made explicitly by the designer—and evaluate their desirability. For example, it can evaluate the quality of a yet undesigned window in the kitchen, based on the wall area available for locating the window and the adjacent appliances. Both the selection of the wall and the need for a window are inferred from the current state of the design.

These examples demonstrate the complexity of evaluation's multicriteria and multilevel modalities and some of the methods and the tools that have been developed to support them. A tool that can support both modalities is yet to be developed. It will involve not only a collection of criterion-specific tools, each capable of multilevel evaluation, but also the means needed to develop a composite assessment of the design at every abstraction level. In addition, such a tool will also require means that will facilitate composite assessment across different levels of abstraction, which will help the designer choose design solutions that may appear deficient in one aspect at one level of abstraction only to emerge as superior overall later on.

Bibliography

Hartkopf, V., V. Loftness, P. Mill, and M. Siegel. "Architecture and Software for Interactive Learning about Total Building Performance." In *Evaluating and Predicting Design Performance,* ed. Y. E. Kalay, 183–194. New York: Wiley Interscience, 1992.

Jockusch, P. R. A. "How Can We Achieve a Good Design?" In *Evaluating and Predicting Design Performance,* ed. Y. E. Kalay, 37–50. New York: Wiley Interscience, 1992.

Karpak, B., and S. Zionts. *Multiple Criteria Decision Making and Risk Analysis Using Microcomputers.* Berlin: Springer-Verlag, 1989.

Keeney, R., and H. Raiffa. *Decisions with Multiple Objectives: Preferences and Value Tradeoffs.* New York: John Wiley and Sons, 1977.

Manning, P., and S. Mattar. "A Preliminary to Development of Expert Systems for Total Design of Entire Buildings." In *Evaluating and Predicting Design Performance,* ed. Y. E. Kalay, 215–238. New York: Wiley Interscience, 1992.

Schmitt, G. "Design for Performance." In *Evaluating and Predicting Design Performance,* ed. Y. E. Kalay, 83–100. New York: Wiley Interscience, 1992.

Evaluating Quantifiable Qualities 19

To perform an evaluation, three conditions must be met:

- There needs to be an *object,* or a representation of one, to be evaluated.
- There needs to be a set of *objectives,* or benchmarks, that state the desired level of performance.
- There needs be a *method* for comparing the two.

Many building-related performance characteristics meet these conditions and are, therefore, amenable to evaluation. They include the structural performance of a building, how well it meets its occupants' functional needs (sizes, proportions, adjacencies, and so forth), its overall cost, the level (and cost) of thermal comfort it provides to its occupants, and the level of acoustical insulation it affords. Each of these performance characteristics enjoys an extensive body of research and a host of computational tools that have been developed over the years for its evaluation.

The intent of this chapter is to demonstrate how computational methods can be used to evaluate quantifiable building characteristics for the sake of illustrating the implementation of the principles discussed earlier. It does not presume to provide a comprehensive introduction to any one of these evaluations, each of which requires a tome of its own.

19.1 Structures

The purpose of the structural schema and components of a building are to ensure that the realized design will stand up to gravitational, wind, and seismic forces while supporting the functional goals of the building (including shelter or passage, in the case of bridges) as well as the aesthetics chosen by the architect.

Principles

The structure of a building must resist two general types of loads:

1. *Vertical loads*—generated by gravity as the result of the uses the building is made for ("live" loads) and the weight of the building itself ("dead" loads).
2. *Lateral loads*—generated by wind and seismic forces.

Loads of the first type are countered by building elements that transfer the forces to the ground, such as columns and bearing walls. The second type are countered by elements that stiffen and anchor the building—shear walls, braced frames, tension wires or buttresses—and transfer the lateral loads to the foundations.

In addition to design goals, the structure must contend with natural constraints, such as the properties of the materials used, climatic conditions (e.g., extreme cold), methods of assembly to be used in the construction phase, soil conditions, as well as constraints imposed by building codes and regulations. Wind bracing, for example, is part of the design of every building, but it becomes one of the cardinal design constraints for tall buildings, where up to 10% of the structure's weight and cost goes toward accommodating this constraint. Likewise, the strength of different materials has a direct impact on the structure. Some materials work well for tension loads (e.g., steel) while others can better resist compression loads (e.g., concrete). Steel-reinforced concrete resists both tension and compression loads.

There are many ways to design structural solutions to meet the goals and abide by the constraints. Each of these options will have some advantages and some disadvantages, and the role of evaluation and prediction methods is to help the engineer find out and compare the relative merits of different design options, making it possible to choose the one most suitable for a particular design.

For example, if one solution fails in spanning a distance for a roof or bridging a chasm, other design schemes or materials can be tried. Steel may be used in place of timber, or a combination of structural methods may be used, such as pretensioning and precompression. Yet another level of choice is to design within a given design methodology but to alter the internal system, as in using lightweight trusses in lieu of beams.

Evaluation

Construction methods have varied over time, depending on such factors as the availability of materials, technologies, and the means for achieving stylistic goals. This diversity was driven by economics, politics, even religion. Today, many of these same issues govern options in the construction process. Code restrictions, on-site assembly limitations, and sustainability are additional variables the designer must contend with. In total, multiple factors make every design solution take on a uniqueness of its own, so that no two situations are exactly the same. The structural engineer must juggle all these variables and more without sacrificing the safety of the inhabitants.

Habitual Methods

Designing a structural solution that meets the goals and abides by the constraints of the project involves the acts of calculation, reasoning, simulation, extrapolation, and some guessing. Over the years, engineers have developed analytical and heuristic methods to predict the performance of buildings and to analyze the behavior of given structures.

Typically these methods involve the identification of the forces operating in a structure and designing structural elements that counter them. For hundreds of years engineers have developed structural design methods using hand calculations. These methods, like those we use today, required a strong understanding of mathematics, physics, and materials' properties. However, more important than these was the experience of many years of trial and error that was attainable only through long apprenticeship.

When pressure, shear, and moment (PVM) diagrams were developed, they became the primary communication and analysis tools.

SAP2000

Analytical methods use computational mechanics and finite element analysis to determine and balance the stresses, strains, forces, and displacements that occur in a structure. The governing equation for such analyses is:

$$[K]\{u\} = \{F\}$$

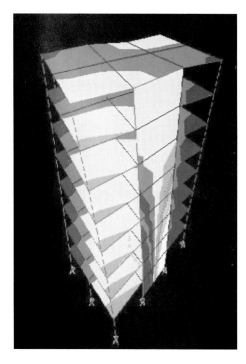

19.1 SAP2000 produces color-coded stress maps showing how the building responds to earthquake and wind loads (Computers and Structures, Berkeley, California). (See color plate 15.)

where $[K]$ is the structural stiffness matrix, $\{u\}$ is the displacement vector, and $\{F\}$ includes concentrated forces, pressures, and thermal or inertial loads.

Analytical computational analysis systems include SAP2000, Design Space, and ANSYS, to name a few. SAP2000, developed by Computers and Structures of Berkeley, California, is a structural engineering computer program based on finite element analysis methods. Through its powerful graphical user interface, the user can create and modify the structural model, execute the analysis, and check and optimize the design.

SAP2000 provides fast equation solvers, force and displacement loading, nonprismatic frame elements, highly accurate shell element calculations, Eigen and Ritz dynamic analysis, multiple coordinate systems for skewed geometry, many different constraint options, the ability to merge independently defined meshes, a fully coupled six-by-six spring stiffness, and the option to combine or envelope multiple dynamic analyses in the same run. It displays the results graphically, including real-time time-history displacements (fig. 19.1).

The SAP2000 PLUS program adds unlimited capacity bridge-analysis capabilities, a complete range of finite elements, time-history analysis options, and ground motion effects with multiple base excitations. The SAP2000 Nonlinear version extends the PLUS capabilities by adding a dynamic nonlinear link element for gaps, hooks, isolators, dampers, and hinges. This nonlinear link element (Nllink) allows engineers to model the dynamic behavior of everything from tension-only braces in buildings to post-yield hinges in three-dimensional frames to elastomeric bearings for bridges and base-isolated buildings. The programs feature powerful and completely integrated design modules for steel and concrete, accessible from within the same interface used to create and analyze the model. The design of steel frame members features initial member sizing and iterative optimization. The design of concrete frame members includes the calculation of the amount of reinforcing steel required.

19.2 Energy

The growing mechanization and industrialization of society causes people to spend most of their time indoors (upward of 95%, according to some estimates).[1] As a result, interest has grown in designing indoor environmental conditions within which people feel comfortable in terms of heat

Evaluation

gain/loss and perspiration. Thermal comfort is influenced primarily by the ambient temperature of the air, its relative humidity, relative air velocity, mean radiant temperature, activity level, and thermal resistance of closing. Buildings gain from and lose energy to the environment. Therefore, geographical location, season of the year, time of day, and local conditions—like topography, proximity to bodies of water, trees, and the effects of other buildings—affect the thermal conditions of buildings. These conditions vary by the day and by the hour. Buildings must be designed to reduce the effect of fluctuating external conditions and to maintain constant comfortable thermal conditions for the inhabitants. This can be achieved by choosing appropriate design parameters in the first place ("passive" environmental controls) and by the judicious deployment of mechanical heating, cooling, and ventilation systems ("active" environmental controls).

The importance of properly designing the environmental control characteristics of buildings goes far beyond thermal comfort. Studies have shown that in the United States, buildings account for roughly 36% of total energy consumption and 64% of electricity consumption.[2] Passive environmental controls contribute significantly to the form of individual buildings, neighborhoods, even entire cities; at the same time they can save much of this energy expenditure.

It is not surprising, therefore, that the importance of energy-conscious design has been recognized for over forty years and was enacted into law in California in 1978 as Title 24.[3] In principle, this recognition ensures that architects, clients, and developers pay attention to the relationship between the context, the form, the materials, the equipment, and the intended use of buildings for the purpose of maximizing the thermal comfort of their inhabitants while minimizing their life-cycle energy consumption.

Principles

The design of energy conscious buildings depends on determining the combined effect of various building components and site conditions on the thermal comfort of the inhabitants. Habitual energy-related design methods and practices are, to a large extent, the result of continual trial and error in shaping and situating buildings and choosing the proper materials for their constructions. The results of trial and error are most clearly evidenced in vernacular architecture, such as closely clustered, thick-walled, and small-windowed Middle Eastern dwellings; airy tropical dwellings; and heavily insulated and wind-protected Eskimo igloos. However, as designers gain ever more control over the process of making habitable environments, and as the demands for "better" controlled environments grows, designers must assume the responsibility for making decisions that improve comfort conditions while minimizing the expenditure of energy to maintain them.[4]

Over the past forty years, much research has been directed toward modeling, predicting, and evaluating the thermal comfort implications of individual buildings, neighborhoods, and cities, for the purpose of designing them to be more energy-efficient yet thermally comfortable.

Most of these models, and the computational tools that implement them, have typically focused on the performance of individual buildings. They simulate expected energy gain/loss, given the climatic context, the building form, orientation, materials, mechanical systems, and patterns of occupancy.[5]

Heat gain/loss in buildings occurs through conduction, convection, and radiation. In steady-state calculations (where time is not factored in), it is typically modeled in terms of thermal conduction and convection (by means of infiltration, especially around windows), although radiation (through direct sun penetration through windows) can contribute a significant additional heat gain/loss. Computation of heat rate transfer is based on the laws of thermodynamics: heat flows from a higher-temperature locus to a lower-temperature locus until a state of equilibrium is reached. The transfer of heat changes the internal energy of both systems involved in the process, which in the case of buildings means that the interior temperature will, over time, rise if the exterior is warmer and will fall if the exterior is cooler. The rate of heat transfer depends on the temperature gradient, the area of contact, and the material properties of the medium through which the heat transfer process occurs:

$$\text{Heat transfer rate} = \text{Area} \times (T_{\text{inside}} - T_{\text{outside}}) \text{ / thermal resistance}$$

Computer programs that can help evaluate the energy gain/loss of buildings must perform such calculations for each part of the building's envelope, including all walls, roofs, floors, and windows (or other openings). They generally fall into one of two categories:

1. Steady-state programs.
2. Dynamic simulation programs.

Steady-state programs ignore the time it takes heat to flow from one side of the wall to its other side. This simplifies the calculation and is appropriate for sites where the external temperature does not fluctuate much during any 24-hour period.

Where the day/night temperatures differ considerably, as in subtropical and desert areas, the heat capacity of construction materials must be taken into account, which requires the use of a dynamic simulation model. Heat capacity is the property of a material that makes it conceptually like a "container," which must be "filled" with heat before it is transferred to the next medium. In the case of buildings, masonry walls have a large heat capacity, compared to frame construction. Hence, there is a lag between the heat build-up during the day outside the building and the time it begins to affect the building's interior. If this lag is long enough to last until the outside temperature begins to drop in the evening, comfortable interior temperature can be maintained by closing the windows during the daytime (and shading them to block heat gain due to solar radiation) and allowing cross ventilation in the evening and at night, when the outside temperature drops. Computer programs that can keep track of the time lag associated with heat capacitance are, necessarily, "dynamic," and must be able to solve time-dependent heat flow equations. Moreover, since thermal capacitance (and conductivity) varies for different building materials (e.g., the roof and the walls typically have very different material properties), such models must solve the heat flow equations simultaneously for all parts of the building's envelope.

DOE-2

DOE-2 is a detailed, multizone, whole-building, hourly simulation program widely used in the United States and other countries for calculating the energy consumption and operating costs of commercial or residential buildings. Originating as an energy evaluation program written for the U.S. Post Office in the late 1960s, it has been continuously developed for the U.S. Department of Energy by the Simulation Research Group at the Lawrence Berkeley National Laboratory ever since.

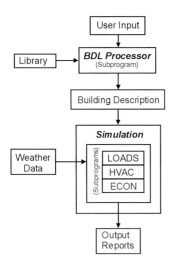

User Input

Library → BDL Processor (Subprogram)

Building Description

Simulation
(Subprograms)
LOADS
HVAC
ECON

Weather Data

Output Reports

19.2 The structure of DOE-2.

DOE-2 has been used in the design or remodeling of such noted buildings as the White House in Washington, the World Trade Center in New York, the Sears Tower in Chicago, the National Library of France, the new Parliament House in Australia, and many others. Users report an average 22% reduction in energy consumption through use of DOE-2. In the U.S. alone, this has led to a savings of approximately $11 billion in energy costs through 1998.[6]

The input to DOE-2 consists of hourly weather information and a description of the building, its HVAC equipment, and the utility rate structure at the building's location. Its output consists of hourly variations in indoor ambient climate conditions, internal heat loads, as well as evaluation of the impact of equipment performance and operating conditions, such as thermostat setbacks.

Written in FORTRAN, DOE-2 comprises a subprogram for translating user-supplied input to DOE-2 internal building description data structure (BDL Processor), and several simulation subprograms that perform specific calculations (fig. 19.2).

DOE-2 has been the basis of books and design guides on energy-efficient buildings and the source of algorithms and calculation techniques used by professional societies and industry groups for research, development, and energy-related impact analysis. It has also been used by federal agencies for developing energy efficiency standards for building design. Its correctness has been validated by comparing its results with thermal and energy use measurements on actual buildings.

Although DOE-2 is one of the most comprehensive building energy simulation programs available, it cannot addresses all situations encountered in commercial office buildings, whose complexity exceeds the capabilities of any one simulation program. For example, many buildings are heated and cooled by systems not described in any one simulation program or whose number exceeds the limits of the program. Or they use new and innovative building automation systems (e.g. for controlling room temperature and lighting) whose impact has not yet been added to the program. The standard version of DOE-2 is a batch program with no interactive user interface, which has made it hard to use, but several graphical user interfaces for DOE-2 have been developed over the years, such as VisualDOE.

DOE-2 has given rise to a host of other energy evaluation programs and hundreds of energy-related software tools.[7] They include such programs as EnergyPlus (a new-generation building energy simulation program based on DOE-2) and BLAST (an energy simulation program developed by the U.S. National Bureau of Standards for use by the Department of Defense). Released in April 2001, the program was developed jointly by the Lawrence Berkeley National Laboratory, the University of Illinois, the U.S. Army Construction Engineering Research Laboratory, GARD Analytics, Oklahoma State University, and others with support from the U.S. Department of Energy, the Office of Building Technology, and a variety of state and community programs.

SustArc

At the neighborhood scale, models have been developed that account primarily for the implications of buildings' height, orientation, and groupings on wind patterns and shading. Their goals are to maximize (or minimize, as the case may be) airflow between buildings, avoid (or provide) shading of open spaces and pedestrian sidewalks, and avoid shading of lower buildings by their tall neighbors. Much like other design variables, the factors that contribute to these performance characteristics are interrelated. For example, proper design can guarantee that each building will get adequate sun exposure, while maintaining high urban density. This interrelationship depends not only on the geometry of the buildings themselves but also on their location along streets and open spaces, on the distances between them, as well as on the geometry of the streets and the open spaces themselves.

The importance of proper shading design was recognized by researchers more than forty years ago.[8] Since the late 1970s cities like San Francisco have formally recognized the importance of "solar rights," which (among other things) guarantee that new buildings do not cast excessive shadows on existing buildings or open spaces.[9]

Software that can help designers and developers locate and orient their buildings in a manner that will maximize airflow and avoid (or provide) shading of designated spaces has been developing since the 1970s. It uses techniques developed for determining shading performances and techniques developed for computational fluid dynamics to determine wind patterns.[10]

SustArc is an example of prediction and evaluation programs that assist in designing urban fabrics that account for solar rights. Developed by Capeluto and Shaviv at the Faculty of Architecture and Town Planning

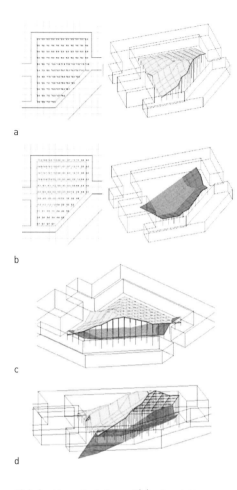

a

b

c

d

19.3 SustArc calculations of (a) solar rights envelope, (b) solar collection envelope, (c) and (d) solar volumes. (I. G. Capeluto and E. Shaviv, "Modeling the Design of Urban Grids and Fabric with Solar Rights Considerations," ISES 1997 Solar World Congress, Taejon, Korea, 1997.)

in the Technion, Israel, it calculates the maximum allowed "solar volume" that can be built without violating the solar rights of adjacent buildings and open spaces during a predefined period of the year.[11] It also calculates the minimal height of windows and solar collectors such that they will be exposed to sun during the winter and shaded during the summer.

The solar volume is determined by combining two envelopes, the "solar rights envelope" (SRE) and the "solar collection envelope" (SCE), each calculated separately using a method developed by Shaviv for the design of external sunshades, discussed in section 13.1.[12] The SRE represents the maximum heights of buildings that do not violate the solar rights of any of the existing buildings during a given period of the year (fig. 19.3a). The SCE represents the lowest possible locus of windows and passive solar collectors on the elevation of the building, such that they will be exposed to the sun during a given period of winter but will be shaded in summer (fig. 19.3b). The solar volume represents the volume included between these two envelopes. This volume contains all the building's heights that allow the sun to reach surrounding buildings and that at the same time are not shaded by the neighboring buildings (fig. 19.3c,d). The results are presented in the form of a nomogram showing the maximum available volume that can be built without violating the solar rights of any existing building—including the one being designed.

PLACE³S

At the urban and regional scale, energy-related evaluation programs such as PLAnning for Community Energy, Economic, and Environmental Sustainability (PLACE³S) focus on issues of economic and environmental sustainability: they are intended to help communities understand the tradeoffs they must make among various planning goals, using energy as a common yardstick for quantifying energy-related, economic, and environmental effects of alternative urban or regional development plans.[13]

PLACE³S is an example of a land use and urban design simulation program.[14] It uses statistical modeling based on geographic information systems (GIS) and database query techniques to assist planners in assessing the urban- and regional-scale energy demands of alternative development plans (fig. 19.4). It is based on correlations and heuristics derived from statistical data concerning energy consumption in residential and

Evaluation

office buildings, transportation habits and costs (translated into miles per gallon) of private automobiles and public transportation, job-to-housing trip averages, average trips generation by businesses, and CO_2 emissions.

For example, a density of three auto-dependent single-family residential units per acre is estimated to require 440 MMBtu/year of residential heating and cooling energy at a cost of $4,800/year, and produce 50 tons/year of CO_2 emissions per household. These figures drop to 360 MMBtu, $4,100, and 47 tons, respectively, when residential density climbs to twenty-four units of low-rise apartments and to 310 MMBtu, $3,700, and 42 tons when it reaches a density of ninety-six high-rise apartments with high transit activity.[15]

PLACE³S comprises two computer-assisted planning tools: INDEX, a proprietary software developed by Criterion, of Portland, Oregon; and Smart Places, a public domain software developed in collaboration with the Electric Power Research Institute. PLACE³S calculates the estimated energy consumption per person, cost of energy per person per year, and CO_2 emissions of alternative development plans, so planners, community leaders, and other stakeholders can choose the plan that best matches their growth goals while minimizing its energy-related impacts.

The objective of using PLACE³S for regional assessments is to identify the region's efficient locations and to ensure that land use, transportation, and infrastructure plans capture the inherent efficiencies of those locations. For example, if an area is close to transit and jobs, it should be zoned for high-density uses. Hence, neighborhoods designed with the assistance of PLACE³S will be compact, with a mix of housing, shops, offices, schools, parks, and other recreation easily accessible by walking, bicycling, public transit, and by car. Based on the assumptions underlying PLACE³S, such neighborhoods are also energy-efficient.

In the mid-1990s, PLACE³S was used by the San Diego Association of Governments to quantify the benefits of their regional energy plan, revealing an energy cost savings of nearly $1.5 billion, the creation of over 5,000 new jobs in energy efficiency services, and the elimination of a half million tons of air pollutants over fifteen years if the plan was fully implemented. In the Eugene-Springfield region of Oregon, the Lane Council of Governments used PLACE³S to evaluate the region's existing policies favoring compact growth and transit use. PLACE³S unveiled annual energy cost savings of about $10 million to the region by 2015.

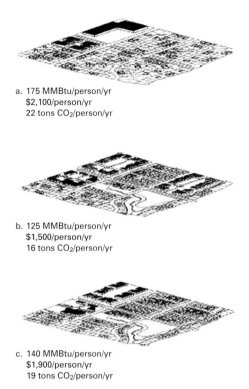

a. 175 MMBtu/person/yr
$2,100/person/yr
22 tons CO_2/person/yr

b. 125 MMBtu/person/yr
$1,500/person/yr
16 tons CO_2/person/yr

c. 140 MMBtu/person/yr
$1,900/person/yr
19 tons CO_2/person/yr

19.4 Alternative urban plans can be evaluated using PLACE³S: (a) existing situation, (b) "optimal" situation, (c) preferred situation. (Center for Excellence for Sustainable Development, Office of Energy Efficiency and Renewable Energy, U.S. Department of Energy, 1996.)

The use of statistical correlations as a basis for quantitative modeling falls under the "weak" methods of predictions discussed in chapter 17. Researchers like Moore and Thorsnes warn that while it is possible to describe the general forces that shape cities, it is not possible to quantify them with enough rigor to derive optimal size or configuration decisions.[16] Rather, systems such as PLACE[3]S can only be used for illustrating order-of-magnitude differences between planning alternatives.

It can be argued that enacting and enforcing strict energy consumption codes, like California's Title 24, can achieve similar savings. Indeed, the California Energy Commission has estimated that the annual energy cost savings from the Title 24 standard was $420 million in 1985, $970 million in 1992, and $1.6 billion in 1999. The cumulative California savings have been estimated to be $4.9 billion (1985–1992) and $13.8 billion (1985–1999).[17] Codes, however, can only prevent the design of buildings and urban developments whose energy performance is truly unacceptable; they do not encourage the design of buildings and urban developments that exceed prescribed energy standards. Predictive design and planning tools of the kind discussed in this chapter have the potential to encourage designers, developers, and policy makers to explore and design buildings and urban developments that significantly exceed minimum energy and environmental standards.

19.3 Acoustics

Acoustics is a branch of physics that deals with the study of sound—small pressure waves in the air (and other media) generated through the movement of a solid boundary such as a loudspeaker or mechanical equipment, measured in terms of time, amplitude, and frequency. Although the scope of acoustics ranges from the high frequencies of ultrasound to the low frequencies of infrasound, architecture is typically interested only in the range that can be detected by the human ear ($20\ \text{Hz} \leq f \leq 20\ \text{kHz}$). Such sound affects the quality of space (both indoors and outdoors) and plays a special role in concert halls and auditoriums, where the quality of the sound is of paramount importance to fulfilling the building's function.

The principles of acoustics derive from the theories of fluid dynamics, which consider gas (and liquids) as a continuum and assume that a "fluid particle" can be defined that is large compared to molecular scales but small compared to other length scales (e.g., the dimensions of a building). Fluid motion can then be described by using the laws of mass, momentum, and energy conservation, applied to the elementary fluid particles. Sound, therefore, can be defined as a pressure perturbation that propagates as a wave.

Sound intensity is measured as the average rate of energy transfer in watts per unit area. Whispering, for example, produces about 10^{-10} watts/m², shouting produces about 10^{-5} watts/m², and a jet airplane at takeoff produces about 10^5 watts/m². The intensity of sound varies as the square of its amplitude. Hence, the ratio of intensities at the two limits of the human auditory capacity is very large (10^{12}). Because of the large range of values involved, and because the human ear has a roughly logarithmic sensitivity, it is more convenient to measure the sound level using the decibel (dB) scale—the term commemorating the work of Alexander Graham Bell—instead of watts; for example:[18]

Sound Level	(dB)
Threshold of pain	140
Near a jet aircraft engine	120
Near a jackhammer	100
Typical factory	80
Normal speech level	60
Quiet living room	40
Quiet recording studio	20
Threshold of hearing	0

Architectural acoustics typically deals with two kinds of problems: (1) blocking off unwanted sound ("noise"); and (2) matching sound qualities (intensity and reverberation time) to the needs of the space (especially in auditoriums and concert halls but also in other social places like restaurants, offices, and factories).

Environmental Sound Prediction and Evaluation

The first type of problem arises both inside buildings (typically as a result of noise generated by mechanical equipment) and outside buildings (typically as a result of noise generated by vehicular or aircraft traffic). Acoustical

NORMAN Y. MINETA
SAN JOSE
INTERNATIONAL
AIRPORT

LEGEND
HOSPITALS,NURSING/
CONVALESCENT HOMES
CHURCHES
SCHOOLS
NON COMPATIBLE
COMPATIBLE
ACT COMPATIBLE
2006
1Q01
◇ RMS

19.5 Airport noise contour map. (Courtesy of San Jose Norman Y. Mineta Airport Authority, California.)

engineering design, in this case, involves reducing the sound level to acceptable levels (often determined by building codes or local regulations). Two characteristics of sound propagation are used to accomplish this goal: distance, and the fact that sound travels (mostly) in a straight line.

Sound level decreases with the square of the distance from the source. Locating the source away from a protected area is a good solution to the noise problem; this is why airports and freeways are often located at some distance from residential areas. When distance cannot be used as a design variable, because of other constraints or because natural population growth brings residences close to noise sources, barriers designed to block off direct sound propagation may be used.

The calculations involved in this type of prediction can and are often handled by means of spreadsheets, after the proper formulae have been programmed into them. In addition to spreadsheets, several programs have been developed specifically to support such prediction. They include the Integration Noise Model (INM) for aircraft noise calculation,[19] developed by the Federal Aviation Administration's (FAA). Since 1978 it has served as the standard evaluation tool for determining the predicted noise impact in the vicinity of airports (fig. 19.5). It uses flight track information, aircraft fleet mix, standard and user-defined aircraft profiles, and terrain as inputs and produces noise exposure contours for land use compatibility maps as output. The model supports sixteen predefined noise metrics that include cumulative sound exposure, maximum sound level, and duration of noise beyond metrics from both weighted and effective perceived noise levels. Aircraft profile and noise calculation algorithms are based on several guidance documents published by the Society of Automotive Engineers (SAE), that address, among other things, atmospheric absorption, temperature profiles, wind gradients, humidity effects, ground absorption, individual aircraft directivity patterns and sound diffraction terrain, buildings, barriers, and noise attenuation. The INM is an average-value model and is designed to estimate long-term average effects using average annual input conditions.

Indoor Sound Prediction and Evaluation

The second type of problem arises from the (relatively) slow speed of sound (344 meters per second in dry air at 20°C) and from the fact that, like other wave phenomena, when the advancing front of the sound wave

Evaluation

encounters a rigid object, some of it is absorbed (depending on the material qualities of the object), some scattered, and the rest bounces off at an angle equal to the angle of incidence. These two factors combine to create the phenomenon of echoes—reverberations due to the delayed arrival of different sound waves that originate at the same source.

Reverberation is a desirable property of auditoriums and concert halls to the extent that it helps to overcome the inverse square law drop-off of sound intensity in the enclosure. However, if it is excessive, it makes the sounds run together resulting in loss of articulation; the sound becomes garbled. The reverberant sound in an auditorium dies away with time as the sound energy is absorbed by multiple interactions with the surfaces of the room. In a more reflective room (e.g., a Gothic cathedral), it will take longer for the sound to die away and the room is said to be acoustically "live." In a very absorbent room (e.g., a recording studio), the sound will die away quickly and the room will be described as acoustically "dead."

The time for reverberation to die away completely depends upon how loud the sound was to begin with and upon the acuity of the listener's hearing. In order to provide a reproducible parameter, a standard reverberation time, RT, has been defined as the time for the sound to decrease to a level 60 decibels below its original level.[20]

For a general-purpose auditorium (intended for both speech and music performances) the desirable RT is 1.5 to 2.5 seconds. For example, the Vienna Musikvereinsaal has an RT of 2.05 seconds, Boston's Symphony Hall has an RT of 1.8 seconds, and New York's Carnegie Hall's RT is 1.7 seconds. A longer reverberation time (3.5 seconds) produces "richer" sound, which helps musical performances sound "smoother"; but the same characteristic makes speech become less articulated and more difficult to understand. Longer RT (5.5 seconds) further aggravates speech. The cathedral of Notre-Dame in Paris is noted for its ultralong RT (8.5 seconds), which produces dramatic effects for its pipe organ.

On the other hand, shorter RT (1 second) produces crisper sound, which is desirable for lecture halls, but not for musical performances. A very short RT (0.3 seconds) makes for "dead" space and is appropriate only for recording studios.

Reverberation can be quantitatively characterized using Sabin's Formula, which established the relationship between the space's geometry and the absorption coefficients associated with the materials it is made of:

$$RT_{60} = (0.16 \; s\,/m) \; \times \; V \; / \; S_e$$

where RT_{60} is the approximated time it takes the reverberation to decrease by 60 dB, V is the auditorium's volume, and S_e is the effective absorption area (the sum of the areas of each exposed material multiplied by its absorption coefficient).

Designers thus aim to predict the RT of a proposed auditorium and adjust its geometry and absorption characteristics to arrive at the desirable RT. However, the fluid dynamics equations of motion are nonlinear. This implies that an exact general solution of these equations is not available. But since sound is a small perturbation of a steady state, second-order effects can be neglected and acoustics can be treated as a first-order approximation in which the nonlinear effects are neglected.

The calculation of such approximations has been computer-assisted by specialized software that generally operates on the same principles as visualization ray-tracing algorithms (see section 9.3): a number of "rays" of sound that emanate from a sound source on the proscenium are "traced" to determine the time it takes them to reach selected points in the audience (e.g., the front row, the back row, the gallery, center seats, side seats, and so forth). Instead of calculating the color of the ray at each reflection point, these algorithms calculate its absorption. Together, the time of travel and the sound level provide the necessary data to predict how well the proposed shape and materials of the auditorium perform (fig. 19.6a).

A number of computer programs were developed specifically to support such ray-tracing-based acoustical prediction, including ODEON—a PC-based software developed at the Technical University of Denmark (starting in 1984).[21] It can be used to predict the interior acoustics of large rooms such as concert halls, opera halls, auditoriums, foyers, subway stations, airport terminals and industrial workrooms, as well as noise propagation generated by large machinery in industrial environments. Input consists of the building's geometry and the properties of surfaces. Output consists of figures, graphs, and "auralizations"—simulations of how speech and music will sound in the simulated environment.

ODEON uses image-source methods for rough estimations and ray-tracing algorithms for accurate simulation of noise propagation, reflection, and absorption. It calculates the binaural room impulse response (BRIR), which allows for three-dimensional presentation of the predicted acoustics

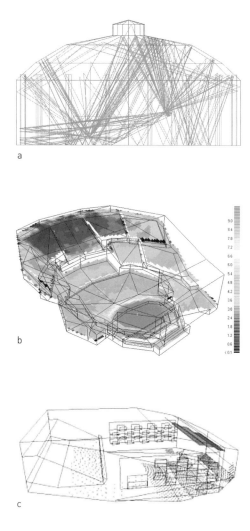

19.6 The outputs of ODEON: (a) ray-traced sound propagation, (b) absorption map, and (c) reflector coverage map. (Courtesy of ODEON, Lyngby, Denmark.) (See color plate 16.)

over headphones. A BRIR is calculated for each typical sound source using more than 100,000 reflections per source. The calculation includes full filtering of each reflection in nine octave bands (the 16 kHz band being extrapolated) and application of a set of head-related transfer functions (HRTFs) for each reflection. In addition to producing decay and reverberation time predictions, this process produces natural-sounding digital sound that can be experienced by donning headphones—the aural equivalent of stereoscopic visualization—hence the term auralization. Auralization allows the evaluation of sound quality, speech intelligibility and clarity, and the elusive but important "feel" of the soundscape. More technically, it provides evaluation of:

- High-order echoes.
- Directivity and frequency response of sources.
- Envelopment (the experience of being surrounded by sound)—an effect produced by lateral reflections arriving more than 80 milliseconds after the direct sound itself.
- Frequency-dependent reverberation time. Usually the sound will get deeper as the sound decays—a very dominant feature of rooms with extreme reverberation times (e.g., cathedrals, mosques).

Room geometries can be imported in DXF format, or modeled parametrically in ODEON's built-in modeling language. The model requires only details that are relevant for acoustics calculation, including appropriate sound sources and receivers, directivity of point sources gain, equalization, and delay. Materials are defined by their absorption coefficients (available from their manufacturers), ranging from 63 to 8000 Hz, and their scattering coefficient (available only from consultants, based on experience and iterative measurements). Graphical displays of the results help to verify the validity of the room's geometry, the location of source and receiver points, as well as decay curves, maps of sound pressure levels, energy parameters or intelligibility (sound transmission index), and reflector coverage (fig. 19.6b,c).

Computational evaluation of the expected performances of design propositions was one of the major reasons for introducing computing in architecture in the 1950s. As such, it has enjoyed continuous study and development for the past half century, the results of which comprise a considerable body of knowledge pertaining to many different areas of building performance. A large number of computer programs make this body of knowledge available to practicing professionals, albeit generally in a manner not integrated with other design activities. This short list of quantifiable evaluations is only intended to serve as examples of this well-developed area of computing in architectural design, rather than a survey of the field.

Bibliography

Berg, R. E., and D. G. Stork. *The Physics of Sound*. 2d ed. New York: Prentice Hall, 1995.

Birdsall, B., W. L. Buhl, K. L. Ellington, A. E. Erdem, and F. C. Winkelmann. *Overview of the DOE-2 Building Energy Analysis Program, Version 2. 1D*. Lawrence Berkeley National Laboratory Report No. LBL-19735, Rev. 1, 1990.

Fenves, S., U. Flemming, C. Hendrickson, M. L. Maher, R. Quadrel, M. Terk, and R. Woodbury. *Concurrent Computer-Aided Integrated Building Design*. Englewood Cliffs, N.J.: Prentice-Hall, 1994.

Halliday, D., R. Resnick, and J. Walker. *Fundamentals of Physics*. 6th ed. New York: John Wiley and Sons, 2001.

Kinsler, L. E., A. R. Frey, A. B. Coppens, and J. V. Sanders. *Fundamentals of Acoustics*. 3d ed. New York: John Wiley and Sons, 1982.

Mahdavi, A., P. Mathew, S. Kumar, and N. H. Wong. "Bi-Directional Computational Design Support in the SEMPER Environment." *Automation in Construction* 6, no. 2 (1997): 353–373.

Mills, G. "The Radiative Effects of Building Groups on Single Structures." *Energy and Building* 25 (1997): 51–61.

Noor, A. K., and S. L. Venneri. "A Perspective on Computational Structures Technology." *IEEE Computer* 26, no. 10 (1993): 38–46.

Rossing, T. D. *The Science of Sound*. 2d ed. Reading, Mass.: Addison-Wesley, 1990.

Salter, C. M., and Associates. *Acoustics: Architecture, Engineering, the Environment*. San Francisco: William Stout Publishers, 1998.

Salvadori, M. *Why Buildings Stand Up: The Strength of Architecture*. New York: W. W. Norton, 1980.

Swaid, H., and M. Hoffman. "Climatic Impact of Urban Design Features for High- and Mid-latitude Cities." *Energy and Buildings* 14 (1990): 325–336.

Wilson, E. L. *Three Dimensional Static and Dynamic Analysis of Structures*. Berkeley, Calif.: Computers and Structures, 1998.

Woodward, P. R. "Interactive Scientific Visualization of Fluid Flow." *IEEE Computer* 26, no. 10 (1993): 13–25.

Evaluating Nonquantifiable Qualities 20

The conditions of evaluation, as stated in chapter 19, require that, in addition to an object (or its representation) to be evaluated, there should also exist a set of benchmarks that state the desired level of performance and a method for comparing the predicted performance to the desired one.

Many building-related performance characteristics meet these conditions and are amenable to evaluation. However, certain important building characteristics lack one or more of these conditions and therefore are not amenable to quantitative evaluation. Two such characteristics are design aesthetics and how humans relate to their built environment: these lack either the benchmarks that define "good" performance or a methodology for determining the performance of a given design proposition. Both raise the question of whether they are at all amenable to computer-aided evaluation; in the case of design aesthetics, even if it were possible, should computers be used to evaluate the aesthetics of buildings?

20.1 Human Factors

Human factors, in the context of architectural design, is a term that describes the relationship between the built environment and its human inhabitants. It is an area that draws on resources from psychology, sociology, ergonomics, and cognitive science, among others, and whose aim is to describe (and evaluate) how people respond to and behave in built environments, under both normal and emergency conditions. Human factors is one of the most difficult building performances to predict and evaluate before construction because it involves many subjective measures, which include:

- *Perception.* How will the building be perceived by its owners, its users, and by the community in which it is situated?

- *Ergonomics.* How will the building affect the ability of its inhabitants to carry out their tasks (learning, working, manufacturing, healing, praying, traveling, and so on)? How will it affect their behavior during emergencies?
- *Impact on social systems.* How will the building impact the formation of connections between its users? How will it affect their behavior? Is it commensurate with their lifestyles, or does it conflict with them?
- *Interpreted meaning.* Will the building acquire a meaning beyond its immediate functional role and become an icon for the community (like the Transamerica Pyramid has for San Francisco and the Sydney Opera House for Australia)?

Post-occupancy evaluation (POE) methods can help analyze human responses to existing buildings. These methods analyze the behavior of people in such settings as office buildings, hospitals, and train stations. Their purpose is to find correlations between a building and the behavior of its inhabitants for the purpose of improving current situations or developing knowledge that can guide the design of new facilities of the same kind. One of the better known such studies has been William Whyte's video documentary of small urban places in New York City, which led to the formulation of municipal design ordinances intended to improve the urban landscape.[1]

Few methods of evaluation exist that address this type of building performance during the design process itself because relatively little is understood about how people react socially, psychologically, and cognitively to their physical environment. Analyzing the human response is complicated by the influence of cultural factors, which are themselves the result of education, social habits, and beliefs; people of different cultural backgrounds might react very differently to the same physical environment. Even the same people may react differently to the same environment at different times.

Evaluating the impact of buildings on their human inhabitants is, therefore, one of the most difficult aspects of preconstruction building performance evaluation. It requires an understanding of human perceptive and cognitive processes and the ability to interpret and evaluate them within complex socio-demographic and cultural contexts.

Norms and Regulations

Knowledge about human factors in architecture has traditionally been represented and transmitted through "norms," in the form of guidelines and regulations: the characteristics of the desired situation are prescribed as codes, generated from precedents, and are applied to new design situations as checklists. For example, the observed behavior of people evacuating a building in emergency situations is the source of fire egress codes, which are enforced through a checklist of safety features (smoke detectors, sprinklers, fire doors, and so on).

This normative approach is relatively easy to implement at an atomic level (i.e., individual norms and rules, such as the required number of fire doors in a building). However, the need to make tradeoffs between competing factors, and the large number of norms that may come into play in any design project, makes building evaluation for code compliance a lengthy and difficult process. The generalized nature of rules and regulations can sometimes be misleading, because their applicability in the context of a specific design situation depends on the evaluator's interpretation and judgment (e.g., the building inspector).

NUDA—a system that can assist designers in generating and evaluating layouts for nursing units in long-term care facilities—is an example of the computational implementation of this approach (fig. 20.1).[2] It enforces compliance with all relevant building codes for emergency egress, habitability, and accessibility for people with disabilities. However, the program does not let the designer assign room dimensions that make sense in specific situations, even though they exceed or fall short of those specified by the building codes.

Although normative approaches are relatively easy to implement, they are only effective for improving design quality if the knowledge base used to generate them is accurate and complete. In the case of human factors, serious questions can be raised about the extent and accuracy of our knowledge: although building codes have many norms related to human factors, the knowledge used as the basis for the codes is often obsolete or unsubstantiated.[3]

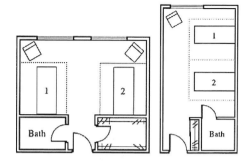

20.1 Alternative nursing room layouts permitted by NUDA. (G. Lima, "NUDA—Nursing Unit Design Assistant," Technical Report, Department of Architecture, State University of New York at Buffalo, 1988.)

Case Studies and Precedents

Even when they are not codified into law, architects rely heavily on experiences when evaluating their work in progress. Case studies and precedents (discussed in section 17.4) provide a rich, empirically validated, anecdotal basis for evaluating human factors. By comparing the emerging design to similar buildings in similar contexts, the designer can project expected behavioral patterns. Much like norms and regulations, case studies are convenient but potentially misleading when the context of the case study differs from the context of the design. Unlike norms and regulations, case studies also suffer from selectivity: the ones used in a particular design situation are those with which the designer is most familiar. There may, of course, exist cases that are more applicable, but are outside the sphere of knowledge of the designer. Case-based reasoning systems, discussed in chapter 14, were developed to overcome this very deficiency.[4]

Moreover, deriving human factors–related experiences from case studies is subject to human experience. The same spatiotemporal contexts in which case studies are embedded and that are essential for their interpretation also affect the experience of the observer. Thus, the very richness of these experiences may hinder their reuse as predictors of behavior in new design contexts.

Direct-Experience Behavior Simulation

The best apparatus for evaluating the impact of an environment on its inhabitants is, of course, the human users themselves. This is the rationale for market-testing full-scale cars, model homes, toys, human-computer interfaces, and many other artifacts. Employing human beings as a testing apparatus requires that the environment that is being evaluated is already built—at least in a prototypical form that allows humans to interact with it on a somewhat realistic basis. Such full-scale mock-ups are expensive and can only be justified if they lead to large production runs (as is the case in full-scale modeling of cars) or if the reality they simulate is too dangerous to allow even the slightest failure (as is the case with control rooms of nuclear reactors and aircraft control towers).

The built environment, in most cases, cannot justify full-scale modeling, because it often produces one-of-a-kind artifacts whose failure from a human factors point of view may be regrettable but not outright dangerous.

20.2 *Sunset Magazine*'s 1999 "Idea House," designed by South Coast Architects of Newport Beach, California, and built in Palo Alto, California, to be directly experienced by potential home buyers and builders. (Courtesy of Jay Graham, photographer.)

Evaluation

In some cases, when a subunit of the whole will be repeated many times, evaluating its human factors by direct experience may be justified. Such are model homes, model offices, or model bathrooms and kitchens (fig. 20.2).

As an alternative to experiencing the actual building, a full-scale mock-up or a virtual model of the building can be used. Such models are an attempt to simulate and evaluate the human response to an emerging design proposal—as if the users were already inhabiting the spaces designed for their use.

Direct-experience behavior simulation offers the most flexibility in terms of evaluating the response of different user populations to the proposed design solution and can be tuned to the specific context of the design. It is also the most difficult approach to evaluating human factors because it implies the ability to create realistic mock-ups that encourage suspension of disbelief on the part of the human testers, who must behave as if the environment they visit was the "real" one.

Experience-based modeling is further complicated by the subjectivity of the users. For example, an experiment often done by the Optometry School at UC Berkeley asks students to experience blindness by walking blindfolded, in pairs, around the campus. Since these students are not actually blind and therefore have neither the motivation nor the heightened environmental sensitivities of blind people, the results of such experiences do not actually convey to them the real feeling of blindness. A similar experiment was conducted by Pastalan and his colleagues. In this case, young, able-bodied researchers donned specially prepared eyeglasses, earplugs, and skin coatings that were intended to simulate the reduced visual, auditory, and tactile sensitivities of older persons.[5]

One way to overcome both the difficulty of developing full-scale realistic models and the difficulty of tuning the perceptual system of the observers to match specific age groups or abilities has been found in the use of virtual reality—a technology that allows people to interact with computer-generated environments in ways that approximate real environments (see section 9.3). Virtual reality uses the modeling power of computers to generate a simulated environment in digital form that can be "inhabited." Virtual environments that help evaluate human response and, at the same time, train them for emergency conditions, have been employed, for example, by the Federal Aviation Administration for the design of aircraft control towers (fig. 20.3).

20.3 Simulation of San Francisco air traffic control tower, to test human factors and train air traffic controllers. (Courtesy of Charles Ehrlich and Greg Ward, 1997, Lawrence Berkeley National Laboratory.)

Indirect-Experience Behavior Modeling

Although direct experience is the best way to evaluate human factors, it is hard for designers, or their clients, to avoid using their own preferences and personal judgment when evaluating a design, even when they are not its intended inhabitants.

The problem of personalizing the evaluation can be avoided through the use of computer programs programmed to simulate the "average" user's response to the built environment. Such programs must represent not only the perceptive and cognitive processes used by humans when confronted by an environment but also their judgmental processes. Their development has often been limited to some well-defined areas of human activities, where considerable empirical research is available to help develop the requisite cognitive models. Some of the areas for which such cognitive models have been developed are access and exposure, fire egress, and wayfinding.

Visual access and exposure refers to the desire of people to be in visual control of their environment while at the same time sheltered from (or conversely, exposed to) the view of others. Such feelings drive people, for example, to seek sheltered park benches when they are on their lunch break, or to seek well-lit routes at night when they feel threatened. Possibly the best example of using the principles of visual access and exposure for controlling behavior can be found in the design of prisons that use the panopticon scheme. The correctional officer sits in the center of a circular cell block, where the walls of the cells facing the center are transparent (made of steel bars or reinforced glass). The officer can, therefore, easily observe the inmates. The officer's station, on the other hand, is made of "privacy" glass, so the inmates cannot see him or her. The result is that inmates never know if they are being observed, but they know that the officer can see them. Their behavior, overall, is improved compared to cell blocks where inmates can hide from view.

Computer programs that can predict the visual access and exposure behavior of people in designed environments have been developed by John Archea and others.[6] Specific programs that incorporate additional behavioral aspects have been developed for the purpose of predicting wayfinding behavior and emergency egress in complex buildings.

Complex public facilities, such as libraries, hospitals, governmental buildings, airports terminals and railway stations, often present problems to visitors who must find their way through them. Research has shown that difficulty in wayfinding has severe cost implications, in terms of wasted time (of the visitors themselves and the workers whom they ask for directions), public safety (especially during emergencies like fire or earthquakes), and stress—as a result of being lost. However, it is often only after the building has been constructed that it will develop a reputation for being easy or difficult to navigate.

Several computer programs have been developed that can predict wayfinding behavior, based on different models of human cognition related to wayfinding.

One such approach relies on the "cognitive map" model, according to which people store information about the layout of the built environment in a kind of "map in the head."[7] According to this model, spatial information is organized in the brain by temporal contiguity; spaces that are experienced close together in time will become associated in memory. The overall schema resembles a network of "choice points," which are akin to milestones on the way to the destination (fig. 20.4a). These choice points, which correspond to corridor intersections or turns and are marked by physical architectural features, help orient a person going from a starting node of the network to a destination node (goal).

NAPS-PC is a wayfinding prediction program, developed by O'Neill,[8] that is based on the cognitive map model. It uses neural-network technology that, given as input a building's floor plan, generates a corresponding graph consisting of nodes and the links between them and can predict the routes that are most likely to be traversed. Since typically there are many possible routes that lead from the starting node to the destination node, the program initially performs a "blind" search, going down corridors that do not lead to the destination. Each route traversed that does lead to the destination is marked by increasing "strength," and subsequent searches favor "stronger," more familiar routes, representing the learning process experienced by repeat visitors (fig. 20.4b).

A different approach to wayfinding, which uses a system of conditions and actions, was adopted by Kuipers in his TOUR program,[9] and by Leiser and Zilbershatz in their TRAVELLER program.[10] They represent conditions, which correspond to (physical) decision points (e.g., intersections of corridors), and actions, which encode the knowledge of what to do when a particular condition is encountered (i.e., when you see view V1, take action A1 [e.g., turn]). Unlike the cognitive map model, which

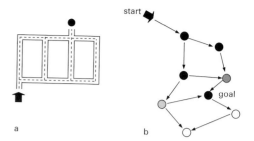

20.4 Navigating a small library: (a) starting point and destination; (b) a network representation of route selection. (After M. J. O'Neill, in *Evaluating and Predicting Design Performance*, ed. Y. E. Kalay [New York: Wiley Interscience, 1992].)

is symmetrical in terms of the relationships between the nodes of a given route, TOUR and TRAVELLER account for the phenomenon of being able follow a route in one direction but not in the reverse direction. However, since their knowledge bases are location-specific, they must be reprogrammed for each new building, based on empirical observations or predicted actions of users' behaviors.

Virtual Users

A more radical approach to simulating human response to the built environment was proposed by Kalay in collaboration with Steinfeld, Irazàbal, and Yan.[11] This approach is based on a technology called artificial life— an interdisciplinary field of study that attempts to model living biological systems through a variety of programming techniques (e.g., genetic algorithms, rule-based systems, and neural networks). Its application to human factors evaluation calls for inserting virtual users (VUsers, for short) into CAD models of buildings.

VUsers resemble, through their shape and size, the intended users of a specific environment (fig. 20.5). To perceive their environment in a manner that simulates human perceptions, they are equipped with simulated "sensors," endowing them with physical and social awareness, including spatial awareness (the capacity to determine their location in space, relative to obstacles and other VUsers); physical awareness (the capacity to perceive environmental states and determine environmental comfort regarding heat, light, humidity, and so forth); psychological awareness (the capacity to perceive and react to environmental conditions that in humans are considered to be the product of psychological phenomena, such as exposure, agoraphobia, and claustrophobia); and social awareness (the capacity to perceive social conditions and to react to them according to stated social and cultural behavioral patterns).

Their "personalities" are represented by means of a set of rules and a set of goals that provide the means to generate or modify their behavior within given social and physical contexts: given a particular social or physical stimulus, the VUser generates a response based on its goals and modified by the rules. For example, an agoraphobic VUser, while en route from point A to point B, that finds itself in a wide open space will make it a strong subgoal to seek and move to a less exposed place.

Evaluation

The intent of VUsers-based behavioral simulation is to help determine the suitability of a given design to the needs of particular populations, including ones having different physical abilities or disabilities. Physical disabilities are modeled by placing constraints on the range of motions available to specific joints, or by placing the VUser in a wheelchair. Mental disabilities are modeled by suitable programming of the responses to external stimuli. Age-related disabilities are simulated by placing limits on sensory input.

By "packaging" personality and physical traits into the VUser, along with a set of goals that represent a certain degree of "free will," their motions and activities need not be individually choreographed and animated by the designer, nor must their specific actions in a given environment be predetermined. Instead, VUsers behave as dictated by the environment itself, by the presence (or absence) of other VUsers, and by their own "personalities" and their specific goals. As such, they make it possible to observe objectively the physical and behavioral dynamics of the interaction between the "hardware" and the "wetware" and provide feedback on the appropriateness of the designed space as a stage, or container, of the intended activity. (See more about VUsers as autonomous rational agents in chapter 22.)

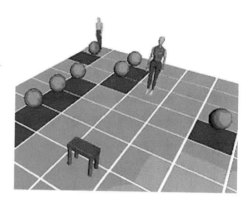

20.5 Virtual Users (VUsers), simulated through H-Anim—an international standard for modeling humans. (W. Yan and Y. E. Kalay, "Simulating the Behavior of Users in Built Environments," Technical Report, University of California, Berkeley, 2002.)

20.2 Aesthetics

Aesthetics is another characteristic that defies conventional evaluation methods. While there may be an actual building to be evaluated (or a representation of the building, in the form of a model or a rendering), there are neither agreed-upon aesthetic "standards" to which it can be compared (although each architect may develop one for himself or herself) nor methods that will compare the building to such standards. Rather, the aesthetic qualities of buildings are typically evaluated subjectively, a practice that makes their methodological study rather difficult.

Nonetheless, over the years, architects, critics, and artists have repeatedly tried to come up with objective methods for evaluating this quintessential nonquantifiable quality, both in order to achieve what they considered beautiful buildings and to help them "defend" these qualities when challenged by quantifiable qualities such as cost, constructability, and maintenance.

Aesthetics is the study of perceived form, independent of the meaning of the object it belongs to—a controversial dichotomy that has dogged the study of aesthetics for centuries.[12] It attempts to understand what features of an object's shape provoke a sense of profound experience and pleasure in the viewer and how new objects (including buildings, cars, even chairs and toasters) can be endowed with form qualities that will elicit such experiences. It is not surprising, therefore, that architects in particular have had an ongoing, prolonged relationship with this subject matter. Following in the footsteps of Vitruvius—who in book III of his *De architectura* claimed that temple building, being a serious matter, was subject to many kinds of rules and regulations to make temples worthy of being houses for the gods—many architects, including Alberti, Palladio, and Le Corbusier, gave considerable attention to compositional principles that produce beautiful buildings.

The formal study of aesthetics dates back at least to the ancient Greeks, who found an analogy between architecture and other forms of art, especially dance and music, where the abstract concept of beauty was made tangible through harmonious arrangements of notes and regularized movement. In particular, the principles of rhythm, proportion, and symmetry have played an important role in shaping the notion of beauty in Greek and Roman architecture, and hence in the architecture of the Western world.

Rhythm (from the Greek word *rhythmos*) was originally associated with the idea of movement in dance. The flowing steps of a talented dancer evoke a sense of beauty in the eyes of the observer. Hence, the argument goes, beauty can be found in the repetition at regular intervals of architectural elements like columns, arches, or windows (fig. 20.6).

Proportion is a mathematical concept that was formalized by the Pythagoreans (disciples of the great Greek philosopher and mathematician), who around 500 BC found that the pitch of the note sounded by plucking a string of a musical instrument was proportional to its length: harmonious combinations of notes resulted when the length of the strings formed certain ratios of whole numbers, e.g., 1:2 (octave), 2:3 (fifth), and 3:4 (fourth). The Pythagoreans where so impressed by this observation that they ascribed ratios to all kinds of things, proclaiming a universal correlation between beauty and ratios of numbers.

20.6 Marin County Civic Center, California (Frank Lloyd Wright, 1958–1962).

However, while the Pythagorean and the Vitruvian concept of divine proportion relied on ratios of whole numbers, it was the irrational number phi (φ = 1.6180339887498948482 . . . or, more precisely $(1+\sqrt{5})/2$) that became one of the most famous aesthetic concepts in art and architecture. Known as the golden ratio, it is considered to be the "most beautiful proportion possible." It was called "the mean and extreme ratio" by the Greeks and the "divine proportion" or "golden section" in the Renaissance.[13] The golden ratio is derived from a string being divided into two (unequal) parts m and M, such that the ratio of their lengths can be expressed by the equation $m{:}M = M{:}(M + m)$. The aesthetic value of this mathematical construction derives from its combination of elegance and simplicity. Although the ratio is one of the most irrational numbers in number theory (i.e., it cannot be derived by dividing two integers), it is found easily and abundantly in nature, because it corresponds to the Fibonacci number series (1, 1, 2, 3, 5, 8, 13, 21, 34, 55 . . .), generated by the rules:

$$f_1 = f_2 = 1$$
$$f_{n+1} = f_n + f_{n-1}$$

Renaissance architects' interest in systems of proportioning rules began with Alberti's treatment of the facade of Santa Maria Novella in Florence, which was based on simple geometric relationships (fig. 20.7). His approach, which was widely adopted, differed markedly from the Gothic approach of the late Middle Ages, whereby the individual parts of the building had no fixed ratios within themselves or with respect to the overall measurements of the building. Rather, they depended on an arcane geometric formula, jealously guarded by the master builder, who consulted it as needed on the site as the building went up.

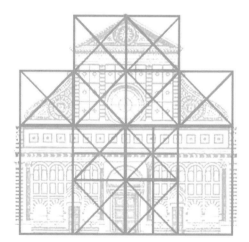

20.7 Alberti's treatment of the facade of Santa Maria Novella in Florence, Italy, inspired many Renaissance architects to use a proportional system to organize their designs.

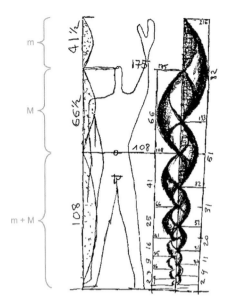

20.8 Le Corbusier's Modulor is a dimensioning system based on the golden ratio ($m:M = M:[M + m]$).

Interest in proportional systems was revived in the 1950s, when Le Corbusier proposed his Modulor system (fig. 20.8), based on the golden ratio. It was intended to provide a rational system for arranging all parts of a building:

My dream is to set up, on the building sites which will spring up all over our country one day, a "grid of proportions," drawn on the wall or made of strip iron, which will serve as a rule for the whole project, a norm offering an endless series of different combinations and proportions; the mason, the carpenter, the joiner will consult it whenever they have to choose the measure for their work; and all the things they make, different and varied as they are, will be united in harmony. That is my dream.[14]

Symmetry, in everyday use, typically refers to bilateral symmetry—the kind of symmetry possessed by the human body. Bilateral symmetry was an important principle of classical composition, and is found in virtually all Greek temples. In the first century BC, Vitruvius states in book I, chapter 2 of his treatise *De architectura*:

Uniformity is the parity of the parts to one another; each corresponding with its opposite, as in the human figure. The arms, feet, hands, fingers, are similar to, and symmetrical with, one another; so should the respective parts of a building correspond.

In the fifteenth century (for obvious reasons), Leon Battista Alberti, in his *Ten Books of Architecture*, recommended that buildings be symmetrical, "much like a man's left hand is symmetrical to his right hand, otherwise he would be considered deformed." As a consequence, symmetry became a hallmark of Renaissance architecture and a trend that carried through the nineteenth century's Beaux-Arts style.

Habitual Methods of Evaluating Aesthetics

Over the years, two approaches to aesthetics have emerged: the "objective" approach, which draws on mathematical principles to describe how the parts of an object relate to its overall configuration; and the "subjective" approach, which draws on psychological and cognitive principles to explain how form is perceived. The two approaches are well represented in Kant's definition of form (not to be confused with shape, which for Kant meant a property of the object itself): "A construction in the human mind which is based on a priori concepts that are imposed onto a perceived thing."[15]

Habitual modes of dealing with aesthetics in architectural design have evolved along a similar dichotomy, with a *prescriptive* approach and a *descriptive* approach.

Prescriptive methods of evaluation are applied *before* the design has commenced and are used to guide the architect in the development of his or her design. They come in the form of design guidelines, stylistic principles, patterns, or concepts borrowed from nature and from other disciplines, which encode "good taste."[16]

Unlike prescriptive methods, which precede the design process, descriptive methods of evaluation are used most commonly by architects and architectural critics to examine the built form *after* it has been designed or built. They consist mostly of textual narratives and correspond to observation and analysis of the artifact according to general, often subjective, aesthetic principles. Such critiques are often published in newspapers and in professional journals. They are similar to critiques of movies, stage plays, concerts, and other forms of art. Because they often lack an objective basis for their evaluation, their authority flows from the respect in which the critic is held. Thus, people with "good taste" are empowered to publish their opinion on works of art, movies, even restaurants, as well as architecture. Their critiques shape the way in which buildings are perceived by society at large; they also impact society's expectations and thereby influence how the architect him- or herself thinks about design.

For example, Minoru Yamasaki, the New York World Trade Center's principal architect, wrote when the Port Authority of New York and New Jersey commissioned him to design the complex that he sought "a beautiful solution of form and silhouette which fits well into Lower Manhattan" while giving it "the symbolic importance which it deserves and must have." However, the noted architectural critic Paul Goldberger, writing about the WTC in the September 24, 2001, issue of the *New Yorker* magazine, used the words "gargantuan and banal, blandness blown up to a gigantic size."

The criteria applied by such critics to establish the "goodness" of a specific design come from the cultural framework and historical period in which they are formulated. Since these criteria do not rely on quantitative methods for determining a minimum standard of quality but rather on some abstract notion of appropriateness, it is typically hard to draw from them conclusions that can help to improve the (aesthetic) performance of buildings. Still, such narratives, and even more so the images that accompany them, have traditionally helped to develop and shape architectural taste. They establish a standard that, although not precisely defined, can be used to measure other designs. For example, Marc-Antoine Laugier's highly dogmatic treatise *Essai sur l'architecture*,[17] which articulates the "correct" rules for designing buildings, can only be understood in the context of eighteenth-century Enlightenment, alongside the ideas of rationalist thinkers like Voltaire, Newton, Descartes, Pascal, and Rousseau (see section 12.4 for details). Similarly, the paradigm of modernity was shaped as much by the advent of architectural photography of Julius Shulman and others as by the buildings themselves and the words used to describe them.[18]

Computational Methods of Evaluating Aesthetics

Computational methods for dealing with aesthetics in architecture—or more generally the issue of form (as distinct from shape)—also follow the dichotomy of prescriptive versus descriptive approaches. Prescriptive methods are, to a large degree, a direct computational embodiment of the formal methods developed by Vitruvius, Palladio, Frank Lloyd Wright, and Le Corbusier, with the exception that rule-based techniques have replaced textual or graphical narratives.

One of the early implementations of this approach have been shape grammars (discussed in section 14.4), where the compositional principles of the works of such master architects as Palladio and Frank Lloyd Wright were analyzed and extracted to form the rules that govern computational algorithms. Such methods are capable of producing results that show a remarkable semblance, in style, to the corpus of work from which they were derived. However, to produce works in a different style their entire rule base must be rewritten.

Computational methods that follow the descriptive approach have been based on analyzing the form of buildings to discover their underlying compositional characteristics and compare them to known generalized rules of rhythm, proportion, and symmetry. Such methods rely on feature extraction—a technology that looks for geometric and topological characteristics of an image, like repeating groups of lines, their orientations, color similarity, and so on.[19]

A computational approximation of "acquired taste" and the use of visual metaphors in evaluating aesthetics in architecture has been attempted through the use of neural networks (discussed in section 15.4). Neural networks, derived from the cognitive theory of connectionism, are signal processors rather than symbolic processors—machines that process patterns rather than execute explicit instructions consequutively.[20] As such, they do not require that the features, comprising the elements of a form relevant to an evaluation, or the rules they are measured against be explicitly defined. Instead, they can be "trained" to translate input patterns into output patterns in predictable ways.

Training consists of presenting the network with examples of input patterns and their corresponding output patterns and adjusting the weights and thresholds of the nodes of the network such that it will, once the training is complete, produce the desired output patterns for given inputs (fig. 20.9).

By avoiding the need to explicate the relationship between input patterns and output values, neural network are eminently useful when this relationship is difficult to explicate, as in the case of recognizing and evaluating aesthetic features. A neural network can be shown examples of "beautiful" buildings and be expected to adapt its network weights so it will evaluate similarly to humans when shown similar images.

Parallel Distributed Processing Analogical Architectural Modeler (PDP-AAM), discussed in section 15.4, is a neural network that has been designed to demonstrate such aesthetic evaluation capabilities of buildings designed in the GIMS system.[21] Its "evaluation" consists of a list of semantic attributes in the form of a semantic differential matrix (fig. 15.8).

A semantic differential matrix is table in which each row reflects the user's preference, on a sliding scale, between two propositions. For example, the first row in the semantic differential matrix depicted in figure 15.8 provides five settings between the two extremes "exciting" and "boring." By choosing one of the five boxes during the training session, it is possible to "teach" the program to evaluate the building depicted on the left as

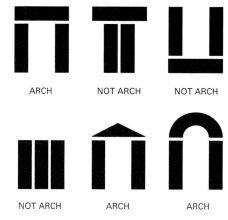

20.9 Sample inputs to train a neural network to recognize an arch.

very exciting, moderately exciting, neither exciting nor boring, moderately boring, or very boring. A similar indication can be made for all the other descriptors alongside the matrix. Together, the matrix tells the computer how to evaluate the building. After the training is completed, the program will produce such a semantic differential matrix for a new building it is shown.

As stated in section 15.4, the network does not "understand" what it does, concepts of beauty, or anything else for that matter. It simply applies the transformation it has been trained to perform, matching an input pattern to some output. Still, in a sense, it can be said that the translation itself contains the "knowledge" of the network.

The two areas of nonquantifiable qualities that have been discussed in this chapter are similar, to some extent, in that both rely on psychological and cognitive human abilities that are difficult to express in computationally convenient terms. This difficulty, however, must not be confused with inability to evaluate. Rather, they indicate areas where computers have yet to catch up to human knowledge and capabilities, which—some experts believe—is only a matter of time.[22]

Bibliography

Andel, J. van. "Behavior Modeling and Urban Design: Graphic vs. Non-Graphic Information about Environment-Behavior Relations." Technical Report, Department of Social Sciences, Eindhoven University of Technology, The Netherlands, 1994.

Andel, J. van. "Expert Systems in Environmental Psychology." In *International Association for People-Environment Studies (IAPS) 10 Conference* (Delft, The Netherlands, 1988).

Archea, J. "Puzzle-Making: What Architects Do When No One Is Looking." In *Computability of Design*, ed. Y. E. Kalay, 37–52. New York: Wiley Interscience, 1987.

Bosselmann, P. *Representation of Places: Reality and Realism in City Design*. Berkeley: University of California Press, 1998.

Darley, J. M., and D. T. Gilbert. "Social Psychological Aspects of Environmental Psychology." In *Handbook of Social Psychology*, 3d ed., ed. G. Lindzey and E. Aronson, 2:949–991. New York: Random House, 1985.

Gross, M. D., and C. Zimring. "Predicting Wayfinding Behavior in Buildings: A Schema-Based Approach." In *Evaluating and Predicting Design Performance*, ed. Y. E. Kalay, 367–378. New York: Wiley Interscience, 1992.

Ozel, F. "An Intelligent Simulation Approach in Simulating Dynamic Processes in Architectural Environments." In *Computer Aided Architectural Design Futures '91*, ed. G. N. Schmitt, 177–190. Wiesbaden, Germany: Vieweg Verlag, 1992.

Rapoport, A. *The Meaning of the Built Environment: A Nonverbal Communication Approach.* Tucson: University of Arizona Press, 1990.

Steinfeld, E., and Y. E. Kalay. "The Impact of Computer-Aided Design on Representation in Architecture." *ARCC Conference on Representation and Simulation in Architectural Research and Design.* Minneapolis, Minn., 1990.

Future V

Forecasting the future, especially in a technologically fast-paced field like computing—which is at the midst, if not at the beginning of the "information revolution"—is a rather foolhardy endeavor, destined to failure and early obsolescence. Nonetheless, or perhaps because we are witnessing only the early effects of the new technology on the processes and products of architecture, it is necessary to venture a prognostication, or rather—an informed indication of a direction for further development. To reduce the risk, the following chapters will only deal with trends rather than specific developments, and only in areas where the new technology promises to have major impacts—the trend toward a more intelligent, distributed process of architectural design; the automation of construction technologies and buildings themselves; and the emergence of an alternative inhabitable cyberplace.

Social evolution is closely related to technological revolutions. In almost every generation society has invented new tools, methods, and techniques to manufacture and distribute the products needed for its survival and growth. Most of these inventions are incremental refinements of earlier technologies, such as new and better crops, stronger and more efficient machines, and better means of locomotion and communication. But a few inventions have been "revolutionary" in the sense that they have caused major economic, political, and social changes.

The agricultural revolution, beginning some 10,000–12,000 years ago, was technologically manifested by the invention of the wheel, farming, and the domestication of livestock. These technological advances diminished the role of hunting and gathering as the primary means of food production and replaced their associated nomadic lifestyle with permanent settlements, which, together with a substantial growth of population due to more efficient (and reliable) food supply, led to the invention of new modes of settlement (villages, towns, and cities), new modes of governance, the invention of bookkeeping (including arithmetic and writing), codification of legal systems, and other social and cultural developments that we have come to associate with civilization itself.[1]

The adaptation of a winepress used in the Rhine Valley in Germany into the movable-type printing press by Johannes Gutenberg in about 1455 automated the production of books. Within three decades, printing spread across Europe and became one of the chief means by which the ideals of the Renaissance were transmitted from culture to culture. The printed book became a means of scientific, religious, and political revolutions—the technological means underlying the rise of Protestantism, vernacular languages, scientific and literary culture, and the French and other democratic revolutions of the eighteenth century.[2]

The technological invention underlying the first Industrial Revolution in the eighteenth century was the powered machine, which substituted inanimate (water, heat) power, precision, and regularity for human power and skill. By concentrating labor in factories—the locus of powered machines—in place of spread-out "cottage" industries, the Industrial Revolution supplanted the feudal system with a new social order and a new class—the bourgeoisie—along with new systems of governance, locomotion, and redistributed national power and wealth.[3] It also changed the nature of families, the nature of work, and even the sense of time itself. Unlike earlier periods of prosperity, which were soon consumed by the rising population, these benefits of the Industrial Revolution were widespread and sustainable, fueled by increased productivity, increased income per capita, and better health. With them came expectations for even more and better advancements—changing the ways of thinking as much as the ways of doing.[4]

The second industrial revolution, which started after World War II, was based on the inventions of the semiconductor, the integrated circuit, and the computer—machines that extend, multiply, and leverage mental and communication abilities, rather than physical ones.[5] This revolution transformed mechanical industries into information-based industries, where knowledge is the new capital. Not only did this revolution lead to the development of new types of products, services, and modes of production, but it also changed organizational structures, including the roles played by employees, customers, suppliers, and partners. In this so-called new economy the value of products no longer depends on the amount of material resources necessary to produce them, but rather on the amount of knowledge required to design them. One of the largest current industries—the software industry—requires no raw materials and produces no tangible goods: information itself has become the product.[6] Moreover, Henry Ford's celebrated "mass production" process has been transformed into a process of "mass customization," where consumers can customize, to a smaller or greater extent, the products they purchase. This relatively new mode of production is already on its way to be replaced with "mass personalization," where the production of highly customized products, combining the effort of multiple manufacturers, are economically (and technically) feasible.

Architecture has undergone two revolutionary changes in the past 2,500 years. First was the codification of "style," invented by the Greeks and established by the Romans. It created a professional body of knowledge that could be formally taught and improved upon—as distinct from an ad hoc collection of techniques—thereby creating the *discipline* of architecture. The second revolution, in the fifteenth century, was promulgated by the invention of scale drawings and the separation of design from construction. This revolution created the *profession* of architecture, elevating its practitioners to the status of artists rather than craftsmen.

Together, these two revolutions transformed architecture from a hands-on, building-related enterprise, where a "master builder" directly marshaled people and materials to form a physical artifact, into one that manipulates information. Using their disciplinary knowledge base and skill, architects interpret the needs of their clients and develop plans that, once executed by other people, are expected to meet those needs—subject to environmental and other constraints.

It is because of this "infocentric" nature of architecture that computing—a technology that affects the core processes and products of architecture—will have a "revolutionary" effect on the profession and the discipline of architecture. Computing technology has made the production, manipulation, and dissemination of information cheap and easy. It has made information more accessible, hence eminently shareable. It has also made it possible to redefine the traditional sequences of information production and reassign the responsibilities for its production and the privileges of owning it.

The technologies underlying the computing revolution have been growing exponentially since the end of World War II. In 1965 Gordon E.

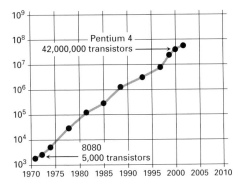

A.1 Moore's Law predicts that the data density on computer chips will double every 18 months. (http://www.intel.com/research/silicon/moores-law.htm)

Moore, cofounder of Intel Corporation, observed that the number of components on integrated circuits had been doubling every year and predicted that this rate of progress would continue. Although since 1970 the rate of increase of physical components on a silicon chip has slowed down somewhat, the data density they handle has continued to double approximately every eighteen months (fig. A.1). Many experts expect this trend, which has come known to be known as Moore's Law, to hold for at least another two decades, sustained by technological innovations and business competition (fig. A.2).

Computing, especially its telecommunication aspects, will transform what is now a strictly hierarchical design process into a vertically disaggregated market by distributing the design process across multiple professions, organizations, and geographic locations, creating a *network* of design, manufacturing, marketing, and distribution organizations.[7] Accessibility will transform the sequential process into an interleaved one, where decisions will be made in a distributed, often asynchronous manner. It will accentuate and promote the configurational principles underlying architecture (the integration of disparate standardized products and services into a unique whole), transforming custom designing to mass-customization, thereby lowering costs without sacrificing quality.

By embedding interconnected computational devices in both the building components themselves and the means of assembling them, the process of construction and its products will become more "intelligent." They will be able to respond to the changing needs of the occupants without redesign, take advantage of economies of scale, and reduce waste and duplication of efforts.

Finally, the advent of the Internet—an alternative "space" in which more and more activities "take place" (learning, shopping, entertaining, transacting business, and so on)—will promote a new kind of architecture, in its most cherished sense of "place making," though dressed in a different physical "cloth"—a *virtual* architecture, unburdened by the laws of nature.

Some of these changes are already evident today, albeit in a rather primitive, tentative, even bungled manner. Most computational applications are still in the "horseless carriage" phase—emulating older techniques and methods, like computer-aided drafting and modeling. Yet, in spite of its early, humble manifestations, computing technology promises

	1997	1999	2001	2003	2006	2009	2012
Process (microns)	0.25	0.18	0.15	0.13	0.10	0.07	0.05
Wafer diameter (mm)	200	300	300	300	300	450	450
Lithography	Deep UV	DUV	DUV	Extreme UV x-ray e-beam	(same)	"innovative technology"	(same)
Metal interconnect levels (DRAM)	2 to 3	3	3	3	3 to 4	4	4
Metal interconnect levels (logic)	6	6 to 7	7	7	7 to 8	8 to 9	9
DRAM	256Mb	1Gb	1Gb	4Gb	16Gb	64Gb	256Gb
Logic (transistors)	4M	6M	10M	18M	39M	84M	180M
Frequency (MHz)	600	958	1570	1768	2075	2574	
Maximum I/O pins	1089	1493	1824	2228	3008	4060	5480

A.2 Technological advances driving the microelectronics industry. (Semiconductor Industry Association *InfoWorld*, November 16, 1998.)

to become a *revolutionary* rather than evolutionary development in the history of architecture. Like other revolutions, it will take time to explore, develop, and accept the new possibilities.[8] Their effects will likely be felt by the professionals who have traditionally been entrusted with the design and construction of buildings—and by the society that uses them.

Distributed, Collaborative Design 21

The need for collaboration arises when the limits of their individual abilities prevent people from completing a given task on their own (due to the lack of knowledge, power, or resources) or when collaboration can help them complete the task more quickly and more effectively than they could otherwise. In addition to helping individuals undertake larger and more complex tasks, a collaborative arrangement can help them gain a perspective on the shared enterprise they would not have been able to perceive on their own, learn from others, and be motivated by them. Collaboration, as such, is an enabling force. At the same time, it can also be a restrictive force, in the sense that the action best suited to satisfy the goals and needs of one collaborator may not also be best suited to satisfy those of another, thereby raising potential conflicts and the need to compromise or even to yield to the will of others.

Collaboration, therefore, is a highly complex and challenging task. It has been the subject of study in virtually every field—sociology, psychology, politics, science, technology, and professional practices such as law, medicine, and engineering. Yet collaboration in A/E/C is different from collaboration in other fields. First, it involves individuals representing often fundamentally different professions who, perforce, hold different goals, objectives, and even belief systems. Unlike collaborators in medicine or jurisprudence, who share a common educational basis, architects, structural engineers, electrical engineers, clients, contractors, suppliers, property managers, and other professionals who comprise a design team, rarely share a common educational foundation. Second, it involves what has been termed "temporary multi-organizations"—teams of independent organizations that join forces to accomplish a specific project. While they work together to achieve the common, short-term goals of the project, each organization also has it own long-term goals, which might be in conflict with some of the goals of the particular project, thereby introducing issues that are extraneous to the domain of collaboration.[1] These may include financial, legal, ethical, professional, and other issues. Third, although short-term in comparison to the life of the participating organizations, collaboration in A/E/C tends to stretch out over a prolonged time, possibly outlasting the original participants. Yet the decisions and actions that have been taken by them when they were part of the project team may still impact and constrain the freedom of action of other participants.[2]

21.1 The Essence of Collaboration

History shows evidence of two closely linked and parallel trends related to the provision of professional services: (1) the trend toward collaboration, which brings people together for the purpose of combining their physical, mental, and financial powers to achieve greater goals than they could separately; and (2) the trend toward specialization, or division of labor, where individuals assume specific roles within the collective enterprise.

The first trend has been fueled by the limits of individual physical, mental, financial, and other abilities—from the Paleolithic collective hunting parties 40,000 years ago, in which individuals joined forces to hunt large animals, to construction of the great pyramids of Egypt 4,000 years ago, in which thousands of workers were mobilized to erect monuments for their rulers; from the construction of cathedrals in the Middle Ages by communities that combined their financial and labor resources to build communal places of worship, to the modern corporation, with its multitudes of technical, administrative, legal, financial, and other specialists who come together for the purpose of developing, marketing, and servicing some product.

Collaboration fostered specialization. Individuals working collectively soon found out that division of labor improves productivity.[3] Specialization exploded with the advent of the (first) Industrial Revolution: the substitution of mechanical power for human (and animal) labor, and the commensurate development of efficient distribution networks (railways and waterways), meant that it was no longer necessary—even desirable—for each community to produce all the goods it consumed. Factories (or, rather, "manufactories") could produce goods in one location, where natural or human resources favored the production of that type of product, and export them for consumption at other locations, while importing goods produced elsewhere.[4] The evolving patterns of trade created demand for additional goods and thus fueled the creation of additional manufacturing capacity, and in turn additional specialization.

At the microeconomic scale, individuals found it advantageous to specialize, so they could capitalize on what they did best. Such specialization, which was first known as craftsmanship and later as professionalism, conferred upon its members economic and social benefits commensurate with rendering specialized services. The attainment of such professional status required acquisition of specialized knowledge or know-how, a process that became formalized through the medieval guild structure (fraternities of masters, journeymen, and apprentices who controlled access to, the conduct of, and competition among the practitioners of a particular industry) and later through schools and universities such as the French Ecole des Ponts et Chaussées (1747), which was followed by the Ecole Polytechnique (1794)—the first institution to award the title "engineer."

To maintain their privileged status, the professions had to continuously develop new specialized knowledge. The model to emulate became medicine, which developed a successful research-educate-apply process. New knowledge was created at an ever accelerating rate by medical research centers, who passed it on to students, who applied it in the practice of medicine, where its successful application created expectations and demand for even more research, and so on. Thus, specialization, enforced through professional education, fostered the pursuit of knowledge, which in turn strengthened the profession.

The relentless pursuit of knowledge increased not only its quality but inevitably also its quantity. As a profession's knowledge base grew, it took longer to master. There are, however, limits to how long individuals are willing to train before the rewards of their training begin to be realized. It has been estimated that once a profession reaches the point where it takes ten years to master, it tends to break up into specializations.[5] Therefore, professions like medicine, law, and engineering, that once were comprised of general practitioners, now bustle with dozens, even hundreds of specialists. Even architecture, the most "generalist" of all disciplines, has yielded to specialization, as evidenced by the proliferation of professional interest areas (PIAs) within the American Institute of Architects—health care, codes and standards, construction management, housing, and so on.

Professional specialization thus leads to a symmetry of ignorance: the comprehensive knowledge of the mythical "Renaissance man," who knew

21.1 The symmetry of ignorance can cause architectural objectives to be compromised by structural considerations, and vice versa (a temporary building at the University of California, Berkeley).

about many things and could use knowledge from one domain to help solve problems in another, or at least avoid causing them, can no longer be attained (if indeed it ever could).[6] Rather, as the professional specializes, she or he trades depth for breadth, potentially loosing sight of the whole enterprise. As a result, while solving a narrowly defined problem, the expert can inadvertently cause or aggravate other problems, which may have a larger negative effect on the enterprise as a whole than the benefits of the individual expert's own contribution. For example, it can cause architectural objectives to be compromised by structural considerations (fig. 21.1).

The solution to the problems generated by increasing specialization is *collaboration*—joining forces with fellow experts, whose knowledge complements one's own, to solve problems too large for an individual. This has become the norm in complex medical cases, where an oncologist may team up with a surgeon and a family doctor to treat a patient with cancer; in complex legal cases, where the defense "dream team" may include a litigator, a DNA expert, and a jury consultant; and in architecture, where architects routinely team up with structural engineers, mechanical engineers, contractors, suppliers, and many other specialists to design a complex facility.

21.2 Types of Collaboration

Professional collaboration can be defined as "the agreement among specialists to share their abilities in a particular process, to achieve the larger objectives of the project as a whole."[7] This rather broad definition can be interpreted in different ways. Three main types of collaboration can be readily identified (fig. 21.2). It may be an *association* of experts who represent complementary skills in a professional group for the purpose of rendering a wider range of allied services than any one of them could render individually. It may be a *team* of experts assembled to handle a specific task, such as winning a football game; the members of the team contribute their expertise to accomplish the desired overall result. Finally, the collaboration may be *creative,* the experts joining together to solve a specific problem or discover new knowledge.

Future

Association

Association can be considered the simplest form of collaboration—the joining together of persons with different expertise for the purpose of expanding the range of related services beyond those which individuals can render on their own. Such collaborations have become the norm in the healthcare industry, where a group of doctors, each representing a different specialty, form a "providers group" or "network." Their association is aimed at providing patients with a variety of healthcare services. Often one of the professionals, typically the family doctor, assumes the role of coordinator, although this role may be limited to the initial referral. After that, each specialist assumes responsibility for the patient's well-being, informing the family doctor of treatment but not requesting permission to undertake medical procedures related to his or her own area of specialization.

A professional association is typically formed for business purposes, when independent but professionally compatible individuals find that they can realize better economic benefits by belonging to the group than by practicing on their own. This incentive is relatively weak, and members may leave if they find better opportunities elsewhere. Hence, their association is relatively loose, imposing few mutual constraints on members. The participants enjoy a relatively great degree of autonomy, since the actions of the individuals are largely independent of one another. Each of the participants typically maintains his or her own identity or business, with doctors often maintaining their own offices. Often, a separate management organization takes on the role of coordinating the association, a task typically too large and outside the domain of expertise of the participating professionals.

Given that the collaboration, in this case, is not problem-specific but is rather a business arrangement, it may be long lasting. When irreconcilable conflicts arise, or when an individual ceases to enjoy the benefits of the association, she or he may leave the group, often with little consequences to the group itself (they can usually recruit someone else) or to the individual (who can join another group, or practice alone).

	association	teamwork	creative collaboration
purpose	economic advantage	division of labor	problem solving, discovery
inter-dependence	little	considerable	considerable
management	external	internal	leadership, not management
duration	long term	long term	short term

21.2 Types of collaboration.

Teamwork

A more developed form of collaboration than the association is the team of specialists. Examples of such collaborations include symphony orchestras, which are comprised of individuals who are experts in playing different instruments, and professional sports teams, whose members may play different roles. Similar collaborations can be seen in surgical teams, where a surgeon collaborates with an anesthesiologist and other professionals to perform a complex medical procedure. More recently, the practice has been extended to law, where lawyers with different expertise come together for the purpose of litigating a complex case. In the construction industry, teams are formed between the owner, the architect, and the builder (the contractor). Each of these specialties may in turn be comprised of other teams of experts, such as the owner's team of lawyers and accountants, the architect's team of engineers and other consultants, and the contractor's team of subcontractors and suppliers.

Unlike in an association, the actions of individual team members depend on one another; they can enhance one another's efforts or interfere with them. Hence, a team collaboration requires greater coordination of the participants' individual contributions than the association does. In the case of the orchestra, the coordinator is the conductor, who keeps the beat and indicates with a baton who should play when, how fast, and how loudly. In the case of a professional football team, the coordination is multilayered and includes the coaching staff and the quarterback. In the construction industry, coordination depends on the magnitude of the project. In small projects, the owner (the client) may assume the role of coordinator. In larger projects it may be assumed by one of the participating professionals (often the architect or the contractor) or by a specialist (the construction manager).

The purpose of team collaboration is primarily division of labor: each specialist is responsible for one small part of the overall enterprise. Each looks after his or her own part only and tries to maximize personal rewards from the joint project, making sure that his or her professional (and legal) standards are not compromised. The coordinator's task is to ensure that the individual contributions do indeed add up and include all those needed to complete the task and that they do not interfere with one another.

The coordinator's task, therefore, is mostly one of scheduling and of resolving conflicts.

Teams may be formed for short or for long periods. Short-term teams are typically project-oriented, assembled to resolve a particular problem (e.g., a specific trial, surgery, or building project). As soon as the task is completed, the team dissolves. Long-term teams are ones that are formed to handle recurring, specific, well-defined tasks. For example, sports teams are long-term teams, as are orchestras and flight crews. In each case, every member of the team has a well-defined role, for which she or he is educated and regularly trains. Individual members of the team may change, but the long-term team continues to operate.

Like association, teamwork is a management strategy for handling, in an orderly and predictable manner, the division of labor among individuals. The division of labor makes teamwork productive, but it may also have negative side effects. Since each team member's responsibilities are well defined and compartmentalized, they cannot easily be adjusted to accommodate unforeseen circumstances, including those created by other team members. It is possible, therefore, that the actions of individual participants will conflict with one another, even though they appear to be the correct actions from the individual's own point of view. For example, it is possible that the architect, attempting to create a large unobstructed space, will compromise the efforts of the structural engineer who must support the roof. Conversely, the structural engineer may place supports where the architect intended to have unobstructed space. In both cases, the professionals try to maximize the value of their own part of the project, unaware of the negative side effects such actions may have on other parts of the same project. Team-type collaboration thus requires conflict resolution mechanisms as part of its management strategy.

Creative Collaboration

In its most developed state, collaboration is a process of shared creation, where the exchange of ideas among the participants helps to stimulate and enrich their own creativity, to the extent that the solution they arrive at is novel and unique. Collaboration, in this case, becomes a creative process, whose results are not predictable. For example, by listening to each another, sensing where the music is heading and adjusting their own playing accordingly, a group of talented jazz players can improvise and create music that has never been heard before. Likewise, the famous collaboration between James Watson and Francis Crick, who discovered the double helix structure of the DNA, was characterized by one of the two scientists suggesting a new idea, and the other testing its validity, back and forth.[8]

In this sense, collaboration can be considered an extension of the creative process that Donald Schön called "reflection-in-action": each of the participating professionals is attentive to the emerging solution and to the intents and actions of fellow collaborators, reflects upon them, and critiques them.[9] The input received from fellow collaborators may trigger new, innovative solutions, or combinations not seen earlier. In this form, collaboration becomes an instrument for the creation of new knowledge.

Such collaborations have no inherent "management" structure, but they do require a coordinator, or a leader, who will inspire and motivate other participants, keep them focused, and make decisions when deadlocks or conflicts occur. This role need not be assigned: any one of the participants may assume the role of a leader, and different participants may do so at different times. In fact, the absence of a conventional management structure is what makes such creative collaboration possible; it removes the shackles of authority, and replaces them by mutual respect and trust. Only then can the individual participants feel free to venture untested ideas and risk failure—which is a possible result of trying new approaches. Creative collaboration is thus a risky business: its results are not guaranteed. But when it succeeds, the rewards can be much greater than any other collaborative arrangement can deliver.

The duration of creative collaborations is limited. Once the task for which they were formed has been accomplished, the collaboration is dissolved. Hence, when the building project is completed, the solution to the problem found, or a discovery made, the partnership is terminated. While this may seem regrettable, it is often welcomed by the participants themselves, for the collaboration may be intense, contentious, and heated. It may lead to personal conflicts among the participants, even animosity and dislike (as was the case in 1947 in the collaboration between Shockley, Brattain, and Bardeen at Bell Labs, when they invented the transistor). Termination of the collaboration may bring closure to the creative process.

21.3 The Characteristics of Creative Collaboration

Experts form collaborative arrangements for different reasons: associations are formed for economic reasons. Teams are formed for division of labor. Creative collaborations, on the other hand, are formed to tackle a more difficult mission—finding a solution to the problem of creating something new. Consequently, they operate under different conditions and require different tools for their support. Although creative collaborations are unique, they share some common characteristics that help to direct them toward successful completion of their tasks. These characteristics include uniqueness and unpredictability, shared understanding, communication, and joint decision making.

Uniqueness and Unpredictability

Creative collaborations are unique: they are initiated for the explicit purpose of finding or creating a solution to a particular, new problem. There is no need for creative collaboration if the problem is routine, such as winning a football game or treating a well-known disease. Only new, unique problems, for which there are no established solutions, and which are too complex for one expert to solve individually, require creative collaborations. Architectural design falls into this category. Every building project is unique due to the specific requirements it must meet, the constraints it must abide by, and the context in which it is embedded. And the problem is always too complex for one professional to solve.

The uniqueness of the problem means that both the process of collaboration and its results are unpredictable: it is not known ahead of time which specific contributions will be needed to complete the task, what their effects might be, and when the need to involve additional contributors may arise. New problems will be discovered in the course of solving the original problem, requiring more time to resolve, and new ideas will be generated that will cast the problem in a new light. Decisions that were made earlier will have to be modified, entire courses of action may even have to be scrapped. These will result in unpredictable schedules, budgets, and ultimately—in unpredictable results of the collaborative effort.

Shared Understanding

The symmetry of ignorance implies that the collaborators must complement each other, not duplicate each other. Accordingly, there is typically only one representative from each area of knowledge relevant to solving the problem. Yet, to be of use to the project, these representatives ought to be able to share their knowledge with one another and understand one another's needs and contributions well enough to be able to respond to them constructively.

Understanding is hard to come by, since it implies a deeper cognitive state than mere knowing, which is the ability to apply standardized knowledge to solving routine problems. Understanding adds a measure of critical reflection, which helps one to appreciate the extent of the knowledge and its relationship to one's values and beliefs. It permits one to discern appropriate knowledge from inappropriate knowledge, gauge its usefulness and its limitations, and instill the necessary confidence needed to discard invalid or old knowledge for the sake of new or improved propositions.

The cognitive filtering and internalizing mechanisms that transform knowledge into understanding are different from one individual to another. They depend on the individual's values and beliefs as well as on his or her educational and social background. Specialization, which as discussed earlier is the result and reason for collaboration, is a powerful force working to counter shared understanding. It instills in its disciples not only the specialized knowledge needed to solve certain problems, but also a world-view and often an unshakeable belief in the truth of its validity.[10] Therefore, it is unlikely that two individuals, especially highly specialized ones, will have the same understanding of the same situation.

Still, because all the specialists who participate in a creative collaboration are expected to contribute to solving the same problem, they must posses a measure of shared understanding. It is not enough for them to be able to answer questions raised by other contributors, for those contributors may not know which questions to ask. Hence, for a collaboration to qualify as creative, the individuals must actively proffer their advise, insight, and criticism, even (or especially) when not asked. Such activism can have disastrous consequences for the project (and the individual), unless it is done from a standpoint of mutual respect and trust.

Shared understanding allows each of the participants to comprehend, critique, debate, adopt, or incorporate the propositions made by the other participants into the emerging collective creation. Like the jazz musicians who "feel" the music, and therefore can contribute harmoniously to it, so must architects, engineers, owners, and contractors share the "vision"—for lack of a better term—of the collective enterprise, as must authors who collaborate on writing a joint manuscript or scientists who collaborate in research.

Having a shared understanding does not mean that the collaborators must embrace one another's positions; they may very well "agree to disagree." However, their differences must be based on substantively understanding one another's positions, not merely their styles of presentation. Without such shared understanding, disagreements may lead to irreconcilable conflicts or to resolutions where one of the participants unwillingly yields to the position of another—two options that do not add value to the project. In contrast, disagreements based on shared understanding have the potential to produce novel solutions, ones that none of the participants has envisioned before. Metaphorically speaking, the sparks of disagreement may ignite the creative flame. Hence, for example, a structural engineer would have to *understand* the architect's sensitivities and position with regard to a building project, not merely accept it as given, and vise versa. Likewise, the architect must understand and respect the engineer's position. Only then will they be able to contribute constructively to the joint experience (fig. 21.3). Without such understanding, the engineer is bound to see the architect's proposition as a "problem" to be solved rather than as an edifice to be improved upon, and the architect will view the engineer as an "obstructionist" to fulfilling his or her "dream."

21.3 The Dives in Misericordia church, near Rome, Italy, is the result of creative collaboration between architect Richard Meier, who conceived its shape, structural engineer Professor Antonio Michetti, of the University of Rome "La Sapienza," who designed a double-stressed concrete structure that made the shape possible, and Italcementi, the Italian construction company, which developed a special concrete mix and a construction robot to realize it.

Communication

Creative collaboration is an *interactive* effort. It requires interaction among the participants for the purpose of exchanging ideas, not only information. It is this give-and-take of ideas that enriches and contributes to the shared understanding of the problem and to its successful resolution. By making suggestions, critiquing others, and simply by responding to one another's ideas, the participants receive the necessary feedback to their own ideas, as well as the inspiration needed to form them in the first place.

Such interactive exchange need not be real-time. It works just as well, albeit more slowly, through correspondence, e-mail, or leaving notes on a blackboard. But it requires an active respondent. Reading the work of a nonresponsive author does not qualify as exchange, for then there is no way to validate the understanding the reader derives from the reading; nor can the author's work be adapted to the particular circumstances of the new project. Hence, building upon the discoveries of the past is not collaboration. Creative collaboration requires argumentation: positions must be proposed, challenged, supported, debated, and allowed to inspire new ideas—all of which requires active participation.[11]

Joint Decision Making

In addition to these "technical" characteristics, creative collaboration also has social and behavioral characteristics. Collaborators must trust and respect one another (although they do not necessarily have to like one another). They must be committed to solving the problem, not only to performing their task as team members in work-for-hire mode. And most importantly, they must be willing to accept and contribute to a joint decision-making process.

Sharing the decision-making process is, however, often difficult for design professionals, who are trained to evaluate and to judge—and immediately seek the action that follows from their observations—while discarding information that appears to be irrelevant. They are trained to search for congruence between what they observe and the theoretical constructs of their respective professional worldviews, which they have come to accept as truth. Professionally, experts are not rewarded for suspending judgment or for allowing other worldviews to alter their own. The suspension of judgment increases their professional vulnerability and risk of failure. It can only be justified if the risks taken lead to the attainment of desirable objectives which, in the case of a collaborative enterprise, are shared—and hence negotiated—as well.[12]

Negotiated goals and objectives are as much a result of the personalities of the participants as of their professional standing. Personalities play an important role in collaborative relationships, as they do in most other work relationships. Professional collaboration therefore can be—and often is—an intense, demanding, even contentious, process.

21.4 How Can Creative Collaboration Be Facilitated?

Association- and teamlike collaborations can be facilitated by relatively simple computational means, which help inform the collaborators of one another's contributions, and—to a limited extent—provide a forum to recognize and resolve conflicts when they arise. To facilitate creative collaboration, however, it is necessary to cope with the related problems of uniqueness and unpredictability, to engender shared understanding among the participants, and to facilitate communication and joint decision making. In addition, it is necessary to instill in the participants a commitment to solving the problem, along with trust and respect.

The first set of problems is technical in nature. The problems are, therefore, amenable to computational or organizational assistance. The second set is social and behavioral. While the problems are not less important for creative collaboration than those in the first set, they can be more appropriately handled by educational and behavioral science methods. To complicate matters, the two types of problems are thoroughly intertwined: addressing one affects the other.

Habitual Methods of Collaboration

Professional practices in A/E/C have recognized the need for creative collaboration and have generally adopted one of two methods to address it: hierarchical decision making or temporal partitioning of responsibilities.

Hierarchical decision making among professionals comprising an A/E/C design team takes the form of contractual arrangements, in which one of the participants (often the architect) is appointed team leader and the rest are considered subcontractors or consultants.[13] While this arrangement may be efficient in terms of process (i.e., getting the job done), it introduces the risk of diminishing the overall performance of the product by reducing the commitment of subcontractors who may feel they have less "ownership" of or influence on the product. The overall result, therefore, is often less than optimal.

Temporally partitioning responsibilities represents the typical over-the-wall practice of transferring responsibility for the project from one design professional to the next as it moves along the design-build-use process. Thus, the responsibilities of the architect end when construction begins, and the construction manager's responsibilities end when the facilities manager takes over. While this method, too, is efficient in terms of process and has the added benefit of compartmentalizing legal and other responsibilities, it is detrimental in terms of quality. The carefully considered knowledge applied in earlier design phases is lost when the responsibilities are transferred, along with all the assumptions underlying them. Moreover, knowledge that resides in "downstream" participants is not available to the "upstream" participants (e.g., the availability of better methods or products than those specified by the "upstream" participant, or the unavailability or incompatibility of those specified).

Thus, accepting either one of the first two collaboration management strategies, while superficially efficient, may result in overall failure of the project or, at best, less-than-optimal overall performance. Truly effective collaboration requires the ability to make joint decisions that will promote the overall performance of the product over individual disciplinary concerns. Yet the piecemeal nature of hierarchically or temporally partitioned habitual collaboration makes it almost impossible to recognize the existence of such higher-level objectives or distributed knowledge, let alone develop a shared view of the project.

Educational Approach to Collaboration

An obvious solution to overcoming professionally induced fragmentation is to address the educational process through which architects, engineers, and construction managers (as well as other professionals involved in the construction process) are socialized into their respective worldviews. By informing students of the views, beliefs, and methods of their peer disciplines, they may become more aware of and sensitive to the issues held dear by their future partners in the design process.

It is impractical, however, to try to cross-educate students in more than one discipline. The very problem of fragmentation is the result of the explosive growth of knowledge in each and every discipline. It *is*, however, practical—even desirable—to try to sensitize students (as well as professionals) to the issues, objectives, and concerns of their peer disciplines.[14] While there is evidence that all the students who participate in such cross-disciplinary courses gain valuable insight into the value systems used by their peers, by and large such courses serve more to elucidate the differences between the disciplines than to reconcile them.[15]

Computational Methods of Collaboration

Several computational methods, aimed mostly at facilitating the communication aspects of collaboration in A/E/C, have been proposed over the past two decades. They can be classified into three generic types of methods:

- *Product-sharing* methods use common data exchange formats to facilitate the transfer of project information among the participating professionals (e.g., ID'EST, EDM, COMBINE).[16] Communication efforts in this area have focused on the development of sharable product models of the kind discussed in section 8.5 and databases of increasing sophistication that include factual information about the objects they describe, with particular emphasis on solving issues of concurrency, data integrity, and data-sharing.[17] These methods assume that the readers of the data will interpret it correctly, using their own professional knowledge. This, however, is a risky assumption for reasons of the social and professional orientation discussed earlier. Therefore, while these efforts have made *communication* easier and more efficient, they have not, in and of themselves, improved *shared understanding*, which is fundamental for collaborators to make joint decisions and negotiate trade-offs. In particular, product-sharing methods cannot handle the uniqueness and unpredictability of the design process.

- *Performance evaluation* methods combine individual, discipline-specific performance evaluations into a composite or an overall performance assessment of the evolving design solution (e.g., BDA and IBDE, discussed in chapter 18).[18] Generally, performance-based collaboration methods tend to emphasize the *technological* aspects of the evolving solution (energy, lighting, cost, and so on), while largely ignoring the *human* aspects of design collaboration. They suffer, therefore, from the same limitations as the habitual collaboration methods, namely—compartmentalization of worldviews and a tendency to communicate the results of evaluations without the objectives they strive to accomplish or the assumptions they rely upon. They are, however, capable of dealing with unpredictable situations, since their role is to evaluate, rather than to generate them.[19]

- *Process-based* methods emphasize the deliberative aspects of design decision-making processes in terms of design intents, assumptions, and arguments, in favor of or against proposed design actions. The theoretical underpinning of deliberative methods were proposed by Rittel in his IBIS method,[20] and implemented in case- and knowledge-based networked hypermedia systems such as MIKROPLIS, PHIDIAS I and II, and Janus (see section 11.2).[21] Agent-based systems that support argumentation were developed by Pohl and his colleagues.[22] These systems have helped researchers to understand the deliberative nature of the design process but suffer from the inherent difficulty of encoding design knowledge in computational constructs, such as expert systems and "agents" (discussed in chapter 22). Therefore, they tend to work well in restricted domains such as load planning for military ships (ICADS and ICDM systems) or NASA's lunar habitat module (PHIDIAS II).

21.5 A Network-Based Approach to Design Collaboration

Habitual modes of collaboration in architectural design—and the computational tools that support them—have focused on controlled data management, that is, the organized transfer of information among the participants, subject to centralized control. They are similar to the modes of operation used in other complex supply-chain business enterprises, like the automotive and retail industries. [23] One of the participants is entrusted to be the "controller" of the enterprise (although this role may transfer from one participant to another throughout the process), who prescribes and schedules the contributions of the other participants. For example, it is typically the architect who is in control of the design process, determining what input is needed from each one of the engineers, consultants, and other participants, and when that input is needed. Traditional architectural communication technologies—in the form of drawings and specifications—have been designed to support this mode of collaboration, facilitating the transfer of information along with the clear indication of responsibilities.

Information technology can certainly support these traditional models—as well as disrupt them.[24] But it can also afford new modes of collaboration that can support, or at least accommodate, the uniqueness and unpredictability of creative design processes (as well as other network-like organizational relationships). For example, collaborative product commerce (CPC) tools use the Internet as a virtual marketplace, where information is readily available and control is distributed.[25] The underlying technology comprises high-speed, reliable, secure communication, browser-based standardized user interfaces, object-oriented product descriptions, URL-style location transparency, secure business tools for bidding, billing, and servicing (updating) products, and business models that are more flexible than traditional contracts (e.g., pay for use without licensing the product). Utilization of such tools substitutes accessibility for the transfer of information (the information resides at its owner's location, where all authorized participants can view it, rather than being shipped to the controller's location). It also distributes ownership and responsibility for conforming to one another's needs and to the overall needs of the project among the participants, binding them in appropriate contractual relationships (i.e., it specifies who may update what parts of the information) instead of work-for-hire relationships. The controller is replaced by a facilitator, a coordinator, or a "configurator," whose responsibility is to make sure that individual contributions are made on time and that the overall process progresses toward meeting its goals. Decisions concerning the overall direction of the project are still made by one of the participants (e.g., the client or the client's representatives), but they are transmitted to the affected parties as constraints on their individual contributions rather than as instructions to be fulfilled.

An example of such collaborative procurement model was pioneered by Wal-Mart Stores, the world's largest retailer of general merchandise goods, and was quickly implemented by its competitors. Instead of automating only the order-processing means between its stores and its suppliers, Wal-Mart's Efficient Consumer Response (ECR) initiative uses an eChannel supply-demand product called MyVision (made by Stonebridge, a Pleasanton, California, company) to collect data at the checkout counter from each transaction, compare it to inventory levels, and—when inventories fall bellow a prescribed level—notify the respective supplier. It is then the supplier's responsibility to restock the indicated store with its products. Thus, Wal-Mart always has the right level of inventory for each product in each store, without assuming the responsibility for producing, inventorying, and delivering the products, which it has successfully transferred to the suppliers. The overall result is minimizing the total cost of the retail supply chain.

Similar approaches have been adopted in the construction management of the A/E/C enterprise, where lean construction—a notion adopted from the automotive industry—has made the organization of the building process more efficient.[26] The automotive industry itself has adopted such a supply-chain networking approach to afford lean production, as did the computer industry, both of which are now able to tailor each product (within well-defined limits) to the needs of their customers.[27]

It is not at all clear at this time that the architectural design process is amenable to similar techno-organizational changes, nor how exactly this new environment will look. It will likely be structured around a high-bandwidth communication network, which will link location-transparent, distributed data sets, each representing the individual contribution of one participant. The data formats need not—indeed cannot—be the same, for each discipline has developed its own tools and representations that are most appropriate for its domain. Nonetheless, these data sets will be tagged through XML or similar cross-platform standards so critical attributes can be recognized across disciplines. If collaborative product commerce (CPC) methods are indicative of a trend, then the participants will be organized as a network of service and product suppliers, who will offer alternative solutions for their part of the collaborative project, subject to goals and constraints established by other collaborators. These solutions will be reviewed by other collaborators for conforming to the overall needs of the project, and for their impact on each collaborator's own domain of expertise. The process will not be completely linear, as it is now, nor will it be parallel, because the solutions provided by one collaborator serve as input, or at least as guidelines, to others. The envisioned process will be fluid, dynamically negotiated, and mutually stimulated—providing the participants with a greater stake in the results and therefore a greater commitment to its success.

21.6 Consequences of Collaboration for the A/E/C Industry

The most important impacts of a network-based collaborative approach on architectural design will be its transformation from a hierarchical, linear process into a distributed, interleaved process, where the sequence of inputs is not predetermined but rather opportunistic. It means that opportunities can be recognized and acted upon in time to make the most of them, and problems can be spotted earlier, when they arise, because more specialists will have access to the evolving product: they will not have to wait their turn to be consulted, at which time it may be too late to recognize an opportunity or to avoid a problem. The avoidance of problems will lead to reduced design time, and greater satisfaction of all parties involved.

The roles of the individual participants stand to change as well, much as they changed during the fifteenth century, when the profession of architecture was instituted, and in the eighteenth century, when factory-based production supplanted cottage industries. The traditional role of the architect as the lead player in the design process may diminish, while the respective roles of other specialists—like consultants and suppliers—may increase. Although the administrative roles of the architect may erode, his or her contribution will not. Design will still need the overall creative vision provided by architects, which is different from solving technical problems associated with its realization. On the other hand, other participants in the design process will become contributors rather than problem solvers, increasing their commitment to the project.

Overall, the hierarchical structure of the process—and the organizations engaged in it—may "flatten out," changing from "command and control" to "coordination and communication"—a structure Robert Reich (secretary of labor in the Clinton administration) calls "collective entrepreneurship." It makes the process less bureaucratic and more able to respond to opportunities and to changing needs (which are inevitable in design processes).

Such a transformation depends on, and is shaped by technology, which provides a means of communication among the specialists and helps them individually gain access to knowledge and databases. However, it is not a simple addition of information technology to an existing process and organizational method. Rather, it is a combined techno-organizational change, where the respective roles and links among the participants change along with the technology.[28]

Bibliography

Blau, J. R. *Architects and Firms: A Sociological Perspective on Architectural Practice.* Cambridge: MIT Press, 1984.

Coovert, M. D. *Computer-Supported Cooperative Work: Issues and Implications for Workers, Organizations, and Human Resource Management.* Thousand Oaks, Calif.: Sage, 2001.

Fischer, M. D., and A. Finkelstein. "Social Knowledge Representation: A Case Study." In *Using Computers in Qualitative Research,* ed. N. G. Fielding and R. M. Lee, 119–135. London: Sage, 1993.

Heller, F., E. Pusic, G. Strauss, and B. Wilpert. *Organizational Participation: Myth and Reality.* Oxford: Oxford University Press, 1998.

Jacky, J., and D. Schuler. *Directions and Implications of Advanced Computing (Diac–87).* Norwood, N.J.: Ablex, 1993.

Kalay, Y. E., L. Khemlani, and Jin Won Choi. "An Integrated Model to Support Collaborative Multi-Disciplinary Design of Buildings." *Automation in Construction* 7, nos. 2–3 (1998): 177–188.

Lander, S. E. "Distributed Search and Conflict Management among Reusable Heterogeneous Agents." Ph.D. diss., Graduate School of the University of Massachusetts, Amherst, 1994.

March, J. G., and H. A. Simon. "Organizations." Technical Report, Graduate School of Industrial Administration, Carnegie Institute of Technology, Pittsburgh, 1959.

Rittel, H. "Reflections on the Scientific and Political Significance of Decision Theory." Technical Report No. 115, Center for Planning and Development Research, University of California, Berkeley, 1969.

Schrage, M. *No More Teams! Mastering the Dynamics of Creative Collaboration.* New York: Doubleday, 1989.

Valkenburg, R. C. "Shared Understanding as a Condition for Team Design." *Automation in Construction* 7, nos. 2–3 (1998): 111–121.

Intelligent Design Agents 22

Much of computer-aided design technology has been devoted to supporting individual design professionals, helping them do their job more effectively and more efficiently. There are many ways in which such support can be manifested. The simplest form of support is tools—implements that enhance the individual's power (physical or mental) in some way. A calculator is a tool, much like drafting and modeling systems. Even design synthesis and evaluation software, of the kinds discussed in parts 3 and 4 of this book, consists mostly of tools, albeit sophisticated ones. What characterizes tools is their complete passivity. They must be instructed, step by step, how to carry out their assigned tasks. Thus the buttons of a calculator must be punched one digit at a time, and the arithmetic operators must be entered in the correct sequence before the tool can add or multiply two numbers. Likewise, computer-aided drafting and modeling systems must be instructed line by line, operator by operator, before they can help the designer produce a drawing or a model.

A more advanced form of support is assistants—semiautonomous tools (as well as people) who can take an instruction and carry it out, even when the task involves multiple steps and some judgment. An example of a computer-aided design assistant is a space allocation program of the kind discussed in section 13.2, or an expert system of the kind discussed in section 14.3. These programs have preset behaviors, coded in the form of algorithms or rules, that enable them to perform limited judgments that affects their actions.

An even more advanced form of support is agents—completely autonomous entities (they can no longer be called tools) that can not only respond intelligently to some instruction but initiate actions on their own. In the human world, this is the kind of behavior we expect from travel agents, real estate agents, even secret agents. Agents can still be considered "support" mechanisms, because their actions come on behalf of someone else—a business executive who needs to make travel arrangements but

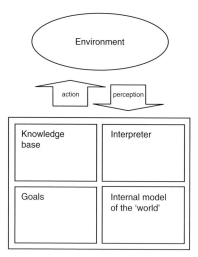

22.1 The basic structure of a software agent.

does not have the time to do it himself, a homeowner who wants to sell her house but cannot afford the time to show it and extol its virtues to prospective buyers, or a government that wants to collect information about another country and needs to do so covertly. Yet, while the "strategic" initiative, or motivation for their action comes from outside the agent, the "tactical" decisions—how to fulfill the mission—are the agents' own, carried out independently of the supervision of their employers.

22.1 Artificial Agents

"Artificial agents" are software equivalents of human agents: they are task-specific, autonomous programs that can communicate with their "senders," perceive the environment in which they operate, and use their built-in knowledge and judgment to accomplish some predefined goals. In addition, software agents are able to learn from their experiences, so their actions under the same conditions may differ from time to time.

Artificial agents, much like human agents, must be invoked into action. Such invocation may be explicit, through a command (equivalent to the homeowner calling a real estate agent), or based on some environmental stimulus for which the agent is programmed to look out. Once invoked, the agent continues to perceive its environment and interpret it according to its knowledge base. It can then choose the best course of action available to it, such that the action will cause a change in the environment that best suits the agent's goals. A record of the two activities—perception and action—is added to the agent's memory, thereby modifying its knowledge base in a manner akin to learning.

Types of Agents

The first characteristic that affects the agent's effectiveness is the its internal structure (fig. 22.1), which classifies artificial agents into different types.

A rational agent is one that chooses actions that will maximize its goal function. The term "rational" is taken here to mean that the agent's performance is measured by the degree of the *expected* success of its action, given what has been perceived, rather than the *actual* success of its action (which may not be entirely under the agent's control). In other

Future

words, a rational agent is not expected to take action in response to conditions it cannot perceive nor ones it can perceive but is not equipped to handle (a simple game-playing agent, for example, will select the next best move it can find from among the current options presented by the game board).[1]

More sophisticated agents can keep track of the history of their "world." They construct a more complete description of their environment than the input tools allow for by "remembering" changes that were made to it through the agent's own prior actions. This calls for *persistent* world models that are constructed and stored incrementally and updated every time new input is received or action taken. In so doing, the most recent input is combined with the old internal model to generate an updated description of the current state of the world. Such incremental world models, coupled with a knowledge of the actions that contributed to the change, help agents choose more judiciously the best action available to them (thus a more sophisticated game-playing agent will recognize previously played game patterns and select a move that may not appear the best, but which has historically led to better results than other, more apparent moves).

In addition to keeping track of the state of its world, an agent needs a goal or set of goals describing desirable situations to be achieved through its actions. Thus, a goal-based agent also maintains information about the result of possible actions so it can choose from among alternative actions the one that will best achieve the desired goals.

Utility-based agents not only keep track of the possible results of their own actions but can construct hypothetical models of the resulting state of the world after each possible action has been taken. This helps them look for a preferred world state from among possible alternatives and choose their action accordingly. Each possible world state is given some utility index, which maps the state, or sequence of states, to a number describing the degree of satisfaction derived by achieving it. This helps the agent decide on the preferred course of action in case there are conflicting goals only some of which can be achieved (i.e., when tradeoffs need to be considered); and when there is uncertainty about whether goals can be achieved through the agent's actions, in which case the utility function provides a means for weighing possible success against the importance of each goal.

Types of Environments

The second characteristic that determines the effectiveness of artificial (and human) agents is the environment in which they operate. It provides stimuli to the agent, which the agent acts upon. There are different kinds of environments in which an agent might perform. An *accessible* environment is one where the agent's sensors provide it with complete knowledge of the state of the environment. In this case, the agent does not need to maintain an internal model to keep track of the world. Game-playing agents enjoy this type of environment. Design agents, on the other hand, do not. The state of the design is often too complex for any one agent to comprehend (much as it is too complex for one human designer to know all that happens in a complex building project). In such cases an internal model of that part of the world that affects the agent, and is affected by it, must be maintained by the agent, possibly with additional information derived from the agent's own knowledge of similar conditions elsewhere— what human agents call "experience."

An environment is considered to be *deterministic* when the next state of the world is completely determined by its current state and by the actions of the agent. The opposite of a deterministic environment is an *episodic* environment, where the state of the world does not entirely depend on the actions taken by the agent itself but also on actions taken by others. Game-playing agents operate in an episodic environment: the state of the game depends as much on the actions of the opponent(s) as on the actions of the agent itself.

An environment is considered to be *static* when it does not change while the agent is deliberating what action to take. If, on the other hand, it does change, it is known as a *dynamic* environment. Chess is an example of a static environment. Collaborative design is an example of a dynamic environment: other actors may change the state of the project while the design agent contemplates its next move.

The environment is considered to be *discrete* when there are a limited number of distinct and clearly defined states of the world and a limited number of actions that can be taken on the environment, as is the case in chess, for example. Obviously, design is not a discrete environment: the number of possible changes is infinite.

22.2 Properties of Agents

Both human and software agents assume the responsibility that has been entrusted to them by their client-user. To uphold this trust, they must have certain qualities, including the ability to communicate, capability, autonomy, and adaptability: they must be able to understand the goals, preferences, and constraints of their senders; they must have the ability to carry out the task and do so with little or no supervision; and they must be able to learn from their successes and failures.

Communication

Effective communication between the agent and its client-user is of paramount importance because the agent is expected to infer from a short goal statement the needs and wishes of the client. To do so, it must share the client's knowledge and preferences and have an understanding of the domain of inquiry. For example, a purchasing agent entrusted to find doors that meet the project's needs and the architect's preferences must know something about doors, about the project, and about the architect's preferred style or other door-related attributes.

In the case of human agents, shared understanding is established through prolonged relationships between the agent and the client. In the case of software agents, this knowledge must be provided explicitly. One way to do so is through an ontology—a formal definition of the body of knowledge that is pertinent to the agent's domain of expertise. An ontology is essentially a taxonomy of class and subclass relationships, coupled with definitions of the relationships between objects, concepts, and their attributes, and some inference mechanism that can traverse the classification hierarchy and retrieve the requested information. An example of such an ontology for doors is depicted in figure 22.2.

Although a machine-readable ontology allows the computer to access and manipulate the terms used in the ontology—terms that make sense to human users as well—the computer of course does not "understand" the information in any deep sense of the term. Still the ontology can provide a form of communication between the user and the computer, which in turn enables the software agent to act on behalf of its user.

22.2 An ontology of doors, including a classification hierarchy and definitions of attributes. (L. Khemlani et al., in *Automation in Construction* 8, no. 1 [1998].)

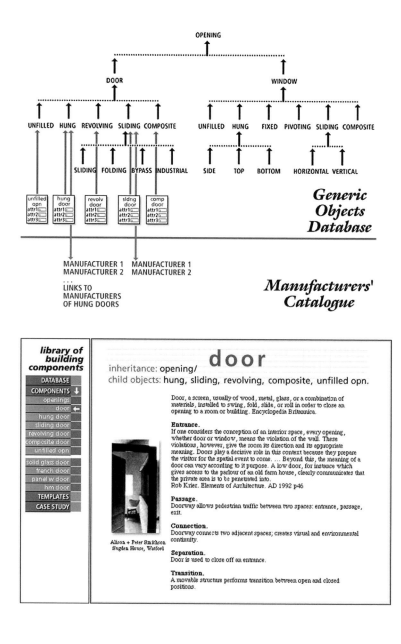

Future

Capability

For an agent to be of service, it must be able to take action on behalf of its client. For example, a door-purchasing agent must be able not only to find the appropriate door(s) for the project, but also to negotiate prices and delivery dates, arrange for payments, service contracts, and all the other details one would expect from a purchasing agent.

Such software agents have been developed for some low-level transactions (e.g., buying nuts and bolts for manufacturing purposes),[2] but are yet to be developed for more complicated transactions of the kind needed in architectural design, where there may not be any products that match exactly the specified needs. The negotiations, in such cases, affect not only the terms of the transaction itself but also the designed product as a whole (for example, if the desired doors are not available, the architect may have to change the design to match what is available on the market or initiate a custom design procurement process).

The advent of Internet-enabled standards such as XML for general purpose tagging of attributes,[3] and the International Alliance for Interoperability's (IAI) Industry Foundation Classes (IFC),[4] provide "hooks" that software agents can use to recognize specific information which they need for their actions.

Autonomy

The main difference between an assistant and an agent is autonomy. A person or software that can help make wise decisions but needs constant supervision to keep it on track may be a useful advisor but falls short of the help that an agent is expected to provide. To be truly effective, an agent needs to be able to operate on behalf of its client with little or no supervision. Relinquishing control to either a human or a software agent is, of course, a matter of controversy. On one hand, too much independence may produce undesirable results. On the other hand, too little autonomy demotes the agent to the status of an assistant or a tool.

Enabling autonomy is not a difficult programming task (as has been proved by software viruses). Controlling the degree and effects of autonomous action is. It depends on the context in which the agent operates and on operational parameters established for its operation. For

22.3 KAAD is a mixed-initiative agent that "watches over the designer's shoulder" and informs him or her of incompatibilities between the design and the stated goals and constraints. (G. Carrara et al., in *Automation in Construction* 3, nos. 2–3 [1994].)

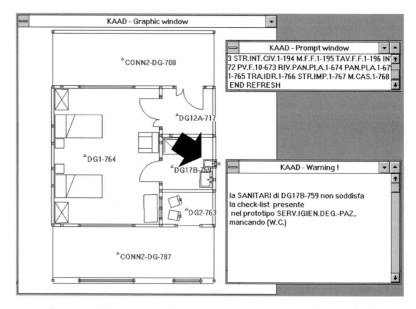

example, a travel agent may be given the autonomy to book a flight if it meets the parameters established by the client; whereas for most home buyers it would be a considerable leap of faith to allow their real estate agent to purchase a house for them without further consultation. For human agents the level of autonomy is often defined by law or by custom. For software agents it is much less clear.

One possible solution to the autonomy problem is the so-called mixed-initiative approach, or partnership paradigm.[5] In such systems the software agent's autonomy varies, based on factors like cost, the resources needed, or other variables the user has chosen to delegate to the system. Sometimes the system is in charge—preauthorized to make decisions or suggest alternatives. Other times, the user is in charge, taking control and steering the decision-making process. An example of such mixed-initiative autonomy is ALEX, a single-family house design system that was discussed in section 13.3.[6]

Expert systems are another kind of mixed-initiative agent that essentially "looks over" the user's shoulder. Such systems monitor (and understand) the user's actions and might make suggestions as to which options to choose or point out which options that were chosen are incompatible with the rules that make up the agents' knowledge base. This is the approach that has been implemented in KAAD,[7] an expert system for the design of health-care facilities discussed in section 4.1 (fig. 22.3).

Adaptability

The best way for a software agent, like a human agent, to find the appropriate balance between aiding a user and overstepping its bounds is to learn the user's preferences. A truly useful agent should be able to adapt its behavior to a combination of user-feedback and environmental factors. Such adaptive behavior can be achieved in a number of ways. Microsoft's Windows, for example, presents menu options based on the frequency of their use: if a particular menu option has not been used over some predefined period of time, it will no longer appear on the pull-down menu, unless the user persists by keeping the menu open for a few seconds. After it has been used, Windows "assumes" that the user will be interested that option again and continues to show it in the pull-down menu.

More sophisticated "learning" has been implemented over the Internet through the use of "cookies"—small programs that are embedded on the user's computer and consulted by a Web site when the user visits that site. The cookie stores the user's preferences, such as the password needed to access some site, credit card and shipping information, even his or her interests. Web sites like Amazon.com can then present their customers only with items they may be interested in, rather than waste their time by looking at items they are not (obviously, cookies can be misused by malicious Web sites to implant unwanted or even destructive instructions on the user's computer).[8]

22.3 Examples

Software agents with all the desired capabilities are difficult to develop. Those that have been developed are primarily experimental systems, running in research labs, and must overcome a number of challenges before they are ready for professional use. Foremost among them are knowledge and autonomy. An agent that is truly useful must have a lot of knowledge about its problem domain and must have enough autonomy to perform the task on behalf of its client. The problems are related: if the agent has less knowledge, its client will be reluctant to let it operate autonomously. The difficulties associated with these capabilities grow with the complexity of the domain within which the agents operate. Still, a number of promising test case studies have been developed that illustrate these capabilities, even if they are not yet ready for practical use.

Fenestration Agent

The Fenestration Agent, developed by Gustavo Llavaneras, is a mixed-initiative agent intended to support an architect in choosing the right windows for a given project.[9] Its knowledge base comprises a database of commercially available windows, along with their cost, energy, and acoustical performance attributes. Its environmental awareness includes the conditions of the site in which the project is located, in terms of views, orientations, and noise sources (fig. 22.4a), as well as the nature of the project itself. The site conditions are provided as input by the designer, selected from a menu. The design solution itself, in the form of a room, is also provided by the designer, through a built-in graphical user interface. Once the environment has been specified and the room laid out, the designer can indicate the locations and sizes of the windows and choose specific windows from a list (fig. 22.4b). The Fenestration Agent checks to see if the chosen windows meet the specified design constraints and goals in terms of cost, heat gain/loss, daylighting, and noise transmission. The results are presented to the designer in aggregate form (fig. 22.4c), with specific recommendations to make changes that will improve the overall performance of the design. If the designer chooses to delegate the

22.4 The fenestration agent helps to design windows that meet a number of performance characteristics. (G. J. Llavaneras, "The Fenestration Intelligent Design Assistant," Ph.D. diss., University of California, Berkeley, 1996.)

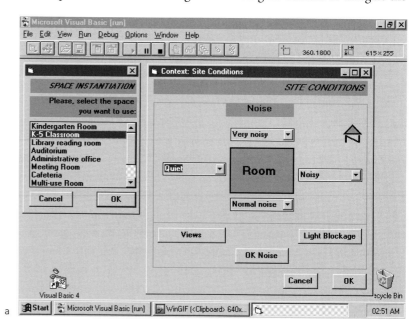

a

Future

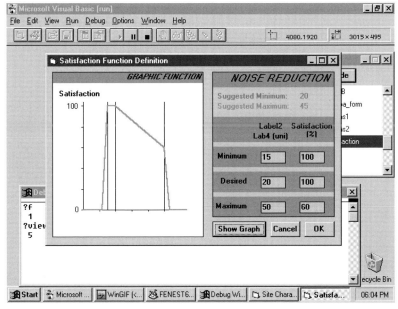

b

c

22.5 REA is an artificial real estate agent that can converse in English and by gesture with a human "client." (Courtesy of the Gesture and Narrative Language Group, the MIT Media Lab, Cambridge, Massachusetts.)

responsibility to the program, the Fenestration Agent can pick specific windows from the list that will meet the specified requirements in the optimal way. To that end, the system includes built-in evaluation and tradeoff functions and display capabilities for presenting the results to the designer.

REA

Developed by Justine Cassell and her students in the Gesture and Narrative Language Group at MIT's Media Lab, REA is an artificial real estate agent that can converse in English and by gesture with a human "client" (fig. 22.5). REA plays the role of a salesperson who interacts with prospective home buyers to determine their needs, shows them around virtual properties, and attempts to "sell" them a house. Her human form and ability to communicate using both verbal and nonverbal modalities provides a human-computer interface with which users can interact naturally, without training, since they already know how to engage in face-to-face conversation with other people. The real estate sales personality was chosen because it provides opportunities for both task-oriented and socially oriented conversation, thus providing a platform for exploring theories of human communicative behavior.

Human gestures are sensed through video cameras. They undergo "gesture recognition," which, along with speech recognition, provide REA with the input needed to generate her own responses. These are synthesized, based on a grammar, a lexicon, and the communicative context, and include speech and accompanying hand gestures.

Creating a synthetic conversational human is a large undertaking that introduces a wide range of hard research issues, including the recognition of user hand gestures, the synthesis of hand gestures intended to communicate pragmatic information, and the planning of mixed-initiative dialog including non-task-oriented "small talk" and conversational storytelling.

VUsers

The virtual users (VUsers) that were discussed in section 20.1 are a kind of rational agent, intended to simulate how humans behave in spatio-social environments, while representing specific human traits.[10] As such, they posses the ability to perceive and interpret their social environment as well as the physical one and act upon it by adjusting their own behavior. This, in turn, affects the environment perceived by other VUsers and thus affects their behavior as well, and so on.

The VUser agent possesses a set of goals that defines its "mission" (e.g., get to the other side of the plaza), and an extensive set of physical and social rules that determines its physical and psychosocial responses to external stimuli (e.g., collision avoidance, shortest path selection, preference for walking in the shade, preferential treatment of women, curiosity, and so on). A control mechanism interprets the environment from the VUser's point of view at each clock cycle and selects the most appropriate rules to helps it accomplish its goal(s).

The physical appearance of the VUsers is modeled through component-based programming methods, which allow for defining body parts as fully articulated, independent objects (fig. 20.5). Several representation tools that can simulate animated human figures have been developed, including Jim Blinn's "Blobby Man," Magnenat and Thalman's ACTORS, and H-Anim (a standard developed by the WEB3D Consortium).[11]

Overall control of the VUser resides in several linked modules that coordinate the sequence of perception-reaction, as depicted in figure 22.6.[12] They collect the information from the sensors, interpret it, and generate the appropriate response. They also perform conflict-resolution to reconcile goals and constraints for the particular behaviors or personality variables defined for each VUser. For example, VUsers representing women have priority over VUsers representing men when it comes to finding a bench to sit on. This constraint may, at times, conflict with a goal that directs VUsers to go to the closest bench available. Thus, even though "Bob" may be closer to the left-most bench in figure 22.7, it will go to the further bench, and let "Nancy" occupy the closer one.

A VUser perceives two types of stimuli: stimuli that come from the socio-physical space in which it is immersed and is captured by its sensors, and stimuli that come from its "mission" script. The environmental sensors inform the VUser of its whereabouts at any given time, of the configuration of the space, the environmental conditions (e.g., sun, shade, wind), the presence of other VUsers around it, the activities they are engaged in, and so on. The "mission" scripts let the designer ascribe different missions to individual VUsers. These missions are translated into more specific goals by the "mission" interpreter, which drives the response

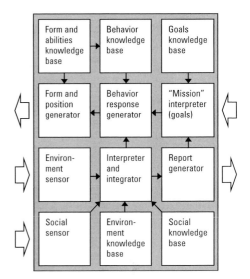

22.6 The architecture of the VUser as a rational learning agent. (C. Irazàbal, "Towards a Computer-Aided Design Assistant: A Virtual User," master's thesis, University of California, Berkeley, 1995.)

22.7 The VUsers' decision control mechanism is guided by built-in behavior characteristics and external environmental circumstances, allowing it, for example, to give preference to female VUsers when seeking a bench to sit on: "Bob" will go to the further bench. (W. Yan and Y. E. Kalay, "Simulating the Behavior of Users in Built Environments," Technical Report, University of California, Berkeley, 2002.)

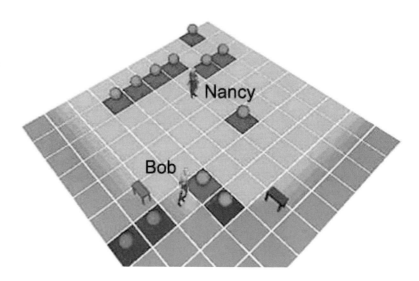

generator. A general goal describes the ultimate state toward which the VUser is directed in the environment (e.g., cross the plaza, find a place to sit). Subgoals help the VUser achieve certain intermediate states in the progress toward the main goal. The subgoals vary, depending on the perceptions the VUser obtains from the social and environmental states of the world. Once the goals are known for the next stage of the VUser response, behavioral and physical responses are activated through the physical and the behavioral response generators, which are informed by the physical and behavioral knowledge bases.

The combination of built-in intelligence and externally scripted "mission" endows VUsers with the ability to react to changes in the simulated environment in which they are immersed with a certain degree of autonomy but also with purposefulness needed to simulate different design situations. The VUser's actions are based on both its own experience and the instructions used in the particular environment in which it operates. A learning mechanism adds to the VUser's built-in knowledge bases, expanding and modifying them with accrued experience. The results of the generators are reflected in the form, type of motion, specific behaviors and any other performance attributes with which the VUser reacts to its environment.

Future

22.4 Agencies

Agents can act together in order to achieve more complex goals than any one agent can achieve on its own. A group of agents acting together was termed an *agency* by Minsky.[13] In the domain of architecture, a group of software agents can represent the different disciplines that comprise the design process, resembling the collaboration of (human) experts discussed in chapter 21. Assigning to each agent responsibility for only one part of the overall process makes it easier to develop an agency than a single, comprehensive agent. However, management and conflict resolution issues that arise from the multiplicity of goals and solutions becomes a major obstacle to the development of a society of agents.

ICADS

One of the first design systems to include a group of software agents was ICADS, developed by Jens Pohl and his CADRC group at the California Polytechnic and State University, in San Luis Obispo (fig. 22.8).[14] The

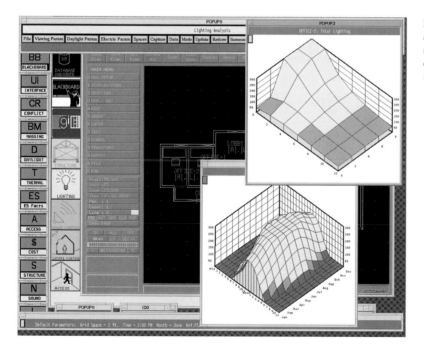

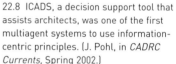

22.8 ICADS, a decision support tool that assists architects, was one of the first multiagent systems to use information-centric principles. (J. Pohl, in *CADRC Currents,* Spring 2002.)

system consists of a host of design agents, each responsible for one aspect of the design. Operating within a narrow domain of expertise, each agent provides two kinds of support: intermittent responses to requests for information and assistance initiated by the designer, and continuous background monitoring and evaluation of the evolving design solution. A central coordination and control mechanism, which has its own multidomain knowledge base, guides the evolving design solution within the context of the design problem space, acting in an iterative consultative mode. The actions of the agents are transparent to the designer unless a conflict arises that requires his or her attention.

An agent is triggered when an object in which it has interest is created or modified by the designer or another agent. For example, when the designer creates a space object, an appropriate agent would be "awakened" and announce its "arrival" to the other active agents. The announcement includes information about the agent's needs, capabilities, and interests. The agent would then proceed to examine the attributes of the space object and its links to other objects (e.g., other spaces). If warranted, it would issue warnings and suggest changes, or even make the changes that are within its purview (e.g., change the shape of the space object to align it with existing walls).

ICADS was conceived as a cooperative decision-making system, comprising multiple agents (possibly executing on separate machines) and communicating through a message passing facility. The concepts it pioneered have been applied to naval logistics, through such systems as SEA-WAY-LOGGY (for logistic planning) and IMMACCS (for command and control), each of which comprises a number of agents responsible for one issue each.[15] For example, one agent in the SEAWAY-LOGGY system is responsible for calculating the fuel consumed by a helicopter in transporting supplies from a sea base to an inland supply point. Other agents are responsible for selecting the best mix of different kinds of helicopters to transport a wide range of supplies to multiple supply points within requested time windows, subject to weather and other constraints. These agents rely on objective data (e.g. the capabilities of each type of helicopter), as well as input received from other agents, and use heuristic and algorithmic methods to arrive at possible solutions.

The cooperative nature of these systems makes their recommendations unpredictable, because they are derived from the interaction of many collaborating agents. It also reduces the need for any one agent to be "intelligent"; instead, intelligence is distributed among all the agents that make up the system.

Intelligent Design Assistants—IDeAs

A similar collaborative arrangement was implemented in the P3 system,[16] through a society of agents called intelligent design assistants (IDeAs) (fig. 22.9). These are semiautonomous computational constructs that are able to carry out high-level instructions, perform tests and make suggestions on their own accord. They represent discipline-specific operators, each with its own discipline-specific knowledge base. Unlike ICADS agents, IDeAs are intelligent agents, independent from the evolving design object database. As such, each has a "global" view of the project and is able to access information that is scattered among several (perhaps all) the objects that comprise an evolving design solution. For example, they can calculate the overall cost of a project, its thermal and structural properties, and so on. In addition, each IDeA can participate, at the same time, in several different design projects, comprising part of an ad hoc "agency," much like human experts often participate in multiple projects at the same time.

IDeAs do not purport to replace the human designers. Rather, their role can be likened to highly skilled "junior" designers, financial analysts, or even secretaries, who have limited authority in making decisions. They are, nonetheless, able to interpret the (sometimes abstract) instructions given to them by human designers. For example, given a general description of a single-family house, they are able to look up standard room sizes and their desired relationships and transform the instruction into a detailed floor plan that conforms to the client's goals. The extent of their action depends on run-time circumstances, including the disposition of the human designer. It can range from simply providing information to the designer, all the way through creating a complete design solution for consideration by the client.

An IDeA is comprised of a semantic interpretation module, a user interface, and several knowledge bases (fig. 22.10). The semantic interpreter, which is essentially a decision-action system, is responsible for the communication between the project database and the knowledge bases of which the IDeA is comprised. For example, it can search the project data-

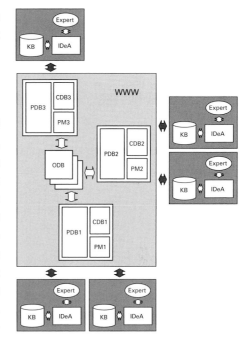

22.9 The P3 system comprises multiple independent agents, called IDeAs, that can cooperate in developing multiple design projects. (Y. E. Kalay, in *Automation in Construction* 8, no. 1 [1998].)

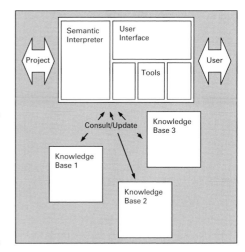

22.10 The structure of an IDeA. (Y. E. Kalay, in *Automation in Construction* 8, no. 1 [1998].)

base for the information needed to perform thermal calculations and use its own knowledge bases to perform the evaluation. Alternatively, it can decide to consult an external energy evaluation program, in which case it will translate the project data into the format required by that evaluator, perform the necessary communication, and interpret the results for the designer (much like the BDA system does, as described in section 18.2). The user interface, in turn, provides a means to control the actions of the IDeA, and to present to the user the results of the consultation.

A couple of examples of the IDeAs approach have been implemented, for cost estimation and energy evaluation of buildings.[17] The Fenestration Agent described earlier is one such IDeA.

Other Collaborative Agent-Based Systems

Federation of Collaborative Design Agents (FCDA) is a system that facilitates communication among designers in A/E/C.[18] It allows five designers and engineers (in different locations) to concurrently perform some of the design tasks and transparently exchange design information and changes via their software applications in a coordinated manner. Although it is considered to be an agent-based system, the agents in FCDA are the (human) end-users themselves. FCDA itself is, basically, an intelligent information management tool, built around a very sophisticated facilitator, which performs a wide range of tasks including the intelligent routing of information based on its content, the selection of agents to accomplish certain tasks, the semantic translation of different information models, support of delayed notifications and requests, dynamic discovery of information, and management of communications across the network. The FCDA system thus comprises a framework for design communication and provides tools to present design solutions and a mechanism to exchange them. But it does not address the conflict management issues themselves, leaving them for the (human) end-users to detect and resolve.

SEED (Software Environment to Support Early Phases in Building Design),[19] introduced in chapter 14, is a system that employs distributed multi-agent approach to support multidisciplinary building design process, especially in its early, exploratory phases. It employs three major agents, an architectural programming agent (SEED-Pro), a schematic layout agent (SEED-Layout), and a structure-massing agent (SEED-Config).

SEED creates and elaborates design states comprising functional units and design units. It solves design problems by generating and testing design solutions, until it reaches an acceptable solution.

PERSUADER is a system that acts as a mediator between a company and a labor union.[20] The quality of the resolution it produces is a function of the utilities of independent agents. Agents act as adversaries whose local goals are strongly interrelated. They cannot accurately predict or model the beliefs or utility values of other agents. In general, the problems they tackle are overconstrained, so complete goal satisfaction is impossible. The basic PERSUADER system generates an initial compromise, repairs and improves a rejected compromise, and persuades the parties to change their evaluation of a compromised solution. It uses case-based reasoning, preference analysis, and situation assessment for its problem-solving methods. Case-based reasoning is used to form initial compromise proposals when suitable precedents are found; otherwise preference analysis is applied. Once a solution is proposed, the possible responses to rejection are: (1) to persuade other agents to accept the proposal by getting the agents to change their utilities; or (2) to modify the proposal to better meet the agents' goals, although this may result in rejection by other agents. PER-SUADER generates counterproposals by changing the agents' preferences, modeled as weights, and the utility values of goals.

DESIGN FUSION is an agent-based concurrent design software, built on a blackboard architecture.[21] It maintains a shared object representation and a constraint management system. Each agent is allowed to create its own local representation, but it communicates with other agents through a shared representation (a translation and a mapping). Constraints within an agent remain in the local perspective as long as the global design does not violate the constraint. When a constraint is violated, it is posted to the global constraint management system (the blackboard), which builds a global constraint network. Each agent is responsible for evaluating the constraints posted on the global constraint blackboard. Conflict detection is managed by individual agents.

22.5 Intelligent Agents versus Direct Manipulation

The progress that has been made over the past two decades in understanding what sorts of capabilities are needed to provide meaningful assistance to computer users has raised the question of whether such assistance ought to take the form of direct manipulation, which affords greater comprehensibility, predictability, and control over the task through advanced user interfaces, or whether users can be better served through indirect manipulation, where control is delegated to software agents.

Proponents of direct manipulation, which takes the form of graphical user interfaces and visual representations of the objects and actions that are relevant to some task, agree that relinquishing control over some processes to a software agent may save time.[22] However, when users can directly specify what they want through actions selected from a visual display, they can accomplish their goals more rapidly, maintain control over the process, and gain satisfaction from its accomplishment.

Proponents of indirect manipulation,[23] which takes the form of software agents, point out that computers, unlike other tools such as automobiles and toasters, require much more training to operate, let alone to master (they often mention the programming of a VCR as an example).[24] Such training can only be justified when the task is critical to one's mission or is often repeated. Most people could learn how to make real estate transactions or travel arrangements but choose not to bother if the task occurs only once every few years and when accomplishing the task in a short time is more important than controlling all its details.

The agent metaphor assumes that users can trust their agents to satisfactorily carry out the task on their behalf. In the physical world, such trust is enforced through financial rewards (repeat business) and legal penalties (lawsuits). In the information world, it is enforced through loyal users, the lack of whom has doomed many Internet companies (and other types of software ventures). Attempts to dress up artificial agents in humanlike form, as is the case with REA and with VUsers, are intended to enhance this trust, putting users at ease even when they are unable to control the systems they use.

The need for software agents arises from the ability of computers to respond only when a person gives them commands through a keyboard, a mouse, or an audiovisual user interface. Nothing happens without external stimulus, and the computer provides little help for complex tasks. In fact, the more complex the task, the more user attention and skill are needed. If untrained users are to employ future computers and networks effectively, and if experts are to use them to facilitate their own jobs (rather than become experts in operating complex software products), direct manipulation will have to give way to some form of delegation. Such delegation of responsibility depends on the ability of software agents to automatically ascertain their users' intentions and take action based on a vague statement of goals. Opponents are skeptical that user intentions can so easily be determined or that vague statements can affect desired results. Certainly, better direct manipulation interfaces are in order and will lead to user interfaces that are more comprehensible, predictable, and controllable. However, as tasks become more complex, and as more (untrained) people begin to use computers, they will have to relinquish complete control (and responsibility) for every move the computer makes on their behalf, much as people have embraced automatic transmission in automobiles in lieu of manual shifting, even though the car may perform less efficiently than when controlled by a skilled driver.

Success stories for advocates of adaptive indirect manipulation systems include a few experimental systems that have been extensively studied and carefully refined to give users appropriate feedback for the errors that they make. Generalizing from these systems has proved to be more difficult than advocates hoped.

Still, the widespread dissemination of agents can have enormous social, economic, and political impact. Agents can help narrow the gap between the millions of untrained users and their sophisticated microprocessors, thus "democratizing" the use of computers. They have the potential to make the use of computers as easy as using a toaster or a TV set. Almost anyone will have access to information currently enjoyed only by a few privileged people with enormous support staff. As a result, they will be able to process large amounts of information and engage in several different activities at once. The ultimate ramifications of this change are impossible to predict.

Bibliography

Boden, M. "Agents and Creativity." *Communications of the ACM* 37, no. 7 (1994): 117–121.

Cheek, M. "Intelligent Agents Gaining Momentum." *IEEE Computer* 27, no. 8 (1994): 8–9.

Edmonds, E., et al. "Support for Collaborative Design: Agents and Emergence." *Communications of the ACM* 37, no. 7 (1994): 41–47.

Genesereth, M., and S. Ketchpel. "Software Agents." *Communications of the ACM* 37, no. 7 (1994): 48–53.

Guha R., and D. Lenat. "Enabling Agents to Work Together." *Communications of the ACM* 37, no. 7 (1994): 126–142.

Minsky, M., and D. Riecken. "A Conversation with Marvin Minsky about Agents." *Communications of the ACM* 37, no. 7 (1994): 22–29.

Russell, S., and P. Norvig. *Artificial Intelligence: A Modern Approach.* Prentice Hall, Englewood Cliffs, N.J., 1995.

Swerdloff, L. M., and Y. E. Kalay. "A Partnership Approach to Computer-Aided Design." In *Computability of Design,* ed. Y. E. Kalay, 315–336. New York: Wiley Interscience, 1987.

Werkman, K. "Multiple Agent Cooperation Design Evaluation Using Negotiation." In *Artificial Intelligence in Design,* ed. J. S. Gero, 161–180. Dordecht, The Netherlands: Kluwer Academic Publishers, 1992.

Additionally, since this is a relatively new topic, some of the best resources about agent-based systems can be found on the World Wide Web. These resources are also subject to rapid change and update:

The Ariadne Project at the Information Sciences Institute, <www.isi.edu/ariadne>.

The European Community Agentlink project, <www. agentlink. org/>.

The MIT Media Laboratory Agents Research group, <agents.www.media.mit.edu/groups/agents/>.

The National Research Council of Canada Agent resource list, <ai.iit.nrc.ca/subjects/Agents. html>.

The University of Maryland Baltimore County (UMBC) Laboratory for Advanced Information Technology (LAIT) Agent Web, <www.cs.umbc.edu/agents/>.

The University of Washington "Softbots" Project, <www.cs.washington.edu/research/projects/softbots/www/softbots. html>.

Building and Construction Automation 23

It may seem that the automation of construction processes and of the buildings themselves has little to do with the process of design. After all, by the time construction begins, and even more so—once the building is completed—the process of design is long done. While it is true that the design phase precedes construction and use of the building, it is the later two phases that inform the design phase what it can and ought to do as much as the design phase informs the other two phases of the building's life cycle.

Examples of how construction technologies impact the design of buildings are abundant in history. The adaptation of the Etruscan keystone arch enabled Roman engineers to build extremely strong and durable bridges and led to the invention of the dome as early as 27 BC.[1] The invention of the flying buttress, which receives the gravitational thrust of the roof, allowed medieval master builders to develop the Gothic cathedral, replacing the romanesque's massive walls and columns by relatively thin, tall walls and soaring vaulted ceilings. Since the walls were relieved of much of the burden of the roof, they could accommodate large stained glass windows, which transformed the interior from a dark and confined space into a light-filled, spacious cathedral.

Henry Bessemer's invention of mass-produced steel in 1855, coupled with Elisha G. Otis's invention of the safety elevator in 1853 and Werner von Siemens's invention of the electric elevator in 1880, allowed the design and construction of skyscrapers, such as Daniel Burnham's 285-foot-tall Flatiron Building in New York (1902).

Thus technological innovations—often several of them coming together at the same time—have always had a significant impact on the design of buildings. The advent of computer-assisted construction technologies and of computer-controlled buildings promises to have as much of an impact on the design process and its products as these earlier technological advances had.

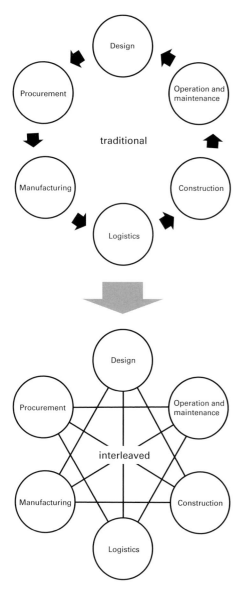

traditional

interleaved

23.1 Interleaving removes the classical sequencing of the division of labor between the different phases of the building's life cycle. (After B. Benne, "Redefining the Construction Industry's Value Chain: New Business Rules for Collaboration and Procurement," Technical Report, Haas School of Business, University of California, Berkeley, 2000.)

On the construction side, computing facilitates a much tighter and better-controlled information transfer between the design team and the builders, permitting the design of complex structures that could not have been built at all, or would have cost too much to build, without computational assistance.

On the building operation side, computing allows for finer control of buildings, making it possible to design dynamically stabilized structures that are lighter, taller, and more economical than statically stabilized structures. Computing makes the control of the interior environment more responsive to changing needs, such as different light levels during the day and different heating and cooling needs over the year. By making them more efficient, computers allow architects to design buildings that clients would have balked at due to maintenance and life cycle costs.

23.1 The Building Procurement Process

The key to understanding the link between technological innovations and the design, construction, and use of buildings is an understanding of the building procurement process as a whole, integrative process, where changes in one component affect and are affected by others. Figure 23.1 depicts this interrelationship, showing how computational advances in manufacturing affect the logistics of the procurement process (e.g., larger and more complex parts can be prefabricated and shipped to the construction site) and how manufacturers are contracted to participate in the project. These, in turn, affect the design process (what designs can be built) and the construction process (how the parts are assembled into a whole building). They also affect the use and maintenance of the building, which in turn affects its design.[2] Together, this transformation constitutes a change from a largely sequential process into an *interleaved* process.

Interleaving

Interleaving is a term whose origin comes from the bookbinding industry, where blank pages were sewn in between existing pages of a book to strengthen the volume.[3] Its relevance to design derives from the interconnectedness of the processes that make up the building life cycle, which comprise an inherently multi-agent networked system, as discussed in chapters 21 and 22. In such systems, each agent—be it human or computational—is responsible for one part of the overall enterprise. Yet that part is intimately connected to, affects, and is affected by other parts.

The traditional way of orchestrating complex projects has been through partitioning it into tasks, scheduling their execution (in sequence or in parallel), and then integrating them into a composite whole. Such compartmentalization facilitated the management of the process at the expense of the quality of its products: it has virtually enshrined the symmetry of ignorance in an assembly line–like process, guaranteeing that the integrated composition of the individual solutions—each of which may have been optimized for its own purposes—will not be overall optimal. Lean construction techniques, which were borrowed from the automotive industry,[4] have helped streamline one part of the building procurement process, but they have not improved its integration with the design or use phases of the building's life cycle.

As the rate of change affecting each component of the process—induced by advancements in knowledge, practices, and tools (including information technology tools)—accelerates, it has become impractical to maintain the classical compartmentalized approach. By following a rigid compartmentalization of design and construction steps, each agent runs the risk of developing a plan of action that is not valid because changes that affect other parts of the process conflict with some preconditions or assumptions it has made in its ignorance. Instead, each agent needs to continuously exchange information with other agents who are responsible for other parts of the project.[5]

Such exchange of information, whether it is done dynamically (as the need arises) or a priori (when one agent learns of the capabilities of another agent prior to engaging in its own part of the process), amounts to interleaving—the weaving together of design and execution plans based on the *actual* capabilities of the participants rather than on some preconceived notions that may be inaccurate or out of date.

Interleaving is thus a flexible way of interconnecting different participants for design or business purposes.[6] It has ramifications for *how* design and procurement are done and for *what* can be done. By exchanging information as problems arise and as solutions are developed, it is possible not only to assemble a design-build team that can support innovative design ideas but to conceive such ideas in the first place. It is likely that one (or

23.2 Frank O. Gehry & Associates'
Experience Music Project in Seattle,
Washington, is an example of an interleaved design-build process, where the
close integration of technological capabilities in different fields contributed to the
ability to design and construct the building. (Courtesy of the Experience Music
Project, Seattle, Washington.)

more) of the participants has capabilities that will allow others to come up with design or procurement solutions they are unlikely to conceive on their own.

That is precisely how Frank O. Gehry & Associates, an architectural firm in Santa Monica, California, has been able to design and build some of the most innovative buildings in the last few years.

The Experience Music Project

Frank O. Gehry & Associates is an architectural practice known for its innovative, sometimes controversial buildings, likened by some critics to ad hoc pieces of functional sculpture based on "deconstructed aesthetics."[7] Among the best-known examples of Gehry's buildings are the Guggenheim Museum in Bilbao, Spain (1997), the Disney Concert Hall in Los Angeles, California (1989–2003), and the Experience Music Project in Seattle, Washington (1999–2000).[8]

It is not only Gehry's buildings that are unique but also (and of greater relevance to the discussion here) the interleaved process of their design and construction. In fact, it can be argued that without using an interleaved approach, it would have been impossible for Gehry to design his unique buildings in the first place (or rather, they would have remained paper projects, which could not be realized for technical or economical reasons).

The Experience Music Project (EMP) illustrates this approach (fig. 23.2). It was commissioned by Paul Allen, one of Microsoft's cofounders and an avid fan of guitarist Jimi Hendrix (1942–1970), who was known for smashing guitars as much as for his music. The inspiration for the 140,000-square-foot interactive music museum, celebrating creativity and innovation as expressed through rock 'n' roll and other forms of American popular music, came from Hendrix's own music and from electric guitars, their shapes, colors, and strings. This exuberance of form renders the EMP different from all other structures and required a different approach to its design and construction.

Most curvilinear structures—including others by Frank Gehry—use flat planes that have been bent in just one direction or are based on curves that are symmetrical in some aspect. The EMP, on the other hand, is totally freeform: it is nonsymmetrical and curves at every point in many directions at once.

Gehry shaped the building using cardboard, tin foil, and wood (fig. 23.3a). These physical models were digitized into CATIA, a 3D modeling software developed by Dassault Systemes in France (marketed and supported worldwide by IBM). The resulting 3D database, whose development took over three months, formed the core of the design and fabrication process (fig. 23.3.b). It enabled Gehry and his design team to accurately model and test the shapes chosen for the building and to optimize the surface curvatures such that they maintained the desired form but had better buckling capacity than some of Gehry's original shapes did.

Supporting the complex form was not amenable to standard structural solutions. Instead, Skilling Ward Magnusson Barkshire—the structural engineers for EMP—developed a steel structure that stiffens the concrete shell of the building by adapting bridge construction technologies, which produced a ribcage-like structure comprising 240 ribs (fig. 23.3c). Each rib was created by welding three steel plates together to form an I-shaped member. Each plate was cut by computer-controlled torches, deriving its data directly from the 3D model, and molded into the required shape by means of computer-controlled rollers.

The steel and aluminum shell that clads the building was adapted from automotive technologies (fig. 23.3d). It comprises 3,000 steel and aluminum plates, each made of seven uniquely shaped and cut shingles.

In addition to the cladding, the building is "draped" by 621 pieces of $3/4$-inch laminated glass, representing broken guitar strings. These were manufactured by the Italian company Permasteelisa Cladding

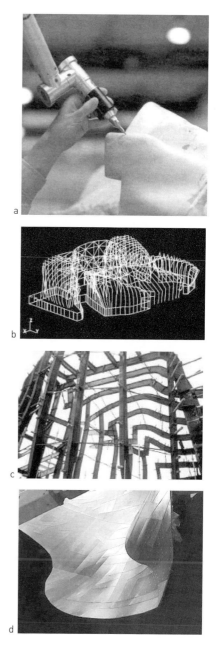

23.3 The participants in the design and construction of the Experience Music Project communicated through a 3D digital database, to which each contributed its own technological innovations. (Courtesy of the Experience Music Project, Seattle, Washington.)

23.4 The NASDAQ MarketSite Tower in Times Square, New York, is draped in a 10,800-square-foot cylindrical media wall, which transforms the building into an active participant in the environment. (See color plate 3.)

Technologies using the same 3D project database that was used for the structure and the skin. Each prefabricated glass component, weighing in excess of 200 pounds, was installed from a tower crane and was positioned using laser-guided surveying instrumentation.

It was the combination of all these technologies and skills that made this structure feasible. Technological innovations developed independently were sought and adapted for the needs of this project. Their complexity precluded the use of typical design-bid procurement practices. Instead, consultants and contractors were brought onboard early, making suggestions and affecting the design through their contributions. For example, A. Zahner Company—the Kansas City, Missouri, cladding contractor—was instrumental in determining the allowable curvatures of the building's skin at the design phase. Columbia Wire & Iron Works—the Portland, Oregon, steel fabricator—was instrumental in determining the manufacturable curvatures of the steel structure. The common denominator for all the participants was the CATIA 3D model, which was used to connect and inform all the parts of the project, as well as for virtual walkthroughs, interference checks, quantities takeoffs, steel detailing, cutting the components of the steel ribs, dimensions, setting the concrete formwork and embeds, and defining survey points.

23.2 Smart Building Materials

The impact of information technology on the products of architectural design—the building itself—will come through enhancing the "intelligence" of the materials from which buildings are made and facilitating their responsiveness and adaptability to changing needs.

The properties of the materials from which buildings are made have always been an inseparable part of the process of architectural design: pozzolana cement, from Pozzuoli, on the slopes of Mt. Vesuvius in Italy, allowed the Romans to build their baths, the Coliseum, and the Pantheon. Iron- (and later steel-) reinforced concrete, invented in nineteenth century, allowed the design of longer span bridges and taller buildings. And the industrialization of plate glass production made possible the "glass box" International Style architecture of the first half of the twentieth century.[9]

It was not, however, until the second half of the twentieth century that "smart materials"—ones that can adapt themselves to the changing needs of

446

the building or its environment—emerged. Unlike traditional materials, such as stone and wood, whose properties determine what the building looks like and how it behaves once and for all, smart materials can be engineered to fit the needs of the building, even when these needs change over time. This, in turn, determines not only *how* buildings are designed, but also *what* can be designed. Instead of designing the building for a finite state, designers who use smart materials can design their buildings for a *sequence of behaviors*. For example, the eight-story NASDAQ MarketSite Tower at 4 Times Square in New York City is wrapped in an 10,800-square-foot cylindrical media wall, which is made of more that 18 million LEDs embedded in black rubber-based compound. They comprise eight display screens that operate simultaneously, driven by one video processor each and an array of 800 digital switching power supplies. This $37 million electronic billboard, developed by Saco SmartVision of White Plains, N.Y., operates like a curved television screen with 170-degree viewing angle: it transforms the building into a "live" entertainment and advertising center for thousands of Times Square daily (and nightly) visitors (fig. 23.4).

While the media wall of the NASDAQ building may not qualify strictly as a "smart material," it does conform to the general definition of such materials as ones that can change their shape or other characteristics in response to some externally applied stimulus. The change may involve the material's shape, transmissivity, viscosity, or luminescence, as is the case with media wall. The input stimulus can be electrical, mechanical, thermal, chemical, or radiant. The effect occurs at the material's molecular level, where it can either change the properties of the material itself, or convert the input energy from one form into another (in the case of the NSDAQ media wall, from electrical stimulus to light output). For smart materials, these changes are reversible: when the input stimulus is removed, the material reverts back to its original properties.

Some materials respond by converting the external stimulus into strain, which elongates the material. Others produce electrical output when mechanical strain is applied to them. Such materials can be used as sensors and actuators and have found use in detecting stress in walls and foundations, even stiffening them as a response to earthquakes or wind conditions. Such actuation or sensing is, of course, picked up and directed by computers that regulate the building's response according to some predetermined program.

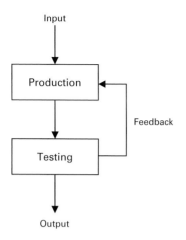

Input

↓

Production

Feedback

Testing

↓

Output

23.5 The feedback principle underlies the concept of automation.

23.3 Intelligent Buildings

The significance of smart materials for the design phase of buildings comes from changing the building (or its surfaces) from a static entity into a dynamic one: it can be made an active participant in the environment in which it is embedded rather than a backdrop "prop" for other actors' activities.

The responsiveness of buildings to their environments is not limited to their surfaces. Other building systems can be made responsive, or automated, in three ways:

- Through feedback regulated adaptability.
- Through model-based adaptability.
- Through total environmental adaptability.

Automation

Automation is a logical extension of the mechanization of labor that began with the Industrial Revolution in the eighteenth century. It adds control and self-correcting abilities to machines, thereby eliminating the need for continuous human supervision and intervention.

Automation is based on the feedback principle, where the output of a machine is linked to its input and compared against some intended performance measures. Departure from the desired condition triggers adjustments in the performance of the machine, hence its output (fig. 23.5). The ubiquitous thermostat demonstrates this principle. As the HVAC system heats (or cools) the air inside a building, the thermostat monitors the air's temperature. When that temperature reaches the thermostat's set point (the desired temperature), it sends an electrical signal to the HVAC plant, shutting it off. When the air cools below the set point (or, conversely, heats up beyond it), the thermostat sends a signal which turns the HVAC plant on, and so on.

Applications of the feedback principle have been around for centuries. But only during World War II was the significance of the feedback principle realized by Norbert Wiener, who developed it into a science he called cybernetics.[10] Computers have extended the ability to capture, measure, compare, and control the actions of machines: the combination of computers with machines has come to be known as robotics. [11]

Feedback-Regulated Adaptability

Enabling the building to sense and respond to changing needs takes many forms. The simplest application is based directly on the feedback loop, where some action occurs in response to an external stimulus:

- Thermostats turn HVAC equipment on/off based on sensing the current temperature and comparing it to the preset temperature.
- Automatic doors open when their sensors inform them that a person approaches.
- External sun shading devises can be controlled by means of sensors that respond to direct sunlight.
- Lights can be turned on/off as required by the presence of people and the level of outside illumination.
- Security systems can respond to the presence of intruders by sensing motion.
- Elevators are dispatched to floors where large number of people wait to be picked up, as indicated by video cameras and pattern recognition systems.

This is a relatively simple approach to automation, which has been implemented in areas of control, regulation, and supervision of electrical, mechanical, and climatic control equipment. It has been around since World War II and reached a state of maturity as evidenced by the proliferation of commercial products and companies that support them (e.g., Johnson Controls of Milwaukee, Wisconsin). The role of computers in this kind of automation is mostly to control and coordinate the various systems and keep a log of their operation.

Model-Based Adaptability

Adding a functional model to networked building systems and appliances allows for a more far-reaching responsiveness and adaptability approach to automation: it helps to regulate the environment in expectation of events, rather than in response to them. In a functional model of a building behavior patterns are programmed in advance, based on learning the typical behavioral preferences of the occupants, so the building environment can anticipate and position itself to support recurring events, not only to respond to them.

For example, elevator schedules can be automatically adjusted by the system to meet peak demand in the morning by stationing empty cars close to the building's entrance. In the afternoon, when the traffic is reversed, the empty cars can be stationed at the top floors of the building, thus saving the trip time an empty elevator must make to reach those floors from its station at the bottom of the shaft. Similarly, a house equipped with such a model-based adaptability system could optimize household operations, for example by turning on the water heater an hour before the washer is scheduled to be used, thus ensuring that there is plenty of hot water available by the time it is needed and avoiding wasting energy when hot water is not needed.

The networking of different household appliances and systems can be hard-wired or supported by wireless technologies and communication protocols like Bluetooth—a communication standard based on short-range radio frequency (RF) technology, which can be embedded cheaply in almost every product that uses electrical power.[12]

A habitable environment equipped with model-based adaptability has been demonstrated by MIT's Intelligent Room project,[13] which is intended to integrate computers seamlessly in ordinary environments so they can take care of mundane, everyday activities. The interaction with these computing systems is done by voice, gesture, and context rather then through keyboards and mice. As such, the intelligent room is equipped with sensors (video cameras, microphones), connected to image-understanding and speech recognition systems that enable it to "know" where people are in the room and what they are doing. The system can not only perceive but also interact: it can talk back and perform actions on behalf of the inhabitants (even when not explicitly told to do so). For example, upon entering the room, the visitor might be recognized as the habitual occupant of the room and greeted by name. The room would then proceed to tell the office owner of the messages waiting to be answered, contact people as required, or schedule a mutually convenient meeting time with their own intelligent offices.

The origin of such model-based adaptability systems is Xerox euroPARC's influential Digital Desk project,[14] which was built around an ordinary, physical desk. A video camera, mounted above the desk pointing down at the work surface was interfaced to a vision recognition system. It could recognize the documents that were placed on the desk and detect where the user was pointing, using an LED-tipped pen. A more advanced version included a computer-driven projector mounted above the desk, enabling electronic objects to be projected onto real paper documents, removing the burden of having to switch attention between a computer screen and the paper. Additional gesture-based user-interaction techniques allowed the user to control the system.

What makes MIT's Intelligent Room and Xerox's Digital Desk systems possible is the advent of computer vision and speech recognitions systems and the ubiquity of cheap-yet-powerful computers. The major hurdle is, in fact, the integration of many independent systems into one composite, interoperable system, in which each component supports and enhances the others—a problem that is similar to the difficulties encountered in developing collaborative, multi-agent systems discussed in chapters 21 and 22.[15] For example, identifying the combination of speech and gesture—a common human action—requires identifying the speaker from among several people in a room, the fact that she or he is pointing at something, and the direction of that gesture. The context, which is necessary to interpret both speech and gesture, is provided through the model-based adaptive environment, in the form of predefined scenarios.

Total Environmental Adaptability

In his influential book *Soft Architecture Machines*, Nicholas Negroponte proposes that an intelligent, self-cognizant environment could replace all the professional functions of the architect and better serve the occupants. He asks whether architects are unnecessary, perhaps even detrimental, middlemen between the users and the fulfillment of their needs, agents who dictate the decisions to be made by their clients in matters the clients know better.[16] Instead, he proposes that the environment itself will be made responsive to the ever-changing needs of its inhabitants. It will not "help" humans design their habitat, but rather "be" the habitat itself.

Such total environmental adaptability is no longer a matter of science fiction or speculation: it has been demonstrated by the University of Colorado's Adaptive Control of Home Environments (ACHE) project.[17]

In a house that was specifically equipped for the purposes of this project (by running five miles of low-voltage cables), researchers explicitly avoided using sophisticated user interfaces. Instead, the environment itself monitors how the inhabitants use ordinary appliances and apply those observations—in combination with sensors that monitor the state of the house's environment—as training indicators of the inhabitants' preferences. As the house becomes better "trained," it can anticipate the users' preferences and adjust the operation of devices accordingly, gradually freeing the inhabitants from the chores of manually controlling their environment. For example, the "house" can automatically maintain the preferred room temperature given the preferences of particular occupants, their activities, and the time of year. It can choose different patterns of lighting for different activities, and schedule the heating of water for anticipated bath or washing clothes. The house's operations are transparent to the inhabitants, other than the fact that they do not have to worry about managing the various devices in the home. The house, in effect, has become an intelligent agent of the kind discussed in chapter 22, which infers the inhabitants' desires from their actions and behavior.

Specifically, ACHE controls twenty-two banks of lights (each with sixteen intensity levels), six ceiling fans, two electric space heaters, a water heater, and a gas furnace. It includes about seventy-five sensors, which measure intensity setting of the lights, the status of fans, the status of a digital thermostat, ambient illumination, room temperature, sound level, the status of one or more motion detectors (on or off), and the status of doors and windows (open or closed). In addition, the system receives global information, such as the water heater temperature and outflow, outdoor temperature and insulation, energy use of each device, gas and electricity costs, time of day, and day of week.

The objectives of the system are to anticipate the inhabitants needs and to save energy. Achieving either one of these objectives alone is straightforward. Their combination, however, requires trade-offs and judgment. ACHE uses an optimal control framework, in which failing to satisfy each objective has an associated cost. A "discomfort" cost is incurred if ACHE fails to anticipate inhabitant preferences. An energy cost is incurred based on the use of gas and electricity. ACHE's goal is to minimize the combined costs of discomfort and energy.

To do so, ACHE must be able to predict inhabitant lifestyle patterns and preferences and to model the physics of the environment *before* it takes action. For example, it must predict the cost of running the furnace for a given amount of time and the indoor temperature this action will produce, given current outdoor and indoor air temperatures. It must also predict the inhabitants' expected use of the house when the set temperature has been reached, and determine the level of comfort (or rather discomfort) this will achieve. To arrive at this decision, ACHE uses neural network–based predictors of the inhabitants use patterns (derived from previous use patterns) and a model of the thermal properties of the house. ACHE depends on sufficiently robust statistical regularities in the inhabitants' behavior and on techniques of reinforcement learning. It first errs in favor for saving energy. If the inhabitants "complain" by way of changing some setting (temperature, light level), ACHE learns and adapts.

The consequences of these progressively more responsive buildings on the design process will be profound. Much like smart materials transform the building from a passive object into an active participant in its environment, building automation techniques will transform it from a passive container into a responsive "partner" in the process of inhabitation. The architect's role will be transformed from designing an object to choreographing the responses of a "living" machine. The transformation has technical, economic, social, even legal effects. (Whose fault will it be if the intelligent house fails to summon help when an elderly inhabitant falls down and cannot get up to reach the phone herself?)

Bibliography

Brodey, W. M. "Soft Architecture: The Design of Intelligent Environments." *Landscape* 17, no. 1 (1967): 8–12.

Coen, M. "Building Brains for Rooms: Designing Distributed Software Agents." In *Ninth Innovative Applications of AI Conference,* 971–988. Menlo Park, Calif.: AAAI Press, 1997.

Coen, M. "Design Principles for Intelligent Environments." *Fifteenth National Conference on Artificial Intelligence,* 547–554. Menlo Park, Calif.: AAAI Press, 1998.

Mitchell, W. J. *City of Bits: Space, Place, and the Infobahn.* Cambridge: MIT Press, 1995.

Mitchell, W. J. *e-topia: "Urban Life, Jim—but Not as We Know It."* Cambridge: MIT Press, 1999.

Negroponte, N. *The Architecture Machine.* Cambridge: MIT Press, 1970.

Negroponte, N. "Aspects of Living in an Architecture Machine." In *Design Participation: Proceedings of the Design Research Society's Conference,* ed. N. Cross, 63–67. London: Academy Editions, 1972.

Negroponte, N. *Being Digital.* New York: Vintage Books, 1995.

Negroponte, N. *Soft Architecture Machines.* Cambridge: MIT Press, 1975.

Schön, D. A. *Technology and Change.* New York: Delacorte Press, 1967.

Virtual Places

The advent of computers and computer-based telecommunication has opened up a new opportunity for architects that did not exist in the past—the opportunity to inhabit a different kind of space, the *information space*. Cyberspace, as the information space was dubbed by William Gibson in his 1984 novel *Neuromancer*, has become accessible in the 1990s through the World Wide Web.[1] Cyberspace is quickly becoming an alternative "space," where everyday economic, cultural, educational, and other human activities "take place."

Making places for human inhabitation is, of course, what architects, landscape architects, town planners, and interior designers have been doing in physical space for hundreds of years. Yet cyberspace designers have not yet capitalized on the theories, experiences, and practices that have been guiding physical place making. Rather, they adopted the document metaphor, which has guided computer-human interface design since it was invented by Xerox PARC ("the document company") in 1975. But, as the Web matures, and as it assumes more fully its role as a *space* rather than as means of communication, there is a growing need and opportunity to design it according to place-making, rather than document-making, principles.

This chapter explores the possibility of organizing cyberspace into spatial settings that not only afford social interaction but also, like physical places, embody and express cultural values. At the same time, because cyberspace lacks materiality, is free from physical constraints, and because it can only be "inhabited" by proxy, these "places" need not resemble their physical counterparts.[2]

24.1 Place Making

Architecture, above all its other virtues and accomplishments, is the art of making places. Places differ from mere spaces in that they embody social and cultural values in addition to spatial configurations. It is the concept of place, not space, that connects architecture to its context and makes it responsive to given needs. Places are made of objects and spaces. However, these are only the building blocks of places—necessary, but not sufficient components.

"Places" are created through inhabitation. People imbue spaces with social and cultural meaning, transforming a mere space into a place: it is a sense of *place*, not space, that makes it appropriate to be naked in the bedroom but not in the classroom, and to sit at our windows peering out but not at other people's windows peering in. Places frame our actions by providing cues that organize social behavior in the world. People rarely sing or dance when they present conference papers, although conference halls and theaters share many similar spatial features (e.g., lighting, orientation, acoustics). Conversely, the same space—with no changes to its layout—may function as a theater at a different time, when the presentation of a scholarly paper would be considered "out of place" (but not "out of space").[3] To qualify as a place, space must be defined and ordered in meaningful ways. Such meaning is not part of the space itself; rather, it is an added quality, acquired through the adaptation and appropriation of the space by its inhabitants, through their actions and conceptions.[4]

So what is the significance of "place making"? What is a "place," anyway? How does it differ from "space"? What would happen to architecture if the space being ordered and defined was not the traditional physical space but rather the information space of cyberspace? Can cyberspace be made into "places"? What would that mean? How would "cyberplaces" be different from ordinary Web sites, or even 3D virtual worlds? Those are some of the questions explored in this chapter.

What Is a Place?

According to Martin Heidegger (1958), "*Place* places man in such a way that it reveals the external bounds of his existence, and at the same time the depth of his freedom and reality." More conventionally, a place is a setting that affords the entire spectrum of human activities, including physical, economic, and cultural activities, while affecting and being affected by social and cultural behavior. According to Chastain and Elliott:

The word place is often used to describe the larger territory that we build. The boundaries of this territory are defined by a sense of being inside—inside a region, a town, a neighborhood. The boundary is identified not by a demarcation of its edge but by the feeling of coherence of the spaces and the buildings within it, which give rise to a competence in the way a place is built and inhabited. We value such places for their qualities as extended environments and the support they give to our inhabitation. We value the feeling of being somewhere as opposed to just anywhere.[5]

Place is thus as much a psychological phenomenon as it is a physical one. It is rooted in human social action and cultural conceptions: a *place* is a *space* activated by social interactions and invested with culturally based understandings of behavioral appropriateness. Or as Bertrand Russell proclaimed (1914): "Indeed the whole notion that one is always in some definite 'place' is due to the fortunate immobility of most of the large objects on the earth's surface. The idea of 'place' is only a rough practical approximation: there is nothing [physically] logically necessary about it, and it cannot be made precise."

If "place-ness" is the consequence of the activities and conceptions of the inhabitants of a space, then space, or the physical attributes that frame those activities, provides a *socially shareable setting* for the activities, in the form of cues that organize and direct appropriate social behavior in that particular place. Figure 24.1 shows how some objects and spaces, combined with the activities and conceptions of people, transform an ordinary parking lot into a place for dining: the retaining wall serves as a table, or a bench to be straddled; the wall may be leaned on. The solitary diner in figure 24.1b occupies the triangular space defined by a diagonally parked car and the retaining wall, which together define a relatively enclosed and protected space with the proper dimension for one person engaged in the activities of dining and viewing passers by.

These places are not imaginary, nor are they a matter of personal interpretation: it is due to the fact that the spatial organization offered by these physical objects—and by the spaces they define—are the same for *all* the actors, that several people can engage in similar activities. They have a *shared* sense of place. This shared understanding helps them to orient themselves with respect to the space they occupy and with respect to

24.1 Dining in the parking lot—group behavior versus space for one. (Courtesy of Z Smith, 2000.)

a

b

Future

one another, thereby establishing cultural and social references that direct their behavior in a way that gives meaning to their activities. Figure 24.1a shows how they form separate groups of diners who interact internally, while projecting separateness externally. They are connected to the street, but at the same time detached from it.[6]

Place, of course, has many more qualities than affording a shared social setting and directing behavior. Place is *unique*: there are no two places that are alike, no matter how similar they may look. Their uniqueness comes from internal characteristics (location) and from external characteristics (situation)—their relatedness to other socio-spatial determinants (economics, geography, and so on). Although unique, places are not detached: they are *connected* physically and conceptually to other places. It is this connectedness that allows us to know how to behave, for example, in a fast food restaurant in Des Moines, Iowa, even if we have never visited that particular establishment before. Places have a *past*, a *present*, and a *future*. They grow, flourish, and decline, along with the site and the culture in which they are embedded. The "dining place" in figure 24.1 would most likely not exist if the store next to it was not the source of the food consumed by the diners. The solitary diner in figure 24.1b would most likely feel uncomfortably exposed if the car defining the triangular space moved away.

Most of all, places have *meaning*, which is based on the beliefs people associate with them. It is this meaning that determines the expectations of human behavior in a place (which, when violated, is considered to be "out of place"). These meanings arise over time as practices emerge and are transformed within the cultures that use them. Different cultures may have different understandings of similar places and similar concepts, which contribute to the feeling of estrangement when visiting foreign countries, where the same cues have acquired different meanings than back home.

What Is Place Making?

Places are the product of human intervention. They have to be *created*, through practice and appropriation, and made to fit into the culture of society. Place making is the conscious process of arranging or appropriating objects and spaces to create an environment that supports desired activities while conveying the social and cultural conceptions of the actors

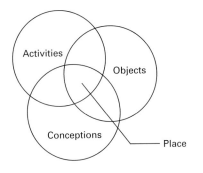

24.2 Place making is the confluence of activities, space, and conceptions. (After C. Canter, *The Psychology of Place* [New York: St. Martin's Press, 1977].)

and their wider communities (fig. 24.2).[7] This is what architects, landscape architects, town planners, and other environmental design professionals have been practicing for centuries.

Designers do not control all aspects of a place. While the objects that define and fill a space are largely (though not exclusively) under their control, the activities that occur in the place are mostly determined by its users. And the conception of the place is typically created by society and by the context in which the place is embedded or by the inhabitants. An architect can design a house, but only the family who inhabits it can make it a home.[8]

Place making, therefore, is a process of creating conditions that afford and encourage the emergence of a particular sense of place. While designers may not be able to create a sense of place directly, the spaces and the objects they create can help, or hamper, its creation. A closed office door may be a physical arrangement intended to keep out noise, but it also sends the message "no visitors." Locating executives in corner offices may improve their task lighting, but it also broadcasts social cues of status and relative importance.

Appropriately arranged forms can support the creation of a sense of place. "Appropriateness" means forms that support the desired functions of their users, and match their conceptions of such places:

- *Functional appropriateness* is a measure of the fit between the activity and the objects or spaces that support it. For example, Philip Johnson's famous Glass House, in New Canaan, Connecticut, is known for its simple, modern functional interior arrangement (fig. 24.3a). Functional appropriateness is, in many cases, the easier component to define because it lends itself to analytical reasoning, either quantifiable or nonquantifiable, as discussed in chapters 19 and 20.

- *Conceptual appropriateness* is a measure of the fit between the form (or environment) and the inhabitants' expectations. Such expectations are a matter of social conventions, cultural norms, education, and ethnicity—what is knows as "acculturation." When confronted with objects (or activities) that conflict or disagree with our expectations, we feel "out of place." Johnson's Glass House, for all its functional appropriateness, is conceptually inappropriate for most visitors: its all-glass enclosure provides no privacy—a cardinal expectation for a

Future

private residence. While Johnson may well have intended to create this conceptual conflict and has been willing to accept it (aided, no doubt, by the 40-acre wooded estate in which the house is located), he nevertheless designed the guest house, on the same estate, to meet more conventional conceptions (fig. 24.3b).

How Is It Done?

As discussed in chapter 12, in the physical world places are often designed by "borrowing" function, form, and conception from precedents, symbols, and metaphors. This approach is based on the assumption that a form that proved to be "appropriate" in earlier circumstances will, with proper adjustments for the new context, continue to be so again for the same activity and conception. Researchers call this approach designing from patterns, case-based design, or more recently, object-oriented design—the instantiation, or judicious adaptation, of a "source" template, archetype, or precedent to fit the specific needs and circumstances of a "target" context.[9]

If no appropriate precedent can be found, symbols and metaphors may be used to engender some inherent quality embedded in the "original." In this case, the fit may be more tenuous and require some explanation. Alternatively, altogether new forms may be developed that, if found to be functionally and conceptually "appropriate," may acquire their own status as precedents (e.g., Frank O. Gehry's curvilinear forms, discussed in chapter 23).

Although the intent of both adaptation and invention is to give *form* to the designed place, they also confer on it certain conceptions that are associated with the metaphorical sources (e.g., shaping the facade of the U.S. Supreme Court like a Greek temple confers upon it the conception of the court as a "temple" of justice).

It is easy to understand, therefore, why cyberspace has, to a large extent, been given the form of "pages": the two main metaphors of the Web—as the "mother of all publishing houses" and as mail-order retail (or e-tail) outlet—have been shaped by the forms and conceptions that worked so well, for so long, in physical space. They were borrowed from scholarly papers and from product catalogs, which proved so successful in selling mail-order goods for Montgomery Ward, Sears Roebuck,

a

b

24.3 Philip Johnson's Glass House (top) and Guest House (bottom), in New Canaan, Connecticut (1949). (Photographs by Michael Moran, New York, 2000.)

JCPenney, as well as countless other retailers. A similar logic guided cyber-worlds that purport to support "meetings" and have, therefore, borrowed the physical conference room metaphor.

The shortcoming of the "borrowing" approach, and the most common cause for its failure, is of course assuring that the "source" and the "target" are similar enough to justify using similar formal solutions and conceptions. It is questionable, for instance, whether Philip Johnson was justified in borrowing the Chippendale furniture design for crowning his AT&T building in New York City, thereby unleashing postmodernism. Likewise, one must question whether cyberspace is similar enough to physical space to justify the borrowing of its forms and conceptions, even functions, which were developed explicitly for the "real" world. To investigate this issue, we must first gain a better understanding of cyberspace and its origins.

24.2 Cyberspace

The stuff of science fiction as recently as 1984,[10] cyberspace became a reality in the early 1990s with the advent of the World Wide Web (WWW). The WWW is only the most recent utility that was added to the Internet, which was initiated in 1973 by the U.S. Defense Advanced Research Projects Agency (DARPA) and whose stated purpose was to develop communication protocols that would allow networked computers to communicate transparently across multiple, linked packet networks.[11]

The WWW was the brainchild of Tim Berners-Lee and his colleagues at CERN, in Geneva, Switzerland, who, in 1989 identified a need for sharing information in support of collaborative work. Since this work involved text, images, graphs, and other forms of information, Berners-Lee developed a hypertext-based user interface, modeled after the well-known and successful way of presenting and linking information that was developed by Xerox PARC and made popular by Apple Computers. He developed the HyperText Transmission Protocol (HTTP)—the language used for requesting and transmitting Web files and documents that Web servers and browsers can understand—and Hyper-Text Markup Language (HTML) for writing the shared documents themselves.

By December 1990 CERN had developed a Web server and a text-based browser for NExTStep Computers. In March 1991 the software for the text-based browser was made available to a limited audience. In January 1992 an updated version of the browser (version 1.1) was made freely available on the Internet. By January 1993 there were fifty Web servers in existence, and free graphical browser software had been made available for the Apple Macintosh. By February 1993 the Web was accounting for 0.1 percent of all Internet traffic.

In September 1993 Marc Andreessen and his colleagues at the National Center for Supercomputer Applications (NCSA) at the University of Illinois in Urbana-Champaign released versions of a graphical Web browser called Mosaic, for Microsoft Windows running on PCs, Apple Macintosh, and Unix computers running X Windows. This software handled files with images and text interspersed in the same document, allowing organizations to create visually exciting documents that could be viewed in very similar formats on the three main types of computers in use at that time.

In 1994 Andreessen cofounded Netscape Communications, which developed Netscape Navigator, a Web browser that quickly became the de facto standard for Web communication.[12]

The success of Netscape, and later Microsoft's Internet Explorer, can be attributed, in part, to their emulating the document metaphor: the World Wide Web looks like a glossy magazine, or catalog, not much different from paper-based products that fulfill the same function, namely communicating information about a company's products or a scholar's papers.

But the Web quickly proved that it was no poor cousin of the paper journal: it could be made interactive! Netscape Communications was the first to develop methods that enabled two-way communication, including getting information from consumers, which led to a rapid growth in companies using the Web for electronic commercial transactions.

It took about a year to set standards and make the first 3D browser for the Web available. Virtual Reality Markup Language (VRML) was born at the First International Conference on the World Wide Web in May 1994 at CERN in Geneva. Its conceptual origins were based on the science fiction literature of Gibson and Stephenson,[13] and mainstream 3D computer graphics (especially SGI's Open Inventor format). A draft for VRML 1.0 was presented at the second WWW conference in fall 1994 in Chicago. In April 1995 SGI presented WebSpace, the first publicly available VRML browser. Since VRML was a relatively simple format built

24.4 "Satellite" maps of activeworlds.com's AlphaWorld in 2001 (overall and partial image). (Copyright 2002 Activeworlds, Inc. All rights reserved.)

upon a well-defined standard, very quickly a number of modeling tools and converters also became available, and several proprietary Web-based 3D modeling environments and tools were established (e.g., Adobe Atmosphere, ActiveWorlds, and Second Life).[14]

Why Make Cyberplaces?

With the advent of VRML, spatial models are becoming increasingly more popular in the design of Web environments (fig. 24.4). These designs are based on the assumption that, since many aspects of our social and cultural behaviors are organized around spatial elements of the physical world, we can carry over these patterns of behavior to virtual environments by designing them to have the same affordances for interaction and meaning that the physical world exhibits.

While this hypothesis seems plausible, current implementations do not yet exhibit the sense of environmental quality or sociocultural significance that could confirm it. Therefore, it is not yet possible to gauge the effect of cyberplace-ness on the economic, educational, or cultural activities for which the Web is used. The only area in which cyberplaces seem to have established themselves at present is multiuser digital games, like Sony's EverQuest.[15]

What can be gained by adopting place-making principles for the design of cyberspace? What are the inherent advantages of cyber*places* versus cyber*spaces*? In the physical world, the effect of culturally rich environments can be seen in how people vacation and shop. Excluding economic constraints, many people prefer to spend their limited leisure time in environmentally and culturally rich places like Tuscany, Venice, and Paris, or even Disneyland. Similarly, it is not the level of service alone that differentiates a luxury hotel from a cheap roadside motel: environmental, social, and cultural richness—and the sense of place they engender—play a key role in determining their appeal.

The physical design of shopping centers is a good case in point. It has changed from merely locating two anchoring department stores on the ends of a long wide corridor into creating visually and emotionally rich environments. Retail-based shopping centers like strip malls, which were popular in the 1970s, are now criticized as sterile and placeless environments (fig. 24.5a). Current shopping center design still utilizes the con-

Future

cept of anchors, be they department stores or movie theaters, but puts an intense emphasis on rich environments that borrow the metaphor of the "village" (fig. 24.5b). The sense and quality of place they create makes people want to go there and stay there for longer periods of time. In Las Vegas, "themed" hotels and casinos, like the Venetian Hotel, go even further, borrowing their theme from historically significant places (fig. 24.5c).

In the realm of digital gaming, the initial constraints of the technology led to the design and marketing of games with visually crude graphics and simple 2D environments, like PacMan and Tetris. But the advent of games like Myst and Riven revolutionized the industry. They created a clear sense of place at both the larger "world" scale as well as the room scale. These environments are familiar yet futuristic and unique, which makes the games intensely attractive. While the mystery/puzzle plot of the game is quite clever, it would hardly come off without the rich place-based environments that serve as its context. They are able to create places people actually want to be in rather than the environmentally shallow "dungeon" games, where the crude nature of the context hinders the game.

24.3 Cyberplaces

It is logical to assume that designing places in cyberspace can, indeed must, be informed by the principles that have been guiding physical place making for centuries, for the sake of environmental, social, and cultural richness. This transformation, however, is not a matter of simply emulating physical form in electronic environments. Cyberspace cannot be "specialized" by appropriating physically based spatial metaphors: objects and spaces that are functionally and perceptually "appropriate" in the physical world lose their appropriateness in cyberspace.[16] On the other hand, having been conditioned from birth to function and perceive the physical world, we carry the expectations and sense of "appropriateness" to cyberspace. For example, while it is unnecessary to use a table to support objects in cyberspace, we are rather uncomfortable when objects simply "float" in cyberspace. And while the lack of gravity permits us to walk on the walls or on the ceiling (if they exist at all), the impression such freedom produces is quite surreal (as has been so aptly illustrated by the Dutch artist M. C. Escher; see figure 1.1).

a

b

c

24.5 The evolving placeness of shopping malls, from (a) strip malls to (b) shopping malls to (c) "themed" malls, demonstrates the importance of place and context for the activity of shopping.

On the other hand, the digital realm offers place-making opportunities that do not exist in physical space. Distances lose their meaning—they can be traversed in an instant—as do spatial boundaries. Even time can be easily manipulated: we can visit cities that no longer exist or do not yet exist. Choosing the right balance to engender the desired sense of place—without falling into the traps of indiscriminate "borrowing" from physical space nor discarding everything we learned from it—is the challenge facing cyberplace making.

Much can be learned from the attempts that were made over the past decade to navigate this narrow, uncharted path. These attempts can be classified into four categories of environmental "shells" for developing placelike environments in cyberspace:

- Hyperreality cyberspaces.
- Abstracted reality cyberspaces.
- Hybrid cyberspaces.
- Virtual spaces.

Hyperreality

Hyperreality attempts to mimic the physical world in every detail. The degree of quality required for believability is rather high and not easily achieved. The test is the inability of the viewer to find telltale flaws in both the completeness of the imagery and its attention to such details as gravity, wind, weather, sunlight, natural materials, dust, dirt, and the aging of materials and surfaces. Technologically, this has been readily achieved using ray tracing and radiosity in still imagery (as discussed in chapter 9), but achieving it in dynamically updated imagery—either on stand-alone or networked computers—is still limited by the speed and storage capacity of computers.

Hyperreality environments can be used to recreate places that no longer exist or have never existed (e.g., Kent Larson's Hurva Synagogue [fig. 24.6], and Takehiko Nagakura's Danteum and Palace of the Soviets) or places that do not yet exist (e.g., the Virtual Museum of Arts El País, fig. 24.7).[17]

The advantages of hyperreality environments, in terms of place making, derive from the richness of experience, familiarity, and visual comfort they convey. The environment is easy for people to understand and relate to, since it contains such familiar implements as walls, ceilings, stairs, lights, doors, and even simulated materials. But it never rains in cyberspace; therefore 3D worlds have no use for roofs (although ceilings might help provide a boundary for spaces). There is no gravity, hence no weight in cyberspace, therefore no need for columns and beams. Even windows lose their role as sources of air and light and function only as portals. Distances are elastic to the extreme: one can hyperjump from place to place without having to visit points in between. Hence roads, walkways, and elevators are silly constructs, unless they assume their alternative meaning as transitional places that afford serendipitous encounters, views,

24.6 Exquisite computer rendering of Louis Kahn's Hurva Synagogue, which was never built, demonstrates hyperreality's attention to detail. (Courtesy of Kent Larson, MIT.)

24.7 Virtual Museum of Arts El País. (Courtesy of MUVA Virtual Museum of Arts El País, Uruguay, 2002.) (See color plate 17.)

"Conference building"

"Lobby"

"Conference room"

24.8 University of Sydney virtual conferencing center. (Courtesy of M. L. Maher, University of Sydney, Australia, 2000.)

and mid-journey changes of destination, or function as "props" that support the creation of a context.

Abstracted Reality

Abstracted reality obeys enough laws of nature to engender believability but does not attempt to create a "perfect" reality. Objects and textures are abstracted, not perfectly rendered, but there is an attempt to avoid disorientation or the unfamiliar. For example, one could not walk through walls, and one needs to "ride" an "elevator" or ascend a flight of stairs to go from floor to floor. Stylistically, the imagery might be "cartoon-like" or image-processed (e.g., run through a watercolor filter). Video games like Myst and Riven are examples of digital abstracted realities, much like Disneyland in the physical world. There is quite a bit more artistic freedom in abstracted reality than in hyperreality, which allows for stretching, or accentuating, place-making qualities such as scale and time.

Most current cyber-environments fall into the abstracted reality category, by default, and 3D multi-user domains (MUDs) are probably their best example. They employ a strong spatial analogy, with the explicit intent to facilitate multiuser (i.e., social) interaction. Like textual MUDs (chat rooms), they typically use "rooms"—a convenient mechanism to restrict the visitor's attention to activities in one "place" at a time. To change activities, the user must "change rooms": in some systems users can jump from one room to another, whereas in others they must "walk" to their destination, passing through points in between.

The Virtual Campus of the University of Sydney, for example, employs an architectural, campuslike MUD (fig. 24.8).[18] Visitors "enter" the "conference building," go "up" the "elevator" to their selected conference "room," where they find a conference "table" flanked by "chairs."

It is, however, a strange sense of place that such virtual environments may engender. They have topology (connectedness) but no orientation. The user has no real experience of moving up and down when "riding" the elevator. A visitor cannot sit on one of the available chairs or put his or her notes on the table. The space can accommodate many more participants than can be assumed from its size.

So in fact abstracted realities do not always exhibit the spatially based place-ness they purport to engender. While the spatial metaphor is an

Future

important contributor to facilitating interaction and engagement, it is not enough. Our sense of place is determined by the cultural or communally held appropriateness of behavior and interaction, not by the spatial metaphor alone.

Hybrid Cyberspace

Hybrid cyberspace freely mixes "real" and "virtual" experiences. It does not pretend to obey the laws of nature. One could, for example, move through walls or fly. The range of artistic expression is limitless, and unusual juxtapositions could easily become surreal. Many elements of the site may be unbuildable in the physical world. One could assume, for example, the form of a blue caterpillar, and sit on top of a mushroom the size of a person, smoking a long hookah—as described in Lewis Carroll's classic stories *Alice's Adventures in Wonderland* and *Through the Looking Glass* (1862–1864). Fellow participants could appear in the form of realistic or unrealistic avatars, even in symbolic representation, such as talking chess pieces or playing cards.[19] Objects could behave in unusual ways, changing size, texture, and form over time. The challenge for the designer is to strike the right balance between the real and the unreal, wherein the experience is aesthetically rich yet not so disorienting or sterile as to destroy the sense of place. Disorientation becomes a major issue, as perceived experiences may conflict with learned or expected ones. The surrealism of Carroll's *Alice's Adventures in Wonderland* adds much to the story, but Alice's experiences are often disorienting and somewhat inhospitable.

Hypervirtuality

Hypervirtuality drops all relationship to the physical world and the laws of nature. It generally avoids the familiar. In fact the uniqueness and innovativeness of the experience, to the intentional exclusion of the familiar, is of primary importance. Each virtual world creates its own set of rules, which could challenge our sense of reality, materiality, time, and enclosure of space. Common building elements such as walls, doors, windows, or floors have no meaning there. Examples of hypervirtuality are the space travel sequence toward the end of Stanley Kubrick's 1968 movie *2001: A Space Odyssey* and Char Davies's *Éphémère* (fig. 24.9).[20]

24.9 "Bones"—digital frame captured in real time through HMD (head-mounted display) during live performance of immersive virtual environment *Éphémère*, by Char Davies (1998). (Courtesy of Immersense, Inc.)

Of the four types of cyberspace, hypervirtuality seems the most fertile relative to the opportunities offered by the digital medium but also the furthest away from "place" experiences derived from everyday life experiences. There is a potential to expand the realm of sensory experiences by taking advantage of the computer's ability to organize time, data, and space, completely unbounded by the laws of nature. However, by completely discarding the physical spatial metaphor, hypervirtuality also loses any sense of familiarity, along with the social and cultural cues that derive from it. The unlimited freedom offered by hypervirtuality, along with its complete rejection of place-making principles, makes this type of cyberspace a form of place-less art.

24.4 Criteria for Cyberplace Making

The hypothesis underlying this chapter is that the need for place making in the digital world is critical to creating a lively and socioculturally progressive environment. But all four types of digital environments listed above fall short of doing so; they are all deficient to some extent or another. Like the first generation of digital games, these early attempts to create cyberplaces have often been too realistic, too virtual, too literal, or too surreal in their imagery. They do not engender cultural experiences, nor do they facilitate social interaction. What would it take to make "good" cyberplaces?

The following criteria of place making, adapted from physical place making, may help guide the creation of placelike cyber-environments:

1. Places are settings for complex and rich *events*. They provide a *reason* and a *purpose* for being there. In digital games the purpose may be to slay the enemy, to conquer territory, or to ascend to "higher" levels of the game. In physical space, the event may be to shop, to be educated or entertained, to conduct business, or simply to meet other people.
2. Places involve some kind of *engagement* with objects or with people. Thus they require *presence*. Presence can be participatory, as in a game or in a MUD, or remote and voyeuristic. Either way, place exposes the actor to social norms, cultural customs, and the scrutiny of others.[21]
3. Places provide *relative location*. They let visitors know where they are, where they came from, and where they might be going in the

future—spatially, temporally, and socially. Their relative locations provide places with a sense of uniqueness and a character of their own that helps to differentiate one place from another. Location creates a *context* for the activity, a sense of "outside" relative to some "inside," in much the same way as one sees the world through the living room window: perhaps one sees only the front lawn and the road, but that road also implies a connection to other roads, to highways, to a city center, located in a certain state and country. It provides not only a geographical location but also a sociocultural one.

4. Presence and location promote a sense of *authenticity*. It allows the visitor to know that she or he is participating in a "real" event rather than viewing a previously recorded one. It is the sense one gets by actually *being* at a ball game or a concert. The telltale signs of an authentic place are *change* and *serendipity*—the traces of other people's presence and the chance of seeing something no one else has seen before.

5. A place must be *adaptable*, so as to allow appropriation to the specific needs of the user and to foster an ability to make it personal. Well-designed places foster a sense of ownership and a sense of control—and at the same time a shared responsibility and access. It is such adaptability by others, who leave their mark on a place, that makes a place authentic. Adaptability could be through the placement of objects, or symbols, both personal and communal, by rearrangement of the objects, or by addition and subtraction of objects.

6. Digital places, unlike their physical counterparts, afford a *variety of experiences*. They can provide multiple different points of view, different scales, different levels of abstraction, even different temporal perspectives. These experiences can be simultaneous, or they can evolve autonomously or interactively.[22]

7. The choice and control over *transitions* in cyberspace from place to place offers much greater richness than physical space affords. One can hyperjump or use the journey as an event in and of itself.

8. Finally, well-designed places are inherently *memorable*. They are places people want to be in, to stay in, and to come back to. They are visually and emotionally rich, inviting spaces that can create a sense of belonging, safety, and acceptance, or, conversely, a sense of adventure and danger.

It is quite obvious that these criteria are neither exhaustive nor independent of one another. They blend principles learned from place making in the physical world and from the new affordances offered by the digital world. These added affordances may enhance the place-making experience, but they could also easily detract from it by overwhelming the viewer with disorienting imagery. A judicial and careful blend is needed.

As cyberspace becomes more commonplace, there will be a growing need to design it like a place rather than as a document or even a space. Environmental quality and sense of place matter as much in cyberspace as they do in physical space. They can have the same beneficial and detrimental effects on visitors of cyberspace that a physical environment has on its users.

The difficulty in making cyberplaces is that there are currently very few metaphors and precedents to guide their development, and few, if any examples to assess the effect of richer environmental quality and place-ness on users. Nonetheless, making places in cyberspace can borrow from the principles developed by architects, landscape architects, and town planners. At the same time, cyberplace making must adopt the abilities offered by the new technology, which allows designers to exercise more freedom in place making than physical places afford. The challenge is to blend these two opposite needs—not to stifle cyberplaces by making them too hyperrealistic while at the same time not making them hypervirtual to the point of renouncing all sense of place.

By looking at physical architecture as a case study and as a metaphor for organizing space into meaningful places, designers of cyberplaces can develop spatial settings that are not only visually rich, but, like physical places, afford social interaction and express cultural values.

The creation of cyber*places* should not be confused with the creation of cyber*spaces*. Places, in the physical world, are filled not only with artifacts, tools, and representations of our work but also with other people and the signs of their activities. The sense of other people's presence and the ongoing awareness of their activity allow us to structure our own activities and to seamlessly integrate them with those of others. They give *meaning* to our own actions and behaviors. That is why we choose to go to live concerts, where we must put up with uncomfortable seating and the coughing and rustling of the audience, rather than stay at home and listen to perfect recordings of the music. That is why we still like to browse for books in physical bookstores, even though we can buy all that we need at virtual bookstores like Amazon.com. That is why we visit physical museums, even though we can visit them on the Web.

As a greater number of social, cultural, economic, and other activities move into cyberspace, architects must work to make it socially and culturally appropriate, so that it can support our rich, place-based, real-world behaviors. Cyberplaces must support, not undermine, the very things that make places work—their activities, uniqueness, the shared understandings of their appropriate use, and the interpretation of social and cultural cues in the physical environment. Without them, they cannot accommodate all the social and behavioral skills we spend a lifetime to learn and that contribute so much to enriching our culture.

The evolution of cyberplaces, in turn, will affect physical architecture, as virtual bookstores and virtual universities are already demonstrating. By providing an alternative to activities that heretofore could only take place in the physical world, they provide users with options, and designers with the need to differentiate one from the other. What is the added value of physical bookstores? Of brick-and-mortar universities? As the place quality of cyberspace continues to evolve, these questions will become more difficult to answer, and may contribute to the evolution of new architectural forms and conceptions.

Bibliography

Campbell, D. A. "Design in Virtual Environments Using Architectural Metaphor." Master's thesis, University of Washington, Seattle, 1996.

Chermayeff, S., and C. Alexander. *Community and Privacy: Toward a New Architecture of Humanism.* New York: Doubleday Anchor Books, 1963.

Donath, J. S. "Inhabiting the Virtual City: The Design of Social Environments for Electronic Communities." Ph.D. diss., Massachusetts Institute of Technology, 1996, <smg.media.mit.edu/people/Judith/Thesis>.

Heidegger, M. *The Question of Being,* trans. W. Kluback and J. Wilde. New Haven: Yale University Press, 1958.

Jones, M. L. W. "Collaborative Virtual Conferences: Using Exemplars to Shape Future Research Questions." Human Computer Interaction Group (HCI-G), Cornell University, Ithaca, N.Y., 2000.

Lynch, K. *The Image of the City.* Cambridge: MIT Press, 1960.

Marcus, C. C., and C. Francis, eds. *People Places: Design Guidelines for Urban Open Space.* New York: John Wiley and Sons, 1964.

Moore, C., and D. Lyndon. *Chambers for a Memory Palace.* Cambridge: MIT Press, 1996.

Munro, A. J., K. Höök, and D. Benyon. *Social Navigation of Information Space.* London: Springer-Verlag, 1999.

Rheingold, H. *The Virtual Community: Homesteading on the Electronic Frontier.* Reading, Mass.: Addison-Wesley, 1993.

Sommer, R. *Personal Space: The Behavioral Basis of Design.* Englewood Cliffs, N.J.: Prentice-Hall, 1969.

Conclusion

The uneasy relationship between novel computational principles, methods, and tools, on one hand, and the ancient discipline of architecture, on the other, can be interpreted according to two different paradigms. The first is that of "forcing a square peg into a round hole," which implies that the use of the new tools is misdirected or at least poorly fits the processes that have traditionally been part of architectural design. As a result, the practice of architecture suffers. The second paradigm describes a state of transformation where the new technology is viewed through the lens of the current, obsolescent practice and labeled in essentially "backward" terms, much like the automobile was viewed as a "horseless carriage" in the early days of the twentieth century. It implies a lack of appreciation for the potential of emerging technology to change the nature of the task to which it is applied.[1]

25.1 Techniques, Tools, and Practices

Technologies are not planned: they emerge as culture evolves. Perhaps that is why their effect on established practices is rarely guided by reflection. More often, as traditional tools are transformed by new technology, it is the practices themselves that must adapt to the changing context. Gradually the effect of these adaptations becomes known, but by then the practices have been irreversibly changed, often with unintended consequences. Even their purposes and values may be displaced by the qualities and capabilities afforded by the new technologies.

In this regard, design technology is no different. Therefore, half a century after the introduction of computers into architecture, it is appropriate to reexamine the premises and purposes of the new tools, so that we may assess what has been displaced, what has been gained, and what has been adapted. This examination may help to realign the tools with the goals of the practice and to realign the practice with the abilities (and shortcomings) of the new tools.

It is the intent of design technology to help architects work more intelligently, more responsibly, more efficiently, more effectively, and more carefully. Representational methods and tools, which comprise a large part of this technology, are employed to assist in the reasoning and communication acts required in designing. They allow designers to reason about the world's events, places, and materials—either real or imagined—without their being present. Designers can reason with a representation because it embodies the qualities of the actual experience. For example, scale drawings represent actual dimensions, and study models indicate the volumetric qualities of the actual building. Both allow for a quick comparison of the spatial qualities of design alternatives while maintaining a consistent building vocabulary—even if that vocabulary is largely diagrammatic.

But the representational technology that is used to help us explore abstract design ideas is not neutral: it interposes itself between the idea and its presentation by appropriating our "logistics of perception."[2] It blurs the distinction between the designer's intent and what has been accomplished through the technological means used to express that intent. As the mediator, technology serves not only to communicate some knowledge but also to determine what is knowable.

One measure of the influence that technology, as a mediator, has on the task it is employed to assist is its affordance—the potential of the technology to enable the assertive will of its user.[3] For example, designs derived from working primarily in scale drawings can result in an architecture that is less expressive three-dimensionally than that which result from working with massing models.[4] Thus, scale drawings and physical models have certain potentials that emphasize different qualities of the idea at the expense of others. Because the affordance of the tool influences, channels, and even directs the reasoning that goes on during the design process, it must be chosen carefully to match the task at hand. A crude diagrammatic model, which affords flexibility of interpretation, is a valuable tool early in design thinking, whereas the strict drawing conventions of contract documents, which afford little ambiguity, are crucial in communicating the design to the contractor.

The introduction of computing technologies into the design process provides new affordances. The efficiency, control, and intelligence afforded by these tools have become increasingly essential to architectural practices. CAD tools make the production of contract documents more efficient and better coordinated. Similarly, computer modeling has reduced the production costs associated with making physical models while increasing the options for their end use. But while it is clear that these needs have dominated the development and adoption of CAD in the profession of architecture, it is less obvious how, increasingly, this technology is influencing its practice beyond production. In many cases, the influence is misunderstood or goes undetected at all. As designers embrace the new technology for all its benefits, they must also become increasingly more cognizant of its less obvious impacts on their work and its products. And, since the tools themselves are man-made, their makers too must be made cognizant of the influence they wield in shaping not only their own products but the practices and products of their end users.

25.2 Two Paradigms

The relationship between a technology, its affordance, and a practice can be described in terms of two different paradigms. The square-peg-in-a-round-hole paradigm describes toolmaking as a problem of adapting a new technology to current practices. As a new technology is introduced into a practice, a dysfunctional relationship can develop between the tools and a task, either because the task is poorly understood or because the process of displacing a traditional technology is largely one of the substitution of habitual tools with new ones that have the wrong affordances. Such inappropriate use of the technology results in a poorer practice. For example, using precise drafting tools such as AutoCAD early in the design process—where ambiguity and flexibility are needed more than preciseness—requires the designer to decide issues whose time has not yet come, thus interfering with the evolution of design ideas. Moreover, it can mislead the viewer of the design (including the architect) to read more precision in the design than it deserves. Understanding this paradigm (and resolving the dysfunction it brings in its wake) requires a clear identification of the different actions that comprise the design process and developing computational tools that can truly be of assistance. This amounts to "rounding off" the square peg.

The horseless carriage paradigm views technology as a means to alter the self-perception of a practice as it is transformed by a new technology. When the term horseless carriage was used at the turn of the twentieth century, transportation was being described through the lens of an old technology, without the realization that travel had dramatically changed. Understanding this paradigm requires asking a different question than that demanded by the first one. The question is not how can the new tools *assist* designers, but rather how do the affordances they provide *change* the practice of design itself? Do we understand how having more precision early in the process affects our reasoning about design options? Do we understand how communication via digital files and video screens fundamentally changes the culture of the practice? How does knowledge, once invested only in the designer but now ingrained in the tools, affect the practice of design? This paradigm, like the first one, assumes that the fundamental task does not change (i.e., the task of designing of a building). But unlike the first paradigm, it assumes that the practice of design is not only assisted, but is changed through the influence of the new technologies.

In both paradigms, the tools are connected to an image of practice.[5] This image is a description of methods, habits, organization, knowledge, and culture of design in relationship to a task. Architects often hold such an image of their practice—but not always explicitly. They may know *how* something is done but are less aware of the *values* implicit in a particular way of working.

Toolmakers (including makers of software tools) also hold an image of design practice. Not being architects themselves (with few exceptions), their image of the practice of design is articulated in the assumptions they make about the kinds of affordances needed within that practice. Both paradigms require an *explicit* understanding of a tool's affordance in relationship to design actions. But, according to the second paradigm, toolmakers also have the added responsibility to understand the implicit embodiment of the values associated with the practice of design in the tools they make and their influence on shaping the emerging practice.

Affordances and Actions

Mapping the range of qualities afforded by a tool results in a set of paired qualities organized as opposite poles of a continuum, as depicted in figure 25.1.

These qualities, when connected to design actions, can be assessed in terms of their appropriateness—at least in the square-peg sense.

The range of affordances offered by drawings demonstrates this issue. A sketch is an abstract, typically conceptual representation; it is more concerned with *exploring* rather than with *describing* a solution and implies more than it defines. It contains configurational knowledge that structures the exploration of variations and moves within the design—as opposed to a definitive description of the plan.[6] As Arnheim puts it, the sketch reduces "a theme visually to a skeleton of essential dynamic features."[7] The semantic openness and abstraction inherent in a sketch serves to aid in the analogical reasoning processes used in early design phases.[8]

As more is known about the design, drawings need to reflect and communicate with more precision to limit possible misinterpretations. The ability to collaborate and direct the action of others in the construction process requires concreteness, explicitness, and agreement about what is represented in the drawings. These requirements are met through the affordances provided by the shared conventions of contract drawings.

While design tools are not always so simple or linear in their relationship to the polar affordances listed in figure 25.1, this range of qualities is useful for evaluating them in relationship to design tasks. More importantly, as a method of mapping, figure 25.1 describes the compression, overlap, and restructuring provided by new computational tools. The practice, the affordances, and the emergence of new forms of representation demonstrate this transformation.

Abstract ↔ Precise
Implicit ↔ Explicit
Semantically poor (open) ↔ Semantically clear (closed)
Conceptual ↔ Concrete
Ideation (exploration) ↔ Descriptive

25.1 Attributes afforded by design tools.

25.3 Design Technologies

Drawings, which have come to be recognized as the traditional tools of the profession of architecture, are in fact relatively new inventions. In the Middle Ages, buildings were often constructed from a simple schema or by use of the master builder's trick of deducing the elevation from the plan by the application of a simple system of proportions, based on a triangle or a square. The "discovery" of the texts of Vitruvius during the Renaissance, with their emphasis on proportions, symmetry, and harmony, and their use of the classical orders, made it necessary to draw up a whole set of plans before construction could commence. Drawings became exact scale representations, with dimensions marked. Specific types of drawings were invented, such as the section (to elucidate the vertical stacking of the spaces and the structure of the building), the orthogonal elevation (to show the true proportions of the building), and the perspective view (to show how the building would look from an eye-level point of view).

These inventions were used as a means for planning or "designing" the building and allowed for analysis of its form and structure. They also formed a means of communication that had major consequences. The architect ceased to be a technician who operated at the construction site and became a designer who spent his or her time at the "studio" drafting rather than building.

Thus, the practice of architecture was transformed, in part, through the introduction of a new design technology, gradually moving away from direct construction toward the theoretical, and in the process it gained status and respect. Among the symbols of status was the new name of the professional—he was now an architect rather than a master mason. The separation of theory, or "design," from practice placed an ever-growing emphasis on drawings as the means of communication to others involved in the actual construction of the building.

The separation of the architect from the actual construction of the building introduced a discontinuity in the design-build process. This discontinuity had many benefits, such as the ability to consider the whole building before construction was begun, allowing for more complex and sophisticated designs. It also introduced problems, including a potential for miscommunication and misinterpretation of information and the increasing abstractness with respect to the architect's experience, with the result that some design decisions had to be delegated to the builder (the contractor). The reliance on means of communication such as drawings, and to a lesser extent, scale models in bridging this discontinuity gap transformed the practice of architecture. It produced an image of practice tied to drawing and raised new issues of competence in the use of design tools, in particular, issues concerning the degree of explicitness of the representation and the designer's control over it.

Drawings

By being explicit about some aspects of the conveyed information, a representation is also inexplicit about other aspects. Drawings, for example, are explicit about the form and relationships of the components of a building, but not about its materiality. Materials are typically specified in accompanying texts, which lack form and relational information.

Drawings provide a parsimonious notational means of conveying both referential and frame-of-reference (context) information, in the form of floor plans, sections, elevations, and details. However, much of the information that is conveyed by drawings is implicit and relies heavily on interpretation. For example, the interpretation of any symbol, such as a "door" or a "wall," is vested in the reader, who must rely on his or her own knowledge of how floor plans are read—knowledge acquired independently from the particular drawing being read. Likewise, the relationship between the walls and the space they enclose is a matter of interpretation, as is the disciplinary frame of reference that determines whether the drawing is read as an architectural plan or as a structural plan. Additional symbols, annotations, and specifications help narrow the range of interpretability, but they cannot completely eliminate it.

This heavy reliance on interpretation, and the need to augment the explicit information with implicit assumptions, hinders the effective use of drawings as a means to engender shared understanding—a precondition for collaborative action, as discussed in chapter 21. The frame-of-reference information that is conveyed by drawings is limited to the immediate physical context of the project and does not include the cultural, economic, and other types of contextual information. Hence, drawings lack the ability to accommodate changing frames of reference or the ability to identify and to propagate such changes; they are completely passive instruments. Instead, the effectiveness of this type of representation relies on information embodied in them through a practice. Accordingly, much of the architect's education is spent learning how to create and interpret drawings. This education includes learning to reason with lines and understanding the drawing as a shared convention of the practice. Ultimately a student's judgment depends on his or her ability to interpret the drawings of projects on the desk and on exhibit in design reviews.

The introduction of computer-aided design tools has accentuated the gap between explicit and implicit information. In manual drawings it is often hard, if not impossible, to tell whether a line designates the "solid" part of the building or its "void" (the space). This is intentional, for in fact walls are intended to both bound space and provide structure. In CAAD, lines and shapes clearly designate "solid" objects (Yessios's early work being the exception).[9] The decision to focus the representation on "solids" in CAAD has been made by the toolmakers—the vendors who design these tools. It shows an understanding of the explicit attributes of the traditional tool—lines representing elements—but lacks the sensibility implicitly embodied in the use of drawings as a practice.

Product Databases

Information technology has provided the means for other forms of representation, such as databases and knowledge bases, with new arrays of affordances. These tools are not simply an extension of drawings but instead work to express the knowledge contained in the practice of design—again, however, structured by the toolmaker rather than the designer.

In an effort to provide more complete information than merely the form and relationships between the objects of the design, or separate materiality information, researchers and vendors have been developing product databases. This approach assumes that by providing a single representation there will be less need for individual disciplinary interpretations. Interpretation will also be enhanced if the semantic relationships between the various objects and their attributes are represented explicitly. Such approaches (discussed in section 8.5), include IPAD, the Interoperability Alliance's foundation classes, EDM, and BDA.[10]

While product databases are informationally more comprehensive and complete than other types of representation, they can provide only part of all the information needed to interpret the project. For example, they typically do not include contextual information, which may change the meaning of the objects that are being considered.[11] Moreover, product databases require making choices, on the part of the designer, of what information to include, what can be omitted, and what relationships to represent. As such, although they are more complete than other representations, product databases too are subject to the choices of their makers.

Rule-Based Expert Systems

Attempts to explicate and share the interpretive knowledge itself have mostly taken the form of Experts Systems, a computational framework borrowed from artificial intelligence (AI) research (see section 14.3). These methods rely on packaging accepted disciplinary knowledge in the form of small modules, known as "rules," which represent the smallest units of experts' knowledge. Their modularity allows developers to focus on the content of the knowledge base one chunk at a time and to build it up incrementally.

In the context of architectural design, rules typically capture and make operational "special-case reasoning characteristic of highly experienced professionals."[12] What constitutes such "special-case reasoning," how its applicability is determined, and how conflicts are resolved are highly variable: they depend on broad disciplinary know-how, good practices, and personal judgment of the system developer. What may appear to be a "rule" to one professional may not be so for another professional within the same discipline and is likely to be completely incomprehensible for someone from another discipline.

Thus, while rule-based expert systems may appear attractive for capturing design knowledge due to their modularity, they are, in fact, highly personalized, arbitrary expressions of knowledge and operational practices. Although some rule-based systems are successful at what they were intended to do, they must often be accepted as "black boxes," which are difficult if not impossible to evolve, modify, and adapt by anyone other than their authors. Even more serious is such systems' sensitivity to changing contexts, which they are ill equipped to handle due to the rigidity of the rules in the face of changing circumstances.

25.4 Images of Practice

Computing has had only a few decades of experience with the practice of architecture, and drawing has a long history. Therefore it is not surprising that the fit between design paractice and the affordances offered by computing technology is more problematic than for drawings. The question for toolmakers is how to understand those affordances and evaluate the impact of their tools.

The first paradigm offers one approach—smoothing off the square peg. This begins by observing what designers do. As Gero argues, studying human designers leads to richer theories of designing, which in turn lead to making more appropriate tools.[13] This is an empirical approach,

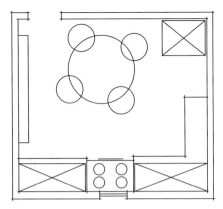

25.2 Typical CAD drawing of a kitchen.

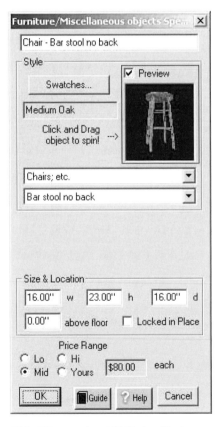

25.3 Object catalog of 3D Kitchen (Books That Work, Palo Alto, California).

which implies an emphasis on the cognitive aspects of designing, rather than an analytical approach to the design process, which is more "convenient" and less "messy" from a computational point of view. The empirical approach is supported by protocol analyses that attempt to capture the reasoning associated with design actions. These studies have provided insight into issues of emergence, analogy, visual reasoning, and the use of representations in design. The connection between these insights and new tools ought to help improve the fit between their affordances and design actions—between the peg and the hole.

The second paradigm, though, is more fundamental and critical to the understanding of where the profession of architecture is heading. In approaching computational tools as a horseless carriage, the observation shifts to include the practice as well as the tool. The promise afforded by the new tools includes the ability to represent in the "drawing" what was formerly held in the practice. As such, the tools contain the toolmaker's understanding of the explicit aspects of the representation, but also, more than ever, they include the implicit understanding of the values held in the practice. And as has happened when drawings were first introduced into the practice of architecture, the organization of the work itself changes, along with the identity of the designer and the image of practice.

Tales from the Kitchen Designer

The design of a kitchen, while not a complex problem, turns out to be a good example of how a tool represents and transforms a practice. The practice of dwelling design (whose practitioners include builders, designers, and architects) has by necessity included a competence in the design of kitchens. Rules of thumb concerning allowable distances between major work areas, knowledge of work surface dimensions and activity requirements, knowledge of cabinetry and its assemblage, principles of organizing access to work areas, and familiarity with materials and their cost—all comprise a fundamental competence in kitchen design. As reflected in the growing number of televised home remodeling shows and magazines aimed solely at kitchen and bath design, the demand for such design services has increased in recent years, due in large part to the perceived economic value of kitchens and bathrooms as part of the overall value of a house. This demand has given impetus to new kitchen design tools and practices. While most kitchens are still designed by practitioners using "traditional" techniques, increasingly their knowledge is represented in design tools used by homeowners or sales people in building supply stores.

Figure 25.2 is a simple drawing of a kitchen layout constructed in a typical CAAD program. The drawing is constrained by the geometric capabilities afforded by the drawing program, but the designer is free to construct any shape desired. The elements of the drawing can be arranged and shifted around, but the representation holds no knowledge about their existence as objects: only the designer does. While the drawing is diagrammatic, it is sufficient to reason about initial organizational concerns. Its simplicity might even be helpful in that it allows for alternative schemes to be generated and assessed only in terms of how the activities are arranged—without the burden of resolving other issues such as materials and costs. According to the affordances listed in figure 25.1, this can be seen as a semantically poor, but "open," drawing.

Figures 25.3 and 25.4 are from a design tool named 3D Kitchen, developed by Books That Work, of Palo Alto, California. It is intended to help homeowners design their own kitchens. With this tool the design is constructed from defined objects, such as cabinets, appliances, walls, and doors, rather than with lines and circles. Thus the designer—who is intended to be a novice kitchen designer—manipulates well-defined objects. Furthermore, the objects are connected to a rich database that allows them to be associated with specific materials and a cost, which can be examined by clicking on the object (fig. 25.3). The tool can, therefore, keep track of the running cost of the construction and alert the designer when the stated budget has been exceeded. At no point in the process does the tool allow for ambiguity: each design "move" is completely defined in terms of its expected results. Thus, if the designer changes his or her mind and wishes to replace one type of cabinet with another, the first one must be deleted and the new one inserted; simply changing the label associated with the cabinet is not enough. Since the program uses well-defined objects, the plan can be easily translated into a three-dimensional view of the kitchen. Overall, this representation contains much of the knowledge held within a kitchen design practice. But this tool is still not very "intelligent." It does not know what a cabinet really is, hence it might allow one to be stretched to be 20 inches long and 2 inches wide.

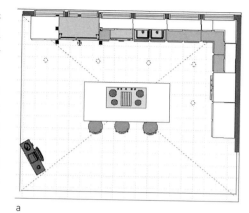

a

b

25.4 Plan (a) and perspective view (b) of a kitchen from 3D Kitchen (Books That Work, Palo Alto, California).

Figure 25.5 shows some cabinets from the KraftMaid catalog—a commercial cabinet manufacturer from Middlefield, Ohio. These cabinets can be ordered through building supply stores. The kitchen designer in the store uses a computer program, provided by the manufacturer, to help customers select and order the cabinets to form a complete kitchen.

Like 3D Kitchen, this program too works with defined objects, not lines. But it is even more "knowledgeable" than 3D Kitchen: it knows not only about cost and form, but also about availability and delivery dates, and it will not allow the cabinets to be resized, because they represent actual manufactured products. This tool introduces even more precision at the beginning of the design process in determining costs and material orders. In both cases, the effect is to introduce early in the design process more affordances for concreteness, precision, and description than found in the CAAD drawing. But the lack of ambiguity may obscure possible alternative choices early in the process by accepting the constraints built into the representation. The cabinet suppliers' design tool limits the designer's choices to what is available in the catalog. Other geometries, dimensions, or storage options are not presented at all. The "completeness" of the tool has the tendency to close the process around conventions in the representation, excluding other types of geometries (e.g., curvilinear cabinets). According to the affordances in figure 25.1, this can be seen as a semantically rich but "closed" kitchen design tool.

For the competent designer, this distance is overcome through experience. A kitchen designer knows that the lines on the paper or the screen represent cabinets that contain dimensional constraints and, with enough experience, the designer ought to be able to estimate costs even from a schematic drawing. For the experienced practitioner, the ambiguity afforded by the schematic drawing can be helpful, if not instrumental, in promoting creative ways of approaching the design. A professional kitchen designer knows the practice and can use the appropriate tool throughout a design process. She might begin with a series of quick sketches to generate different layouts and then move on to a more explicit representation to test them out and might even return to sketching to reason further about organizational options—in effect, squaring off the round hole.

But the critical implication of the kitchen design tool is not in its support of the designer but in its transformation of the practice. The second and third tools are aimed at people who would typically not be considered

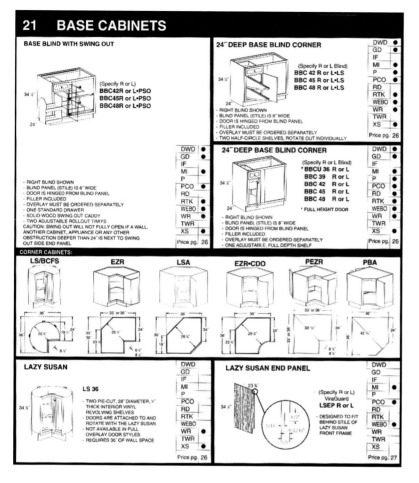

25.5 Page from KraftMaid Cabinetry catalog, Middlefield, Ohio. (Courtesy Kraftmaid, 2002.)

professional designers—homeowners and sales people. These new tools contain a knowledge that heretofore was the province of trained designers. Along with the object-oriented representation, the kitchen design tool also holds lessons about "rules of thumb" and design concepts for the naive designer. In essence, it represents and formalizes a kitchen design practice. With this design tool, anybody, trained or not, can make reasonable decisions about cabinet layout, use of patterns, and costs. The fact that more kitchens are designed using these tools than by professional kitchen designers is testament to their power.[14]

The affect of the tool is to shift the design practice from traditional designers to others, much as the arrival of scale drawings allowed dilettantes, rather than craftsmen, to be in charge of architectural design. This displacement is more understandable within the horseless carriage paradigm of toolmaking, where the affordances of the new technology work to transform the practice. In this case, the affordance of precision, semantic richness, and concreteness allow the knowledge of the practitioner to be represented in the tool, which can now be used by a novice.

Aside from the relative merits of this transformed design practice, two observations can made. First, that the practice has been changed by the technology. And second, that change has been brought about by the tool's ability to represent the practice.

Informing Toolmaking

The implications for the makers of design tools are clear. In the square-peg-round-hole paradigm, observing the cognition and behavior of the designer is critical. If architects are to have better (more effective) design tools, the toolmakers need to examine the way designers reason and work. By matching affordances with design actions, the tools can support, in a more inclusive manner, design reasoning and promote wisdom in their use. But they need to make the distinction between *designer* and *design practice*. While the cognitive ways designers work will not radically change due to their use of computational tools, the practice of design will. The horseless carriage paradigm tells us that, through technology, current practices will be displaced. The questions are how and how much. The kitchen design tool transformed kitchen design by representing an *image* of that practice, albeit incomplete.

Along with knowledge about the task, a practice also contains *values* that are often communicated only in the design itself. A kitchen designer must know about the constraints inherent in the cabinetry but also hold certain values about efficiency and size as they relate to the activities in the kitchen. These values, which are not absolute—they depend on the context—shape the design through decisions that are both overt and fundamental. Does the image of practice represented by the horseless carriage paradigm contain these values? It does, but those are the values of the toolmaker, not the designer. As the design practice shifts to others, will the embedded values behind the design decisions become as explicit as the knowledge of what we know about cabinetry? While we can assess the effectiveness of a tool by understanding its use by a designer, we must also understand the values it promotes within a practice. Although it is not possible to anticipate all the changes that computers will bring to the practice of design, it is already clear that at least some of these changes will be brought about by the toolmakers who participate in the transformation of the practice, rather than by the designers who use these tools. This requires us to examine the practice as well as the designer and to argue for embedding values that reflect our image of practice in the tools that will ultimately direct our design efforts. Whose knowledge comprises that image of practice? What values are displaced? These are some of the questions raised by architecture's new media that are yet to be solved.

25.5 Conclusion

This book has attempted to illustrate how information technology has in the past, does in the present, and will in the future affect the practice of architecture—much like it has affected every other discipline it has touched. The change can be perceived both as a "square peg in a round hole," when it changes older methods, or as a "horseless carriage," when it transforms the practices themselves that use the new technology. Both paradigms are the result of the work of toolmakers who are not necessarily architectural designers themselves. They have the power to develop round pegs in round holes, which will enhance the practice of architecture, or to repackage and transform the practice itself. Much like the transformation brought about by the introduction of drawings in the fifteenth century, which created the office of the architect, computational tools are creating new "design" professionals—the toolmakers. While we may argue about the impact of these "designers" on the practice of architecture, the fact remains that they have transformed the practice itself and created a new horseless carriage.

Bibliography

Abbott, A. D. *The System of Professions: An Essay on the Division of Expert Labor.* Chicago: University of Chicago Press, 1988.

Agre, P. E., and D. Schuler. *Reinventing Technology, Rediscovering Community: Critical Studies in Computing as a Social Practice.* Norwood, N.J.: Ablex Publishing, 1997.

Argyris, C., and D. A. Schön. *Theory in Practice: Increasing Professional Effectiveness.* New York: Jossey-Bass, 1977.

Cuff, D. *Architecture: The Story of Practice.* Cambridge: MIT Press, 1991.

Foucault, M. *The Order of Things: An Archaeology of the Human Sciences.* 1966. Reprint. London: Routledge, 2001.

Graham, S., and S. Marvin. *Telecommunications and the City: Electronic Spaces, Urban Places.* London: Routledge, 1996.

Kuhn, T. S. *The Structure of Scientific Revolutions.* Chicago: University of Chicago Press, 1962.

Resnick, M. "New Paradigms for Computing, New Paradigms for Thinking." In *Computer and Exploratory Learning,* ed. A. DiSessa, C. Hoyles, and R. Noss, 31–34. Berlin: Springer-Verlag, 1995.

Notes

Preface

1. J. Archea, "Puzzle-Making: What Architects Do When No One Is Looking," in *Computability of Design*, ed. Y. E. Kalay (New York: Wiley Interscience, 1987), 37–52.
2. H. W. J. Rittel and M. M. Webber, "Dilemmas in a General Theory of Planning," *Policy Sciences* 4 (1973): 155–169.
3. A. Bijl, T. Renshaw, D. Barnard, S. Wyatt, and D. Burney, "Application of Computer Graphics to Architectural Practice," in *ARU CAAD Studies Report*, Project A25/SSHA-DOE, Architectural Research Unit, Edinburgh University, 1971.
4. Minsky M., *Semantic Information Processing* (Cambridge: MIT Press, 1968).
5. With some notable exceptions, such as Frank O. Gehry's Guggenheim Museum in Bilbao, Spain, and his Experience Music Project in Seattle, Washington, which only serve to emphasize the predominance of buildings whose design has *not* been affected by information technology.

Part I

1. J. Bronowski, *The Origins of Knowledge and Imagination* (New Haven: Yale University Press, 1978).
2. H. A. Simon, *The Sciences of the Artificial* (Cambridge: MIT Press, 1969).
3. H. W. J. Rittel and M. M. Webber, "Dilemmas in a General Theory of Planning," in *Policy Sciences* 4 (1973): 155–169.
4. B. Edwards, *Drawing on the Right Side of the Brain* (Los Angeles: J. P. Tarcher, 1979).
5. C. Alexander, *Notes on the Synthesis of Form* (Cambridge: Harvard University Press, 1964).
6. The term "cyberspace" was coined by William Gibson to denote the virtual "space" of the Internet. W. Gibson, *Neuromancer* (New York: Ace Books, 1984).
7. M. D. Gross, "The Electronic Cocktail Napkin—Working with Diagrams," *Design Studies* 17, no. 1 (1996): 53–69.

Chapter 1

1. For a fictional but fact-based account of a master mason's life in the Middle Ages, see K. Follett, *Pillars of the Earth* (New York: Signet, 1996).

2. B. Jestaz, *Architecture of the Renaissance: From Brunelleschi to Palladio* (New York: Harry N. Abrams, 1995).

3. In 1447 Brunelleschi was buried in a prominent place in the Duomo of Florence, along with a statue and an inscription composed by the chancellor of the Florentine republic.

4. J. C. Jones, *Design Methods: Seeds of Human Futures* (New York: John Wiley and Sons, 1980).

5. C. Alexander, *Notes on the Synthesis of Form* (Cambridge: Harvard University Press, 1964).

6. L. H. Sullivan, *Kindergarten Chats and Other Writings* (1918; reprint, New York: Dover Publications, 1979).

7. L. March and P. Steadman, *The Geometry of Environment* (Cambridge: MIT Press, 1974).

8. A. Drexler, *The Architecture of the Ecole des Beaux-Arts*, 2d ed. (London: Secker and Warburg, 1984).

9. According to Kuhn, problem solving would be considered a paradigm rather than a theory or a method, because it is sufficiently open-ended to admit a broad range of problems and attract an enduring group of adherents away from competing modes of scientific activity. T. S. Kuhn, *The Structure of Scientific Revolutions* (Chicago: University of Chicago Press, 1962).

10. "Satisficing" is a term coined by Herbert A. Simon in his book *The Sciences of the Artificial* (Cambridge: MIT Press, 1969), to indicate solutions that are both satisfactory and sufficient to achieve the goals and abide by the constraints of the problem.

11. A. Newell and H. A. Simon, *Human Problem Solving* (Englewood Cliffs, N.J.: Prentice-Hall, 1972).

12. A. Newell, *Unified Theories of Cognition* (Cambridge: Harvard University Press, 1990).

13. J. Laird, P. Rosenbloom, and A. Newell, *Universal Subgoaling and Chunking* (Boston: Kluwer Academic Publishers, 1986).

14. See, for example, P. H. Winston, *Artificial Intelligence* (Reading, Mass.: Addison-Wesley, 1977), or N. J. Nilsson, *Principles of Artificial Intelligence* (Palo Alto, Calif.: Tioga Publishing Co., 1980).

15. M. D. Gross, S. Ervin, J. Anderson, and A. Fleisher, "Designing with Constraints," in *Computability of Design*, ed. Y. E. Kalay (New York: Wiley Interscience, 1987), 53–83.

16. G. Steele and G. J. Sussman, "CONSTRAINTS—A Language for Expressing Almost-Hierarchical Descriptions," *Artificial Intelligence* 14 (1980): 1–39.

17. F. S. Budnick, R. Mojena, and T. E. Vollmann, *Principles of Operations Research* (Homewood, Ill.: Richard D. Irvin, 1977).

18. Adapted from W. J. Mitchell, *Computer-Aided Architectural Design* (New York: Petrocelli/Charter, 1977).

19. See Book V of Vitruvius, *De architectura* (c. 28 bc), trans. Morris Hicky Morgan as *The Ten Books on Architecture* (Cambridge: Harvard University Press, 1914).

20. G. da Vignola, *Regola delli cinque ordini d'architettura* (1562), published in a modern edition by Alberto Pratelli as "*Architettura* del Baroccio da Vignola: concernente i cinque ordini" (Bologna, Italy: Cooperativa Libreria Universitaria Editrice Bologna, 1984).

21. C. Alexander, S. Ishikawa, M. Silverstein, M. Jacobson, I. Fiksdahl-King, and S. Angel, *A Pattern Language* (Oxford: Oxford University Press, 1977), 115.

22. J. S. Gero, "Design Prototypes: A Knowledge Representation Schema for Design," *AI Magazine* 11 (1990): 26–36.

Chapter 2

1. D. Schmandt-Besserat, *The History of Counting* (New York: Morrow Junior Books, 1999).

2. A modern desktop computer is at least a thousandfold faster, has three orders of magnitude more memory, is a thousand times smaller, and costs 1/1000 of the price of the UNIVAC.

3. Thomas Watson Sr., the head of the IBM corporation—one of the few companies that manufactured computers at that time—forecast in 1946 a need for no more than six computers to handle all the needs of the entire world.

4. D. E. Rumelhart and J. L. McLelland, *Parallel Distributed Processing: Explorations in the Microstructure of Cognition* (Cambridge: MIT Press, 1986).

5. W. McCulloch and W. Pitts, "A Logical Calculus of the Ideas Immanent in Nervous Activity," *Bulletin of Mathematical Biophysics* 7 (1943): 115–133.

Chapter 3

1. A. M. Turing, "On Computable Numbers, with an Application to the *Entscheidungproblem*," *Proceedings of the London Mathematical Society* 2, no. 42 (1936): 230–265.

2. F. P. Brooks, *The Mythical Man Month: Essays on Software Engineering* (Reading, Mass.: Addison-Wesley, 1978).

3. Arthur C. Clark's HAL 9000 computer, the hero of his book *2001: A Space Odyssey* (New York: Penguin/Putnam, 2000), originally published in 1968, is often held up as the model of future "intelligent" machines.

4. R. Kurzweil, *The Age of Spiritual Machines* (New York: Penguin Books, 1999).

Chapter 4

1. Where the size of objects was determined by their relative importance, rather than their geometric relationships.
2. S. Coons, "An Outline for the Requirements for a Computer-Aided Design System," *AFIPS Spring Joint Computer Conference* 23 (1963): 299–304.
3. J. W. Dawson, "The Computer in Building Design," *Architecture and Engineering News* 3, no. 12 (1961): 14–19. See also J. P. Eberhard, "A Computer-Based Building Process: Its Potentials for Architecture," *Architecture and Engineering News* 4, no. 12 (1962): 16–18.
4. C. Alexander, *Notes on the Synthesis of Form* (Cambridge: Harvard University Press, 1964).
5. J. J. Souder and W. E. Clark, "Computer Technology: A New Tool for Planning," *AIA Journal* 52 (October 1963): 97–106.
6. For more details see, for example, A. Baer, C. M. Eastman, and M. Henrion, "Geometric Modeling: a Survey," *Computer-Aided Design* 11, no. 5 (1979): 253–271.
7. N. Negroponte, *The Architecture Machine* (Cambridge: MIT Press, 1970).
8. P. Richens, "OXSYS-BDS Building Design Systems," *Bulletin of Computer-Aided Architectural Design* 25 (1977): 20–44.
9. Non-Uniform Rationale B-Splines—a mathematical form of representing certain types of curves and surfaces.
10. Y. E. Kalay, "WORLDVIEW: An Integrated Geometric-Modeling/Drafting System," *IEEE Computer Graphics and Applications* 2, no. 7 (1987): 36–46.
11. G. Carrara, Y. E. Kalay, and G. Novembri, "Knowledge-Based Computational Support for Architectural Design," *Automation in Construction* 3, nos. 2–3 (1994): 123–142.
12. J. Pohl and L. Myers, "A Distributed Cooperative Model for Architectural Design," *Automation in Construction* 3, nos. 2–3 (1994): 177–185.
13. U. Flemming, "Case-Based Design in the SEED System," *Automation in Construction* 3, nos. 2–3 (1994): 123–133.
14. K. Papamichael, J. LaPorta, and H. Chauvert (1998), "Building Design Advisor: Automated Integration of Multiple Simulation Tools," *Automation in Construction* 6, no. 4 (1998): 341–352.
15. R. Kurzweil, *The Age of Intelligent Machines* (Cambridge: MIT Press, 1990).
16. W. Gibson, *Neuromancer* (New York: Ace Books, 1984).
17. In *Everybody's Autobiography,* the 1937 sequel to her famous "autobiography" of Alice B. Toklas, Gertrude Stein wrote, "There is no there there," to express her dismay at not finding her childhood home on her visit to Oakland, California.

Part II

1. M. McLuhan, *Understanding Media: The Extensions of Man* (New York: McGraw-Hill, 1964).

Chapter 5

1. The first demonstration of electronic transmission of speech by Alexander Graham Bell, on March 10, 1876.
2. A term coined by psychologist J. J. Gibson in his study of human perception to indicate the perceived capacity of objects, or the relationships between objects, for some action. J. J. Gibson, *The Ecological Approach to Visual Perception* (Hillsdale, N.J.: Lawrence Erlbaum, 1979).
3. C. van Doren, *History of Knowledge* (New York: Birch Lane Press, 1991).
4. M. R. Cohen, *A Preface to Logic* (New York: Henry Holt, 1944), 47.
5. E. C. Cromley, "Sleeping Around: A History of American Beds and Bedrooms," *Journal of Design History* 3, no. 1 (1990): 1–17.

Chapter 6

1. H. W. J. Rittel and M. M. Webber, "Dilemmas in a General Theory of Planning," in *Policy Sciences* 4 (1973): 155–169.
2. J. Archea, "Puzzle-Making: What Architects Do When No One Is Looking," in *Computability of Design*, ed. Y. E. Kalay (New York: Wiley Interscience, 1987), 37–52.
3. C. Alexander, *Notes on the Synthesis of Form* (Cambridge: Harvard University Press, 1964). See also J. C. Jones, *Design Methods* (London: John Wiley and Sons, 1980).
4. D. A. Schön, *The Reflective Practitioner: How Professionals Think in Action* (New York: Basic Books, 1983).
5. H. A. Simon, "The Structure of Ill-Structured Problems," in *Developments in Design Methodology*, ed. N. Cross (New York: John Wiley and Sons, 1984).
6. D. A. Schön, "Designing: Rules, Types, and Worlds," *Design Studies* 9 (1988): 3.
7. P. Lloyd and P. Deasley, "Ethnographic Description of Design Networks," *Automation in Construction* 7, nos. 2–3 (1998): 101–110.
8. G. Goldschmidt, "Criteria for Design Evaluation: A Process-Oriented Paradigm," in *Evaluating and Predicting Design Performance*, ed. Y. E. Kalay (New York: Wiley Interscience, 1992), 67–79.
9. R. Mohsini, "On Measuring Project Performance: Some Problems of Aggregation," in *Evaluation and Prediction in Design,* ed. Kalay, 239–250.
10. B. Jestaz, *Architecture of the Renaissance: From Brunelleschi to Palladio* (New York: Harry N. Abrams, 1995).

11. Extract from a letter to Pope Leo X, in ibid., 138–140.

12. P. L. Berger and T. Luckmann, *The Social Construction of Reality* (New York: Anchor Books, 1967).

13. A. K. Boulding, *Conflict and Defense* (New York: Harper and Row, 1962).

14. T. S. Kuhn, *The Structure of Scientific Revolutions* (Chicago: University of Chicago Press, 1962).

15. D. G. Pruitt, *Negotiation Behavior* (New York: Academic Press, 1981). See also H. Raiffa, *The Art and Science of Negotiation* (Cambridge: Harvard University Press, 1982).

16. R. Axelrod, *The Evolution of Cooperation* (New York: Basic Books, 1984).

17. G. Serag-Eldin, "Applying a Human Conflict Management Model to Architectural Design Collaboration" (Ph.D. diss., University of California, Berkeley, 2003).

18. J. P. Protzen and H. Dehlinger, "Debate and Argumentation in Planning: An Inquiry into Appropriate Rules and Procedures," Technical Report, Institute of Urban and Regional Development, University of California, Berkeley, 1972.

19. W. Kunz and H. W. J. Rittel, "Issues as Elements of Information Systems," DMG Fifth Anniversary Report, Design Methods Group Occasional Paper No. 1, University of California, Berkeley, 1972, 13–15.

20. G. T. Fechner, "Zur Experimentellen Aesthetik," *Abhandlungen der Königliche Sachsische Gesellschaft der Wissenschaften Mathematisch-Physische Klasse* 9 (1871): 555–635.

21. A. Musso and H. Rittel, "Measuring the Performance of Buildings," Technical Report, Washington University, St. Louis, Mo., 1967.

Chapter 7

1. C. G. Ramsey and H. R. Sleeper, *Architectural Graphic Standards* (New York: John Wiley and Sons, 1994).

2. B. M. Smith, "IGES: A Key to CAD/CAM Systems Integration," *IEEE Computer Graphics and Applications* 11, no. 3 (1983): 78–83.

3. J. Bronowski, *The Origins of Knowledge and Imagination* (New Haven: Yale University Press, 1978).

4. When photographed, models become two-dimensional representations, and share the drawbacks of renderings and other two-dimensional graphics.

5. Architects typically use generalized "rules of thumb" to determine if their designs can be furnished. These rules often look for limiting factors that may hinder furnishing the space, rather than opportunities that will promote better configuration of the space itself.

Chapter 8

1. Polyhedral shapes are solids that are bounded by planar faces.
2. S. A. Coons, "Surfaces for Computer-Aided Design of Space Forms," Technical Report MAC-TR-41, MIT (Cambrige, 1967).
3. J. H. Alberg, E. N. Nilson, and J. L. Walsh, *The Theory of Splines and Their Applications* (New York: Academic Press, 1967).
4. Polygons are finite, contiguous regions in some two-dimensional space, bounded by edges and vertices.
5. R. Goldstein, "Defining the Bounding Edges of a SYNTHAVISION Solid Model," *Eighteenth Design Automation Conference*, IEEE/ACM, Las Vegas, Nev. (1981).
6. Points on the boundary itself can be classified as being either *inside* or *outside* the shape, depending on certain circumstances. See Y. E. Kalay, *Modeling Objects and Environments* (New York: Wiley Interscience, 1989), 369–379.
7. The process is somewhat more complicated if the shape is not convex, in which case the orientations of the triangles forming the tetrahedrons must be accounted for. See Y. E. Kalay, *Modeling Objects and Environments,* 28–30.
8. Kalay, *Modeling Objects and Environments,* 143–146.
9. E. F. Codd, "A Relational Model of Data for Large Shared Data Banks," *Communications of the ACM* 13, no. 6 (1970): 377–387.
10. B. M. Smith, "IGES: A Key to CAD/CAM Systems Integration," *IEEE Computer Graphics and Applications* 11, no. 3 (1983): 78–83.
11. B. M. Smith, *AutoCAD Customization Manual*, AutoDesk Publication 100891-01, San Raphael, Calif. (1992).
12. W. F. Danner and Y. Yang, *STEP Development Methods: Resource Integration and Application Interpretation*, ISO TC1184/SC4/WG5 N31 (1992).
13. C. M. Eastman, *Building Product Models: Computer Environments Supporting Design and Construction* (Boca Raton, Fla.: CRC Press, 1999).
14. G. Augenbroe, "An Overview of the COMBINE Project," in *Product and Process Modeling in Building Industry,* ed. R. J. Scherer (Rotterdam, The Netherlands: A. A. Balkema, 1995).
15. G. Carrara, Y. E. Kalay, and G. Novembri, "Knowledge-Based Computational Support for Architectural Design," *Automation in Construction* 3, nos. 2–3 (1994): 123–142.
16. C. M. Eastman and A. Siabiris, "A Generic Building Product Model Incorporating Building Type Information," *Automation in Construction* 3, no. 4 (1995): 283–304.

Chapter 9

1. D. Morris, *The Naked Ape* (London: Jonathan Cape, 1967).
2. J. Bronowski, *The Origins of Knowledge and Imagination* (New York: Yale University Press, 1978).

3. It is in fact a standard exercise in computer graphics courses to develop algorithms that fill in a figure that looks like a cat or a penguin . . .

4. In practice, additional restrictions apply, such as the distance of the light source, the distance of the observer, and the nature of the surface. For a full discussion of the method see J. D. Foley, A. van Dam, S. K. Feiner, and J. F. Hughes, *Computer Graphics: Principles and Practice* (Reading, Mass.: Addison-Wesley, 1987).

5. H. Gouraud, "Continuous Shading of Curved Surfaces," *IEEE Transactions on Computers* C-20, no. 6 (1971): 623–629.

6. The normal of a vertex can be computed from the geometric model of the object or by averaging the normals of all the polygons converging on that vertex.

7. B. T. Phong, "Illumination for Computer Generated Pictures," *Communications of the ACM* 18, no. 6 (1975): 311–317.

8. E. Catmull, "A Subdivision Algorithm for Computer Display of Curved Surfaces" (Ph.D. diss., 1974), Report UTEC-CSc-74-133, University of Utah, Salt Lake City.

9. J. F. Blinn and M. E. Newell, "Texture and Reflection in Computer Generated Images," *Communications of the ACM* 19, no. 10 (1976): 542–547.

10. J. F. Blinn, "Simulation of Wrinkled Surfaces," *SIGGRAPH '78* (1978): 286–292.

11. The calculation of refraction is further complicated by *dispersion*—the phenomenon whereby different wavelengths refract differently (which is manifest in the scattering of light by a prism), and by the fact that in some materials the angle of refraction is larger than 90 degrees, causing total refraction and hence the complete disappearance of the refracted object from view.

12. Although all reflections are modeled as diffuse, the emission of light sources can be specified by their directional characteristics and intensity. In this way, luminaires ranging from spotlights to diffuse ceiling panels can be simulated.

13. Note that the area of the patches is not important, because they affect each other in a reciprocal manner. This makes it possible to tailor the calculation to the desired degree of accuracy by controlling the number of surface subdivisions.

14. D. S. Immel, M. F. Cohen, and D. P Greenberg, "A Radiosity Method for Non-Diffuse Environments," *SIGGRAPH '86* (1986): 133–142.

15. J. R. Wallace, M. F. Cohen and D. P. Greenberg, "A Two-Pass Solution to the Rendering Equation: A Synthesis of Ray Tracing and Radiosity Methods," *SIGGRAPH '87* (1987): 311–320.

16. C. Cruz-Neira, D. Sandin, and T. DeFanti, "Virtual Reality: The Design and Implementation of the CAVE," *SIGGRAPH '93* (1993): 135–142.

Chapter 10

1. Ö. Akin and E. F. Weinel, *Representation and Architecture* (Silver Spring, Md.: Information Dynamics, 1982).

2. D. A. Schön, *The Reflective Practitioner* (New York: Basic Books, 1983).

3. Y. E. Kalay, "Redefining the Role of Computers in Architecture: From Drafting/Modeling to Knowledge-Based Assistants," *Computer-Aided Design* 17, no. 7 (1985): 319–328. See also L. M. Swerdloff and Y. E. Kalay, "A Partnership Approach to Computer-Aided Design," in *Computability of Design*, ed. Y. E. Kalay (New York: Wiley Interscience, 1987), 315–336.

4. Object-oriented programming is the practice of combining data and the operators that manipulate it in one "encapsulated" representation, called the "object." See, for example, B. J. Cox, *Object Oriented Programming: An Evolutionary Approach* (Reading, Mass.: Addison-Wesley, 1987).

5. Parametric design is the practice of making the values of several attributes of an object dependent upon a common parameter, so they will all be automatically updated when the value of that parameter is changed. See, for example, C. M. Eastman, *Building Product Models: Computer Environments Supporting Design and Construction* (Boca Raton, Fla.: CRC Press, 1999), 370–379.

6. G. Carrara and G. Novembri, "Constraint-Bounded Design Search," in *Computer-Aided Architectural Design Futures,* ed. A. Pipes (London: Butterworths, 1985), 146–157.

Part III

1. In his *Physics*, Aristotle identified four causes for the existence of anything: *material* cause (what something is made of); *formal* causes (how something is made); *efficient* causes (what activity produced it); and *final* causes (why something is made).

2. E.-E. Violet-le-Duc, *Entretiens sur l'architecture* (1858–1863), trans. B. Bucknall as *Discourses on Architecture,* 2 vols. (New York: Grove Press, 1968).

3. L. H. Sullivan, *Kindergarten Chats and Other Writings* (1918; reprint, New York: Dover Publications, 1979).

4. A. Drexler, *The Architecture of the Ecole des Beaux-Arts,* 2d ed. (London: Secker and Warburg, 1984).

5. C. Alexander, *Notes on the Synthesis of Form* (Cambridge: Harvard University Press, 1964).

6. E. Shaviv, "Generative and Evaluative CAAD Tools for Spatial Allocation Problems," in *Computability of Design*, ed. Y. E. Kalay (New York: Wiley Interscience, 1987), 191–212.

7. U. Flemming, R. Coyne, T. Glavin, and M. Rychener, "A Generative Expert System for the Design of Building Layouts—Version 2," in *Artificial Intelligence in Engineering: Design,* ed. J. S. Gero (Amsterdam: Elsevier, 1988).

8. U. Flemming, "The Role of Shape Grammars in the Analysis and Creation of Designs," in *Computability of Design*, ed. Y. E. Kalay, 245–272.

9. J. Gero, "Creativity, Emergence, and Evolution in Design," *Second International Round-Table Conference on Computational Models of Creative Design* (Sydney, Australia, 1992).

Chapter 11

1. For example, the problem of "being hungry" can be solved by eating—it is not considered a "design" problem. H. A. Simon, *The Sciences of the Artificial* (Cambridge: MIT Press, 1969).

2. H. W. J. Rittel and M. M. Webber, "Dilemmas in a General Theory of Planning," in *Policy Sciences* 4 (1973): 155–169.

3. D. A. Schön, *The Reflective Practitioner: How Professionals Think in Action* (New York: Basic Books, 1983).

4. P. R. A. Jockusch, "How Can We Achieve a Good Design?" in *Evaluating and Predicting Design Performance*, ed. Y. E. Kalay (New York: Wiley Interscience, 1992), 37–50.

5. C. Alexander, *Notes on the Synthesis of Form* (Cambridge: Harvard University Press, 1964); N. J. Habraken, J. T. Boekholt, A. P. Thijssem, and P. J. Dinjens, *Variations: The Systematic Design of Supports* (Cambridge: MIT Press, 1981); W. Peña, *Problem Seeking* (Boston: Cahners, 1977); H. W. J. Rittel and M. M. Webber, "Dilemmas in a General Theory of Planning," *Policy Sciences* 4 (1973): 155–169.

6. R. G. Shibley and L. Schneekloth, "Risking Collaboration: Professional Dilemmas in Evaluation and Design," *Journal of Architecture and Planning Research* 5, no. 4 (1988): 304–320.

7. See <http://www. exploratorium. edu/learning_studio/history/index. html>.

8. M. F. Schmertz, "Musical Excavation (Harris Hall)," *Architecture Magazine* (December 1993): 62–69. See also "Music Underground," *New Yorker*, 6 September 1993.

9. W. Kunz and H. W. J. Rittel, "Issues as Elements of Information Systems," DMG Fifth Anniversary Report, Design Methods Group Occasional Paper No. 1, Department of Architecture, University of California (1972), 13–15.

10. J. Conklin, M. Begeman, "gIBIS: A Hypertext Tool for Exploratory Policy Discussion," *Conference on Computer-Supported Cooperative Work* (New York: ACM, 1988), 140–152. See also J. Lee, "SYBL: A Tool for Managing Group Decision Rationale," *Conference on Computer-Supported Cooperative Work* (New York: ACM, 1999), 79–92.

11. R. McCall, "PHIBIS: Procedurally Hierarchical Issue-Based Information Systems," *International Congress on Planning and Design Theory* (New York: American Society of Mechanical Engineers, 1987).

12. R. Hitchcock, "Improving Life-Cycle Information Management through Documentation of Project Objectives and Design Rationale" (Ph.D. diss., Department of Civil Engineering, University of California, Berkeley, 1996.)

13. D. Noble and H. W. J. Rittel, "Issue-Based Information Systems for Design," in *ACADIA '88,* ed. P. J. Bancroft (Ann Arbor, Mich., 1988), 275–287.

14. S. Chermayeff and C. Alexander, *Community and Privacy: Toward a New Architecture of Humanism* (New York: Doubleday Anchor Books, 1963), 152–156.

15. C. Alexander, S. Ishikawa, M. Silverstein, M. Jacobson, I. Fiksdahl-King, and S. Angel, *A Pattern Language* (Oxford: Oxford University Press, 1977).

16. C. Alexander and M. L. Manheim, "HIDECS 2: A Computer Program for the Hierarchical Decomposition of Systems which have an Associated Linear Graph," Research Report R 62-2, Civil Engineering Systems Laboratory, MIT (Cambridge, 1962).

17. M. A. Milne, "CLUSTER: A Structure-Finding Algorithm," in *Emerging Methods in Environmental Design and Planning,* ed. G. T. Moore (Cambridge: MIT Press, 1970).

18. See, for example, <http://www. designmatrix.com>—a company that provides design services based on tools similar to the HIDECS.

19. G. Carrara, Y. E. Kalay, and G. Novembri, "Knowledge-Based Computational Support for Architectural Design," *Automation in Construction* 3, nos. 2–3 (1994): 123–142.

20. S. A. Gregory, "Morphological Analysis: Some Simple Explorations," in *Design Methods in Architecture,* ed. G. Broadbent and A. Ward (New York: Witternborn, 1969).

21. F. S. Budnick, R. Mojena, and T. E. Vollmann, *Principles of Operations Research for Management* (Homewood, Ill.: Richard D. Irwin, 1977).

22. The amount of time patrons spend sitting at a table is a design variable: fast food corporations have found that this time can be shortened—hence turnaround time increased—if uncomfortable, plastic furniture is used, in combination with strong primary colors (the "eat it and beat it" paradigm). In contrast, when the length of time a patron spends at the establishment is directly related to how much money is spent, as in coffee shops or book stores, the furniture is made more comfortable, and the colors more accommodating.

Chapter 12

1. C. Alexander, *Notes on the Synthesis of Form* (Cambridge: Harvard University Press, 1964).

2. L. H. Sullivan, *Kindergarten Chats and Other Writings* (1918; reprint, New York: Dover Publications, 1979).

3. G. Goldschmidt, "The Dialectics of Sketching," *Creativity Research Journal* 4, no. 2 (1991): 123–143.

4. R. Coyne, "Creativity as Commonplace," *Design Studies* 18, no. 2 (1997): 135–141.

5. Most design methods are intended to produce adequate solutions, not exceptional ones. Creative solutions, on the other hand, are generally left to artists, architects, scientists, engineers, managers, entrepreneurs and educators, at their best. There are, however, a few computational methods, discussed in chapter 15, that were designed explicitly to generate solutions that would be considered "creative."

6. Alexander, *Notes on the Synthesis of Form*.

7. Vitruvius, *De architectura* (c. 28 bc), trans. Morris Hicky Morgan as *The Ten Books on Architecture* (Cambridge: Harvard University Press, 1914).

8. A. Palladio, *I quattro libri dell'architettura di Andrea Palladio* (1570), trans. Sir Isaac Ware as *The Four Books of Architecture* (1738; New York: Dover Publications, 1965).

9. Although, as observed three hundred years later by Marc-Antoine Laugier, this noncritical approach codified "faults" as readily as it codified "proper" forms. M.-A. Laugier, *Essai sur l'architecture* (1753), trans. Wolfgang Herrmann and Anni Herrmann (Los Angeles: Hennessey and Ingalls, 1977).

10. R. Wittkower, *Architectural Principles in the Age of Humanism* (New York: Wiley Academy Editions, 1949).

11. L. B. Alberti, *De re aedifictoria* (1443–1452).

12. M. A. Laugier, *Essai sur l'architecture,* trans. Wolfgang Herrmann and Anni Herrmann.

13. Ibid, 33.

14. J.-N.-L. Durand, *Précis des leçons d'architecture* [Summary of Architecture Lessons Given at the Royal Polytechnic School] (Paris: 1813).

15. E. E. Violet-le-Duc, *Dictionnaire raisonné de l'architecture française du XI au XVe siècle* [Dictionary of French Architecture from the Eleventh to the Fifteenth Century] (Paris: 1854–1868).

16. E.-E. Violet-le-Duc, *Entretiens sur l'architecture* (1858–1863), trans. B. Bucknall as *Discourses on Architecture,* 2 vols. (New York: Grove Press, 1968), 1:267–268.

17. R. H. Clark and M. Pause, *Precedents in Architecture* (New York: Van Nostrand Reinhold, 1985).

18. C.-N. Ledoux, *L'architecture considérée sous le rapport de l'art, des mœurs et de la législation* (1804), cited in H.-R. Hitchcock, *Architecture: Nineteenth and Twentieth Centuries* (New York: Penguin Books, 1958).

19. H. A. Simon, "Style in Design," in *Spatial Synthesis in Computer-Aided Design,* ed. C. M. Eastman (New York: John Wiley and Sons, 1975).

20. A. Tzonis, "Hütten, Schiffe, und Flaschengestelle" [Huts, Ships, and Bottleracks), *Archithese* 20, no. 3 (1990): 16–27.

21. E. Sekler, "Formalism and the Polemic Use of History," *Harvard Architectural Review* 1 (1980): 33–39.

Chapter 13

1. J. C. Jones, *Design Methods: Seeds of Human Futures* (London: John Wiley and Sons, 1980).
2. J. Archea, "Puzzle-Making: What Architects Do When No One Is Looking," in *Computability of Design*, ed. Y. E. Kalay (New York: Wiley Interscience, 1987), 37–52.
3. E. Shaviv, "A Method for the Design of Fixed External Sun-Shades," *Build International* 8 (1975): 121–150.
4. E. Shaviv, "Design Tools for Solar Rights and Sun-Shades Determination," *Proceedings of the Ninth National Passive Solar Conference* (Columbus, Ohio: American Solar Energy Society, 1984).
5. W. J. Mitchell, J. P. Steadman, and R. S. Liggett, "Synthesis and Optimization of Small Rectangular Floor Plans," *Environment and Planning B* 3 (1976): 37–70.
6. G. C. Armour and E. S. Buffa, "A Heuristic Algorithm and Simulation Approach to Relative Location of Facilities," *Management Science* 9, no. 2 (1968): 294–309; B. Whitehead and M. Z. Eldars, "An Approach to Optimal Layout of Single Story Buildings," *Architects' Journal* 17 (1964): 1373–1380; R. B. Lee and J. M. Moore, "CORELAP—Computerized Relationship Layout Planning," *Journal of Industrialized Engineering* 18, no. 3 (1967): 195–200; O. M. Agraa and B. Whitehead, "Nuisance Restriction in the Planning of Single Story Layout," *Building Science* 2 (1968): 291; E. Shaviv and D. Gali, "A Model for Space Allocation in Complex Buildings," *Build International* 7, no. 6 (1974): 493–518.
7. N. Cross, *The Automated Architect* (London: Pion, 1977), 29–59.
8. T. Willoughby, W. Paterson, and G. Drummond, "Computer-Aided Architectural Planning," *Operational Research Quarterly* 21, no. 1 (1970): 91–98.
9. G. C. Armour and E. S. Buffa, "A Heuristic Algorithm and Simulation Approach to Relative Location of Facilities," *Management Science* 9, no. 2 (1968): 294–309; E. S. Buffa, G. C. Armour, and T. E. Vollmann, "Allocating Facilities with Craft," *Harvard Business Review* 42, no. 2 (1964): 136–158; E. Shaviv and D. Gali, "A Model for Space Allocation in Complex Buildings," *Build International* 7, no. 6 (1974): 493–518.
10. C. E. Nugent, T. E. Vollmann, and J. Ruml, "An Experimental Comparison of Techniques for the Assignment of Facilities to Locations," *Operations Research* 16, no. 1 (1968): 150–173.
11. Y. E. Kalay and C. H. Séquin, "Designer-Client Relationships in Architectural and Software Design," in *ACADIA '95*, ed. B. Johnson (Seattle, Wash., 1995).
12. Shaviv and Gali, "A Model for Space Allocation in Complex Buildings."

13. Consider, for example, the needs of a corporation that must accommodate 1,400 workers in seven buildings around town in a manner that will satisfy all their space needs, maximize ease of communication and material flow among them, achieve coherence within work groups and contiguity of closely interrelated groups, minimize fixed operating expenses, minimize wasted or unused space, accommodate locational preferences of key workers and managers, and be responsive to spatial rearrangements induced by reduction and growth over time. See J. M. Hamer, *Facilities Management Systems* (New York: Van Nostrand Reinhold, 1988).

14. S. R. Liggett, "Designer-Automated Algorithm Partnership: An Interactive Graphic Approach to Facility Layout," in *Evaluating and Predicting Design Performance*, ed. Y. E. Kalay (New York: Wiley Interscience, 1992), 101–123.

15. B. Auger, *The Architect and the Computer* (London: Pall Mall Press, 1972).

16. N. Cross, *The Automated Architect,* 39.

17. F. S. Budnick, R. Mojena, and T. E. Vollmann, *Principles of Operations Research* (Homewood, Ill.: Richard D. Irvin, 1977).

18. M. D. Gross, S. Ervin, J. Anderson, and A. Fleisher, "Designing with Constraints," in *Computability of Design,* ed. Y. E. Kalay, 53–83.

19. G. Weinzapfel and S. Handle, "IMAGE: Computer Assistant for Architectural Design," in *Spatial Synthesis in Computer-Aided Building Design,* ed. C. M. Eastman (New York: John Wiley and Sons, 1975), 61–93.

20. A classical tool of mathematics for choosing values for the unknowns in underconstrained systems of linear equations that minimizes the sum of the squared errors in the system.

21. Y. E. Kalay, "ALEX: A Knowledge-Based Architectural Design System," in *ACADIA '85,* ed. P. McIntosh (Tempe, Ariz., 1985).

22. H. A. Simon, *The Sciences of the Artificial* (Cambridge: MIT Press, 1969).

23. E. Shaviv and D. P. Greenberg, "Funicular Surface Structures: A Computer Graphics Approach," *Bulletin of the International Association for Shell Structures,* no. 37 (1970).

Chapter 14

1. M. Minsky, *Semantic Information Processing* (Cambridge: MIT Press, 1968).

2. A. Newell, J. C. Shaw, and H. A. Simon, "Empirical Explorations of the Logic Theory Machine," in *Proceedings of the Western Joint Computer Conference* (1957), 218–239. Also reprinted in E. A. Feigenbaum and J. Feldman, eds., *Computers and Thought* (New York: McGraw-Hill, 1963), 109–133.

3. Written by Arthur C. Clark and directed by Stanley Kubrick in 1968, the main character of this movie is an intelligent computer named HAL 9000, whose abilities—which are yet to be realized—guided the work of many AI researchers. See D. G. Stork, *HAL's Legacy: 2001's Computer as Dream and Reality* (Cambridge: MIT Press, 1996).

4. G. Carrara, Y. E. Kalay, and G. Novembri, "Knowledge-Based Computational Support for Architectural Design," *Automation in Construction* 3, nos. 2–3 (1994): 123–142.

5. L. March and P. Steadman, *The Geometry of Environment* (Cambridge: MIT Press, 1974), 263–284.

6. A. Schwartz, D. M. Berry, and E. Shaviv, "Representing and Solving the Automated Building Design Problem," *Computer-Aided Design* 26, no. 9 (1994): 689–698.

7. H. Watanabe, "IC Layout Compaction Using Mathematical Optimization" (Ph.D. diss., University of Rochester, 1983).

8. A. Witkin and D. Baraff, "Physically Based Modeling: Principles and Ppractice," *SIGGRAPH '97 Course Notes* 19 (1997).

9. S. A. Arvin and D. H. House, "Modeling Architectural Design Objectives in Physically Based Space Planning," *Automation in Construction* 11, no. 2 (2002): 213–225.

10. Consider, for example, the evolution of the home, as described in W. Rybczynski, *Home: A Short History of an Idea* (New York: Penguin, 1987), from a single space that housed the family, its servants, and livestock in the Middle Ages, to the highly differentiated modern house.

11. C. K. Riesbeck and R. C. Schank, *Inside Case-Based Reasoning* (Hillsdale, N.J.: Lawrence Erlbaum Associates, 1989).

12. J. L. Kolodner, "Improving Human Decision Making through Case-Based Decision Aiding," *AI Magazine* 12, no. 2 (1991): 52–68. See also E. A. Domeshek and J. L. Kolodner, "A Case-Based Design Aid for Architecture," in *Artificial Intelligence in Design,* ed. J. S. Gero (Boston: Kluwer Academic Publishers, 1992), 497–516.

13. U. Flemming, "Case-Based Design in the SEED System," *Automation in Construction* 3, nos. 2–3 (1994): 123–133.

14. J. S. Gero, "Design Prototypes: A Knowledge Representation Schema for Design," *AI Magazine* 11 (1990): 26–36.

15. M. L. Maher and D. M. Zhang, "CADSYN: Using Case and Decomposition Knowledge for Design Synthesis," in *Artificial Intelligence in Design,* ed. J. S. Gero (Oxford: Butterworth-Heineman, 1991).

16. Flemming, "Case-Based Design in the SEED System."

17. E. Do and M. D. Gross, "Reasoning about Cases with Diagrams," in *ASCE Third Congress on Computing in Civil Engineering,* ed. J. Vanegas and P. Chinowsky (Anaheim, Calif., 1996), 314–320.

18. M. D. Gross, "The Electronic Cocktail Napkin—Working with Diagrams," *Design Studies* 17, no. 1 (1996): 53–69.

19. R. C. Schank and R. P. Abelson, *Scripts, Plans, Goals, and Understanding* (Hillsdale, N.J.: Lawrence Erlbaum Associates, 1977); R. Schank and R. Osgood, *A Content Theory of Memory Indexing* (Evanston, Ill.: Institute for Learning Sciences, Northwestern University, 1990).

20. R. Oxman, "Precedents in Design: A Computational Model for the Organization of Precedent Knowledge," *Design Studies* 15, no. 2 (1994): 141–158.

21. F. Hayes-Roth, "Rule-Based Expert Systems," *Communications of the ACM* 28, no. 9 (1985): 921–932.

22. Inductive reasoning—the predominant mode of inference used by science, where new rules are derived from examining the facts—has still not been successfully implemented computationally (except in some trivial cases).

23. U. Flemming, R. Coyne, T. Glavin, and M. Rychener, "A Generative Expert System for the Design of Building Layouts—Version 2," in *Artificial Intelligence in Engineering: Design,* ed. J. S. Gero (Amsterdam: Elsevier, 1988).

24. U. Flemming, "Artificial Intelligence and Design: A Mid-Term Review," in *Knowledge-Based Computer-Aided Architectural Design,* ed. G. Carrara and Y. E. Kalay (Amsterdam: Elsevier, 1994), 1–24.

25. R. Oxman, "Multiple Operative and Interactive Modes in Knowledge-Based Design Systems," in *Evaluating and Predicting Design Performance*, ed. Y. E. Kalay (New York: Wiley Interscience, 1992), 125–143.

26. G. Stiny, "Introduction to Shapes and Shape Grammars," *Environment and Planning B* 7 (1980): 343–351.

27. T. Knight, "Shape Grammars in Education and Practice: History and Prospects," *International Journal of Design Computing* 2 (2000), <www.arch.usyd.edu.au/kcdc/journal/>.

28. G. Stiny and W. J. Mitchell, "The Palladian Grammar," *Environment and Planning B* 5 (1978): 5–18.

29. H. Koning and J. Eizenberg, "The Language of the Prairie: Frank Lloyd Wright's Prairie Houses," *Environment and Planning B* 8 (1981): 295–323.

30. U. Flemming, "The Role of Shape Grammars in the Creation and Analysis of Designs," in *Computability of Design*, ed. Y. E. Kalay (New York: John Wiley and Sons, 1987), 245–272.

Chapter 15

1. U. Flemming, "Artificial Intelligence and Design: A Mid-Term Review," in *Knowledge-Based Computer-Aided Architectural Design,* ed. G. Carrara and Y. E. Kalay (Amsterdam: Elsevier, 1994), 1–24.

2. P. McCorduck, *Aaron's Code: Meta-Art, Artificial Intelligence, and the Work of Harold Cohen* (New York: W. H. Freeman, 1991).

3. See <www.scinetphotos.com/aaron.html>.

4. M. Fineman and D. Eggers, *When Elephants Paint* (Berkeley, Calif.: Berkeley Museum of Art, 2002).

5. M. Boden, *The Creative Mind, Myths, and Mechanisms* (London: Wiedenfeld and Nicholson, 1991); S. H. Kim, *Essence of Creativity* (Oxford: Oxford

University Press, 1990); R. Sternberg, *The Nature of Creativity* (Cambridge: Cambridge University Press, 1988); R. W. Weisberg, *Creativity: Genius and Other Myths* (New York: W. H. Freeman, 1986).

6. Named after the British mathematician Alan Turing, who proposed it, the Turing test is a hypothetical means to establish machine intelligence—if the answers to some questions produced by a human and by a machine are indistinguishable, then—according to Turing—the machine ought to be considered "intelligent." A. M. Turing, "Computing Machinery and Intelligence," *Mind* 59, no. 236 (1950): 433–460.

7. R. D. Coyne, M. A. Rosenman, A. D. Radford, and J. S. Gero, "Innovation and Creativity in Knowledge-Based Design," in *Expert Systems in Computer-Aided Design,* Proceedings of IFIP WG 5. 2 Working Conference, Sydney, Australia (New York: North Holland, 1987), 435–465.

8. Ö. Akin, "How Do Architects Design?," in *Artificial Intelligence and Pattern Recognition in Computer-Aided Design,* ed. J. C. Latombe (New York: IFIP, North Holland, 1978).

9. N. J. Habraken, *The Appearance of the Form* (Cambridge, Mass.: Atwater Press, 1985).

10. D. A. Schön, *The Reflective Practitioner: How Professionals Think in Action* (New York: Basic Books, 1983). See also R. Oxman, "The Thinking Eye: Visual Re-Cognition in Design Emergence," *Design Studies* 23, no. 2 (2002): 135–164.

11. G. Goldschmidt, "The Dialectics of Sketching," *Creativity Research Journal* 4, no. 2 (1991): 123–143.

12. Ibid.

13. J. S. Gero and V. Kazakov, "Evolving Building Blocks for Design Using Genetic Engineering: A Formal Approach," in *Advances in Formal Design Methods for CAD*, ed. J. S. Gero (London: Chapman and Hall, 1996), 31–50.

14. T. Schnier and J. S. Gero, "From Mondrian to Frank Lloyd Wright: Transforming Evolving Representations" (Key Center for Design Computing, University of Sydney, 1997).

15. R. Jagielski and J. S. Gero, "A Genetic Programming Approach to the Space Layout Planning Problem," in *CAAD Futures '97*, ed. R. Junge (Dordrecht: Kluwer, 1997), 821–830; J. S. Gero and V. A. Kazakov, "Evolving Design Genes in Space Layout Planning Problems" (Key Center of Design Computing, University of Sydney, 1998).

16. Critics of GAs use the example of the eye as a structure impossible to achieve by evolution. It consists of many interdependent parts—the iris, the retina, the cornea, the lens—all of which rely on the correct functioning of all other elements for the eye to work as a whole. Hence, incremental improvements in each part alone have no meaning on their own and cannot stimulate incremental changes in others. Even Darwin himself is said to have expressed con-

cerns about the difficulties the eye cast on his theory of evolution. However, Oxford University zoologist Richard Dawkins, in his book *Climbing Mount Improbable* (London: W. W. Norton, 1997), showed how the eye could evolve gradually from local improvements.

17. P. Bentley, *Aspects of Evolutionary Design by Computers* (Intelligent Systems Group, Department of Computer Science, University College London, 2002).

18. The computational nature of neural networks was discussed in section 2.2, where non–von Neumann computers were introduced. Here we deal with their abilities to recognize creative design solutions.

19. K. Gurney, *An Introduction to Neural Networks* (London: UCL Press, 1997).

20. D. B. Fogel, *BLONDIE24: Playing at the Edge of AI* (San Francisco: Morgan Kaufmann, 2002).

21. I. Petrovic, "On Some Issues of Development of Computer-Aided Architectural Design Systems," in *Knowledge-Based Computer-Aided Architectural Design,* ed. Carrara and Kalay, 269–301.

22. The semantic differential matrix is simply a list of opposing characteristics (e. g., "exciting" versus "boring," "hot" versus "cold," etc.), with an indicator of the preferences of the assessor among the two.

23. J. Archea, "Puzzle-Making: What Architects Do When No One Is Looking," in *Computability of Design*, ed. Y. E. Kalay (New York: Wiley Interscience, 1987), 37–52.

Part IV

1. G. Goldschmidt, "Criteria for Design Evaluation: A Process-Oriented Paradigm," in *Evaluating and Predicting Design Performance*, ed. Y. E. Kalay (New York: Wiley Interscience, 1992), 67–79.

2. P. R. A. Jockusch, "How Can We Achieve a Good Design?" in *Evaluating and Predicting Design Performance*, ed. Kalay, 37–50.

3. P. Manning and S. Mattar, "A Preliminary to Development of Expert Systems for Total Design of Entire Buildings," in *Evaluating and Predicting Design Performance*, ed. Kalay, 215–238.

4. C. Alexander, *Notes on the Synthesis of Form* (Cambridge: Harvard University Press, 1964).

5. J. C. Jones, *Design Methods: Seeds of Human Futures* (London: John Wiley and Sons, 1980).

6. N. Cross, *The Automated Architect* (London: Pion, 1977).

7. G. Carrara, Y. E. Kalay, and G. Novembri, "Multi-Modal Representation of Design Knowledge," *Automation in Construction* 1, no. 2 (1992): 111–122.

Chapter 16

1. H. W. J. Rittel and M. M. Webber, "Dilemmas in a General Theory of Planning," in *Policy Sciences* 4 (1973): 155–169.
2. H. A. Simon, *The Sciences of the Artificial* (Cambridge: MIT Press, 1969).
3. Y. E. Kalay, "Performance-Based Design," in *CIB-ASTM-ISO-RILEM Third International Symposium on Application of the Performance Concept in Building,* ed. R. Becker (Tel Aviv, 1996).
4. A. Wiezel and R. Becker, "Integration of Performance Evaluation in Computer-Aided Design," in *Evaluating and Predicting Design Performance,* ed. Y. E. Kalay (New York: Wiley Interscience, 1992), 171–182.
5. S. R. Liggett, W. J. Mitchell, and M. Tan, "Multilevel Analysis and Optimization of Design," in *Evaluating and Predicting Design Performance,* ed. Kalay, 251–269.
6. M. Asimow, *Introduction to Design* (Englewood Cliffs, N.J.: Prentice Hall, 1962).

Chapter 17

1. A. Toffler, *Future Shock* (New York: Bantam Books, 1970).
2. B. J. Cox and F. W. Horsley, *Square Foot Estimating Methods,* 2d ed. (Kingston, Mass.: R. S. Means, 1996).
3. M. Beard, "Why Did the Bridge Wobble So Much? F = K x V," *The Independent* [a Web-based forum for the debate of environmental issues] (2001).
4. B. Jog, "Evaluation of Designs for Energy Performance Using a Knowledge-Based System," in *Evaluating and Predicting Design Performance*, ed. Y. E. Kalay (New York: Wiley Interscience, 1992), 293–304.
5. L. A. Zadeh, "Commonsense Knowledge Representation Based on Fuzzy Logic," *IEEE Computer* 16, no. 10 (1983): 61–67.
6. Fuzziness of classification also has implications for the operators that we normally associate with set theory, such as subset, union, intersection, and complementation. For example, members of subset A of the universal set U can be considered also members of subset B of U when their degree of membership in B is at least as strong as their degree of membership in A (i. e., it crosses some predefined threshold).
7. H. A. Simon, *The Sciences of the Artificial* (Cambridge: MIT Press, 1969).
8. This problem is common in designing large office buildings (although it is usually expressed in terms of the area needed to accommodate the cafeteria) and is similar to other queuing problems such as the optimal number of security gates in airports, platforms in a train station, checkout counters in a supermarket, and so on.
9. Fast food establishments use their knowledge, gained from many prior experiences, to determine the number of seats they provide in a new restaurant.

10. E. Shaviv and Y. E. Kalay, "Combined Procedural and Heuristic Method to Energy Conscious Building Design and Evaluation," in *Evaluating and Predicting Design Performance*, ed. Kalay, 305–325.

11. Building and Fire Research Laboratory, National Institute of Standards and Technology, <www. fire. nist. gov/fire/fires/fires. html>.

12. G. Lakoff and M. Johnson, *Metaphors We Live By* (Chicago: University of Chicago Press, 1980).

13. H. Gardner, *The Mind's New Science: A History of the Cognitive Revolution* (New York: Basic Books, 1985).

14. J. Hirshberg, *The Creative Priority: Driving Innovative Business in the Real World* (New York: Harper Business, 1998).

15. G. Goldschmidt, "Criteria for Design Evaluation: A Process-Oriented Paradigm," in *Evaluating and Predicting Design Performance*, ed. Kalay, 67–79.

16. D. A. Schön, *The Reflective Practitioner: How Professionals Think in Action* (New York: Basic Books, 1983).

Chapter 18

1. The Energy Efficiency Standard for Residential and Nonresidential Buildings—known as Title 24—was established in 1978 in response to a legislative mandate to reduce California's energy consumption. The standard is updated periodically to allow consideration and possible incorporation of new energy efficiency technologies and methods.

2. G. S. Golany and T. Ojima, *Geo-Space Urban Design* (New York: John Wiley and Sons, 1996).

3. S. R. Liggett, "Designer-Automated Algorithm Partnership: An Interactive Graphic Approach to Facility Layout," in *Evaluating and Predicting Design Performance*, ed. Y. E. Kalay (New York: Wiley Interscience, 1992), 101–123.

4. G. Schmitt, "Expert Systems in Design Abstraction and Evaluation," in *Computability of Design*, ed. Y. E. Kalay (New York: Wiley Interscience, 1987), 213–244.

5. A. Wiezel and R. Becker, "Integration of Performance Evaluation in Computer-Aided Design," in *Evaluating and Predicting Design Performance*, ed. Kalay, 171–182.

6. R. Becker, "A Method for the Generation of Weight Factors for Performance Evaluation Systems," *Building and Environment* 20, no. 4 (1985): 195–200.

7. F. J. Fenves, U. Flemming, C. Henderson, and M. L. Maher, "Performance Evaluation in an Integrated Software Environment for Building Design and Construction," in *Evaluating and Predicting Design Performance*, ed. Kalay, 159–170.

8. Nii H. P., "Blackboard Systems: The Blackboard Model of Problem Solving and the Evolution of the Blackboard Architectures," *AI Magazine* 7 (1986): 28–53.

9. G. Schmitt, "ARCHPLAN—An Architectural Planning Front End to Engineering Design Expert Systems," in *Expert Systems for Engineering Design,* ed. M. D. Rychener (New York: Academic Press, 1988).

10. U. Flemming, R. Coyne, T. Glavin, and M. Rychener, "A Generative Expert System for the Design of Building Layouts—Version 2," in *Artificial Intelligence in Engineering: Design,* ed. J. S. Gero (Amsterdam: Elsevier, 1988).

11. E. J. Hacfoort and J. Veldhuisen, "A Building Design and Evaluation System," in *Evaluating and Predicting Design Performance*, ed. Kalay, 195–211.

12. K. Papamichael, J. LaPorta, and H. Chauvert, "Building Design Advisor: Automated Integration of Multiple Simulation Tools," *Automation in Construction* 6, no. 4 (1998): 341–352.

13. DOE-2 calculates the hourly energy use and energy cost of a commercial or residential building given information about the building's climatic location, construction, operation, utility rate schedule and heating, ventilating, and air-conditioning (HVAC) equipment.

14. DElight is a simulation engine for daylight and electric lighting systems in buildings. It calculates interior illuminance levels from daylighting, and the subsequent contribution required from electric lighting to meet a desired interior illuminance.

15. E. Shaviv and Y. E. Kalay (1992), "Combined Procedural and Heuristic Method to Energy Conscious Building Design and Evaluation," in *Evaluating and Predicting Design Performance*, ed. Kalay, 305–325.

16. R. E. Johnson, "Design Inquiry and Resource Allocation," in *Evaluating and Predicting Design Performance*, ed. Kalay, 51–66.

17. B. Jog, "Evaluation of Designs for Energy Performance Using a Knowledge-Based System," in *Evaluating and Predicting Design Performance*, ed. Kalay, 293–304.

18. E. Shaviv and Y. E. Kalay, "Combined Procedural and Heuristic Method," in *Evaluating and Predicting Design Performance*, ed. Kalay, 305–325.

19. S. R. Liggett, W. J. Mitchell, and M. Tan, "Multilevel Analysis and Optimization of Design," in *Evaluating and Predicting Design Performance*, ed. Kalay, 251–269.

20. R. Oxman, "Multiple Operative and Interactive Modes in Knowledge-Based Design Systems," in *Evaluating and Predicting Design Performance*, ed. Kalay, 125–143.

Chapter 19

1. L. N. Kalisperis, M. Steinman, and L. H. Summers, "A Human Thermal Comfort Response Design Model for Non-Orthogonal Surfaces," in *Evaluating and Predicting Design Performance*, ed. Y. E. Kalay (New York: Wiley Interscience, 1992), 273–292.

2. *Environmental Building News,* <www.ebuild.com>.

3. See <www. energy. ca. gov/title24>.

4. C. Alexander, *Notes on the Synthesis of Form* (Cambridge: Harvard University Press, 1964).

5. See <www.eren.doe.gov/buildings/tools_directory/>.

6. According to the U.S. Government Accounting Office.

7. See <http://www.eren.doe.gov/buildings/tools_directory>.

8. A. Olgyay and V. Olgyay (1957), *Solar Control and Shading Devices* (1957; reprint, Princeton: Princeton University Press, 1976). See also R. L. Knowles, *Sun Rhythm Form* (Cambridge: MIT Press, 1981).

9. Act of 1978—California Civil Code 714.

10. A. Yezioro and E. Shaviv, "A Design Tool for Analyzing Mutual Shading Between Buildings," *Solar Energy* 52, no. 1 (1994): 27–37.

11. I. G. Capeluto and E. Shaviv, "Modeling the Design of Urban Grids and Fabric with Solar Rights Considerations," ISES 1997 Solar World Congress, Taejon, Korea (1997), 148–160.

12. E. Shaviv, "A Method for the Design of Fixed External Sun-Shades," *Build International* 8 (1975): 121–150.

13. See <http://www.sustainable.doe.gov/pdf/places.pdf>

14. Center of Excellence for Sustainable development, Office of Energy Efficiency and Renewable Energy of the U. S. Department of Energy, 1991.

15. USDOE Annual Energy Outlook, 1994.

16. T. Moore and P. Thorsnes, "The Transportation/Land Use Connection," Planning Advisory Service Report Number 448/449 (American Planning Association, Chicago, 1994).

17. Lawrence Berkeley National Laboratory, "From the Lab to the Marketplace," Technical Report, 1995.

18. Charles M. Salter Associates, San Francisco, Calif.

19. See <http://www.aee.faa.gov/noise/inm/>.

20. Sixty decibels has been chosen because it corresponds to the dynamic range of orchestral music—the difference between the loudest crescendo (about 100 dB) and a typical room background (about 40 dB).

21. ODEON is a Greek term: unlike the large, open-air theater, the odeon was a more intimate, roofed-over venue for music performance (a place to sing "odes"), which is the first known instance of the construction of concert halls.

Chapter 20

1. W. H. Whyte, *The Social Life of Small Urban Spaces* [video] (Municipal Art Society of New York, 1984).

2. G. Lima, "NUDA—Nursing Unit Design Assistant," Technical Report, Department of Architecture, State University of New York at Buffalo, 1988.

3. S. Margulis, B. R. Archea, M. Connel, D. Hattis, and E. Steinfeld, *Symposium on Building Regulations,* Seventeenth Annual Conference of the Environmental Design Research Association, Washington, D.C. (1986).

4. C. M. Zimring, E. Do, E. Domeshek and J. Kolodner, "Supporting Case-Study Use in Design Education: A Computational Case-Based Design Aid for Architecture," in *Computing in civil engineering,* ed. J. P. Mohesen (New York: American Society of Civil Engineers, 1995), 1635–1642.

5. L. A. Pastalan, E. Steinfeld, G. Weisman, U. Cohen, and P. Windley, "Empathic Model Project," Annual Meeting of the Gerontological Society, Houston, Texas (1971).

6. J. Archea, "The Place of Architectural Factors in Behavioral Theories of Privacy," *Journal of Social Issues* 33 (1977): 3. See also D. C. Glaser and H. E. Cavallin-Calanche, "Representations and Meanings: Cognitive Models for Simulations of Architectural Space," in *Fourth International Design Thinking Research Symposium on Design Representation,* ed. W. Porter and G. Goldschmidt (Cambridge, Mass., 1999).

7. S. Kaplan and R. Kaplan, *Cognition and Environment: Functioning in an Uncertain World* (New York: Prager, 1982).

8. M. J. O'Neill, "A Neural Network Simulation as a Computer-Aided Design Tool for Evaluating Building Legibility," in *Evaluating and Predicting Design Performance*, ed. Y. E. Kalay (New York: Wiley Interscience, 1992), 347–366.

9. B. Kuipers, "The Cognitive Map: Could It Have Been Any Other Way?" in *Spatial Orientation,* ed. H. L. Pick Jr. and L. P. Acredolo (New York: Plenum, 1983).

10. D. Leiser and A Zilbershatz, "The TRAVELLER: A Computational Model of Spatial Network Learning," *Environment and Behavior* 21, no. 4 (1989): 435–463.

11. E. Steinfeld, "Toward Artificial Users," in *Evaluating and Predicting Design Performance*, ed. Kalay, 329–346; C. Irazàbal, "Towards a Computer-Aided Design Assistant: A Virtual User" (master's thesis, University of California, Berkeley, 1995); W. Yan and Y. E. Kalay, "Simulating the Behavior of Users in Built Environments," Technical Report, University of California, Berkeley, 2002.

12. R. Weber, *On the Aesthetics of Architecture: A Psychological Approach to the Structure and the Order of Perceived Architectural Space* (Aldershot: Avebury, 1995).

13. M. Livio, *The Golden Ratio: The Story of Phi, the World's Most Astonishing Number* (New York: Broadway, 2002).

14. Le Corbusier, *Le Modulor and Modulor 2,* English ed. (Switzerland: Birkhauser, 2000).

15. I. Kant, *Critique of Judgment* (1790), trans. J. H. Bernard (New York: Prometheus Books, 2000).

16. Ö. Akin, "How Do Architects Design?," in *Artificial Intelligence and Pattern Recognition in Computer-Aided Design,* ed. J. C. Latombe (New York: IFIP, North Holland, 1978).

17. M.-A. Laugier, *Essai sur l'architecture* (1753), trans. Wolfgang Herrmann and Anni Herrmann (Los Angeles: Hennessey and Ingalls, 1977).

18. P. Serraino and J. Shulman, *Modernism Rediscovered* (New York: Taschen, 2000).

19. M. Suwa, B. Tversky, J. S. Gero, and A. T. Purcell, "Seeing into Sketches: Regrouping Parts Encourages New Interpretations," in *Visual and Spatial Reasoning in Design II,* ed. J. S. Gero, B. Tversky, and T. Purcell (Sydney: Key Centre of Design Computing and Cognition, University of Sydney, 2001), 207–219.

20. D. E. Rumelhart and J. L. McLelland, *Parallel Distributed Processing: Explorations in the microstructure of cognition* (Cambridge: MIT Press, 1986).

21. I. Petrovic, "On Some Issues of Development of Computer-Aided Architectural Design Systems," in *Knowledge-Based Computer-Aided Architectural Design,* ed. G. Carrara and Y. E. Kalay (Amsterdam: Elsevier Science, 1994), 269–301.

22. R. Kurzweil, *The Age of Spiritual Machines* (New York: Penguin Books, 1999).

Part V

1. M. Weber, *The Theory of Social and Economic Organization* (New York: Free Press, 1957).

2. D. Schön, *Technology and Change* (New York: Delacorte Press, 1967).

3. D. S. Landes, *The Wealth and Poverty of Nations: Why Some Are So Rich and Some So Poor* (New York: W. W. Norton, 1998).

4. A. Smith, *An Inquiry into the Nature and Causes of the Wealth of Nations,* ed. J. E. Thorold Rogers, 2d ed. (1776; Oxford: Clarendon Press, 1880).

5. R. Kurzweil, "The Second Industrial Revolution," in *The Age of Intelligent Machines* (Cambridge: MIT Press, 1990), 3–9.

6. M. Castells, *The Rise of the Network Society,* vol. 1 (Oxford: Blackwell Publishers, 1996).

7. B. Benne, "Redefining the Construction Industry's Value Chain: New Business Rules for Collaboration and Procurement," Technical Report, Fisher Center for Information Technology and Market Place Transformation, Haas School of Business, University of California, Berkeley, 2000.

8. D. Norman, *The Invisible Computer: Why Good Products Can Fail, the Personal Computer Is So Complex, and Information Appliances Are the Solution* (Cambridge: MIT Press, 1998).

Chapter 21

1. R. Mohsini, "On Measuring Project Performance: Some Problems of Aggregation," in *Evaluating and Predicting Design Performance*, ed. Y. E. Kalay (New York: Wiley Interscience, 1992), 239–250; see also chapter 6 in J. P. Womack, D. T. Jones, and D. Roos, *The Machine That Changed the World: The Story of Lean Production* (New York: Harper Collins, 1990), 138–168.

2. P. R. A. Jockusch, "How Can We Achieve a Good Design?" in *Evaluating and Predicting Design Performance*, ed. Kalay, 37–50.

3. A. Smith, *An Inquiry into the Nature and Causes of the Wealth of Nations*, ed. J. E. Thorold Rogers, 2d ed. (1776; Oxford: Clarendon Press, 1880).

4. D. S. Landes, *The Wealth and Poverty of Nations: Why Some Are So Rich and Some So Poor* (New York: W. W. Norton, 1998).

5. H. A. Simon, *The Sciences of the Artificial* (Cambridge: MIT Press, 1969).

6. H. W. J. Rittel and M. M. Webber, "Dilemmas in a General Theory of Planning," in *Policy Sciences* 4 (1973): 155–169.

7. R. W. Hobbs, "Leadership through Collaboration," *AIArchitect* 3 (1996): 11.

8. J. D. Watson, *The Double Helix* (New York: W. W. Norton, 1980).

9. D. A. Schön, *The Reflective Practitioner: How Professionals Think in Action* (New York: Basic Books, 1983).

10. P. L. Berger and T. Luckmann, *The Social Construction of Reality* (New York: Anchor Books, 1967).

11. W. Kunz and H. W. J. Rittel, "Issues as Elements of Information Systems," DMG Fifth Anniversary Report, Design Methods Group Occasional Paper No. 1, University of California (1972), 13–15.

12. R. G. Shibley and L. Schneekloth, "Risking Collaboration: Professional Dilemmas in Evaluation and Design," *Journal of Architecture and Planning Research* 5, no. 4 (1988): 304–320.

13. D. Cuff, *Architecture: The Story of Practice* (Cambridge: MIT Press, 1991).

14. R. Fruchter, "The Virtual Atelier," in *Bridging the Generations*, CAE Workshop, Carnegie Mellon University (Pittsburgh, 1994).

15. Y. E. Kalay and G. Black, "Berkeley's A/E/C Collaborative Design Studio," in *ASCE ICCCBE-VIII Eighth International Conference on Computing in Civil and Building Engineering*, Stanford University (Palo Alto, Calif., 2000).

16. I. Kim, T. Liebich, and T. Maver, "Managing Design Data in an Integrated CAAD Environment: a product model approach," *Automation in Construction* 7, no. 1 (1997): 35–53; C. M. Eastman and A. Siabiris, "A Generic Building Product Model incorporating Building Type Information," *Automation in Construction* 3, no. 4 (1995): 283–304; G. Augenbroe, "An Overview of the COMBINE Project," in *Product and Process Modeling in Building Industry*, ed. R. J. Scherer (Rotterdam: A. A. Balkema, 1995).

17. M. Sun and S. R. Lockley, "Data Exchange System for an Integrated Building Design System," *Automation in Construction* 6, no. 2 (1997):

147–155. See also P. Galle (1995), "Towards Integrated, 'Intelligent,' and Compliant Computer Modeling of Buildings," *Automation in Construction* 4, no. 3 (1995): 189–211.

18. K. Papamichael, J. LaPorta, and H. Chauvert, "Building Design Advisor: Automated Integration of Multiple Simulation Tools," *Automation in Construction* 6, no. 4 (1997): 341–352; S. Fenves, U. Flemming, C. Hendrickson, M. L. Maher, R. Quadrel, M. Terk, and R. Woodbury, *Concurrent Computer-Aided Integrated Building Design* (Englewood Cliffs, N.J.: Prentice-Hall, 1994).

19. Y. E. Kalay, "Performance based design," in *CIB-ASTM-ISO-RILEM Third International Symposium on Application of the Performance Concept in Building,* ed. R. Becker (Tel Aviv, 1996).

20. D. Noble and H. W. J. Rittel, "Issue-Based Information Systems for Design," in *ACADIA '88,* ed. P. J. Bancroft (Ann Arbor, Mich., 1988), 275–287.

21. R. McCall, "Issue-Serve Systems: A Descriptive Theory of Design," *Design Methods and Theories* 20, no. 3 (1986), 443–458; R. McCall, P. Bennett, and E. Johnson, "An Overview of the PHIDIAS II HyperCard System," in *ACADIA '94,* ed. A. Grin and M. Fraser (Washington University, St. Louis, Mo., 1994), 63–76; R. McCall, G. Fischer, and A. Morch, "Supporting Reflection-in-Action in the Janus Design Environment," in *The Electronic Design Studio,* ed. M. McCullough et al. (Cambridge: MIT Press, 1990), 247–259.

22. J. Pohl and L. Myers, "A Distributed Cooperative Model for Architectural Design," *Automation in Construction* 3, nos. 2–3 (1994): 177–185.

23. J. P. Womack, D. T. Jones, and D. Roos, *The Machine That Changed the World: The Story of Lean Production* (New York: HarperCollins, 1990).

24. The introduction of e-mail in rigidly hierarchical companies, making it possible to easily reach across levels of hierarchy, can be disruptive to corporate standards and etiquette. See, for instance, A. Andia, "Managing Information Technology in Architectural Design," *Journal of the Design Management Institute* 6, no. 4 (Cambridge: Harvard Business School, 1995).

25. Aberdeen Group, "Collaborative Product Commerce: Delivering Product Innovations at Internet Speed," *Market Viewpoint* 12, no. 9 (1999).

26. G. A. Howell, "What Is Lean Construction," *Seventh Annual Conference of the International Group for Lean Construction,* IGLC-7 (Berkely, Calif.: University of California, 1999), 1–10.

27. See <www.dell.com/us/en/gen/corporate/vision_directmodel.htm>.

28. B. Benne, "Techno-Organizational Models to Support Construction Industry Work Processes" (Ph.D. diss., University of California, Berkeley, 2004).

Chapter 22

1. D. B. Fogel (2002), *Blondie24: Playing at the Edge of AI* (San Francisco: Morgan Kaufman).

2. J. Gebauer and A. Segev, "Changing Shapes of Supply Chains—How the Internet Could Lead to a More Integrated Procurement Function," Working Paper 01-WP–1041, Fisher Center for Information Technology and Marketplace Transformation, Haas School of Business, University of California (Berkeley, Calif., 2001).

3. W. Behrman, "Best Practices for the Development and Use of XML Data Interchange Standards," CIFE Technical Report No. 131, Stanford University, Palo Alto, Calif., 2002.

4. See <www. iai-international. org>.

5. Y. E. Kalay, "Redefining the Role of Computers in Architecture: From Drafting/Modeling to Knowledge-Based Assistants," *Computer-Aided Design* 17, no. 7 (1985): 319–328.

6. Y. E. Kalay, "ALEX: A Knowledge-Based Architectural Design System," in *ACADIA '85,* ed. P. McIntosh (Tempe, Ariz., 1985).

7. G. Carrara, Y. E. Kalay, and G. Novembri, "Knowledge-Based Computational Support for Architectural Design," *Automation in Construction* 3, nos. 2–3 (1994): 123–142.

8. Other forms of machine learning technologies are currently being explored. Several interesting examples of learning agents have been developed by Carnegie Mellon University's Text Learning Group. See <www.cs.cmu.edu/afs/cs/project/theo–4/text-learning/www/index. html>.

9. G. J. Llavaneras, "The Fenestration Intelligent Design Assistant" (Ph.D. diss., University of California, Berkeley, 1996).

10. W. Yan and Y. E. Kalay, "Simulating the Behavior of Users in Built Environments," Technical Report, University of California, Berkeley, 2002.

11. J. F. Blinn, "Nested Transformations and Blobby Man," *IEEE Computer Graphics and Applications* 7, no. 10 (1987): 59–65; N. Magnenat-Thalman and D. Thalman (1991), "Complex Models for Animating Synthetic Actors," *IEEE Computer Graphics and Applications* 11(5):32–44. On H-Anim see <www. web3d. org/>.

12. C. Irazàbal, "Towards a Computer-Aided Design Assistant: A Virtual User" (master's thesis, University of California, Berkeley, 1995).

13. M. Minsky, *The Society of Mind* (New York: Simon and Schuster, 1986).

14. J. Pohl and L. Myers, "A Distributed Cooperative Model for Architectural Design," *Automation in Construction* 3, nos. 2–3 (1994): 177–185; J. Pohl, "What Is Meant by an Information-Centric Computer-Based Environment?" California Polytechnic and State University, San Luis Obispo, *CADRC Currents* (Winter 2002).

15. J. Pohl, "Agents Create Virtual Copy of Human Society through Collaborative Intelligence," *CADRC Currents* (Spring 2002).

16. Y. E. Kalay, "P3: Computational Environment to Support Design Collaboration," *Automation in Construction* 8, no. 1 (1998): 37–48.

17. L. Khemlani, A. Timerman, B. Benne, and Y. E. Kalay, "Intelligent Representation for Computer-Aided Building Design," *Automation in Construction* 8, no. 1 (1998): 177–188.

18. T. Khedro, M. Genesereth, and P. Teicholz, "FCDA: A Framework for Collaborative Distributed Multidisciplinary Design," in *AI in Collaborative Design,* ed. J. S. Gero and M. L. Maher (Menlo Park, Calif.: AAAI, 1993), 67–82.

19. U. Flemming, "Case-Based Design in the SEED system," *Automation in Construction* 3, nos. 2–3 (1994): 123–133.

20. K. Sycara, "Resolving Goal Conflicts via Negotiation," *Seventh National Conference on Artificial Intelligence* (St. Paul, Minnesota, 1988), 245–250.

21. M. S. Fox, S. Finger, E. Gardner, D. Navin Chandra, S. A. Safier, and M. Shaw, "Design Fusion: An Architecture for Concurrent Design," in *Knowledge-Aided Design,* ed. M. Green (London: Academic Press, 1992), 157–195.

22. See, for example, the publications of the Human Computer Interaction Lab at the University of Maryland, <www. cs. umd. edu/hcil>.

23. See, for example, the publications of MIT Media Lab's Software Agents Group, <agents. media. mit.edu/index. html>.

24. D. A. Norman, *The Design of Everyday Things* (New York: Doubleday, 1990).

Chapter 23

1. The Pantheon, in Rome, Italy, (re)built by Hadrian in 117–125 AD, was the largest covered structure at its time, with a dome spanning 142 feet (43. 3 m) in diameter.

2. B. Benne, "Redefining the Construction Industry's Value Chain: New Business Rules for Collaboration and Procurement," Technical Report, Fisher Center for Information Technology and Market Place Transformation, Haas School of Business, University of California, Berkeley, 2000.

3. *The American Heritage Dictionary* (Boston: Houghton Mifflin, 1985).

4. J. P. Womack, D. T. Jones, and D. Roos, *The Machine That Changed the World: The Story of Lean Production* (New York: Harper Collins, 1990).

5. M. Paolucci, O. Shehory, and K. Sycara, "Interleaving Planning and Execution in a Multiagent Team Planning Environment," CMU-RI-TR–00–01, Robotics Institute, Carnegie Mellon University, Pittsburgh (2000).

6. Aberdeen Group, "Collaborative Product Commerce: Delivering Product Innovations at Internet Speed," *Market Viewpoint* 12, no. 9 (1999).

7. R. A. M. Stern, *Modern Classicism* (New York: Rizzoli International Publications, 1988).

8. F. Dal Co, K. Forster, and H. S. Arnold, *Frank O. Gehry: The Complete Works* (New York: Monacelli Press, 1998).

9. H.-R. Hitchcock and P. Johnson, *The International Style* (1932; New York: DIANE, 1995).

10. N. Wiener, *Cybernetics: the Control and Communication in the Animal and the Machine*, 2d ed. (Cambridge: MIT Press, 1965).

11. R. Kurzweil, *The Age of Intelligent Machines* (Cambridge: MIT Press, 1990).

12. See <www. bluetooth. com>.

13. M. Coen, "Design Principles for Intelligent Environments," *Fifteenth National Conference on Artificial Intelligence* (AAAI Press, 1998), 547–554.

14. P. Wellner, "Interacting with Paper on the DigitalDesk," *Communications of the ACM* 36, no. 7 (1993): 86–96.

15. R. Hasha, "Needed: A Common Distributed-Object Platform," *IEEE Intelligent Systems* (March/April 1999): 14–16.

16. N. Negroponte, *Soft Architecture Machines* (Cambridge: MIT Press, 1975), 102.

17. M. C. Mozer, "The Neural Network House: An Environment that Adapts to Its Inhabitants," in *AAAI Spring Symposium on Intelligent Environments,* ed. M. Coen (Menlo Park, Calif.: AAAI Press, 1988), 110–114.

Chapter 24

1. W. Gibson, *Neuromancer* (New York: Ace Books, 1984).

2. This chapter has been adapted, with permission, from a paper coauthored with John Marx, titled: "Architecture and the Internet: Designing Places in Cyberspace," presented at *ACADIA '01,* ed. W. Jabi (Buffalo, N.Y., 2001).

3. A *sense of place* was defined by Steven Moore as the "intersubjective construction of conditions experienced [by the inhabitants of a particular locale, through] intersubjective realities that give a place . . . its 'character' or 'quality of life.'" S. A. Moore, "Technology, Place, and the Nonmodern Thesis," *Journal of Architectural Education* (February 2001): 130–139. See also S. Harrison and P. Dourish "Re-place-ing space: the roles of place and space in collaborative systems," *Proceedings of CSCW '96* (ACM, 1996).

4. F. D. K. Ching, *Architecture: Form Space and Order* (New York: John Wiley and Sons, 1996).

5. T. Chastain and A. Elliott (1998), "Cultivating Design Competence: online support for beginning design studio," in *ACADIA '98,* ed. S. van Wyk and T. Seebohm (Quebec City, Quebec, 1998).

6. Z. Smith, "Evaluation and Prediction: Vibrancy of Plazas," Technical Report, University of California, Berkeley, 2000.

7. C. Canter, *The Psychology of Place* (New York: St. Martin's Press, 1977).

8. S. Harrison and P. Dourish, "Re-place-ing Space: The Roles of Place and Space in Collaborative Systems," in *Proceedings of CSCW'96* (ACM, 1996).

9. C. Alexander, S. Ishikawa, M. Silverstein, M. Jacobson, I. Fiksdahl-King, and S. Angel, *A Pattern Language* (Oxford: Oxford University Press, 1977); R. D. Coyne, M. A. Rosenman, A. D. Radford, M. Balachandran, and J. S. Gero, *Knowledge-Based Design Systems* (Reading, Mass.: Addison-Wesley, 1990).

10. W. Gibson, *Neuromancer* (New York: Ace Books, 1984).

11. See Barry M. Leiner et al., "A Brief History of the Internet," ver. 3.31, <http://www.isoc.org/internet/history/brief.shtml> (Internet Society, 4 August 2000).

12. In 1999 Netscape Corp. was acquired by America Online, Inc.

13. N. Stephenson, *Snow Crash* (New York: Bantam Books, 1992).

14. See <http://www.adobe.com/products/atmosphere/>; <http://www.activeworlds.com>; <http://www.secondlife.com>.

15. See <http://everquest.station.sony.com/>.

16. P. Anders, *Envisioning Cyberspace: Designing 3D Electronic Spaces* (New York: McGraw-Hill, 1999).

17. See <http://architecture.mit.edu/~kll/>, and <http://sap.mit.edu/plan/plan_issues/47/unbuilt/index.html>

18. See < http://www.arch.usyd.edu.au/kcdc/studioMOO/main-backup.html>.

19. L. L. Carroll, *Alice's Adventures in Wonderland* and *Through the Looking Glass* (1862–1964).

20. *Éphémère* (1998) is an interactive, fully immersive, visual/aural virtual art-work, where archetypal, metaphorical elements of "root," "rock," and "stream" recur in a dreamlike "landscape," extended to include body organs such as "blood vessels" and "bones," suggesting a symbolic correspondence between the presences of the interior of the body and the subterranean earth. See <http://www.immersence.com/immersence_home.htm>.

21. Consider, for instance, unsocial behavior like "flaming" (venting one's feelings in rather crude way) in on-line chat rooms (*Wired*, April 2001, 66).

22. In Char Davies's *Éphémère*, for example, a prolonged gaze onto a "rock" reveals an unfolding image of a swirling universe of stars within that "rock."

Chapter 25

1. This chapter has been adapted, with permission, from a paper coauthored with Thomas Chastain and Christopher Peri, titled "Square Peg in a Round Hole or Horseless Carriage? Reflections on the Use of Computing in Architecture," *Automation in Construction* 11, no. 2: 237–248.

2. P. Virilio, *Guerre et cinéma: Logistique de la perception* (Paris: Édition Cahiers du Cinéma, 1984).

3. J. J. Gibson, "The Theory of Affordances," in *Perceiving, Acting and Knowing,* ed. R. Shaw and J. Bransford (Hillsdale, N.J.: Lawrence Erlbaum, 1977).

4. I. Halasz, Introduction to *Processes in Architecture: A Documentation of Six Examples*, Plan 10, MIT School of Architecture and Planning (Cambridge, 1979), 6–7.

5. K. E. Boulding, *The Image: Knowledge in Life and Society* (Ann Arbor: University of Michigan Press, 1956).

6. B. Hillier, *Space Is the Machine* (Cambridge: Cambridge University Press, 1996).

7. R. Arnheim, *Art and Visual Perception: A Psychology of the Creative Eye,* 2d ed. (Berkeley: University of California Press, 1983).

8. G. Goldschmidt, "Visual Displays for Design: Imagery, Analogy and Databases of Visual Images," in *Visual Databases in Architecture,* ed. A. Koutaminis, H. Timmermans, and I. Vermeulen (Aldershot: Avebury, 1995), 53–74.

9. C. I. Yessios, "The Computability of Void Architectural Modeling," in *Computability of Design,* ed. Y. E. Kalay (New York: Wiley Interscience, 1987), 141–172.

10. Boeing Commercial Airplane Co., "Development of Integrated Programs for Aerospace Vehicle Design (IPAD): IPAD Evaluation and Alternatives," Report No. D6-IPAD–70036D, vol. 3 (1980). For the Interoperability Alliance's foundation classes see <http://www.iai-na.org/>. See also C. M. Eastman and A. Siabiris, "A Generic Building Product Model incorporating Building Type Information," *Automation in Construction* 3, no. 4 (1995): 283–304; K. Papamichael, J. LaPorta, and H. Chauvert, "Building Design Advisor: Automated Integration of Multiple Simulation Tools," *Automation in Construction* 6, no. 4 (1998): 341–352.

11. Y. E. Kalay, "Enhancing Multi-Disciplinary Collaboration through Semantically-Rich Representation," *Automation in Construction* 10, no. 6 (2001): 741–755.

12. F. Hayes-Roth, "Rule-Based Expert Systems," *Communications of the ACM* 28, no. 9 (1985): 921–932.

13. J. Gero, "What Are We Learning from Designers and Its Role in Future CAAD Tools," in *CAAD Futures 1997,* ed. R. Junge (Amsterdam: Kluwer Academic Publishers, 1997), 61–70.

14. A label on the shrink-wrapped box of 3D Kitchen says "over 2 million sold" (2000).

Index

Carroll, Lewis, 469

CARTESIANA consortium, 73

Cartesian space, 140

Case-based reasoning (CBR), 23, 73, 202, 256, 261–267, 272, 279, 378, 414, 437, 461

Case law, 23

Cassell, Justine, 430

Cathode ray tube (CRT), 69, 162, 168, 170, 184

CATIA, 445–446

Catmull, Ed, 174

Cave, 185–186

Cave drawings, 193

CD-ROM, 38

CEDAR, 68

Cellular automata, 38

Center of gravity, 146

Central processing unit (CPU), 27, 33, 38, 39, 56

CERN (European Organization for Nuclear Research), 35, 462–463

Certainty factor, 268

Change propagation, 130

Chaos theory, 193

Character recognition, 289

Chastain, Thomas, 456

Checkers, 289, 292

Checklist, 377

Chermayeff, Serge, 213, 215

Chess, 422

Choreography, 181

Chromosome, 283–284, 286

Chunking, 265–267, 270, 346, 349, 482

Circle, 136

CISC, 37

Civilization, 394

Civilization (game), 329

Classical logic, 320–325

Classical orders, 6, 22

Classicism, 230

Classification, 149

Clustering, 215, 289

COBOL, 31, 51, 56, 119

CODASYL, 51

Codd, Edgar F., 151

Cognition, 100, 124, 163–164, 224–255, 281, 287, 380–381, 387–390, 408, 484, 488

Cognitive agency, 332

Cognitive map, 208, 381

Cognitive science, 279, 332, 375–376

Cohen, Harold, 278

Cohen, Morris, 94

Coliseum (Rome), 446

Collaboration, 59, 76, 103, 196, 399–416, 433–436, 451, 462, 479, 481

Collaborative product commerce (CPC), 415–416

Color, 162, 166, 179

Columbia Wire & Iron Works Corporation, 446

Combinatorics, 15, 238–241, 258

COMBINE, 156–157, 413

Commodore International, 33

Common sense, 256, 267, 271

Compartmentalization, 413, 443

Compiler, 46, 49, 52

Completeness, 134, 140–143, 158, 304, 325

Compromise, 111–112, 304

Compugraph, 66

Compurelate, 66, 252

Computability, 47

Computational fluid dynamics (CFD), 329, 365

Computek, 66

Computer-aided design (CAD), 65–74, 134, 154–162, 212, 241, 476, 481–482, 485–486

Computer graphics, 74, 161, 165, 167, 170–171, 193–194

Computerized axial tomography (CAT), 144

Computer program, 47

Computers and Structures (firm), 360

Computer science, 46, 48, 168

Computer vision, 451

Computervision Corporation, 67

Concept, 223

Conception, 8–9, 210, 456–462, 473

Concert hall, 368–372

Concurrency, 105–106, 413, 436–437

Configuration, 396, 415

Conflict and conflict management, 100, 108–114, 158, 206, 211, 242, 248–249, 266, 296, 314, 337–339, 399, 403–411, 421, 431–437, 443, 461

Conic sections, 135

Connectedness, 459

Connectionism, 41, 287, 389

Connection Machine (CM-1), 40

Consistency, 325

Consolidated Engineering Company, 30

Constraint management, 249–251

Constraint propagation, 352

Constraint satisfaction, 17, 19–21, 247

Construction, 8, 9, 10, 441–442

Construction management, 404, 411

Constructive solid geometry (CSG), 143–145, 147

Consultants, 12

Contingencies table, 345

Contract documents, 121

Contradiction, 322–323

Contribution, 407, 414

Control, 131, 448–449

Control Data Corporation, 31

Control points, 140

Control Program for Microprocessors (CP/M), 58

Cookies, 427

Coons, Stephen A., 65

Coordinate system, 135–138, 165, 168, 173

Coordination, 83–84, 343–344, 403–406, 415–417, 431–434, 449, 476

COPLANNER, 66

Industry Foundation Classes (IFC), 425

Inference, 94–95, 268–270, 317, 320–321, 325, 423

Infinite loop, 48

Inhabitation, 455–457

Inheritance, 54, 203

Initial graphic exchange specification (IGES), 121, 155–156

Ink jet printer, 69

Innovation, 285–286, 292

Input/output (I/O) devices, 33, 49, 56, 60, 74

Insight, 15

Instance, 95

Insulation, 352

Integer programming, 219

Integrated circuit (IC), 31–32, 72, 394, 396

Integrated data model, 156

Integrated noise model (INM), 370

Integrated resource library (IRL), 156

Integration, 83, 342–345, 451

Integrity, 413

Intel 4004 (and subsequent chips), 33, 34, 58

Intel 80386, 69

Intel Corporation, 33, 34, 40, 58, 69, 396

Intel iPS C/1 Hypercube, 40

Intelligence, 78, 189, 195–197, 203, 393

Intelligence Artificielle SA, 73

Intelligent buildings, 79. *See also* Smart building materials

Intelligent design assistants (IdeAs), 435–436

Intelligent Room project, 450–451

Intensity, 168, 177

Interaction, 186, 463–464, 469

Intergraph, 67

Interleave, 396, 417, 442–444

International Alliance for Interoperability (IAI), 425, 482

International Business Machines Corporation (IBM), 28–34, 57–58, 69

Internationality, 279

International Standards Organization (ISO), 156

International Style, 446

Internet, 34, 35, 36, 41, 76, 78, 79, 108, 196, 396, 415, 438, 462–463

Internet Explorer, 36, 463

Interoperability, 4, 154–156, 451

Interpolated shading, 173

Interpolation, 140, 173

Interpretation, 46, 88–97, 102, 120, 155, 268, 281, 295, 330–334, 354–355, 376–378, 413, 420, 430–436, 451, 457, 481

Intersection, 143, 145, 147

Intuition, 2, 11, 224, 301, 310, 330, 334

Intuitive leap, 2

Ionic column, 227

IPAD, 482

Irazàbal, Clara, 382

IRIS EXPLORER, 56

Issue-concept-form (ICF), 267

Issues, 112–115, 205–206, 210–216, 267

Italcementi Group, 409

Iverson, Kenneth E., 51

Jacks, Ed, 66

Jacquard, Joseph-Marie, 45

JANUS, 414

Japanese garden, 333

Java, 51, 52, 55

Jazz, 101

Jet Propulsion Laboratory (JPL), 56

Jog, Bharati, 322, 349

Johnson, Philip, 96–97, 460–462

Johnson, Robert, 349

Johnson Controls, Inc., 449

Journeyman, 7, 401

JPLDIS, 56

Judgment, 295–296, 304, 311–312, 330, 334, 377, 380, 410, 419–420, 452, 483

Jurisprudence, 23

KAAD, 73, 76, 158, 425

Kahn, Louis, 23, 467

Kalay, Yehuda E., 352–353, 382, 435

Kant, Immanuel, 387

Kay, Alan, 55

Kemeny, John G., 33, 51

Kilby, Jack, 31

Kildall, Gary, 34

Kinematics, 180

Kinesthetic, in design, 125, 130

Kinnetix, 70

Kirchoff's laws of electricity, 257–258

Kitchen, 89, 355, 484–487

Klein bottle, 146

Kline, Franz, 279

Know-how, 401, 483

Knowledge-based design, 72, 73, 343

Knowledge-based systems, 4, 23, 112, 256, 264, 269–271, 354, 377, 382, 395, 401, 414, 420, 426–428, 432–436, 482–483

Knuth, Donald E., 56

Komar, Vitaly, 278

KraftMaid Cabinetry, 485

Kubrick, Stanley, 469

Kuhn, Thomas S., 109, 111

Kuipers, Benjamin J., 381

Kurtz, Thomas, 33, 51

Lakoff, George, 332

Lambertian diffuse reflector, 178

Language, 8, 85, 87, 99, 117–118, 123, 272–274

LARC, 31

Large-scale integration (LSI), 32

Larson, Kent, 466–467

Las Vegas, 333, 465

Laugier, Marc-Antoine, 229, 388

Lawrence Berkeley National Laboratory (LBNL), 73, 347, 363, 365

Lean construction, 416, 443

Lean production, 416